MAGNIFICENCE & GRANDEUR OF THE ROYAL HOUSES IN EUROPE

N° d'édition : L. 05EBAN000275
ISBN SKIRA : 9788857211176
ISBN ESFP : 9782081264519

MAGNIFICENCE & GRANDEUR OF THE ROYAL HOUSES IN EUROPE

GRIMALDI FORUM MONACO

SKIRA

The present volume is published on the occasion of the exhibition
Fastes et grandeur des cours en Europe
at the Grimaldi Forum Monaco,
from July 11 to September 11 2011.

This exhibition has benefited from the support of

d'Amico

CIRIBELLI

CREDIT SUISSE

GRIMALDI FORUM MONACO

10, avenue Princesse Grace
MC 98000 Monaco
www.grimaldiforum.com

Jean-Claude Riey
President

Sylvie Biancheri
General Director

Catherine Alestchenkoff
Director of Cultural Events

Guy Caruana
Director of Building

Gérard Nouveau
Director of Events

Marc Rossi
Administration and Finance Director

Hervé Zorgniotti
Director of Communication

Nathalie Varley
Cécile Valentin
Communication managers

Alfonso Ciulla
Assistant to the Director of Cultural Events

Monaco
His Excellency Michel Roger, Minister of State
Paul Masseron, Government Advisor for the Interior
Marco Piccinini, Government Advisor for Economy and Finance
José Badia, Government Advisor for Foreign Relations,
As well as the consular and diplomatic corps of the Principality of Monaco

EXHIBITION

General curator
Catherine Arminjon
General curator of the French Heritage

Curator
Patricia Bouchenot-Déchin
Historian, associate researcher at the Centre de Recherche du Château de Versailles

Guest curator overseeing the Russia section
Wilfried Zeisler
PhD student, teaching assistant in Art History at the University of La Sorbonne-Paris IV

Curatorial Assistant
Sophie Vergne
PhD in Art History

Exhibition design
Métaphore{s : François Payet
assisted by **Alix de Rozières**
and **Pierre-Antoine Racle Pauchant**

Audiovisual documentation
Marie-Nicole Feret

General coordination
Catherine Alestchenkoff
assisted by **Céline Vacquier**

Registrar
Thierry Vincent
assisted by **Christian Selvatico**

CATALOGUE

General editor
Catherine Arminjon

Publishing assistants
Céline Vacquier
Sophie Vergne

ÉDITIONS SKIRA-FLAMMARION

Senior Editor,
Director of the Illustrated Books Department
Sophie Thompson

Editor
Sophie Laporte

Publishing coordination
Alexandre Curnier

Production
Bénédicte Gaudin

–

Publishing coordination
Audrey Gregorczyk

Graphic design
Agnès Rousseaux

Translation of the texts from French to English
David Radzinowicz

Translation of the text from Danish to English
Joan F. Davidson

Translation of the notices from French to English
Jonathan Slysa

Copy-editing
Chrisoula Petridis

Proofreading
Sarah Kane

ACKNOWLEDGMENTS

We would hereby like to express our deepest gratitude to all those who have offered generous assistance in realizing the present exhibition, in particular to:

H.M. Queen Elizabeth II of the United Kingdom of Great Britain and Northern Ireland
H.M. Queen Margrethe II of Denmark
H.M. King Carl XVI Gustaf of Sweden
H.M. King Juan Carlos I of Spain
H.M. Queen Beatrix of The Netherlands
H.M. King Harald V of Norway
H.M. Albert II, King of the Belgians
H.R.H. Grand Duke Henri of Luxembourg
H.S.H. Prince Albert II of Monaco

together with representatives from the following prestigious institutions and collections:

AUSTRIA

Vienna, Hofmobiliendepot Möbel Museum Wien and Silberkammer Hofburg Wien
Dr. Ilsebill Barta, Scientific Director
Vienna, Kunsthistorisches Museum
Dr. Franz Pichorner, General Director
Dr. Monica Kurzel-Runtscheiner, Director of the Wagenburg and Monturdepot
Eisenstadt, Esterházy Privatstiftung - Sammlungen der Fürsten Esterházy
Dr. Stefan Ottrubay, General Director
Dr. Stefan Körner, Deputy Director

BELGIUM

Brussels, Palais Royal, Liste civile du Roi
Vincent Pardoen, Steward of the Civil List
Prof. Dr. Christian Koninckx, President of the Association Royale Dynastie et Patrimoine culturel
Brussels, Musée BELvue
An Lavens, Coordinator of the Museum and of the King Baudouin Foundation
Brussels, Musée Royal de l'Armée et d'Histoire Militaire
Dominique Hanson, General Director

DENMARK

Copenhagen, The Royal Danish Collections, Rosenborg Castle & Amalienborg Palace
Niels-Knud Liebgott, Director, Chamberlain
Hillerød, The Museum of National History at Frederiksborg Castle
Mette Skougaard, Director

FRANCE

Rueil-Malmaison, Châteaux de Malmaison et Bois-Préau
Amaury Lefébure, General Curator, Director
Nice, Musée d'Art et d'Histoire, Palais Masséna
Louis Mézin, Chief Curator, Director of the Nice Museums
Nice, Parish of St. Nicolas
Russian Orthodox Cultural Association (ACOR)
Alexis Obolensky, Churchwarden
Paris, Bibliothèque Mazarine
Yann Sordet, Director
Paris, Fondation Napoléon
Thierry Lentz, Director
Saint-Lô, Musée des Beaux-Arts
Hubert Godefroy, Curator
Versailles, Etablissement public du Château, du Musée et du Domaine National de Versailles
Jean-Jacques Aillagon, former Minister, President
Béatrix Saule, General Director

GERMANY

Berlin, Stiftung Preussische Schlösser und Gärten Berlin-Brandenburg
Prof. Dr. Harmut Dorgerloh, General Director
Dr. Samuel Wittwer, Director of palaces and collections
Berlin, Stiftung Preussischer Kulturbesitz
Prof. Dr. h.c. mult. Hermann Parzinger, President
Berlin, Staatliche Museen zu Berlin
Prof. Dr. Michael Eissenhauer, General Director
Berlin, Kunstgewerbemuseum
Dr. Sabine Thümmler, Director
Dresden, Staatliche Kunstsammlungen Dresden
Prof. Dr. Martin Roth, General Director
Grünes Gewölbe and Rüstkammer
Prof. Dr. Dirk Syndram, Director
Porzellansammlung
Dr. Ulrich Pietsch, Director
Gemälde Galerie Alte Meister and Kupferstich- Kabinett
Dr. Bernhard Maaz, Director
Kunstgewerbemuseum
Prof. Dr. Peter Plassmeyer, Director
Gotha, Stiftung Schloss Friedenstein Gotha
Dr. Martin Eberle, Director
Munich, Bayerische Verwaltung der Staatlichen Schlösser, Gärten und Seen
Dr. Johannes Erichsen, President
Dr. Sabine Heym, Director of the Museums Department
Munich, Bayerisches Nationalmuseum
Dr. Renate Eikelmann, General Director

HUNGARY

Budapest, Fine Arts Museum
Dr. László Baán, Director

ITALY

Caserta, Palazzo Reale
Arch. Paola Raffaella David, Soprintendente, Soprintendenza per i beni architettonici, paesaggistici, storici, artistici ed etnoantropologici per le province di Caserta e Benevento
Naples, Museo Archeologico Nazionale
Dott.ssa Teresa Elena Cinquantaquattro, Soprintendente, Soprintendenza Speciale per i beni archeologici di Napoli e Pompei
Naples, Museo Nazionale della Ceramica Duca di Martina
Dott.ssa Luisa Ambrosio, Director
Naples, Museo di San Martino
Dott.ssa Rossana Muzzi, Director

Naples, Museo di Capodimonte
Dott.ssa Lorenza Mochi Onori, Soprintendente, Soprintendenza Speciale per il patrimonio storico, artistico, ed etnoantropologico e per il polo museale della città di Napoli
Dott.ssa Mariella Utili, Director
Intesa Sanpaolo
Parma, Pinacoteca G. Stuard
Prof. Francesco Barocelli (†), Director
Signora Carla Carnerini
San Remo, Museo DAPHNE – Museum of Fashion and Perfume,
Renzo Borsotto, President
Barbara Borsotto, Head of of the Historic Archives
Turin, Palazzo Reale
Dott.ssa Luisa Papotti, Soprintendente, Soprintendenza per i beni architettonici e paesaggistici per le province di Torino, Cuneo, Asti, Biella, Vercelli
Arch. Daniela Biancolini, Director
Turin, Galleria Sabauda
Dott.ssa Paola Astrua, Director
Turin, Consorzio La Venaria Reale
Dottore Alberto Vanelli, Director

LUXEMBOURG

Cour Grand-Ducale de Luxembourg
Pierre Mores, Marshal of the Court of H.R.H. the Grand Duke

MONACO

Palais Princier et Musée des Souvenirs Napoléoniens
Hervé Irien, General Secretary of the Advisory Committee of the Collections of Objets d'Art of his H.S.H. The Sovereign Prince, Coordinator of the Inventory of the Collections of the Prince's Palace
Collection de Voitures Anciennes de S.A.S. le Prince de Monaco
Yves Naquin, Coordinator of the Private Collection of Antique Cars of H.S.H. Prince de Monaco
Musée Océanographique de Monaco
Robert Calcagno, General Director of the Océanographic Institute, Foundation of Albert I, Prince of Monaco
Nouveau Musée National de Monaco–villa Paloma
Marie-Claude Beaud, Director

NORWAY

Oslo, Royal Palace
Ragnar Osnes, Head Steward of the Palace
Ingeborg Lønning, Curator
Oslo, The National Museum of Art, Architecture and Design
Audun Eckhoff, Director
Dr. Widar Halén, Director of Design and Decorative Arts
Oslo, The Norwegian Armed Forces Museum
Torstein Arisholm, Head of the Collections and Documentation Department
Niels Persen, Curator

NETHERLANDS

Apeldoorn, Paleis Het Loo National Museum
Prof. Dr. J.R. ter Molen, Director
The Hague, The Royal House Archives
Drs. Ph. Maarschalkerweerd, Director of the Royal House Archives and the House of Orange-Nassau Collections

POLAND

Cracow, Wawel Royal Castle
Prof. Jan K. Ostrowski, Director
Cracow, Jagiellonian University Museum,
Prof. Stanislaw Waltos, Director
Warsaw, Wilanów Palace Museum
Pawel Jaskanis, Director
Wroclaw, National Museum
Mariusz Hermansdorfer, Director

PORTUGAL

Lisbon, Institute of Museums and Conservation
Prof. João Brigola, Director
Lisbon, Palácio Nacional da Ajuda
Isabel Maria da Silveira Godinho, Director

RUSSIA

Gatchina, State Museum-Reserve of the Palace at Gatchina
Vasiliy Pankratov, Director
Yulia Nikolaenko, Exhibitions Coordinator
Pavlovsk, State Museum-Reserve of the Palace at Pavlovsk
Nicolaï Sergueevitch Tretiakov, Director
Anna Manieva, Exhibitions Coordinator
Pushkin, State Museum-Reserve of Tsarskoye Selo
Olga Taratynova, Director
Iraida Bott, Deputy Director
Ludmila Kanaeva, Exhibitions Coordinator

SPAIN

Madrid, Patrimonio Nacional, Palacio Real
Nicolás Martínez-Fresno y Pavia, President
José Antonio Bordallo Huidobro, General Director

SWEDEN

Stockholm, Royal Palace
Dr. Carin Bergström, Director of the Royal Collections
Lars Ljungström, PhD, Director of the Department of the Collections and Documentation
Stockholm, Nationalmuseum
Prof. Solfrid Söderlind, General Director
Dr. Magnus Olausson, Director of the Collections

UNITED KINGDOM OF GREAT BRITAIN AND NORTHERN IRELAND

London, Victoria & Albert Museum
Sir Mark Jones, Director

Private collections:
Jan Valland Collection, Oslo
Mme de Bailleul-Moltzer Collection

We would especially like to express our gratitude to all those who helped make the present exhibition possible:
Christian Beaufort-Spontin
(Director, Kunsthistorisches Museum, Hofjagd und Rüstkammer, Vienna);
H.E. Claude Giordan
(Ambassador of Monaco to Germany);
Christian Heldt (Federal Ministry of Foreign Affairs, Berlin);
Johann Kräftner
(Director, Liechtenstein Museum);
Bernd Küster (Director, Museumslandschaft Hessen, Kassel);
Lothar Lambacher (Deputy Director, Kunstgewerbemuseum, Berlin);
Andreas von Majewski (Director, Wittelsbacher Ausgleichfonds);
Hans Ottomeyer (Honorary President of the Deutsches Historisches Museum, Berlin);
José Luis Gaspar Sancho
(historian, Patrimonio Nacional, Palacio Real, Madrid);
Lorenz Seelig
(Honorary Chief Curator, Munich)

And also to:
Stefan Adam
Carmo Andrade
Juan Ramón Aparicio
Gina Carla Ascione
Paola Astrua
H.E. Mgr Bernard Barsi
Florian Bayer
Lucia Bellofatto
Jérémie Benoît
Torill Bjordal
Jutta von Bloh
Anne Bouin
Pierre Branda
Cédric Braquetti
Claudia Brink
Maria Burnay
Kirsten Christiansen
Cristina Correia
Ferdinando Creta
Michel Dagnino
Lena Dahlén
Hélène Delalex
Peter Ellis
Sylvia Ferino-Padgen
Angelika Futschek
Edith Gabrielli
Paloma Callejo Garrido
Silvia Ghisotti
Nathalie Giordano-Rosticher
Stefano Gizzi
Gerlinde Gruber
Andreas Gugler
Kerstin Hagsgärd
Per Hedström
Josephine Hildebrand
Karine Huguenaud
Birgit Jenvold
Carolyn Jessen
Kathrin Kempermann
Anne Kjellberg
Peter Kristiansen
Benjamin Labarrère
Patrick Latour
Teresa Maranhas
Céline Meunier
Susanne Netzer
Antonio Ernesto de Nunzio
Hanz Nyström
Martin Olin
Natasja Peeters
Gertraud Perz
Patrick Piguet
Alain Pougetoux
Muriel Prieur
Christian Quaeitzsch
Vanessa Rademacher
Lena Rangström
Sigrid Recknagel
P. H. Rem
Ingrid Roos
Paola Rubino
Valeria San Paolo
Manuela Santana
Catharina Charlotta Scheich
Antje Scherner
Michael Schweller
Claudia Schnitzer
Liesbeth Schotsman
Marie-Louise Törnestam
João Vaz
Lisa Veenstra
Piet Veldeman
Martine Vermeire
Dieter Vorsteher-Seiler
Rebecca Wallace
Ute-G.Weickardt
Ulricke Weinhold
Cornelia Wittig
Johnny Van Wymeersch
Brigitta Zachrison

With thanks to all those who, in various ways, have assisted in the preparation of this exhibition :
Clelia Arnaldi di Balme
Enrico Barbero
Noëlle Bine-Muller
Roland Bossard
Rudiger Busch
Charlotte Caillaux
Jacques Cailleteau
Mª do Carmo Rebello de Andrade
Kirsten Christiansen
Ute Däberitz
Matthias Forster
Philippe Goris
Monika von Hagen
La Collection: Véronique Martingay, Hervé Mouriacoux and Remo Pittiglio
Régis Lécuyer
Jean-Marc Léri
Merete Leth
Fatima Louli
Vega di Martini
Sylvie Messinger (†)
Sibylle Michel
Daniel Mooz
Hanna Nelson
Barbara Nepote
Tânia Olim
Enrica Pagella
Sigrid Recknagel
Lisa Skogh
Emilie Tolsau
Gennaro Toscano
Juliette Trey
Matthias Weniger
Massimo Zanella

AUTHORS

Catherine Arminjon,
General curator of French heritage

Isabel Maria da Silveira Godinho,
Director of the Palacio Nacional da Ajuda, Lisbon

José Luis Gaspar Sancho,
Historian, Patrimonio Nacional, Palacio Real, Madrid

Concha Herrero Carretero,
Curator, Historic Tapestries Department, Patrimonio Nacional, Madrid

Bernard Chevallier,
General Heritage Curator, Former Director of the Musée National de Malmaison et Bois-Préau

Frédéric Lacaille,
Curator of the nineteenth century paintings collection at the Musée National des Châteaux de Versailles et de Trianon

Muriel Prieur,
Curator of the Collections, Court Grand-Ducal, Luxembourg

Gustaaf Janssens,
Head of the Archives Department, Palais Royal, Brussels

Philippe Maarschalkerweerd,
Director of the Archives of the Royal House and the Collections of the House of Orange-Nassau

Peter Kristiansen,
Curator, Royal Danish Collections, Rosenborg Castle and Amalienborg Palace, Copenhagen

Birgit Jenvold,
Curator, Royal Danish Collections, Rosenborg Castle and Amalienborg Palace, Copenhagen

Mogens Bencard,
Honorary Director, Rosenborg Castle, Copenhagen

Widar Halén,
Director of Design and Decorative Arts, National Museum of Art, Architecture and Design, Oslo

Anne Kjellberg,
Chief Curator, The National Museum of Art, Architecture and Design, Oslo

Magnus Olausson,
Director of the Collections, Nationalmuseum, Stockholm

Lena Rangström,
Chief Curator, Livrustkammaren, Stockholm

Lars Ljungström,
Director of the Department of the Collections and Documentation, Royal Palace, Stockholm

Wilfried Zeisler,
PhD student, Art History, University of La Sorbonne-Paris IV

Ludmila Kanaeva,
Curator of the Exhibitions Department, State Museum-Reserve of Tsarskoye Selo

Marta Golabek,
Curator, Art Department, Wilanów palace Museum, Warsaw

Samuel Wittwer,
Director of Palaces and Collections, Stiftung Preussische Schlösser und Gärten Berlin-Brandenburg

Hans Ottomeyer,
Honorary President, Stiftung Deutsches Historisches Museum, Berlin

Dirk Syndram,
Director, Grünes Gewölbe and Rüstkammer, Staatliche Kunstsammlungen, Dresden

Ulrich Pietsch,
Director, Porzellansammlung, Staatliche Kunstsammlungen, Dresden

Jutta von Bloh,
General Curator, Grünes Gewölbe and Rüstkammer, Staatliche Kunstsammlungen, Dresden

Lorenz Seelig,
Honorary Chief Curator, Munich

Uwe Gerd Schatz,
Conservator of the Castles of Ludwig II of Bavaria

Ilsebill Barta,
Scientific Director, Hofmobiliendepot and Silberkammer, Vienna

Stefan Körner,
Deputy Director, Esterházy Foundation

Andrea Merlotti,
Head of Historical Research, La Venaria Reale

Imma Ascione,
Director of the Archives, Naples

Thomas Fouilleron,
PhD (History)Research Coordinator, Palais Princier, Monaco

Jacqueline Carpine-Lancre,
Research Coordinator, Palais Princier, Monaco

Palais de Monaco

July 2011

This year, which sees the celebration of my marriage to Miss Charlene Wittstock, provides an opportunity for Monegasques and all residents of the Principality to unite in joy around our common values. The event also presents an ideal time to take stock of the time-honored bonds we share with so many other great European families.

It is with this in mind that the Grimaldi Forum has decided to stage a truly exceptional exhibition entitled *Magnificence and Grandeur of the Royal Houses in Europe*. Featuring pieces from all over Europe—paintings and other artworks, together with photographs, jewelry, costumes, etc.—the aim of the exhibition is to pay tribute to regal living and statecraft.

Specialists in various eras and nations, a team of art historians address themes such as the origins, monarchs, and treasures of a score of sovereign courts.

Thus, *Magnificence and Grandeur of the Royal Houses in Europe* offers an exploration of the underlying bedrock of our identity. The future and the numerous challenges of modernity can only be envisaged with serenity if we keep uppermost in mind, not only our history and culture, but also the foundations of the civilization that has made us what we are today.

I would hereby like to express my deepest gratitude to all those who have made this remarkable exhibition possible.

Albert de Monaco

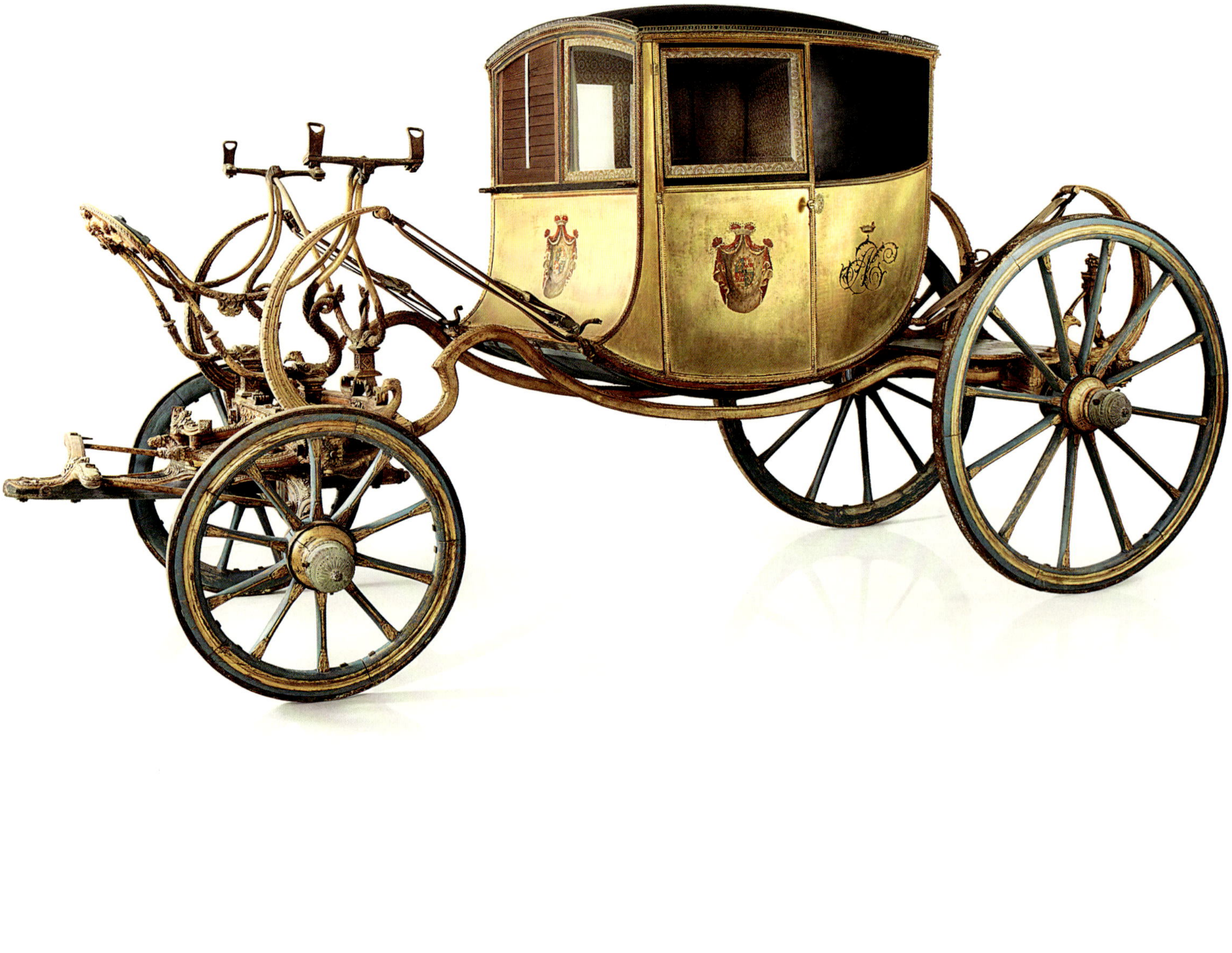

Carriage belonging to the Princes Esterházy
c. 1785
Eisenstadt Castle,
Esterházy Foundation

Around the courts of Europe

Catherine Arminjon

This summer, visitors are invited to Monaco to meet historical royal and princely personages and learn more about seminal events in European history.

This first exhibition dedicated to the courts of Europe will set the stage for some unique encounters. Covering three centuries of European history, it is arranged neither chronologically nor politically, but geographically and builds into a veritable Grand Tour that travels west to Spain and Portugal, before turning north to Scandinavia, through France, Belgium, and England, on to the nations of Central Europe and Russia, then into the Italian peninsula, and finishing in the Principality of Monaco.

The royal personages and princely couples who come to life in this spectacular exhibition were chosen only after close scrutiny by a group of historians and directors of the royal collections of each country.

Out of the twenty European courts on show here, fully half are still existant: England, Spain, Denmark, Sweden, Belgium, Luxembourg, the Netherlands, Sweden, Norway, and Monaco. In the other countries, other modes of government prevail, but all still strive to preserve and perpetuate their past in the great national collections of Portugal, France, Russia, Germany, Austria, Poland, and Italy.

Some of these monarchs, such as Felipe V of Spain, José I of Portugal, and Gustav III of Sweden, are exemplars of the century of the Enlightenment. During the reign of Carlo di Borbone, Naples experienced an upsurge in national feeling in which the establishment of the Borbone dynasty in Naples coincided with the city's drive for independence.

The reigns of other princes are characterized by a desire to obtain kingly status. This is the case with the duke of Savoy, Vittorio Amedeo II, whose efforts were finally crowned with success in 1713, thanks to the support of France and her allies. Likewise, the elector of Saxony, Augustus the Strong, obtained his crown on his election as king of Poland in 1697. A few years later, in 1701, Friedrich of Prussia became the first king "in Prussia," while his grandson, Friedrich II, was to be elevated to the rank of king "of Prussia" only in 1772.

While reigning over their kingdom, monarchs often discover a taste for and an interest in the arts and artworks. In architecture, obviously, in the guise of palaces and monuments. Manufactories, too, presented a prestigious outlet for the natural resources of a nation (as in the elaborate gifts crafted out of amber that the kings of Prussia bestowed on other reigning princes), but they also allowed rulers to vie with one another peacefully. Showcases for the industrial base of a nation, royal porcelain manufactories in particular —be they in Sèvres, Meissen, Vienna, Berlin, or Saint Petersburg, or at Buen Retiro in Spain or Capodimonte in Naples—were pressed into service in creating diplomatic and private presents. Louis XV, for instance, presented the Bleu Céleste Sèvres service to Gustav III of Sweden, while Christian VII of Denmark purchased the Bleu service from the French royal manufactory that now stands in the palace of Amalienborg in Copenhagen. For its part, Saxony also put into practice the principle of offering prestigious services as gifts with its own Meissen porcelain, prime examples being those delivered to Isabella Farnese, queen of Spain.

It is treasures like these that the exhibition presents, together with penetrating portraits, images of official or private life, spectacular collections of objets d'art, and many personal as well as official gifts. But there are also garments and jewels, as well as other more everyday articles that allow visitors to see the real face behind the regal mask, affording a glimpse into some of the key moments in a monarch's existence.

Naturally, such an historical journey through the courts of Europe cannot but take religion into account. For centuries—in Protestant countries, chiefly in the north, as well as in the Catholic nations of the south—not only did faith determine royal marriage arrangements, but it was also a mainspring of national policy, the basis of alliance and conflict alike. And yet, to win the crown of the Catholic land of Poland, the Protestant elector of Saxony, Augustus the Strong, had no hesitation in changing observance. He was not alone: Protestant princesses would also convert to the Eastern Orthodox rite on marrying the Russian czar.

From time immemorial, the lives and nuptials of princely couples have played a significant role in territorial and political relations. Occasionally, however, official demands overlapped with true love. While visiting France, the famous king of Poland, Jan Sobieski, for instance, met a young French aristocrat named Marie Casimire. When she became a widow, Sobieski took her as his consort, admiring her unswervingly for the rest of a happy and successful reign that proved one of Poland's most conspicuous. In Spain, meanwhile, Felipe V and Isabella Farnese formed a particularly close couple, both as private individuals and as rulers, bestowing on the Spanish monarchy the grandeur that characterized it during their reign.

Royal affairs could be more complicated. With Napoleon and Josephine, each played a part in what became a turning point in the history of France. Bonaparte was besotted with Josephine; she quickly grasped the situation and was of immense help to Napoleon as he ascended the rungs of power. The course of Josephine's fascinating life was unusual in that she, unlike other princesses of the age, had never been intended for such elevated status; and yet, once her destiny became clear, she stood by the side of the future emperor and served him with singular grace and intelligence.

The role of women could indeed be determinant, and they could influence politics in the countries whose queen they became. Thus it was with the powerful Isabella Farnese, Felipe V's second wife, who spent her husband's lengthy reign doing her utmost to ensure that her eldest son, Carlo, ruled first as king over Naples and then, after his return to the homeland, over Spain. Sometimes, thanks to her upbringing or her previous way of life, a royal wife could enrich the artistic culture of her adopted country. Today, it is hard to imagine what losing their home must have represented for these consorts who in general would never set eyes on their native land again.

Some of our royal protagonists were no strangers to arts such as painting, drawing, music, and drama. King Gustav III of Sweden for one was hugely fond of the theater and even trod the boards himself in Drottningholm. Music, too, fulfilled an important role. The Italian Domenico Scarlatti came to the court of Spain and Haydn served at that of his patron, the Prince Esterházy, while Mendelssohn became a great favorite of Queen Victoria's. In another domain, the cultivated and intellectual wife of King Friedrich I, Queen Sophie Charlotte, proved a perceptive observer of the career of the philosopher Leibniz.

Unfortunately, each century was also shaped by war. Almost every reigning prince was sooner or later caught up in conflict, emerging victorious or defeated, and some earned a glowing place in the annals of the military. In 1685, for instance, Jan III Sobieski of Poland repulsed the Turks at the Battle of Vienna, while in 1706 Vittorio Amedeo II of Savoy carried the day at the Siege of Turin. Others strode the battlefield their entire lifetime without ever acquiring the laurels they craved. Their courage though could make them into veritable national heroes, as with Christian IV, who entered Danish legend at the naval battle of Kolberger Heide in 1644, where he continued to fight in spite of serious wounds and the loss of an eye.

A period of upheaval, of industrialization, of political and social movements, and of wholesale changes in daily life, the nineteenth century saw some monarchs embark on novel policies—as in the liberalization program of Czar Alexander II (rightly dubbed the "Liberator") so promptly dropped by his successor. Moreover, when the map of Europe was redrawn following the Congress of Vienna, several wholly new countries, such as Belgium and Luxembourg, came into being.

Royal espousals, however, could still follow more traditional lines. The wedding between Louise d'Orléans, eldest daughter of the king of the French, Louis-Philippe, and the first king of the Belgians, Léopold, is a prime example of a diplomatic union, as it marked the close bond between the fledgling state of Belgium and France, which had done so much to obtain recognition for the new kingdom.

During her long and brilliant reign, Queen Victoria piloted both Great Britain and her colonies through the choppy waters of history as they were buffeted by the great movements of the mid-nineteenth century that affected her realms and Europe generally. Nonetheless, while busying herself in the political, social, economic, and industrial spheres, she was also constructing an idyllic love match with Prince Albert of Saxe-Coburg. Victoria lived to see many of her descendants join in matrimony with other great families, thereby earning herself the moniker "the grandmother of Europe." In Denmark, Queen Louise, wife of King Christian IX, also put into action a matrimonial strategy that was so effective (one of her daughters married the king of England, a second the czar of Russia, and a third the son of the king of Hanover) that her husband became known as "Europe's father-in-law."

The invention of photography in the middle of the nineteenth century—followed by that of cinema—also left an indelible stamp on court life. Not only did several monarchs build up remarkable collections, but the technique also made more readily available informal portraits and scenes revealing a sovereign's family or official life (on vacation, traveling, etc.), his lifestyles and pastimes, bringing them a little closer to their subjects, and making them more popular and better understood.

The early twentieth century witnessed the birth of many constitutional monarchies: in 1905, at the cession of its union with Sweden, Norway gained its independence, a plebiscite electing Carl of Denmark as king with the name Haakon VII of Norway. In the same period, the Netherlands, on the brink of becoming a significant industrial power, was guided by a quite exceptional personality, Queen Wilhelmina. One of the sovereigns who wielded the greatest sway over the history of the country, it was during her reign that the Salic law was abolished. Totally transforming the image of the monarchy, she was also very effective during the great world conflicts.

Whatever the period, the soul of a sovereign is reflected in his or her country. Thus, in the present exhibition, one will encounter women and men whose reign and life story proved decisive, not just for the history of their own country, but for that of Europe as a whole.

PORTUGAL
SPAIN
FRANCE
ENGLAND
LUXEMBOURG
BELGIUM
NETHERLANDS
DENMARK
NORWAY
SWEDEN
RUSSIA
POLAND
PRUSSIA
SAXONY
BAVARIA
AUSTRIA
ESTERHÁZY
TURIN
NAPLES
MONACO

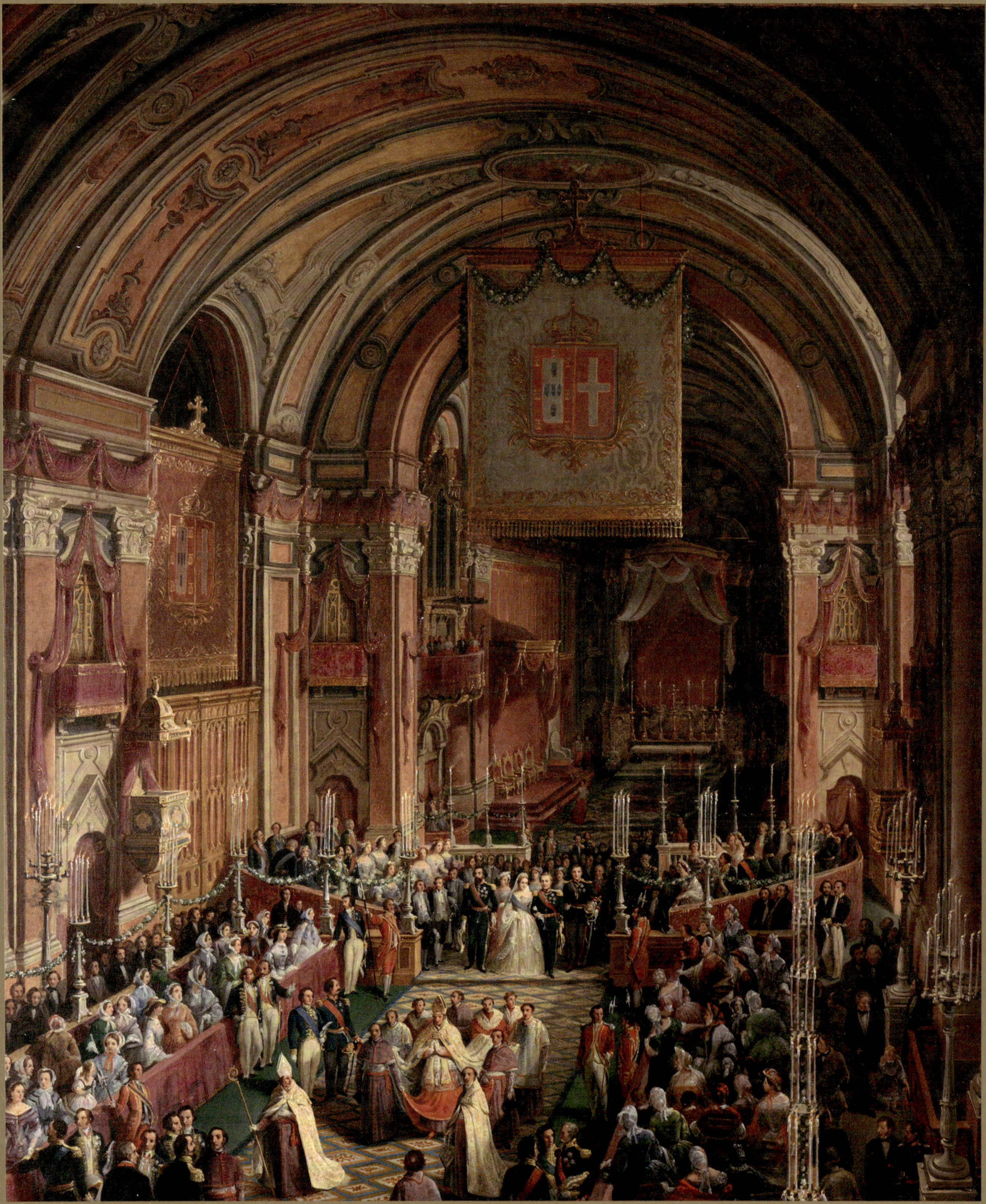

PORTUGAL

Luís I (1838–1889) and Maria Pia (1847–1911)

The Wedding of King Luís I of Portugal and Maria Pia of Savoy
1864
Antonio Manuel da Fonseca
(1796–1890)
Palácio Nacional da Ajuda,
Lisbon

King Luís I and Queen Maria Pia
The court of Portugal in the nineteenth century

Isabel Maria da Silveira Godinho

The outstanding Portuguese reign of the nineteenth century was that of Luís I (1838–1889) and Maria Pia of Savoy (1847–1911), who chose the Ajuda Palace as their principal residence, in Lisbon.

Luís was born in Lisbon on October 31, 1838, in the Palácio das Necessidades. He was the son of Queen Maria II (1819–1853) and Fernando of Saxe-Coburg-Gotha (1816–1885). His elder brother Pedro (1837–1861) was heir to the crown, but at the death of his mother the queen he was still a minor and thus too young to reign. His father, Fernando, acted as regent, while the king only acceded to the throne in 1855 under the name as Pedro V. Still young, he had been well prepared, however, receiving a modern education and traveling throughout Europe with his brother, Luís, duke of Porto, both acquiring an acute perception of the realities in Europe and of the contemporary scene.

Luís chose a career in the navy. Always attracted by the sea, one of his ruling passions, he rose rapidly through the ranks and in 1859 was appointed lieutenant-commander, taking command of the sailing ship *Pedro Nunes* and the corvette *Bartolomeu Dias*, a silver model of which dated 1888 is now in the Ajuda Palace.

In September 1861, Luís, accompanied by his younger brother João, once again traveled around Europe. In Paris he learned of the death of his father Fernando and of the illness of the young king, his brother Pedro V, who died before he was able to return to Lisbon. This sequence of deaths meant he was heir to the Portuguese throne and he was proclaimed king on his arrival in Lisbon on December 22, 1861, to the cheers of the people. Adopting the name Luís I, the king was to reign for twenty-eight years.

His reign proved a peaceful one. Tolerant with the opposition, he respected the different political parties and instituted many reforms and innovations: the construction of railroads, the creation of banks, the abolition of the death penalty in 1867 followed by that of slavery in 1869, reforms in education and legislation, the foundation of an academy of art, and the setting up of the Royal

Luís I (1838–1891), King of Portugal
c. 1865
Attributed to
Michele Gordigiani
(1830–1909)
Palácio Nacional da Ajuda, Lisbon

Maria Pia (1847–1911), Queen of Portugal
c. 1865
Attributed to
Michele Gordigiani
(1830–1909)
Palácio Nacional da Ajuda, Lisbon

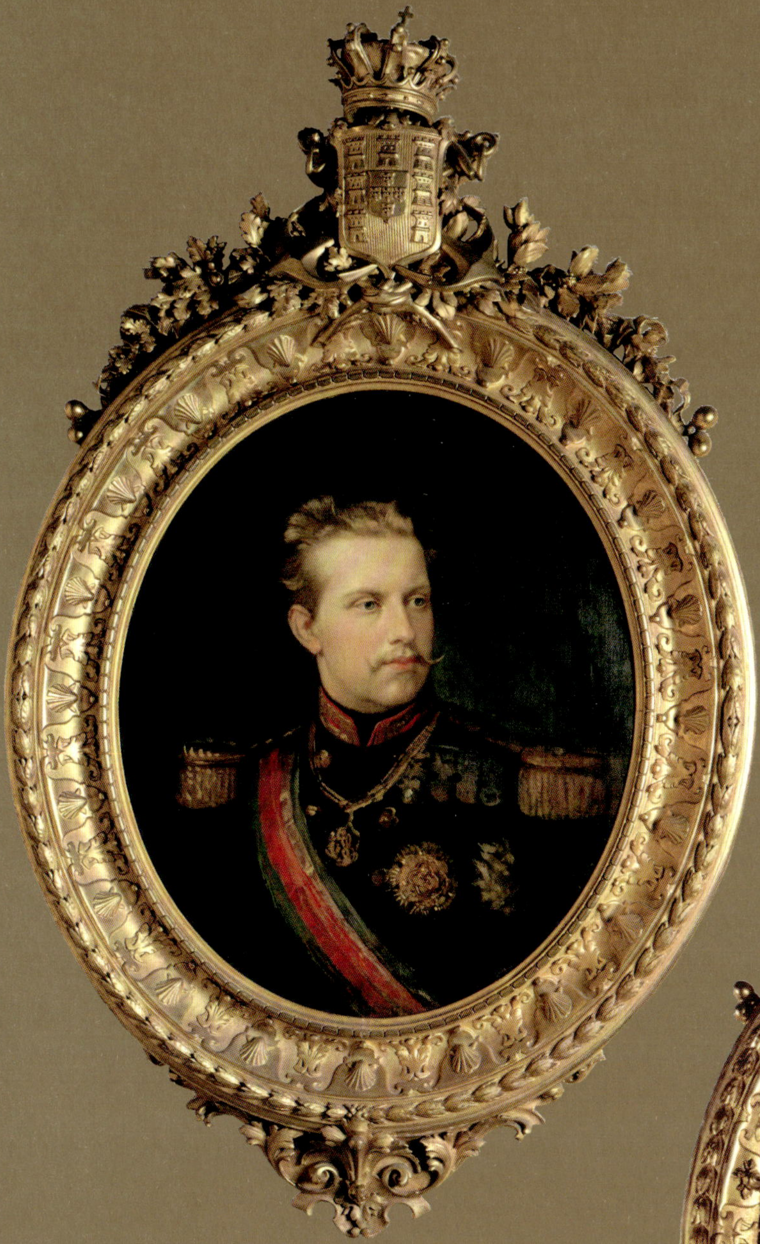

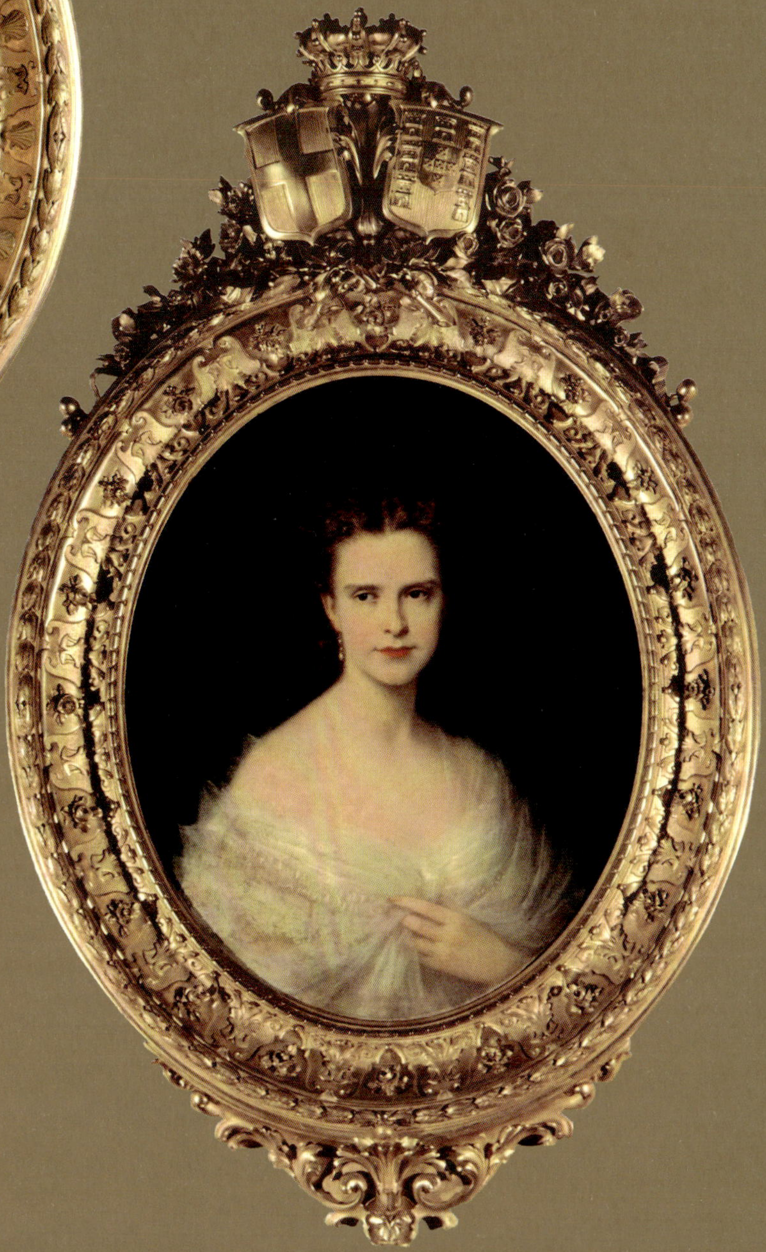

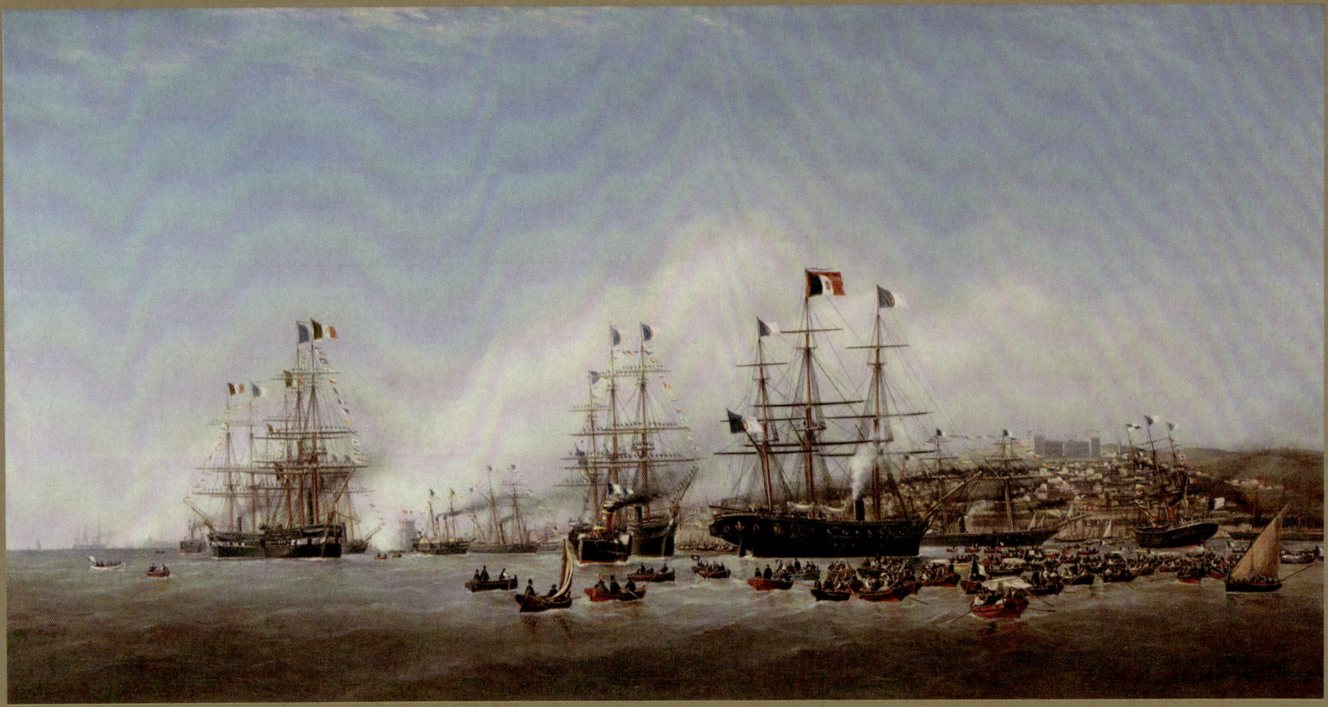

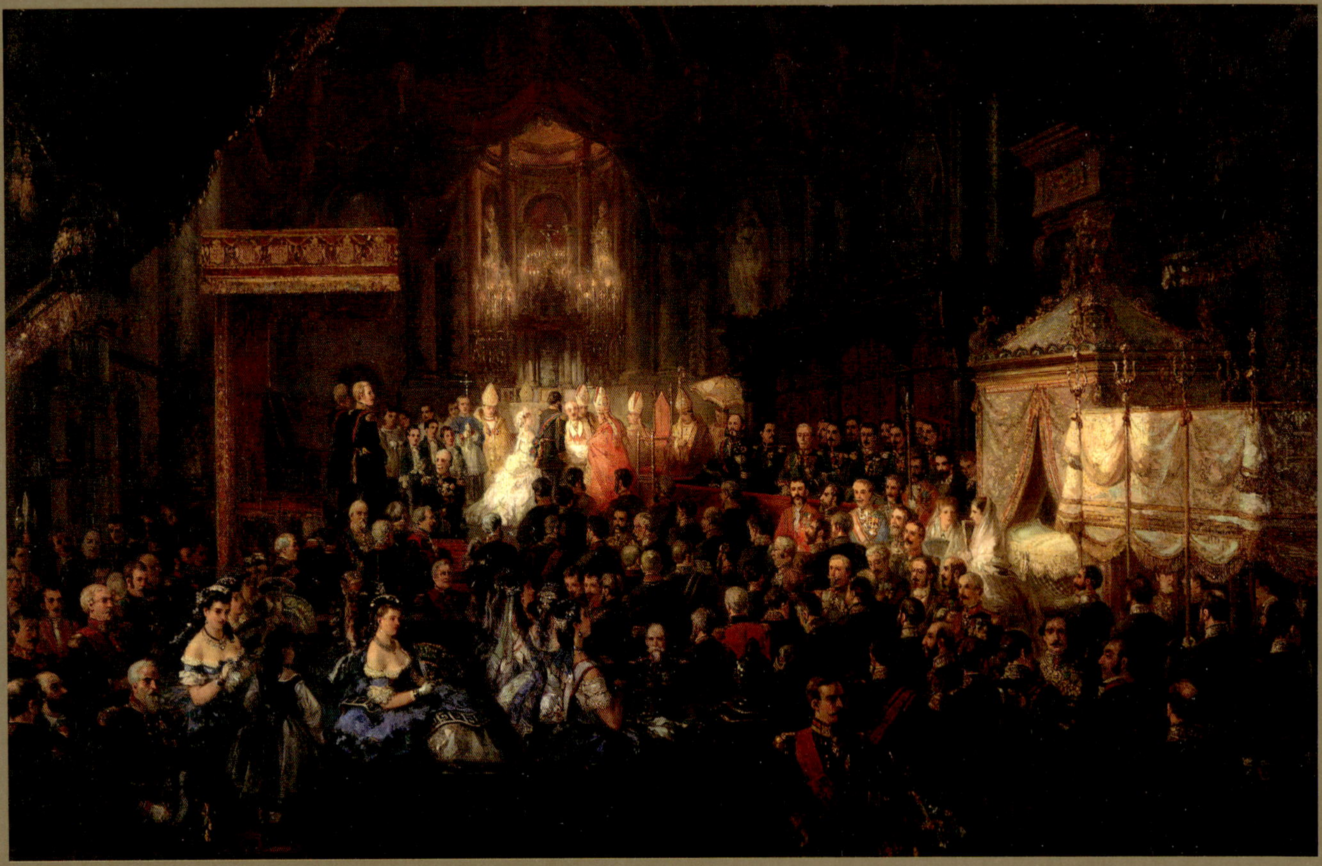

Painting Gallery in the Ajuda Palace, which opened in September 1869. Related to many European monarchs he had met during his travels with his brother, Luís I made use of these family ties to resolve political conflicts and to maintain the neutrality incumbent upon a nation like Portugal.

In Lisbon the royal family lived at the Palácio das Necessidades. The palace, however, had been the scene of so many tragic deaths that the court and the people alike begged the new king to change residence. Thus, although the building required a great deal of work, Luís moved into the Ajuda Palace in Holy Week 1862.

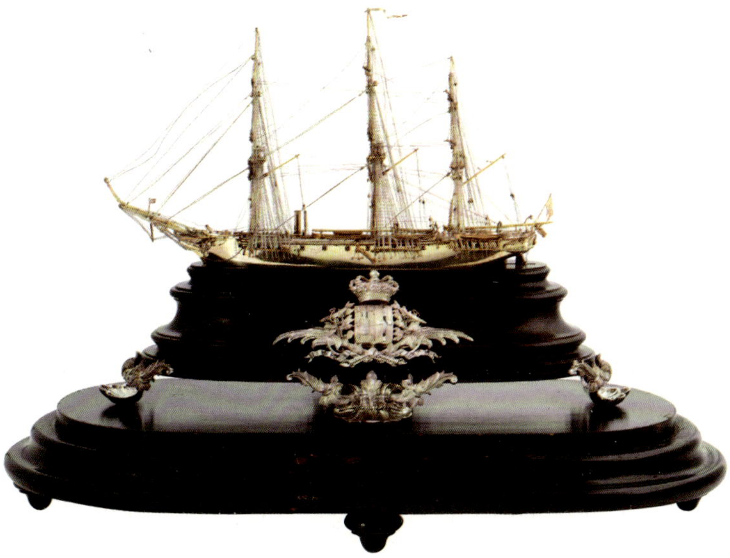

Model of the royal corvette *Bartolomeu Dias*
c. 1881
Palácio Nacional da Ajuda, Lisbon

The absence of an heir for the kingdom turned his mind to marriage. His choice fell on the fourteen-year-old Princess Maria Pia of Savoy, daughter of the unifier of Italy, Vittorio Emanuele II, and Archduchess Maria Adelaide of Austria. The marriage by proxy took place in the chapel of the royal palace of Turin on September 27, 1862, Luís being represented by Prince Eugene of Savoy-Carignan. The union was solemnized in the church of São Domingos in Lisbon on October 6 the same year in the presence of the court and many renowned guests. The ceremony is depicted in a painting dated 1864 by António Manuel da Fonseca (1796–1890), onetime drawing tutor to Princes Pedro and Luís.

The period turned a new page for the House of Braganza. Princess Maria Pia had been born in Turin on October 16, 1847, and was a youngest child. Having lost her mother when only seven, she was brought up by the marchioness Paulina di Pallavicini, lady-in-waiting to her mother, while Countess Carolina Villamarina acted as her lady's companion. As for other princesses of the era, Maria Pia's education centered on the study of languages, grammar, history, geography, music, and drawing; Father Gazelli was her spiritual adviser. She spent her youth in the various Savoy palaces of Piedmont.

Having asked for the hand of the princess and gained the approval of her father, Luís had to prepare the trousseau and organize a retinue to accompany her. The new queen of Portugal arrived in Lisbon on October 5, 1862, aboard the corvette *Bartolomeu Dias* commanded by the king in person. Comprising three Portuguese and three Italian vessels, the flotilla sailed into the Tagus around midday, greeted by salvos of welcome fired from the fortresses of Lisbon. As

***The Arrival of Queen Maria Pia in Lisbon aboard the Corvette* Bartolomeu Dias**
1863
João Pedroso Gomes da Silva
(1825–1890)
Palácio Nacional da Ajuda, Lisbon

Baptism of the Infante Carlos (1863–1908), Future King of Portugal
c. 1865
Pierre-Henri-Théodore Tetar Van Elven
(1828–1908)
Palácio Nacional da Ajuda, Lisbon

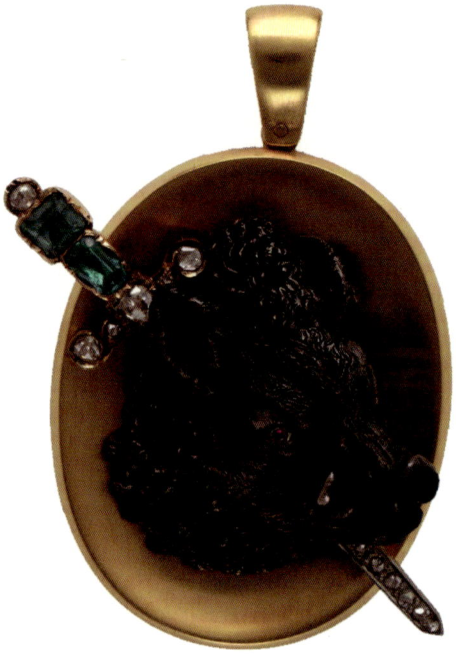

Queen Maria Pia's hunting jewelry
Boar pendant
Late nineteenth century
Palácio Nacional da Ajuda, Lisbon

she dropped anchor, the ship was surrounded by innumerable little boats, a scene painted a year later by João Pedroso da Silva.

Italy also wished to pay homage to its princess, and several cities presented her with sumptuous gifts, many of which remain in the Ajuda Palace. The wedding ceremonies, including opera, ball, and dinners, were magnificent. The atmosphere in Lisbon was festive as it hailed a new queen in whom all the hopes of the people were invested as they prayed for an heir to put the tragedies of the preceding reign behind them.

To receive Maria Pia, the Ajuda Palace, the new royal residence, had to be entirely refurbished. On her arrival, the young queen immediately began modernization works, summoning many decorators to transform the chilly palace into a practical, up-to-date, and comfortable family dwelling. Throughout her life, Maria Pia showed great passion for interior design, an interest she fueled through travel and purchase. Her efforts transformed the palace into a residence as grand as the royal palace of Turin. In this determination to reflect her position as queen and wife of the king of Portugal, orders for clothing and ornaments, silverware, furniture, glassware, and crockery would be placed solely with the foremost foreign manufacturers and suppliers to other European courts.

Luís's interests focused rather on technology and scientific inventions; he equipped the palace with elevators, first gas and then electric lighting, and telephones. He also had a "megalethoscope" installed—a piece of apparatus invented in 1862 that allowed photographs to be viewed in three dimensions. In 1866 its inventor, Carlo Ponti (1823–1893), was named optician to the royal house of Italy. It is possible that this apparatus was acquired or commissioned by the Portuguese monarchs while on a European tour in 1865.

Diamond diadem belonging to Queen Maria Pia
1863–66
Estevão da Sousa
Palácio Nacional da Ajuda, Lisbon

Diamond necklace belonging to Queen Maria Pia
1865
Estevão da Sousa
Palácio Nacional da Ajuda, Lisbon

The birth of Prince Carlos (1863–1908) was greeted with immense joy throughout the kingdom: finally, an heir to the crown. Carlos's baptism took place on October 19, 1863, in Lisbon. The birth of a second son, Infante Alfonso (1865–1920), secured the future of the dynasty. A demanding mother, Maria Pia chose only the best and most renowned figures to educate the princes. Their childhood progressed happily enough, living in the Ajuda Palace and spending their holidays between Sintra, Queluz, and Mafra. King Fernando II, their paternal grandfather, introduced them to culture, literature, and the arts. Like his

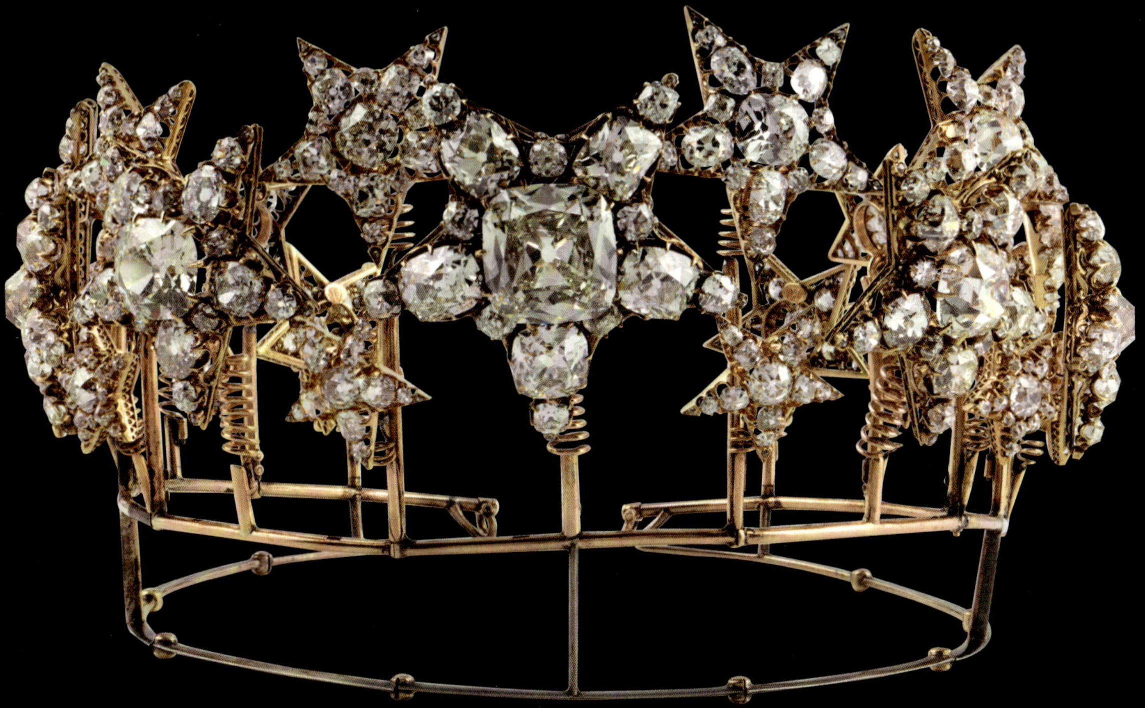

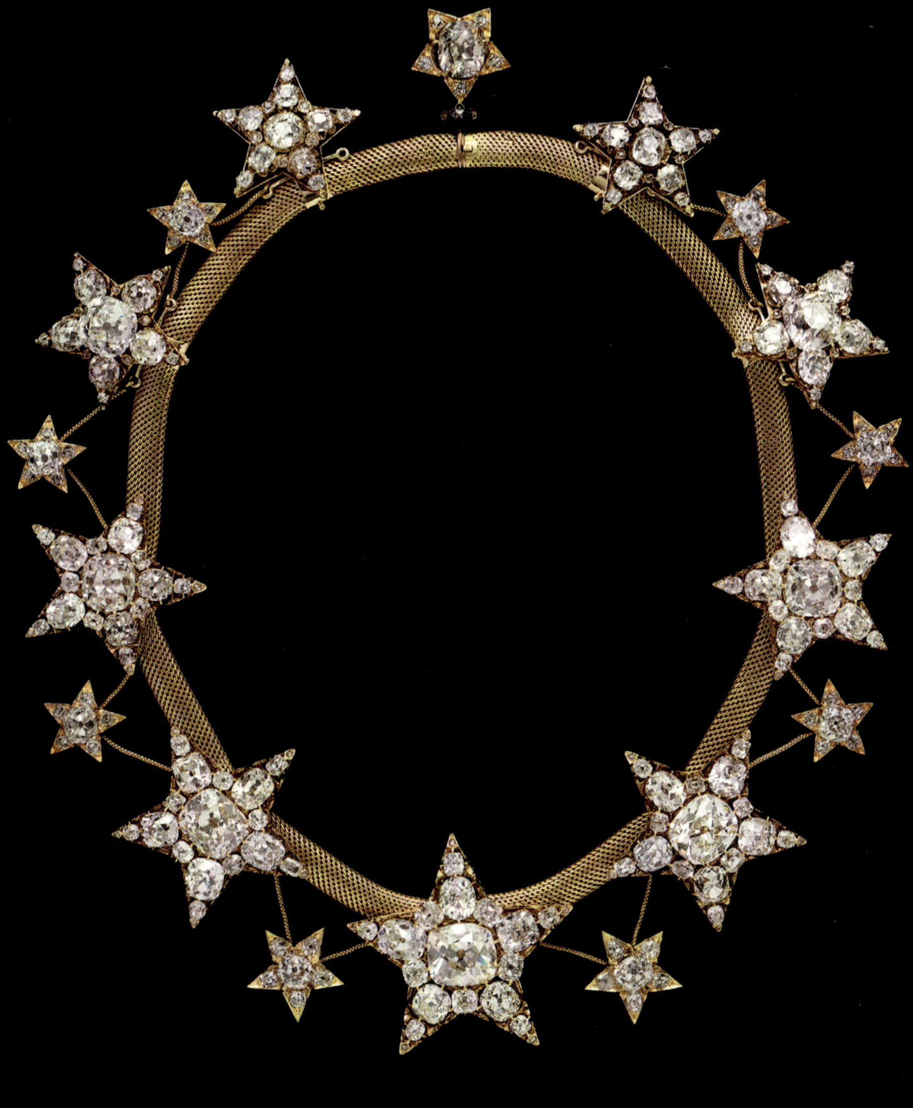

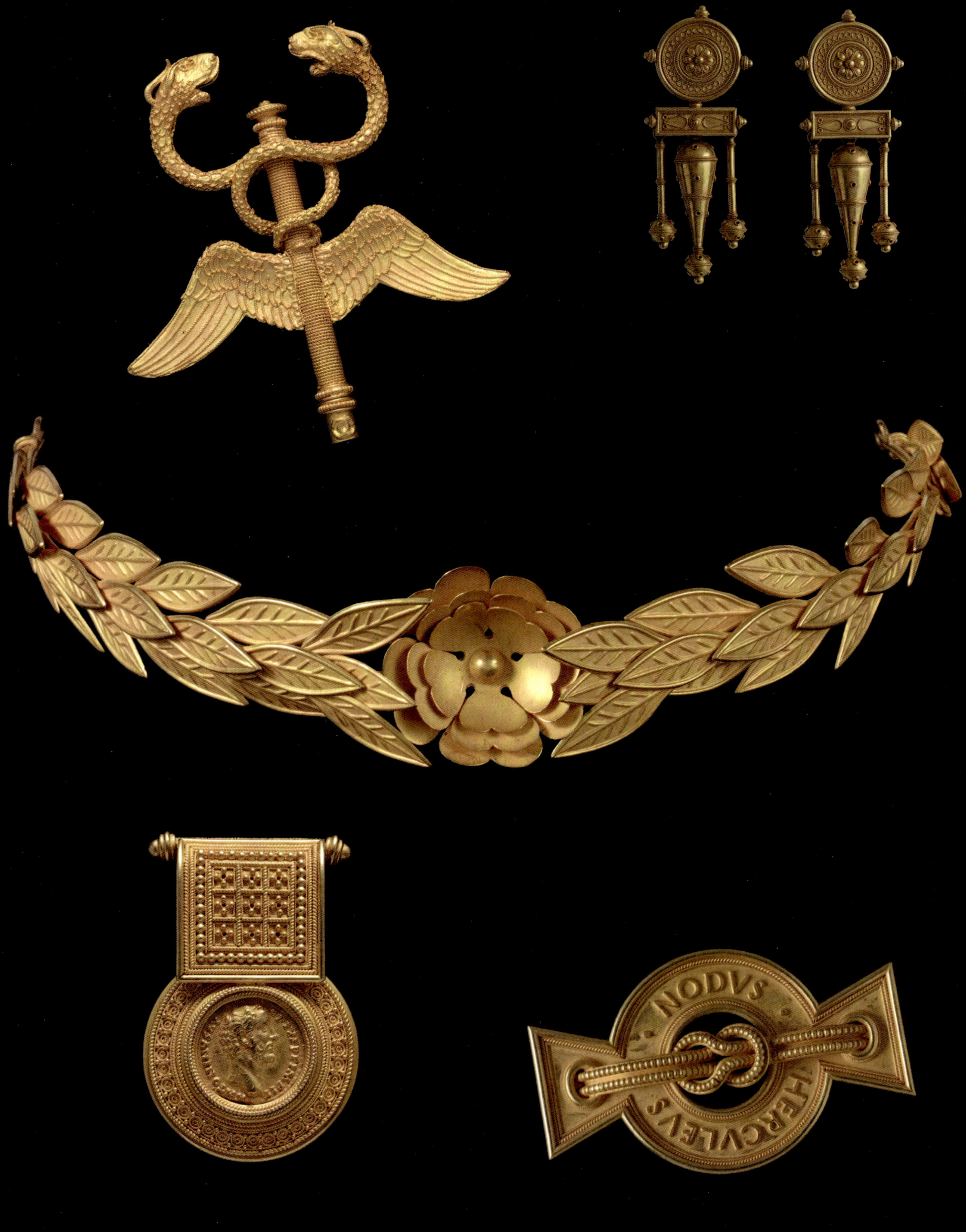
NODVS
HERCVLEVS

father, Carlos enjoyed drawing and painting, and his seascapes acquired a certain reputation, even obtaining a painting prize in Paris.

Headed by monarchs brought up in the values of liberalism, life at the Portuguese court in the second half of the nineteenth century was not very different from that at other European courts, and the royals exerted a measure of influence on the life of the country. They remained, however, intransigent when it came to respecting and maintaining the ideas and political regime for which Pedro IV (1798–1834) had striven. A more reticent figure, Pedro V's view of the country had been critical and intent on change. In addition to taking up his duties as king, Pedro V showed a keen interest in the natural sciences, classical literature, and history, and he kept abreast of the newest theories concerning technology, education, military reform, and modes of communication. His brutally curtailed reign prevented him from putting his ideas into action, leaving the task up to his more expansive as well as more pragmatic brother Luís. Unlike his predecessor, Luís was blessed with a sense of humor that transpired for instance in caricatures in which he poked fun at Portuguese high society. Wide-ranging, his culture was not limited to drawing, painting, and music, but also—as a translator of Shakespeare—extended into literature.

In the political domain, Luís steered the country towards a democratic system based on alternating governments. Although in the end this policy fell short, it did ensure a degree of stability necessary for Portugal's development and paved the way for it to join the European community of nations.

Archaeological jewelry:
laurel diadem, hair pins, pendant, earrings, brooch, necklace, bracelet
c. 1862
Fortunato Pio Castellani (1794–1865)
Palácio Nacional da Ajuda, Lisbon

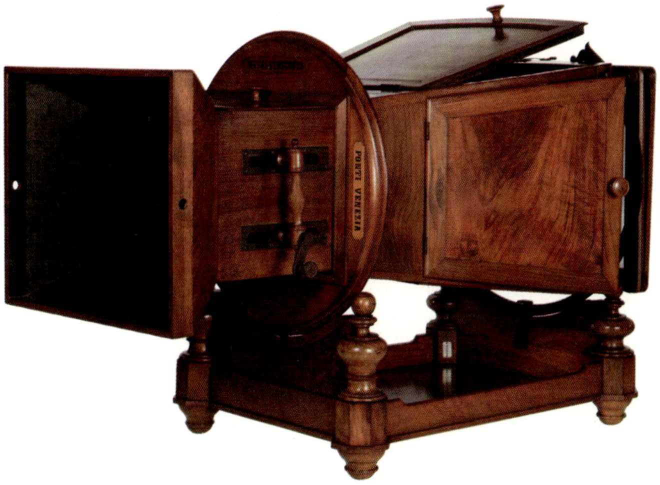

Megalethoscope: a piece of apparatus that allowed photographs to be viewed in three dimensions
1862
Carlo Ponti (1823–1893)
Palácio Nacional da Ajuda, Lisbon

The great silver service of José I (1714–1777), king of Portugal, by François-Thomas Germain (1726–1791)

Spice box
1760–61
Dish cover
1756–62
Terrine and platter
1756–57
Salt cellar
1757–61
François-Thomas Germain
(1726–1791)
Palácio Nacional da Ajuda,
Lisbon

The discovery of immense mines of silver, gold, and gemstones in Brazil in the late seventeenth and early eighteenth centuries swelled Portugal's coffers and significantly increased the resources at the disposal of the Portuguese crown. But the earthquake and fire of 1755 completely destroyed Lisbon and with it the vast royal collections, including the French silverwork King João V had commissioned from Thomas Germain (1673-1748). In 1756 his son, José I, placed an order with the son of the goldsmith François-Thomas Germain, the *orfèvre du Roi* Louis XV working in the galleries of the Louvre, for a large quantity of silver plate. The ensemble is composed of nine hundred pieces in four services for grand banquets, marked with the Portuguese royal coat of arms and engraved with indications of their weight.

The first service included four *terrines* (tureens), four *pots à oille*, and sixteen large dishes with lids. The second and third service featured twenty-five dishes each of various sizes and shapes together with small *hors-d'œuvre* dishes and table candelabra. The fourth and most generously appointed service included plates, cutlery, candelabra, oil servers, spice sets, salt cellars, breadbaskets, etc. The silverware was delivered in several batches beginning in 1757, though the pace slowed down considerably before the goldsmith eventually went bankrupt in 1765. The service was inaugurated at the coronation of Queen Maria, the daughter of José I, on May 13, 1777. Thereafter, the Germain services managed to escape being melted down as they were transported with the Portuguese royal family to Brazil. Most of it was then dispatched back to Portugal in 1821 by King João VI, the grandson of José I.

Although incomplete—above all, because the great centerpiece that was meant to accompany the dessert service was never made—this French silver service, one of the most important in the world and now preserved in the prestigious Portuguese state collections, represented the largest order ever placed by any Portuguese sovereign with the goldsmiths of the kings of France.

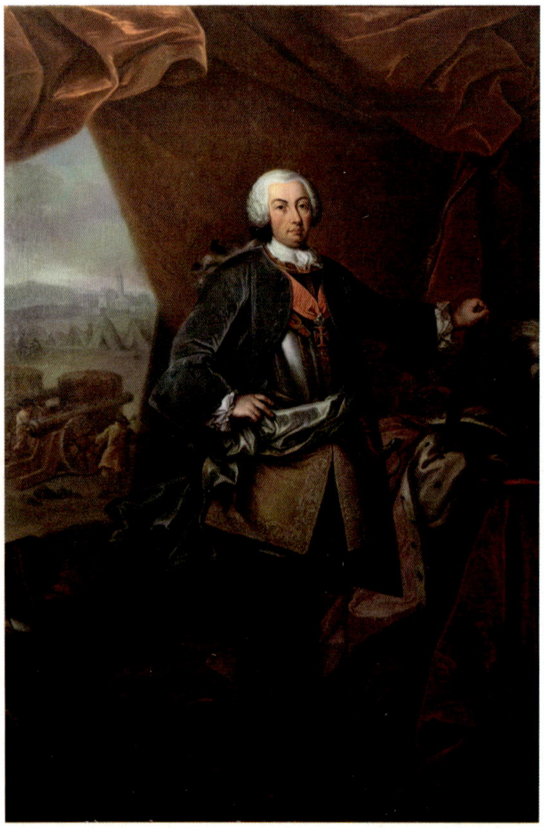

José I (1714-1777),
King of Portugal
Eighteenth century
Palácio Nacional da Ajuda,
Lisbon

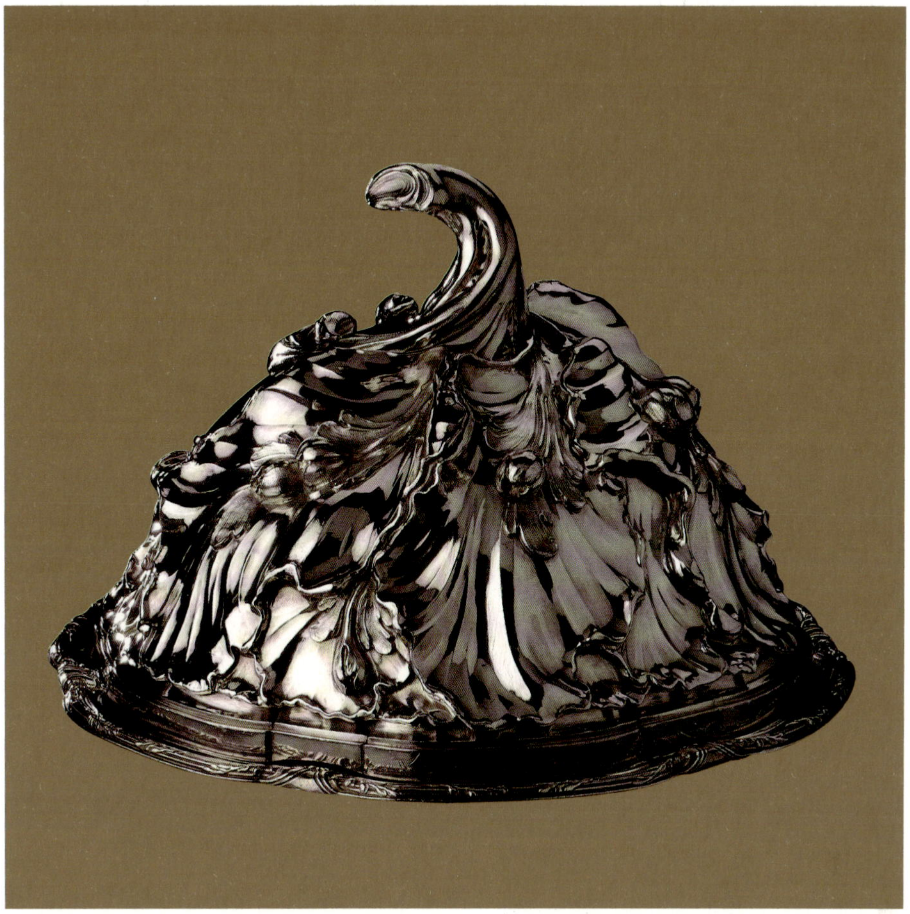
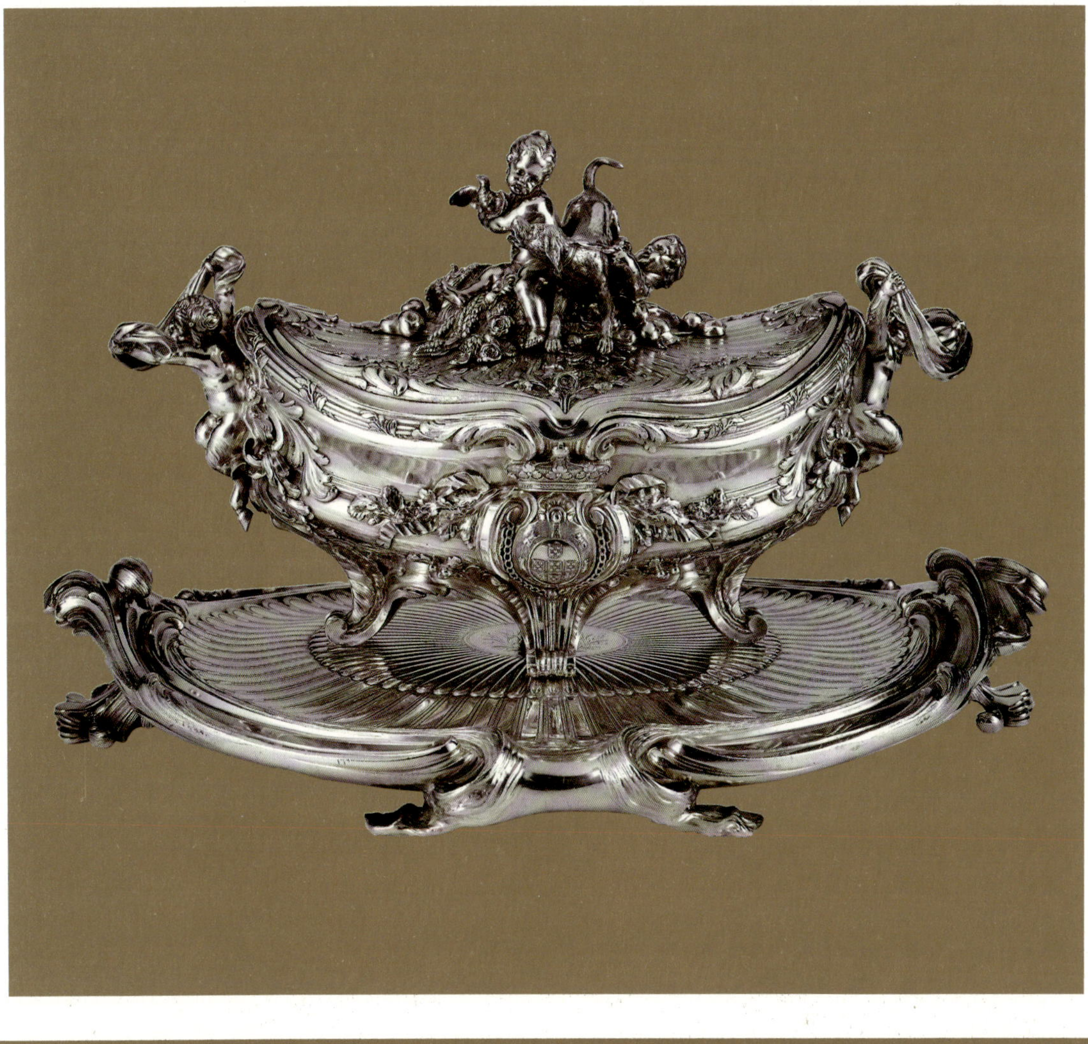
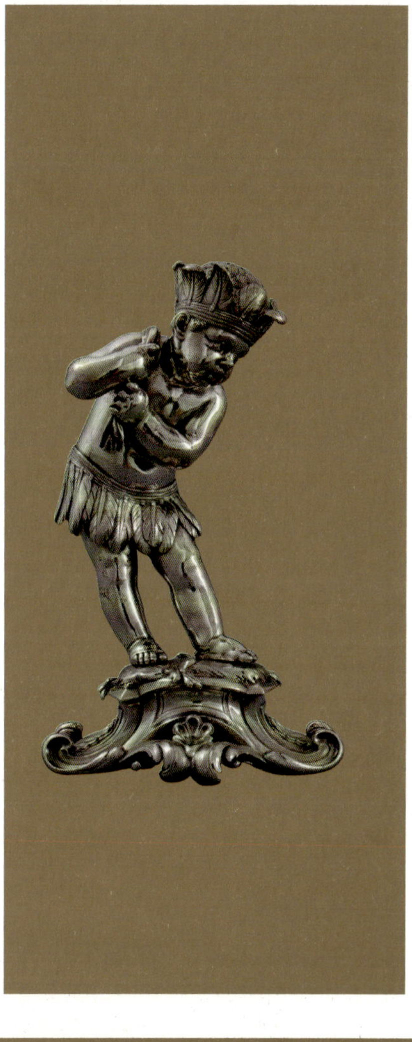

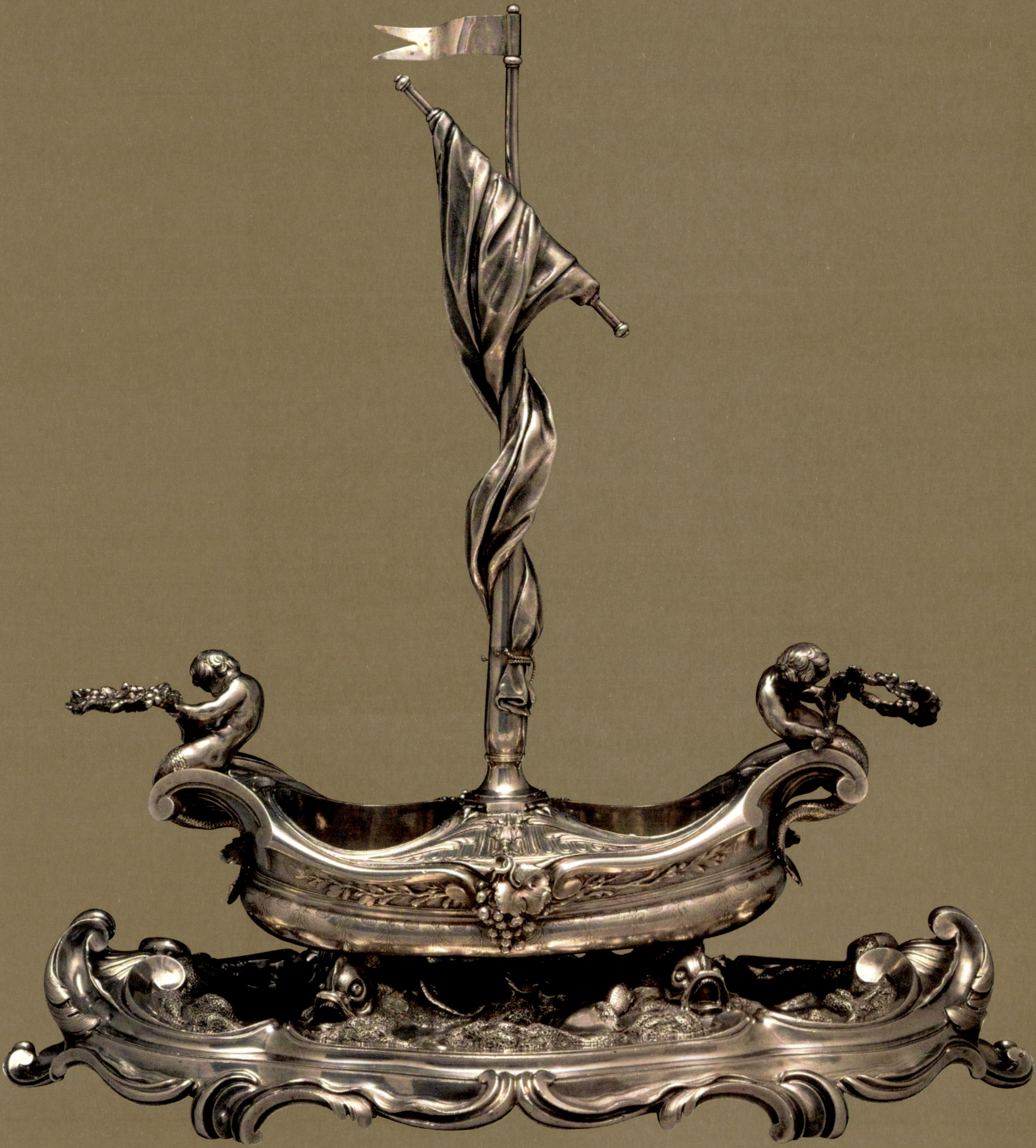

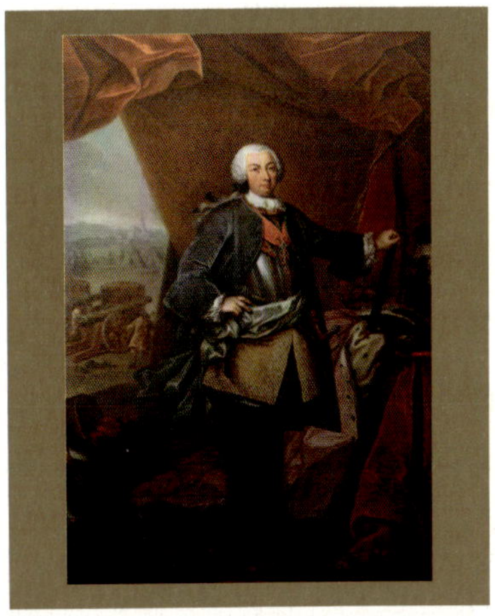

José I (1714–1777), King of Portugal
Eighteenth century
Oil on canvas
321 × 184 cm (inc. frame)
Palácio Nacional da Ajuda, Lisbon
Inv. 3787

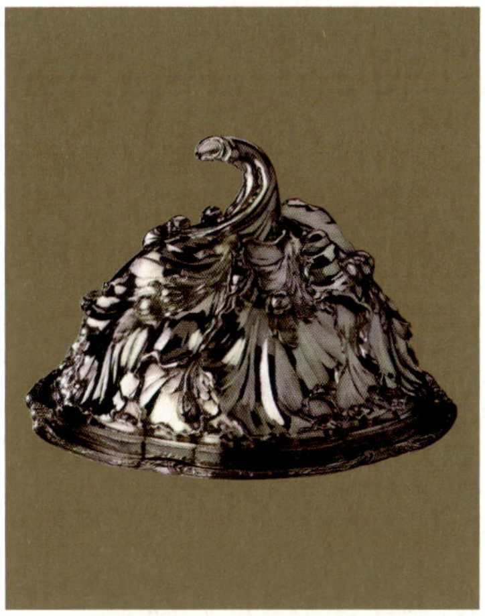

Dish cover
1756
François-Thomas Germain
(1726–1791)
Silver
23 × 37 cm
Palácio Nacional da Ajuda, Lisbon
Inv. 5360-5365

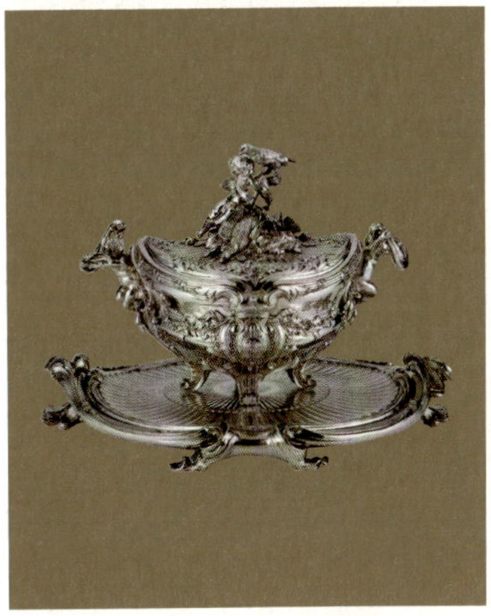

Soup bowl and platter
1756–57
François-Thomas Germain
(1726–1791)
Silver
36 × 46 cm; L. (platter) 59 cm
Palácio Nacional da Ajuda, Lisbon
Inv. 5350-5351

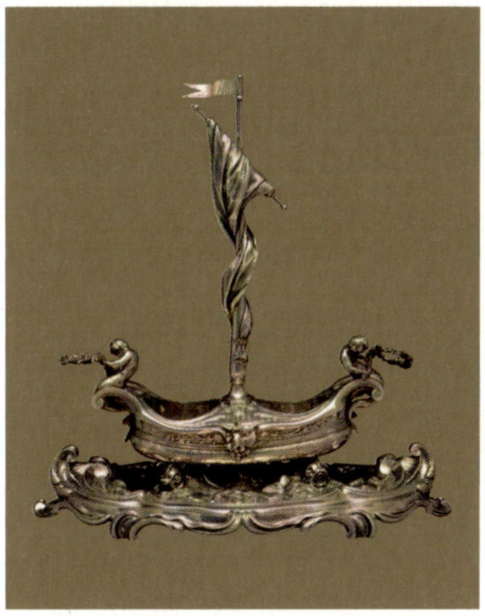

Oil bottle holder
1759
François-Thomas Germain
(1726–1791)
Silver
42 × 39 cm
Palácio Nacional da Ajuda, Lisbon
Inv. 5390

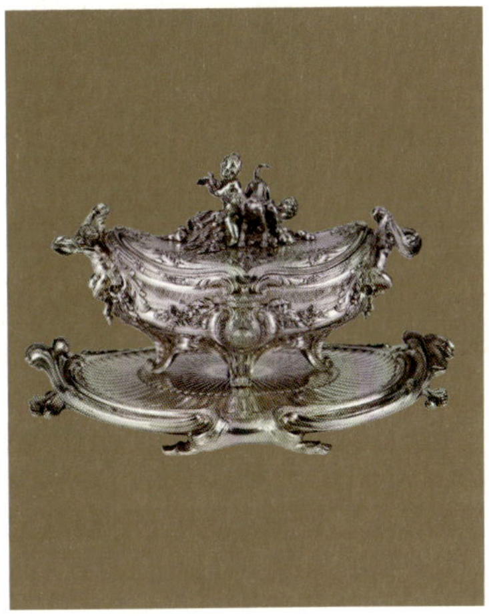

Terrine and platter
1756–57
François-Thomas Germain
(1726–1791)
Silver
H. 29 cm; L. (platter) 58.4 cm
Palácio Nacional da Ajuda, Lisbon
Inv. 5352-5353

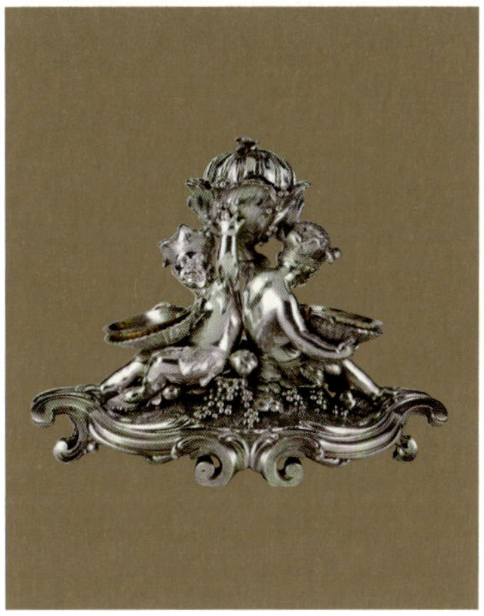

Spice box
1760–61
François-Thomas Germain
(1726–1791)
Silver
24.2 × 31 × 18 cm
Palácio Nacional da Ajuda, Lisbon
Inv. 5386

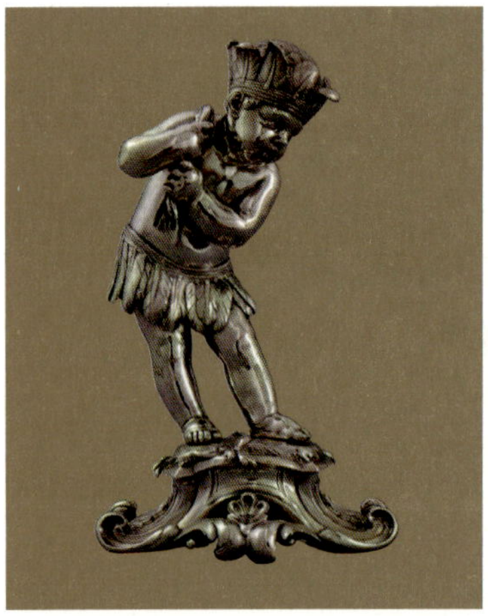

Two salt cellars
1757–61
François-Thomas Germain
(1726–1791)
Silver
20.7 x 12.2 cm
Palácio Nacional da Ajuda, Lisbon
Inv. 5381-5385

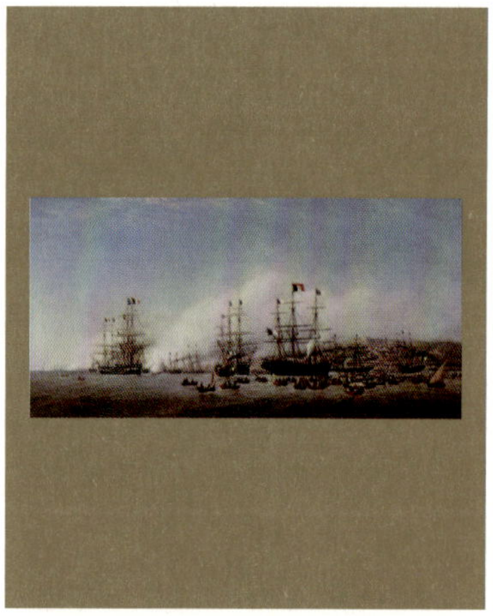

***The Arrival of Queen Maria Pia in Lisbon aboard the Corvette* Bartolomeu Dias**
1863
João Pedroso Gomes da Silva
(1825–1890)
Oil on canvas
103 × 188 cm
Palácio Nacional da Ajuda, Lisbon
Inv. 1334

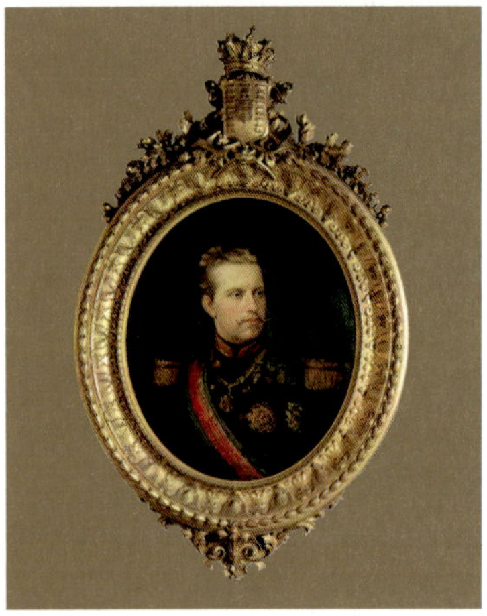

Luís I (1838–1889), King of Portugal
c. 1865
Attributed to Michele Gordigiani
(1830–1909)
Oil on canvas
140 × 88 cm
Palácio Nacional da Ajuda, Lisbon
Inv. 2391

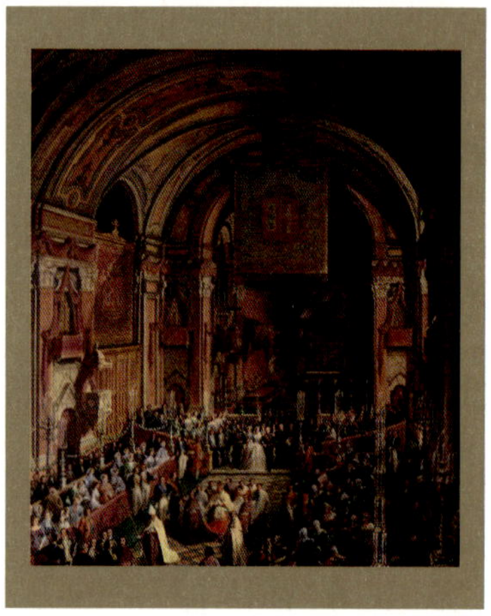

The Wedding of Luís I and Maria Pia
1864
Antonio Manuel da Fonseca
(1796–1890)
Oil on canvas
149 × 127 cm
Palácio Nacional da Ajuda, Lisbon
Inv. 1335

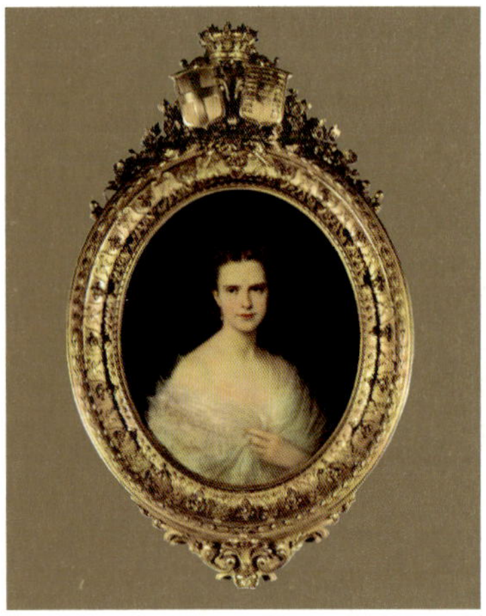

Maria Pia (1847–1911), Queen of Portugal
c. 1865
Attributed to Michele Gordigiani
(1830–1909)
Oil on canvas
140 × 88 cm
Palácio Nacional da Ajuda, Lisbon
Inv. 2390

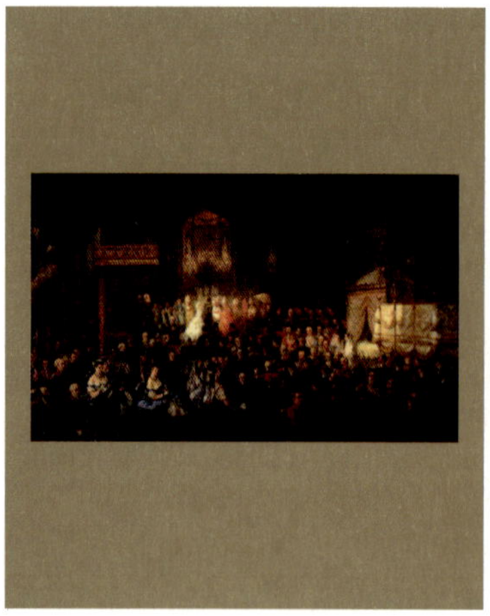

Baptism of the Infante Carlos (1863–1908), Future King of Portugal
c. 1865
Pierre-Henri-Théodore Tetar van Elven (1828–1908)
Oil on canvas
94 × 135 cm
Palácio Nacional da Ajuda, Lisbon
Inv. 1336

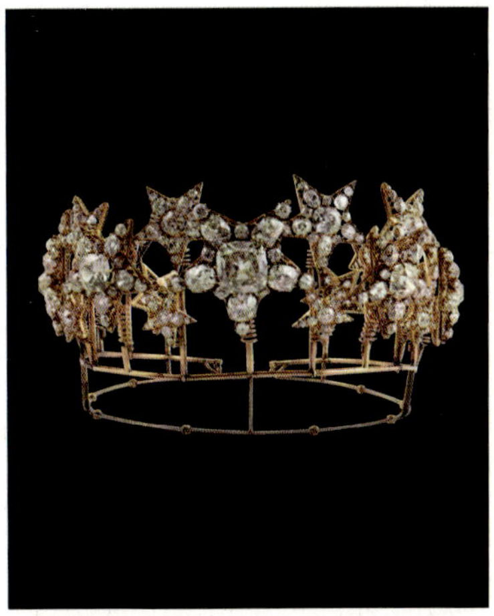

Diamond diadem belonging to Queen Maria Pia
1863–66, Lisbon
Estevão da Sousa
Gold, silver, diamonds, pink diamonds
9.3 × 15 cm
Palácio Nacional da Ajuda, Lisbon
Inv. 4722

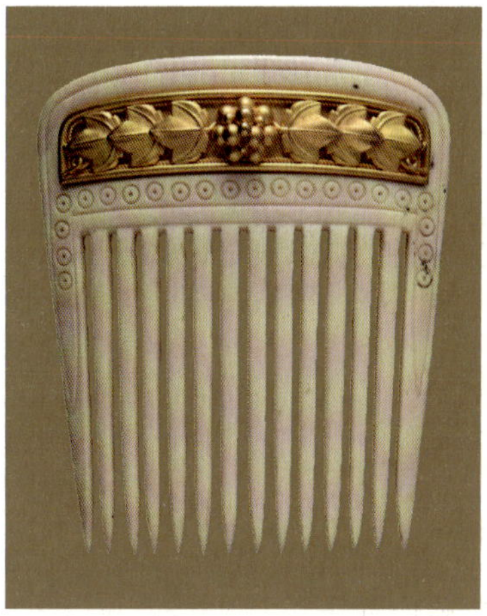

Comb
c. 1861
Gold, ivory
9 × 7.5 cm
Palácio Nacional da Ajuda, Lisbon
Inv. 52565

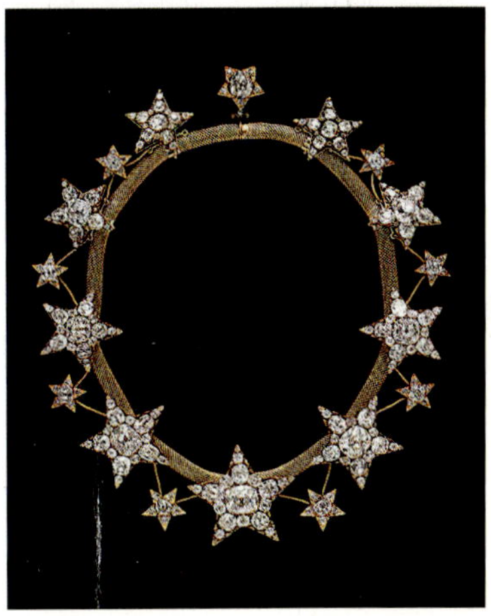

Diamond necklace belonging to Queen Maria Pia
1865, Lisbon
Estevão da Sousa
Gold, silver, diamonds, pink diamonds
42.5 × 3.9 cm
Palácio Nacional da Ajuda, Lisbon
Inv. 4724

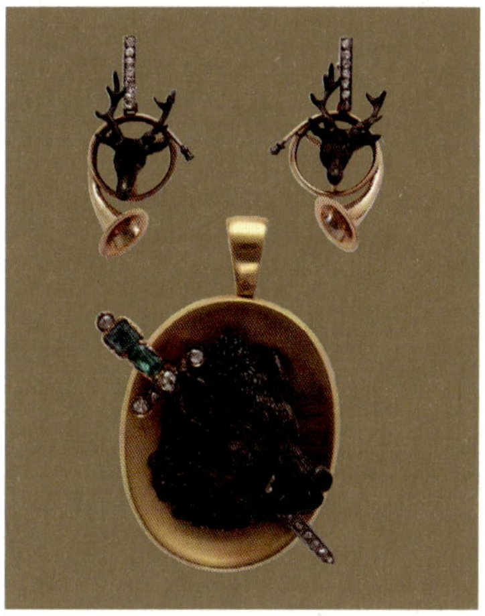

Queen Maria Pia's hunting jewelry
Late nineteenth century
Palácio Nacional da Ajuda, Lisbon
Boar pendant
Gold, ruby, oxidized silver, emeralds, diamonds
Inv. 52147
Pair of stag and horn earrings
Gold, oxidized silver, diamonds
Inv. 52147/A-B

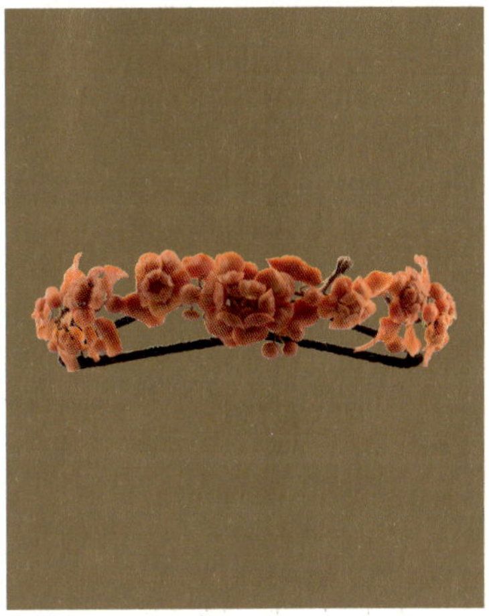

Coral diadem
Mid–late nineteenth century
Gold, coral, velvet
4.5 × 19.8 cm
Palácio Nacional da Ajuda, Lisbon
Inv. 52577

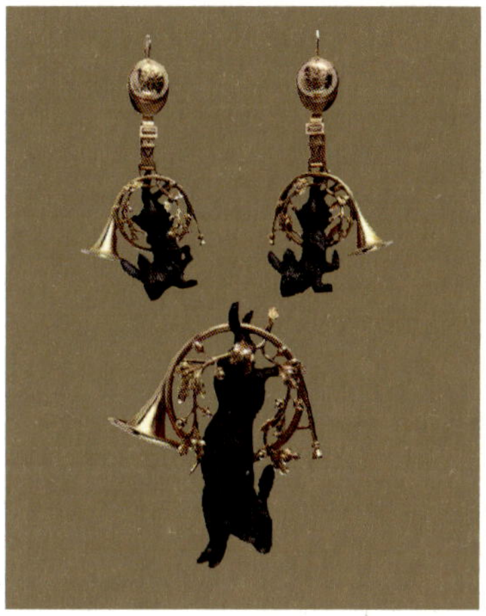

Queen Maria Pia's hunting jewelry
Late nineteenth century
Palácio Nacional da Ajuda, Lisbon
Hare pendant
Gold, oxidized silver, ruby
Inv. 52146
Pair of earrings
Gold, oxidized silver, ruby
Inv. 52146/A-B

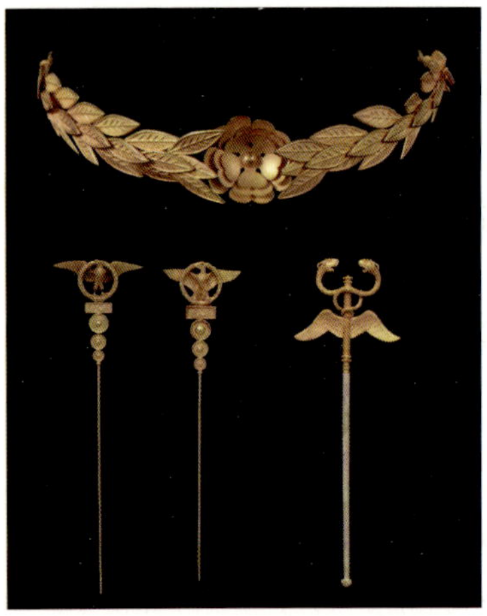

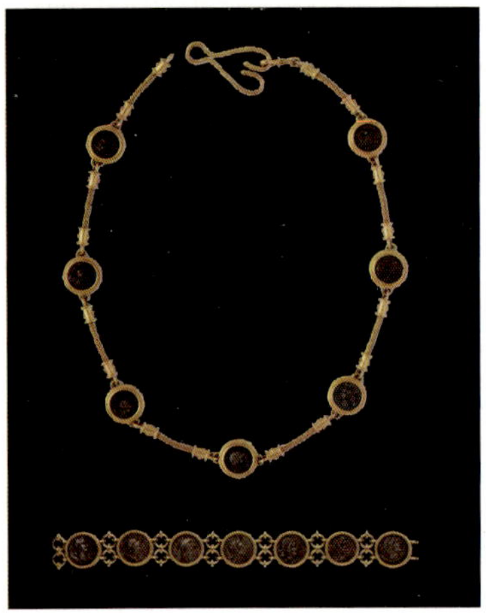

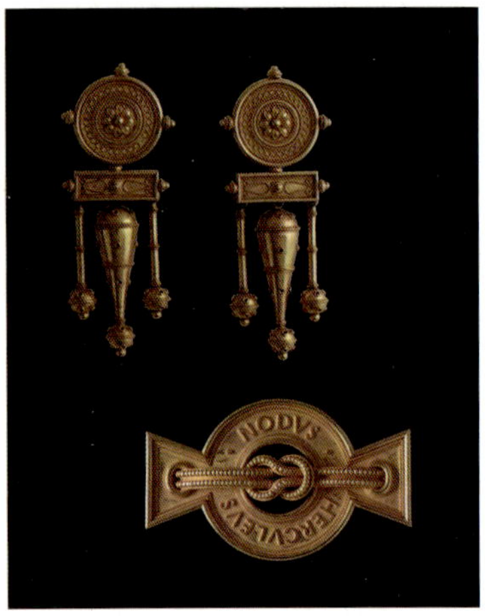

Archaeological jewelry
1862
Fortunato Pio Castellani
(1794–1865), Rome
Palácio Nacional da Ajuda, Lisbon
Laurel diadem
Gold
Inv. 52548
Hair pins
Gold, ivory
Inv. 52569
Two imperial eagle hairpins
Gold
Inv. 52570-52571
Pendant
Gold, bronze, crystal
Inv. 52563
Earrings, brooch, necklace, bracelet
Gold
Inv. 52558-52559 (earrings),
52564 (brooch), 52572 (necklace),
52568 (bracelet)

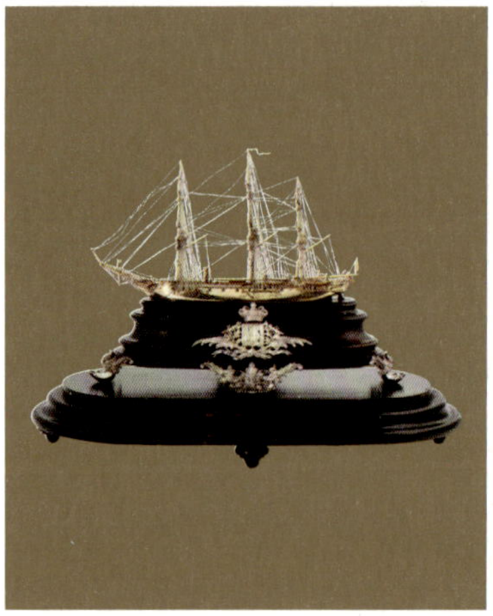

Model of the royal corvette *Bartolomeu Dias*
c. 1881
Silver, wood
35 × 51 cm
Palácio Nacional da Ajuda, Lisbon
Inv. 858

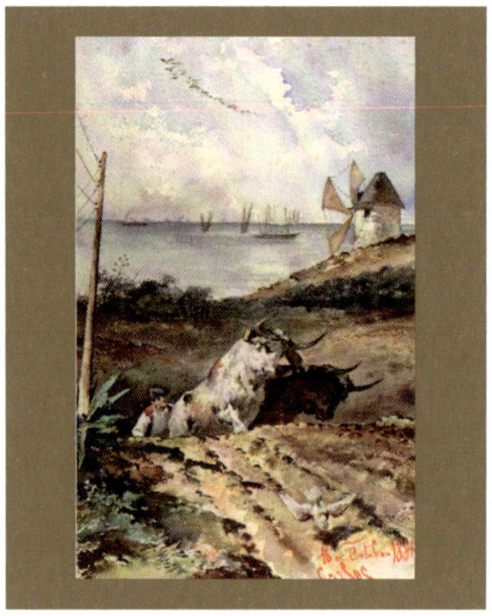

Seascape by Don Carlos
Late nineteenth century
Watercolor
Palácio Nacional da Ajuda, Lisbon

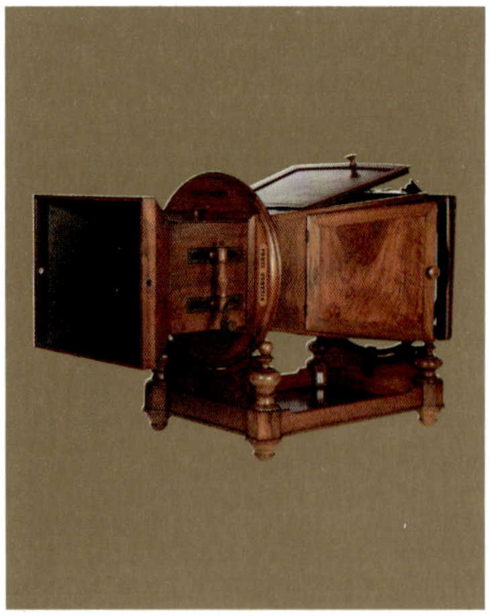

Megalethoscope
1862
Carlo Ponti (1823–1893), Venice
Wood, glass, metal
73 × 90 × 49 cm
Palácio Nacional da Ajuda, Lisbon
Inv. 51282

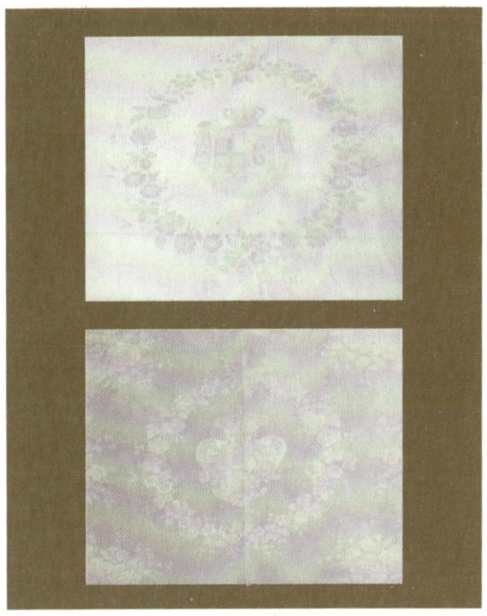

Tablecloth and twelve serviettes with the royal arms of Portugal and Savoy produced for the wedding of Maria Pia
Nineteenth century
250 x 1.39 cm (tablecloth)
Palácio Nacional da Ajuda, Lisbon
Inv. 35078, 37761 to 37772

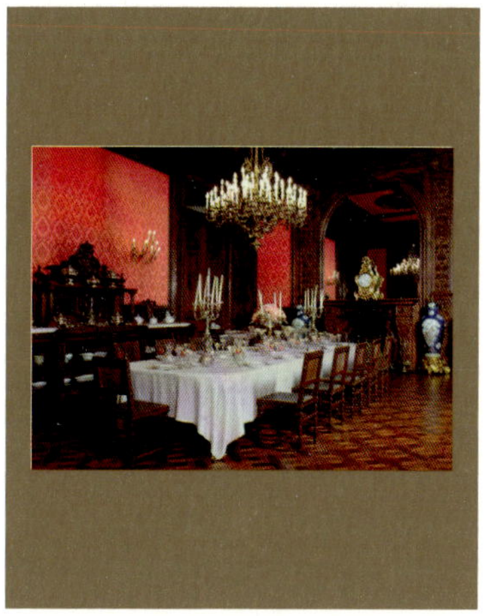

Twelve plates from the "Casquinha" service with flowers, fruits and birds
ca 1824-1840
Edouard Honoré Manufactory, Champoux
D. 22,6 cm
Palácio Nacional da Ajuda, Lisbon
Inv. 54582-85 à 87, 89-90 à 92
Inv. 58232 à 35

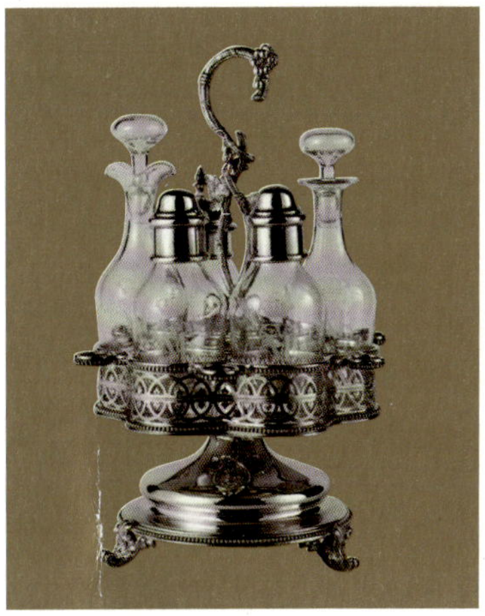

Silver tableware for the wedding of King Luís I and Queen Maria Pia, with the Portuguese royal arms
c. 1862, Paris
Jean-François Veyrat
(1840–late nineteenth century)
Silver
Palácio Nacional da Ajuda, Lisbon
Oil and vinegar set
Inv. 50723 A-F and 50724-50729
Two covered dishes on a stove
Inv. 50706-50709
Mustard pot
Inv. 50704
Two double salt cellars
Inv. 50702-50703
Spice spoon, mustard spoon, and four salt spoons
Inv. 9693-9694 and 9689-9692
Serving cutlery
Inv. 9821-22 and 9825-26
Salad servers
Inv. 9823-24
Asparagus tongs, ladle, and fish slice
Inv. 9818-9820
Cutlery set: spoons, forks, and knives
Inv. 9635-9646, 9647-9676 and 9695-9724
Dessert cutlery set
Inv. 9731-9742, 9743-9754 and 9755-9766
Ice cream spoon set
Inv. 9791-9802
Four carafe coasters
Inv. 50738-50743
Two large fruit bowls
Inv. 50762-50763
Two fruit bowls
Inv. 50758-50761
Two candelabras
Inv. 3771-3772

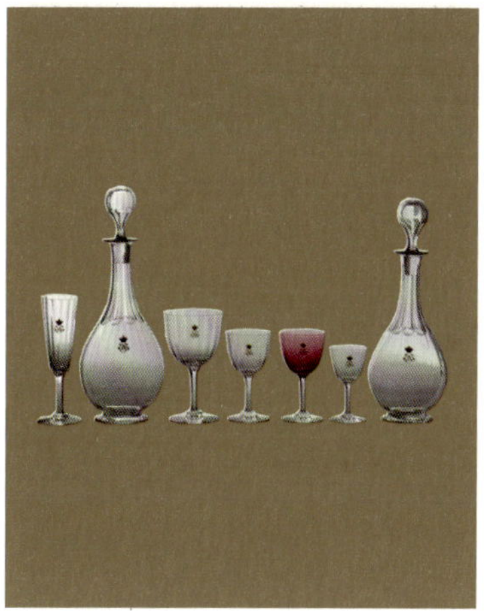

Twelve sets of five glasses and four carafes with the Portuguese royal arms
1880–94
Crystal
Palácio Nacional da Ajuda, Lisbon
Water glasses
H. 15.5 cm
Inv. 22897/108-119
Red wine glasses
H. 12.5 cm
Inv. 22897/144-155
Rhine wine glasses
H. 12.5 cm
Inv. 22897/181-192
Flutes
H. 17.8 cm
Inv. 22897/419-430
Port glasses
H. 10.5 cm
Inv. 22897/234-245
Carafes
H. 33.5 cm and 31.5 cm
Inv. 22897/2-3-36-37
and 22897/80-81-93-101
Four bottle coasters
D. 15.4 cm
Inv. 50724-50727 (base)
and 50738-50741

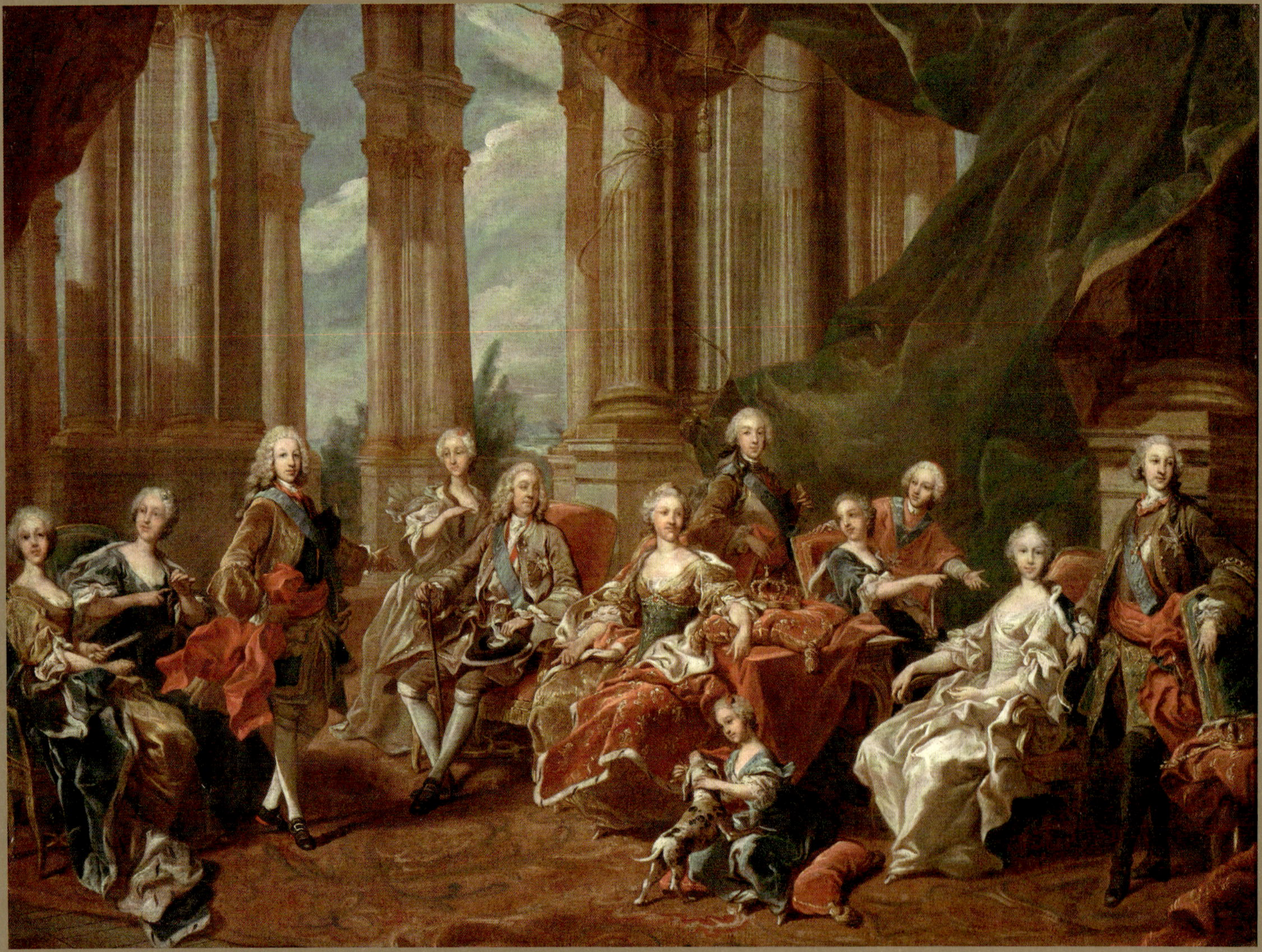

SPAIN

Felipe V (1683–1746) and Isabella Farnese (1692–1766)

King Felipe V of Spain, Isabella Farnese and their Family
c. 1737
Louis-Michel Van Loo
(1707–1771)
Musées des Châteaux
de Versailles et de Trianon,
Versailles

Felipe V and Isabella Farnese
The Spanish monarchy in the first half of the eighteenth century

José Luís Gaspar Sancho

Reigning between 1714 and 1746, Felipe V de Bourbon and his second wife, Isabella Farnese, saw eye to eye both in their private life and with regard to the exercise of their sovereign power, restoring the prestige the Spanish monarchy enjoyed during the Old Regime. They also bequeathed to their country a great number of princes, who ensured not only security and continuity for the Bourbon dynasty in Spain, but also founded new branches in Naples and Parma, and forged international alliances. Bound by a wide range of common interests, both parties considered it their duty to maintain the position of Spain among the chief powers of Europe and also harbored ambitions to regain the lands forfeited in Italy following the War of the Spanish Succession. A point of honor for Felipe V, this goal chimed in perfectly with the dynastic and maternal ambitions of Isabella, who was as concerned for her hereditary rights in Italy as she was for ensuring crowns for her children. Indeed, the existence of three sons born from Felipe's first marriage precluded her or any of her offspring from ever inheriting the Spanish throne.

Felipe (Versailles, 1683–Madrid, 1746), duke of Anjou, was the second son of the Grand Dauphin and thus grandson of Louis XIV; he had been brought up far from the glare of court, under the wing of the duke of Beauvilliers and with Fénelon as tutor. In 1700, the will of Carlos II, the last Habsburg king of Spain, acknowledged him as sole heir to the Spanish monarchy. In ratifying this claim, the Sun King renounced early treaties that partitioned the Spanish territories. This marked the beginning not only of the reign of the first Bourbon king of Spain, but also of a process which, by the end of the war of succession, led to the Peace of Utrecht. In the meantime, Felipe V, king of Spain already acclaimed as the "Catholic King," took the oath in all his territories, and, at the beginning of 1701, settled in Madrid, the seat of the court. The fair-haired, robust young man of seventeen, a fine horseman, wasted no time contracting a worthy marriage.

Due to both his nature—stemming mainly from his Bavarian mother—and his solitary upbringing, Felipe suffered from a tendency to introversion and

Felipe V, King of Spain (1683–1746)
c. 1737
Louis-Michel Van Loo (1707–1771)
Musées des Châteaux de Versailles et de Trianon, Versailles

Isabella Farnese (1692–1766), Queen of Spain, Wife of Felipe V
c. 1737
Louis-Michel Van Loo (1707–1771)
Musées des Châteaux de Versailles et de Trianon, Versailles

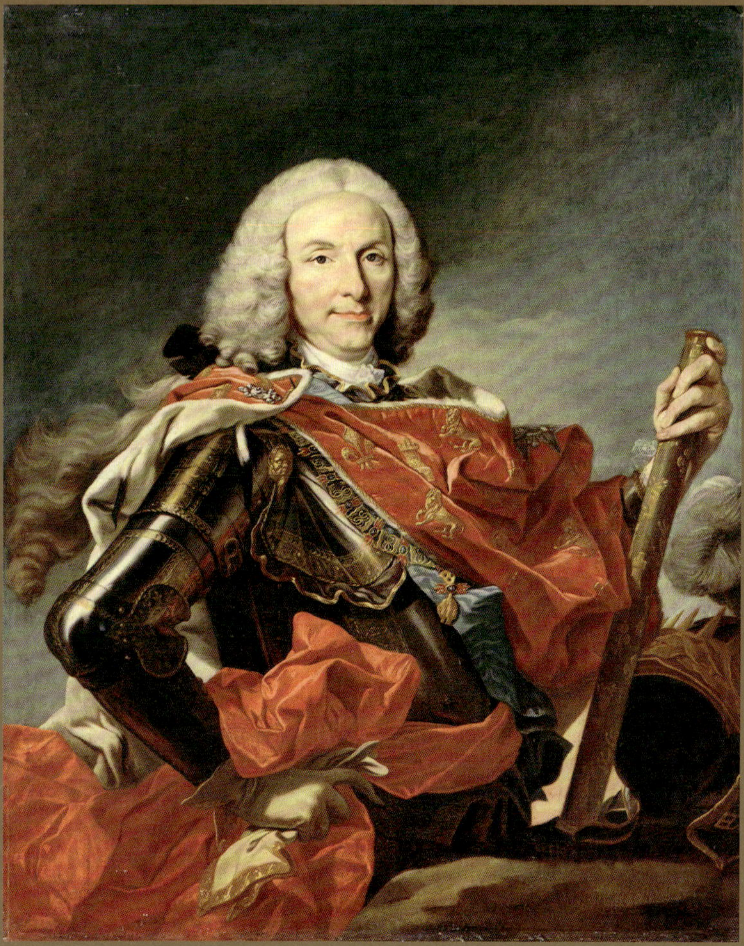

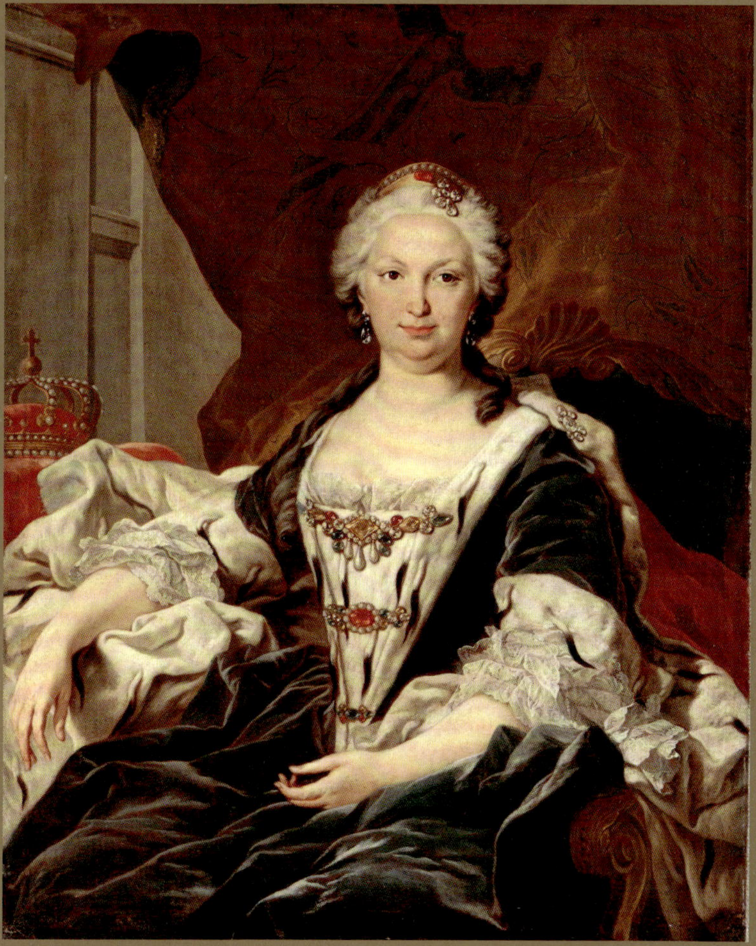

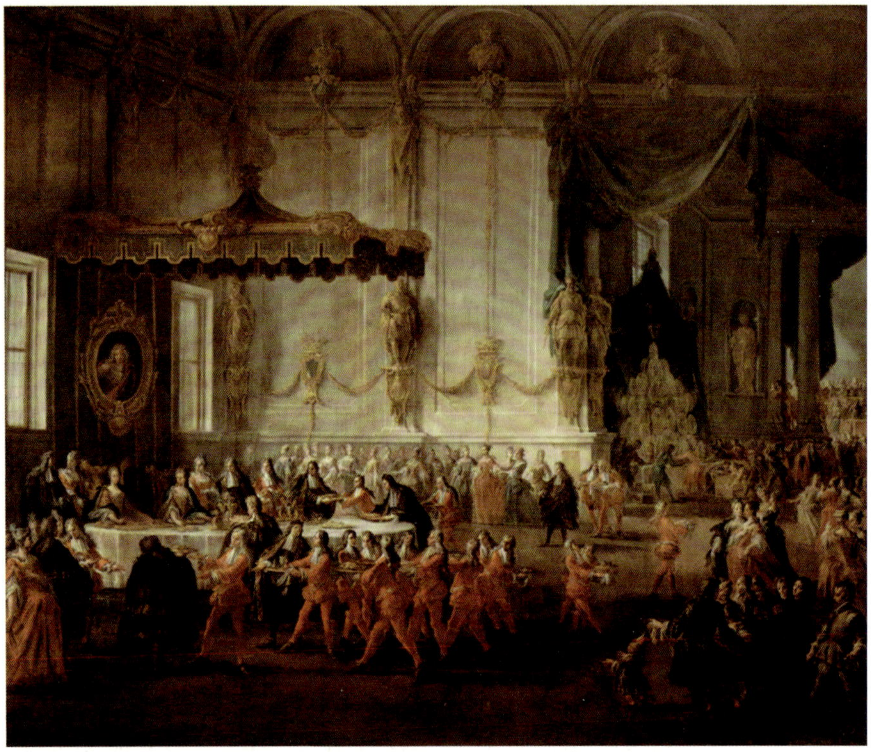

melancholy. His temperament, joined to profound and sincere piety, made him a dyed-in-the-wool monogamist, who trusted his wife implicitly. In 1701, having barely ascended the throne, he married Maria Luisa Gabriella of Savoy (the sister-in-law of his elder brother, the duke of Bourgogne), who at the time was little more than a child. She had been nobly brought up at the court of Turin and once in Spain benefited from the guidance of her lady companion, Marie, princesse des Ursins. The Piedmontese queen proved an exemplary wife during the difficult years of the War of the Spanish Succession. Unfortunately, she never lived to see an upturn in fortunes as she died prematurely on February 14, 1714, after giving Felipe four sons, two of whom died while still young; the other two became the kings Luís I and Fernando VI.

Felipe V was not long in taking another a wife, however, and the very year of Maria Luisa's death, he contracted a marriage with Isabella Farnese, who was not only heiress to the duchies of Parma and Piacenza but also held hereditary rights over Tuscany. In 1716 she gave birth to their first child, Carlos, followed by Mariana Victoria (who wedded the crown prince of Portugal in 1729), Felipe (who, the same year, took as his wife the eldest daughter of Louis XV, becoming duke of Parma in 1748), Maria Teresa (who, in 1744, married the son of Louis XV, the Dauphin, only to die in 1746), Maria Antonia (who wedded the future Vittorio

Banquet for the Proxy Wedding of Isabella Farnese to Felipe V in Parma
1714
Lo Spolverini (1657–1734)
Civiche Raccolte d'Arte del Comune di Parma, Parma

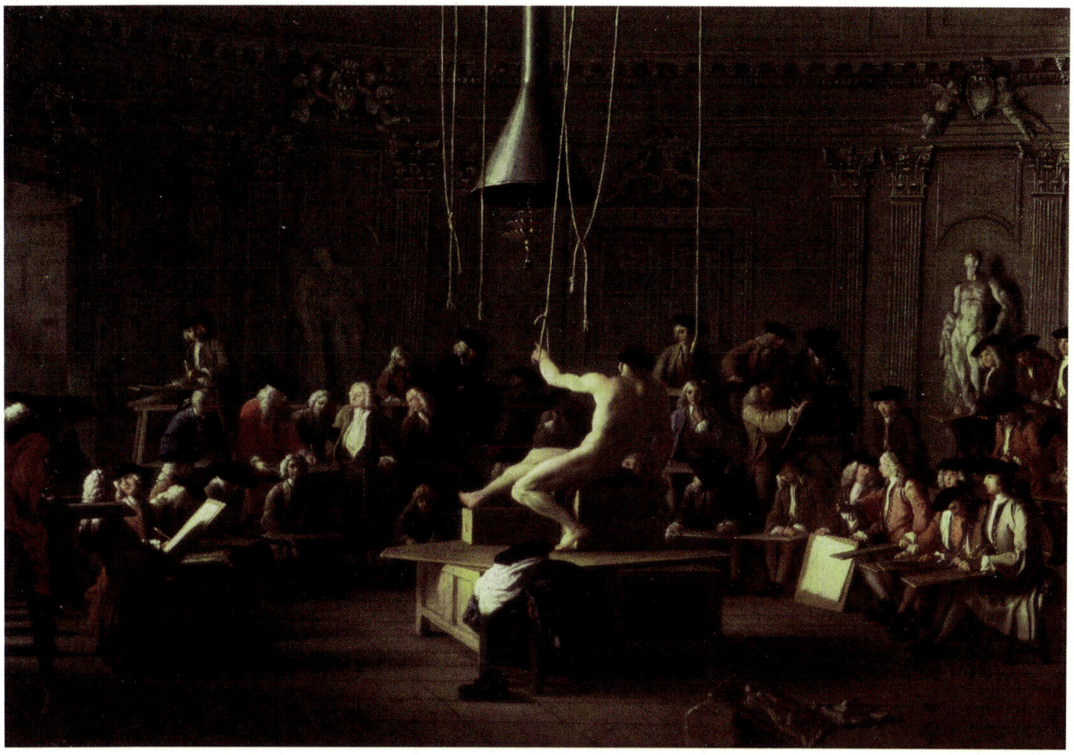

Amedeo III of Savoy in 1750), and finally Luís, known as the Cardinal-Infante.

The political and dynastic ambitions entertained by Felipe V and Isabella Farnese for their children and for their rung on the ladder of power in Europe are clear from the various group portraits by French painters at their court —successively Michel-Ange Houasse, Jean Ranc, and Louis-Michel Van Loo— who all devised ideas for large family pictures. The only composition to be finished, and in any case the most revealing, hangs in the Prado. Both the picture itself, completed in 1743 by Louis-Michel Van Loo, and the preparatory studies (presenting minor compositional variants) depict the complete contingent of the couple's children, together with other members of the family.

On the international stage, the sovereigns succeeded—though at the cost of enormous sacrifices occasioned by armed conflict—in partially rectifying the situation created in Europe by the war of succession, after which the Spanish Crown was shorn of the Netherlands and its Italian territories. Taking their cue for their monarchical government from the French administration, in private and at court, Felipe and Isabella maintained a delicate but effective balance, well-adapted to the problematic character of the king. Their palaces and the works of art that adorned them constituted a perfect backdrop to a way of life essentially regulated by the seasons. They also convey an eloquent image of the might of the

The Drawing Academy
Eighteenth century
MICHEL-ANGE HOUASSE
(1680–1730)
Palacio Real,
Patrimonio Nacional,
Madrid

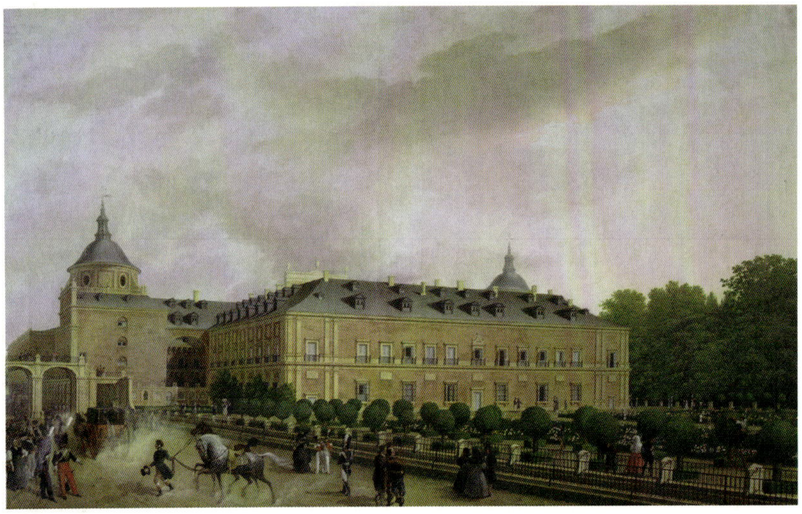

two monarchs, in which cosmopolitan taste, inflected by French and Italian models, reflects both dynastic links and political aspirations.

Felipe's melancholy soon compelled him to retreat from everyday affairs. He built the new royal residence La Granja de San Ildefonso and moved there in 1724, having abdicated on January 10 in favor of his son, Luís I. Scarcely six months later, however, the new king died and the royal couple were obliged to return to the throne. Subsequently, life at the increasingly peculiar court was dominated by the king's mood swings and by the queen's efforts to distract him. The sovereigns, and with them their entire family, servants, and secretaries of state, only spent about eight weeks at various times of year in Madrid, spending the remainder in the various royal residences: spring in Aranjuez, summer in La Granja de San Ildefonso, autumn in the Escorial and winter in the Pardo. They would return to the capital only in December, during Holy Week, and for a fortnight in July. The Habsburgs also frequented these palaces, but at other times of the year and for three months a year in all, spending the remainder of the year, including the summer, in Madrid. This rhythm explains the growth of gardens and palaces dedicated to the court's seasonal existence under Felipe and Isabella. The palace that most clearly shows the imprint of the royal couple is La Granja, whose formal gardens transposed a taste for Louis XIV and the French Regency onto a royal country retreat in the Sierra of Segovia. The fountains were intended to outdo those of Versailles and, with decorations carved by French artists who had worked at Marly, they seem to succeed. Turning their backs on the blooming of a specifically Spanish baroque decorative art, the court opted instead for a more cosmopolitan aesthetics in painting and the applied arts, while the Italian model prevailed in music and architecture. Felipe and Isabella called on the talents of some of the most famous European artists of the time, from the castrato Farinelli to the architect Filippo Juvarra, who in 1735 was commissioned to rebuild the new royal palace in Madrid, its predecessor having burned down in a fire. The royal couple thus imparted an indelible stamp on both court taste and academic art in the second half of the century.

The Royal Palace of Aranjuez
Nineteenth century
Fernando Brambilla
(1763–1834)
Patrimonio Nacional, Madrid

The Pardo Palace
1720–24
Michel-Ange Houasse
(1680–1730)
Palacio Real de Riofrío, Patrimonio Nacional, San Ildefonso

The Monk's Garden at El Escorial
Eighteenth century
Michel-Ange Houasse
(1680–1730)
Palacio de la Moncloa, Patrimonio Nacional, Madrid

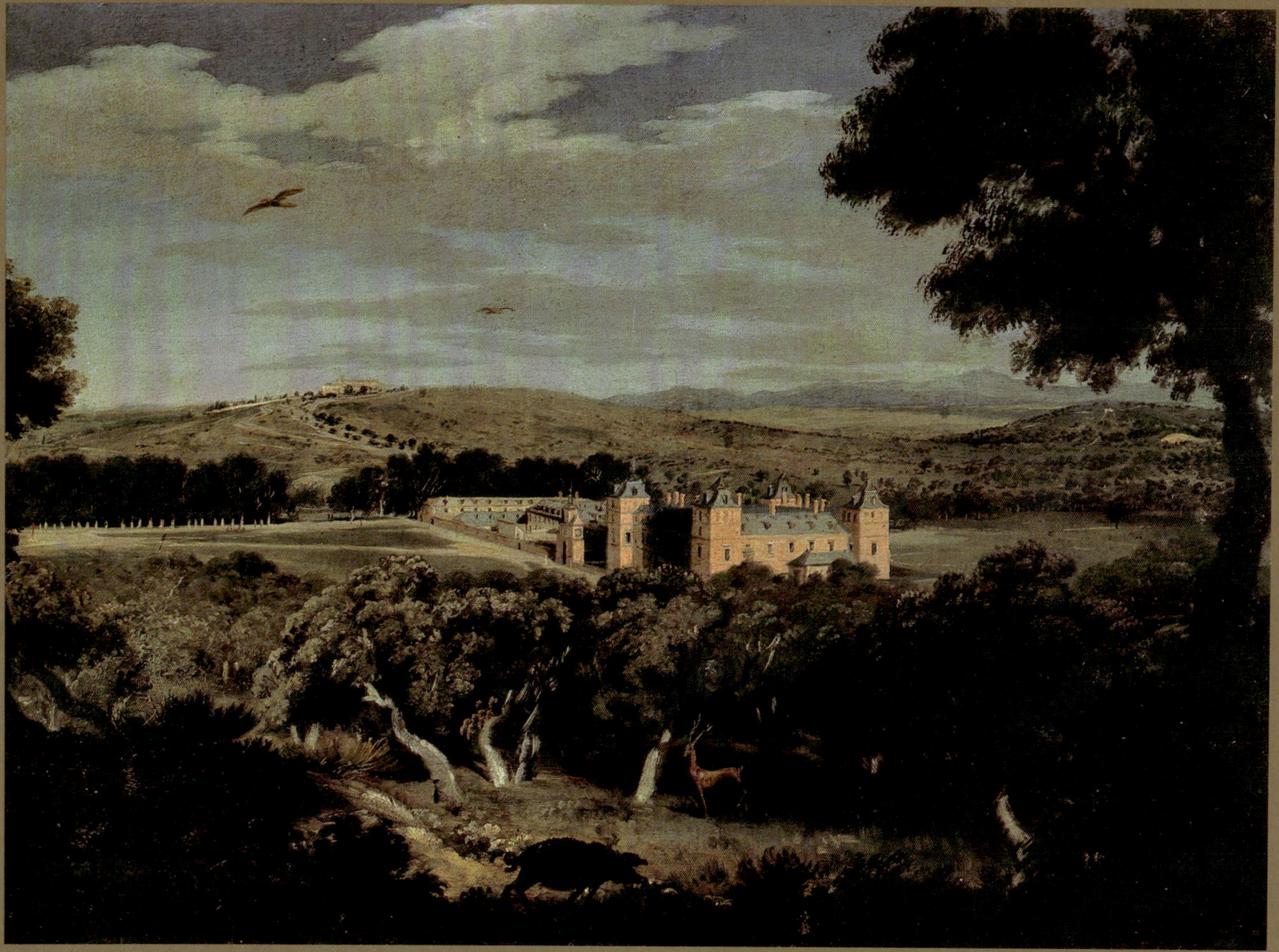

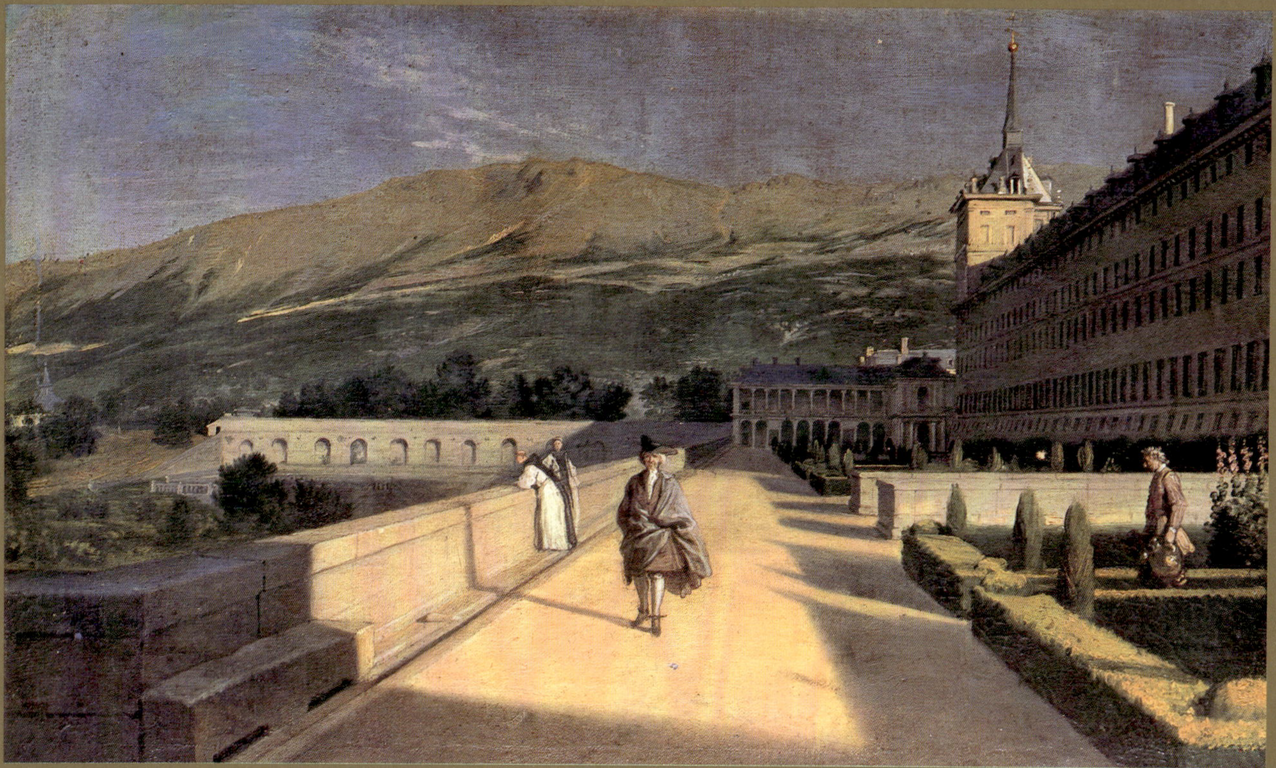

Tapestry of *The Story of Don Quixote* from the Spanish royal collection

Concha Herrero Carretero

The success of *El Ingenioso Hidalgo Don Quixote de la Mancha* by Miguel de Cervantes, its countless editions and translations, have rightly earned the novel a place among the great books in the "library of humankind."

An integral part of the classical repertory of iconography, it was thoroughly explored in the seventeenth century by painters and tapestry cartoon designers and makers, becoming extremely popular in the eighteenth century in many of the most important manufactories of Europe.

It was in England that the tales of the derring-do of the famous love-struck knight-errant were translated for the first time; and it was from England that the oldest woven version comes, in the form of six scenes depicting Cervantes's characters parading over wool and silk. This first tapestry to employ the story of Don Quixote, intended for the anteroom to James II's chamber in Whitehall, was woven in London in 1670 by Francis Poyntz and James Bridges, originally from Arras and Bruges, and is now in the castle at Cawdor, near Nairn, Scotland.

Through sumptuous diplomatic gifts to princes visiting Paris, Louis XV and Louis XVI made the Gobelins *Don Quixote* celebrated throughout Europe. The Manufacture Royale des Meubles de la Couronne (the Crown furniture manufactory), founded in 1667 by Louis XIV in the Faubourg Saint-Marcel, flooded Europe's courts with hangings inspired by the second part of Cervantes's novel and woven after cartoons by Charles-Antoine Coypel (1694–1752).

In his youth, Felipe, duke of Anjou, had shown a keen interest in *Don Quixote*. Not only had he read it, he had also composed a sequel and an imitation in French, and even drawn several scenes from Cervantes's novel. Crowned king of Spain as Felipe V, known as "the Courageous," in 1721 he commanded his *maestro de obras reales* (master of royal works), the Italian Andrea Procaccini (1671–1734), to produce cartoons for a *Story of Don Quixote*. Felipe's idea of ordering a tapestry representing *Don Quixote* from the royal tapestry manufactory in Madrid was inspired by a wide range of factors: a still lively chivalric spirit, the artistic competition then rife between European courts, an enlightened policy that had entailed the establishment of manufactories, and the fact that tapestries were regarded both as one of the most valuable items in a royal treasury and as an antidote to melancholy.

Twenty scenes were woven under the direction of the brothers Francisco and Jacobo Vandergoten after cartoons by Procaccini and his pupil Domingo

Two Tapestries of The Story of Don Quixote: Tilting at Windmills and the Duel with the Basque Servant; The Sheeps Adventure
1721
Royal Tapestry Manufactory, Madrid
FRANCISCO VANDERGOTEN (1704–1774) (tapestry-maker)
Palacio Real, Patrimonio Nacional, Madrid

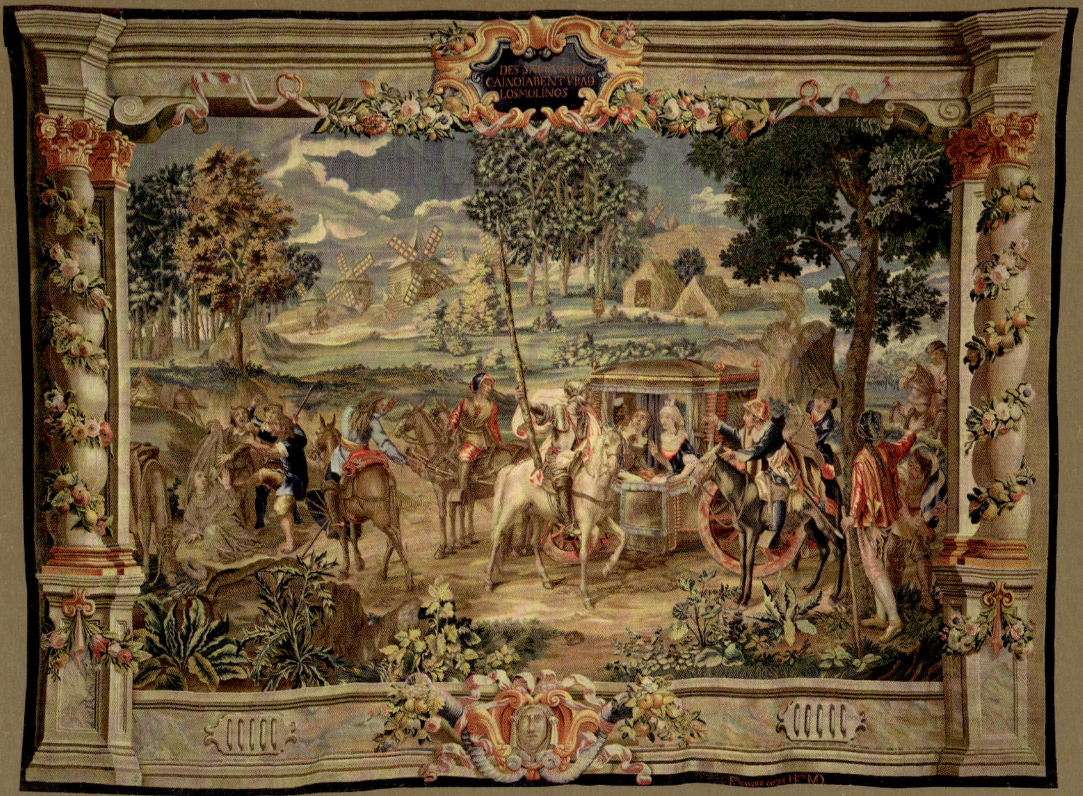
LOSMOLINOS

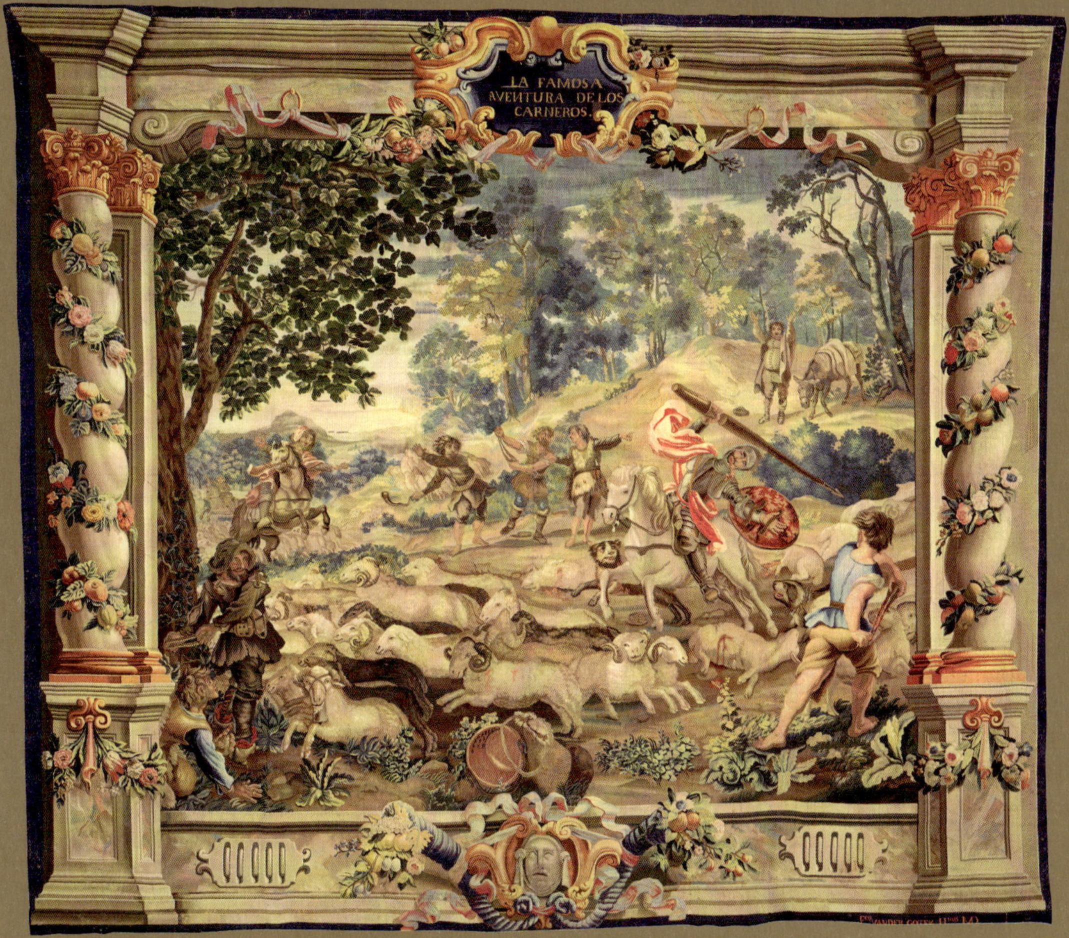
LA FAMOSA
AVENTURA DE LOS
CARNEROS.

María Sani, including nineteen corresponding to the first part of the novel, with only one from the second: *Don Quixote sets out on his adventures; Don Quixote takes arms as a knight; the merchants of Toledo; tilting at windmills, and the duel with the Basque manservant; the fight with the Basque; the Yanguas muledrivers, Maritornes and Don Quixote at the inn; Maritornes puts paid to Don Quixote's illusions; Sancho is tossed in a blanket; the episode with the sheep; the adventure at the fulling mill; Mambrino's helmet; meeting galley slaves; Ginés de Pasamonte steals Sancho's donkey; Beltenebros's penance; Sancho travels to Toboso; the false princess from the kingdom of Micomicon; Don Quixote tied by the wrist; Don Quixote locked up in a cage; the three countrywomen.*

Three tapestries reflect three characteristic aspects of Cervantes's novel: the qualities of the knight-errant, his honor and gallantry in *Tilting at Windmills* and *The Duel with the Basque Servant*; wryly comic situations, such as *Sancho Tossed in a Blanket*; and the sadness, melancholy, and dejection felt in the face of the cruelty of human existence, in *Don Quixote Locked Up in a Cage.* The realistic, approachable features of the protagonists in the Madrid tapestry are readily distinguished from French and Brussels tapestries of the time, in which a comic character prevails. The lively, neat line, the light that floods the exterior scenes—where the foreground is occupied by the main characters and staffage—allow broad expanses of color that gave the tapestry-makers ample opportunity to exploit variations in complexion and attire. The colonnades of twisted columns inspired by Flemish models afford the Spanish tapestry a theatricality and grandeur quite in keeping with the pictorial and decorative values of the finest baroque hangings.

Tapestry of the Story of Don Quixote: Sancho is Tossed in a Blanket
1721
Royal Tapestry Manufactory, Madrid
Francisco Vandergoten (1704–1774) (tapestry-maker)
Palacio Real, Patrimonio Nacional, Madrid

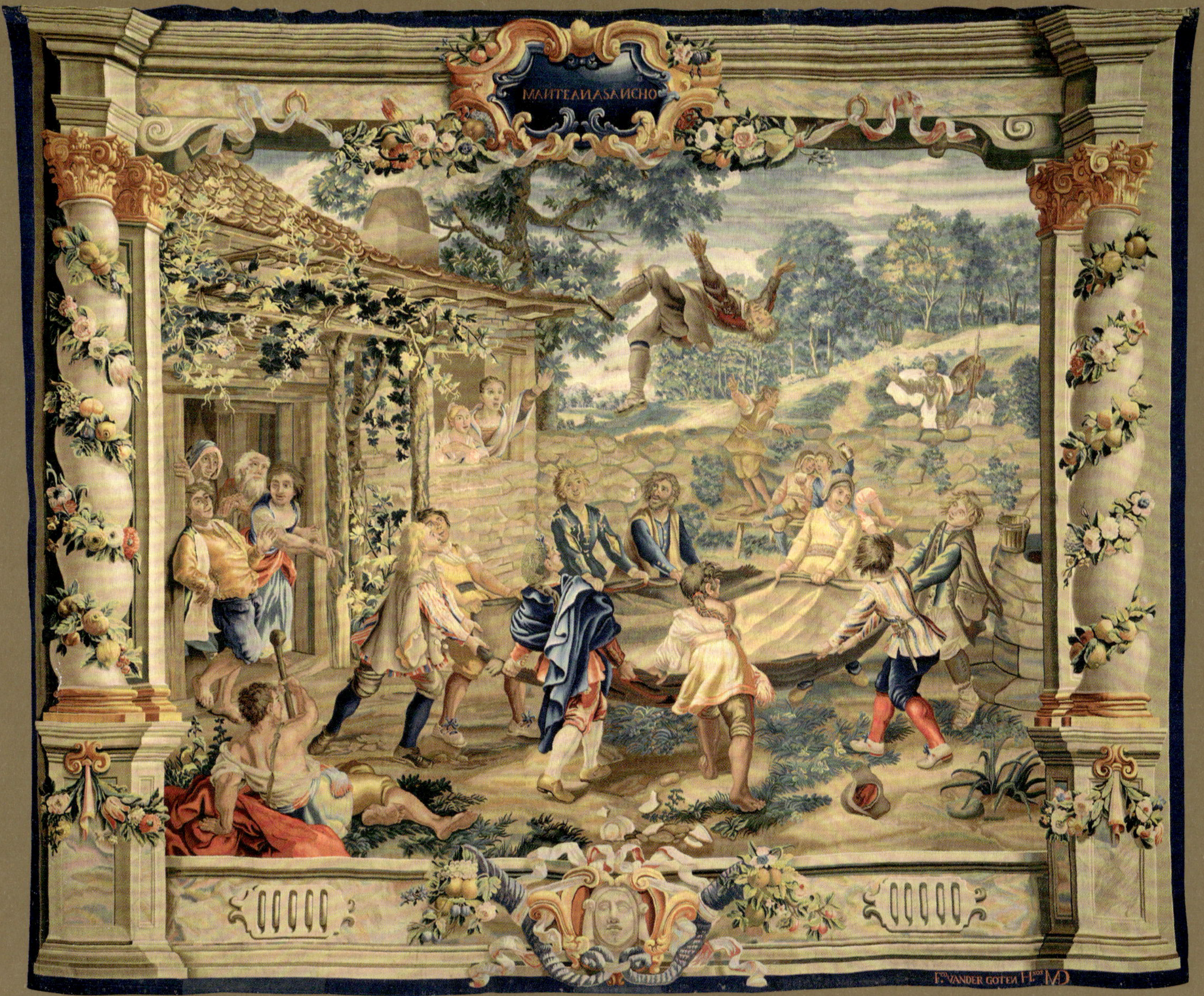
MANTEANAS A SANCHO
F.co VANDER GOTEN H.nos MD

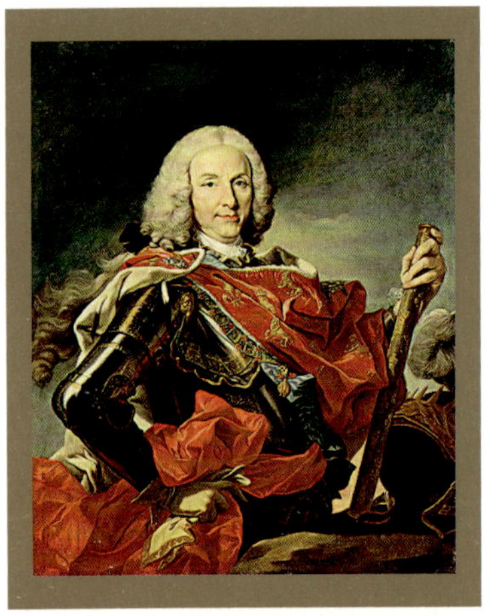

Felipe V, King of Spain (1683–1746)
c. 1737
Louis-Michel Van Loo (1707–1771)
Oil on canvas
107 × 84 cm
Musées des Châteaux de Versailles et de Trianon, Versailles
Inv. MV5884

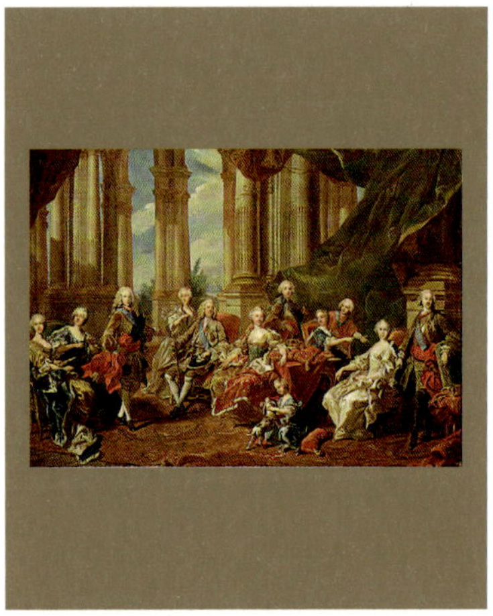

King Felipe V of Spain, Isabella Farnese and their Family
c. 1737
Louis-Michel Van Loo (1707–1771)
Oil on canvas
Modello for the work in the Prado, Madrid; acquired by King Louis-Philippe for the historical galleries of Versailles
96.5 × 102 cm
Musées des Châteaux de Versailles et de Trianon, Versailles
Inv. MV4380

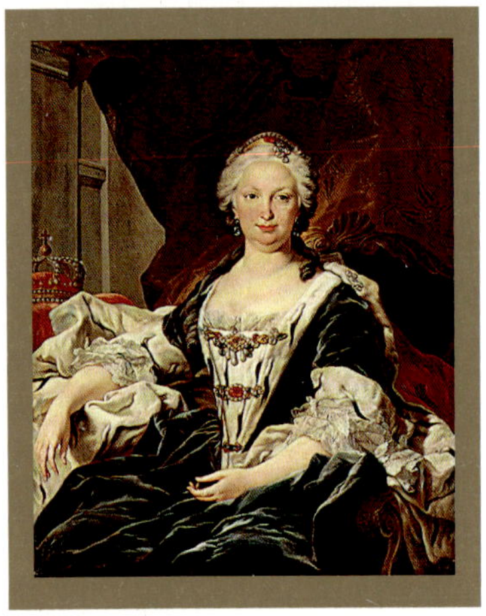

Isabella Farnese (1692–1766), Queen of Spain, Wife of Felipe V
c. 1737
Louis-Michel Van Loo (1707–1771)
Oil on canvas
107 × 84 cm
Musées des Châteaux de Versailles et de Trianon, Versailles
Inv. MV6253

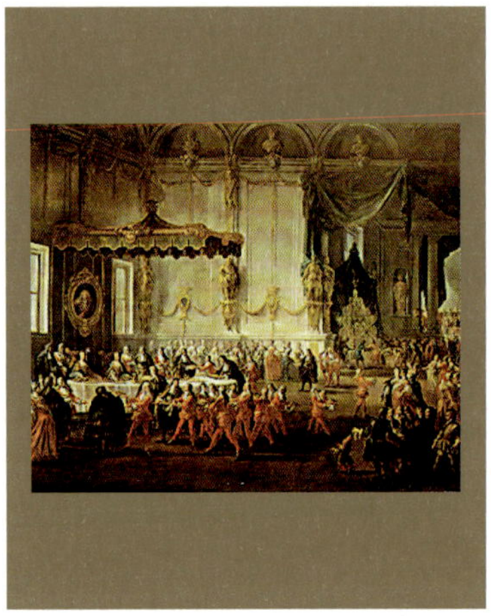

Banquet for the Proxy Wedding of Isabella Farnese to Felipe V in Parma
1714
Lo Spolverini (1657–1734)
Oil on canvas
248.5 × 285 cm
Civiche Raccolte d'Arte del Comune di Parma, Parma

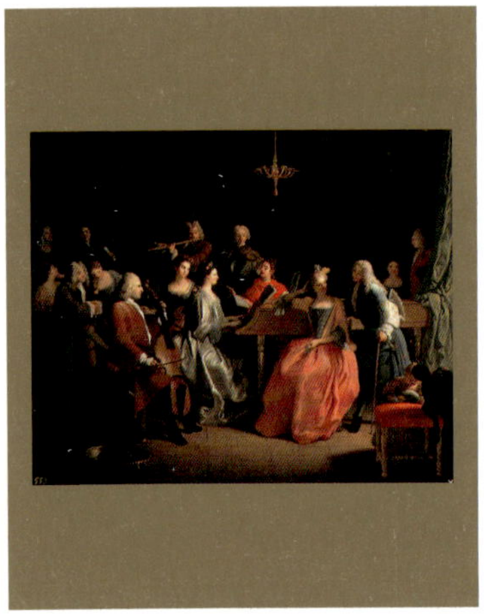

Concert
Eighteenth century
Michel-Ange Houasse (1680–1730)
Oil on canvas
53.5 × 64 cm
Palacio Real de La Granja, Patrimonio Nacional, San Ildefonso
Inv. 10024190

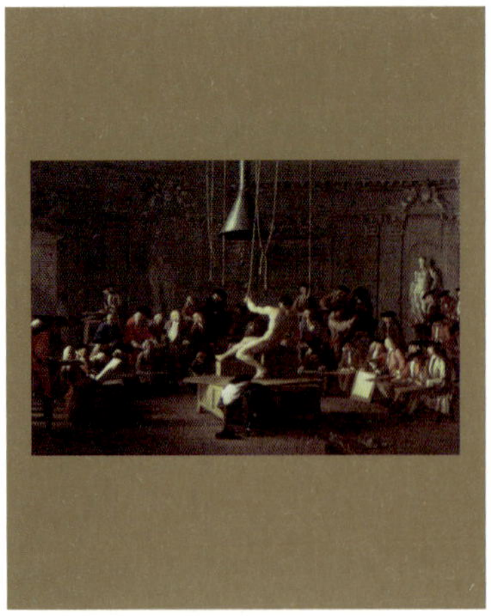

The Drawing Academy
Eighteenth century
Michel-Ange Houasse (1680–1730)
Oil on canvas
51 × 72 cm
Patrimonio Nacional, Madrid
Inv. 10010233

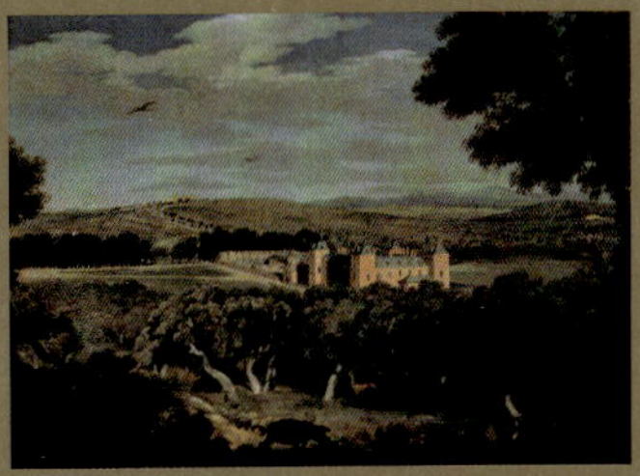

The Pardo Palace
1720–24
Michel-Ange Houasse (1680–1730)
Oil on canvas
37 × 50 cm
Palacio real de Riofrío,
Patrimonio Nacional, San Ildefonso
Inv. 10066775

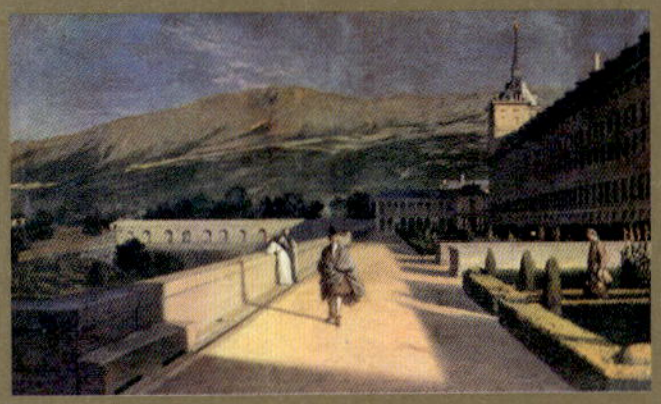

The Monk's Garden at El Escorial
Eighteenth century
Michel-Ange Houasse (1680–1730)
Oil on canvas
51 × 82 cm
Palacio de la Moncloa, Patrimonio
Nacional, Madrid
Inv. 10151674

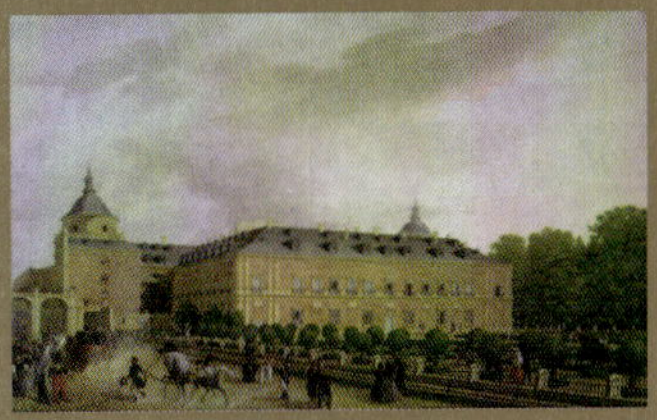

The Royal Palace of Aranjuez
Nineteenth century
Fernando Brambilla (1763–1834)
Oil on canvas
93 × 142.5 cm
Patrimonio Nacional, Madrid
Inv. 10069551

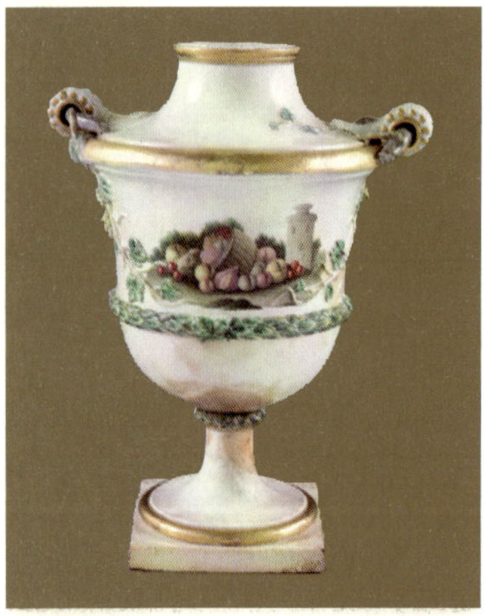

Decorative vase
Mid-eighteenth century
Buen Retiro workshop, Madrid
H. 29 cm
Patrimonio Nacional, Madrid
Inv. 10003263

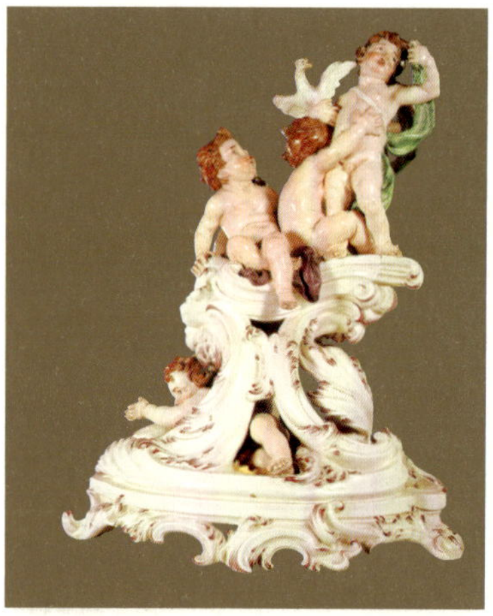

Group of Children
Eighteenth century
Buen Retiro workshop, Madrid
H. 49 cm
Patrimonio Nacional, Madrid
Inv. 10028221

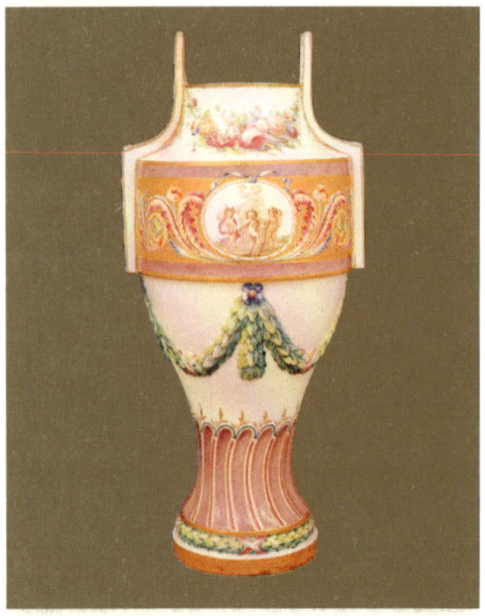

Decorative vase
Mid-eighteenth century
Buen Retiro workshop, Madrid
H. 90 cm
Patrimonio Nacional, Madrid
Inv. 10009772

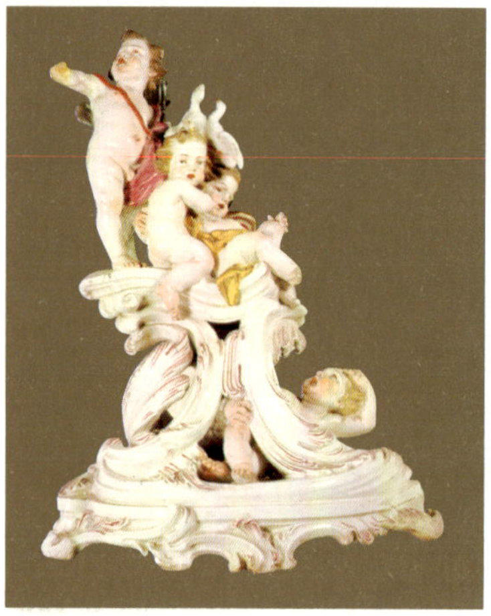

Group of Children
Eighteenth century
Buen Retiro workshop, Madrid
H. 49 cm
Patrimonio Nacional, Madrid
Inv. 10028222

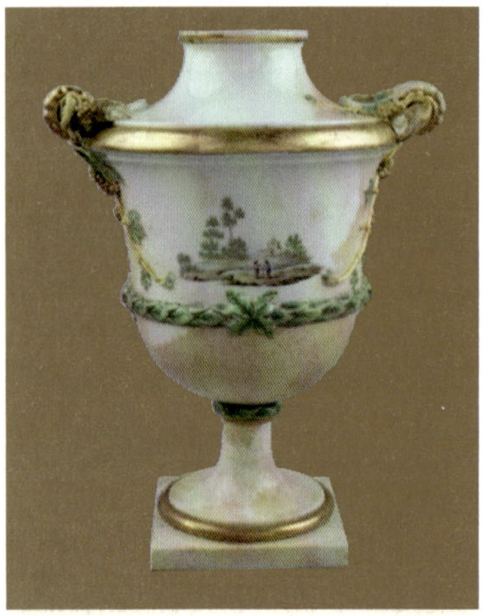

Decorative vase
Mid-eighteenth century
Buen Retiro workshop, Madrid
H. 29 cm
Patrimonio Nacional, Madrid
Inv. 10003264

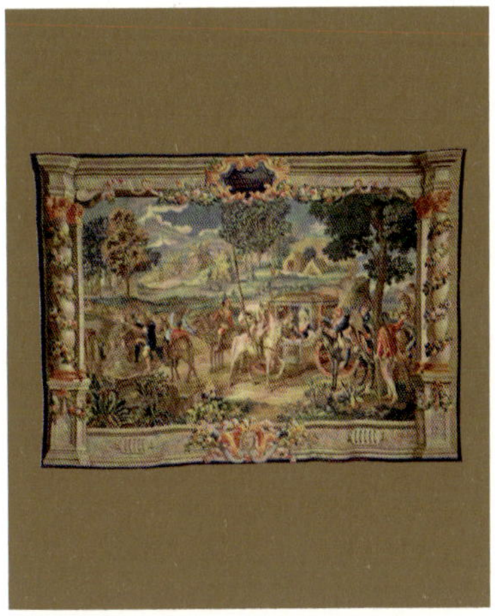

Tapestry of the Story of Don Quixote: Tilting at Windmills and the Duel with the Basque Servant
1721
Royal Tapestry Manufactory, Madrid
Francisco Vandergoten (1704–1774), (tapestry-maker), after cartoons by Andrea Procaccini and Domingo María Sani (1671–1734)
Silk, wool; high-warp tapestry
398 × 530 cm
Madrid, Palacio real, Patrimonio Nacional
Inv. 10007060 (TA-130/3)

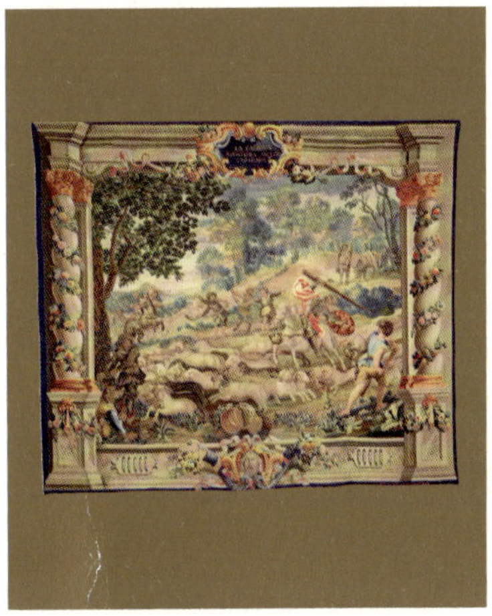

Tapestry of the Story of Don Quixote: The sheeps Adventure
1721
Royal Tapestry Manufactory, Madrid
Francisco Vandergoten (1704–1774), tapestry-maker, after cartoons by Andrea Procaccini and Domingo María Sani (1671–1734)
Silk, wool; high-warp tapestry
369 × 486 cm
Madrid, Palacio real, Patrimonio Nacionall
Inv. 10013121 (TA-77/9)

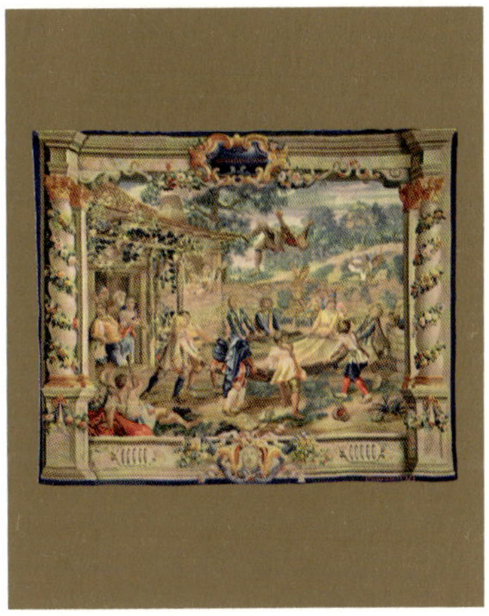

Tapestry of the Story of Don Quixote: Sancho is Tossed in a Blanket
1721
Royal Tapestry Manufactory, Madrid
Francisco Vandergoten (1704–1774), tapestry-maker, after cartoons by Andrea Procaccini and Domingo María Sani (1671–1734)
Silk, wool; high-warp tapestry
380 × 456 cm
Madrid, Palacio real, Patrimonio Nacional
Inv. 10005765 (TA-130/6)

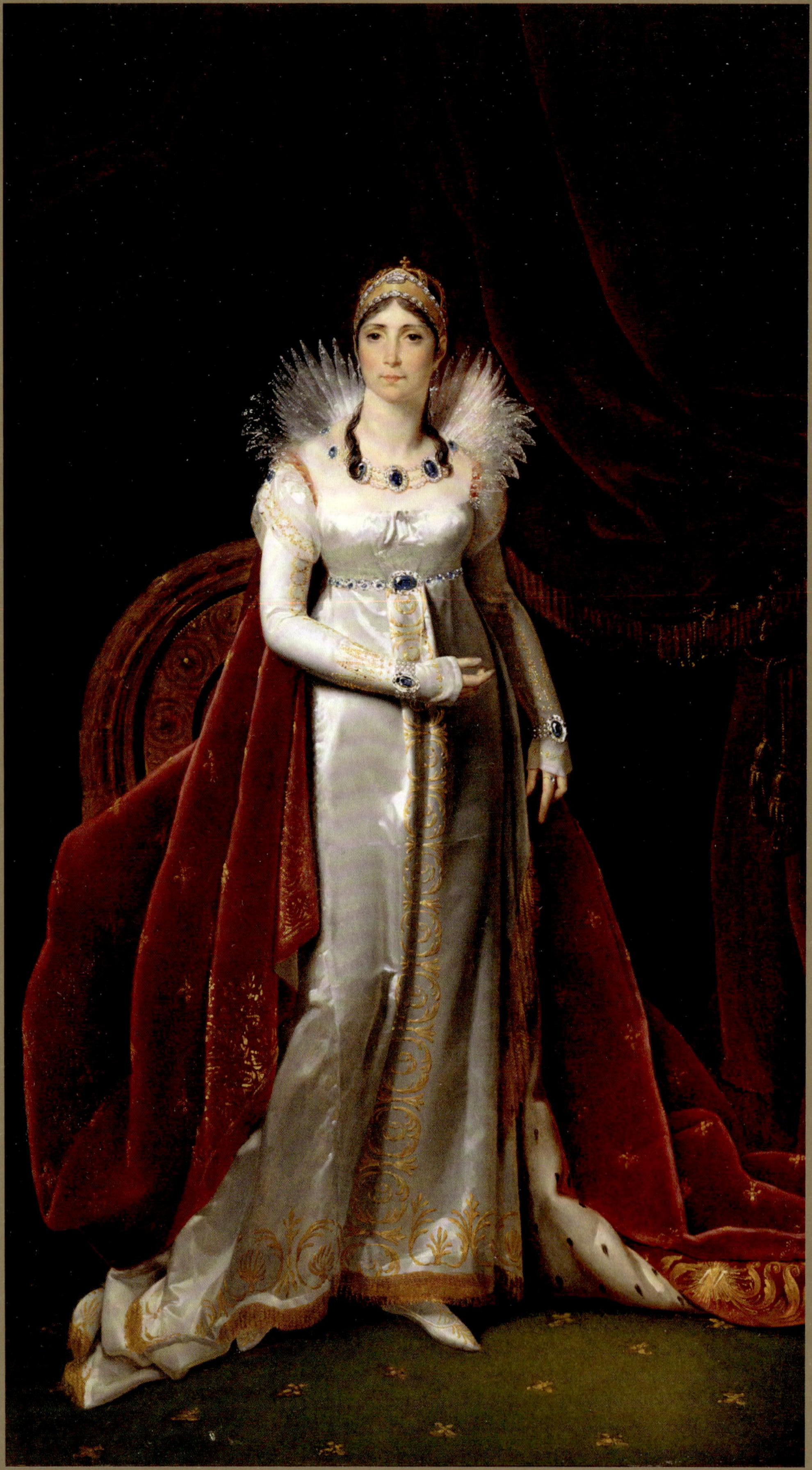

FRANCE

Napoleon (1769–1821) and Josephine (1763–1814)

Empress Josephine in Her Sapphire Parure
1806
Henri-François Riesener
(1767–1828)
Musée National des Châteaux
de Malmaison et Bois-Préau,
Rueil-Malmaison

Napoleon and Josephine

Bernard Chevallier

Josephine came from a family as venerable as it was honorable. The widow of General Beauharnais, who enjoyed his hour of glory in the service of the Republic, she was one of the jewels of high society and gave at least the impression of being extremely wealthy. Thus it was that the viscountess of Beauharnais looked like a good match for General Bonaparte.

Their liaison was not long in taking a passionate turn. Napoleon fell madly in love, while she delighted in the adoration that, at thirty-two, she was apparently still able to inspire. She had an inkling that the general six years her junior might one day prove rather useful. Conversely, he was convinced she had money to burn and her fingers on the political pulse. Their complicity thus stemmed from common interests evident to both sides and carefully considered. Bonaparte was well aware of what he could gain from an alliance with an aristocrat who combined refined manners with natural goodness. The idea of marriage soon coalesced and the banns were published on February 19, 1796. On March 8, the couple signed a marriage contract (prenuptial agreements stipulating that their property be held separately), and on March 9 they were married in Paris at a civil wedding in the town hall of the second arrondissement.

Shortly after the wedding, however, circumstances dictated that Napoleon leave Josephine to take command of the army in Italy. His letters showed him in confessional, tearful mode, constantly begging her to join him. As for Josephine, she could hardly have acted more insensitively. While he called for her plaintively, she, turning a deaf ear to his pleas, preened herself in the *beau monde* surrounded by a posse of fawning men, the most prominent being Hippolyte Charles, an attractive young lieutenant, a sort of devoted knight who followed her around like a dog and whose attentions soon had Parisian tongues wagging. The rumors flew across the Alps and landed in Bonaparte's headquarters. Amplified by distance and maliciously distorted, they sparked the couple's first serious crisis, causing a breach that nothing would ever really repair.

Then there was the question of her sterility, with its attendant effects on her self-image as a woman and on her relationship with Napoleon. Yet here, too, Josephine failed to appreciate the gravity of the situation. Earnestly desiring to

Napoleon I (1769–1821) in Coronation Costume
1805–10
François Gérard
(1777–1839)
Musée National des Châteaux de Malmaison et Bois-Préau, Rueil-Malmaison

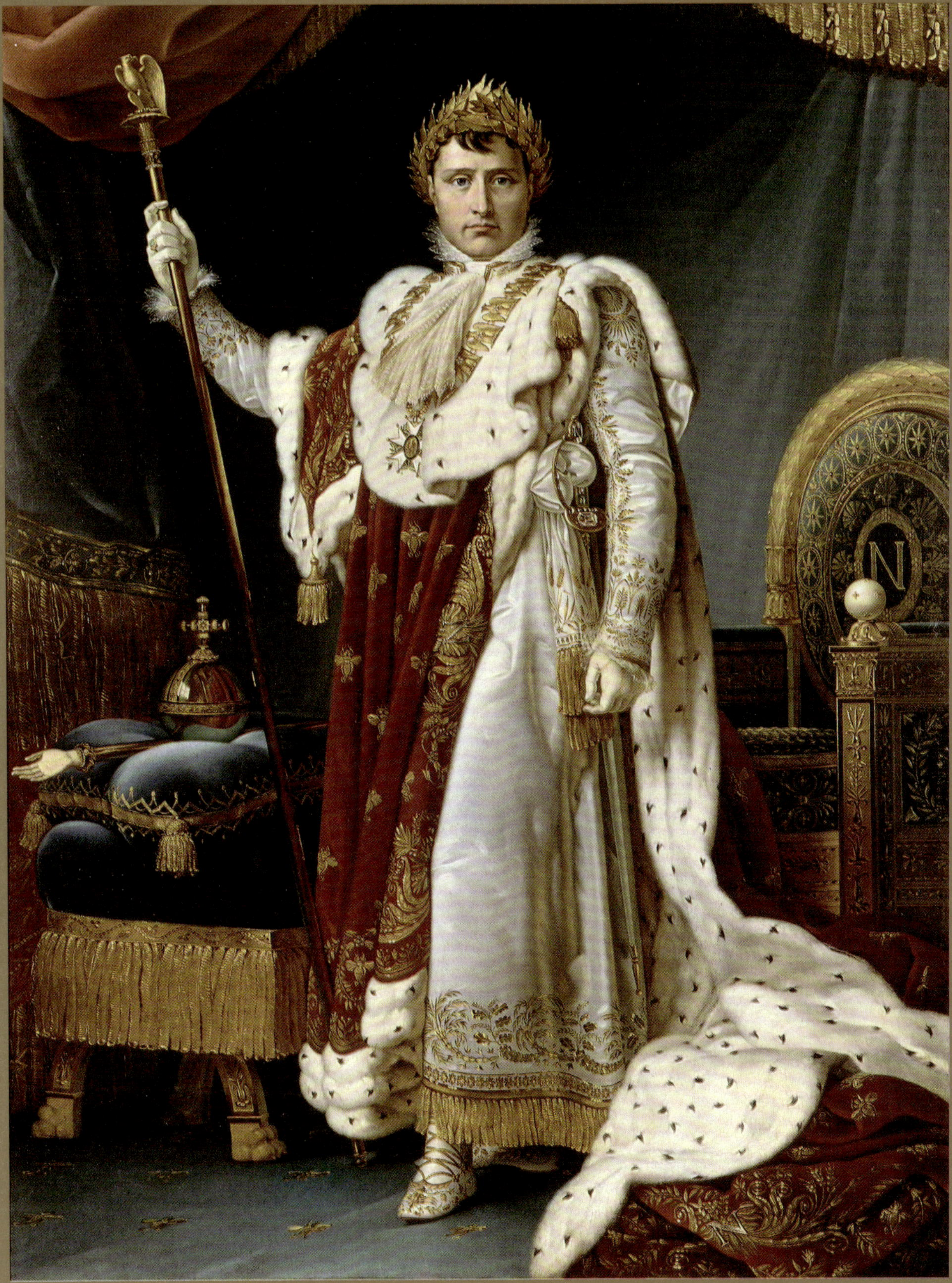

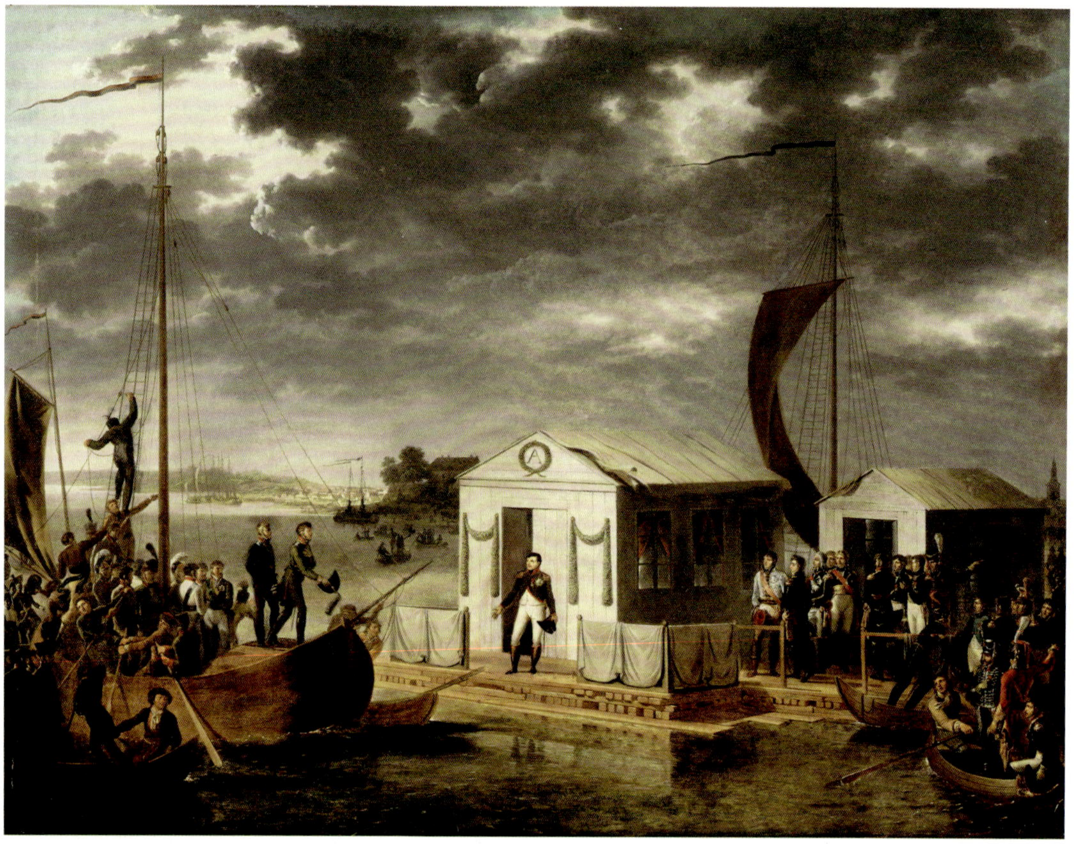

provide him with a son, in the early years of the marriage she never lost faith that she could. Unfortunately, and after trying every available remedy, her hopes were dashed, and eventually she had to face up to the fact that she was no longer of an age to bear children.

Meanwhile, exasperated by his wife's indifference, Bonaparte planned to leave the army and return to Paris. The members of the Directory panicked and Josephine was immediately dispatched to join her husband, accompanied by the inevitable Charles, in whose puns, often of dubious taste, she seemed to delight. Staying in Italy for a year and a half, from June 1796 to December 1797, she acquired a queenly bearing that stood her in good stead when she became empress. The worldly manners she absorbed in her youth made her unflappable even at the most formal functions. She moved into the Palazzo Serbelloni in Milan, but the spouses lived separately due to the enduring military conflict. Henceforth, the husband's correspondence overflowed with recriminations, fiery declarations, and outpourings of jealousy, peppered with stories from the front.

Napoleon I and Czar Alexander I (1777–1825) on the Niemen River
First half, nineteenth century
Adolphe Roehn (1780–1867)
Musées des Châteaux de Versailles et de Trianon, Versailles

When both were back in Paris in December 1797, they spent an unusually protracted period of four and a half months in conjugal proximity until the fleet set sail for Egypt. Informed of his wife's liaison with Charles, however, Bonaparte decided to divorce her as soon as he returned from maneuvers. On her side, Josephine, with no news of her husband, hastened to buy Malmaison on April 21, 1799, but was forced to borrow 15,000 francs from the sellers' own steward for the first installment! It is against this backdrop that she prepared for her husband's return, throwing sumptuous dinners for members of the Directory at the residence. Buttering up Gohier, recently appointed to the Directory, she was comforted by the arrival in the government of Abbé Sieyès, an old friend. With Barras, that made three directors rallied to the cause.

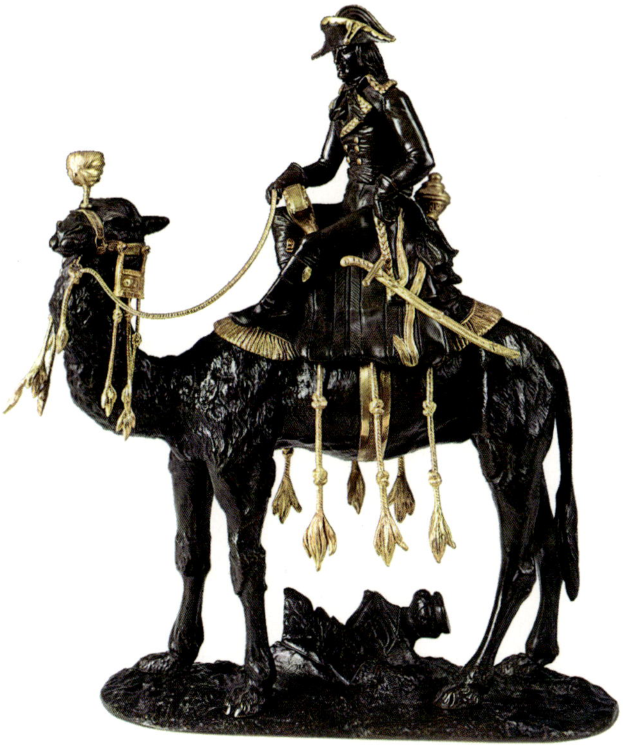

Bonaparte on a Dromedary
Nineteenth century
Fondation Napoléon, Paris

Thus, when, on October 9, 1799, as the bell struck for dinner, she learned that Bonaparte was disembarking at Fréjus, Josephine did not have a moment to lose. Fearing—and with good reason—that his brothers-in-law might arrive first and start telling tales about her to the general, she set out to meet him as quickly as possible. Flying south, she took the Burgundy road, while Bonaparte took a different route, via the province of Bourbonnais, so that, arriving in rue de la Victoire on the morning of October 16, he found the house empty. The Bonaparte clan immediately demanded that he divorce the absentee, and Napoleon locked himself away in the study, swearing never to open the door to his errant wife. Two days later, on October 18, came the famous scene of reconciliation during which, having vainly tried to gain access to her own apartment, Josephine had recourse to her children, who burst into tears and called for their mother. This Bonaparte could not stand and the next morning Lucien Bonaparte had the unpleasant surprise of finding the loving couple in the same bed! Duly reconciled, and as

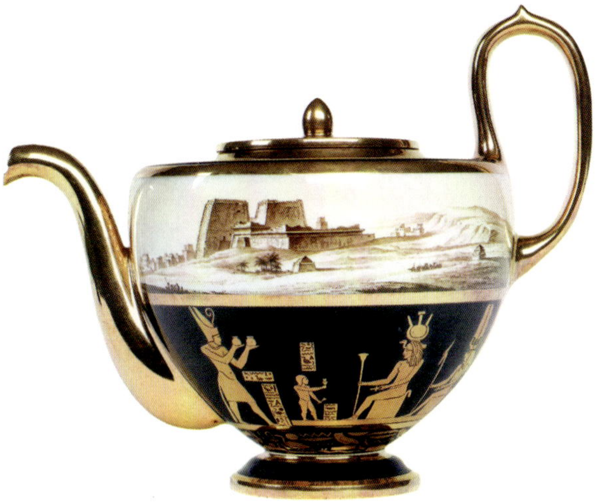

Teapot from the Egyptian tea set
1810
Sèvres Manufactory
Fondation Napoléon, Paris

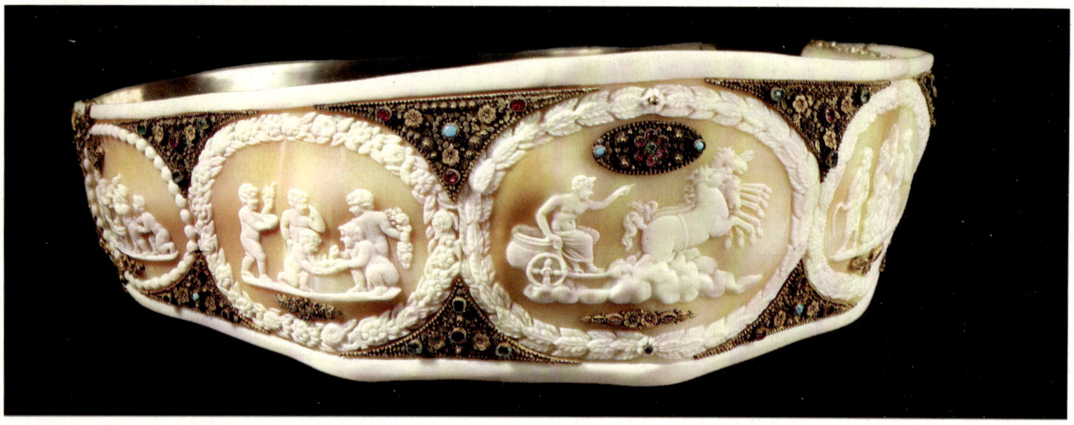

Empress Josephine's diadem, a gift from her brother-in-law, Joachim Murat, king of Naples: the cameos depict Apollo's chariot and the four seasons
1808–14
Musée d'Art et d'Histoire, Palais Masséna, Nice

events gathered pace, Josephine received in her salon all the officers needed to advance Bonaparte's position. On November 9, a coup d'état offered him the possibility of absolute power, with the title First Consul. On November 11, the couple said goodbye to their little house on rue de la Victoire and move into the Luxembourg Palace. General Bonaparte's wife was henceforth to be styled "Consulesse," so becoming France's first "First Lady." Conscious of her new role, Josephine firmly fixed herself to Napoleon's rising star and gave up her former more adventuresome existence.

When, in Saint-Cloud on May 18, 1804, Cambacérès greeted Madame Bonaparte in the name of the French Senate with the title "Empress", Josephine knew that she could never again be her own woman. She was no longer just a wealthy private individual: the peace and tranquility she so valued in the past would have to be sacrificed; Josephine would have to conform to the straitjacket of formal etiquette. Never raising her voice, she obeyed the emperor's diktats without demur. She submitted not because she feared Napoleon's anger, but because she was afraid of jeopardizing the situation by saying or doing something of which he disapproved. She was determined to remain irreproachable and consulted him as to what was appropriate, doing nothing without first receiving permission. Suppressing her own desires, her will was totally subordinated to that of the emperor and she existed solely through and for him. Although, in

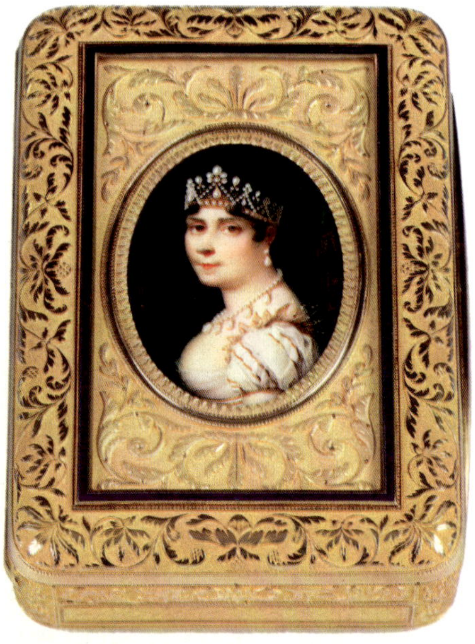

Box with portrait of the empress
Daniel Saint (1778–1847); Pierre-André Montauban, goldsmith (active 1800–20)
Fondation Napoléon, Paris

Malachite parure in its casket: choker, large necklace, diadem, brooch, pendant, four cameo hairpins, and two palmette hairpins
First quarter, nineteenth century
Fondation Napoléon, Paris

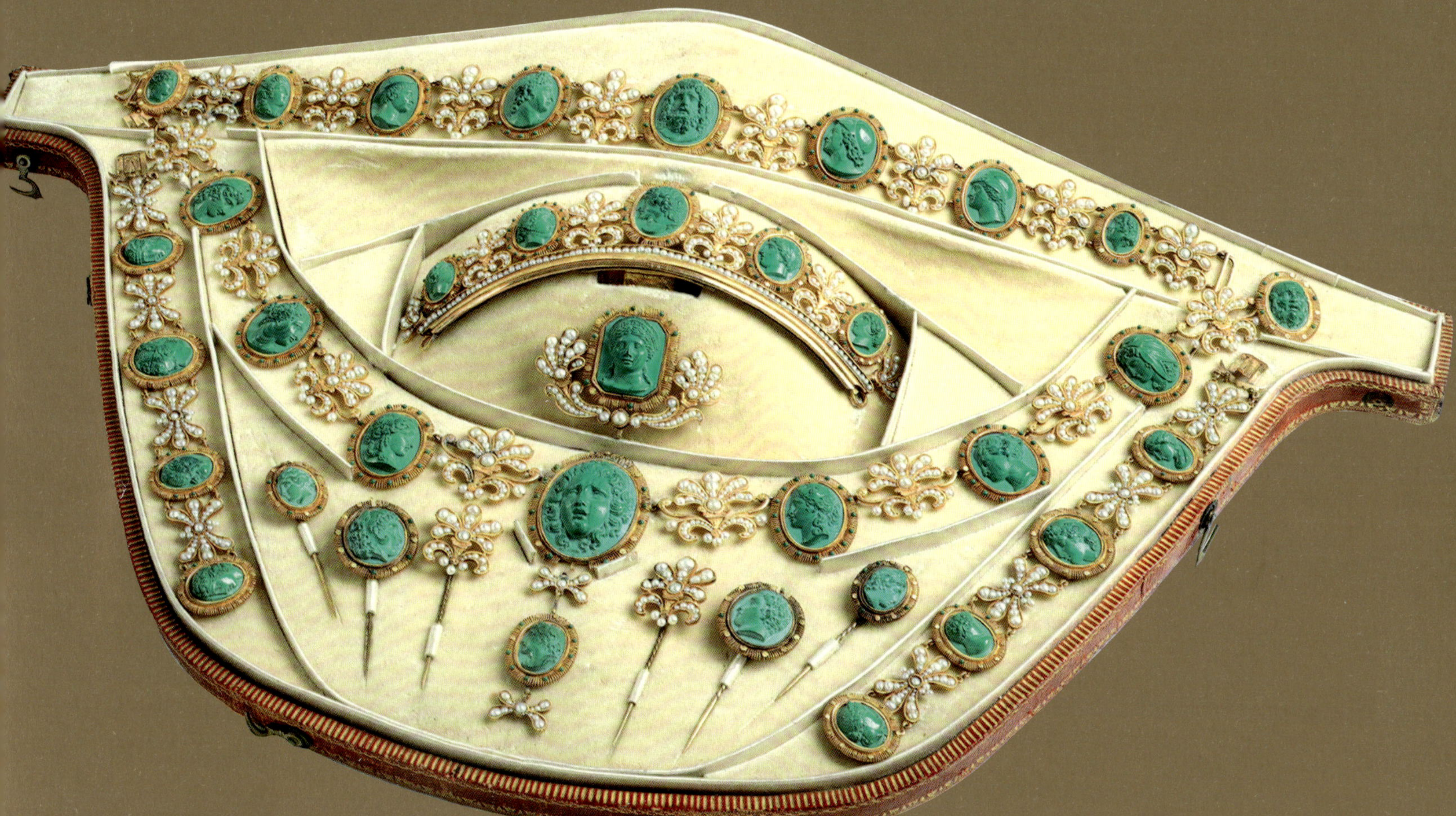

View of Josephine's concert room in Malmaison
ca 1812
Auguste Garneray
(1785-1824)
Musée national
des châteaux de Malmaison
et de Bois-Préau,
Rueil-Malmaison

Napoleon I with Young Princes and Princesses of His Family on the Terrace of the Château de Saint-Cloud in 1810
c. 1830
Louis Ducis (1775–1847)
Musées des Châteaux
de Versailles et de Trianon,
Versailles

accompanying Bonaparte on his meteoric rise she sacrificed liberty and free will, her life acquired meaning. Tied to Napoleon by bonds of friendship, she understood and forgave his faults and knew how to calm his fiery temper, while he, in return, always made it clear that she occupied a special place in his heart. She spent two-fifths of their reign on her own, at Malmaison, in the Tuileries, at Saint-Cloud, on cures, or at best on the steps of empire—at Strasbourg or Mainz—awaiting Napoleon's return. Indeed, from the proclamation of the Empire on May 18, 1804, until her final departure from the Tuileries on December 15, 1809, after the divorce, 2,037 days would pass, during 836 of which she did not see the emperor at all. Accustomed as he was to the woman he had known for nearly fifteen years and whose gentleness and calm suited him so well, for as long as Napoleon thought it was not impossible that she might produce offspring, he hesitated to divorce her, unsure of what to do. But Marie Walewska's pregnancy—since in this case his paternity was not disputed—gave him hope of an heir and he became resolved to contract another union. His determination to dissolve his marriage was now irrevocable: he must have an heir of his own blood.

The ceremony took place on the evening of December 15, 1809, Napoleon declaring before the imperial family: "She has embellished fifteen years of my life. What finer tribute could he make to a woman he never really stopped loving?"

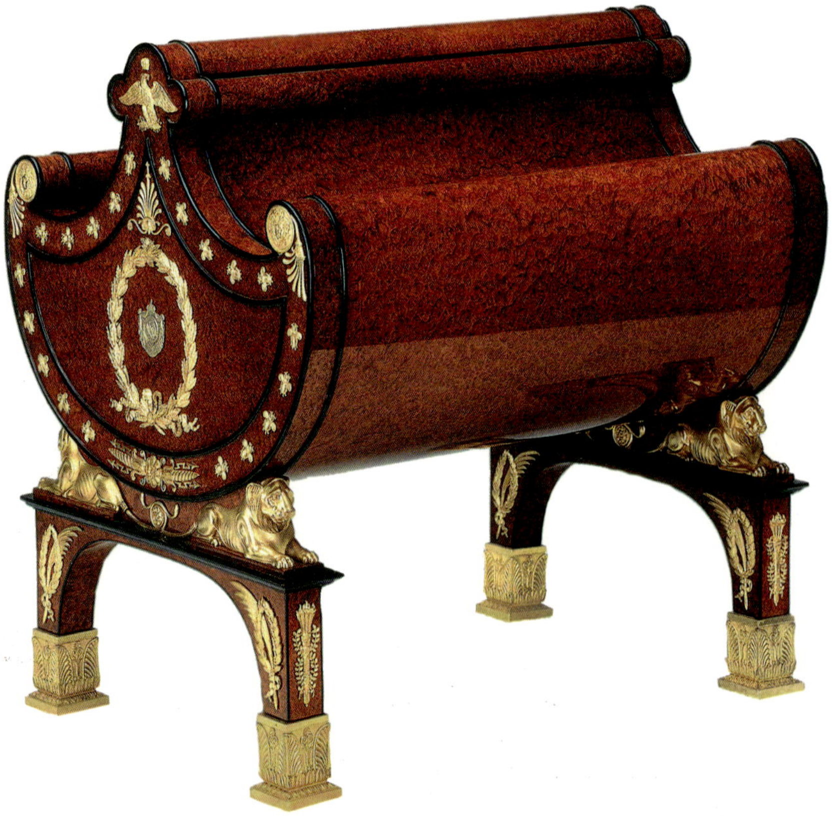

Empress Josephine's paper holder
1805–10
Martin-Guillaume Biennais
(1764–1843)
Fondation Napoléon,
Paris

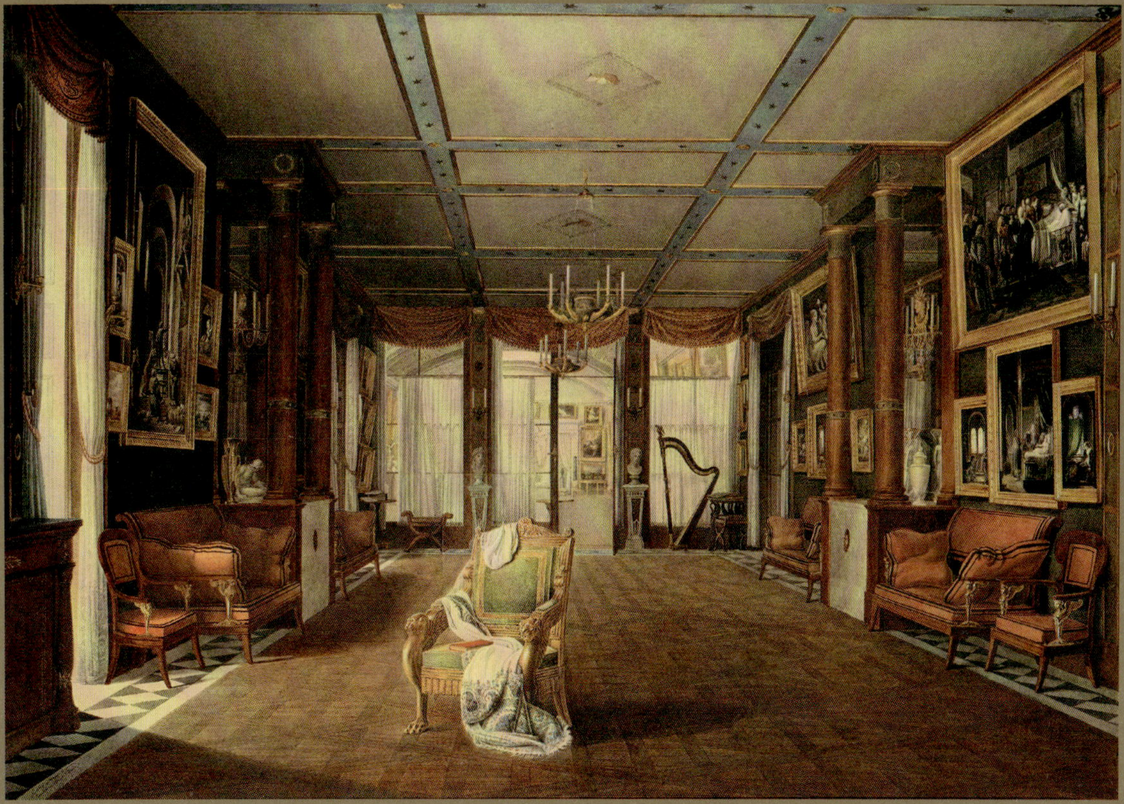

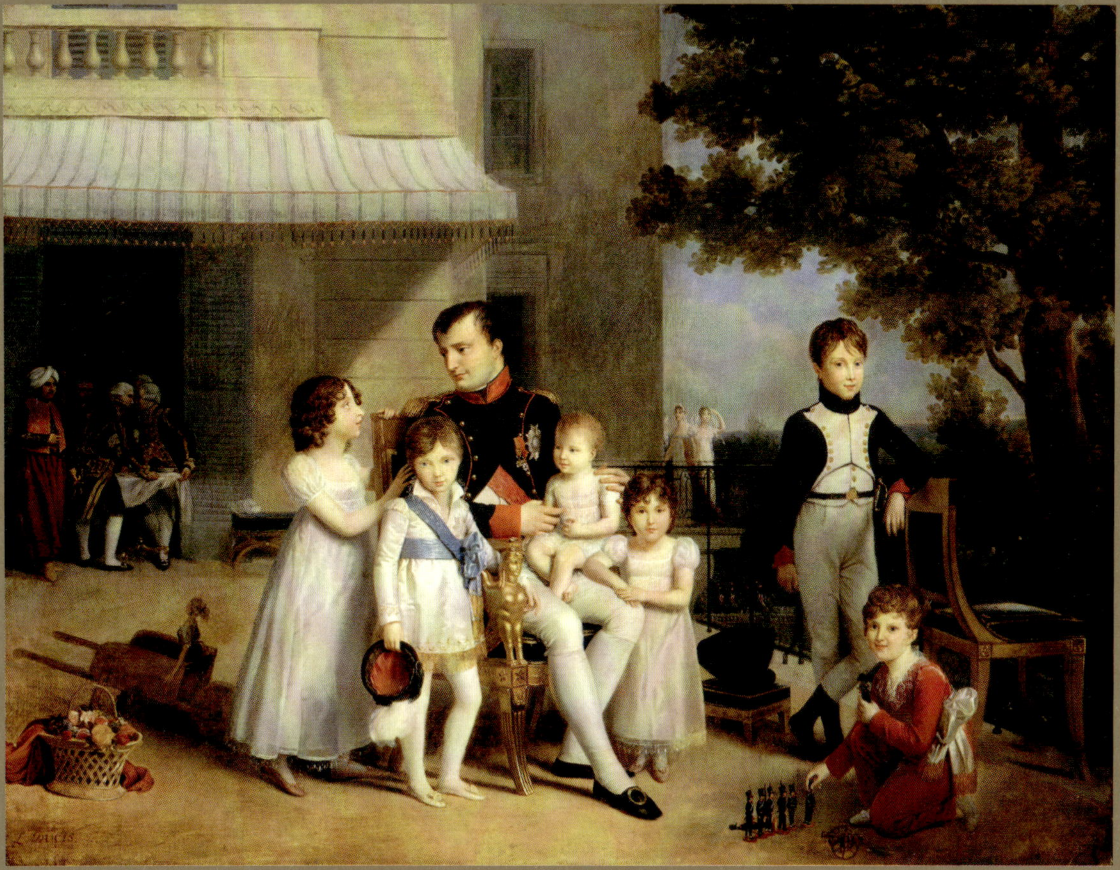

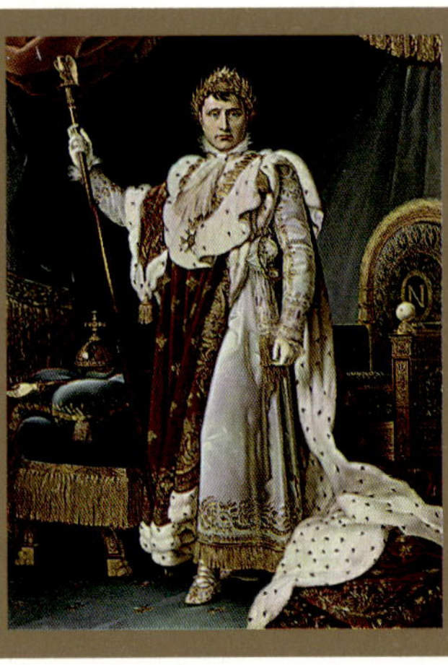

Napoleon I (1769–1821)
in Coronation Costume
1805–10
François Gérard (1777–1839)
Oil on canvas
250 × 150 cm
Musée National des Châteaux
de Malmaison et Bois-Préau,
Rueil-Malmaison
Inv. MM 95-2-1

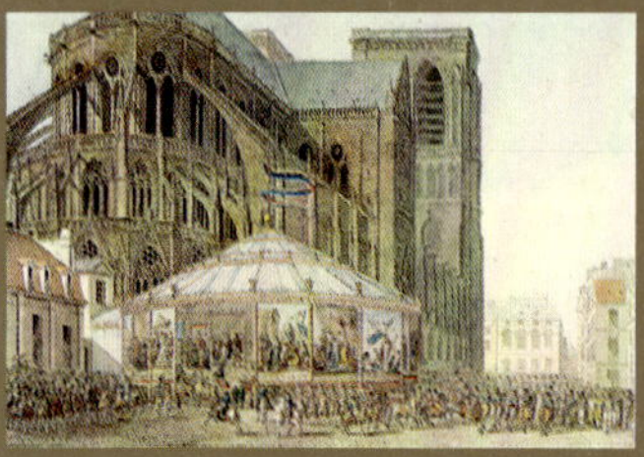

Napoleon's Coronation:
Rotunda Decorated with
Tapestries for the Reception of
Guests on Arrival at Notre-Dame
1804–07
Pierre-François-Léonard Fontaine
(1762–1853)
Pen and ink wash drawing,
watercolors and pencil on laid paper
31 × 44.2 cm
Fondation Napoléon, Paris
Inv. 1150-8

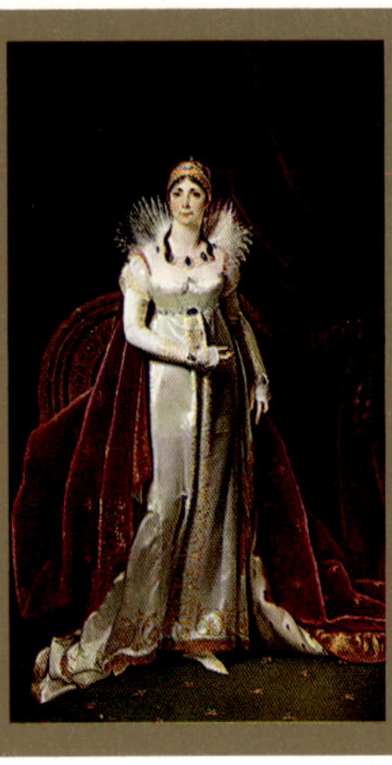

Empress Josephine (1763–1814)
in Her Sapphire Parure
1806
Henri-François Riesener (1767–1828)
Oil on canvas
235 × 130 cm
Musée National des Châteaux
de Malmaison et Bois-Préau,
Rueil-Malmaison
Inv. N 3097

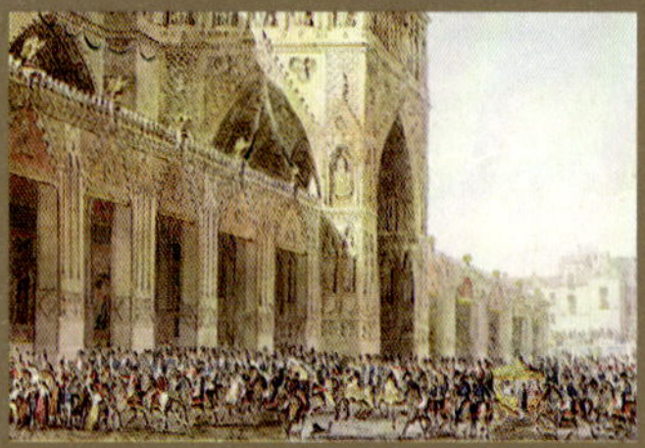

Napoleon's Coronation:
Arrival at Notre-Dame
1804–07
Pierre-François-Léonard Fontaine
(1762–1853)
Pen and ink wash drawing,
watercolors and pencil on laid paper
36 × 52 cm
Fondation Napoléon, Paris
Inv. 1150-2

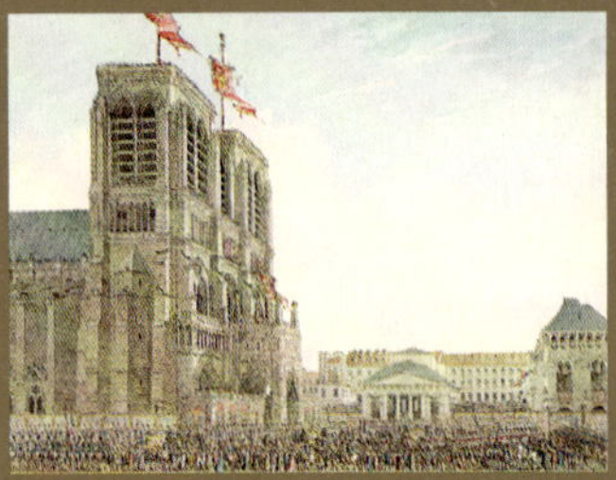

Napoleon's Coronation:
The Façade of Notre-Dame
and Decorative Portico
on the Day of the Coronation
1804–07
Pierre-François-Léonard Fontaine
(1762–1853)
Pen and ink wash drawing,
watercolors and pencil on laid paper
31 × 44.2 cm
Fondation Napoléon, Paris
Inv. 1150-7

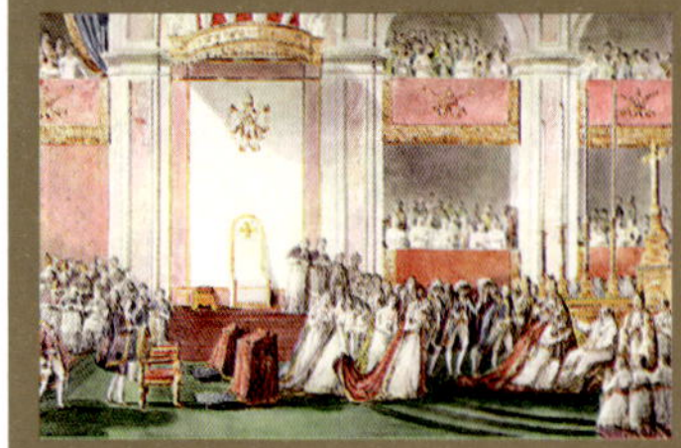

Napoleon's Coronation:
The Unctions
1804–07
Pierre-François-Léonard Fontaine
(1762–1853)
Pen and ink wash drawing,
watercolors and pencil on laid paper
35.5 × 52 cm
Fondation Napoléon, Paris
Inv. 1150-3

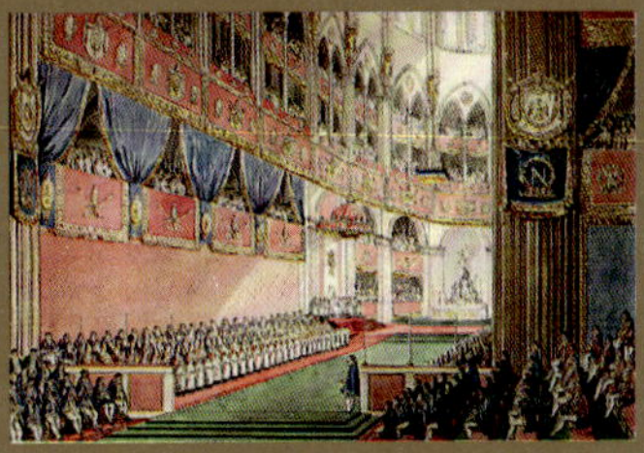

Napoleon's Coronation:
The Nave of Notre-Dame
1804–07
Pierre-François-Léonard Fontaine
(1762–1853)
Pen and ink wash drawing,
watercolors and pencil on laid paper
37 × 53 cm
Fondation Napoléon, Paris
Inv. 1150-4

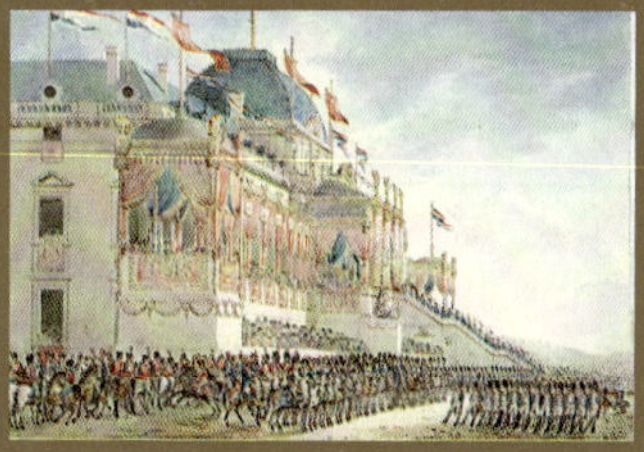

Napoleon's Coronation:
Awards Ceremony
on the Champ-de-Mars
1804–07
Pierre-François-Léonard Fontaine
(1762–1853)
Pen and ink wash drawing,
watercolors and pencil on laid paper
36.2 × 52.8 cm
Fondation Napoléon, Paris
Inv. 1150-6

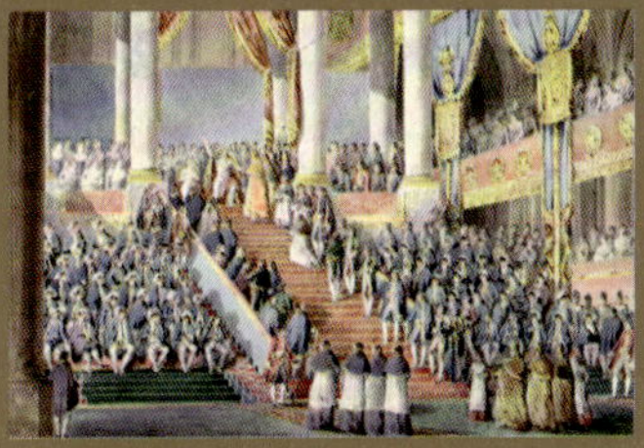

Napoleon's Coronation:
The Oath
1804–07
Pierre-François-Léonard Fontaine
(1762–1853)
Pen and ink wash drawing,
watercolors and pencil on laid paper
36 × 52 cm
Fondation Napoléon, Paris
Inv. 1150-5

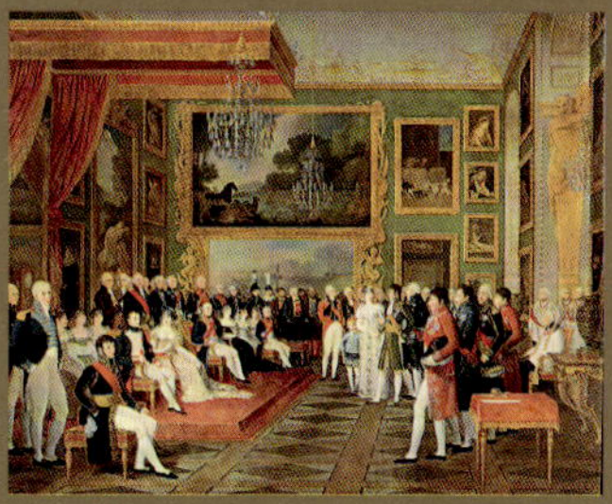

The Wedding of Prince Eugène
de Beauharnais, Viceroy of Italy,
and Princess Augusta of Bavaria
in the Presence of the Emperor
and Empress in the Grand Gallery
of the Palace of Munich,
January 13, 1806
1808
François-Guillaume Menageot
(1744–1816)
Oil on canvas
189 × 230 cm
Musées des Châteaux de Versailles
et de Trianon, Versailles
Inv. MV1716

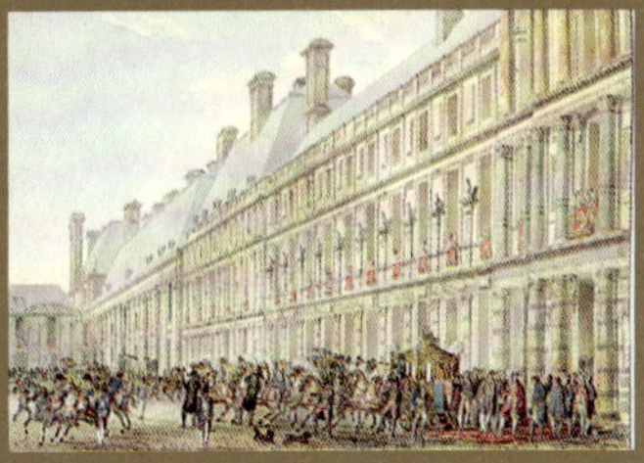

Napoleon's Coronation:
Leaving the Tuileries Palace
1804–07
Pierre-François-Léonard Fontaine
(1762–1853)
Pen and ink wash drawing,
watercolors and pencil on laid paper
38 × 52.5 cm
Fondation Napoléon, Paris
Inv. 1150-1

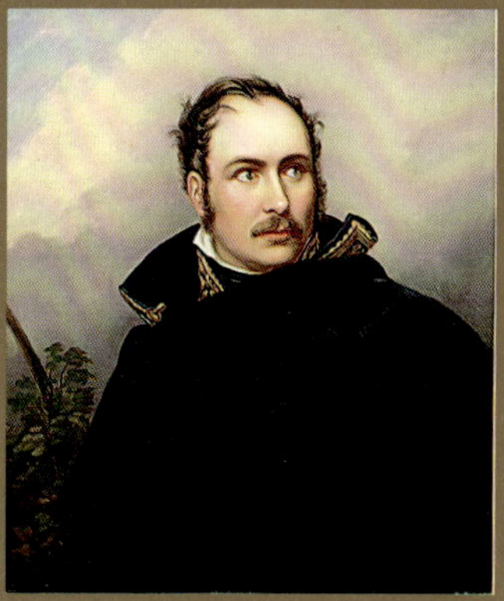

Eugène de Beauharnais
(1781–1824)
1839
Butz (German school), after
Joseph-Karl Stieler (1781–1858),
Munich
Oil on canvas
83 × 71 cm (inc. frame)
Musée National des Châteaux
de Malmaison et Bois-Préau,
Rueil-Malmaison
Inv. MM 97-12-1

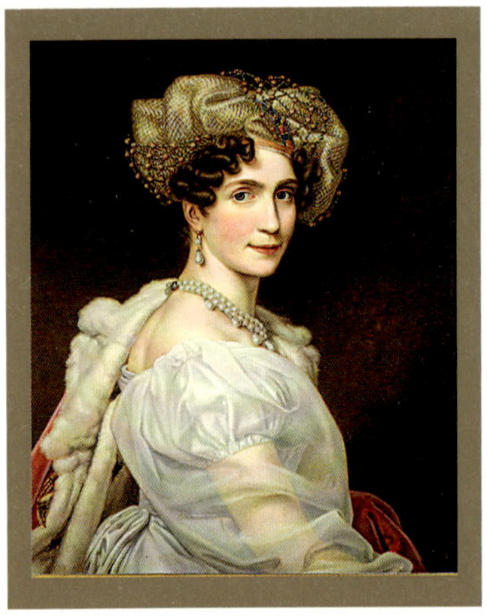

Augusta of Bavaria (1788–1851), Wife of Eugène de Beauharnais, Wearing the Pearl Parure of the Empress Josephine
c. 1820
Joseph-Karl Stieler (1781–1858), Munich
Oil on canvas
73 × 60 cm (inc. frame)
Musée National des Châteaux de Malmaison et Bois-Préau, Rueil-Malmaison
Inv. MM 2008-18-1

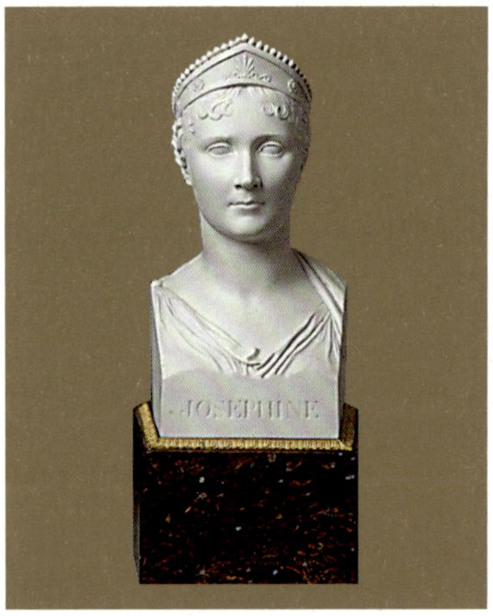

Bust of the Empress Josephine
1808
Sèvres Manufactory
Antoine-Denis Chaudet (1763–1810) and Jean-Jacques Oger (1761–1821?), (after models by Oger)
Bisque porcelain, second order
16 × 18.5 cm
Musée National des Châteaux de Malmaison et Bois-Préau, Rueil-Malmaison
Inv. MM 61-4-2

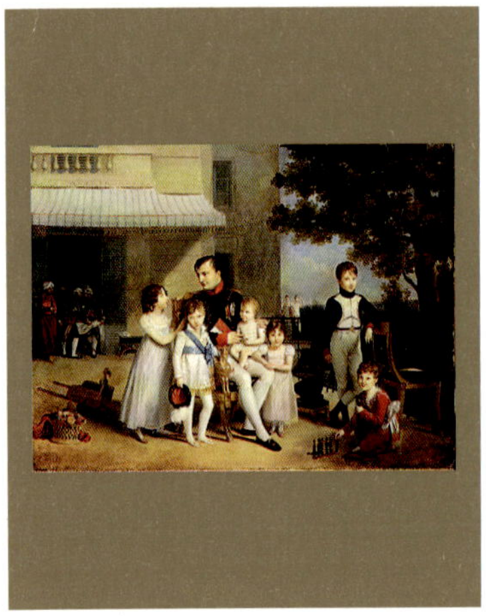

Napoleon I with Young Princes and Princesses of His Family on the Terrace of the Château de Saint-Cloud in 1810
c. 1830
Louis Ducis (1775–1847)
Oil on canvas
105 × 143 cm
Musées des Châteaux de Versailles et de Trianon, Versailles
Inv. MV5147

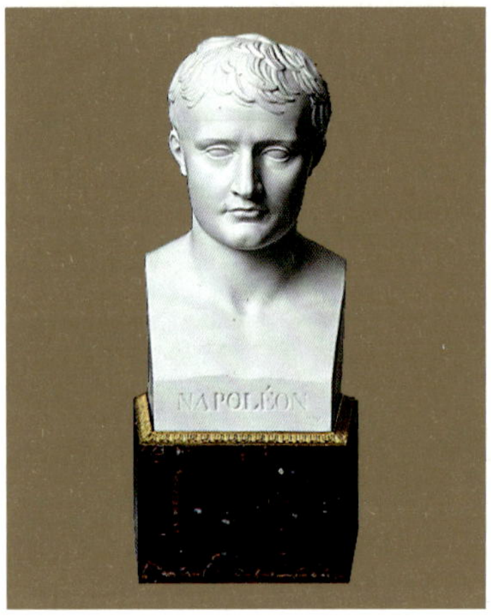

Bust of Napoleon I
1808
Sèvres Manufactory
Antoine-Denis Chaudet (1763–1810) and Jean-Jacques Oger (1761–1821[?]), (after models by Oger)
Bisque porcelain, second order
16 × 18.5 cm
Musée National des Châteaux de Malmaison et Bois-Préau, Rueil-Malmaison
Inv. MM 61-4-1

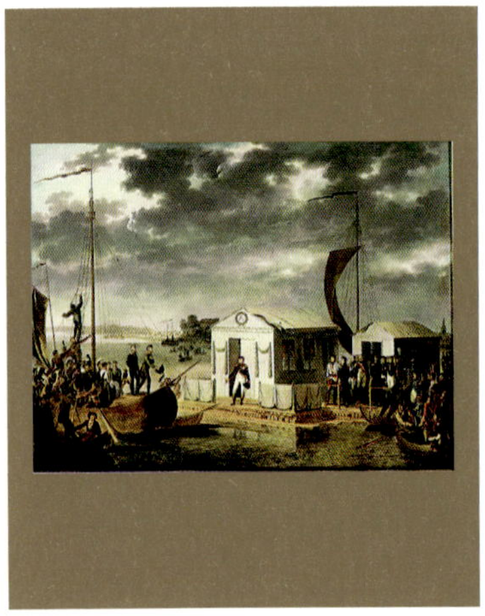

Napoleon I and Czar Alexander I (1777–1825) on the Niemen River
First half, nineteenth century
Adolphe Roehn (1780–1867)
Oil on canvas
125 × 152 cm
Musées des Châteaux de Versailles et de Trianon, Versailles
Inv. MV1728

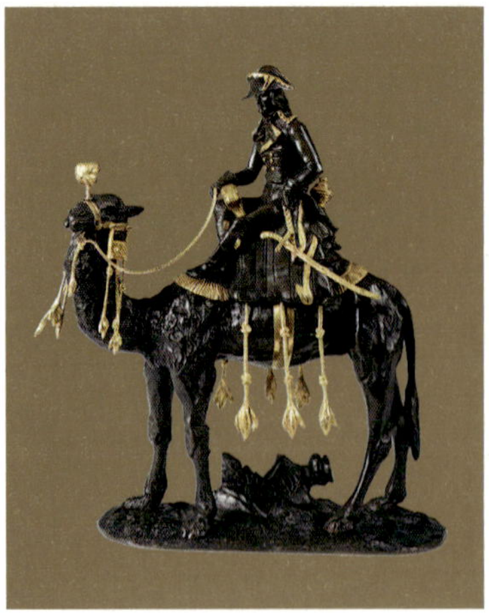

Bonaparte on a Dromedary
Nineteenth century
French school
Patined and partially gilded bronze
37 × 27 × 12 cm
Fondation Napoléon, Paris
Inv. 465 (Lapeyre donation)

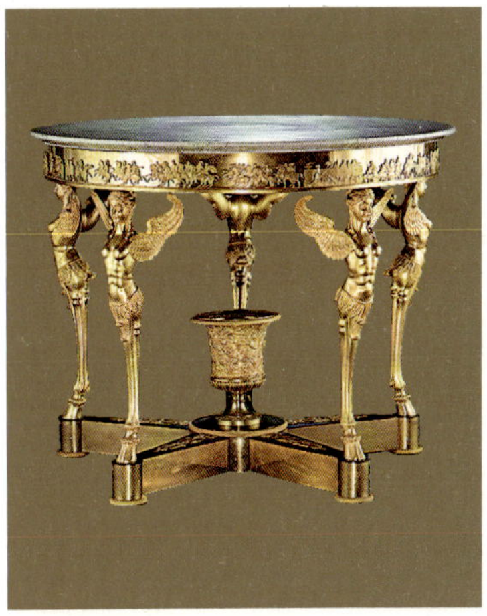

Occasional table with sphinx motifs
1796–1803
François-Honoré-Georges Jacob-Desmalter (1770–1841)
Wood, gilded bronze, marble
97 × 119 cm
Musée d'Art et d'Histoire, Palais Masséna, Nice
Inv. MAH-10256

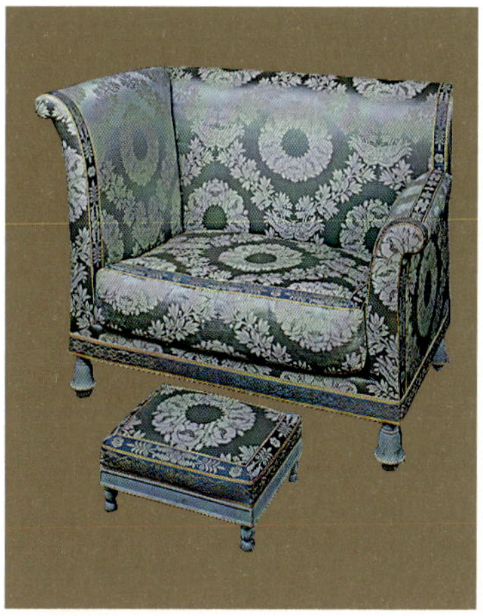

Breakfast room sideboard and footstool from the Grand Trianon
Nineteenth century
François-Louis Castelnaux Darrac (c. 1775–1862) (tapestry-maker); François-Honoré-Georges Jacob-Desmalter (1770–1841)
Painted wood, damask
Sideboard: H. 88 cm, L. 104 cm; stool: H. 17 cm, L. 40 cm
Musées des Châteaux de Versailles et de Trianon, Versailles
Inv. T389 C and T392C

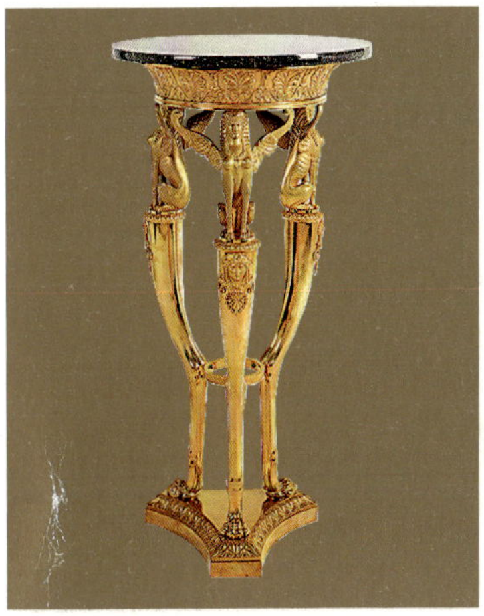

Washstand
First quarter, nineteenth century
Attributed to Pierre-Philippe Thomire (1751–1843)
Gilded bronze
H. 81 cm
Fondation Napoléon, Paris
Inv. 870 (Lapeyre donation)

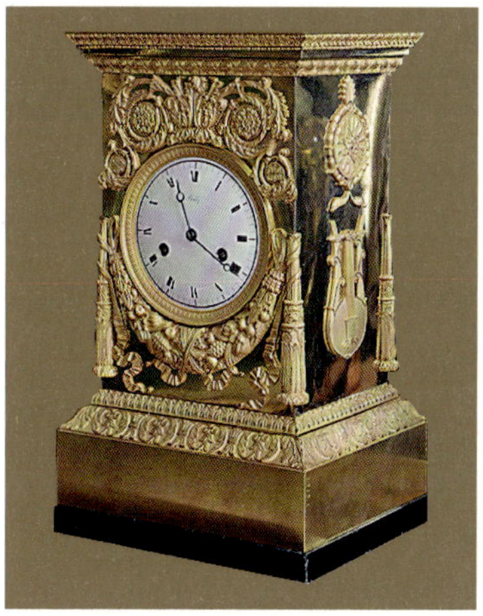

Clock in the emperor's study at the Grand Trianon
1813
Jean-François Bailly (clockmaker)
Gilded bronze, enamel, marble
47 × 26 cm
Musées des Châteaux de Versailles et de Trianon, Versailles
Inv. T380 C

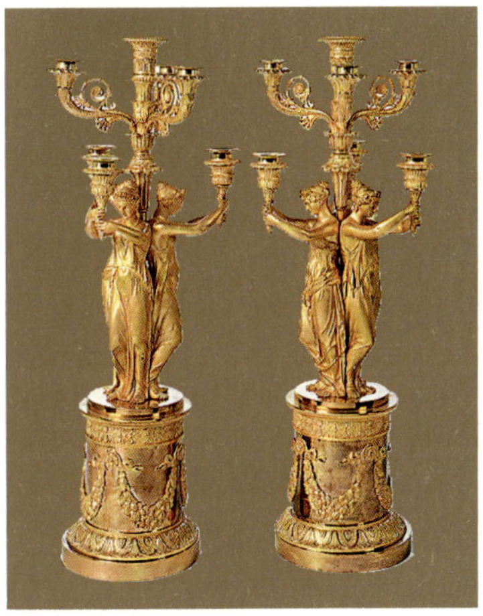

Two candelabras
First half, nineteenth century
Attributed to Pierre-Philippe Thomire (1751–1843)
Gilded bronze, brown porphyry
81 and 65 × 36 cm
Fondation Napoléon, Paris
Inv. 814 and 870

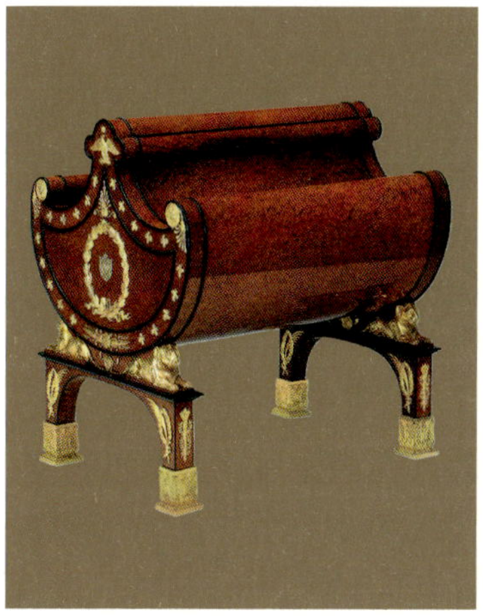

Empress Josephine's paper holder
1805–10
Martin-Guillaume Biennais (1764–1843)
Mahogany magnifying glass, ebony molding, gilded bronze
58 × 52.5 × 45.5 cm
Fondation Napoléon, Paris
Inv. 50

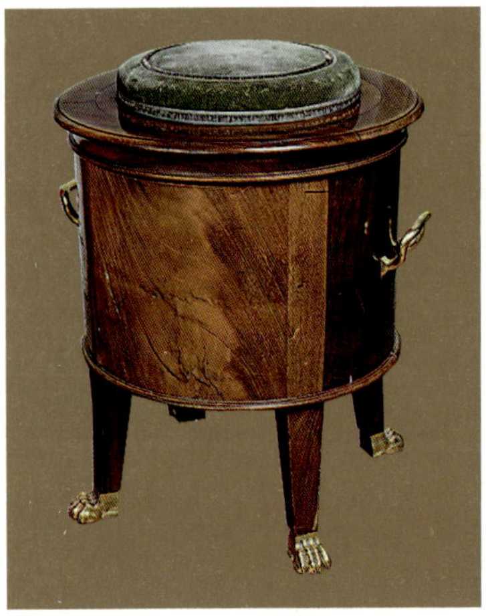

Commode from the Grand Trianon
1809
François-Honoré-Georges Jacob-Desmalter (1770–1841)
Mahogany, gilded bronze, porcelain
47 × 39 cm
Musées des Châteaux de Versailles et de Trianon, Versailles
Inv. T 217

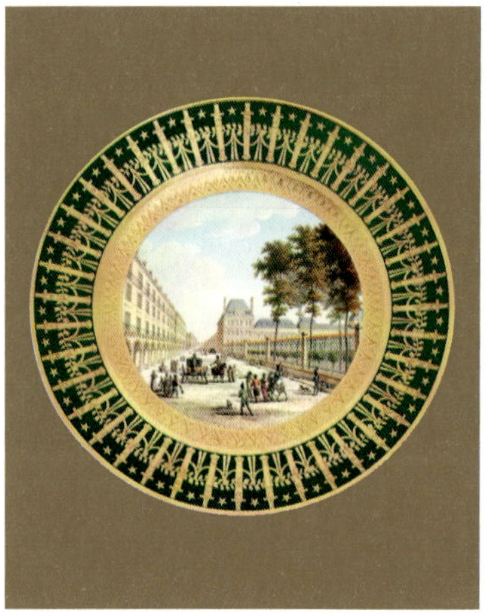

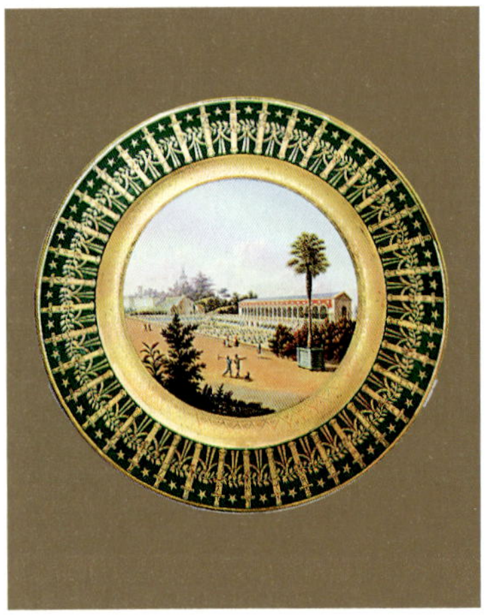

Emperor's personal dining service: four plates
Palais de Saint-Cloud (no. 124)
Les Tuileries (no. 119)
The Jardin des Plantes Orangery (no. 120)
The Lighthouse of Alexandria (no. 108)
1807–11
Sèvres Manufactory
Porcelain
D. 24 cm
Fondation Napoléon, Paris
Inv. 30, 414-418, 792 A-M
(Lapeyre donation)

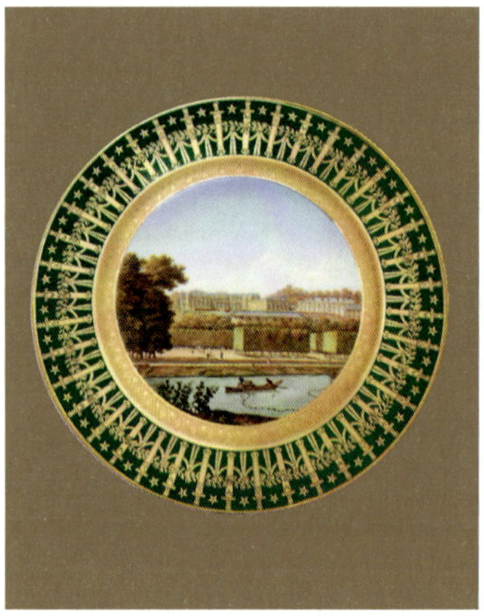

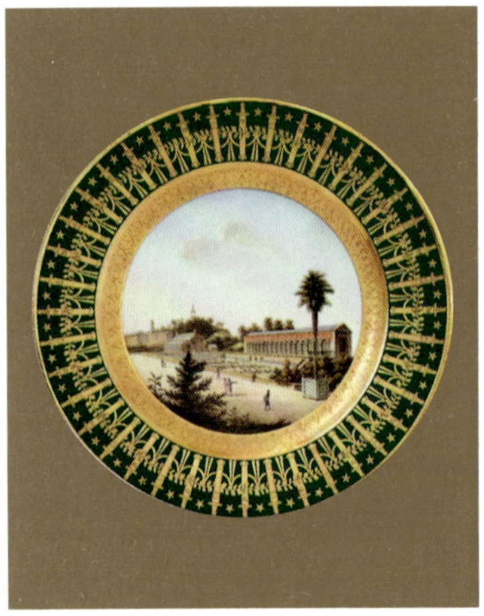

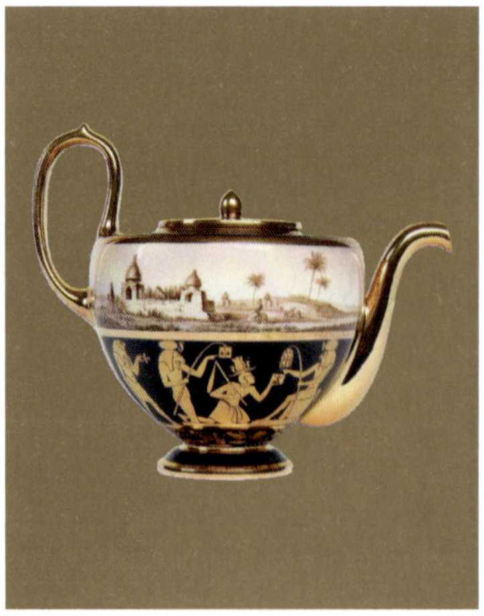

Teapot from the Egyptian Tea set (teapot, nine cups and saucers)
1810
Sèvres Manufactory
Porcelain
H. (teapot) 18 cm; H. (cup) 5 cm; D. (saucer) 13.6 cm
Fondation Napoléon, Paris
Inv. 794

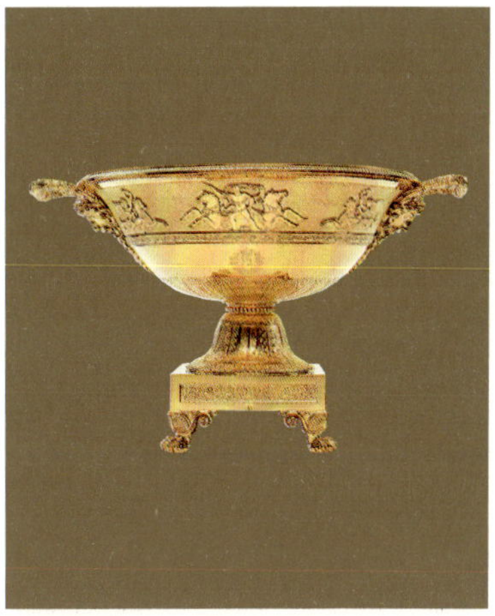

Punch bowl with the empress's arms
1805–10
Martin-Guillaume Biennais (1764–1843)
Gilded silver
25.5 × 32 cm
Fondation Napoléon, Paris
Inv. 567 (Lapeyre donation)

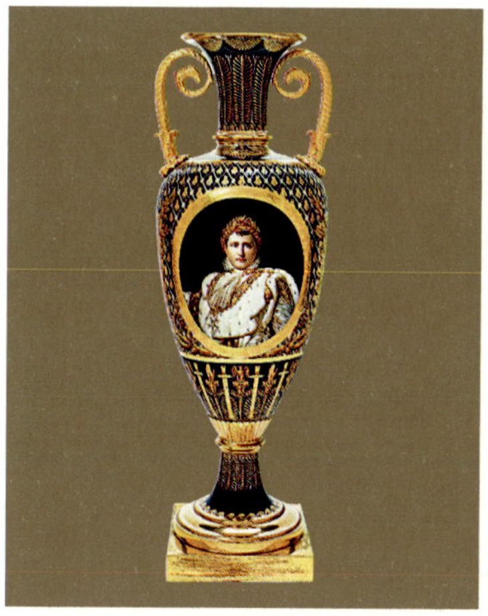

Second order vase with the portrait of the emperor in Coronation Costume
1812
Sèvres Manufactory
Cobalt blue, hard porcelain, gilded bronze
H. 54.5 cm
Fondation Napoléon, Paris
Inv. 1165

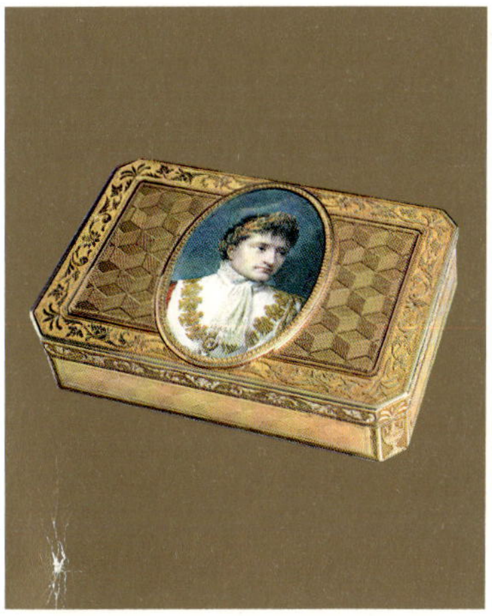

Box with portrait of Napoleon in Coronation Costume
1798-1809
Jean-Baptiste Isabey (1767–1855), signed; Jacques-Félix Viennot, goldsmith (active 1785–1812)
Gold, miniature on ivory
2.2 × 9.8 × 6.5 cm
Fondation Napoléon, Paris
Inv. 1096 (Lapeyre donation)

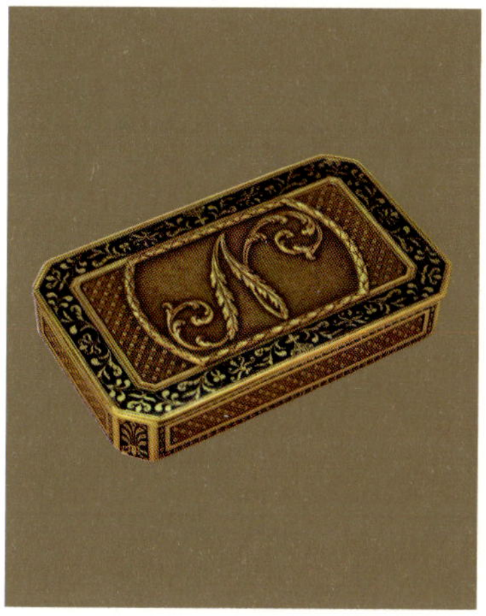

Snuffbox, a gift from the empress to Napoleon
1798–1809
Marguerite, jeweler to the crown, Paris
Gold, enamel
2 × 9 × 5,5 cm
Musée des Souvenirs Napoléoniens et des Archives du Palais Princier, Monaco

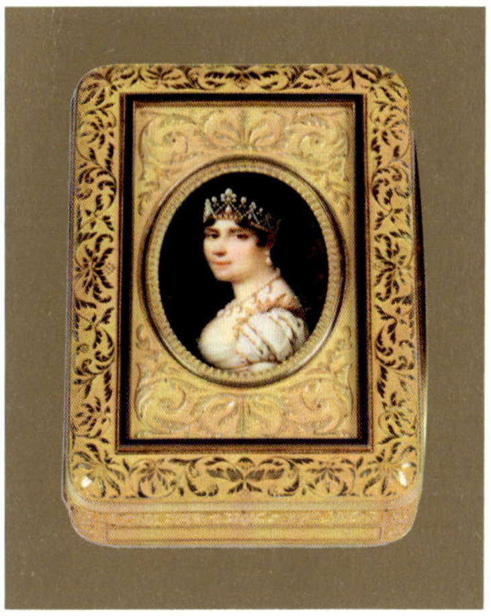

Box with portrait of the empress
c. 1800–20
Daniel Saint (1778–1847); Pierre-André Montauban, goldsmith (active 1800–20)
Gold, enamel, painted miniature on ivory, signed "Saint"
2.2 × 8 × 5.4 cm
Fondation Napoléon, Paris
Inv. 635 (Lapeyre donation)

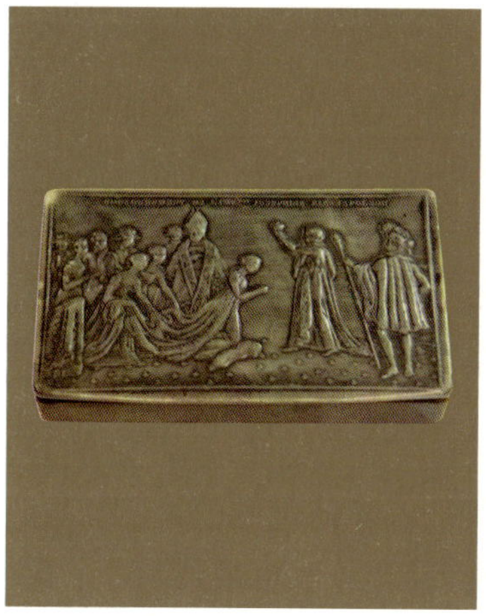

Snuffbox: Napoleon crowning Josephine
Horn, painted miniature on ivory
2 × 10 × 5.7 cm
Musée des Souvenirs Napoléoniens et des Archives du Palais Princier, Monaco

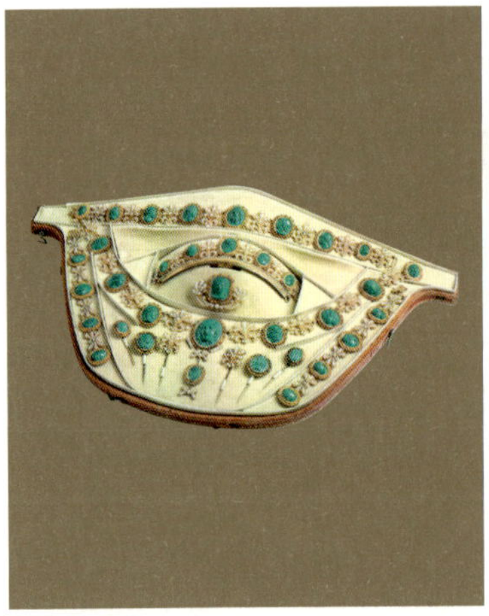

Malachite parure in its casket: choker, large necklace, diadem, brooch, pendant, four cameo hairpins, and two palmette hairpins
First quarter, nineteenth century
Gold, malachite, pearls
L. (casket) 44.5 cm
Fondation Napoléon, Paris
Inv. 973 (Lapeyre donation)

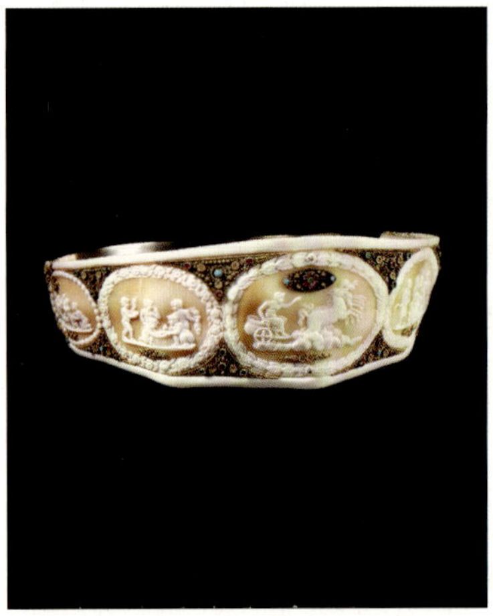

Empress Josephine's diadem, a gift from her brother-in-law, Joachim Murat, king of Naples: the cameos depict Apollo's chariot and the four seasons
1808–14, Naples
Shell cameo, gold, silver, precious stones, mother-of-pearl, and pearls
6.7 × 17 × 20 cm
Musée d'Art et d'Histoire, Palais Masséna, Nice
Inv. CHAP-1360

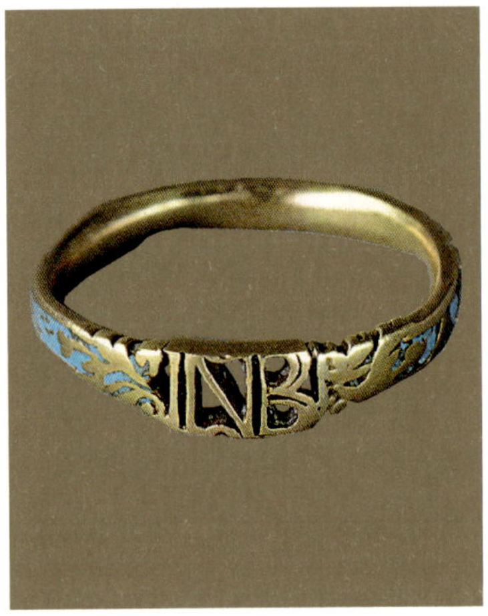

Empress Josephine's ring
Gold, enamel
Musée National des Châteaux de Malmaison et Bois-Préau, Rueil-Malmaison
Inv. MMD.29
(Department of Decorative Arts, Musée du Louvre, Paris, inv. OA 8117)

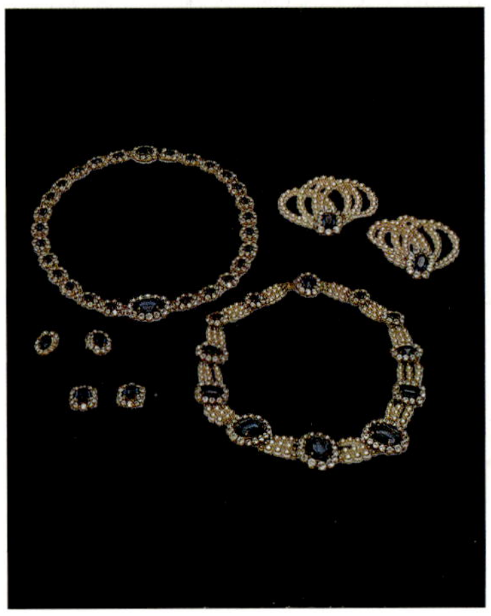

Sapphire parure belonging to Empress Josephine (replica)
Twentieth century
Sapphires, pearls, and diamonds
Musée National des Châteaux de Malmaison et Bois-Préau, Rueil-Malmaison
Inv. M.M.2004.9.1

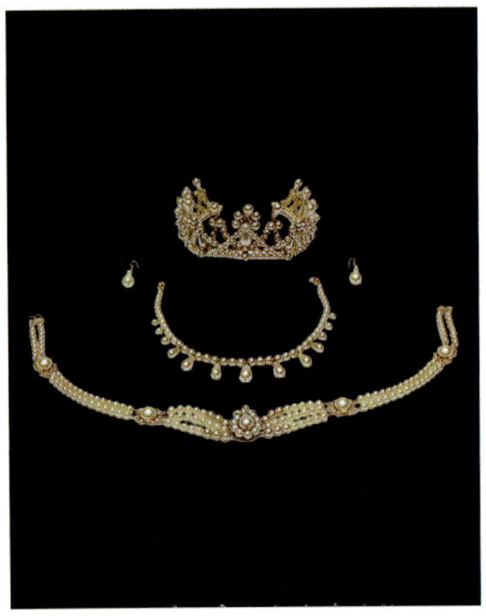

Pearl parure belonging to Empress Josephine (replica)
2003
Privilège Orfèvrerie
D. 17 cm
Musée National des Châteaux de Malmaison et Bois-Préau, Rueil-Malmaison
Inv. MM 2003-6-1

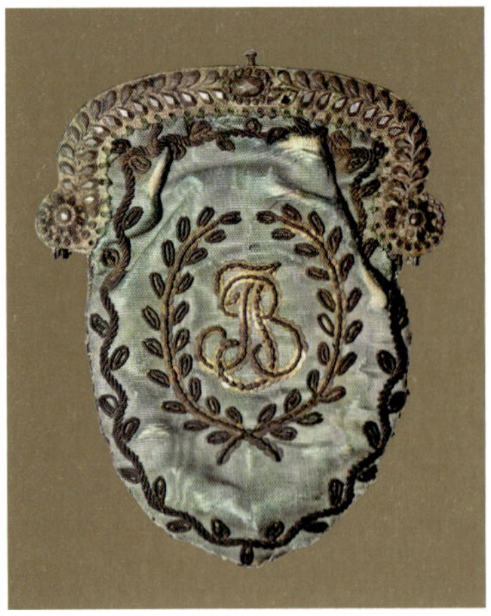

Purse belonging to Empress Josephine
First quarter, nineteenth century
Silver-embroidered silk
1 × 10 × 8 cm
Musée des Souvenirs Napoléoniens et des Archives du Palais Princier, Monaco

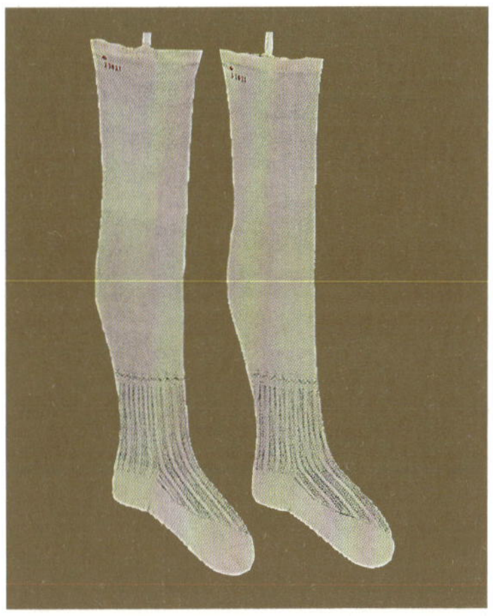

Pair of stockings belonging to Empress Josephine
White cotton
L. approx. 100 cm
Musée National des Châteaux de Malmaison et Bois-Préau, Rueil-Malmaison
Inv. MM 2003-18-1 and 2

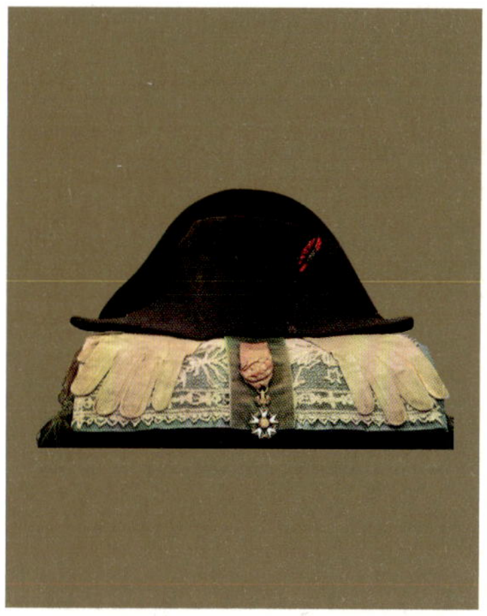

Hat belonging to Napoleon
Black felt, silk lining, no leather band
17 × 23 × 46 cm
Musée des Souvenirs Napoléoniens et des Archives du Palais Princier, Monaco

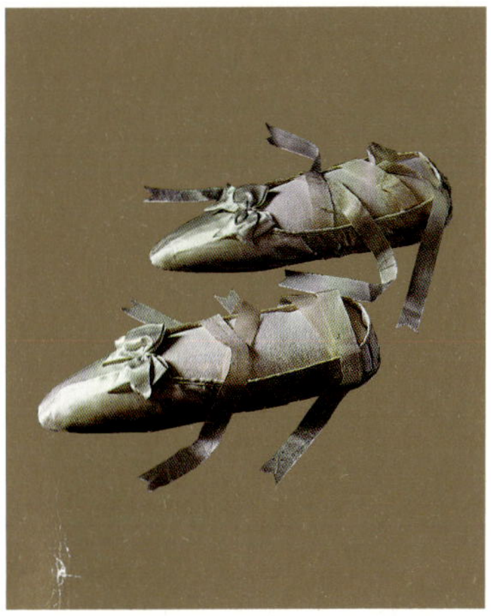

Pair of shoes belonging to Empress Josephine
First Empire
Leather, silk
L. 25 cm
Musée National des Châteaux de Malmaison et Bois-Préau, Rueil-Malmaison
Inv. N 331

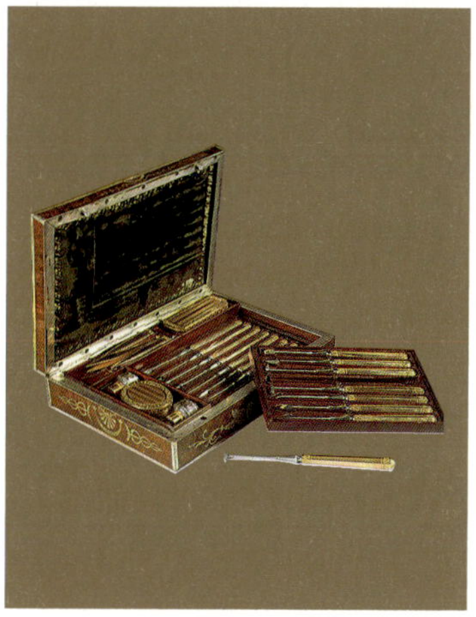

Dental hygiene set belonging to Napoleon
Early nineteenth century
Attributed to Martin-Guillaume Biennais (1764–1843)
Rosewood, mahogany, gold, steel, crystal, velvet
19 × 13.5 cm
Fondation Napoléon, Paris
Inv. 286

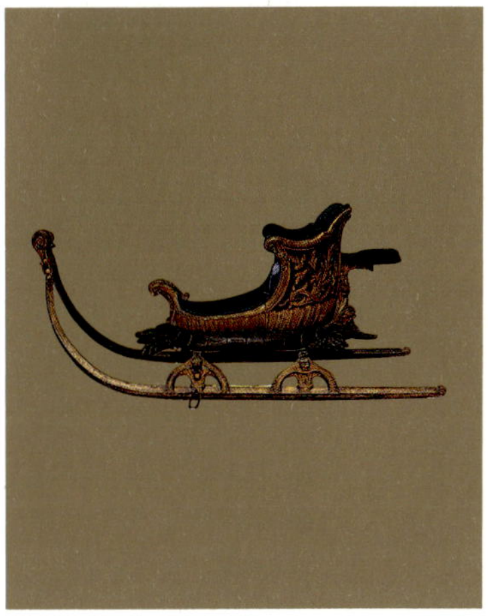

Tortoise sled from the French royal collections
1732, France
Gilded, painted wooden casing with sculpted tortoise; green embossed velvet interior
130 × 285 × 108.5 cm
Musées des Châteaux de Versailles et de Trianon, Musée des Carrosses, Versailles
Inv. MV2006.00.15 CR

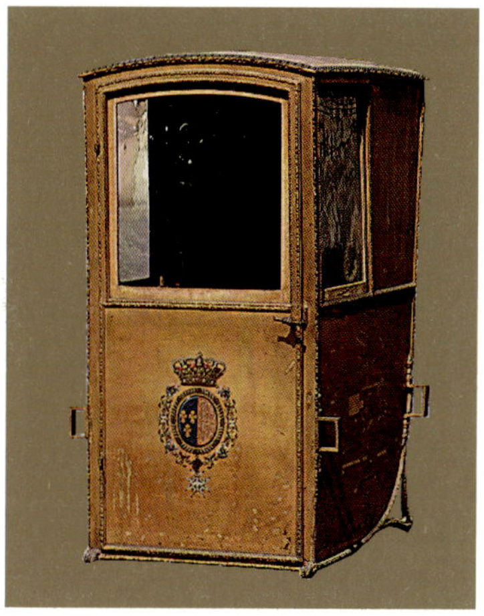

Sedan chair with the arms of France and Navarre
1780
Gilded and painted wood
151.5 × 85.5 × 103 cm
Musées des Châteaux de Versailles et de Trianon, Musée des Carrosses, Versailles
Inv. MV2006.00.23 CR

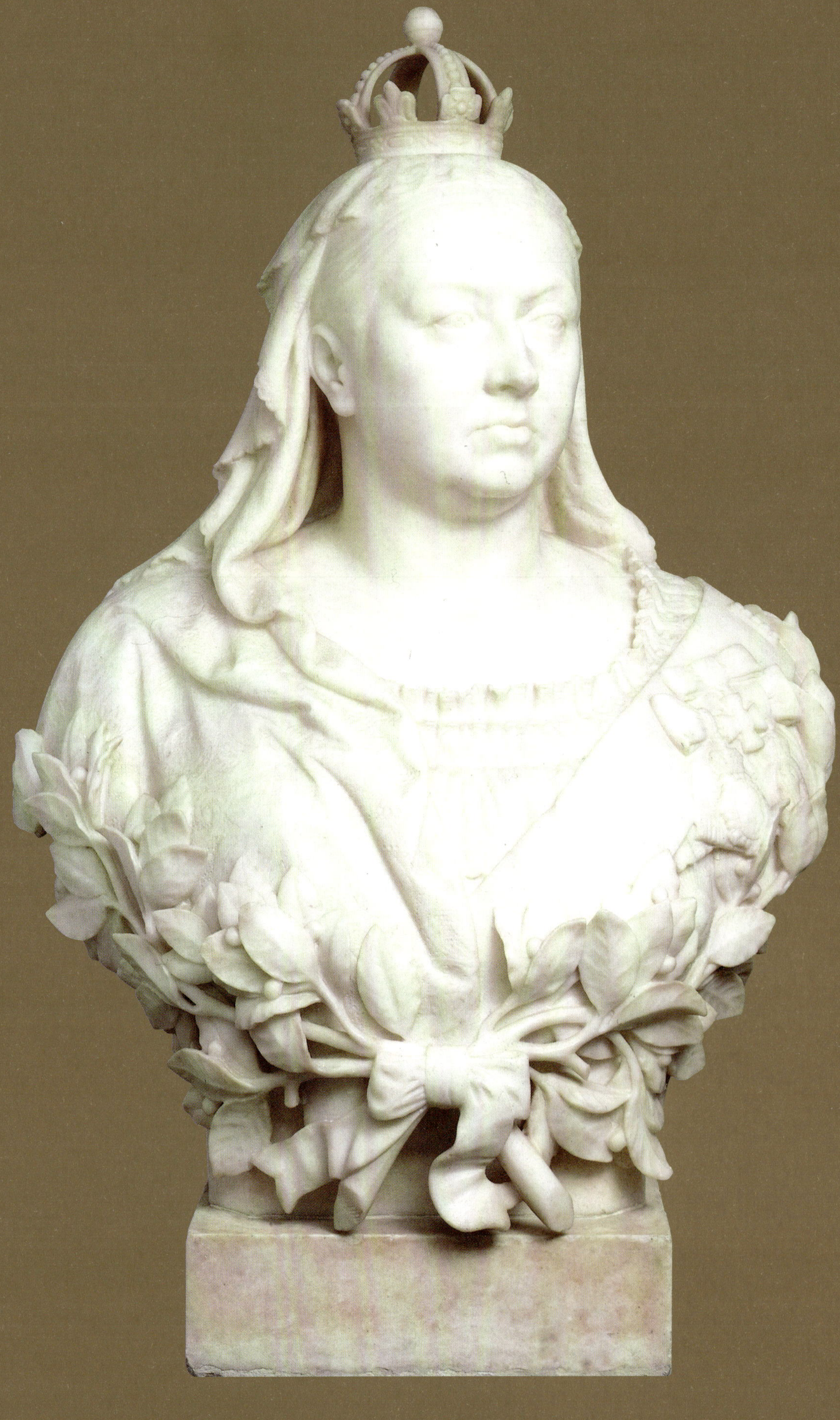

ENGLAND

Victoria (1819–1901) and Albert (1819–1861)

Bust of Queen Victoria
1888
Comte Gleichen (sculptor)
Marble
Victoria and Albert Museum, London

Victoria and Albert
A union sealed by love plays a major European role

Frédéric Lacaille

Nothing seemed to predispose Victoria, when queen-in-waiting of Great Britain, to marital happiness. Born to reign over one of the greatest powers on the planet, then at a turning point in its history and grappling with major upheavals in every field, she was also heiress to a prestigious dynasty recently shaken by scandals that had deeply discredited it in the eyes of its subjects and its European peers. And yet, utterly confident in her destiny, the young princess managed to keep her empire afloat through the choppy seas ahead, to polish the tarnished image of her family by remaining a paragon of flawless virtue and contented fruitfulness, and to enjoy the delights of practically unclouded married bliss for some twenty years.

The birth of Victoria on May 24, 1819, was the outcome of a hurriedly devised matrimonial policy designed to provide heirs for her grandfather, King George III (1738–1820), himself father to fifteen children, including seven boys surviving to adulthood, two of whom were to succeed him. In 1811, the eldest son, George (1762–1830), prince of Wales, had become prince regent to ensure the security of the dynasty when his father started to display incontrovertible signs of lunacy. With his wife Caroline of Brunswick (1768–1821), he had had a daughter Charlotte (1796–1817), who was married off to Prince Leopold of Saxe-Coburg (1790–1865). Thus, though the king's other sons lived disorderly lives—the majority preferring connections with social inferiors to dynastic alliances—the future seemed assured. But the untimely death in 1817 of their niece, Princess Charlotte, while giving birth to a stillborn infant, brought them closer to the crown, sparking a veritable sprint to the altar rail. While the second son, Frederik, duke of York and Albany (1763–1827), could hold out little hope of having a child with his wife Frederica, princess of Prussia (1767–1820), the third, William, duke of Clarence (1765–1837), married Adelaide of Saxe-Meiningen (1792–1849). She provided him with two daughters who died early, before he succeeded his brother to the throne as William IV. The fourth, Edward, duke of Kent (1767–1820), jilting a mistress he had had for many years, married Victoria

Victoria I (1819–1901), Queen of Great Britain and Ireland, Empress of India
1842
Franz Xaver Winterhalter (1806–1873)
Musées des Châteaux de Versailles et de Trianon, Versailles

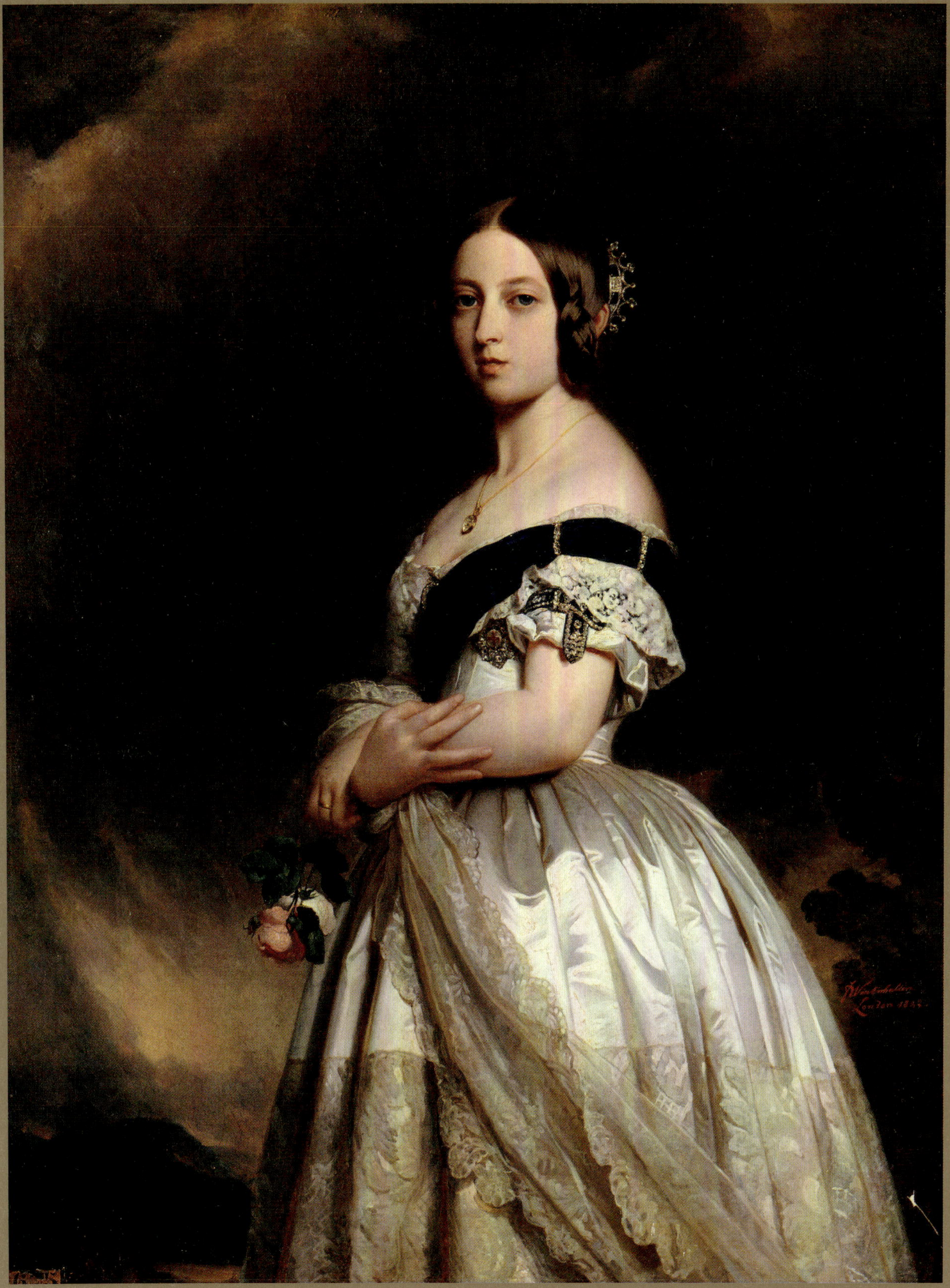

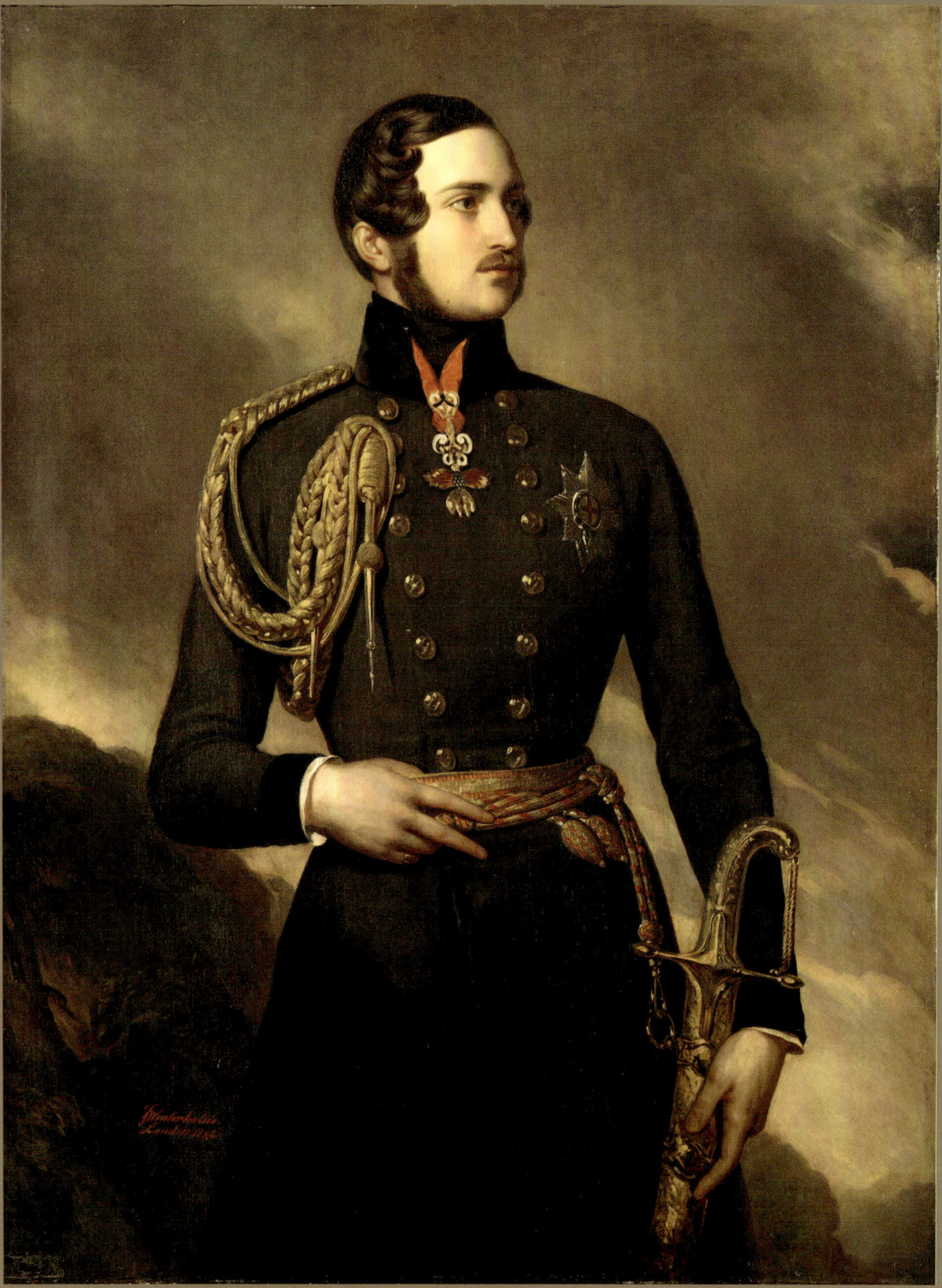

of Saxe-Coburg (1786–1861), a widow, who in 1819 gave him a daughter, later to become Queen Victoria. The fifth son, Ernest (1771–1851), had been removed from the line of British succession, along with his children, as he was king of Hanover, while the sixth, Augustus, duke of Sussex (1773–1843), had similarly been excluded though this time due to his marrying illicitly on no less than two occasions. The last son, Adolphus, duke of Cambridge (1774–1850), married Augusta of Hesse-Kassel (1797–1889), with whom he had several offspring.

Victoria of Kent, who lost her father a few months after she was born, was brought up as heiress to the British throne by her mother, the duchess of Kent, in spite of the public and unalloyed hostility of her uncles. Fortunately, the duchess could count on the well-meaning support of her younger brother, Leopold of Saxe-Coburg, George IV's son-in-law, who had remained in England after his wife's death. After his ascension to the throne in Belgium as Leopold I in 1830, he continued to watch over his niece, sustaining a correspondence with her and keeping an eye out for a husband in the family entourage.

Close to the sons of his brother Ernest (1784–1844), first duke of Saxe-Coburg and Gotha, the Princes Ernest and Albert, he presented them at the English court. The meeting with their first cousin Victoria took place in May 1836, and the young woman was immediately smitten by the charms of Albert, who had been born on August 26, 1819. The time, however, was not yet ripe for marriage.

Reaching her majority on May 24, 1837, Victoria ascended to the throne of her forefathers the following June 20, after the death of William IV. No sooner was her reign underway than Victoria embraced her duties with singular determination, impressing her entourage with her implacable calm and masterful self-control. Crowned in Westminster Abbey on June 28, 1838, she was to marry the man on whom she had set her heart—her cousin Albert—in the chapel at the Palace of St. James on February 10, 1840. Their love would endure until the premature death of Albert on December 14, 1861, the loss of her beloved plunging Victoria into inconsolable grief that continued to her own death on January 22, 1901.

The partnership of Victoria and Albert, founded on a great number of common values and shared interests, remains a model of its kind, the finest example of true love among nineteenth-century European dynasties. Their relationship was not, however, without its ups and downs, due both to Victoria's authoritative personality and the rather austere character of Albert, who was eager to play a political role that his wife refused him—during the early years of their marriage, at least.

It was in the private sphere that Victoria and Albert were closest, sharing similar tastes in the arts in particular. Distrustful of her own judgment, the young

Prince Albert of Saxe-Coburg and Gotha (1819–1861): Prince Consort of Great Britain, Husband to Queen Victoria I
1842
Franz Xaver Winterhalter
(1806–1873)
Musées des Châteaux de Versailles et de Trianon, Versailles

sovereign almost always bowed to her husband's opinions in this area. The British Royal Collection boasts glorious evidence of this joint passion for the arts. Their favorite living artists included the German portraitist Franz Xaver Winterhalter, a painter in the grand manner who also worked for the French crown; he was presented to them in 1842 by the daughter of the French monarch, Louise, queen of the Belgians, now the new spouse of dear old uncle Leopold. For nearly thirty years, Winterhalter would undertake regular sojourns in London a few months a year, turning out some one hundred and fifty pictures and drawings for his royal British patrons. The portraits on show here are replicas of the first official portraits of Victoria and Albert carried out by Winterhalter in London in 1842 and that same year given by Victoria to the French king.

Victoria and Louis-Philippe: First steps on the road to the Entente Cordiale

On the announcement of the death of William IV and the accession of Victoria, the king of the French, Louis-Philippe I, was to be among the first to send letters of condolence and congratulation to the young sovereign. Though inevitably conforming to protocol, the French sovereign also wanted to express his attachment to the British royal family, in remembrance of the friendship that had sprung up between him and the duke of Kent during his long years of exile. Meeting for the first time in 1794, in Canada, where the British nobleman was acting as governor of Halifax, the two men struck up a correspondence that ended only on the death of Kent in January 1820.

Inclined to Anglophilia through education and the course of his early life, Louis-Philippe was keen to engineer a rapprochement between France and Britain, by then venturing beyond the diplomatic isolation in which she found herself since the treaties of 1815. Moreover, the *Trois Glorieuses*, those days in July 1830 that had led to Louis-Philippe taking the throne, had revived the specters of revolutionary violence. He felt it necessary to reassure other European powers and thereby convince them of his legitimacy. Nevertheless, it was Victoria herself who, in 1843, took the initiative in arranging a summit meeting with the French king. To avoid placing her government before a "fait accompli", however, it was decided that the visit should be a strictly private, family affair. The queen would be received at the Château d'Eu, a residence belonging to Louis-Philippe personally, situated inland from the Normandy coast, near Tréport.

As it was to be the first by an English sovereign on French territory since Henry VIII met François I at the Field of the Cloth of Gold in 1520, the symbolic significance of this journey could be lost on no one. Arriving on her yacht the

Louis-Philippe and Queen Victoria aboard the Victoria and Albert Yacht, September 2, 1843
After 1843
François-Auguste Biard (1798–1882)
Musées des Châteaux de Versailles et de Trianon, Versailles

Banquet Held by Queen Victoria in Honor of King Louis-Philippe, October 11, 1844
Attributed to
Édouard-Henri-Théophile Pingret (1788–1875)
Musées des Châteaux de Versailles et de Trianon, Versailles

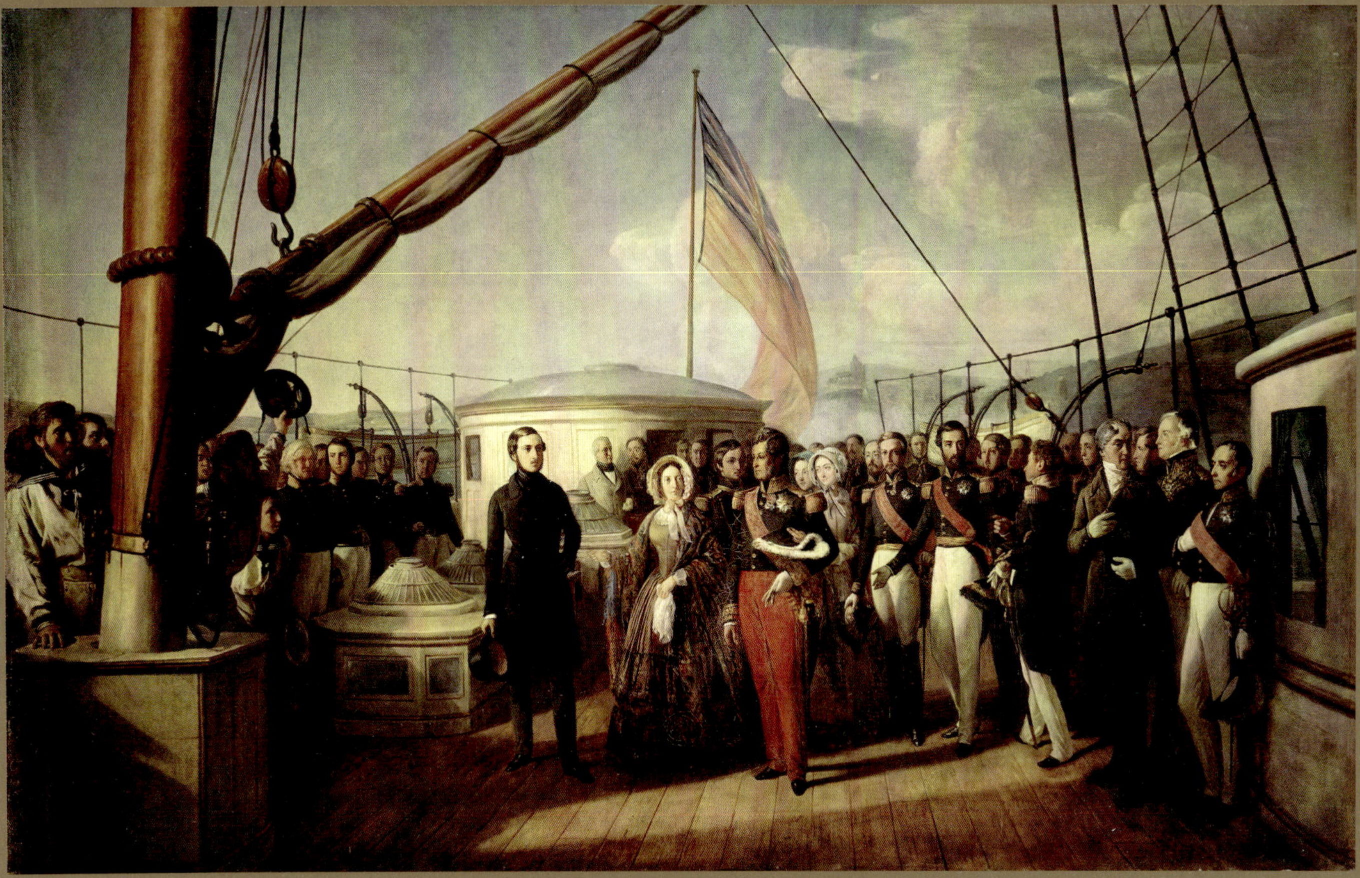

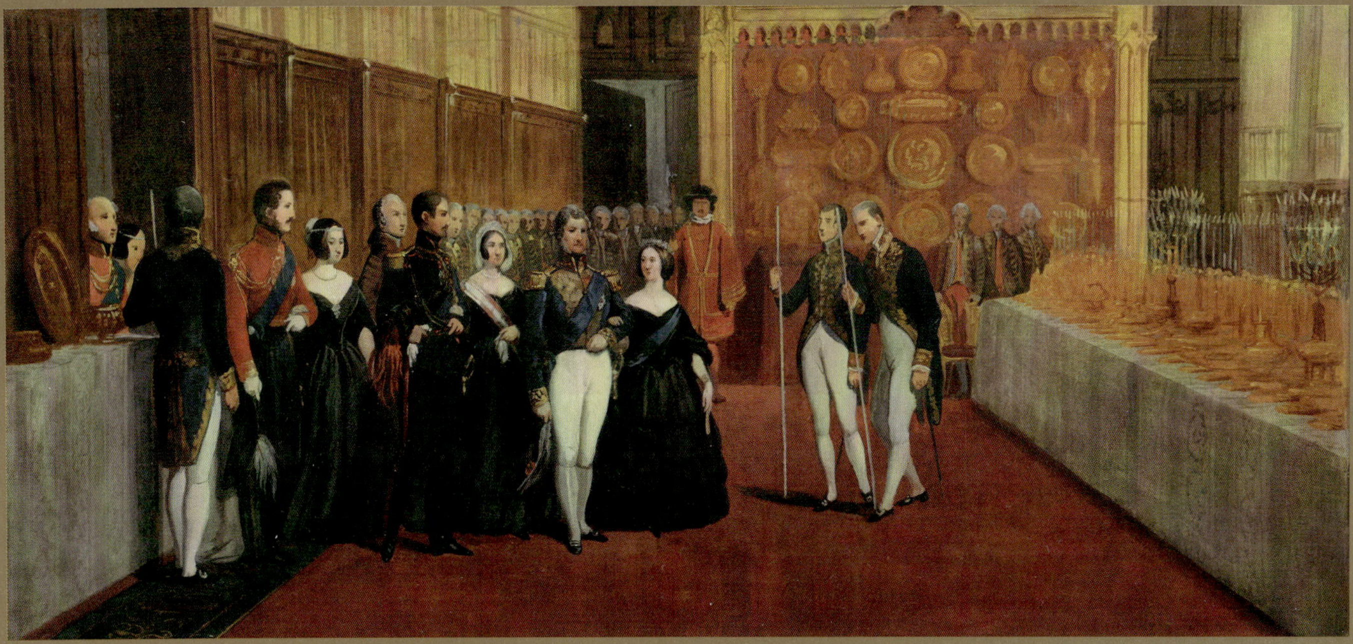

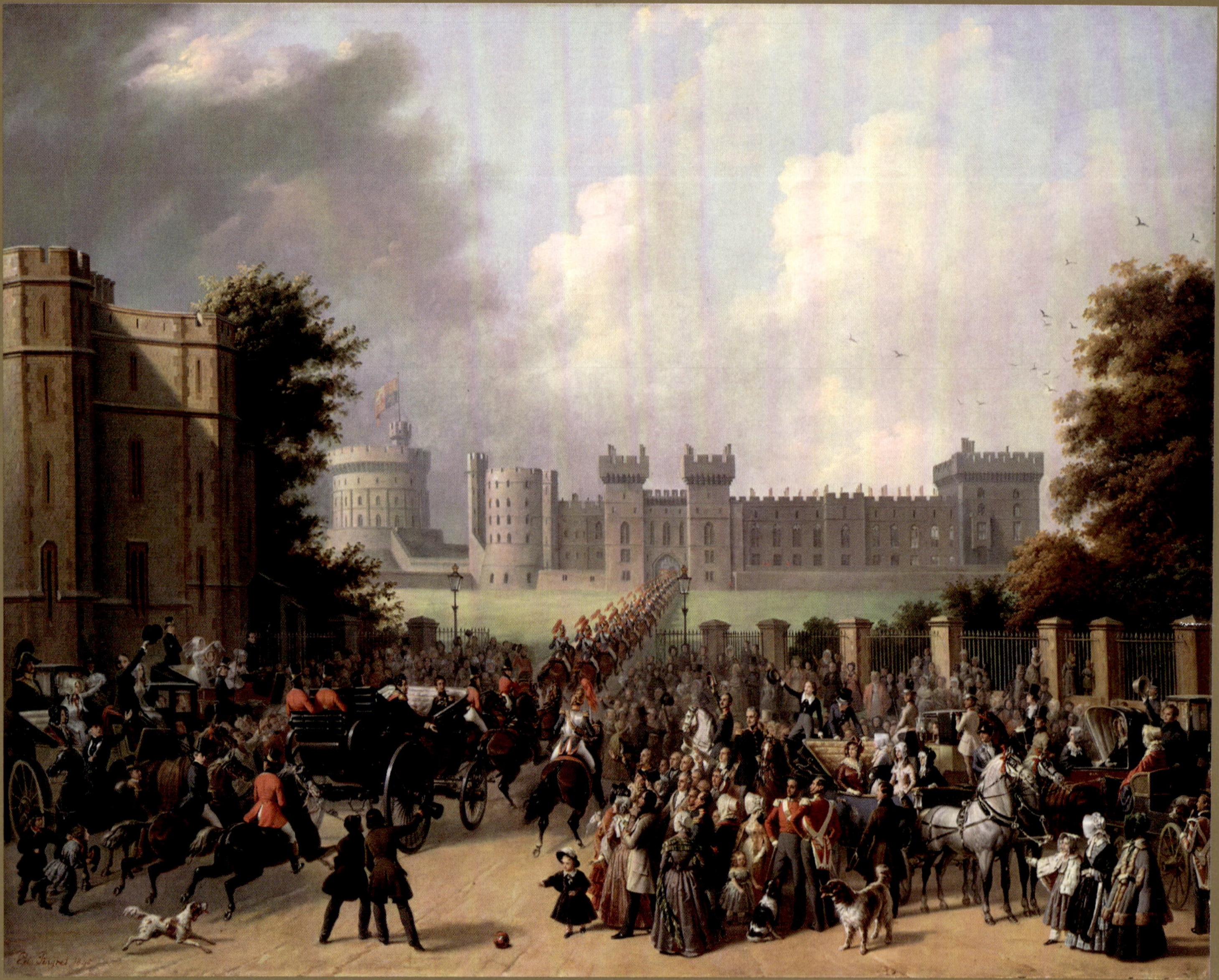

Victoria and Albert with a small English contingent, the queen and her husband disembarked at Tréport on September 2, 1843. Conducted to the Château d'Eu, she remained there until September 7 for a succession of receptions, promenades, and country picnics, during which she became acquainted with the entire French royal family and forged bonds of friendship with both Louis-Philippe and Queen Marie Amélie. On the fringes of the royal meeting, the ministers invited—Guizot for France and Lord Aberdeen for Great Britain—worked to bring their two countries closer together. At the request of Louis-Philippe, each stage in the journey was immortalized by several artists, both in an album of watercolors the king presented to the queen the following year and in a series of pictures that were later to hang in a new gallery devoted to the queen and named after her at the Château d'Eu.

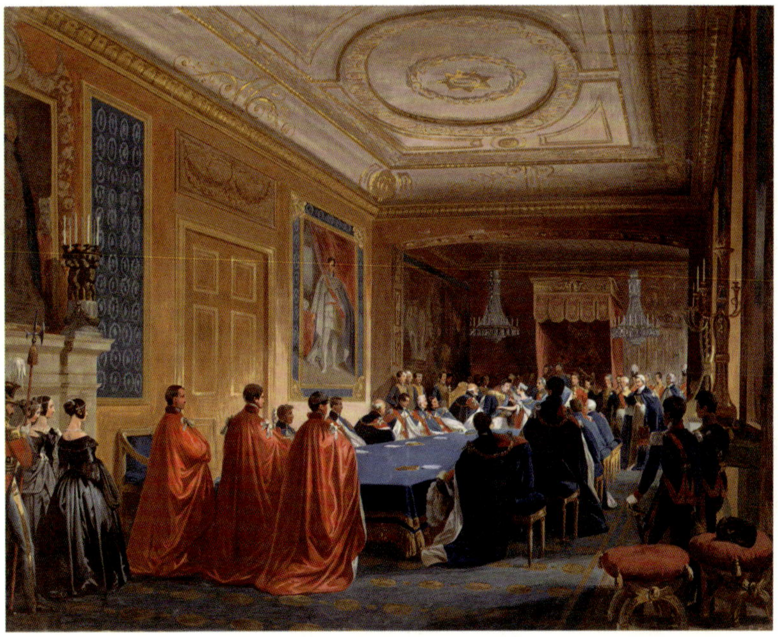

Admittance of King Louis-Philippe to the Most Noble Order of the Garter by Queen Victoria, Windsor Castle, October 11, 1844
Claude, also known as Claudius Jacquand (1804–1878)
Musées des Châteaux de Versailles et de Trianon, Versailles

The following year, from October 8 to 15 1844, it was the turn of Louis-Philippe to make a courtesy call of his own to Great Britain, where he was received by Queen Victoria at Windsor Castle. He was accompanied by his youngest son, the duke of Montpensier, and a substantial entourage, including the faithful Guizot. The major event of the visit occured on October 11, when the French king was awarded the Order of the Garter, a ceremony followed by a great banquet of the knights of the order in St. George's Hall.

Louis-Philippe would have liked such visits to take place once a year, but political events decided otherwise. After her return from a sojourn in Prussia in 1845, Queen Victoria was to make just one further visit to Château d'Eu. Faithful to her political engagements, however, the British sovereign offered asylum to the French king when he was overthrown during the Revolution of 1848. Louis-Philippe was to end his life in 1850 in the great house at Claremont that Victoria had placed at his disposal and which had once been the residence of her uncle Leopold.

King Louis-Philippe's Voyage to England in 1844, the Arrival of the King and His Son, the Duke of Montpensier, at Windsor Castle, October 8, 1844
1845
Édouard-Henri-Théophile Pingret (1788–1875)
Musées des Châteaux de Versailles et de Trianon, Versailles

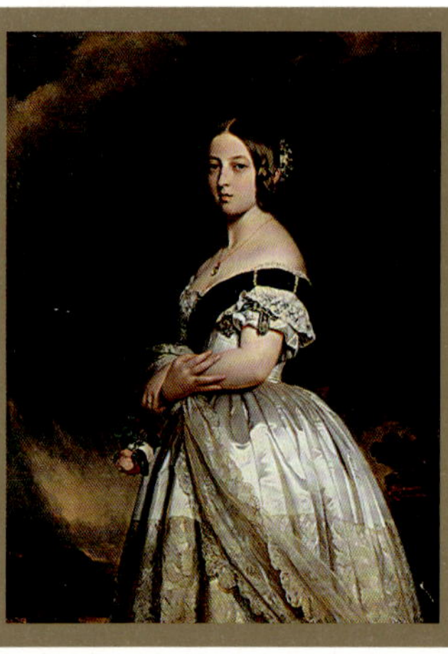

Victoria I (1819–1901), Queen of Great Britain and Ireland, Empress of India
1842
Franz Xaver Winterhalter (1806–1873)
Oil on canvas
146 × 114 cm (inc. frame)
Musées des Châteaux de Versailles et de Trianon, Versailles
Inv. MV4675

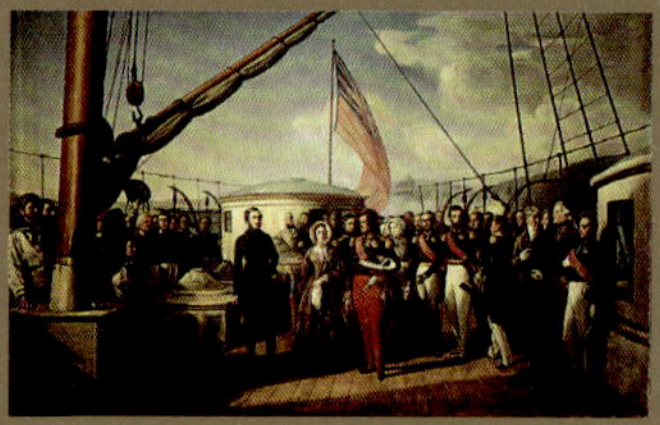

Louis-Philippe and Queen Victoria aboard the Victoria and Albert Yacht, September 2, 1843
After 1843
François-Auguste Biard (1798–1882)
Oil on canvas
148 × 230 cm
Musées des Châteaux de Versailles et de Trianon, Versailles
Inv. MV6883

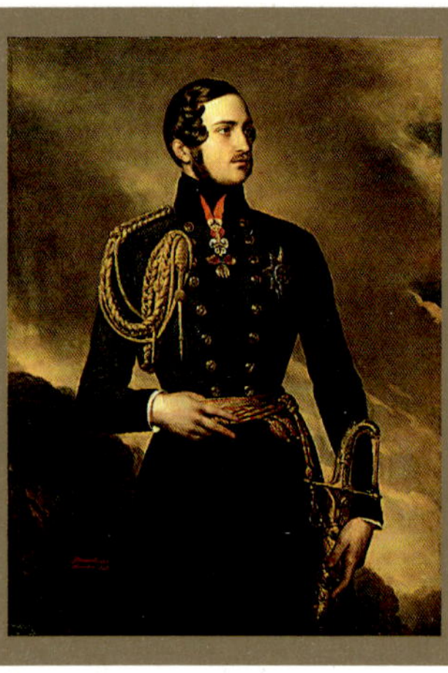

Prince Albert of Saxe-Coburg and Gotha (1819–1861): Prince Consort of Great Britain, Husband to Queen Victoria I
1842
Franz Xaver Winterhalter (1806–1873)
Oil on canvas
150.5 × 115.5 cm (inc. frame)
Musées des Châteaux de Versailles et de Trianon, Versailles
Inv. MV4676

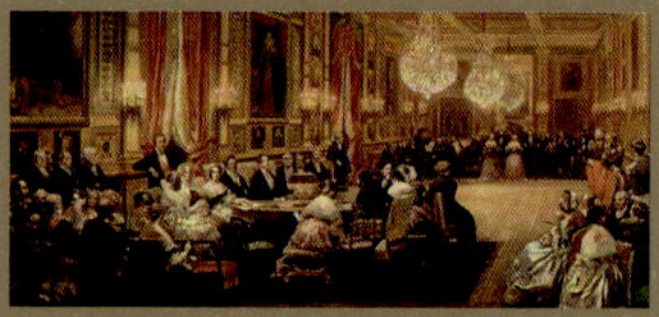

Concert in the Galerie des Guise, Château d'Eu, September 4, 1843, in the Presence of Louis-Philippe, the Royal Family, Queen Victoria, and Prince Albert
After 1843
Eugène Lami (1800–1890)
Oil on canvas
83 × 172 cm
Musées des Châteaux de Versailles et de Trianon, Versailles
Inv. MV6119

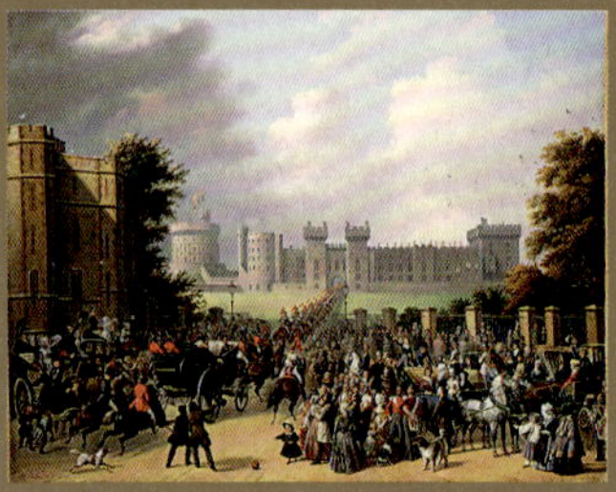

King Louis-Philippe's Voyage to England in 1844, the Arrival of the King and His Son, the Duke of Montpensier, at Windsor Castle, October 8, 1844
1845
Édouard-Henri-Théophile Pingret (1788–1875)
Oil on canvas
128 × 160 cm
Musées des Châteaux de Versailles et de Trianon, Versailles
Inv. MV5127

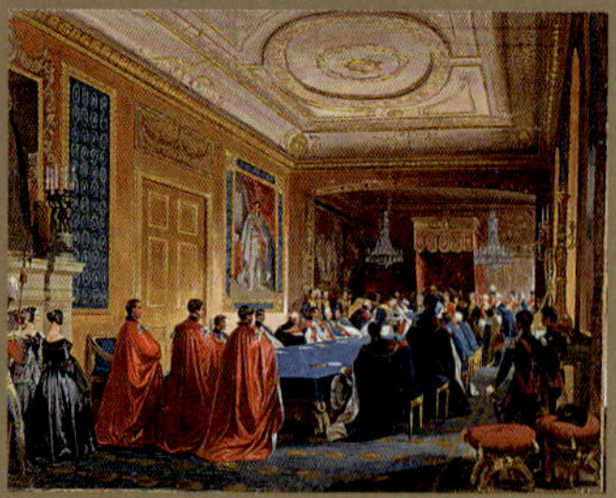

Admittance of King Louis-Philippe to the Most Noble Order of the Garter by Queen Victoria, Windsor Castle, October 11, 1844
Claude, also known as Claudius Jacquand (1804–1878)
Oil on canvas
97 × 145.9 × 5.5 cm (inc. frame)
Musées des Châteaux de Versailles et de Trianon, Versailles
Inv. MV6871

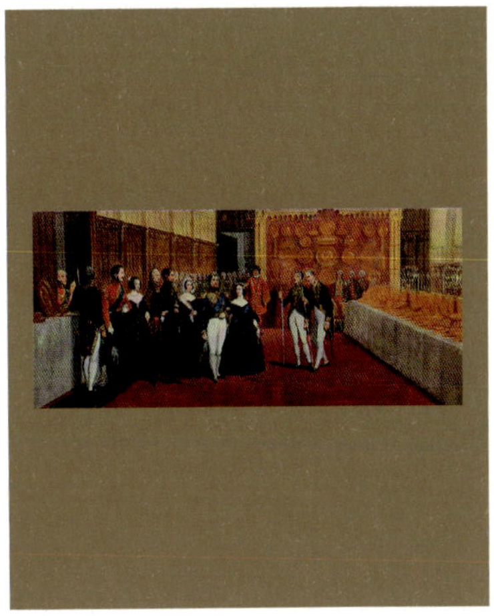

Banquet Held by Queen Victoria in Honor of King Louis-Philippe, October 11, 1844 (Following the Admittance of King Louis-Philippe to the Most Noble Order of the Garter at Windsor Castle)
Attributed to
ÉDOUARD-HENRI-THÉOPHILE PINGRET
(1788–1875)
Tempera
83 × 170 cm
Musées des Châteaux de Versailles et de Trianon, Versailles
Inv. MV8150

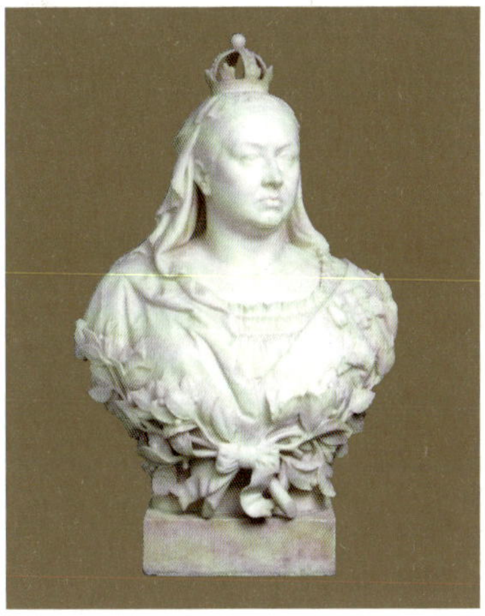

Bust of Queen Victoria
1888
COMTE GLEICHEN (sculptor)
Marble
Victoria and Albert Museum, London
Inv. W.10-1967

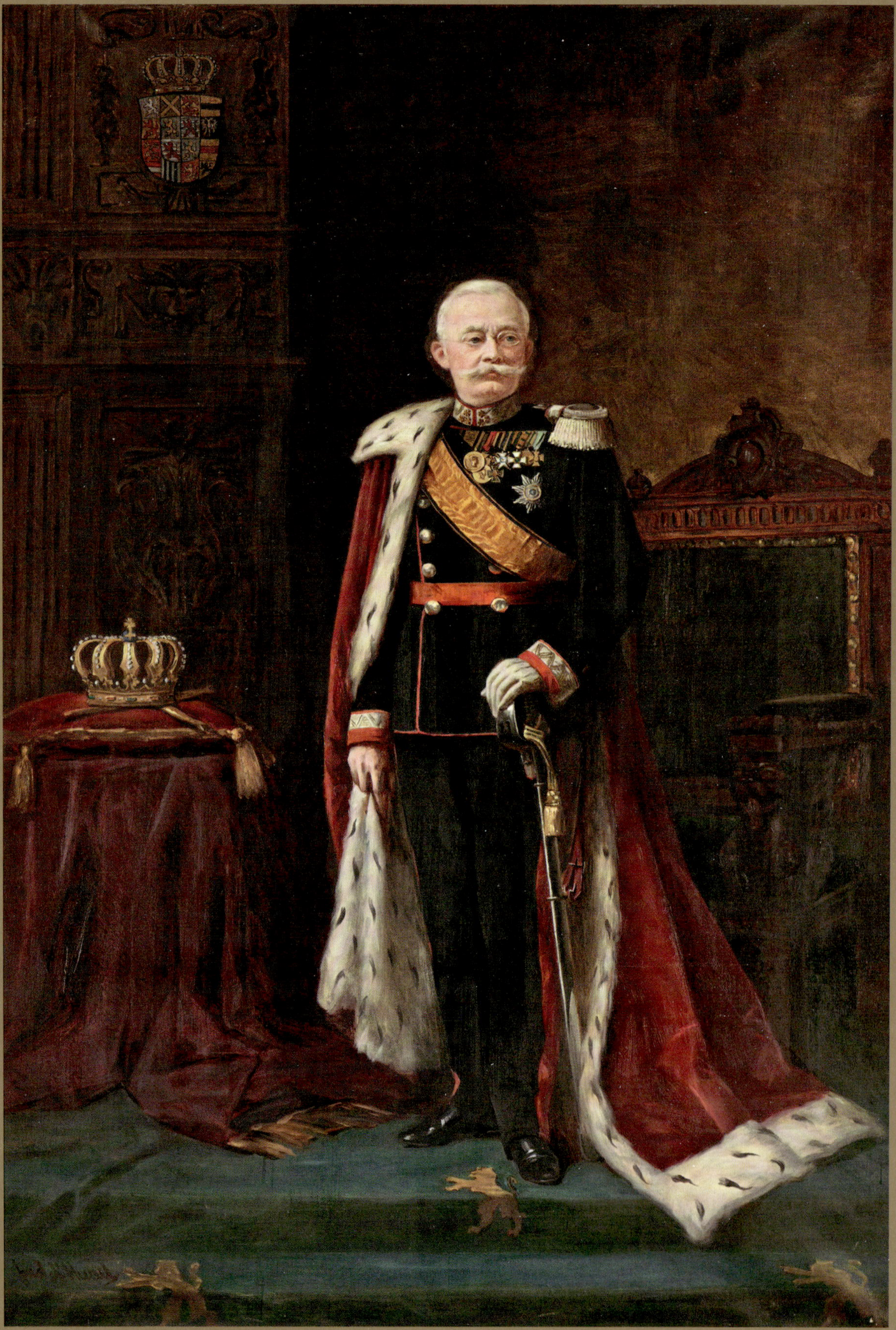

LUXEMBOURG

Grand Duke Adolf (1817–1905)

Grand Duke Adolf
c. 1900
Ferdinand d'Huart
(1857–1919)
Cour Grand-Ducale
de Luxembourg

Adolf, Duke of Nassau and Grand Duke of Luxembourg

Muriel Prieur

The modern-day grand duchy emerged in the late nineteenth century after Luxembourg crossed paths with the Nassau-Weilburg family. It was this encounter that proved decisive for the history of the country, the prime mover being Adolf, duke of Nassau, who became, after 1890, grand duke of Luxembourg.

The Congress of Vienna in 1815, which sought to repair the wounds of a Europe shattered by the effects of the twenty-year period between the French Revolution and the First Empire, also reinstituted a state that had been swallowed up by France. The origins of Luxembourg date back to 963, when Sigefroi, the son of the count of the Ardennes, acquired territory on which he founded a city. He started by building a fortified settlement, Lucilinburhuc, a word meaning "little castle" that gives the country its name. During the Middle Ages, the county experienced the usual vicissitudes, but the sagacious policies adopted by a series of ambitious counts extended its frontiers. By the fourteenth century, the Luxembourgs had risen to become one of the more significant feudal families in Europe. Allied to the kings of France, they also wielded considerable power in the Holy Roman Empire. The kings of Bohemia by marriage, on no less than three occasions their counts rose to become emperor.

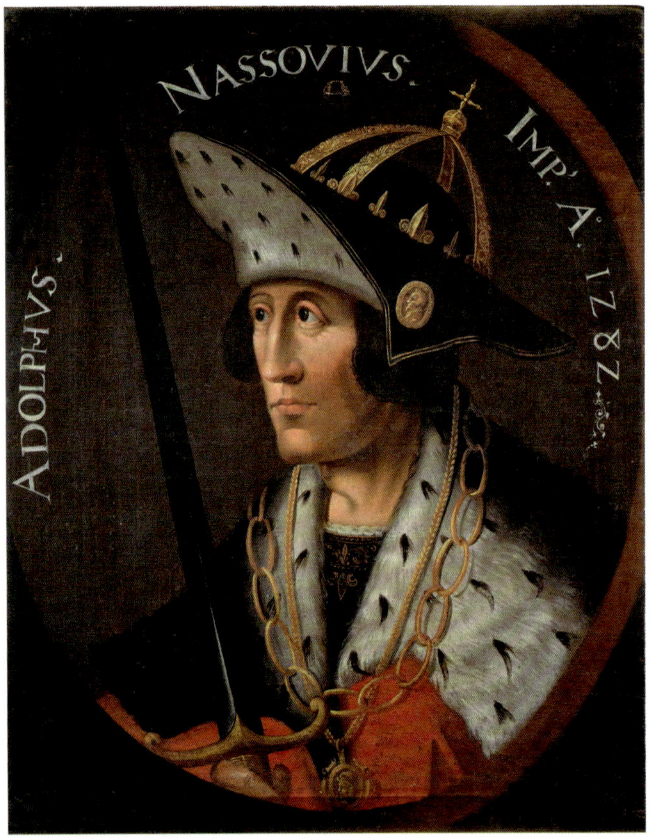

Presumed Portrait of Emperor Adolf of Nassau (1250–1298)
Nineteenth century
Cour Grand-Ducale de Luxembourg

By the second half of the fifteenth century the curtain was coming down on the golden age of Luxembourg, and for several centuries the country was piloted by foreign sovereigns. This was a time of famous ducal

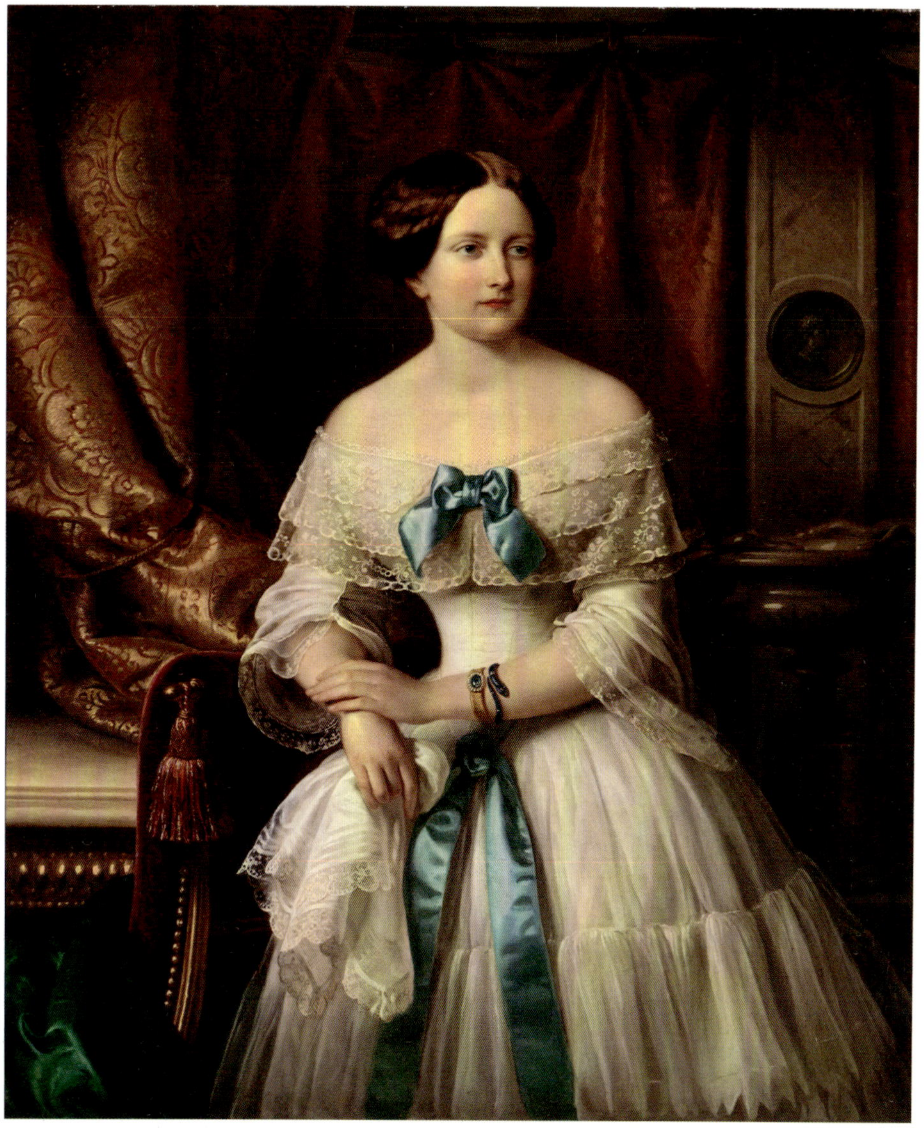

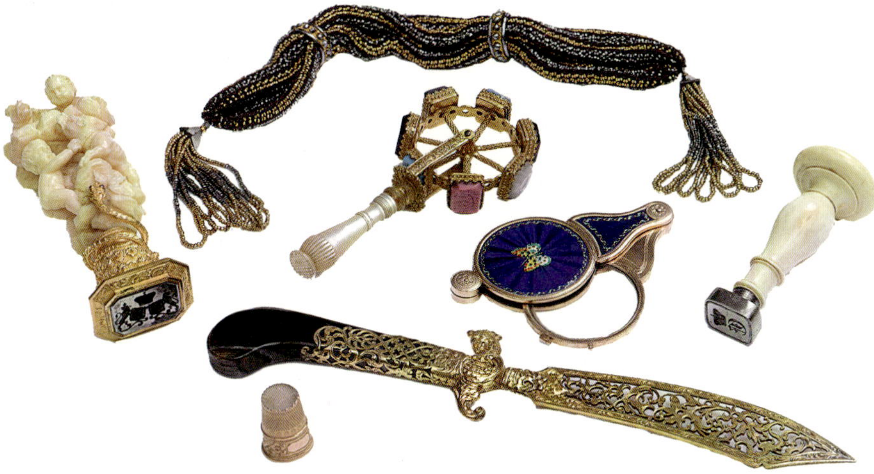

Elizabeth Mikhailovna (1826–1845), Grand Duchess of Russia, First Wife of Grand Duke Adolf (posthumous portrait)
1847
After Carl Ferdinand Sohn (1805–1867)
Cour Grand-Ducale de Luxembourg

Seal, case, bracelet, magnifying glass, paper knife, belonging to the Grand Duchess
Russia
Cour Grand-Ducale de Luxembourg

rulers of Luxembourg, such as Charles V and Empress Maria Theresia of Austria, who, though showing an interest in the outlying duchy, never took up residence there. During the French Revolution and the Empire the county was absorbed as a French department.

In 1815 the state, elevated to the rank of grand duchy, was presented to King Willem I of the Netherlands as compensation for the loss of territories ceded to Prussia. When revolution broke out in Belgium in 1830, however, and the nation attained independence, the fate of Luxembourg was poised on a knife-edge. Forced to yield its French-speaking territories to Belgium, its independence was formally ratified by the 1839 Treaty of London. Willem I of Orange-Nassau remained in place as king of the Netherlands and grand duke of Luxembourg.

The Nassaus were a very ancient lineage and they, like Luxembourg, had been a force to be reckoned with in the Holy Roman Empire. One of their ancestors, Adolphus, had been elected king of the Romans in the Empire in 1292. Split into many branches over the course of the centuries, the Nassaus still wielded influence when, on Napoleon's demand, the Holy Roman Empire was dissolved. As protector of the new Confederation of the Rhine, the latter was instrumental in the establishment of many new principalities, duchies, and kingdoms. The Nassaus rose from princes to dukes in 1806, the first being Frederik August of Nassau-Usingen. A young cousin destined to succeed him, Prince Frederik Willem of Nassau-Weilburg, had the ear of many of the most powerful figures of the time. Showered with gifts by Napoleon, he turned the duchy into a significant player. He died shortly before ascending the throne, however, and it was his son Willem who became second duke of Nassau.

An ally of the czars through his family, Willem's son, Duke Adolf, had married a niece of Nicholas I in 1844. The czar provided the young lady with a sumptuous trousseau, including a silver dinner service and a dowry of 1 million roubles. The duchess, Elisabeth, died in childbed after the birth of her daughter, who also failed to survive. This tragedy left the young duke overwhelmed by what he called the "destruction of his paradise." Honoring the memory of his late wife with a portrait that was later to hang in the study at the grand-ducal palace in Luxembourg, another memento of this union can be seen in the splendid set of silverware ornamented with the Nassau and Romanov coat of arms delivered to the grand duchy years later, well after the death of the duchess.

Eventually, however, in 1851, the duke did remarry a young princess of Anhalt-Dessau, Adelheid-Marie, much vaunted for her charm, intelligence, and love of the arts. Remaining by his side for more than fifty years, she gave him an heir who was to succeed him on the throne of Luxembourg as Willem IV.

Adelheid-Marie d'Anhalt-Dessau (1833–1916), Second Wife of Grand Duke Adolf
1855
Carl Ferdinand Sohn
(1805–1867)
Cour Grand-Ducale de Luxembourg

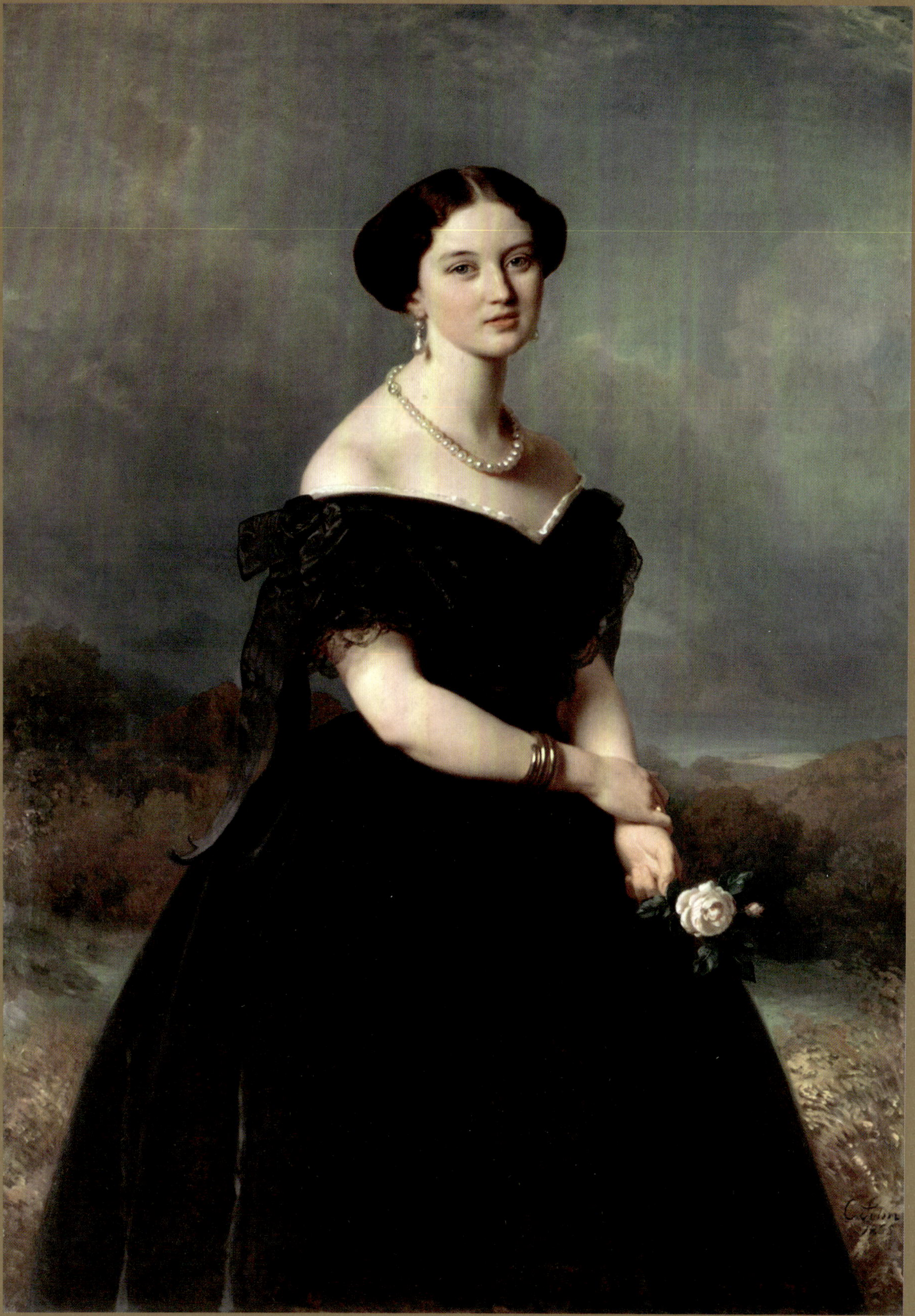

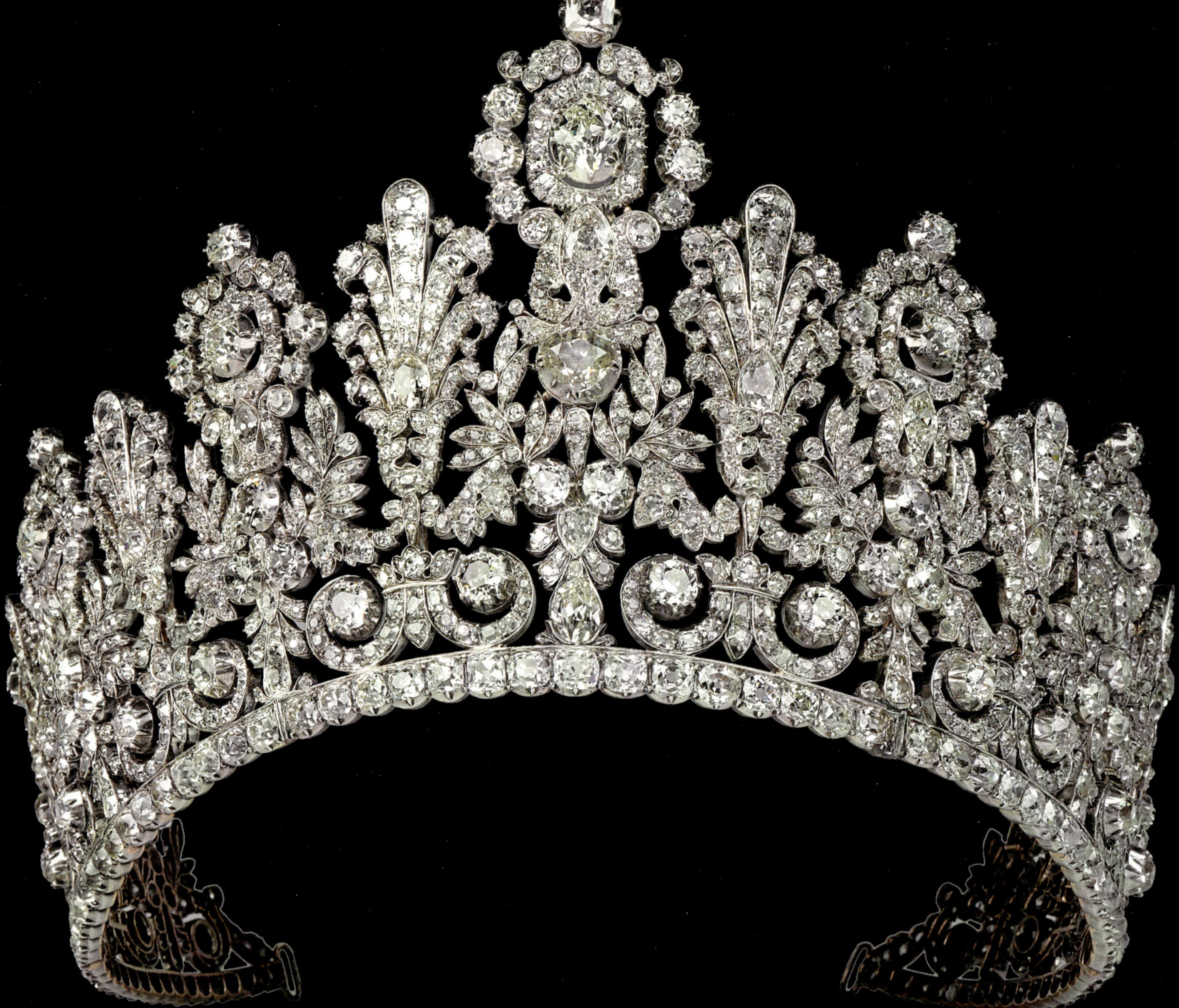

In the Austro-Prussian conflict of 1864, Duke Adolf kept faith with the grand duchy's many bonds with Austria. After his victory, King Wilhelm I of Prussia annexed his lands and Adolf, forced into exile, had to withdraw to a palace in Vienna. Deprived of his territory, but still duke in title, he remained head of the Weilburg family and one of the descendants of the male Nassau line.

As fate would have it, due to the rules of the Nassau Family Pact of 1783, the old duke, then aged seventy-three, inherited the Luxembourg crown as the closest male relative. King-Grand Duke Willem III of Orange-Nassau, following the successive deaths of his three sons, had only his daughter, Wilhelmina, left to succeed him. The Congress of Vienna, however, stipulated that the Luxembourg succession, unlike that of the Netherlands, was to remain agnatic (uniquely through the male line). Adolf thus assumed the regency for the seriously ill Willem III, and, when the latter passed away in November 1890, succeeded him as grand duke. In consequence, Luxembourg obtained its own dynasty, the Luxembourg-Nassaus, and, moreover, a sovereign who would actually reside in the country—unheard of since the fifteenth century.

As his official residence, the new grand duke chose the former sixteenth-century city hall of Luxembourg. Renovating and modernizing it, he added a new wing. Grand Duke Adolf and Grand Duchess Adelheid-Marie moved into their new residence on December 1, 1895, standing on the palace balcony to the acclamation of the people. Although Adolf had attempted to impose his will on his government while in the duchy of Nassau, as grand duke he opted to rely on a prime minister to manage the business of state. Proud to call himself a Luxembourger, thanks to his amenable character and acute sense of responsibility, he quickly won the affection of his new subjects. After his accession to the throne, he saw his role as one of consolidating and defending the independence of the country and promoting its development.

Born in 1817, Adolf survived to become a doyen among European monarchs, reigning until his death in 1905, followed on the throne by his son Willem IV. As the last agnate of Nassau, he confirmed in law a clause in the family pact authorizing—in the absence of surviving male heirs—the succession of a princess. Thus it was that in 1912 he was in turn succeeded by Grand Duchess Adelheid-Marie, then, after the latter's abdication, by Grand Duchess Charlotte in 1919. Much loved, Charlotte inspired the nation and encouraged its resistance during the dark years of occupation.

The Diadem of the Grand Duchess of Luxembourg
1829, Frankfurt
Jacob Tillmann Speltz
Cour Grand-Ducale
de Luxembourg

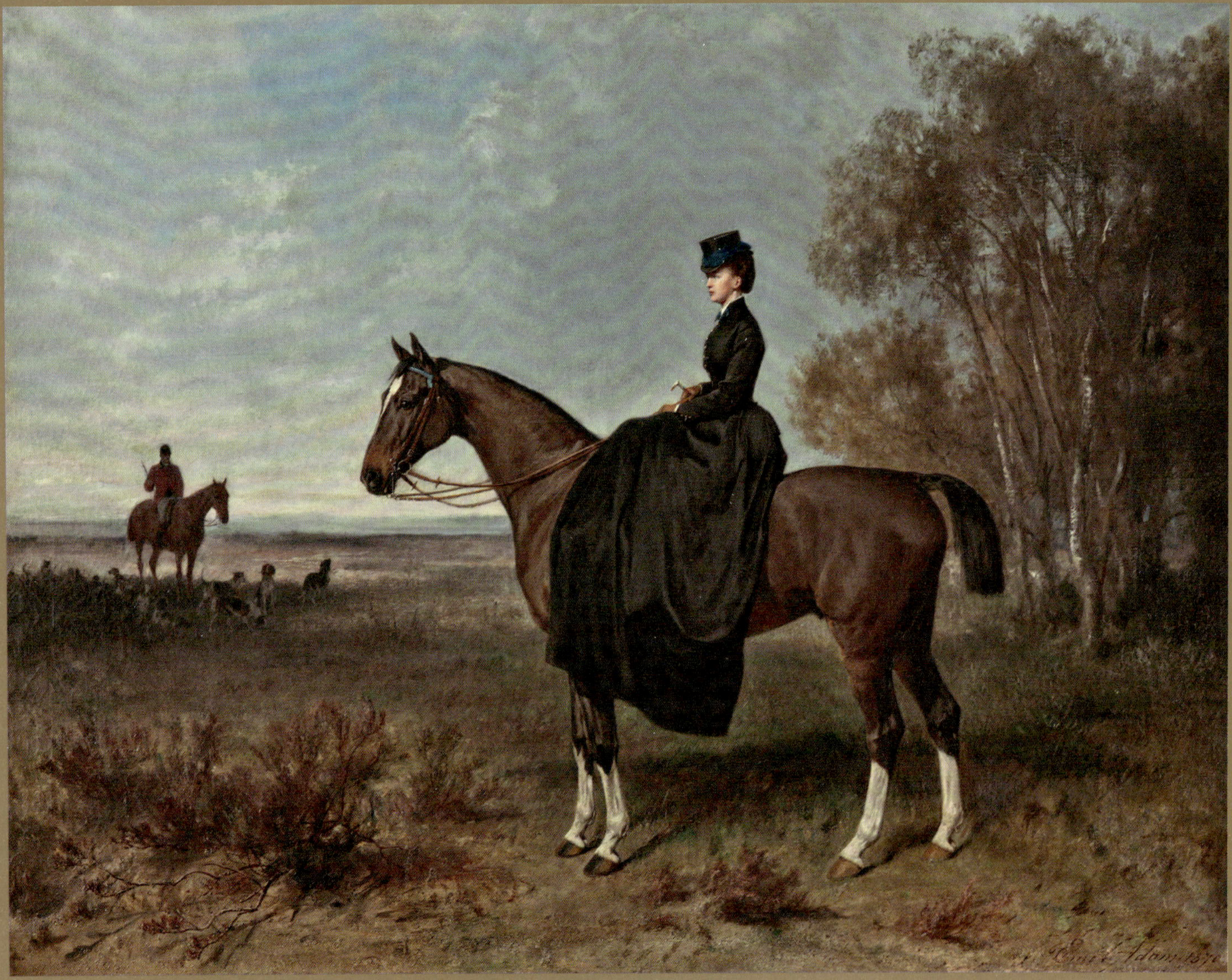

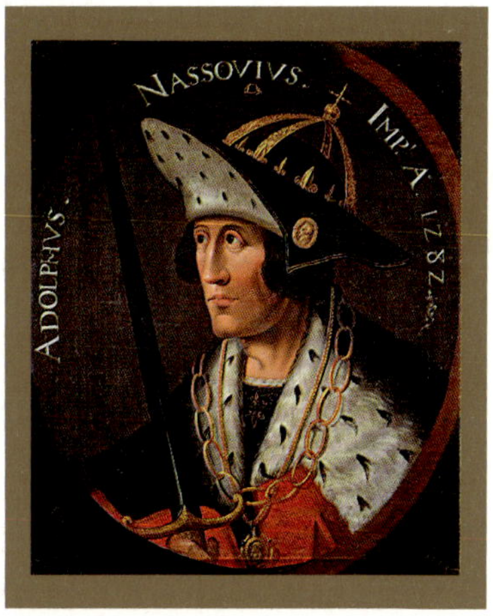

Presumed Portrait of Emperor Adolf of Nassau (1250–1298)
Nineteenth century
Oil on canvas
80 × 60 cm
Cour Grand-Ducale de Luxembourg
Inv. AAN00411001

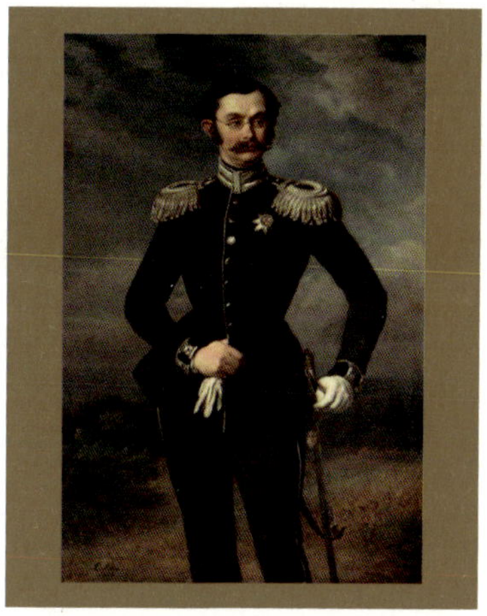

Adolf of Nassau (1817–1905), Grand Duke of Luxembourg
1856
Carl Ferdinand Sohn (1805–1867)
Oil on canvas
182 × 143 cm (inc. frame)
Cour Grand-Ducale de Luxembourg
Inv. AAN00098001

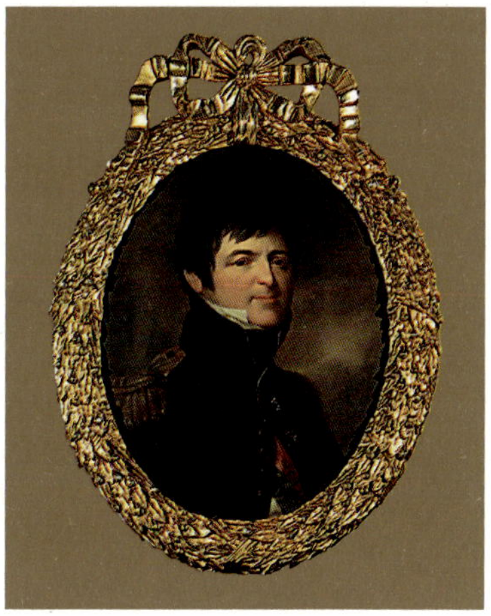

Frederik Willem of Luxembourg (1768–1816), Prince of Nassau-Weilburg
1810
Johann Friedrich August Tischbein (1750–1812)
Oil on canvas
78 × 63 cm (inc. frame)
Cour Grand-Ducale de Luxembourg
Inv. AAN00010001

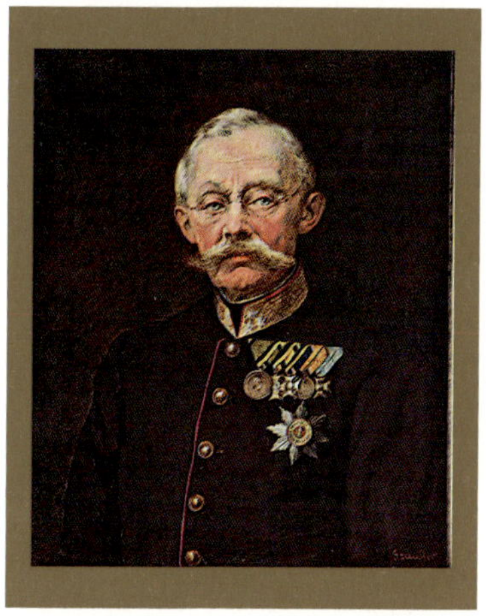

Grand Duke Adolf in Uniform
Second half of the nineteenth century
Viktor Stauffer (1852–1934)
Oil on canvas
104 × 91 cm
Cour Grand-Ducale de Luxembourg
Inv. AMO00665001

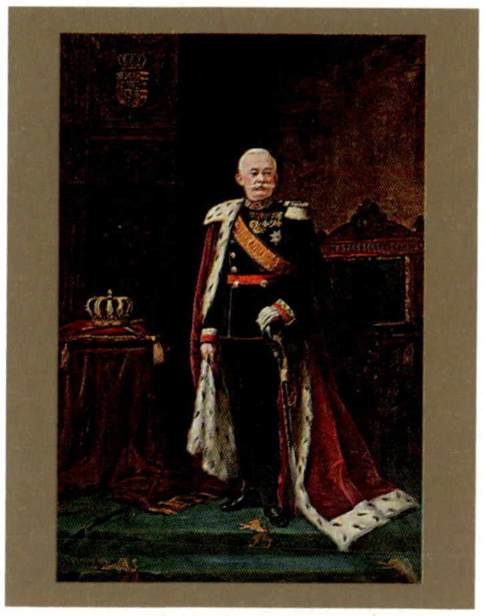

Grand Duke Adolf
c. 1900
Ferdinand d'Huart (1857–1919)
Oil on canvas
165 × 117 cm
Cour Grand-Ducale de Luxembourg
Inv. AMO01321001

Grand Duchess Adelheid-Marie (1833-1916), Second Wife of Grand Duke Adolf, on Horseback
1870
Émile Adam (1843–1924)
Cour Grand-Ducale de Luxembourg

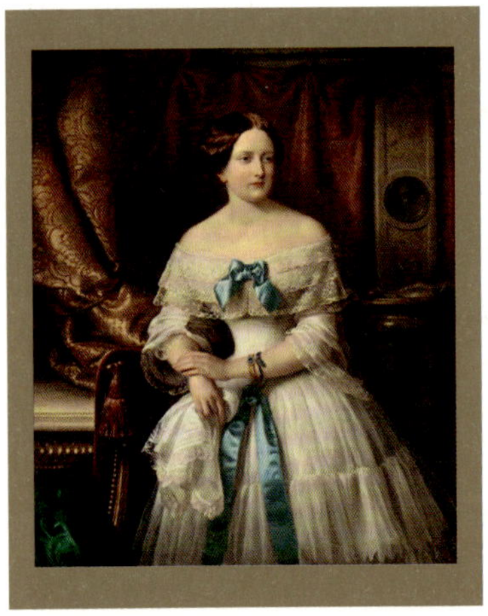

Elizabeth Mikhailovna (1826–1845), Grand Duchess of Russia, First Wife of Grand Duke Adolf (posthumous portrait)
1847
Carl Ferdinand Sohn (1805–1867), after a miniature by
Woldemar Hau (1816–1895)
Oil on canvas
180 × 156 cm (inc. frame)
Cour Grand-Ducale de Luxembourg
Inv. AMO01300001

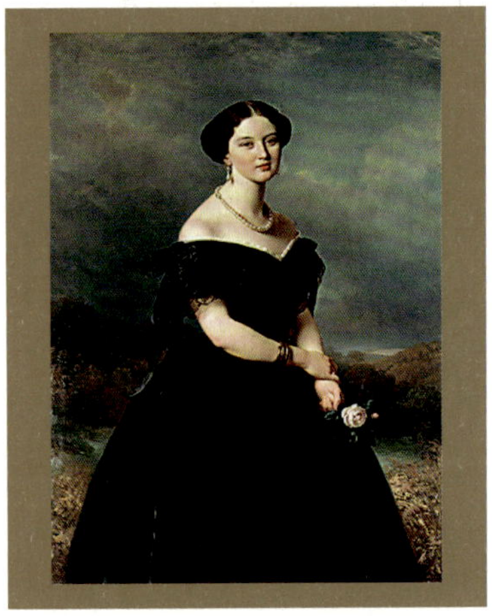

Adelheid-Marie (1833–1916), Second Wife of Grand Duke Adolf
1855
Carl Ferdinand Sohn (1805–1867)
Oil on canvas
200 × 155 cm (inc. frame)
Cour Grand-Ducale de Luxembourg
Inv. AAN00094001

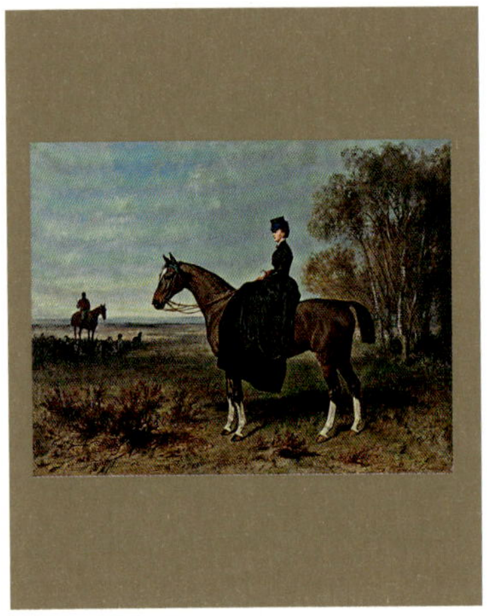

Grand Duchess Adelheid-Marie on Horseback
1870
Émile Adam (1843–1924)
Oil on canvas, gilded wood molding painted in black
99 × 121 cm (inc. frame)
Cour Grand-Ducale de Luxembourg
Inv. AMO01311001

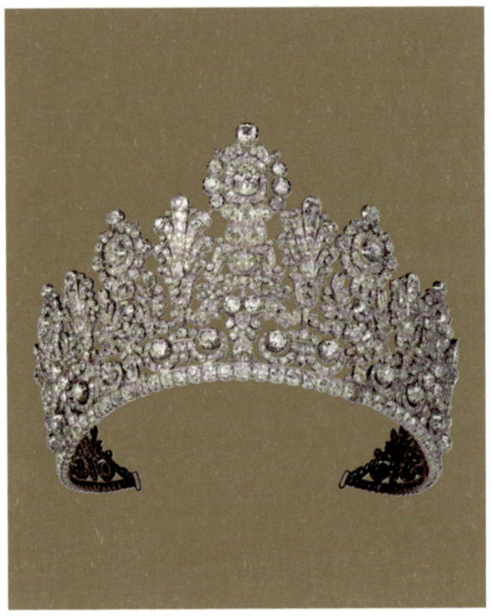

The Diadem of the Grand Duchess of Luxembourg
1829, Frankfurt
Jacob Tillmann Speltz
Silver, gold, rose, cushion, and pear-cut diamonds
D. approx. 30 cm
Cour Grand-Ducale de Luxembourg
Inv. BIJ1

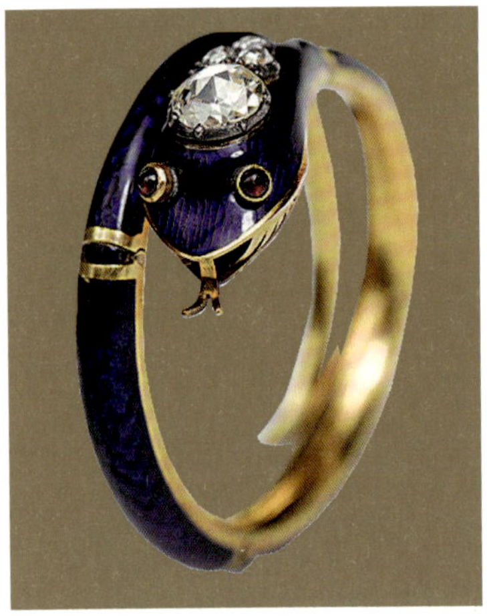

Serpent bracelet
c. 1840
Enamel, rose-cut diamonds
D. approx. 10 cm
Cour Grand-Ducale de Luxembourg
Inv. BIJ JC IX

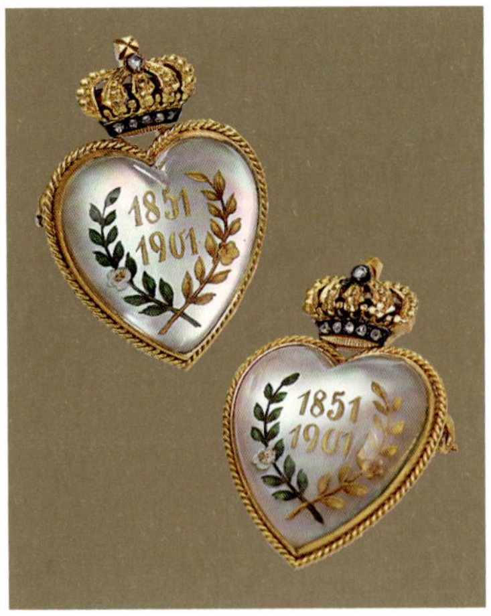

Two heart-shaped brooches, gold wedding souvenirs
1901
Koch, Frankfurt
Gold, diamonds, mother-of-pearl, covered in polished crystal
3.4 × 2.3 × 1.3 cm
Cour Grand-Ducale de Luxembourg
Inv. BIJ00016001-2

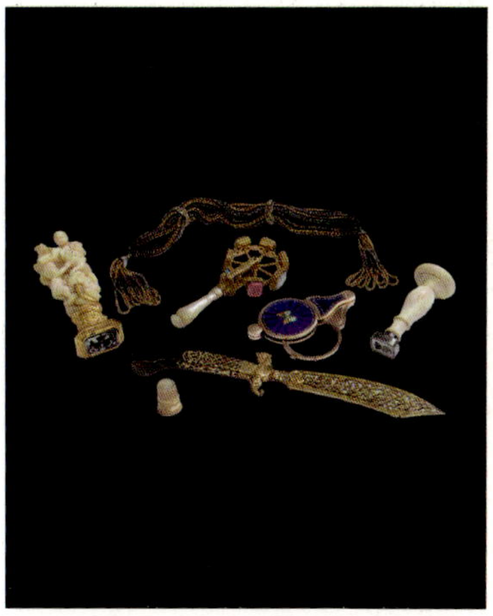

Seal, case, bracelet, magnifying glass, paper knife
Russia
Gold and silver; enamel (magnifying glass); ivory, silver, and precious stones (seals)
Cour Grand-Ducale de Luxembourg

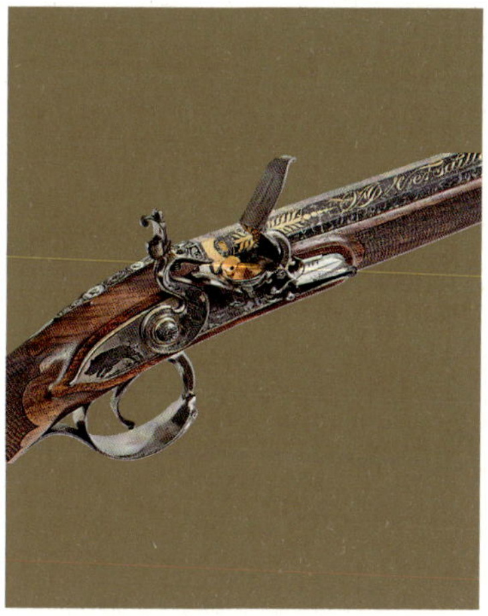

Gun offered by Napoleon to Frederik Willem of Nassau-Weilburg
1805–1810
Nicolas Boutet (1761–1833)
Flintlock gun, walnut (butt), damascening
L. approx. 130 cm
Cour Grand-Ducale de Luxembourg
Inv. ARM00314001

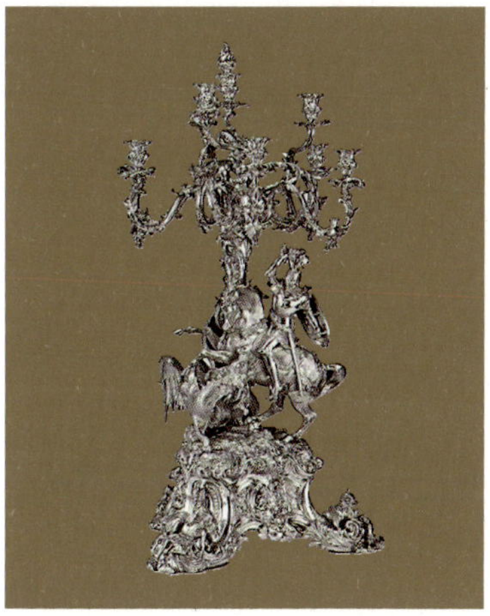

Table centerpiece with the arms of Nassau and two candelabras with the arms of Nassau and Russia
1850–51
J. S. Hunt, London
Silver
H. 122 cm
Cour Grand-Ducale de Luxembourg

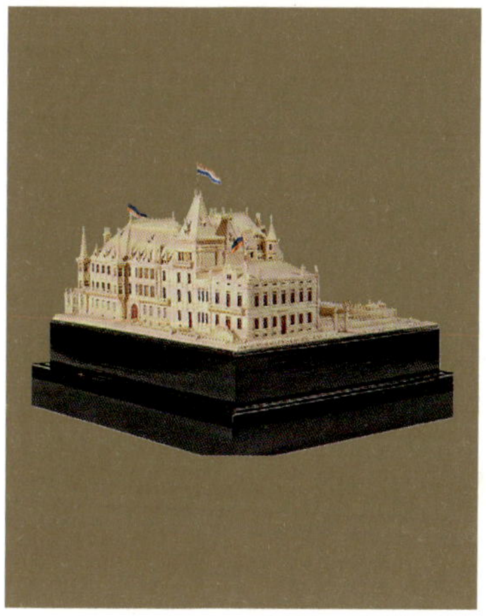

Model of the grand-ducal palace of Luxembourg after transformation in the nineteenth century
Sugar
30.7 × 37.5 cm
Cour Grand-Ducale de Luxembourg

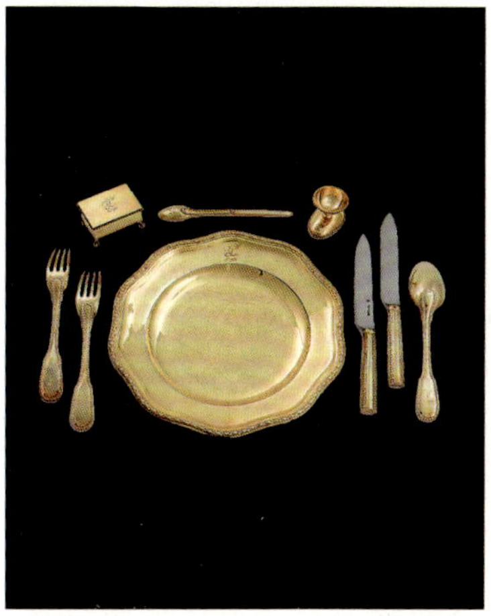

Table service with the arms of Orange-Nassau
1790, Augsburg
Samuel Bardet (1719–1800)
Gilded silver
Inv. OPA00503001
Egg cup
1790, Augsburg
Samuel Bardet (1719–1800)
Gilded silver
Inv. OPA00502001
Plate
1790
Christian II Drentwett (1729–1801)
Gilded silver
Inv. OPA00510001

Cutlery: spoon, fork, knife
1790, Augsburg
Samuel Bardet (1719–1800)
Gilded silver
Inv. OPA00505001, 6001 and 7001
Cour Grand-Ducale de Luxembourg

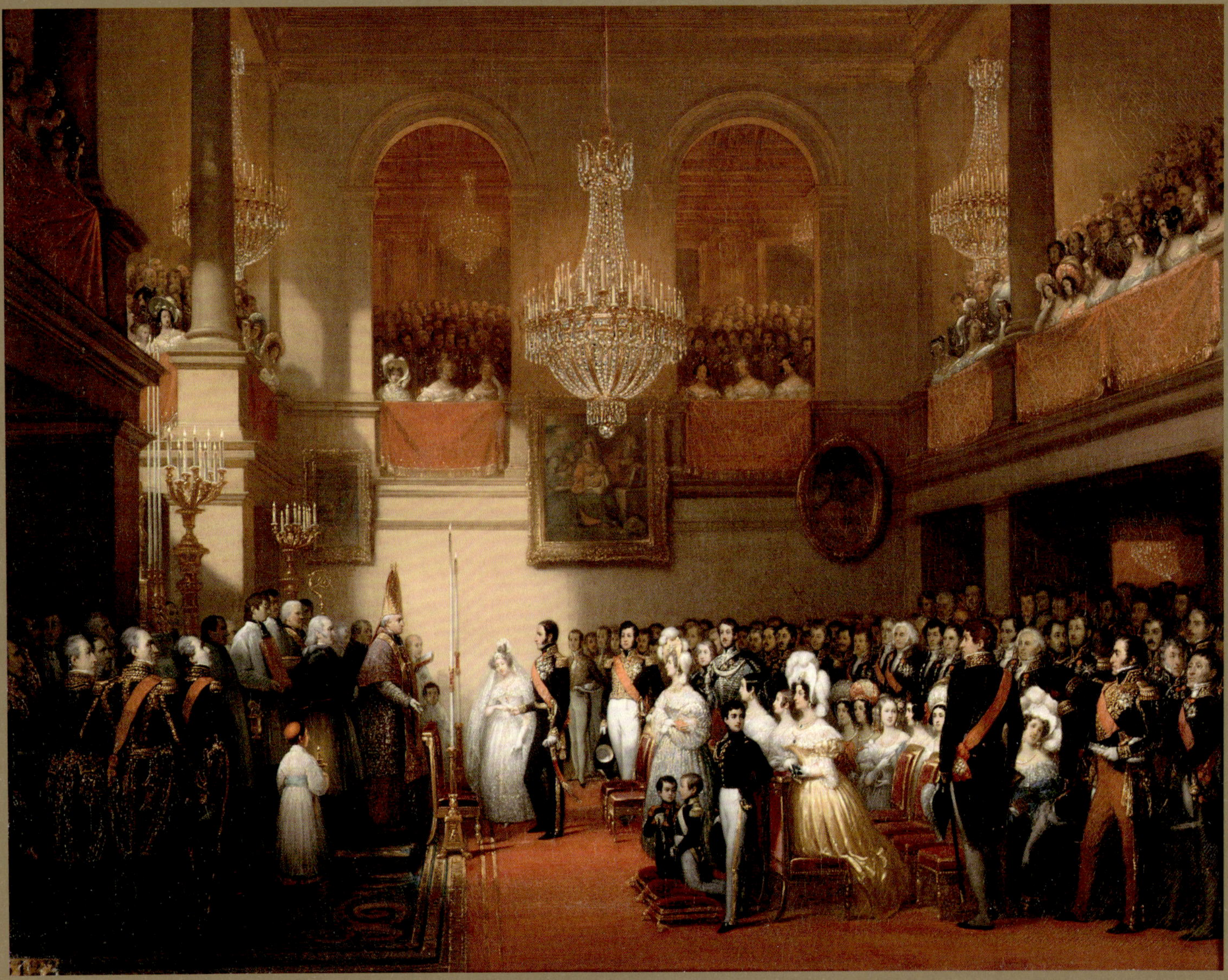

BELGIUM

Leopold I (1790–1865)

The Wedding of Leopold I, King of the Belgians, and Princess Louise-Marie d'Orléans at the Château de Compiègne, August 9, 1832
Nineteenth century
Joseph-Désiré Court (1797–1865)
Musées des Châteaux de Versailles et de Trianon, Versailles

Leopold I, first King of the Belgians and European statesman

Gustaaf Janssens

When, in 1831, Belgian politicians embarked on their search for a head of state for the region separated from the kingdom of the Netherlands in September 1830, their choice finally fell on Prince Leopold of Saxe-Coburg, at the time widower of Princess Charlotte of Great Britain. It was a choice that presented Belgium who had a king with international experience and family ties to almost every other European dynasty.

As head of the fledgling Belgian state, King Leopold I set out to ensure peace in Europe and the welfare of his country, quoting these ideals on July 25, 1831—four days after swearing the oath—in a letter addressed to his sister, Sophie: "I came here to work for the well-being of this country and, by my acceptance of the crown, to preserve the peace of Europe; anything that is able to contribute to these two things I will do; anything that goes beyond this will be harmful."

On August 9, 1832, Leopold I wed Louise d'Orléans (1812–1850), eldest daughter of Louis-Philippe, king of the French. Although the marriage was predicated on the international political situation, and in spite of the fact that Leopold was some twenty-two years older than his wife, the king and the queen were to form a happy couple. It was in the Ardennes, where he had purchased an estate, that Leopold I could share his romantic feelings with Louise. Four children were born including a son, Leopold, his successor, and Charlotte, who was to wed the brother of Emperor Franz Joseph, Maximilian, emperor of Mexico, who met such a tragic end.

Leopold I saw himself as an "apostle of peace," and any compromise of the European balance of power constituted in his eyes a threat to the very survival of the Belgian state. Hence the immense importance he attached to the country's neutrality. According to Leopold's lights, a neutral Belgium must be able to count on military aid from its guarantors and, in the event of pressing danger, ought to be in a position to levy as many men as possible to serve under the flag. As he saw it, the importance of Belgium on the European military chessboard largely depended on the forces the country could muster.

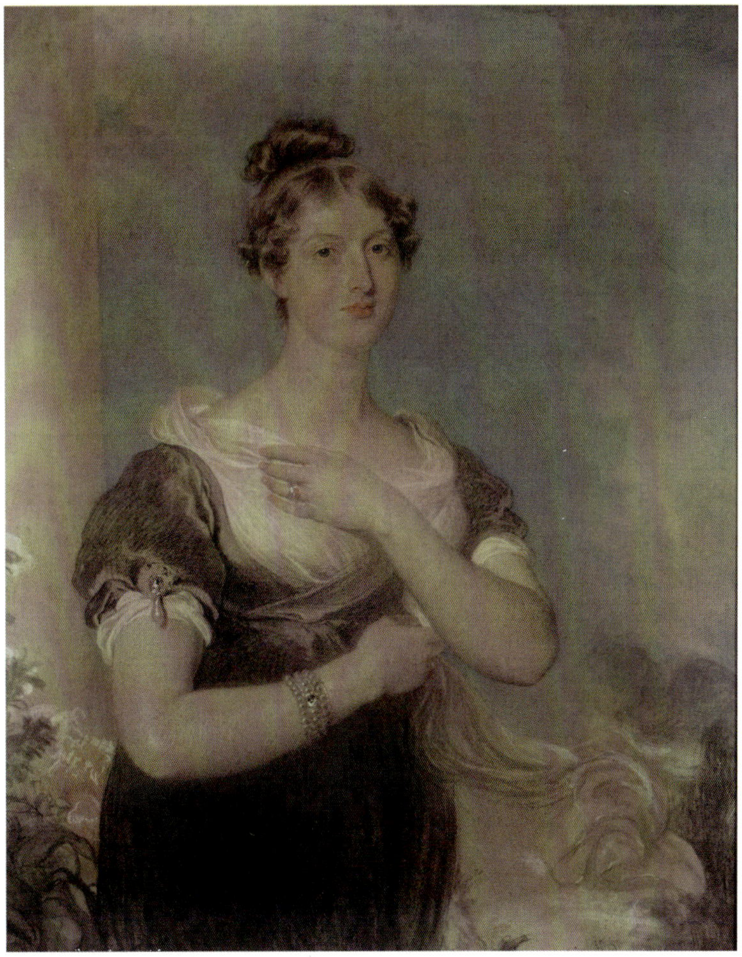

Thus preoccupied by the dynamics of power in Europe and Belgium, Leopold I opposed the formation of overly progressive governments that threatened to undermine the reputation of Belgium on the international stage. The king thus upheld moderation in government policy and favored governments as independent as possible from political parties. Advocating a "unionist policy" to promote solidarity among the citizenry, his approach found itself endangered when liberals and Catholics joined political forces and upset the political equilibrium. King Leopold I was also wary of liberal, anticlerical sectors which, in his eyes, could only ever represent a small fraction of the population. Consequently, the king was all the more pleased to observe that the liberal government in 1858 tried in reality to implement "what it considers useful for the country and that it eschews all exaggeration." He remained vigilant, however, and the growing number and increasing virulence of clashes between militant anticlerical liberals and Catholics worried him greatly. On January 11, 1864, he wrote to his daughter

Princess Charlotte Augusta of Wales (1796–1817), First Wife of Leopold I
Early nineteenth century
Thomas Lawrence
(1769–1830)
Palais Royal, Brussels

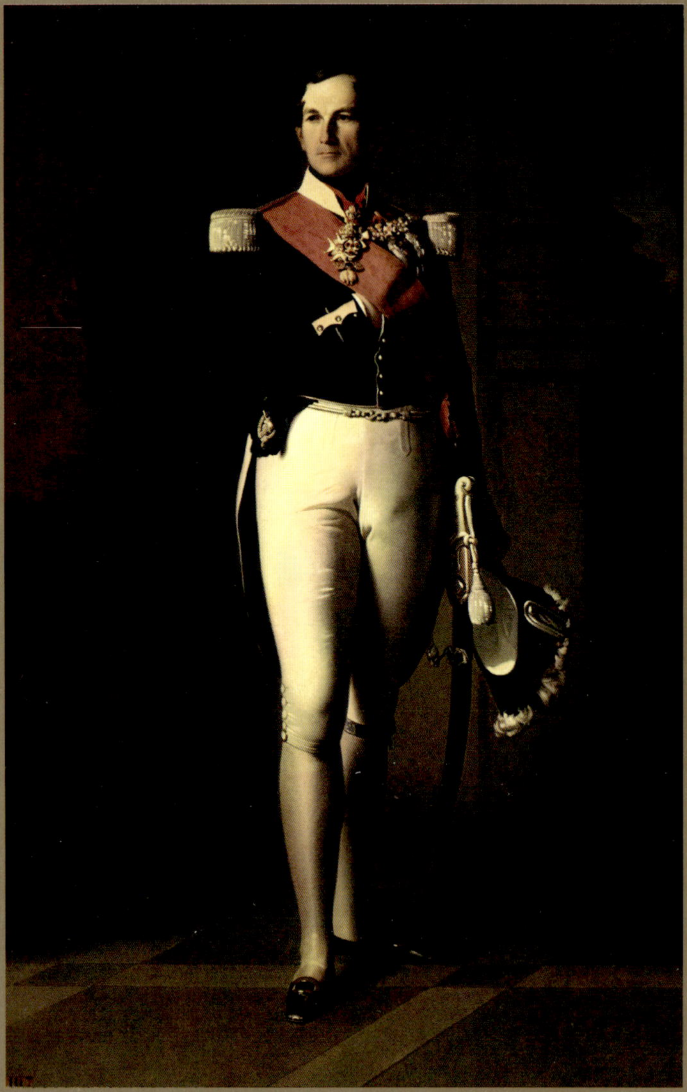

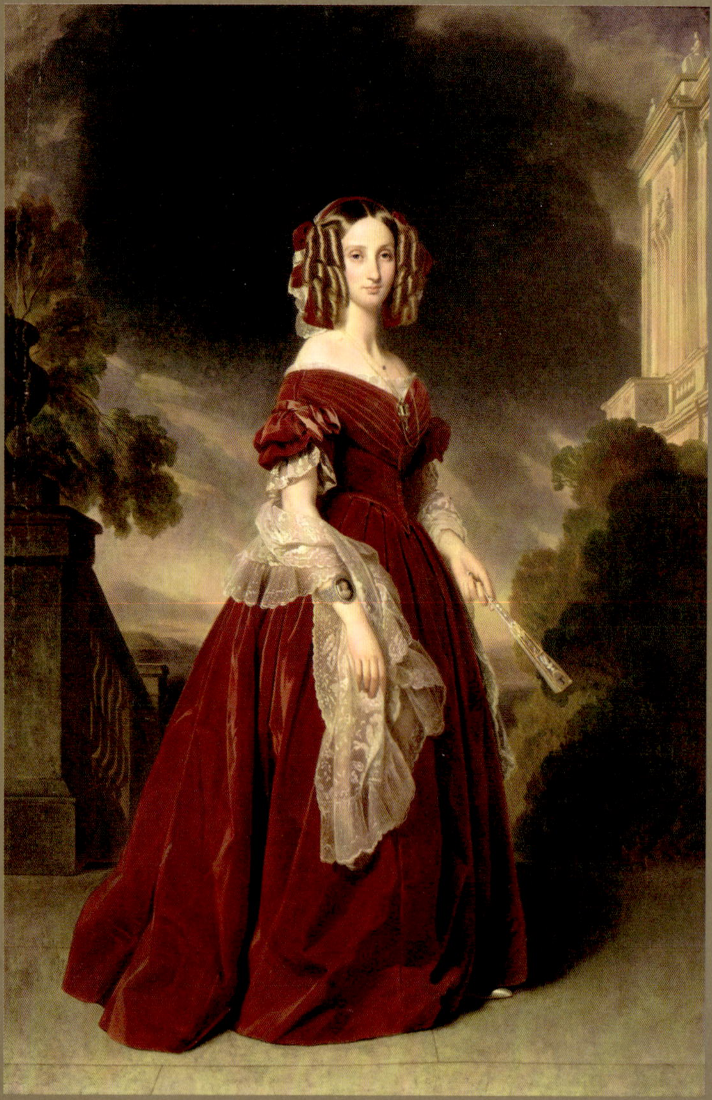

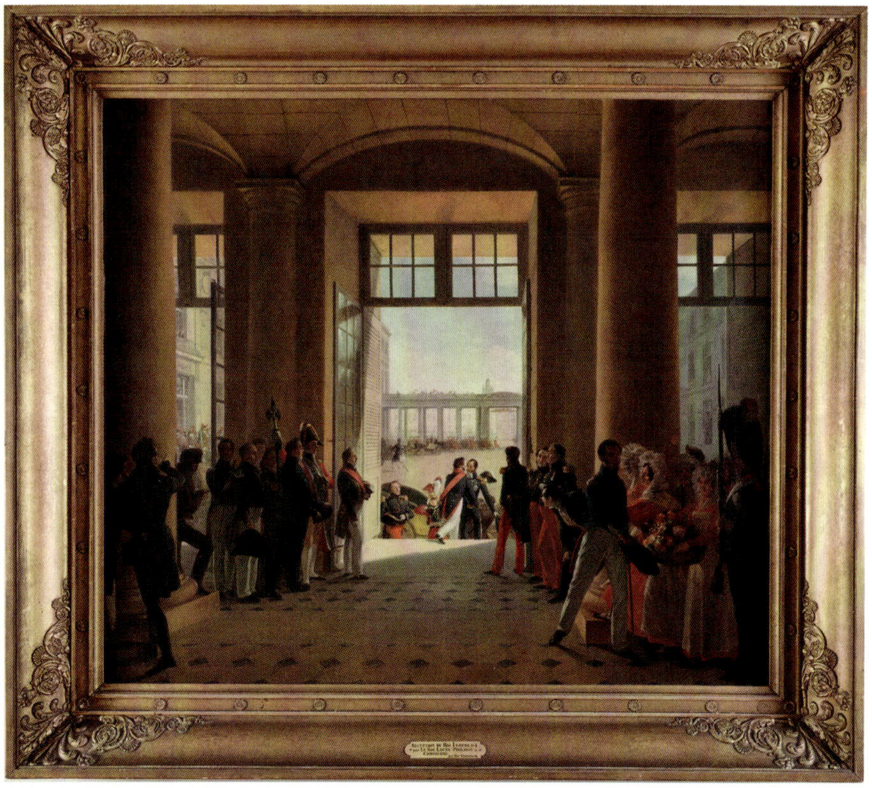

Reception of King Leopold I in Compiègne
c. 1831
Jules van Ysendyck (1836–1901)
Palais Royal, Brussels

Charlotte: "Parties here are of a violence and hatred that can scarcely be imagined. It's the freemasons, ministers, etc. who stir things up, so that the conservative party is totally crushed. . . . How a small country will be able to continue if it remains so divided is a grave question."

The king regarded ministers as his personal collaborators and would often chair the cabinet. Through conversations and discussions, he would inflect policy in directions he favored and made sure that certain issues appeared on the agenda. The king always acted with the greatest discretion and prudence, qualities he esteemed a sovereign needed in abundance, as he expounded to a young Queen Victoria on June 17, 1837.

Foreign affairs were the king's chief theater of operations, averring that mere politicians should not become involved in "great politics." Armed with family ties to various European dynasties, Leopold I regarded himself as a "natural intermediary" destined to bring all parties together. As uncle of both Queen Victoria of Great Britain (her mother was the king's sister) and her husband Prince Albert (son of Ernst, Leopold's elder brother and the reigning duke of Saxe-Coburg and Gotha), Leopold was well placed to be apprised of and to make an impact on European policy.

Leopold I (1790–1865), Duke of Saxe-Coburg and Gotha, King of the Belgians
1840
Franz Xaver Winterhalter (1806–1873)
Musées des Châteaux de Versailles et de Trianon, Versailles

Louise-Marie d'Orléans (1812–1850), Queen of the Belgians
1840
Franz Xaver Winterhalter (1806–1873)
Musées des Châteaux de Versailles et de Trianon, Versailles

As a great matchmaker of dynastic marriages, he brought power and prestige to the house of Saxe-Coburg throughout Europe. Letters from the "devoted uncle" to his "dearest Victoria" testify to this "Coburg diplomacy," and, when war threatened Europe and then when the Eastern question came to a head, Leopold I was to do everything in his power to prevent conflict. Instability in France and more especially tensions between France and Great Britain were a genuine menace to peace in Europe. As Leopold I viewed events, any disturbance to the European apple cart would inevitably jeopardize the survival of the Belgian state.

It is on record that in its early days Leopold I did not view the Belgian Constitution of 1831 with any great warmth. Indeed, on announcing his willingness to accept the crown, he did so in the following terms: "Sirs, you have treated royalty, which was not there to defend itself, rather harshly. Your charter is well and truly democratic; I believe, however, that, assuming goodwill on both sides, it can still work." "Goodwill on both sides": this was a significant phrase for a king—though Leopold I was repeatedly infuriated by the "democratic constitution." Throughout his reign, however, the fact that he found the Belgians ungovernable and the Belgian constitution all too republican did not prevent Leopold I from striving for peace and a balance of power, both at home in Belgium and more widely on the European stage.

It was an attitude that bore fruit in the end. When, in 1848, a wave of revolutions broke over Europe, the situation remained relatively calm in Belgium; indeed, the young Belgian state and its monarchy emerged none the worse for wear from the international crisis. As the king noted, not without pride: "Being undoubtedly the only political doctor in Europe who has succeeded, not only in curing his patient, but also in consolidating and improving his health, has earned me the confidence of most governments and the population at large, which I intend using to my utmost to ensure the welfare of Europe."

The king vented criticism of the liberal Belgian constitution solely in his private correspondence: in public, Leopold I breathed not a word against it. As he declared on September 25, 1850, when laying the foundation stone of the Congress Column: "The experience of twenty years has proved the solidity and wisdom of the actions congress has bestowed on the Nation. The Freedoms enshrined in the national pact, respected and developed, can all be exercised without hindrance, and the greatest praise one can make of the Belgian people is to say that they is worthy of their constitution."

At a later date, there were indications that the king also recognized a positive side to this system of constitutional rule. When, in 1863, a change of government took place in France, Leopold showed himself relieved, as transpired in a letter to

Statue of King Leopold posing hand on the Belgian Constitution
Nineteenth century
Musée Royal de l'Armée, Brussels

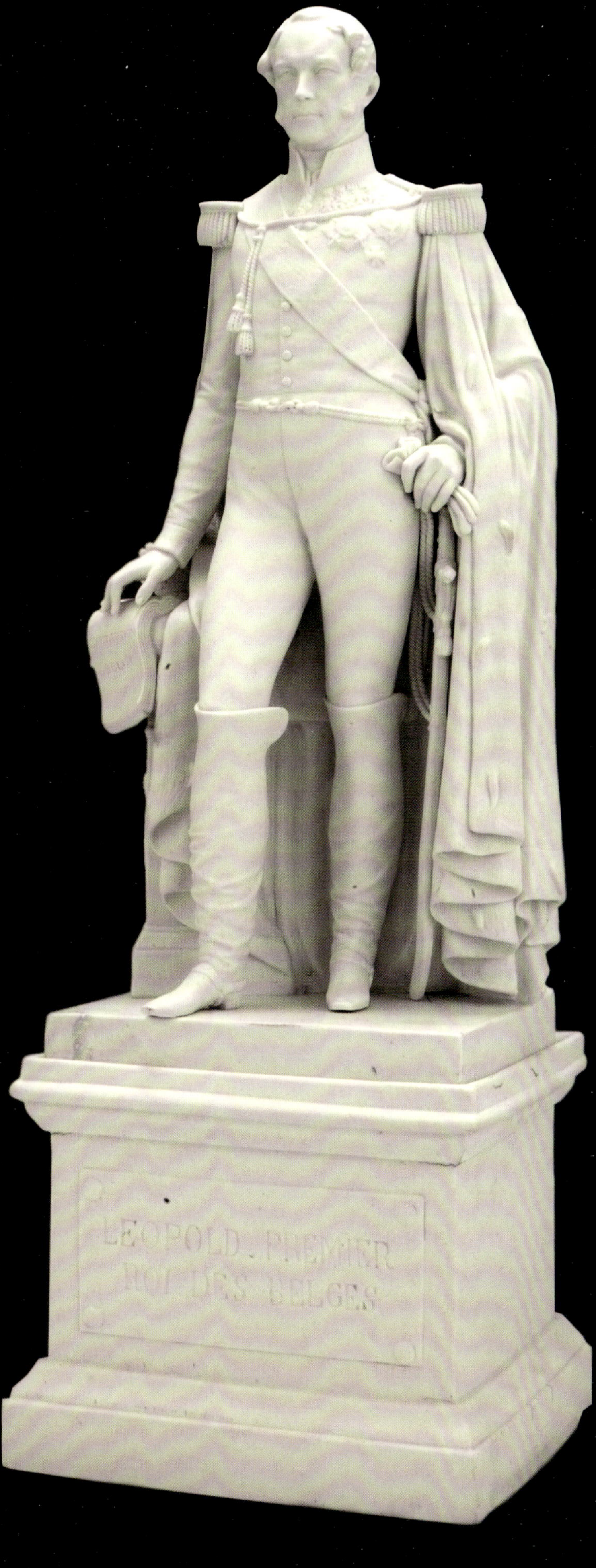
LEOPOLD PREMIER
ROI DES BELGES

Plates depicting Leopold I and Louise d'Orléans
Nineteenth century
Association Royale Dynastie & Patrimoine Culturel, Brussels

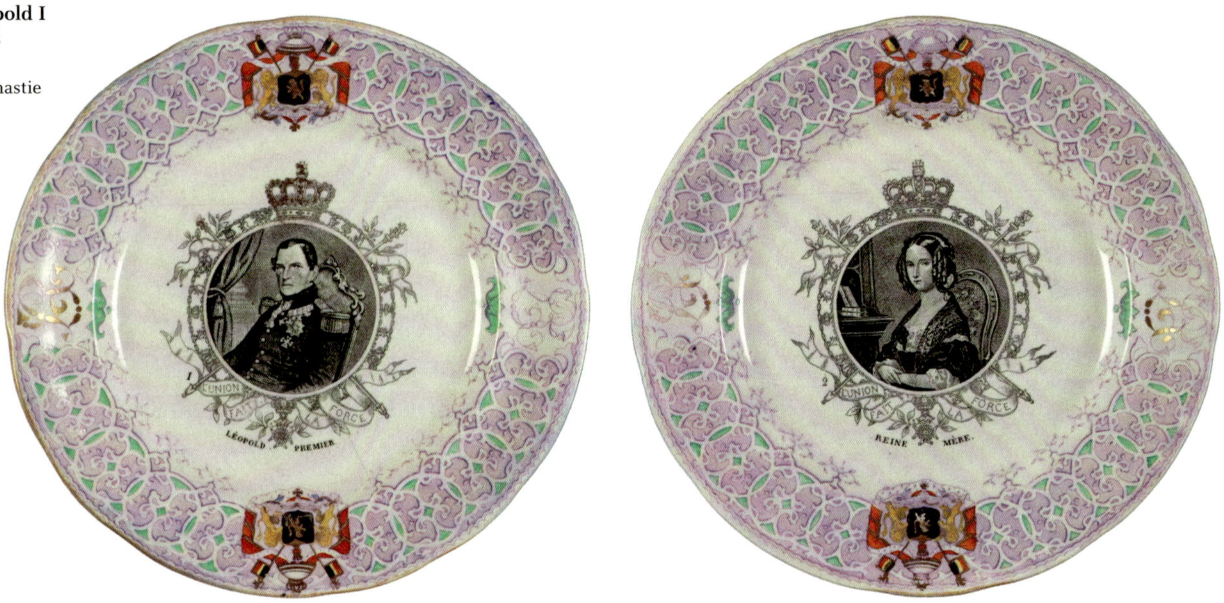

Queen Victoria: "The change of government in France means they are approaching a constitutional regime, the only one applicable in Europe."

Leopold I was a conscientious sovereign who strove for peace and equilibrium, and who possessed an acute sense of duty, which, it may be supposed, he handed down to his children. Certain remarks by his daughter, Charlotte, empress of Mexico, hint at its effects. As she wrote to her brother Philip on March 9, 1865: "We are on this earth to fulfill a duty and to make ourselves as useful as possible."

In what was undoubtedly an exaggerated view, the king was convinced that Belgium owed its existence to him and that the nation survived in the face of foreign powers only thanks to his intervention. As Charles Rogier, the head of the Belgian government and foreign minister, testified during a private conversation on the eve of the king's funeral in 1865: "King Leopold was possessed of a fine and penetrating mind. . . . He allotted too great a part in the consolidation of the kingdom of Belgium to himself. He would often say to me, 'I hold Belgium in my hand.' This is an exaggeration. The Belgian people could look after themselves; the king helped them—that is the truth."

Even taking into account Charles Rogier's rectification, Leopold's lasting image is of a statesman of note who piloted political life in Belgium and Europe for more than thirty years, ensured the survival of the Belgian state, and served as an inspiration for a considerable number of his successors.

Clocks depicting King Leopold I and Queen Louise
Nineteenth century
Association Royale Dynastie & Patrimoine Culturel, Brussels

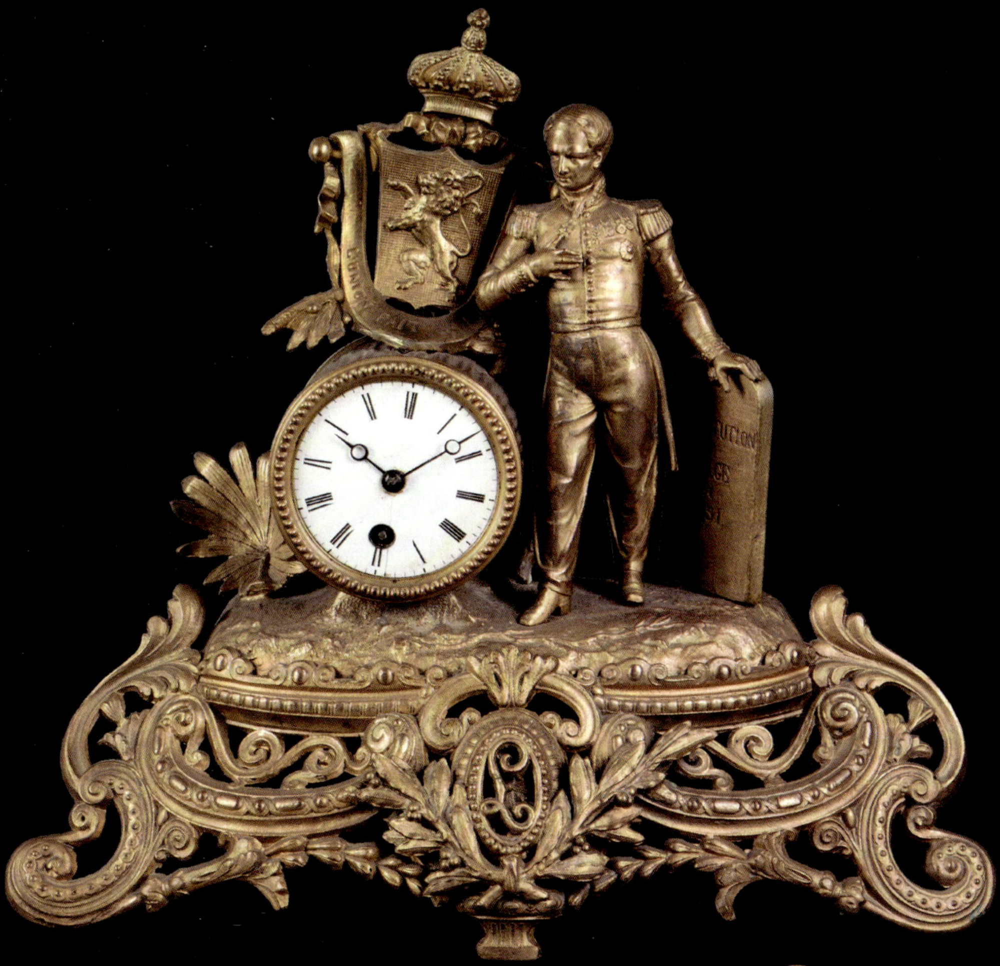

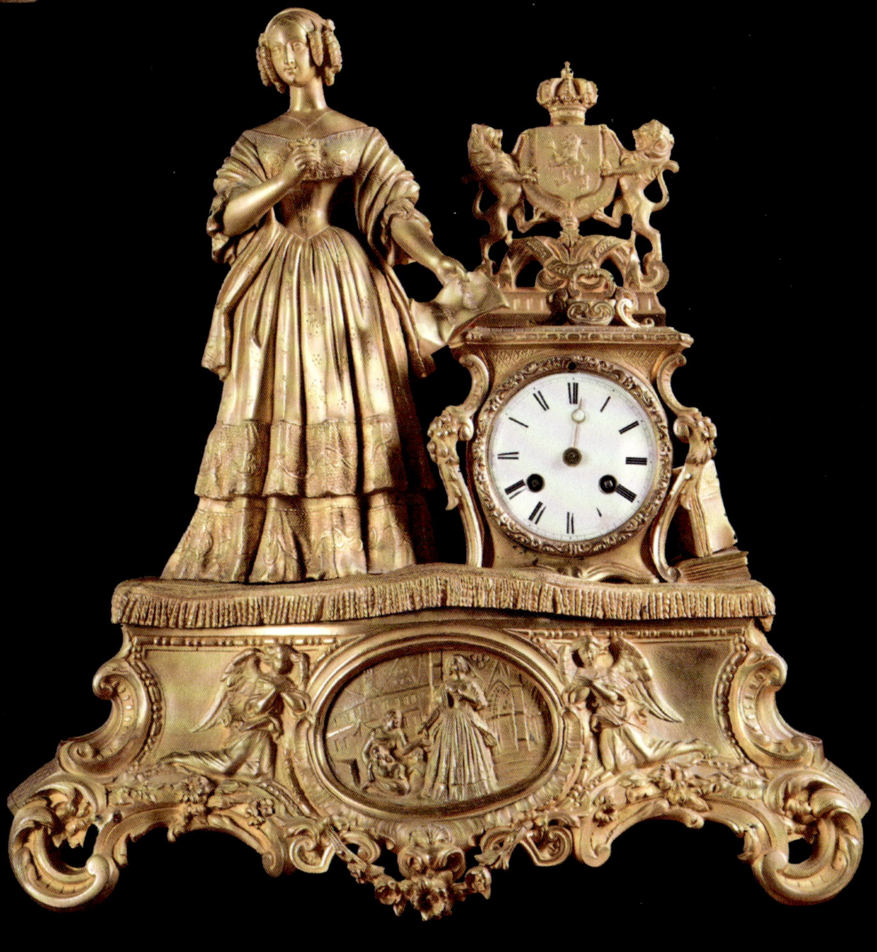

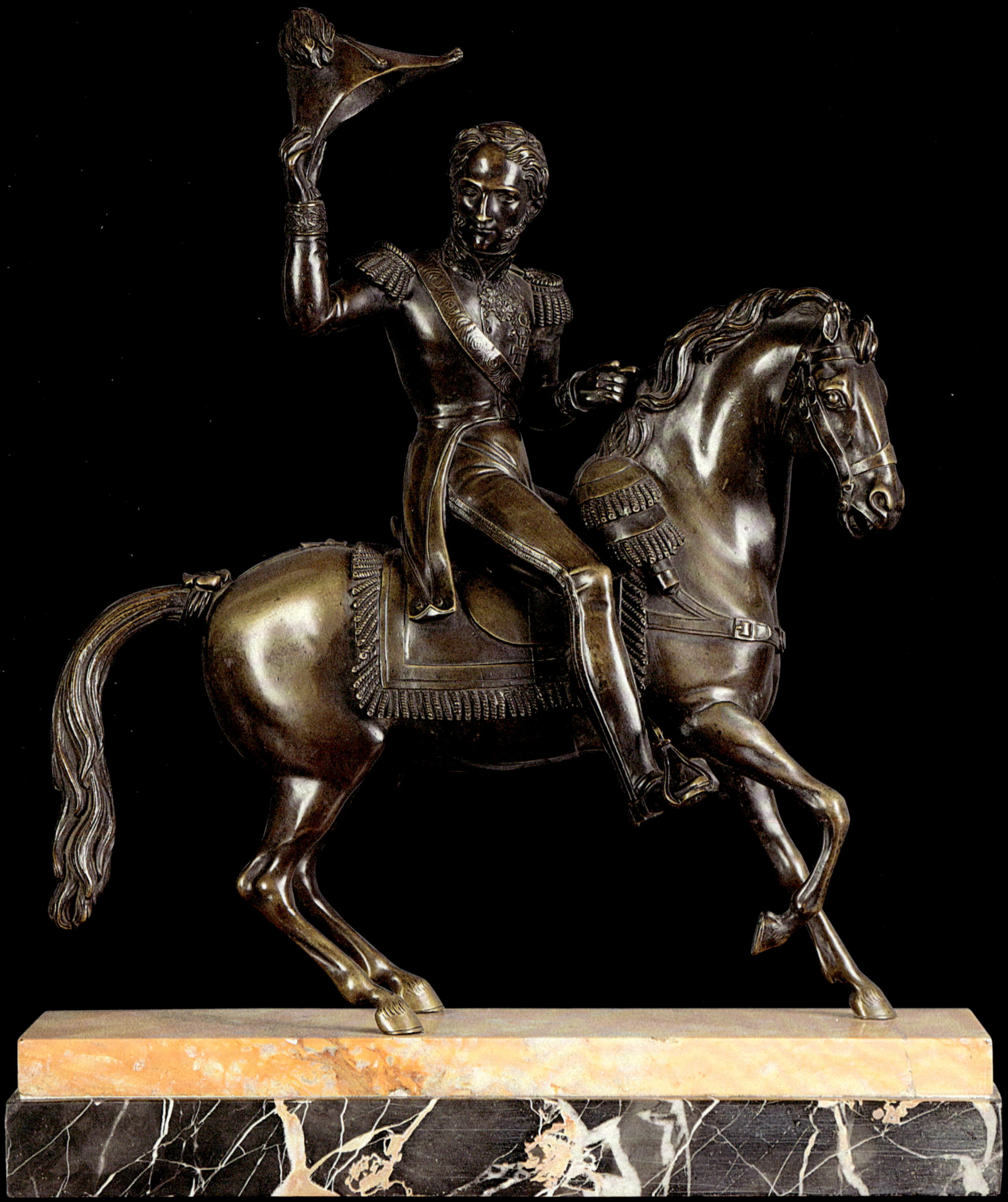

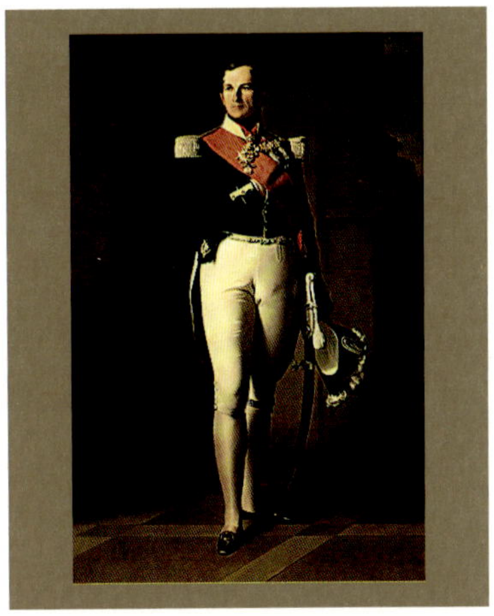

Leopold I (1790–1865), Duke of Saxe-Coburg and Gotha, King of the Belgians
1840
Franz Xaver Winterhalter (1806–1873)
Oil on canvas
227.3 × 147.8 cm (inc. frame)
Musées des Châteaux de Versailles et de Trianon, Versailles
Inv. MV5107

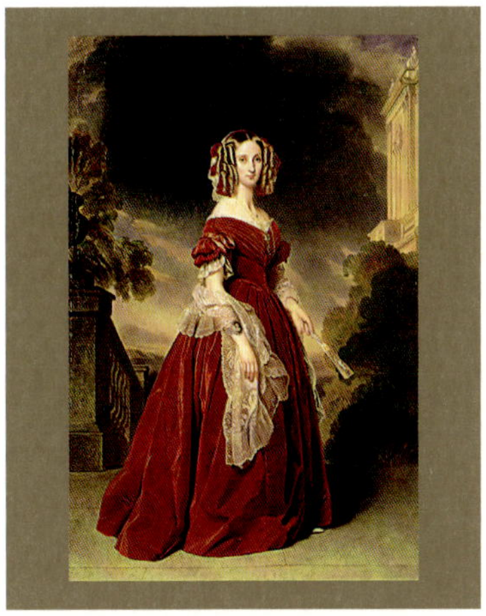

Louise-Marie d'Orléans (1812–1850), Queen of the Belgians
1840
Franz Xaver Winterhalter (1806–1873)
Oil on canvas
227 × 151.8 cm (inc. frame)
Musées des Châteaux de Versailles et de Trianon, Versailles
Inv. MV5110

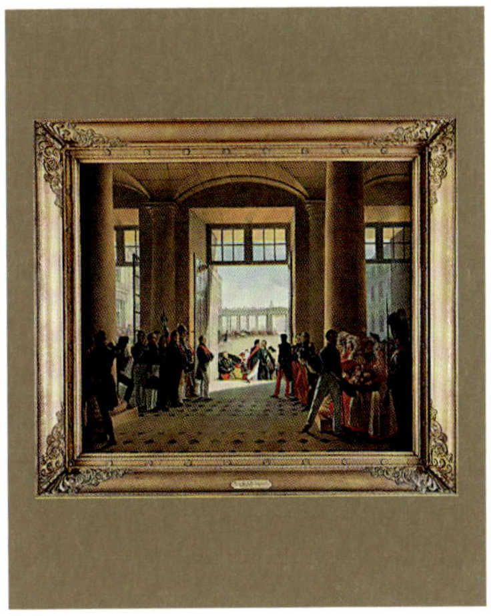

Reception of King Leopold I in Compiègne
Nineteenth century
Jules van Ysendyck (1836–1901)
Oil on canvas
100 × 112 cm
Palais Royal, Brussels
Inv. PB S074-075 TAB

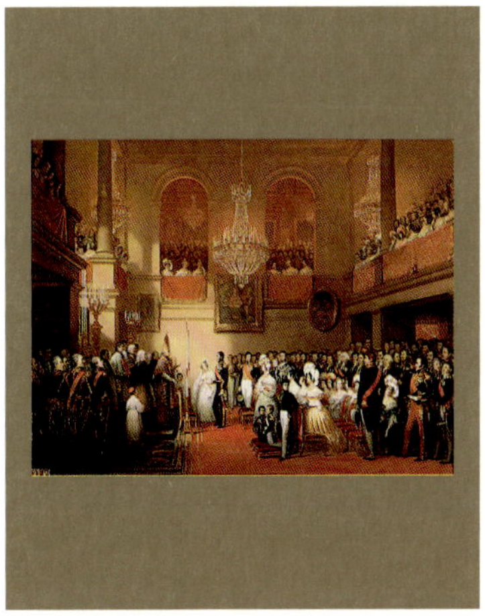

The Wedding of Leopold I, King of the Belgians, and Princess Louise-Marie d'Orléans at the Château de Compiègne, August 9, 1832
Nineteenth century
Joseph-Désiré Court (1797–1865)
Oil on canvas
111 × 135.8 cm (inc. frame)
Musées des Châteaux de Versailles et de Trianon, Versailles
Inv. MV5122

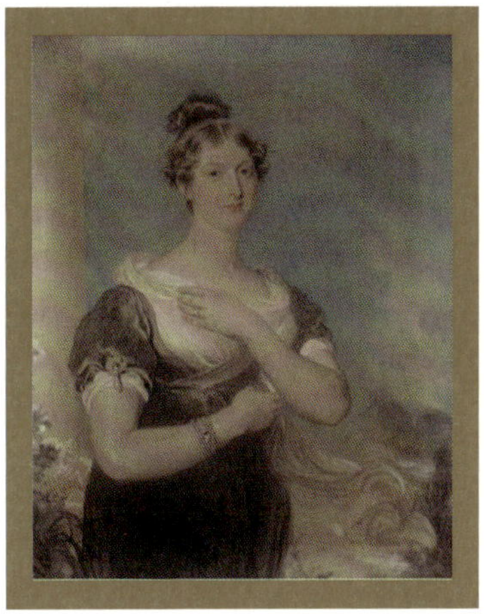

Princess Charlotte Augusta of Wales (1796–1817), First Wife of Leopold I
Early nineteenth century
Thomas Lawrence (1769–1830)
Pencil
125 × 102 cm (inc. frame)
Palais Royal, Brussels
Inv. PB 111-019 TAB

Equestrian statue of Leopold I
Nineteenth century
Association Royale Dynastie & Patrimoine Culturel, Brussels

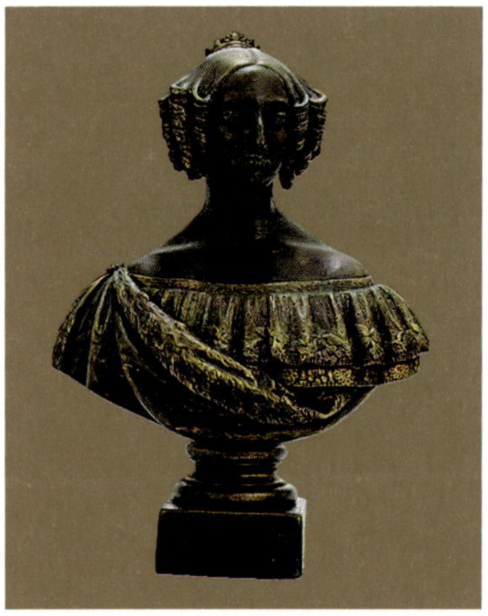

Bust of Queen Louise
Nineteenth century
Patinated plaster
H. 40.5 cm
Musée Royal de l'Armée, Brussels
Inv. 503092

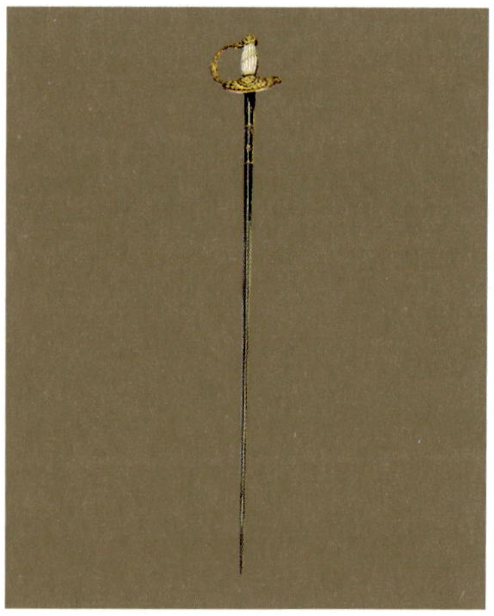

Sword belonging to King Leopold I
Nineteenth century
Iron, mother-of-pearl
L. 97.4 cm
Musée Royal de l'Armée, Brussels
Inv. 11477

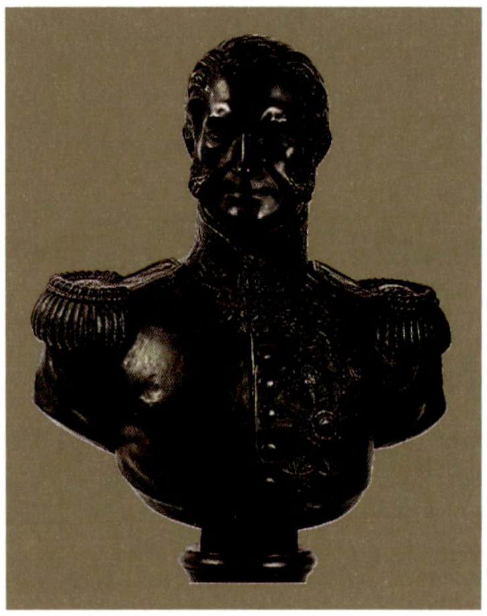

Bust of Leopold I
Nineteenth century
Patinated plaster
H. 58 cm
Musée Royal de l'Armée, Brussels
Inv. 501258

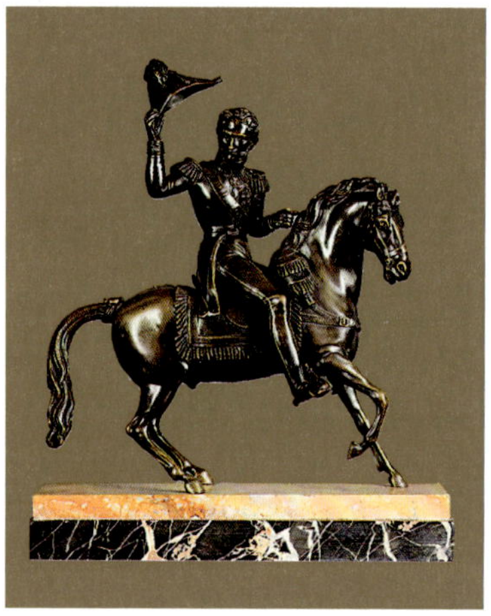

Equestrian statue of Leopold I
Nineteenth century
Patinated plaster
37 × 30 cm
Association Royale Dynastie & Patrimoine Culturel, Brussels
Inv. 2823

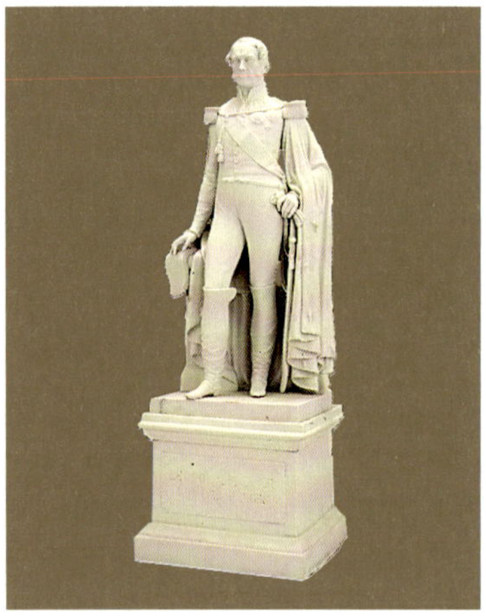

Statue of King Leopold posing hand on the Belgian Constitution
Nineteenth century
Porcelain Bisque
H. 78.5 cm
Musée Royal de l'Armée, Brussels
Inv. 503453

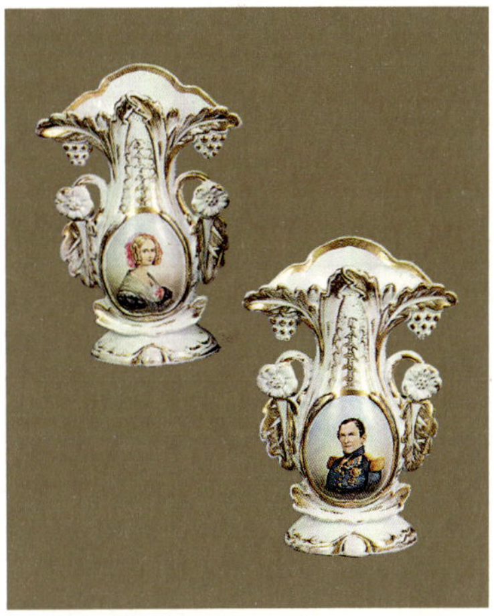

Vases depicting Leopold I and Queen Louise
Nineteenth century
Porcelain
H. 30 cm (each)
Association Royale Dynastie
& Patrimoine Culturel, Brussels
Inv. 2286 and 2287

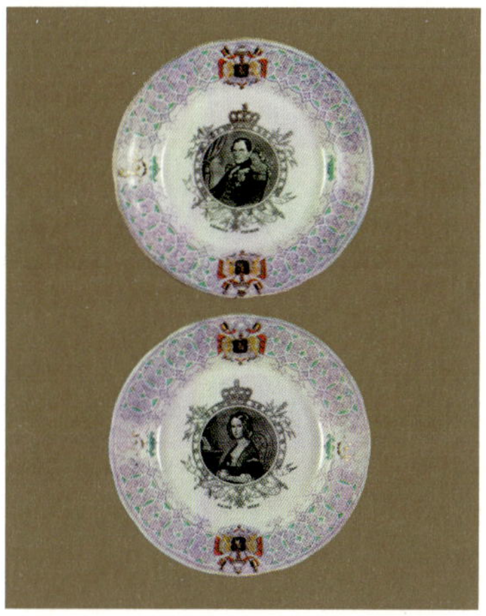

Two plates depicting Leopold I and Louise d'Orléans
Nineteenth century
Faience
D. 25 cm (each)
Association Royale Dynastie
& Patrimoine Culturel, Brussels
Inv. A1262 and A1264

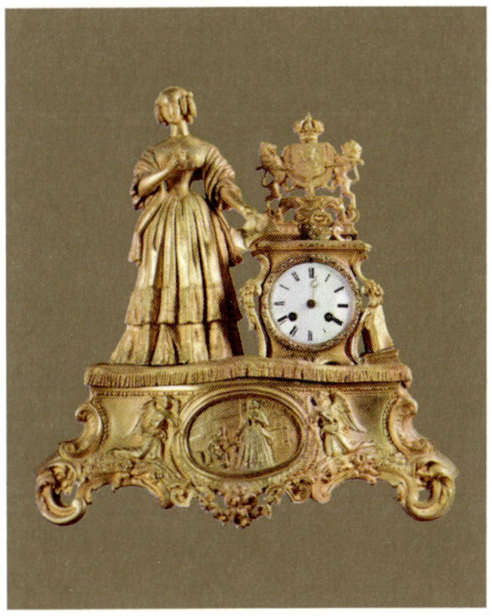

Clock depicting Queen Louise
Nineteenth century
Bronze
H. 65 cm
Association Royale Dynastie
& Patrimoine Culturel, Brussels
Inv. . 2298

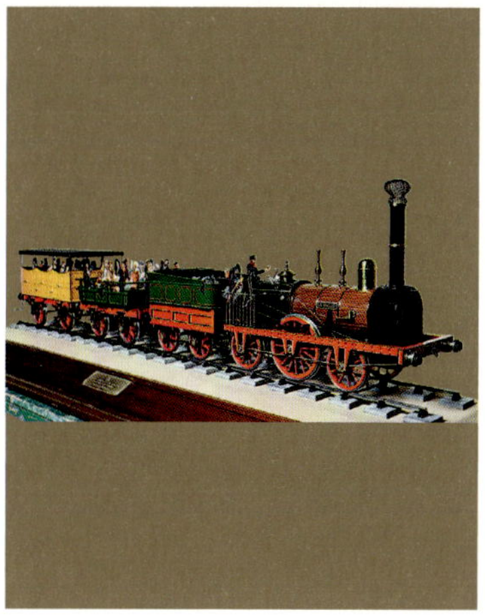

Model of the train *Le Belge* given to Prince Baudouin to celebrate the jubilee in 1938
Alfred Bastien (1873–1955)
Painted iron
200 × 65 cm
Palais Royal, Brussels
Inv. BN0029

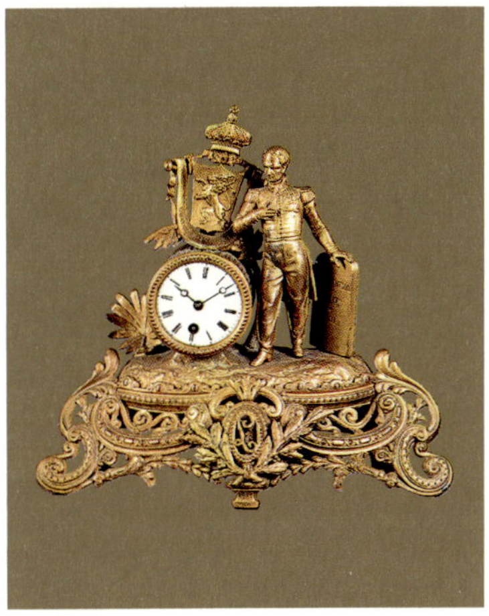

Clock depicting King Leopold I
Nineteenth century
Bronze
H. 40 cm
Association Royale Dynastie
& Patrimoine Culturel, Brussels
Inv. . 2805

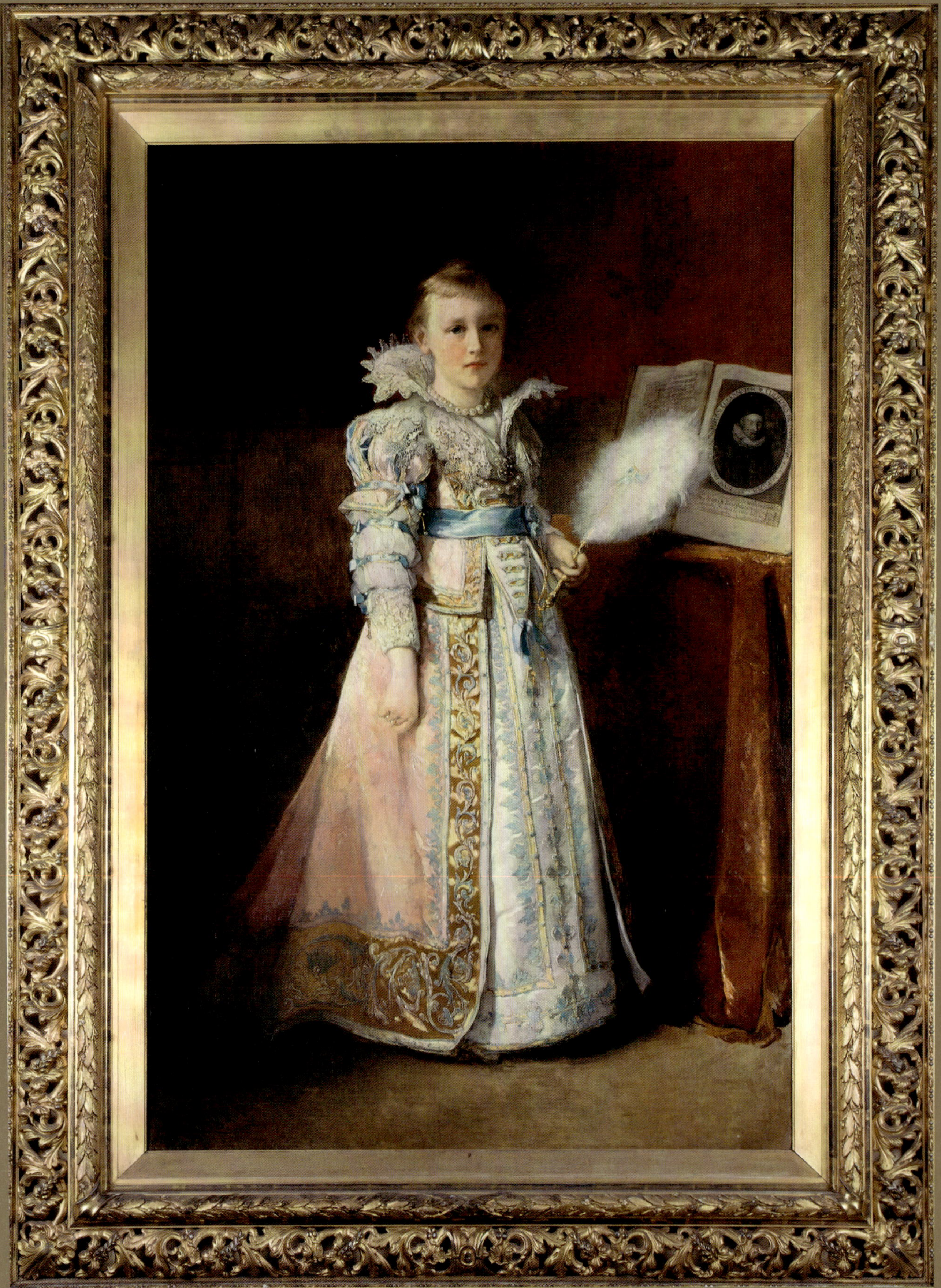

NETHERLANDS

Wilhelmina (1880–1962)

The Young Queen Wilhelmina in Seventeenth-Century Costume
1891
Christoffel Bisschop
(1828–1904)
Dutch Royal Collections

Wilhelmina
The education of a queen

Philippe C. B. Maarschalkerweerd

August 29, 1898

My dearest niece,
I cannot allow this very important day in your life to pass without writing you a few unofficial lines which are to express how truly and warmly I pray that God may bless and protect you and guide you. I was just your age when I ascended the throne and I know all the difficulties and trials which surround a young queen. But you have such a dear wise friend in your beloved mother who has held the reins of government for so many years, that you can always turn to her for advice.
Accept again the assurance of my true affection and friendship and believe me always, your very affectionate aunt and sister.
Victoria R.

It was two days before Wilhelmina's eighteenth birthday on August 31, 1898, and barely a week before the accession of the princess to the throne of the Netherlands that Queen Victoria (1819–1901)—doyenne of the sovereigns of the period—wrote the above words of encouragement to one of her young European counterparts. The British monarch, similarly aged only eighteen when she became queen in 1837, expresses her confidence that Wilhelmina (1880–1962)—with wise guidance from her mother—will be perfectly capable of surmounting the problems which are sure to confront her. In writing this letter, Victoria surely called to mind the visit that Wilhelmina, then fourteen years old, had paid her in May 1895 together with her mother, Queen Emma (1858–1934). The girl, on whom the royal title had in the natural course of things been bestowed after the death of her father in 1890, but who had to wait until she was eighteen before being officially crowned, had made a decent impression on Victoria: "So simple, dignified and pretty with a sweet expression and lovely complexion and pretty figure. She reminds me of myself from her extremely youthful appearance."

Queen Wilhelmina in the Park of Soestdijk Palace
1898
WILLY MARTENS
(1856–1927)
Dutch Royal Collections

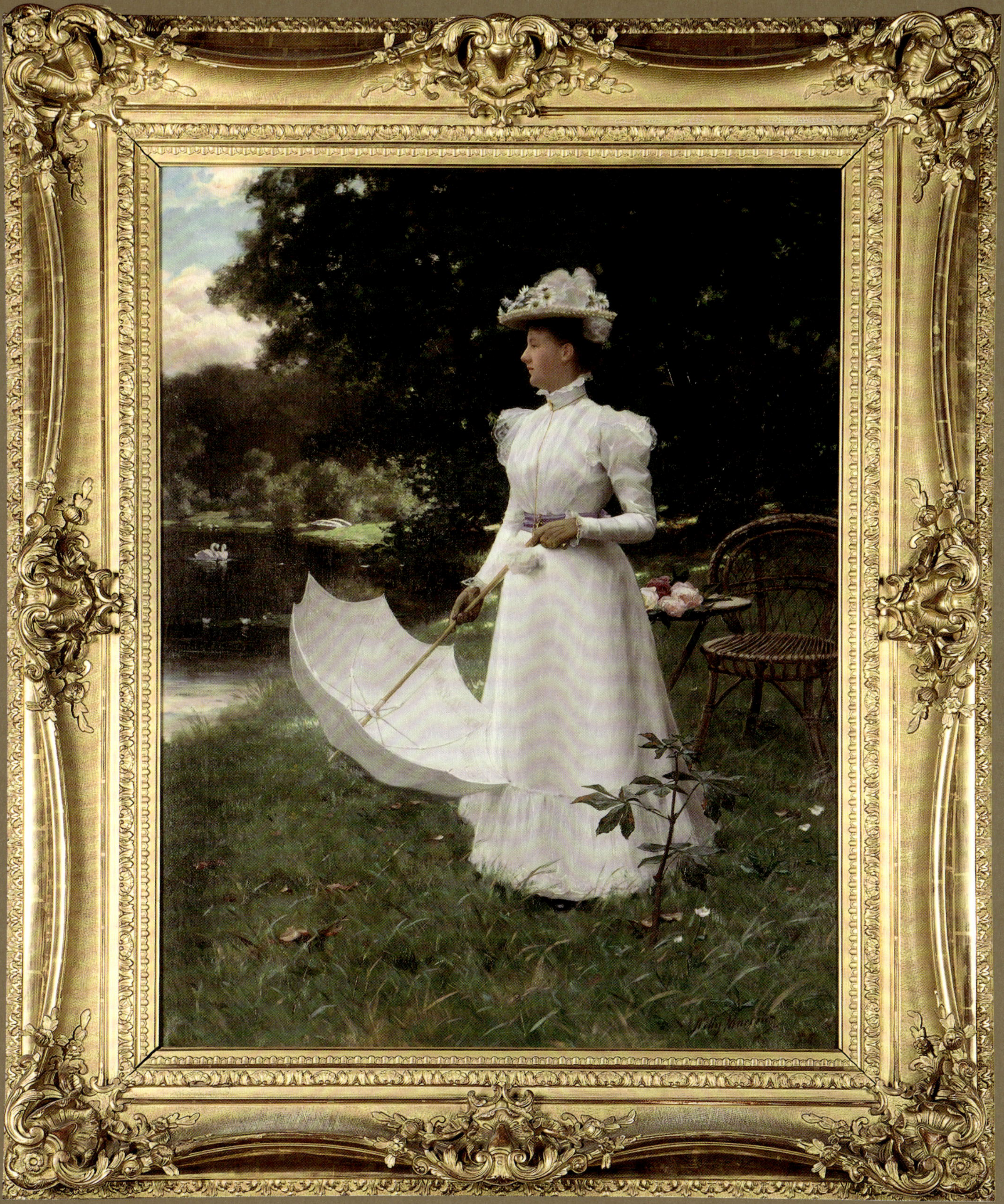

At the time, a photographer from The Hague, attuned to the historical significance of the meeting between two queens, made a montage of their portraits into a picture depicting the event.

A comparison between the two sovereigns reveals several common factors: both were only daughters; both inherited the burden of the crown at eighteen; both enjoyed considerable prestige as a head of state reigning over a major colonial power; and during extremely lengthy reigns (sixty-one years for Victoria, fifty for Wilhelmina), both brought considerable authority to the function they exercised and became living symbols of national unity. Both even present similarities in the physical changes that affected them, as they turned from sylph-like young women into imposing matriarchs.

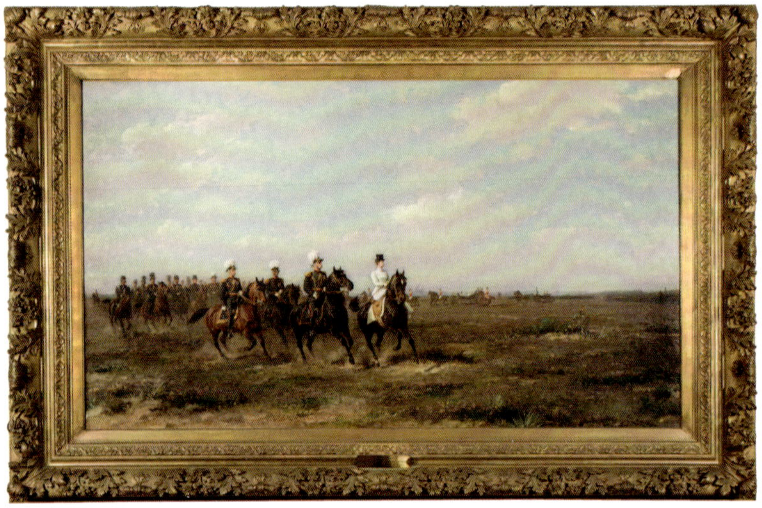

The birth of Wilhelmina in 1880 was of crucial importance to the dynasty. Her father, King Willem III, had had three boys from an earlier marriage to Sophie of Württemberg, but the only survivor proved unsuitable for the monarchy. Widowed, in 1879 the sovereign had remarried Emma de Waldeck-Pyrmont, then twenty-one years old, and was sixty-three by the time Wilhelmina was born. In this era of high infant mortality, the continuity of the dynasty was thus far from assured, not least since, in a relatively short space of time, Wilhelmina's half-brother, as well as an uncle and a great-uncle, had passed away without issue. After the death of Willem III in 1890, everything was done to perpetuate the Orange-Nassau monarchy and to prepare the young Wilhelmina, then just ten years old, for her future role as head of state. It was not what anyone would call a sinecure: the kingdom of the Netherlands had hitherto known only male sovereigns, the most influential positions in Dutch society were all occupied by men (in particular those of a certain age), politics was riddled with antimonarchism, and the royal family had been noted in the past for its fine military—and therefore purely male—traditions.

Emma (an "excellent mother," in the words of Queen Victoria) possessed all the qualities desirable in a regent and tutor. She was of the opinion that Wilhelmina's upbringing should be based on a certain number of fundamental virtues, such as sobriety, perseverance, self-discipline, obligingness, and a love

Queen Wilhelmina during a Military Parade
1898
Otto Eerelman (1839–1926)
Dutch Royal Collections

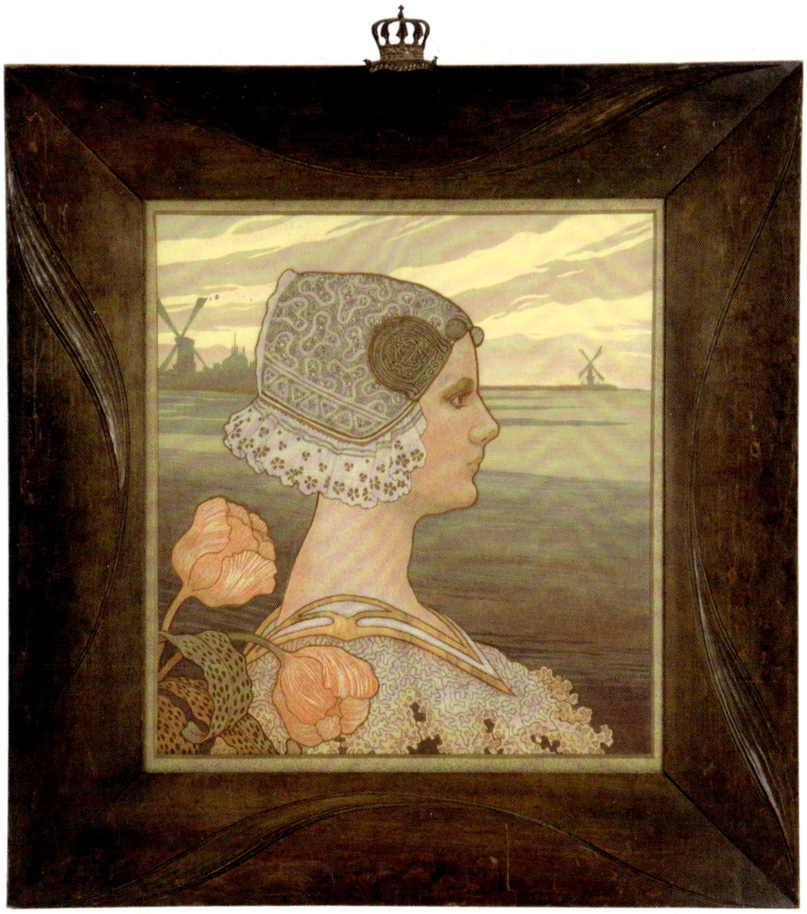

of the homeland. It was essential, as she saw it, to forge the character of her daughter so she could one day become "a noble woman, courageous, strong, and unswerving." On each and every occasion, Wilhelmina was to remind herself that, in order to acquire the necessary degree of authority to effectively discharge her office, she had to embody national unity and be seen to guarantee her country's independence. It was moreover crucial that the young queen keep alive the historical bonds between the Netherlands and the House of Orange, and to reassure all that, in her hands, the dynastic tradition would remain secure. In this context, the portrait of Wilhelmina aged eleven in garb from the time of Amalia van Solms, wife of the victorious and peace-loving prince Frederik Hendrik, prince of Orange-Nassau (1584–1647), speaks volumes. Subsequently, by then a mother in her turn, she was to pose together with her husband and daughter in a similar historical genre picture.

After a regency lasting eight years, Emma, so as to be able to hand over the entire kingdom to an eighteen-year-old girl without qualms, realized that it was imperative that Netherlanders become better acquainted with their future head

Queen Wilhelmina in Friesian Headwear
1901
P. Berthon (1872–1909)
Dutch Royal Collections

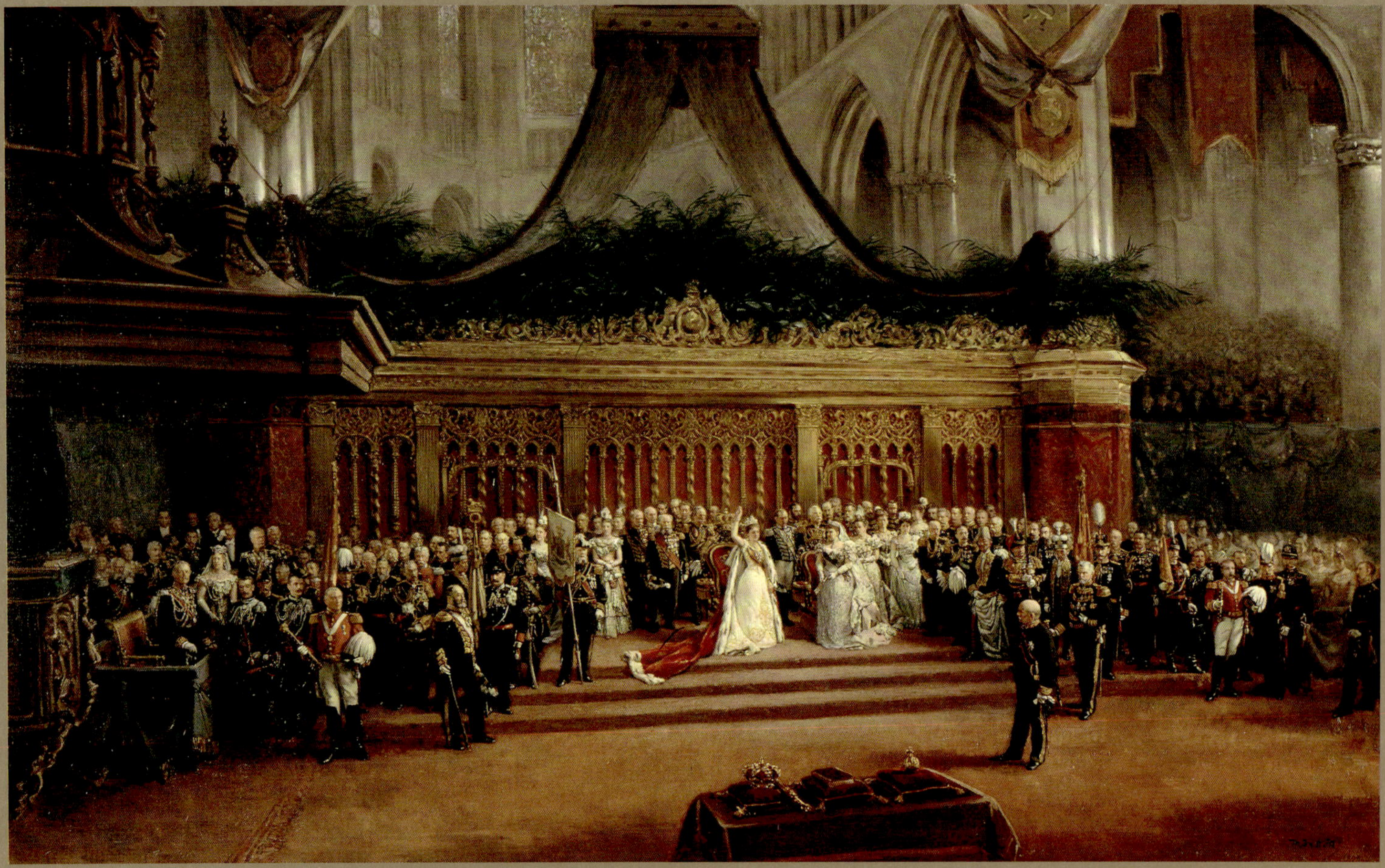

of state and that Wilhelmina learn more about her country and its people. To this end, from 1891 to 1898, mother and daughter crisscrossed the land, meeting local authorities, attending exhibitions, visiting social projects, and participating in official ceremonies, such as the laying of the foundation stone for a new building at the University of Utrecht. In Friesland and Zeeland, the princess was wearing the traditional costume as a sign of her attachment to the people of the region. Emma and Wilhelmina returned laden with gifts from these visits that reflect the consideration in which both queens must have been held.

It was also important to make clear that even with a woman at the helm, the bonds between the head of the state and the army would not be compromised. Efforts were thus made to demonstrate Wilhelmina's interest in things military: when just thirteen, she personally presented an infantry regiment with a new standard. Soon, the army was to become so familiar to her that, many years later, the queen was able to reflect that: "My heart has always been profoundly military, and I feel rather like a soldier at his post."

On September 6, 1898, Wilhelmina swore the oath on the constitution, thus putting the seal on her accession as head of the Dutch state and signaling the end of her mother's regency. Consequently, the new monarch also became head of the House of Orange-Nassau and entered the "family of crowned heads." It is not without reason then that the queen of England styles and signs the letter quoted above in such personal and affectionate terms.

The day she was enthroned, Wilhelmina made clear how she intended to exercise her office by making her own a phrase from the coronation speech of her father in 1863: "There is nothing, no, nothing, that the House of Orange would not do for the Netherlands."

The most important task falling to Wilhelmina after her coronation was naturally enough to ensure the continuation of the dynasty, and this meant arranging a marriage. Rational considerations suggested that the most obvious candidate would be a member of the Protestant nobility of Europe, without close family ties to the bride-to-be, and who would have no chance of one day reigning himself. It was impossible to choose a Briton, because at the time the Boer War opposed the United Kingdom and the Netherlands. A Scandinavian applicant seemed worth considering, but, probably after an exhaustive examination of the ramified aristocratic genealogies of the Germanic territories, the choice finally settled on Heinrich, son of the grand duke of Mecklenburg-Schwerin. Without denying the weight of cool calculation in this, it is undeniable that love also played a role

Enthronement of Queen Wilhelmina of the Netherlands (1880–1962) in the presence of Emma (1858–1934), Queen of the Netherlands
1899
Mari ten Kate (1831–1910)
Dutch Royal Collections

in their union. For once, personal feelings went hand in hand with reason of state. The ambitions of the newlyweds were, however, very different: rather self-effacing, Heinrich cherished a fondness for hunting, life in the great outdoors, and forestry. These preoccupations were perhaps for the best, in that the role of prince consort to the queen of the Netherlands did not provide much scope for those of grand views. He exercised no official function, and Wilhelmina, adhering rigidly to the constitution, had no intention of implicating him in affairs of state.

The wedding was celebrated in The Hague on February 7, 1901, and it was not long before hopes were running high for the birth of an heir. But it was in fact fully eight years later, after several unsuccessful pregnancies, that the royal couple's first and only child came into the world: Juliana (1909–2004). On this occasion, the city of Amsterdam presented Wilhelmina with a cradle which would later be inherited by her granddaughter Beatrix (1938), her great-grandson Willem-Alexander (1967), and his daughter, Princess Amalia (2003). Today, with a continuous line of succession from single heirs, the dynasty of Orange—with Wilhelmina's four grandchildren and fourteen great-grandchildren—finds itself in a far better state than it was fifty years ago.

Queen Wilhelmina with Her Husband, Heinrich of Mecklenburg-Schwerin (1876–1934), and their Daughter, Princess Juliana, in Seventeenth-Century costumes, perpetuating the Historical Relationship between the Netherlands and the House of Orange
1915
Thérèse Schwartze
Dutch Royal Collections, (on deposit to Het Loo Palace)

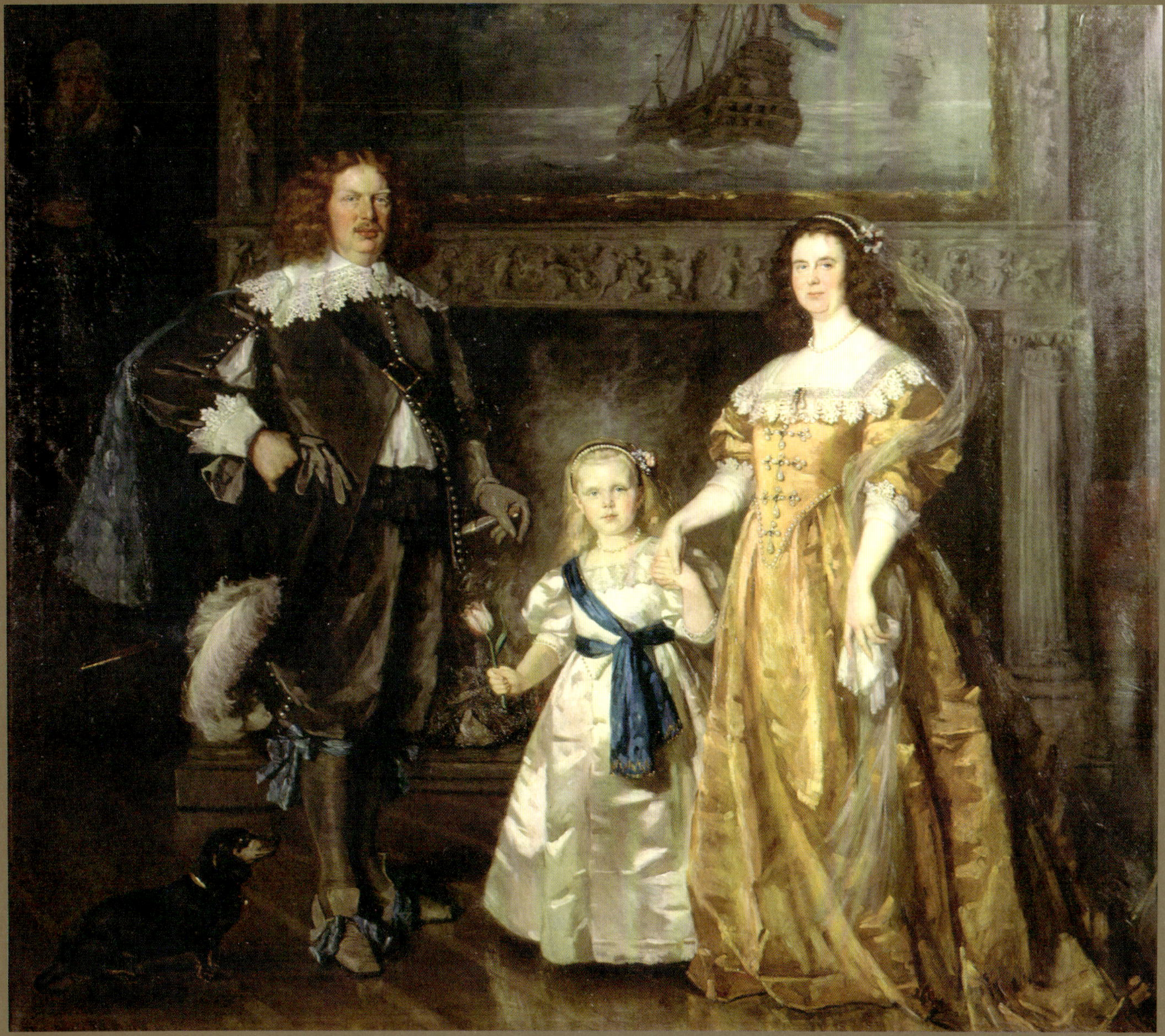

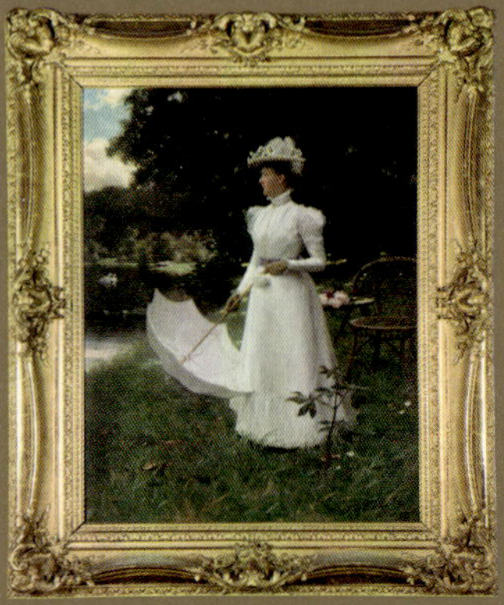

Queen Wilhelmina in the Park of Soestdijk Palace
1898
Willy Martens (1856–1927)
Oil on canvas
98 × 75 cm
Dutch Royal Collections
Inv. SC/0506

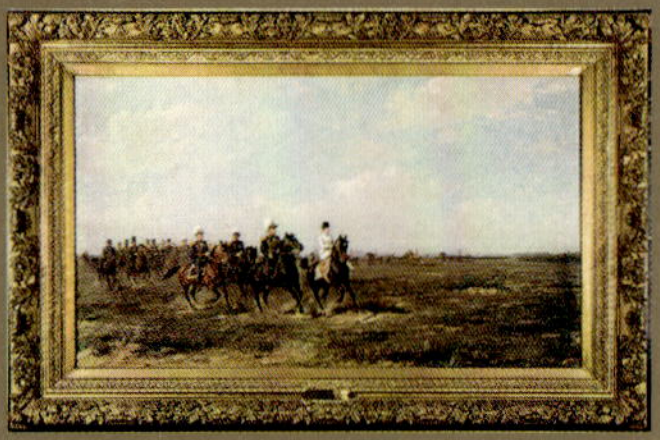

Queen Wilhelmina during a Military Parade
1898
Otto Eerelman (1839–1926)
Oil on canvas
166 × 240 cm
Dutch Royal Collections
Inv. SC/0896

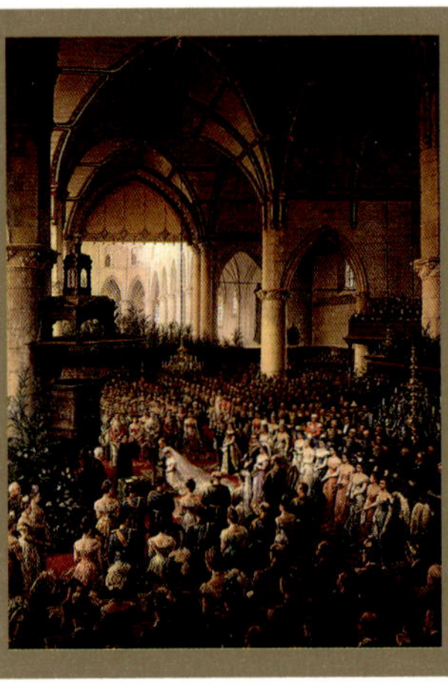

The Wedding of Queen Wilhelmina and Prince Heinrich of Mecklenburg-Schwerin in The Hague, February 7, 1901
1901
Otto Eerelman (1839–1926)
Oil on canvas
136 × 98 cm
Dutch Royal Collections
Inv. SC/0943

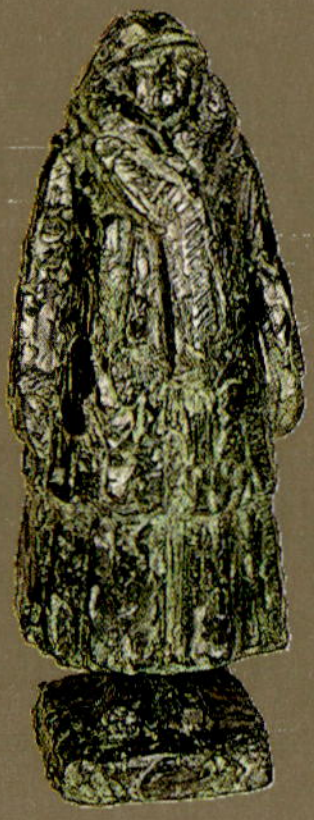

Queen Wilhelmina in Her Robes
1967
Mari Andriessen (1897–1979)
Bronze
H. 57 cm
Paleis Het Loo National Museum, Apeldoorn
Inv. RL2673

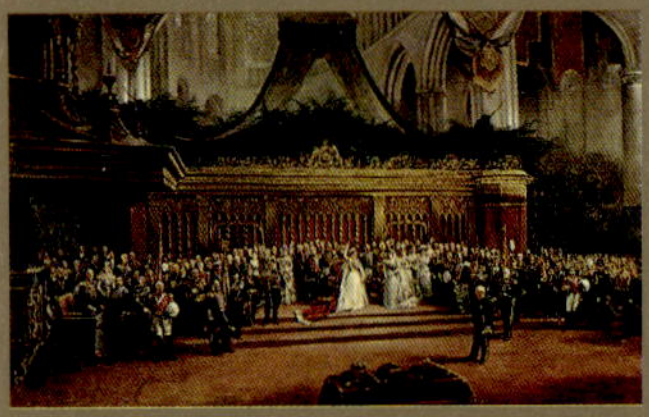

Enthronement of Queen Wilhelmina of the Netherlands (1880–1962) in the presence of Emma (1858–1934), Queen of the Netherlands
1899
Mari ten Kate (1831–1910)
Oil on canvas
84 × 133 cm
Dutch Royal Collections
Inv. SC/0941

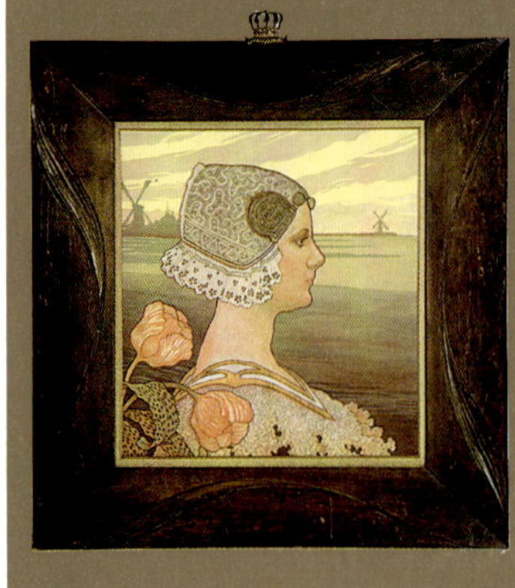

Queen Wilhelmina in Friesian Headwear
1901
P. Berthon (1872–1909)
Oil on canvas
60 × 52 cm
Dutch Royal Collections
Inv. TN/010

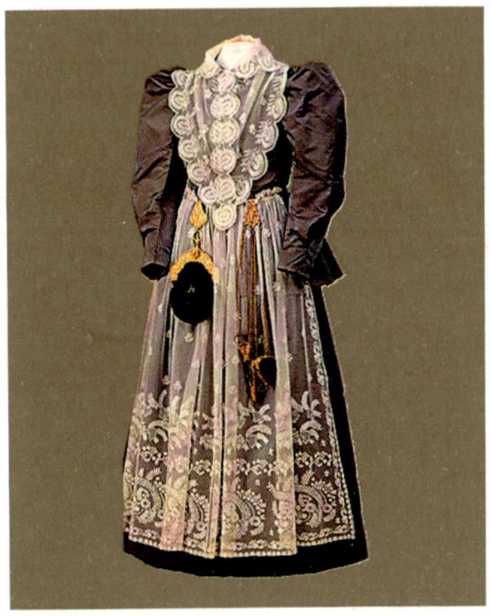

Traditional Friesian robe offered by the women of the province for the young queen's birthday, June 17, 1892
1892
Postma and Smitz (1892), Leeuwarden
Silk, cotton, and lace; gilded headdress with two diamond hairpins; gilded silver chatelaine with scissors and needle case; black velvet bag embroidered with a crowned "W" with the inscription "Friesland June 1892"
Dutch Royal Collections
Inv. MU/4001

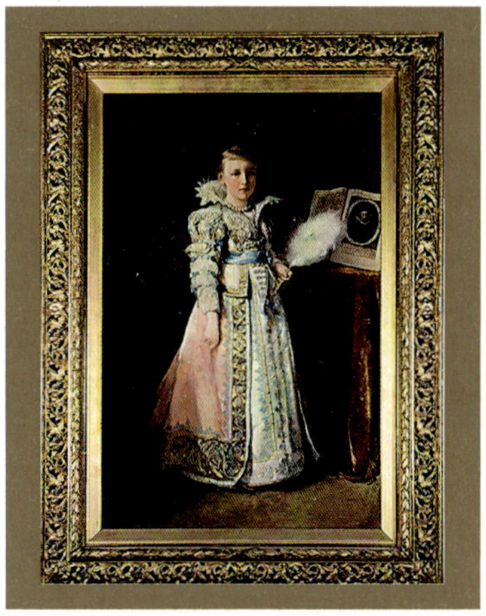

The Young Queen Wilhelmina (1880–1962) in Seventeenth-Century Costume, Known as the Gown of Amalia van Solms
1891
Christoffel Bisschop (1828–1904)
Oil on canvas
218 × 156 cm (inc. frame)
Dutch Royal Collections
Inv. SC/0504

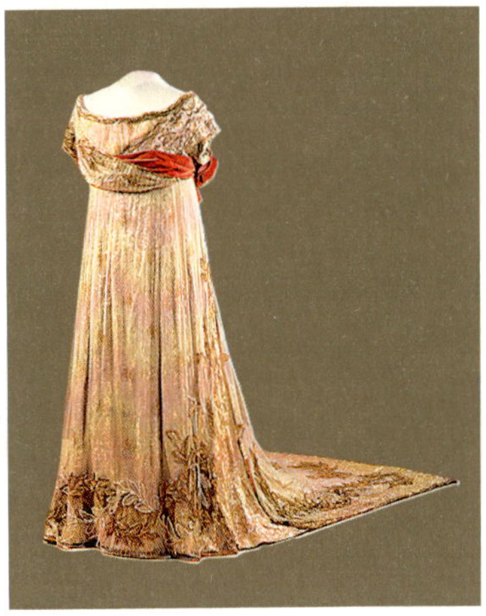

Court robe worn to celebrate twelve-and-a-half years of Queen Wilhelmina's reign
c. 1911
Silk embroidered with gold thread, mother-of-pearl
206 × 43 cm
Dutch Royal Collections,
(on deposit to the Het Loo Palace)
Inv. MU/3980

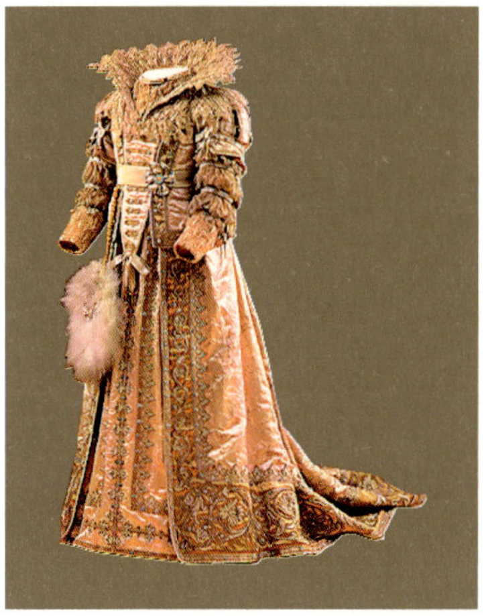

Historical costume, known as the gown of Amalia van Solms, offered by Queen Emma for the eleventh birthday of the young Queen Wilhelmina
c. 1890
Pierre-Eugène Lacoste (1818–1908), theatrical costumer in Paris
(after his models)
Silk embroidered with silver, lace, muslin
120 × 60 cm
Dutch Royal Collections,
(on deposit to the Het Loo Palace)
Inv. MU/3989

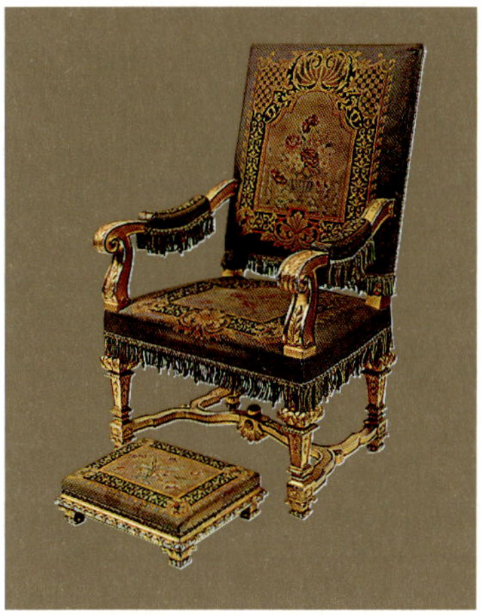

Armchair throne and footrest of Queen Wilhelmina
1900–24
H. F. Jansen and Zonen, Amsterdam
Wood, textile trim
114 × 69 cm
Paleis Het Loo National Museum, Apeldoorn
Inv. L638-a and L637-a

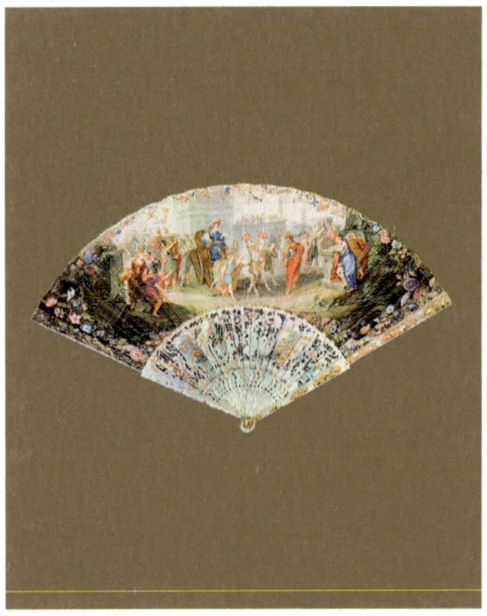

Fan presented by the City of Paris to Queen Wilhelmina in 1912, in accordance with the Parisian tradition of giving a fan to all officially visiting queens
On one side: the entrance of Alexander the Great into Babylon (c. 1750); on the other side: an inscription commemorating the official visit of Queen Wilhelmina to Paris (1912)
Maison Faucon, Paris
Painted silk, mother-of-pearl
26 × 45.5 cm
Dutch Royal Collections
Inv. MU/3167

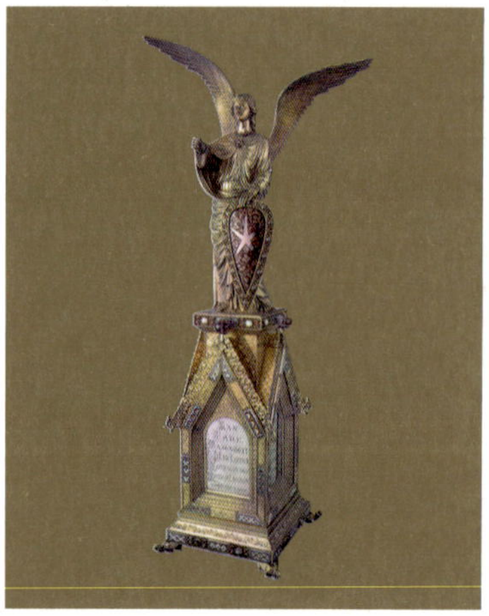

Statue depicting an angel bearing the arms of the City of Maastricht with an inscription on the base: Gift from the City of Maastricht to Princess Wilhelmina during her visit to Maastricht, May 1895
1895
L. Brom (1860–1915)
Gilded silver, enamel
40.7 × 13.6 cm
Dutch Royal Collections
Inv. ID/13

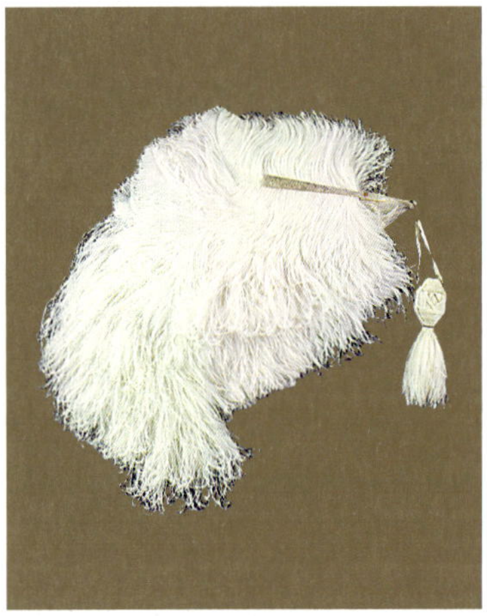

Swan-feather fan of Queen Wilhelmina
c. 1890
Swan feathers, gilded wood
32 × 95 cm
Dutch Royal Collections
Inv. MU/8054

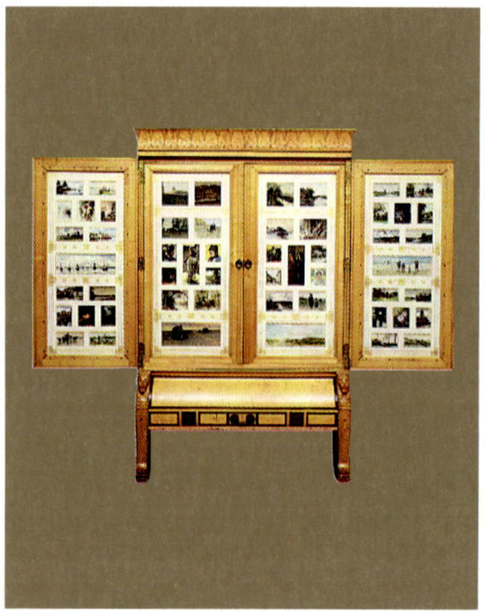

Cabinet, gift for the wedding of Queen Wilhelmina, featuring 116 small watercolors of artists from The Hague, including H. Mesdag (1831–1915), P. Mondrian (1872–1944), and I. Israëls (1865–1934)
1901
Karel Petrus Cornelis de Bazel (1869–1923)
Wood and paper
209 × 132 cm (closed)
Dutch Royal Collections
Inv. W/H/I

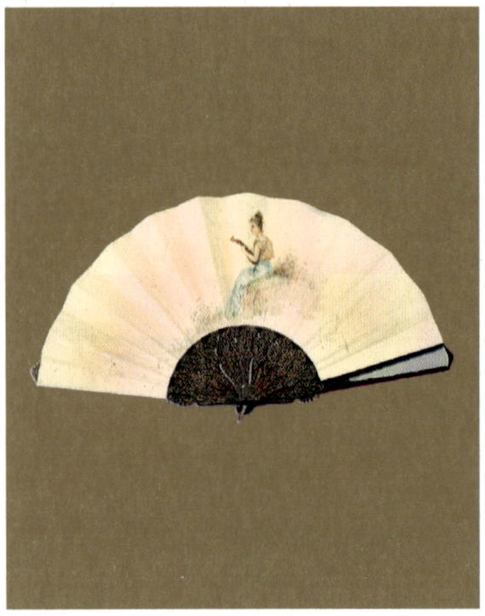

Court fan of Queen Wilhelmina
1888
Mellerio, *dits* Meller, Paris
Diamonds and ruby (mounting); red leather (case); silk painting, signed and dated, "Louis-Robert de Cuvillon 1888"
H. 36.5 cm
Dutch Royal Collections
Inv. MU/8059

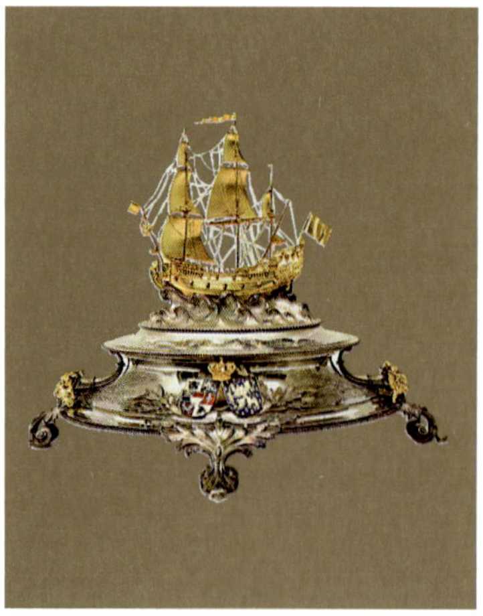

Table centerpiece given to Queen Wilhelmina and Prince Heinrich by the Surinam in 1901
1901
J. M. van Kempen
Partly gilded silver
44 × 37 cm
Dutch Royal Collections
Inv. MU/11051

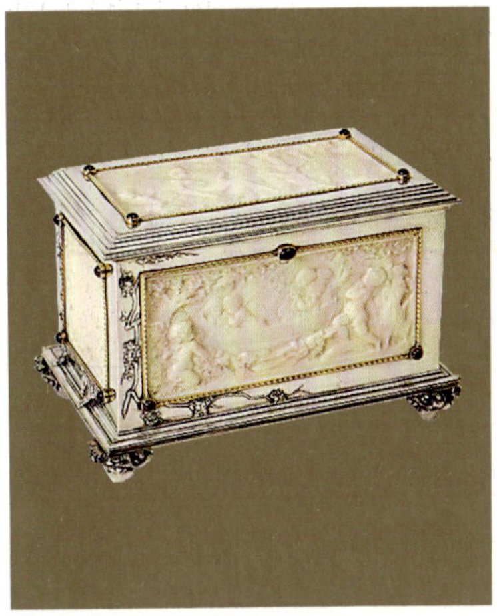

Jewelry case, gift from the Belgian members of the Holland-Belgium Committee to celebrate the birth of Princess Juliana
1874
Philippe Wolfers (1858–1929)
and Isidore de Rudder (1855–1943)
Silver, ivory
13.5 × 18.5 × 12 cm
Dutch Royal Collections
Inv. MU/1320

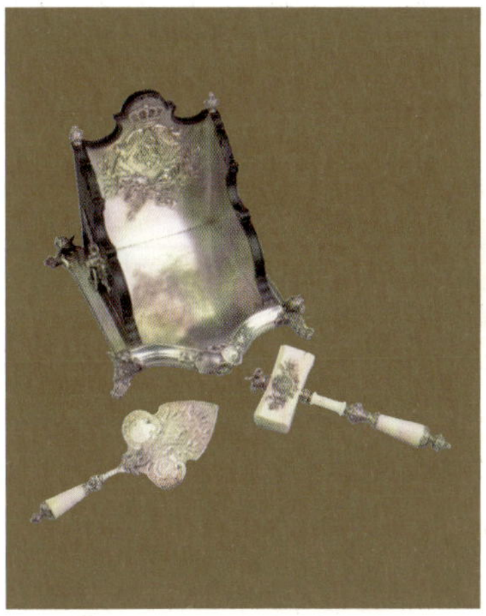

Hammer, trowel, and mortar used for the laying of the cornerstone of Utrecht University, 1892
1891
Gilded silver and mother-of-pearl
H. (mortar) 27 cm;
L. (trowel) 26 cm;
L. (hammer) 25 cm
Dutch Royal Collections
Inv. MU/1101

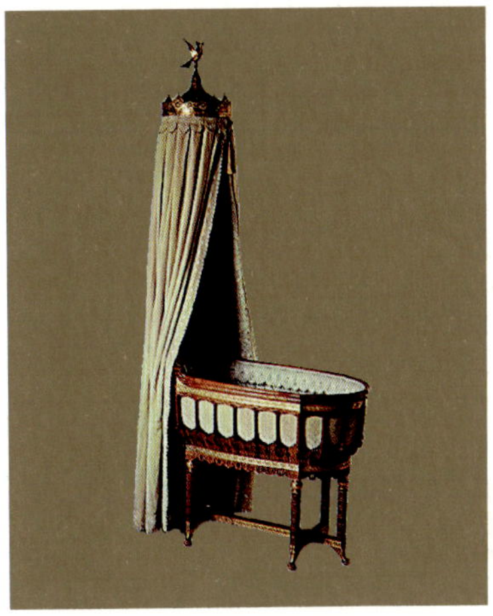

Cradle of Princess Juliana (1909–2004) offered to Queen Wilhelmina by the City of Amsterdam in 1909
1909
Karel Petrus Cornelis de Bazel (1869–1923);
Frans Zwollo (1872–1945)
Marquetry; gilded bronze;
silk and lace garnish
Dutch Royal Collections
Inv. MU/3538

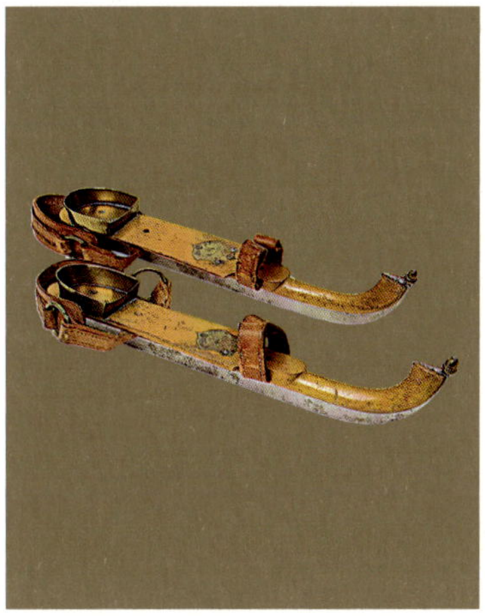

Pair of skis belonging to Princess Wilhelmina
c. 1888
Wood
L. 31 cm
Dutch Royal Collections
Inv. MU/1091

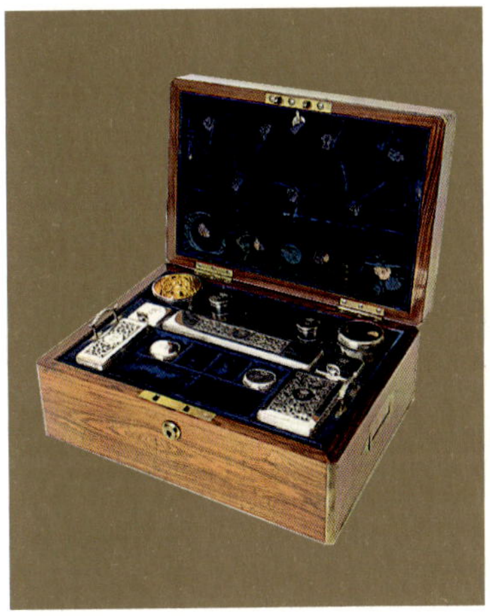

Toilette case belonging to Queen Wilhelmina
c. 1895
Silver
Dutch Royal Collections
Inv. MU/0408

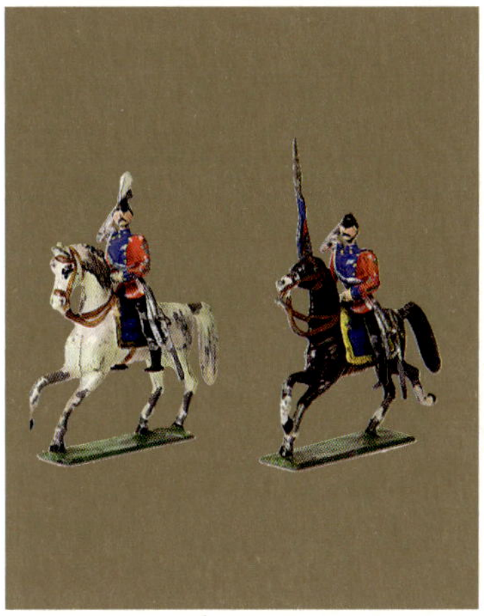

Lead soldiers of the Old Prussian Guard of Princess Wilhelmina
Painted lead
Dutch Royal Collections
Inv. MU/1103

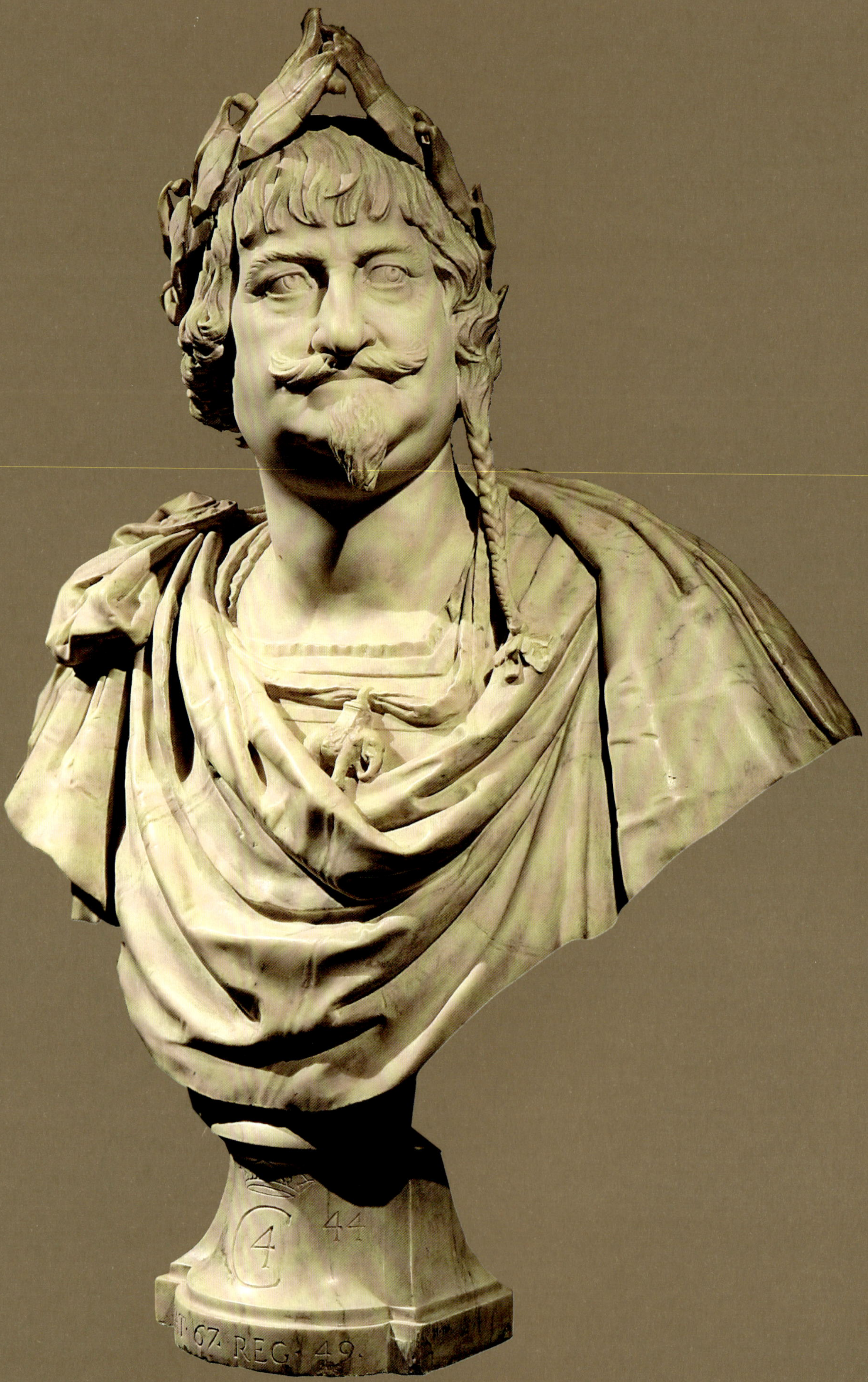
44
REG·49·

DENMARK

Christian IV (1577–1648)
Christian IX (1818–1906)

Christian IV
King of Denmark
1644
François Dieussart
(c. 1600–1661)
Rosenborg Castle,
Copenhagen

Christian IV, King of Denmark and Norway

Peter Kristiansen

Christian IV was born on April 16, 1577, in Frederiksborg Castle in Hillerød. He was the eldest son of King Frederik II of Denmark-Norway and of Sophie, born duchess of Mecklenburg. The celebrated astronomer Tycho Brahe laid out a horoscope that predicted that he would become a well-liked and just king and a great warrior, but that his disposition towards a virtuous life would mean that he was not likely to have children. In this Brahe was badly mistaken!

Frederik II saw to it that Prince Christian received a rounded and useful education, in compensation for the marked deficiencies in his own upbringing by his predominantly German-speaking parents. Christian had the best teachers and was taught Danish, German, French, English, and Latin, but he was also taught many other skills considered appropriate for a future king. Rosenborg Castle contains a portrait of him as a little prince painted around 1585 by Hans Knieper. In 1584, as an expression of the close relationship between father and son, the king gave him a valuable clock.

To Christian's great sorrow, his father died on April 4, 1588; this was eight days before the prince's eleventh birthday. Even though he had become king in principle, it was thought that he was too young and a regency government was set up. Initially, the young dowager queen was involved in this government. According to the Germanic tradition in which she had grown up, she would have been expected to set up minor duchies to provide for Christian's younger brothers, which would mean splitting up the kingdom. The regency powers and the State Council could not accept this, and they managed to have her removed from influence. Meanwhile Christian continued his education at Sorø Academy.

In 1595 the State Council decided that Christian was mature enough to become king. On August 17, 1596, he signed his coronation charter—a contract between the State Council and the king—and on August 29, he was crowned in Copenhagen. The coronation celebration became one of the greatest events in Danish history. All of Copenhagen was buzzing with the excitement of hosting hundreds of guests with their entourages. Tableware, bedclothes, etc. were commandeered from all over the country. And 35,000 drinking glasses were ordered. For the townspeople the fountains ran with wine and spit-roasted beef was

King Christian IV (1577–1648) in Armor
c. 1611
Jacob van Doordt
(c. 1590–1629)
Rosenborg Castle,
Copenhagen

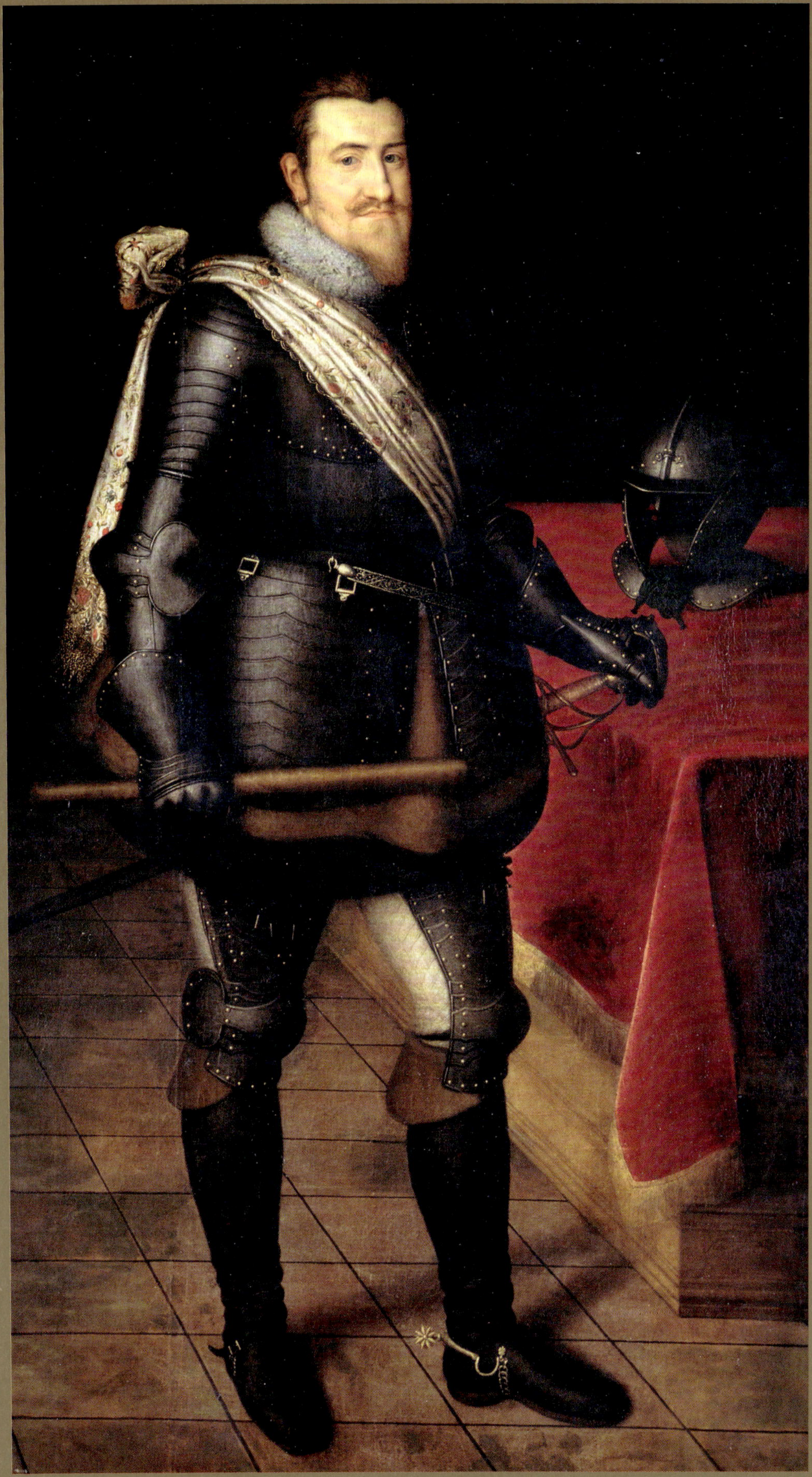

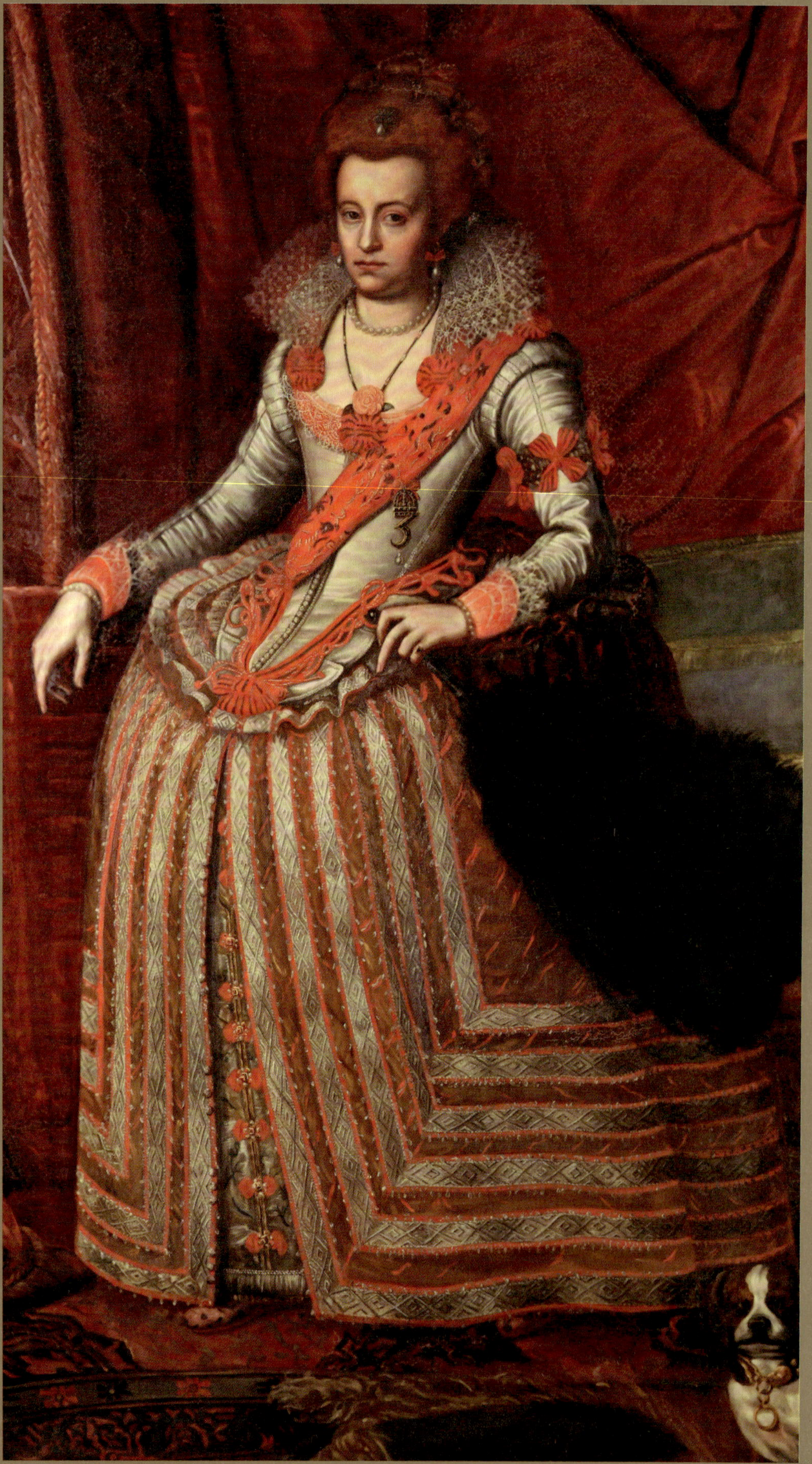

distributed. There were several days of magnificent tournaments, including riding at the ring, celebratory fireworks, and so on.

For the coronation a crown was commissioned from the goldsmith Dirich Fyring in Odense; in spite of many complications the crown is still to be found virtually intact in Rosenborg Castle. The actual shape of the crown—an open crown, presenting the king's head surrounded by radiant gold—would have been old-fashioned at that time, but the crown was also an element in the ongoing disagreement between Denmark and Sweden over the right to use the old coat of arms with three crowns, which Sweden considered to be the Swedish national coat of arms.

The coronation took place in Copenhagen. The king rode to the Cathedral Notre-Dame on a magnificently decorated horse. There the coronation took place in a ceremony lasting several hours, culminating in the actual placing of the crown, held by four noblemen from the State Council, on the king's head. There was to be no doubt that it was the State Council that gave power to the king. When the king left the cathedral he remounted his horse and rode in procession back to the castle, while coins were scattered among the crowd.

Christian IV dreamt of Denmark's glory and of exerting power over the gateway to the Baltic—through controlling the Danish waterways of Øresund, Storebælt, and Lillebælt. He had inherited a long-running conflict with Sweden over the use of the three crowns (Sweden's national coat of arms) in the Danish coat of arms. The conflict arose because the three crowns had been part of the coat of arms of the Kalmar Union, which brought together Denmark, Norway, and Sweden from 1397 onwards. After the dissolution of the union in 1523, it again became the Swedish coat of arms, but at the same time the Danish king claimed the right to use the emblem as part of the Danish coat of arms. Throughout the sixteenth century, the conflict led to continuing feuds between Denmark and Sweden, the most serious of them being the Nordic Seven Years' War (1563–70). The conflict ended with a Danish victory in the Kalmar War of 1611–12, and the subsequent peace treaty of Stettin in 1619, which established that Denmark could use the three crowns as a memorial coat of arms for the Kalmar Union, but without making territorial claims. The three crowns are still to be found in the Danish queen's coat of arms.

In the early 1620s, Christian tried to involve Denmark in what would later become the Thirty Years' War; he wanted to strengthen his position as the major champion of Lutheranism in the Nordic region, naturally in competition with Sweden. The State Council, however, considered it more prudent to avoid conflict with the Catholic Holy Roman Emperor. Their view did not prevail; in March 1625, the king chose to bypass the State Council—his position as duke of Holstein was independent of the Danish crown and thus of the State Council.

Anna Katharina of Brandenburg (1575–1612), First Wife of Christian IV
c. 1895
After Pieter Isaacsz (1568–1625)
Det Nationalhistoriske Museum, Frederiksborg Castle, Hillerød

Kirsten Munk (1598–1658), Second Wife of Christian IV
1623
Jacob van Doordt (c. 1590–1629)
Det Nationalhistoriske Museum, Frederiksborg Castle, Hillerød

After a year of inconclusive fighting, the martial episode came to a sudden end on August 17, 1626, when the king's army was almost eradicated in the Battle of Lutter (northwest of Goslar in southern Lower Saxony). The imperial troops, with General Wallenstein at their head, exploited this victory and, in the following year, Wallenstein invaded and plundered Jutland. It proved possible to reach a peace agreement in 1629, however, on condition that Christian IV promised never to meddle in German affairs again. As a result of the expenses incurred in the war, in 1643 the king found that he had to pawn his royal crown to a merchant in Hamburg, and when he died he had not managed to redeem it. His successor, his son Frederik III, was fortunately able to buy it back, however, so that he could be crowned with his father's old crown; he could not have afforded a new one.

King Frederik III (1609–1670), Son of Christian IV, on horseback with ring game
c. 1650
Jorgen Stichmand
Rosenborg Castle, Copenhagen

In the same year, 1643, the Swedes tried to deal a death blow to Denmark: without a declaration of war, the Swedish field marshal, Lennart Torstenson, invaded Jutland from the south, and Field Marshal Gustav Horn invaded Scania, the Danish territory in southern Sweden, from the north. During this war the sixty-seven-year-old Christian IV led a naval battle, at Kolberger Heide (between Fehmarn and the Bay of Kiel) in 1644. There the king was hit by shrapnel from a cannon and was knocked unconscious. All those around him thought that he was dead. But he struggled to his feet and commanded his men to continue the fight. He had been wounded and lost the sight of one eye. His blood-stained garments from the battle are still preserved in Rosenborg Castle. The battle ended with defeat for the Danes and, when he died in 1648, Christian IV left a ruined country and an unresolved conflict with Sweden.

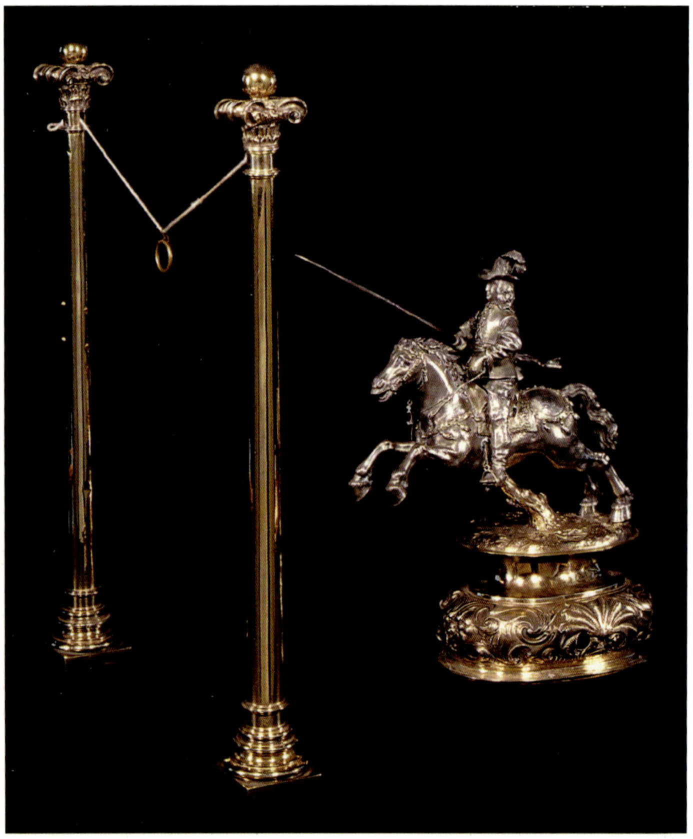

Despite Tycho Brahe's words about the king's disposition towards a virtuous life, Christian was also in this respect a typical Renaissance man. While still young he undertook a journey along the north coast, round the North Cape, to the border fortress in Vardø and all the way to Murmansk in Russia. He traveled incognito as Captain Christian Frederiksen, and in all the places he came to on the way he and his noblemen went out for a good time—there was heavy drinking and many windowpanes

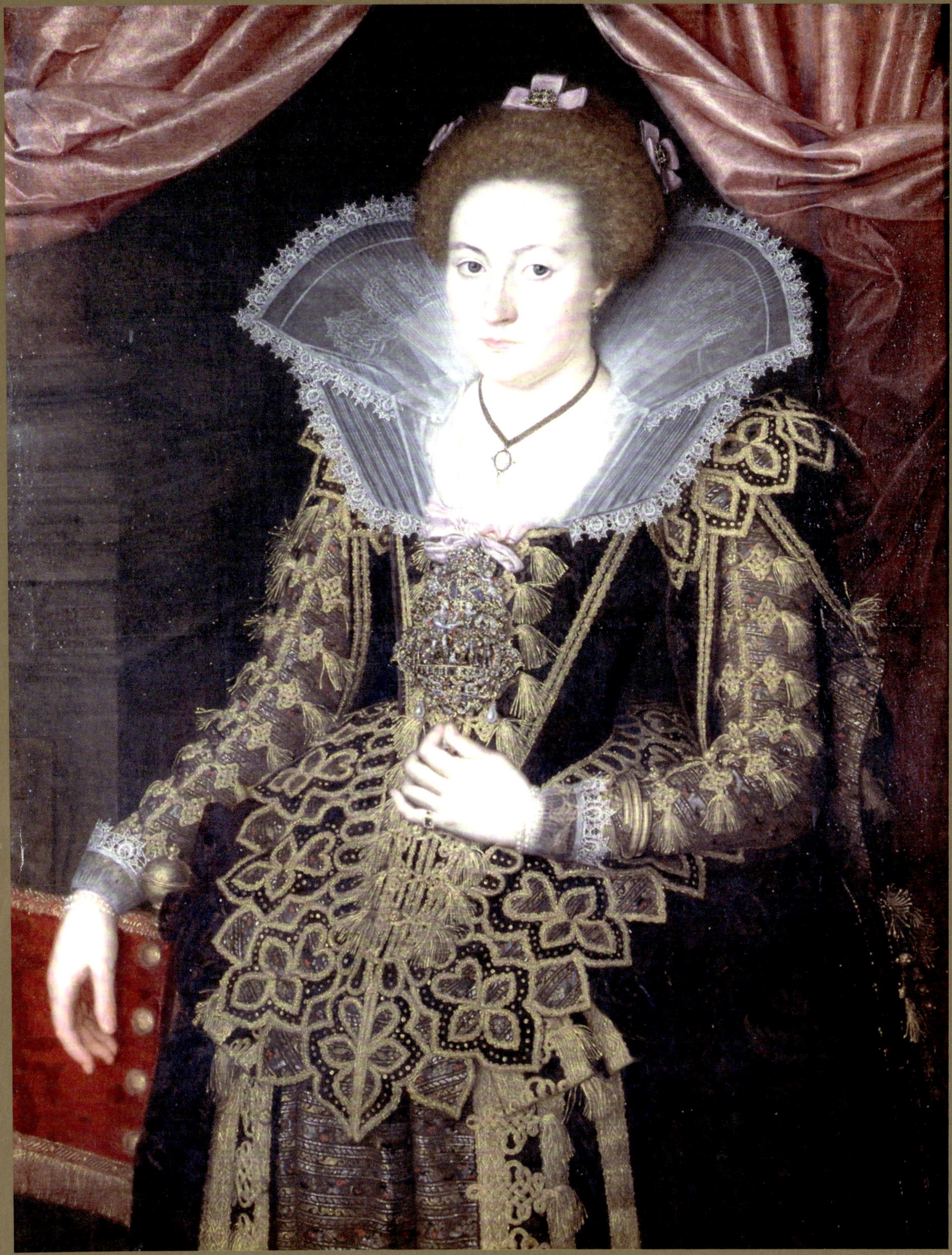

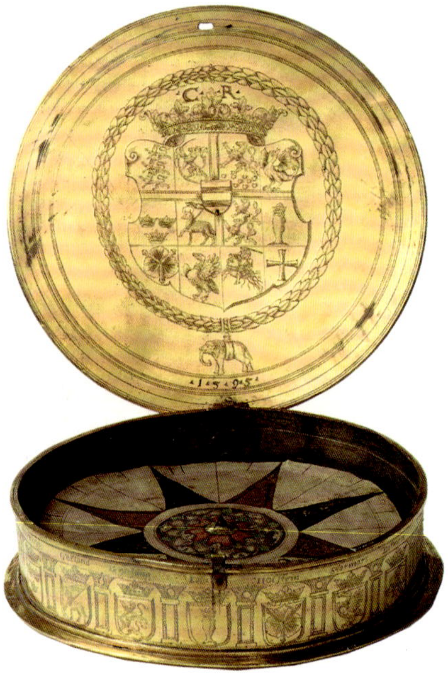

were broken on that trip! One of his companions was the nobleman Sivert Grubbe, who kept a diary throughout the journey. In the margin there are discreet notes with small crosses denoting how heavy the drinking had been. In one place there are three crosses and the supplementary lament, "oh my poor head."

In 1597 Christian IV married Anna Katharina of Brandenburg, with whom he had six children; only one of them, the future Frederik III, outlived him. Anna Katharina died in 1612, and in 1615 Christian was married morganatically to the noblewoman Kirsten Munk, with whom he had ten children. The relationship with Kirsten Munk was tempestuous, and the age difference of twenty-one years between them led to her finding a younger lover in later years. The king threw her out in 1630, but the break-up had a lasting effect on him. In his many letters he returns constantly to complaining of how unfairly she had treated him; she had tried to kill him with poison, she had altered his shirts so that her lover could use them, and she had not treated the many children properly. Christian's final companion was the serving girl Vibeke Kruse, who stayed with him faithfully until his death in 1648. With her he had two children. In addition he had three children with two bourgeois women —making a total of at least twenty-one children with five different women. One of his children, Leonora Christine (1621–1698) had a particularly grim fate. In 1636 she married the nobleman Corfitz Ulfeldt, who became prime minister and minister of finance and found himself in opposition to the new king, Frederik III, and his queen, Sophie Amalie. Ulfeldt saw no way of extricating himself other than by fleeing to Sweden and entering into its service—thereby committing treason. During a visit to Denmark the couple was arrested, but Ulfeldt managed to escape; he died in exile in 1664. Leonora Christine, however, was imprisoned in 1663 and remained in a cell in Copenhagen Castle until her enemy Queen Sophie Amalie died in 1685. She herself died in 1698. But on the whole Christian IV was not keen to involve his sons in the running of the kingdom. The king wanted to do everything himself! He governed from early morning to late at night and intervened in all contexts—from war with the Swedes to questions of missing keys. He was virtually an absolute monarch before the introduction of the absolute monarchy in Denmark, and he was an absolute *pater familias,* if not a household tyrant. It should be said in his defense that he managed to keep up an astounding pace throughout the nearly fifty years of his reign.

Compass with the arms of Christian IV
c. 1595
Rosenborg Castle, Copenhagen

Clock with figures representing the emperor surrounded by the seven electors
c. 1600
Rosenborg Castle, Copenhagen

Cup with base
c. 1650, Hamburg
Hans Lambrecht II
(c. 1600–1670)
Rosenborg Castle, Copenhagen

Covered bowl in the shape of a celestial globe
c. 1650, Hamburg
Heinrich III Lambrecht
Rosenborg Castle, Copenhagen

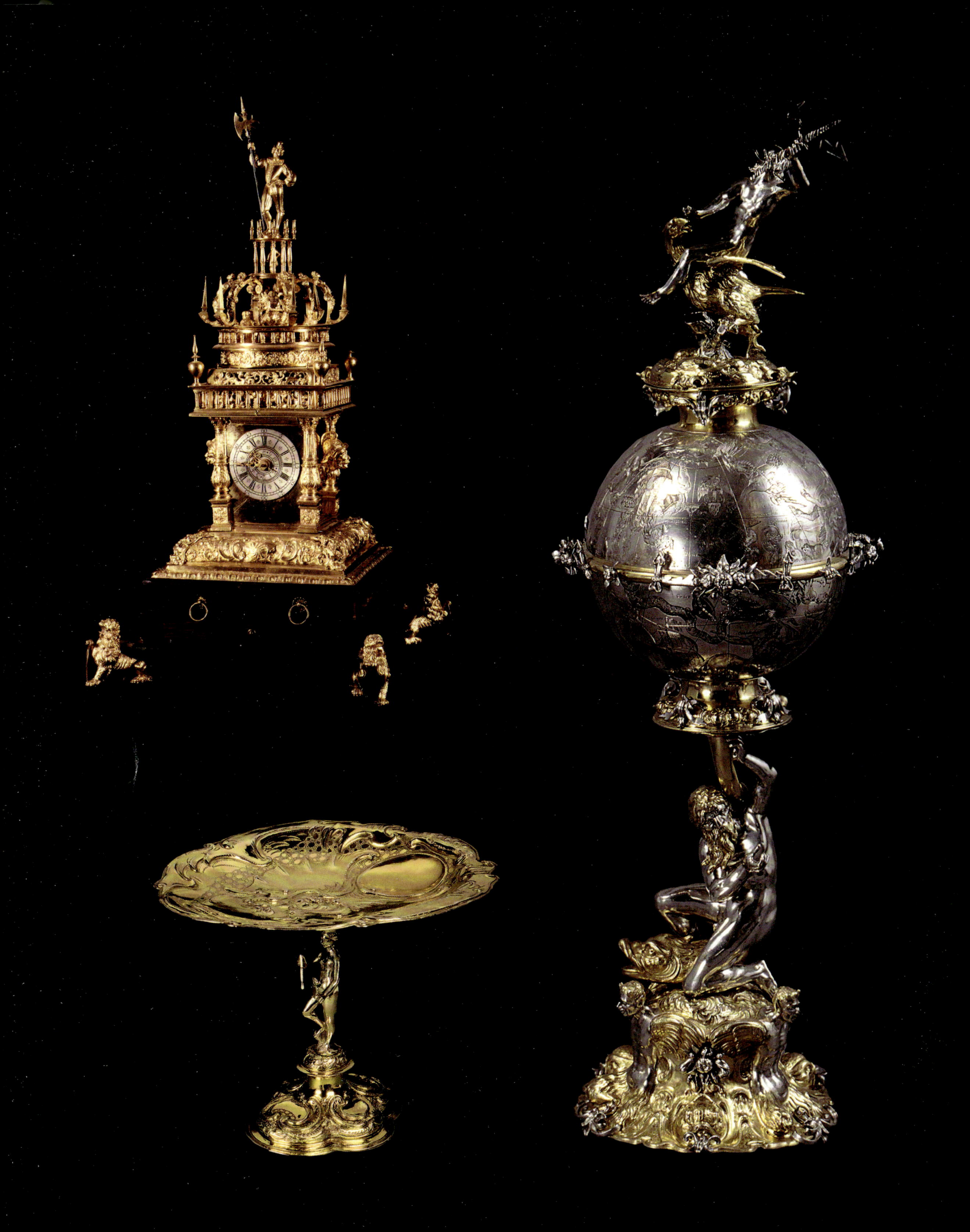

Covered bowl with base
Early seventeenth century
Rosenborg Castle,
Copenhagen

In his youth Christian IV was taught about many things, including art and architecture. The art of building interested him greatly, and it was even thought for a long time that the king was his own architect. That would perhaps be an over-interpretation of his role, but as a commissioner of building works he was certainly knowledgeable and critical, and those who worked on his projects were well-advised not to thwart his ideas. He began his reign by extending Copenhagen to almost double the area of the medieval town. He provided the town with new and fine buildings, some of them still in existence today: the Armory with the naval harbor, Rosenborg Castle, the Børsen (stock exchange), Nyboder (dwellings for naval personnel), the Round Tower (with its observatory) and the adjoining Trinitatis Church, Regensen (the student residence), and renovations and a new tower for Copenhagen Castle. Elsewhere in the country he commissioned a major rebuilding of Frederiksborg Castle in Hillerød, rebuilt Kronborg Castle after a fire, and had the fantastic church in Kristianstad constructed. He was also active in establishing towns and he named most of them after himself—in Denmark, Christianshavn; in Scania, Christianstad; in Blekinge, Christianopel; in Norway, Christiania and Christiansand, and finally, in Holstein, Christianspris, and as the crowning achievement Glückstadt on the Elbe, which was given the hard task of competing with Hamburg. As is now evident, it did not win.

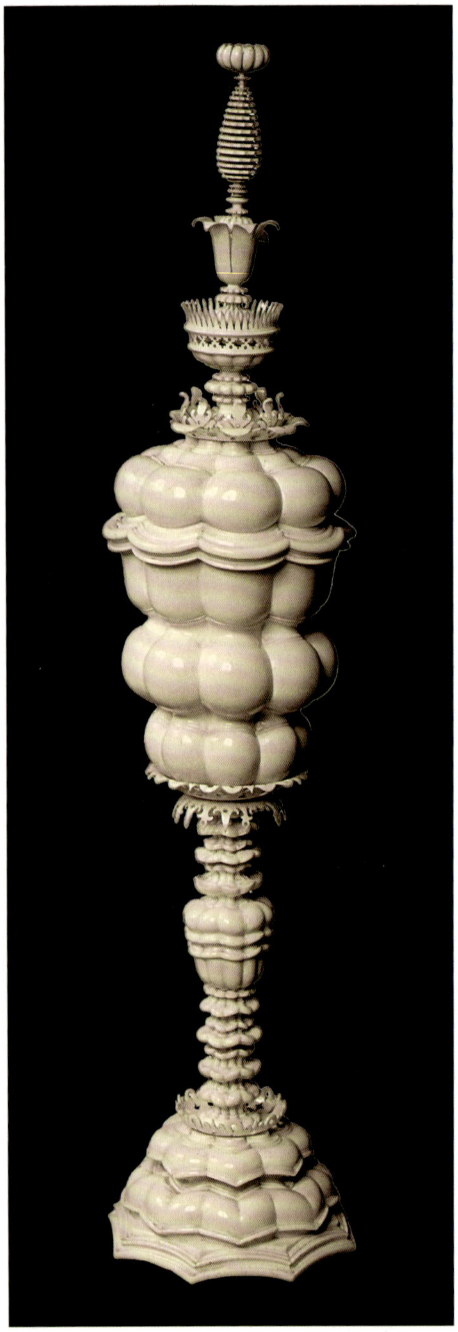

Christian IV worked throughout his life on his "legacy," the posthumous reputation he could hope to achieve, rather in the spirit of the old joke that if you want a good obituary you have to write it yourself. All his life he collected objects that supported the legend of the victorious and self-sacrificing king. Most of these objects he ordered made himself—if he won a battle or a war, he had himself painted as a great warrior, etc. In addition, he was a deeply religious person and experienced two visions, each of them before major war episodes. Both visions were the subject of paintings which can be found today in Rosenborg. During the Thirty Years' War,

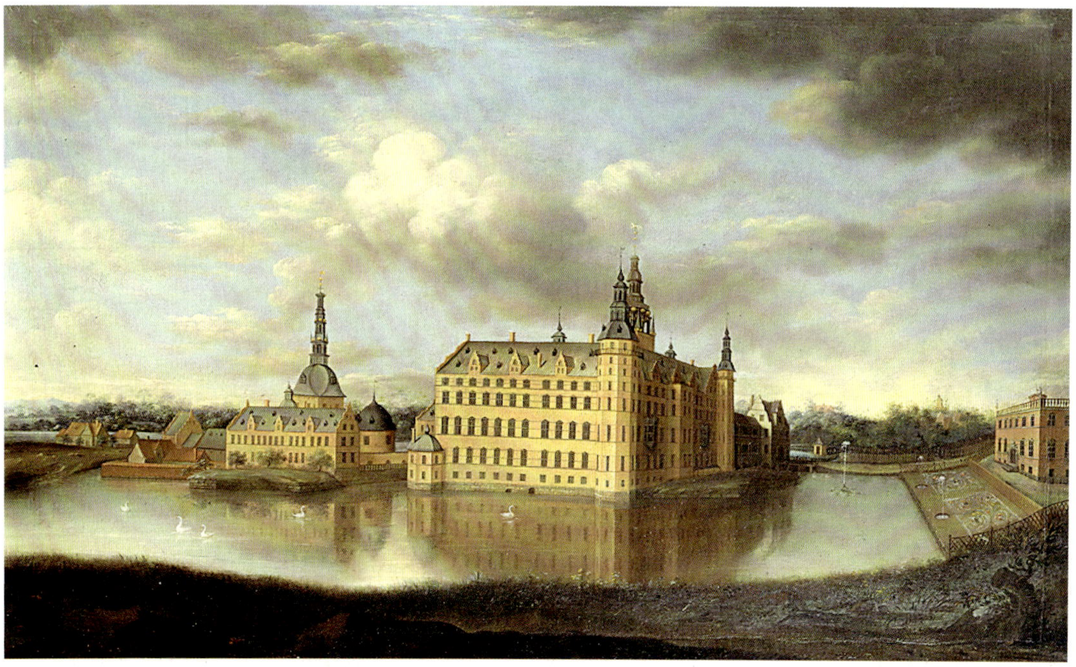

the king made himself available as a mediator and had a portrait painted of himself as the great king receiving humble delegations from all the countries of Europe, led by *Pieta*, holding the hand of *Pax*, asking him to make peace. The painting's content is almost an expression of megalomania.

Christian IV died in Rosenborg Castle on February 28, 1648, aged seventy. Now, 350 years after the king's death, it has to be said that his propaganda has worked. If Danish schoolchildren can name one king, it is Christian IV. He is famous for his Renaissance lifestyle: food, wine, women, and children, for the wars he took part in, and perhaps most of all for his efforts in art and buildings. There is less heard about the other side of the coin—the war efforts that came to nothing, for example, in 1644, when large parts of the country were ravaged by Swedish troops. He also left behind him an unresolved conflict with Sweden, which came to a head in the war of 1658–59 and ended with the old Danish territories east of Øresund—Scania, Halland, and Blekinge—becoming Swedish for good.

Frederiksborg Castle
c. 1690
Det Nationalhistoriske Museum, Frederiksborg Castle, Hillerød

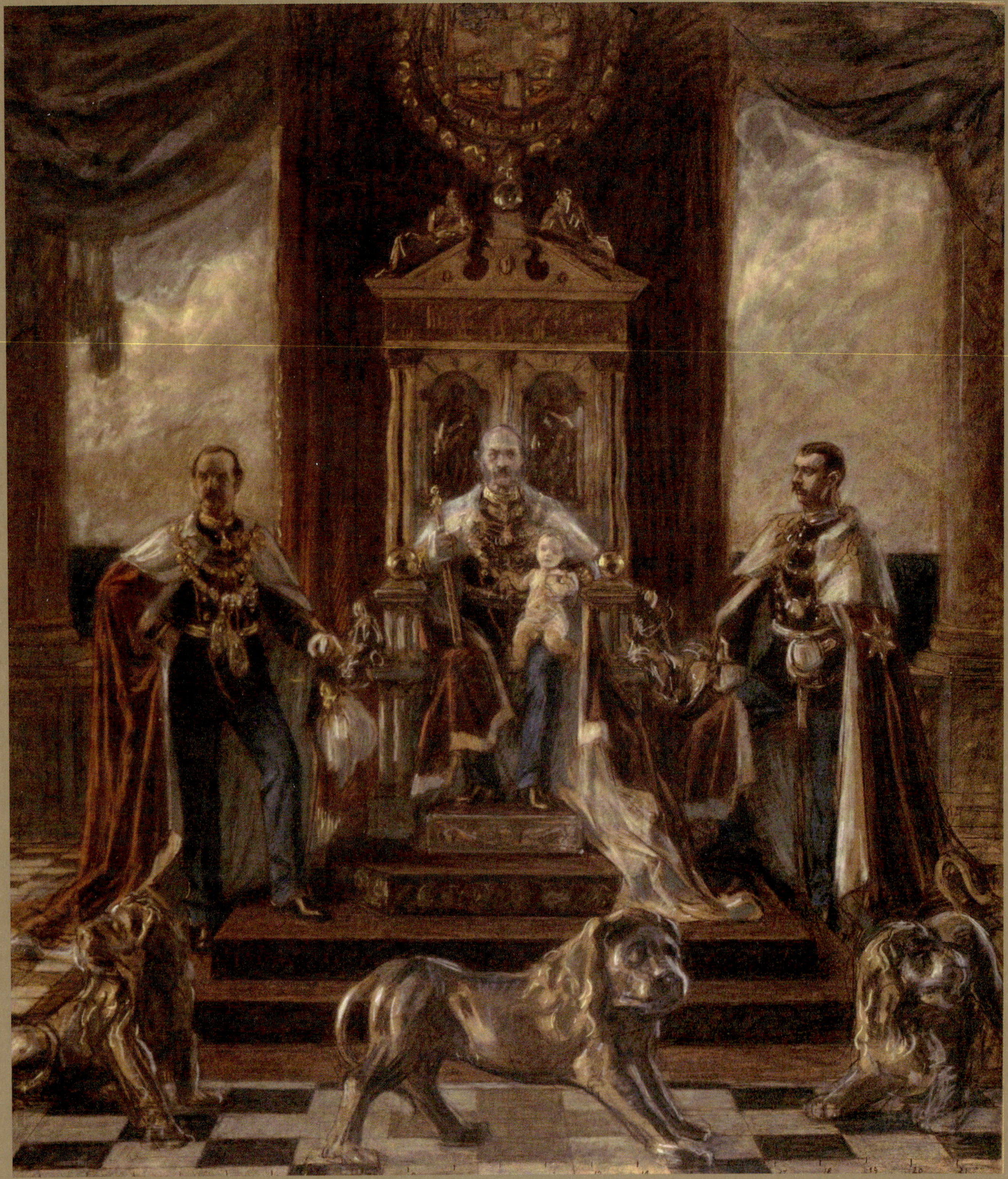

Christian IX of Denmark and Queen Louise, Europe's "parents-in-law"

Birgit Jenvold

The wedding of the great-great-grand parents of Denmark's present queen, H. M. Margrethe II, took place in 1842. Prince Christian of Glücksborg and Princess Louise of Hesse-Kassel both belonged to the distant branches of the Danish royal family, and Christian VIII, Denmark's king, was the godfather of the groom and uncle of the bride (her mother's brother). It had by then become modern, in matters of marriage, to take into account the wishes and feelings of potential partners, and these two young individuals were in love and wanted each other. Prince Christian's salary as a young cavalry officer was modest, but with contributions from the family they were able to have an appropriate lifestyle. Christian VIII provided accommodation for them in the form of a mansion adjacent to his own residence at Amalienborg Palace in Copenhagen.

Prince Christian and Princess Louise had six children, born between 1843 and 1858: Frederik (1843–1912), Alexandra (1844–1925), Wilhelm (1845–1913), Dagmar (1847–1928), Thyra (1853–1933), and Valdemar (1858–1939). Their mother was chiefly responsible for providing them with a suitable upbringing and education, and this included ensuring that the daughters could sew and mend their own clothes, while music and art lessons were also in the curriculum. Their father undertook what was then a very progressive activity: morning gymnastics with the children. This was a well-ordered and by princely standards extremely modest environment. The family thrived together and enjoyed leisure pursuits such as playing card games. The children, who were fun-loving and on occasion noisily unruly, were also charming and polite, as a result of their rather strict but affectionate upbringing. Attention to duty, kindness, integrity, and piety were the basic elements.

In 1848 Christian VIII was succeeded by his son, Frederik VII, who was childless; this meant that the Oldenborg line of the royal house would die out. In 1852, after international negotiations, Prince Christian was chosen as successor to the throne, to become the first king of the Glücksborg line of the royal family. From then on the family's financial situation improved, and more public attention

The Four Generations of the Kings of Denmark
c.1901
Laurits Tuxen (1853-1927)
The Museum of National History at Frederiksborg Castle,
Hillerød

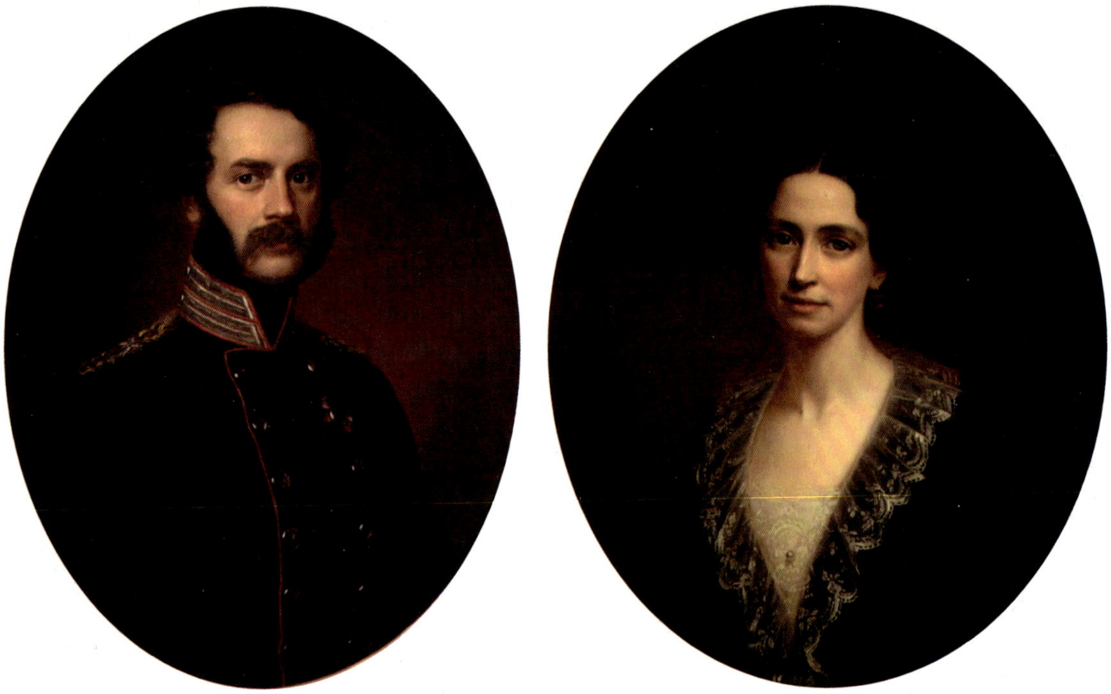

was paid to its members, both in Denmark and further afield in Europe, where other royal houses now started to view the family's many children with great interest. Princely family alliances were given high priority at international level, and in that context Princess Louise was particularly active.

On the death of Frederik VII in 1863, Prince Christian and Princess Louise became Denmark's king and queen. As years passed they became known as "Europe's parents-in-law," since their children had achieved prominent positions through marriages and appointments. Also in 1863 their son Prince Wilhelm was chosen to be king of Greece, under the name George I, and their eldest daughter Princess Alexandra married Queen Victoria's eldest son, the prince of Wales, later Edward VII.

Subsequently, Princess Dagmar married Russia's heir to the throne, Grand Duke Alexander, Crown Prince Frederik married the Swedish Princess Lovisa, King George of Greece married Grand Duchess Olga, Princess Thyra married Duke Ernst August of Cumberland, and Prince Valdemar married Princess Marie d'Orléans.

The Danish public followed the news of these weddings, and of other major events in the royal house, with pleasure and pride. In spite of their royal position, however, Christian IX and Queen Louise still had to exercise economic restraint, and so when Dagmar's wedding took place in St. Petersburg the bride's family was represented only by two of her brothers, George and Frederik. If the Danish king

King Christian IX (1818–1906) and Queen Louise (1817–1898)
1850
August Schiott
(1823–1895)
Amalienborg Palace, Copenhagen

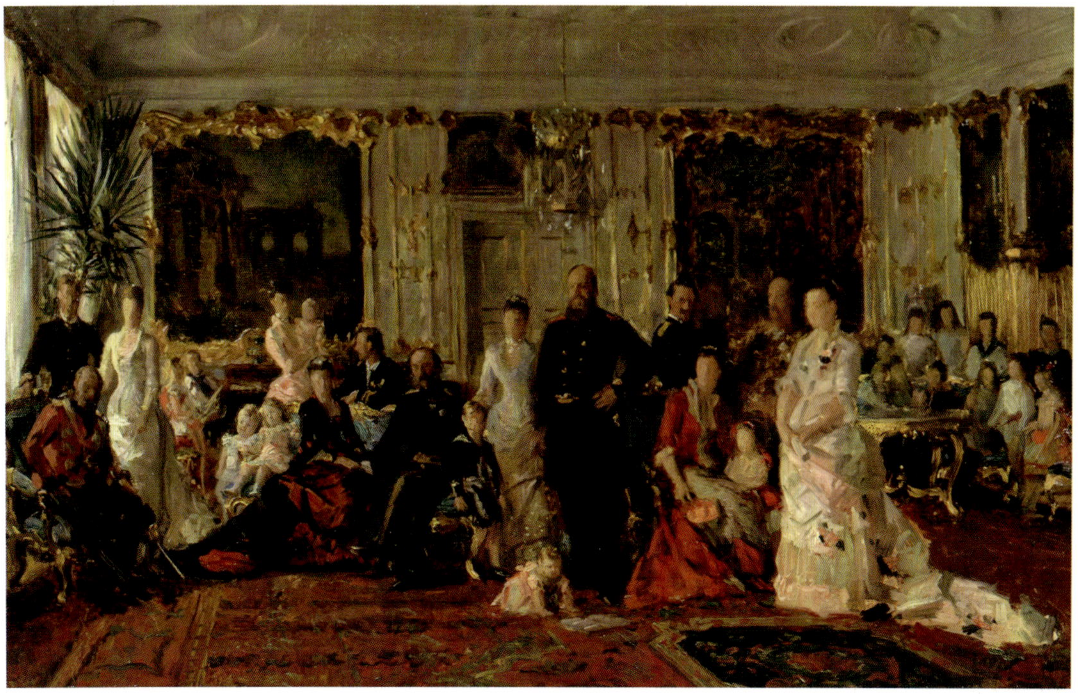

and queen had participated, enormous costs would have been incurred in living up to the splendor of the czar's court, and this could not have been afforded. Instead a gala dinner and celebration was held in Copenhagen on the day of the wedding.

Although scattered across several countries, the royal couple's children kept in close contact with their parents and with each other. Much of their correspondence is preserved—ranging from short telegrams to long letters—and it is full of affectionate greetings and tales of matters great and small, thoughts and deeds, encouragement, comfort, and good advice. The presents that were given at Christmas and for birthdays often consisted of samples of the new medium, photography. Portrait photos meant that one could see those one held dear even when they were far away and opportunities to meet were limited. In Christian IX and Queen Louise's home, family photos were dominant among the objects that surrounded the royal couple in their everyday lives.

It became a tradition that the children, sons- and daughters-in-law, and grandchildren, whenever possible, would gather together to visit Christian IX and Queen Louise in Denmark over a long period in the summer. This became known as the "Fredensborg days," a phenomenon which Chancellor Bismarck of Germany is said to have dubbed "Europe's whispering gallery," since it was suspected that many issues of international politics were discussed and decided on at the Danish royal family gatherings. There is no evidence that this was the

The Royal Family of Christian IX
1868
Laurits Tuxen (1853–1927)
Det Nationalhistoriske Museum, Frederiksborg Castle, Hillerød

Ball gown belonging to Queen Louise
c. 1896
Amalienborg Palace, Copenhagen

Bracelet with two miniature portraits: Czar Alexander III and Empress Maria Feodorovna, born Dagmar, Princess of Denmark
Samuel Arndt (1845–1890)
Amalienborg Palace, Copenhagen

Souvenir locket with miniature portraits of Christian IX and Louise of Hesse-Kassel
1904
Anton Michelsen (1809–1877)
Amalienborg Palace, Copenhagen

case, however; holiday enjoyment and relaxation with the family were clearly the main motivation. Alexander III thoroughly enjoyed his holiday visits to his parents-in-law, both as czarevitch and later as czar—in contrast to his English brother-in-law, the future Edward VII, who found these family reunions boring and escaped from them when he could. The czar enjoyed the freedom of being able to move around Copenhagen incognito, and he was well-loved by the many children in the family as a playful uncle.

Not so much a "whispering gallery," then, but when one knows one's uncle, brother, or cousin well and is on good terms with him, the idea of declaring war on him cannot be other than remote.

Christian IX and Queen Louise's long period as Denmark's reigning couple was perhaps not characterized by magnificence and grandeur. There is every sign that the young couple's love for each other turned into life-long devotion in a good marriage, in which their relationship to their children and their growing flock of descendants was close and fond. The queen constantly supported her husband, and it was a great sorrow for him that she died after fifty-six years of marriage. In everyday speech, one could describe her as a wise and supportive wife.

Royal activities throughout many years were influenced by the fact that in 1864 Denmark suffered defeat in war and had to relinquish the duchies of Schleswig, Holstein, and Lauenburg to Prussia and Austria. The country was thus reduced by about a third of its area, and this defeat was felt bitterly by the royal family as well as the rest of the Danish population. For Christian IX there was an additionally poignant element, in that his childhood home, Glücksborg Castle, was now in "the lost land." There had at first been some skepticism among the Danish public about the royal couple's German background, but they gained sympathy through their suffering over Denmark's loss of the duchies, and as time went on their popularity grew; their role as "Europe's parents-in-law" was a factor contributing to this popularity in an age when contact between the royal house and the public grew closer because of the development of press attention.

Queen Louise died in 1898 and Christian IX in 1906; after that their home at Amalienborg remained intact for a number of years, in accordance with the wishes of their children, who returned to stay there from time to time. Two rooms from their private apartments—full of photos of their dear family—can still be seen in the Amalienborg Museum, looking as if Christian IX and Queen Louise have just left.

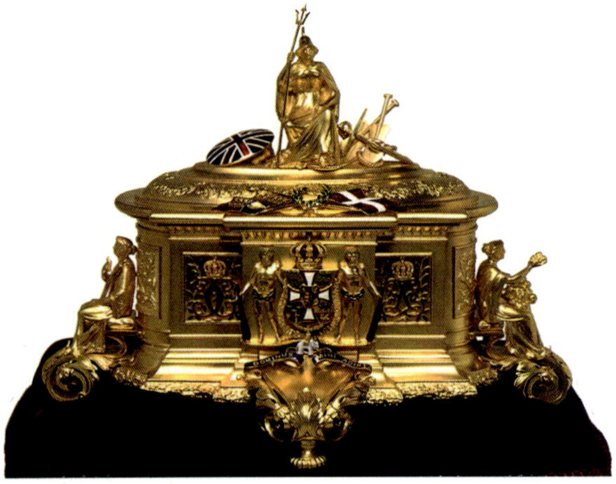

Gift case for the golden wedding anniversary of Christian IX and Queen Louise
1892
Hunt and Roskell / Late Storr and Mortimer, London
Amalienborg Palace, Copenhagen

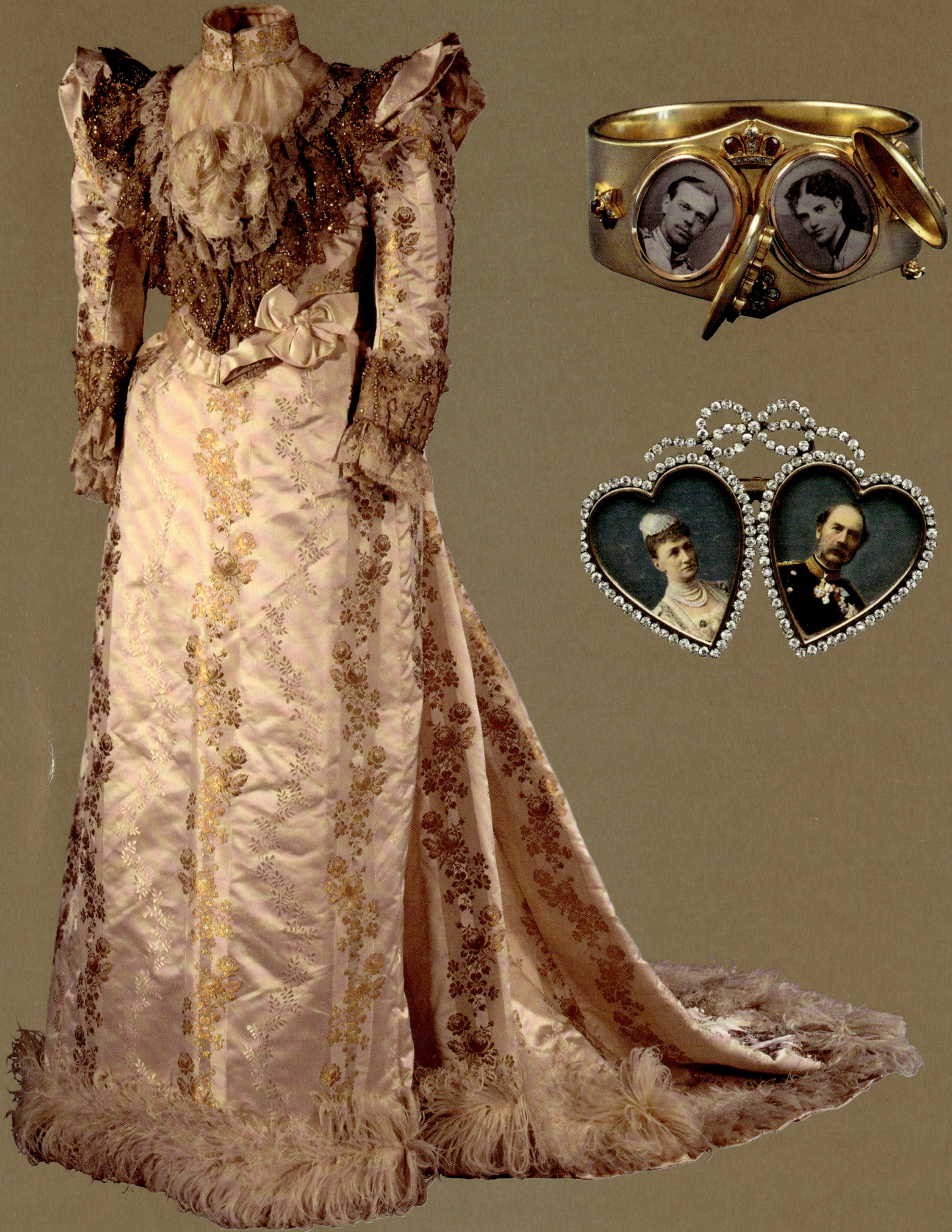

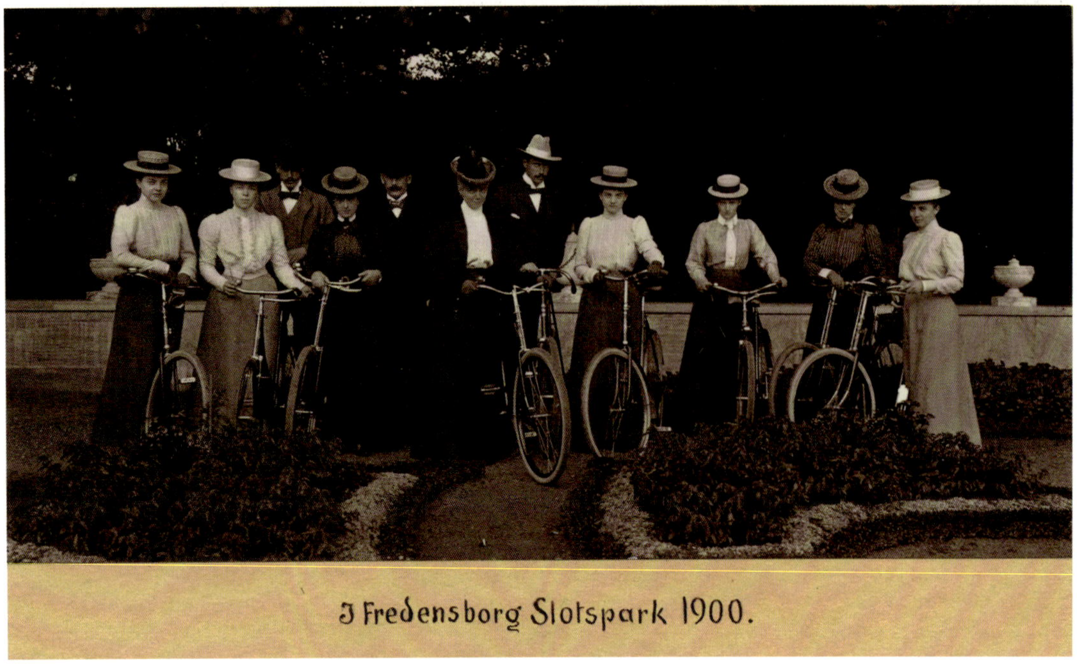

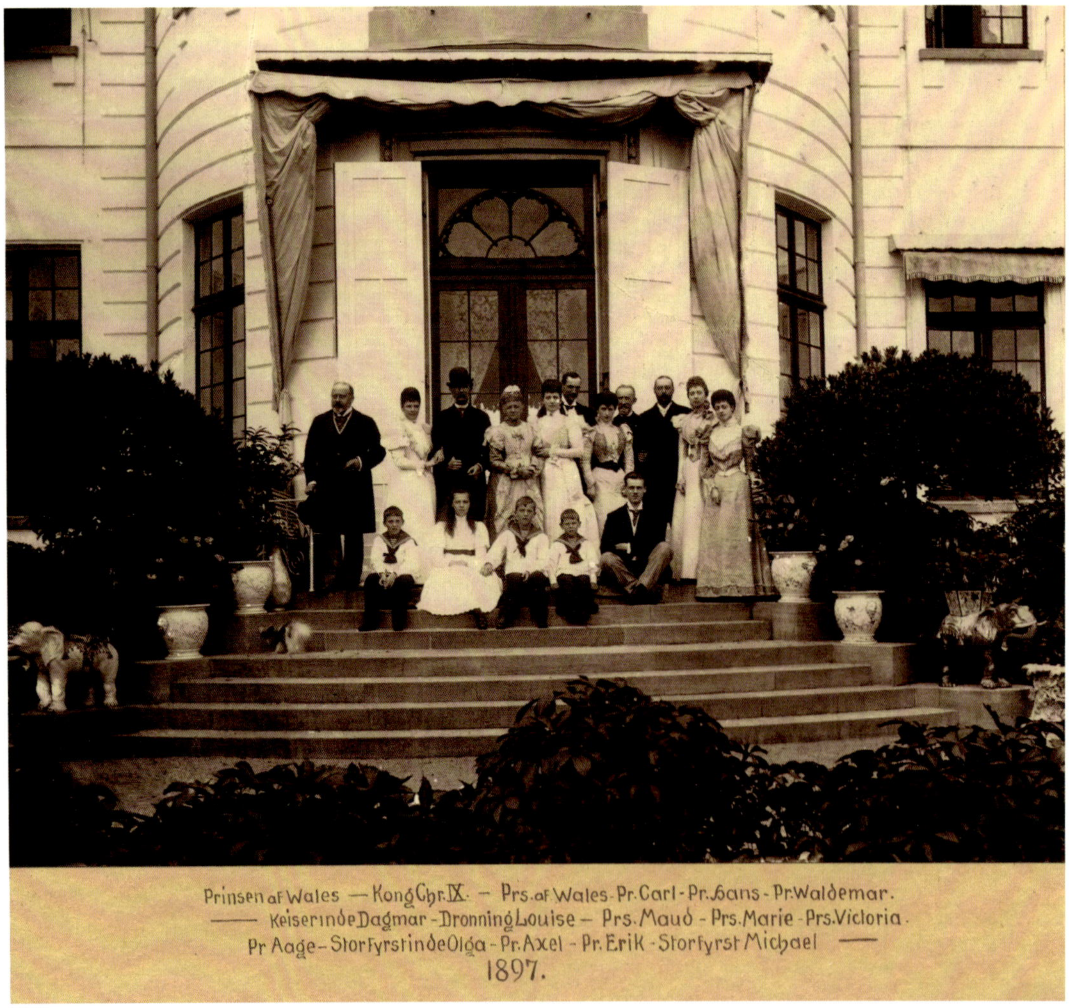

The royal family go cycling, summer 1900, Fredensborg Castle

The royal family on the main steps of Fredensborg Castle: Prince of Wales, King Christian IX, Princess of Wales, Prince Michael, Prince Valdemar, Empress Dagmar, Queen Louise, Princess Maud, Princess Marie, Princess Victoria, Prince Aage, Grand Duchess Olga, Prince Axel, Prince Erik, Grand Duke Michael

The history of the *Flora Danica* service

Mogens Bencard

In 1648 the Danish professor and botanist Simon Paulli (1603–1680) published a survey of Danish plants and their practical use. He gave the book the title *Flora Danica*, which was the first time the Roman goddess had appeared in this context. The idea became internationally popular so that in the following years all similar publications in other countries were entitled "Florae".

This, perhaps, gave Danish botanical science a certain fame, so that when the Danish government decided to establish a new *Flora Danica* in 1752, it was followed by botanists of other countries to such an extent that they initially made the decision to publish their own plants only if they had not been published already in *Flora Danica*. This idea was soon abandoned, but, surviving many political changes, *Flora Danica* continued to be published until installment no. 51, which appeared in 1883.

In the latter half of the eighteenth century, botany was considered the most promising of the natural sciences by the rulers of Europe, who hoped that it would benefit their state economies. Other rulers developed a keen interest in the subject, so there were initiatives similar to that of *Flora Danica* outside Denmark.

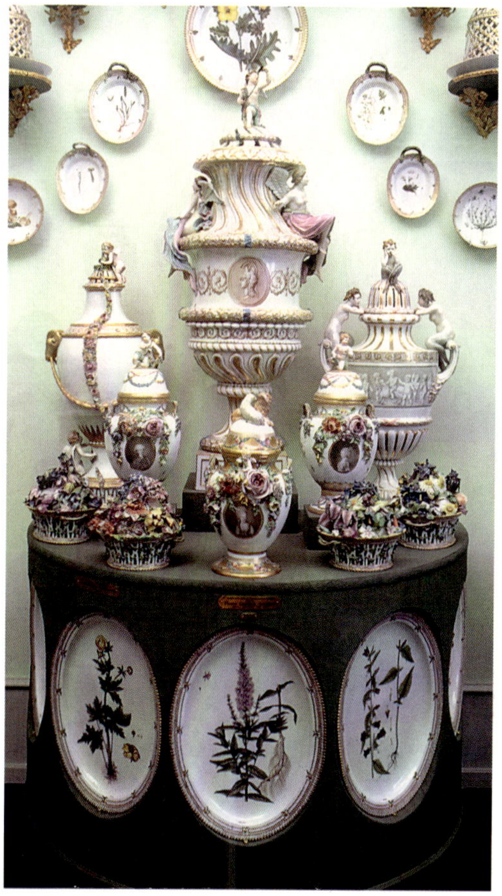

The Flora Danica service in the porcelain cabinet of Rosenborg Castle
1789
Rosenborg Castle, Copenhaguen

One of the interested rulers was Catherine the Great of Russia, and in the *Flora Rossica* one can see that the idea of not publishing plants that had appeared in Flora Danica was carried out.

The situation obviously demanded some sort of action, and the idea of combining porcelain with *Flora Danica* arose. This idea may have come from the dow-ager queen Juliane Marie (1729–1796), one of the important investors in the manufactory. The queen had in her youth seen her family's manufactory, Fürstenberg, being established and prosper, and she seems to have been eager to see the same thing happen in her new homeland. She may also have heard of the tiles produced in Fürstenberg that were decorated with plants, complete with their Latin names.

Another possible inspiration came from the recently appointed director of the factory Theodor Holmskjold (1731–1793), a botanist who published a book on fungi whose charming Latin title may be translated as *Happy Periods of Rest in the Country in the Company of Danish Mushrooms.* The plates for this work were engraved after designs by J. C. Bayer (1738–1812), who prior to his employment at the porcelain factory had made the drawings for the plants for *Flora Danica.* The botanical aspect was therefore in capable and serious hands.

At the manufactory there was a puzzling secrecy about the person for whom the service was being made. Catherine's name is never once mentioned in the archives. Two French visitors in 1790 described the service, but were unable to ascertain when it was started or for whom it was being made. A recently discovered diary by a visiting Scot, dated 1789, features an admiring description of the service, leaving no doubt that he had seen *Flora Danica.* Given the fact that the Danish army had marched back from Sweden in November 1788, it is obvious that the Danish rulers had not been sitting on their hands, but had decided to have the service made already in the beginning of 1789.

Tureen from the Flora Danica dinner service; on the back, mark of the royal factory and inscription giving the name of the represented plant
1784–1801
Rosenborg Castle, Copenhagen

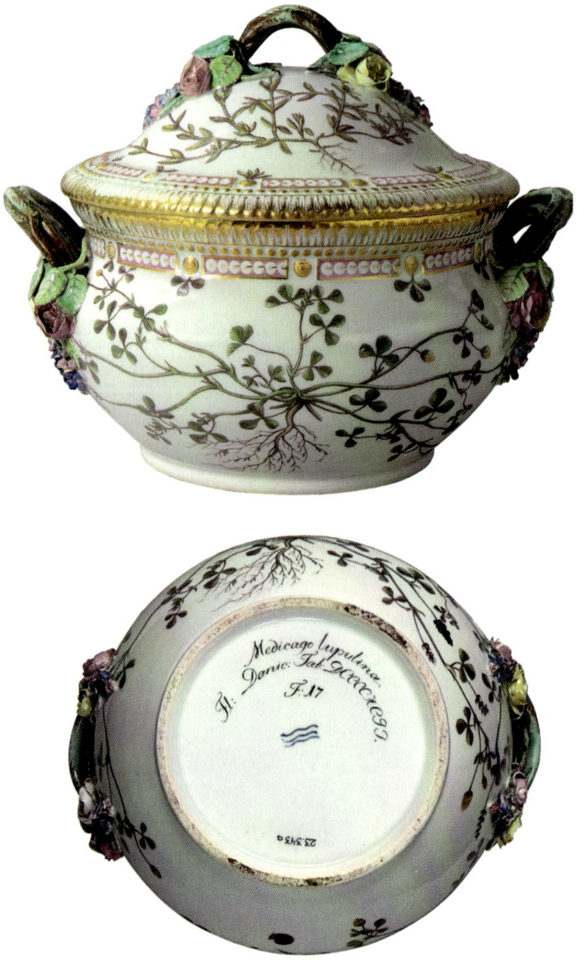

The only contemporary source, which connects the service with the empress, is an entry dated 1794 in a diary by a Dr. Fabricius on the remote island of Born-holm. He had been banished from Copenhagen because of his unruly behavior, which makes the entry somewhat doubtful. He does, however, quote the son of a master at the manufactory, so there seems to be little reason for not believing him. This is corroborated by visitors to Rosenborg Castle, where the service was stored from 1803. They were told by the guides that the service had been intended for Catherine the Great.

Perhaps the reason for the secrecy is that the people at the manufactory did not feel certain that they would succeed and did not want to make public who the recipient was. It was, after all, a large service featuring a complicated decoration. As to the size of the service, it was originally ordered to comprise eighty settings, which was changed by royal order in 1797 to one hundred settings. When in 1802 the production was finally stopped—again by royal order—the number of items belonging to the service was no less than 1,800 pieces, making it one of the largest services in Europe.

The czarina died in 1796, so by the following year the gift had become irrelevant, especially since her son was hostile to Denmark and like his father wished to regain the family dukedom of Holstein-Gottorp.

The order from the crown prince in 1797 to extend the service is puzzling, almost an act of defiance, underlined by the order five years later to stop.

As can be seen the manufactory did not manage to fulfill the order in time. The *Flora Danica* service was much bigger than normal services presented by the royal owners of the factories and this alone may be the reason for keeping its recipient a secret. Mishaps, like misfiring, might so easily delay the project.

A second reason for secrecy—and perhaps the most important one—is the decoration. At the factory they had sufficient knowledge about how long it took to make a decoration of a bouquet of flowers or scattered ones, but they could not know how long it would take to decorate an item based on the botanic drawing. It had rarely been tried before and was undoubtedly particularly demanding. In *Flora Danica and the Royal Danish Court*, Steen Nottelmann wrote: "Pieces reproducing the copper prints with minute accuracy with all the lines and shadows that are the special characteristic of this graphic technique, but with a precision that demanded great self-discipline on the part of the porcelain painter" (1990, p. 184).

Flowers and bouquets of flowers, attractive and charming, are well-known decorative features on porcelain. The Flora Danica decoration features serious, strict and educational depictions, and is fascinating as such. The stem of a plant may be cut in three to fit the surface, details of the flower may be placed next to the plant, on the back is painted the Latin name of the plant and a reference to its place in *Flora Danica*. You may find on the bottom of your soup plate the ugliest of fungi, because all the plants from *Flora Danica* had to be presented. On tureens you may see longer plants with the roots to one side running horizontally round the sides of the bowl. And you may see stiff grass standing on a plate, aesthetically ill-fitting the circular surface.

Originally a set of figures had been planned to accompany the service, but that plan had been abandoned. A number of centerpieces was executed and still exist. They contained all the alluring charm of flowers and porcelain, and consisted of modeled bouquets of flowers in various vessels: four pieces in baskets on pedestals, eight oval baskets, eight round baskets, and four plates. These were executed by Søren Preuss, who worked for the factory from 1784 to 1801. When the service was discontinued in 1802, it consisted of the following pieces: 18 round tureens with lids and dishes, 18 oval tureens with lids, 67 oval dishes, 45 round dishes, 327 flat plates, 86 deep plates, 18 butter containers with lid and dishes, 25 salt cellars, 56 egg cups, 318 knife and fork handles, 16 cruets, 7 cruet stands, 4 mustard spoons,

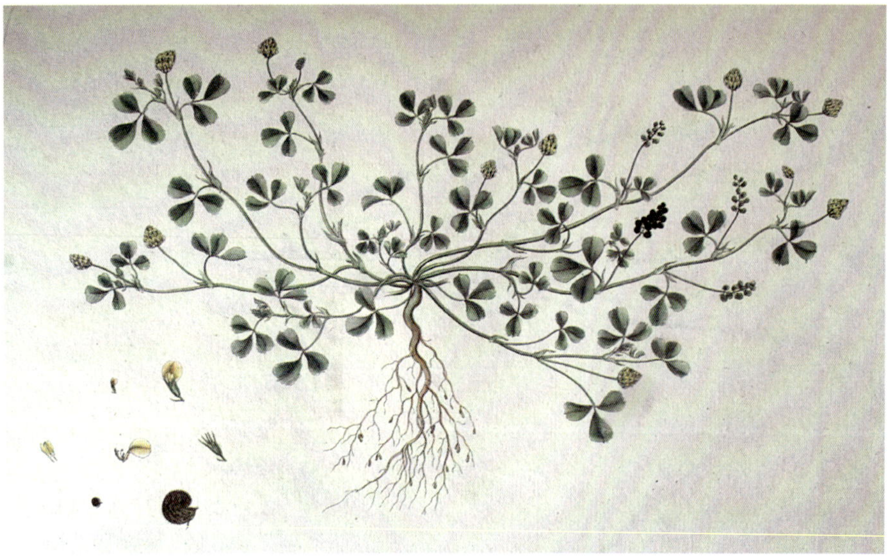

8 sugar bowls with lids and dishes, 8 sugar-sifting spoons, 24 round salad dishes, 16 oval salad dishes, 8 square salad dishes, 12 triangular salad dishes, 12 square serving dishes, 6 oblong serving dishes, 6 monteiths, 8 salad bowls, 14 sauce boats with dishes, 6 fish drainers, 6 round casseroles with lids and handles, 16 oval vegetable dishes with lids, 44 round wine coolers, 12 oval wine coolers, 16 oval fruit baskets with dishes, 12 round fruit baskets, 141 round dessert dishes, 102 deep dessert dishes, 6 ice boxes with casserole and lid, 24 leaf dishes, 36 shell dishes, 4 ice dishes with cover, 4 dishes for custard cups, and 104 custard cups with lid.

Drawing for
a *Flora Danica* plate
Simon Paulli (1603-1680)
Botanisk Centralbibliotek,
Copenhagen

The Danish royal family has guarded the *Flora Danica* service well for 200 years and has only used it rarely over the years, with the happy result that over 1,500 pieces still exist.

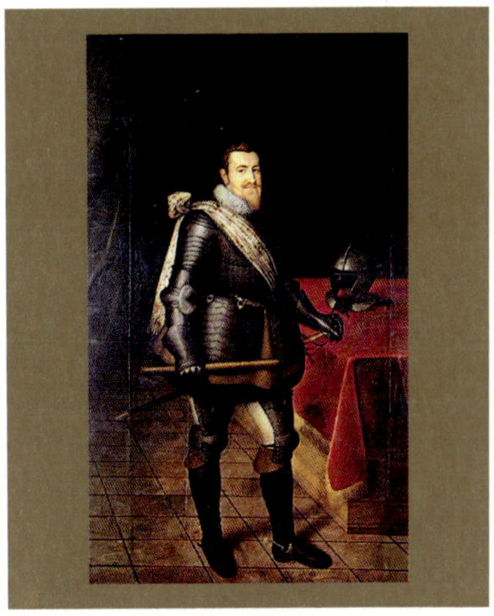

King Christian IV (1577–1648) in Armor
c. 1611
Jacob van Doordt (c. 1590–1629)
Oil on canvas
240 × 143.7 cm
Rosenborg Castle, Copenhagen
Inv. 3-172

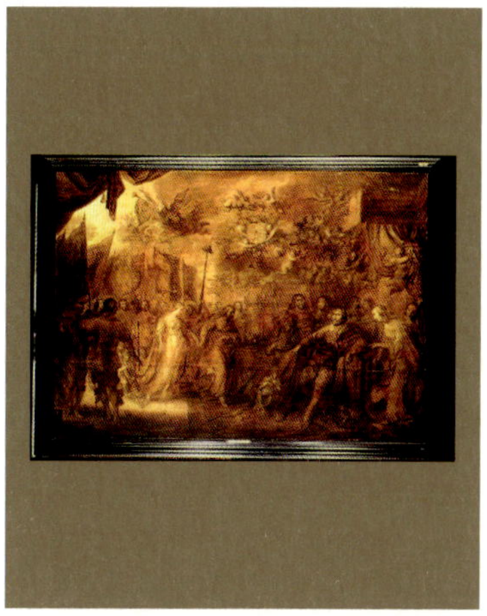

Christian IV as Mediator
c. 1643
Adrian van de Venne (1589–1662)
Oil on canvas, grisaille painting
120.6 × 165.3 cm
Rosenborg Castle, Copenhagen
Inv. 7-12

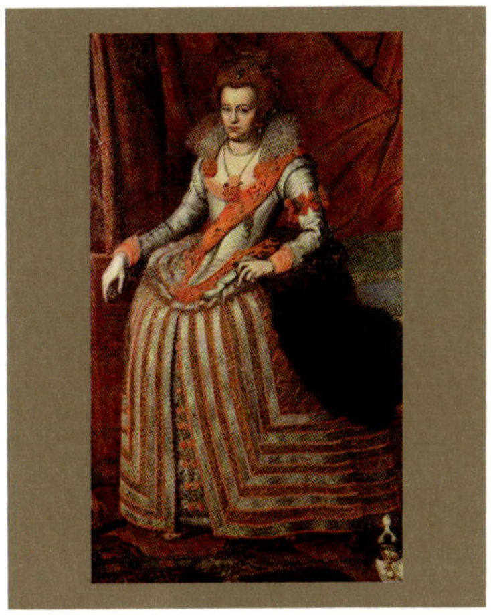

Anna Katharina of Brandenburg (1575–1612), First Wife of Christian IV
c. 1895
After Pieter Isaacsz (1568–1625)
Oil on canvas
approx. 230 × approx. 150 cm (inc. frame); L. (canvas) 128 cm
Det Nationalhistoriske Museum, Frederiksborg Castle, Hillerød
Inv. A 686

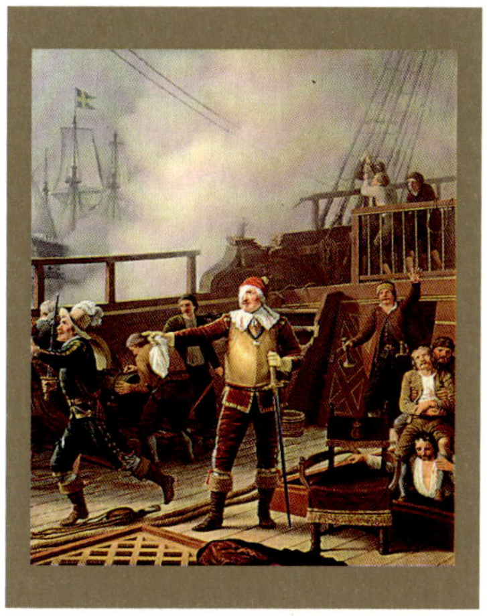

Christian IV, King of Denmark
1832
Christoffer Wilhelm Eckersberg (1783–1853)
Oil on canvas
56 × 48 cm (inc. frame)
Det Nationalhistoriske Museum, Frederiksborg Castle, Hillerød
Inv. A 7210

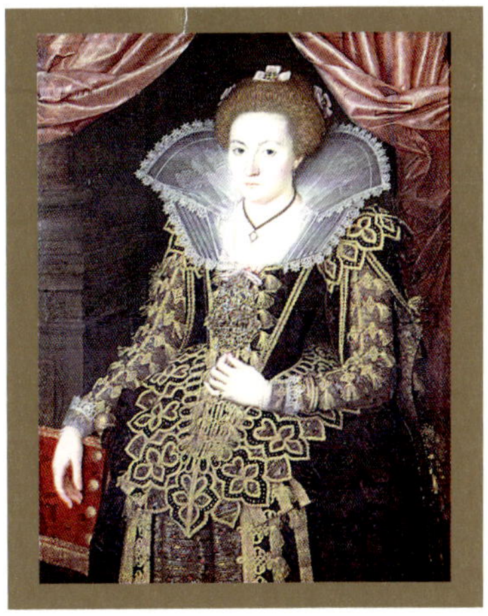

Kirsten Munk (1598–1658), Second Wife of Christian IV
1623
Jacob van Doordt (c. 1590–1629)
Oil on canvas
142.5 × 114.5 cm (inc. frame)
Det Nationalhistoriske Museum, Frederiksborg Castle, Hillerød
Inv. A 7299

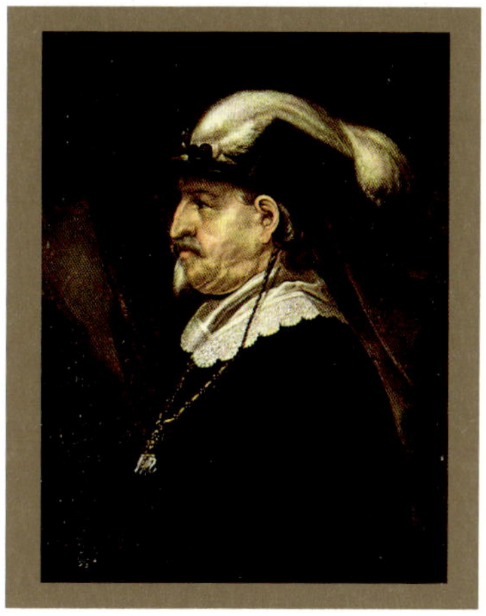

Christian IV in Profile, Blinded in One Eye Following a Battle with Sweden
c. 1645
Karel van Mander the Younger (1577–1648)
Oil on canvas
98.5 × 78 cm (inc. frame)
Det Nationalhistoriske Museum, Frederiksborg Castle, Hillerød
Inv. A 2545

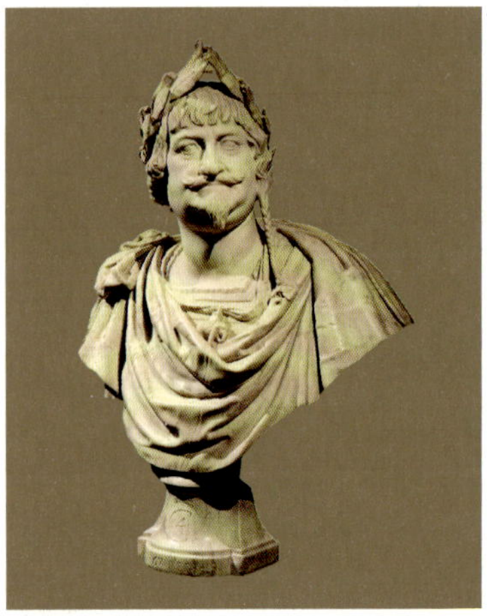

Bust of Christian IV
1644
François Dieussart (c. 1600–1661)
Marble
H. 98 cm
Rosenborg Castle, Copenhagen
Inv. 21-120

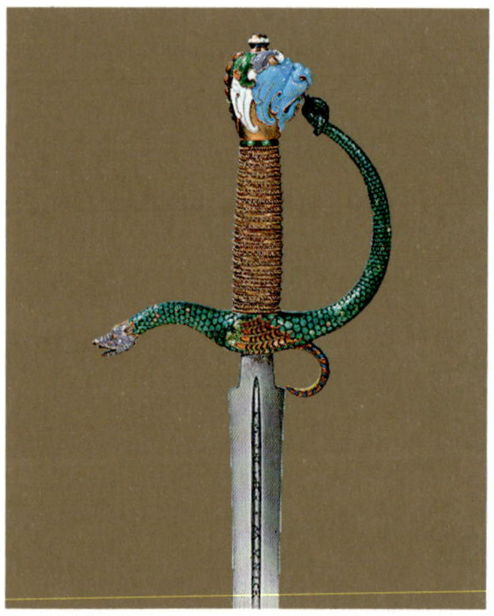

Sword belonging to Christian IV
c. 1634, Paris
Pierre Delabarre (c. 1625–1680)
Steel, iron, gold, enamel
L. 93.3 cm
Rosenborg Castle, Copenhagen
Inv. 7-208

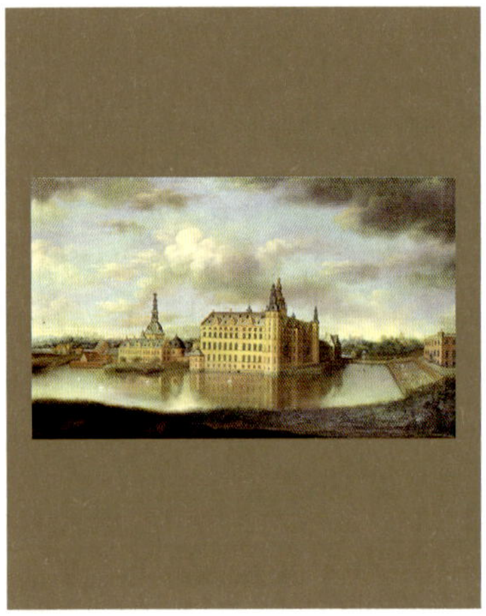

Frederiksborg Castle
c. 1690
Oil on canvas
approx. 100 × 150 cm (inc. frame)
Det Nationalhistoriske Museum,
Frederiksborg Castle, Hillerød
Inv. A 851

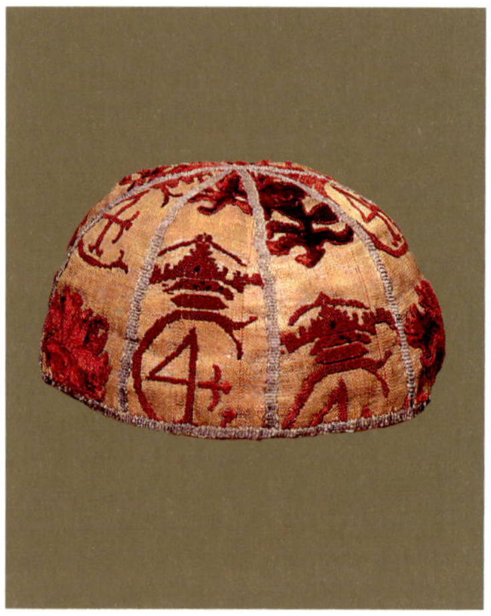

Headgear belonging to Christian IV
Early seventeenth century
Red velvet
approx. 10 × approx. 28 cm
Rosenborg Castle, Copenhagen
Inv. 2-32

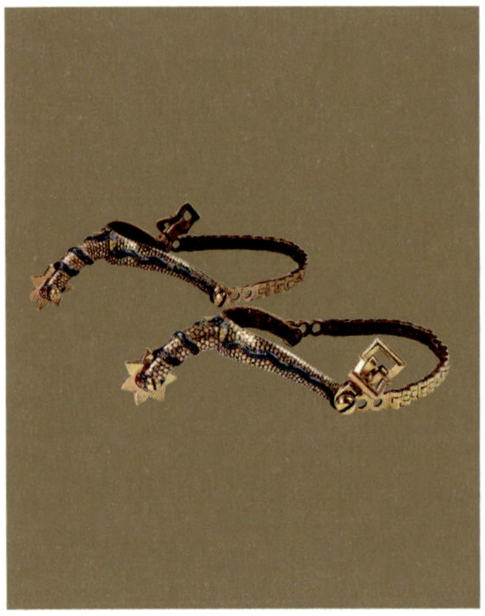

Pair of spurs belonging to Christian IV
c. 1634, Paris
Pierre Delabarre (c. 1625–1680)
Iron, gold, enamel
L. 12.5 cm
Rosenborg Castle, Copenhagen
Inv. 7-220

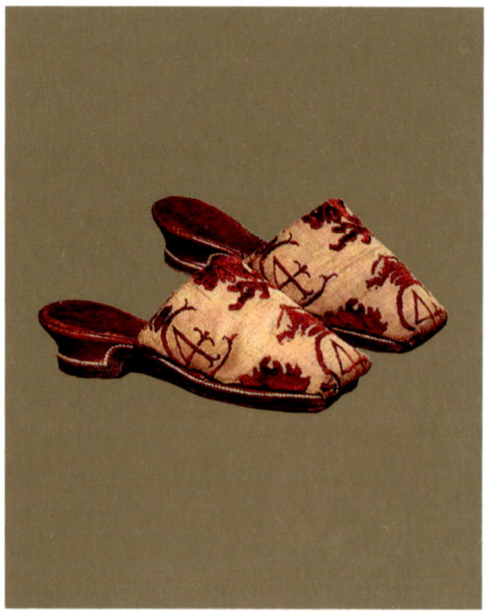

Pair of slippers belonging to Christian IV
Early seventeenth century
Red velvet
approx. 15 × approx. 20 cm
Rosenborg Castle, Copenhagen
Inv. 2-41

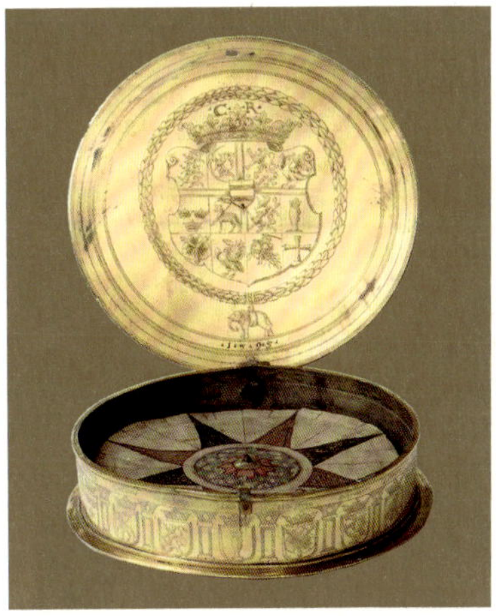

Compass with the arms of Christian IV
c. 1595
Gilded silver
D. 20.9 cm
Rosenborg Castle, Copenhagen
Inv. 1-78

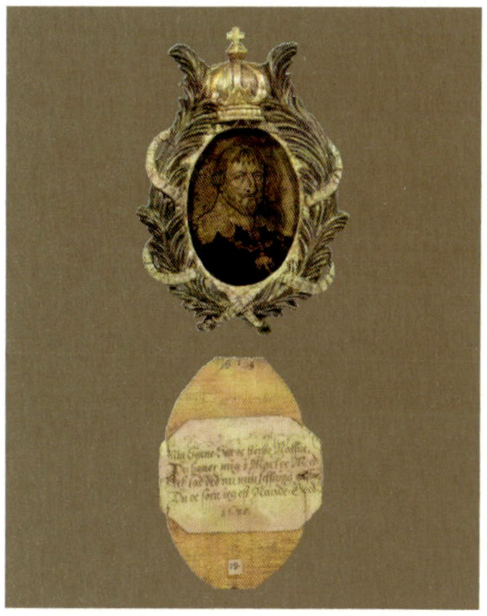

Miniature of Christian IV, with a message from his imprisoned daughter Eleanor Christine, on the reverse side
Early seventeenth century
Painted miniature,
gilded wood frame
H. 18.2 cm
Rosenborg Castle, Copenhagen
Inv. 6-585

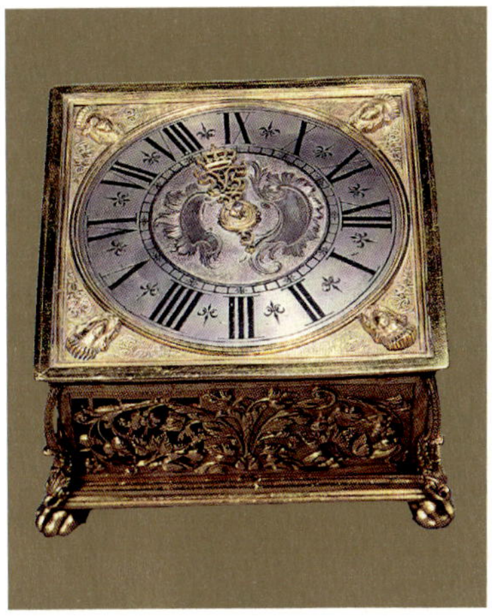

Table clock
1561
Steffen Brenner (1556–1602)
Gilded bronze, enamel;
leather, velvet (case)
13 × 13 cm
Rosenborg Castle, Copenhagen
Inv. 1-102 and 1-71

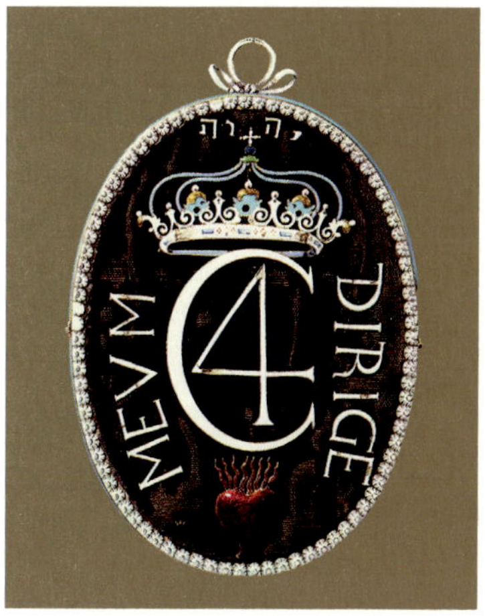

Mirror with Christian IV's initials
1633–48
Enamel on gold
18.2 × 10.2 cm
Rosenborg Castle, Copenhagen
Inv. 1-115

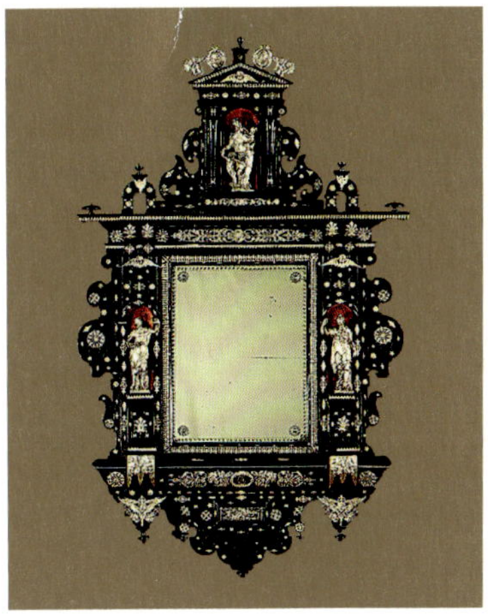

Wall mirror
c. 1610, Copenhagen
Nicolaus Svabe; decoration
and figures after the work
of Jacob van Doordt
Ebony, silver
121.5 × 72.5 cm
Rosenborg Castle, Copenhagen
Inv. 3-36

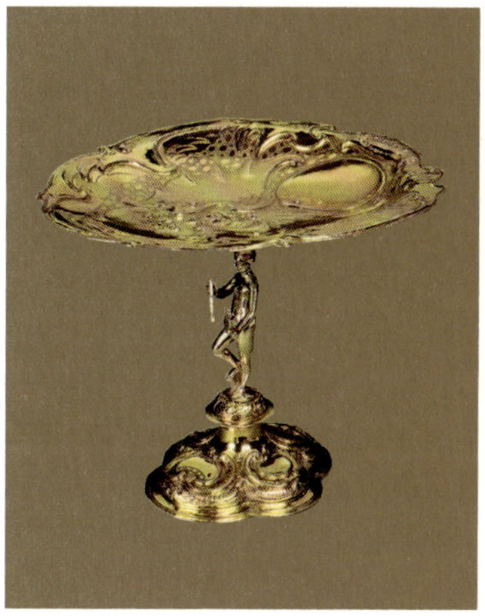

Cup with base
1631–33
Hans Lambrecht II (c. 1600–1670)
Gilded silver
H. 19 cm
Rosenborg Castle, Copenhagen
Inv. 2-84

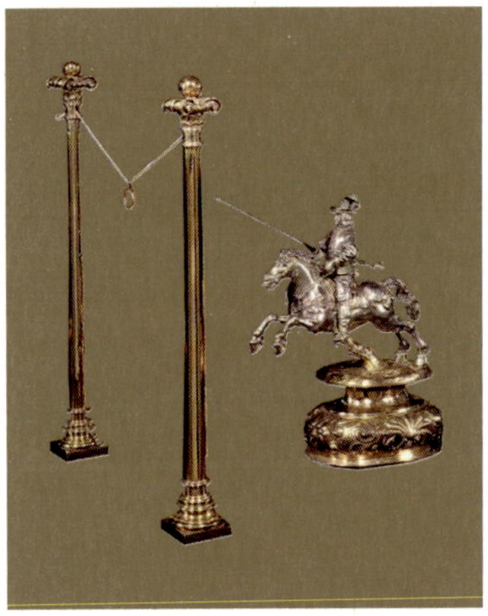

King Frederik III (1609–1670), son of Christian IV, on horseback with ring game
c. 1650, Copenhagen
JORGEN STICHMAND
Gilded silver
H. 42.5 cm
Rosenborg Castle, Copenhagen
Inv. 5-8 a-c

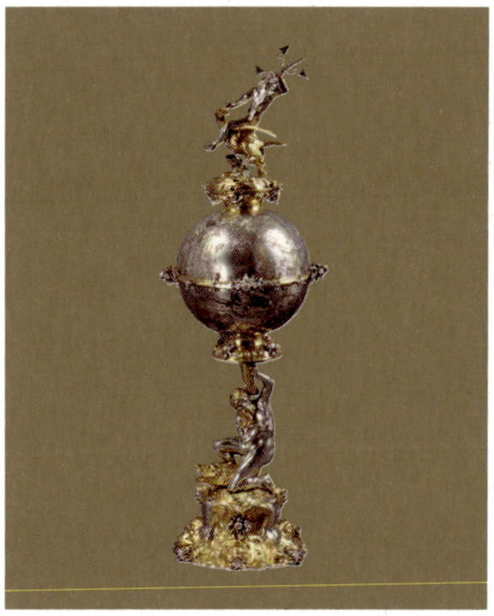

Covered bowl forming a celestial globe
c. 1650, Hamburg
HEINRICH III LAMBRECHT
Gilded silver
H. 89.6 cm
Rosenborg Castle, Copenhagen
Inv. 21-118

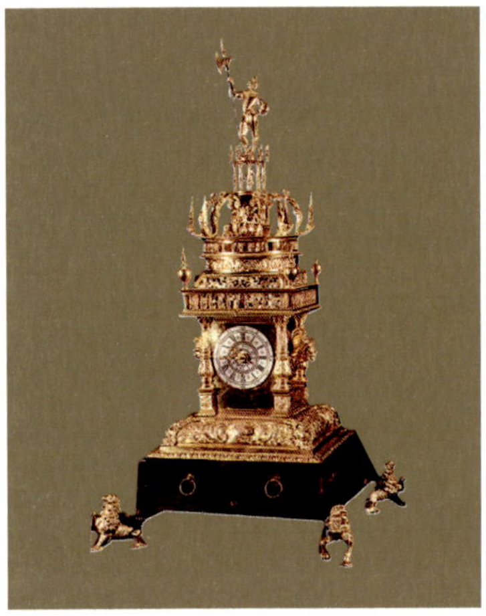

Clock with figures representing the emperor surrounded by the seven electors
c. 1600
Gilded bronze
H. 75.8 cm
Rosenborg Castle, Copenhagen
Inv. 2-44

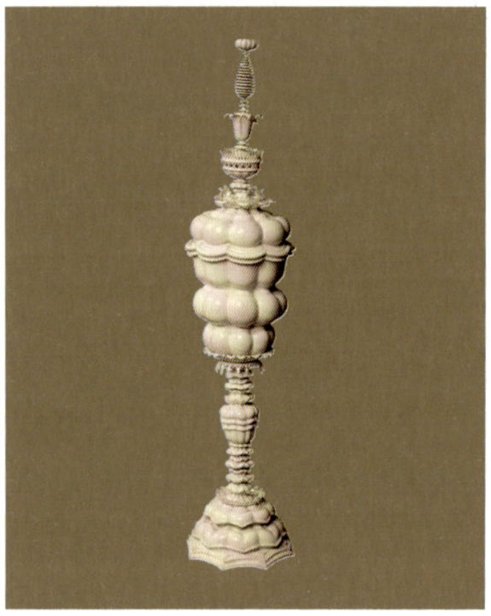

Covered bowl with base
Early seventeenth century
Ivory
H. 52.4 cm
Rosenborg Castle, Copenhagen
Inv. 23-81 ab

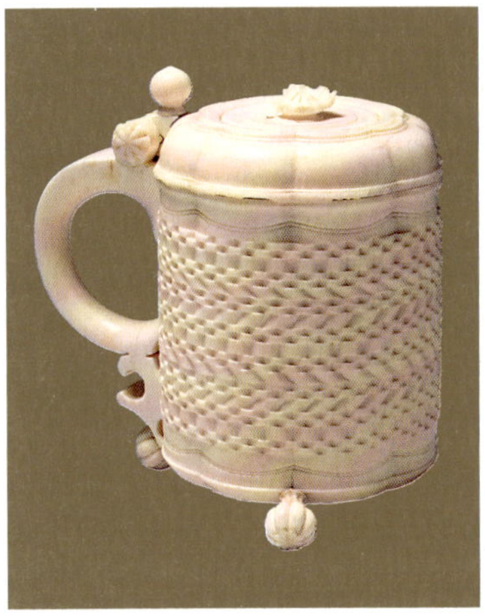

Decorated mug made by Christian IV
c. 1650
Ivory
H. 12.4 cm
Rosenborg Castle, Copenhagen
Inv. 1-162

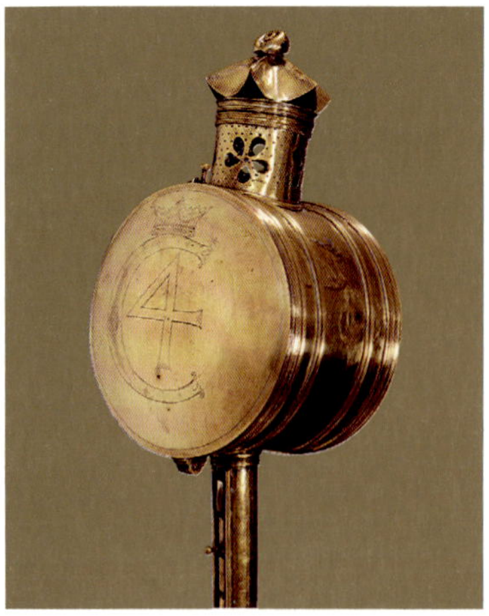

Lantern forming a magnifying glass
1642, Augsburg
JOHANN WRISEL (1586–1662)
Wood and iron
192 × 19 cm
Rosenborg Castle, Copenhagen
Inv. 1-64

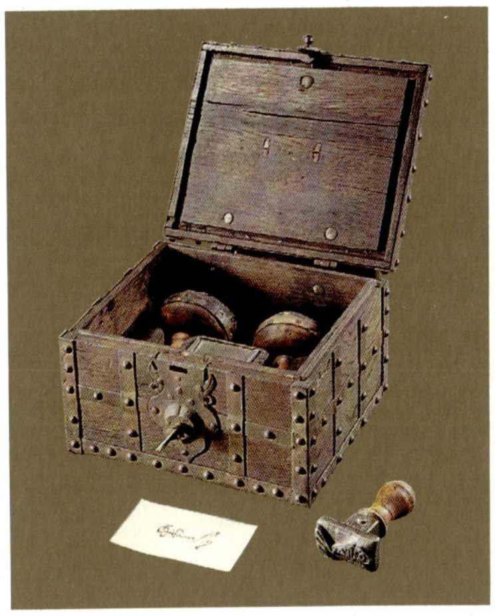

Case containing a seal belonging to Christian IV and facsimiles of his signature
Before 1645
Silver
13.5 × 23.2 cm
Rosenborg Castle, Copenhagen
Inv. 3-147 a-e

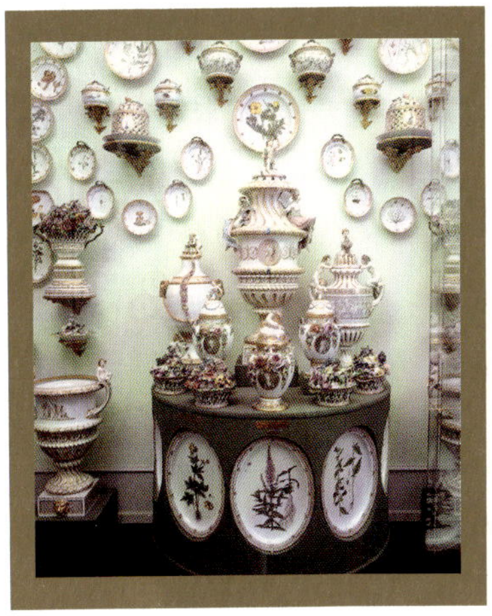

Flora Danica **service**
1784–1801
Søren Preuss
Royal Copenhagen Porcelain
Rosenborg Castle, Copenhagen
Round fruit bowl
H. 16 cm
Inv. 23-313
Round dish
D. approx. 33 cm
Inv. 23-569
Covered sugar bowl and spoon
H. approx. 15 cm
Inv. 23-462 abc
Round bottle cooler
H. 16 cm
Inv. 23-358
Sauceboat with platter
13 × 23 cm
Inv. 23-430 and 23-441
Fruit bowl
D. 23.5 cm
Inv. 23-426

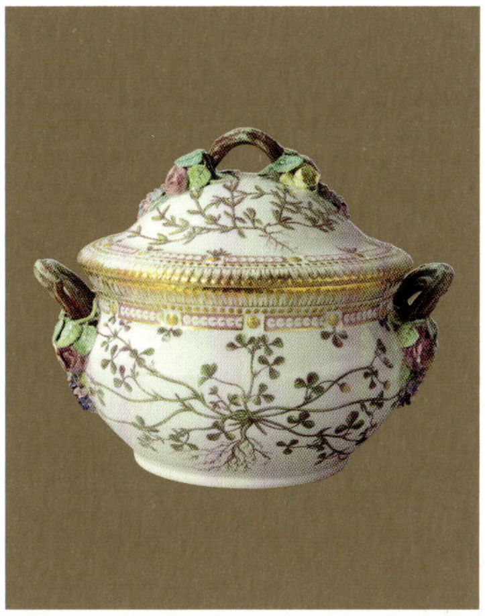

Round soup tureen with cover from the *Flora Danica* dinner service
1784–1801
Søren Preuss
Royal Copenhagen Porcelain
H. 23 cm
Rosenborg Castle, Copenhagen
Inv. 23-343 ab

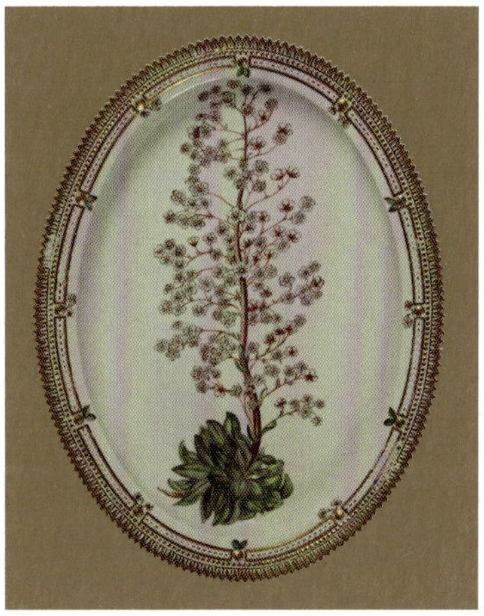

Flora Danica **oval serving dish**
1784-1801
Søren Preuss
Royal Copenhagen Porcelain
L. 50 cm
Rosenborg Castle, Copenhagen
Inv. 23-518

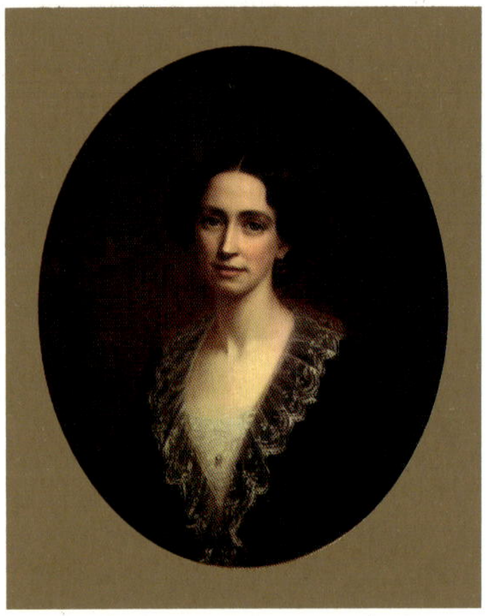

Queen Louise (1817–1898)
1850
August Schiott (1823–1895)
Oil on canvas
82.8 × 66.6 cm
Amalienborg Palace, Copenhagen
Inv. A1-1020

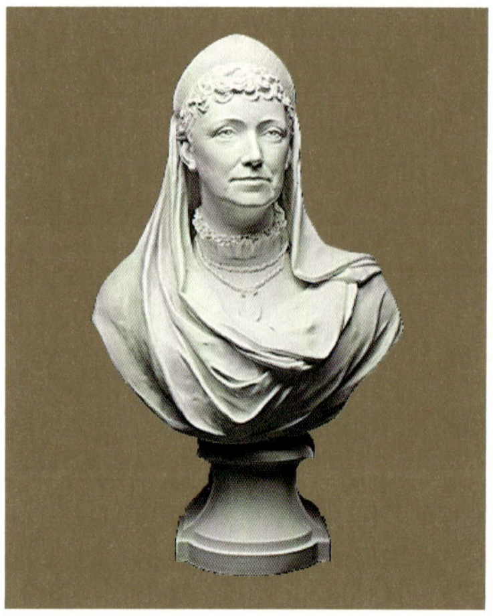

Louise of Hesse-Kassel
Nineteenth century
Marble
H. 66 cm
Amalienborg Palace, Copenhagen
Inv. A3-934

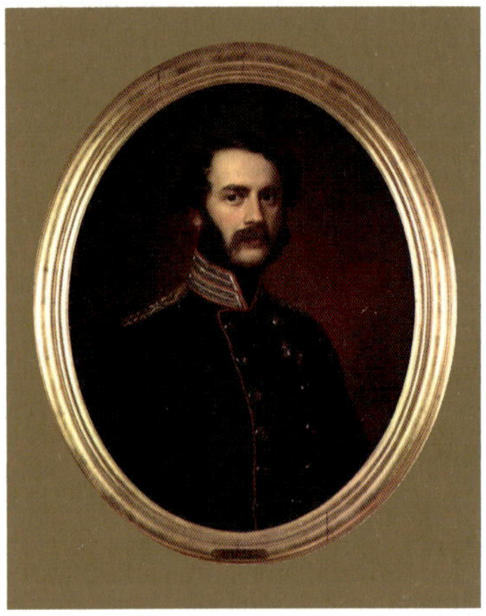

King Christian IX (1818–1906)
1850
August Schiott (1823–1895)
Oil on canvas
82.8 × 66.6 cm
Amalienborg Palace, Copenhagen
Inv. A2-42

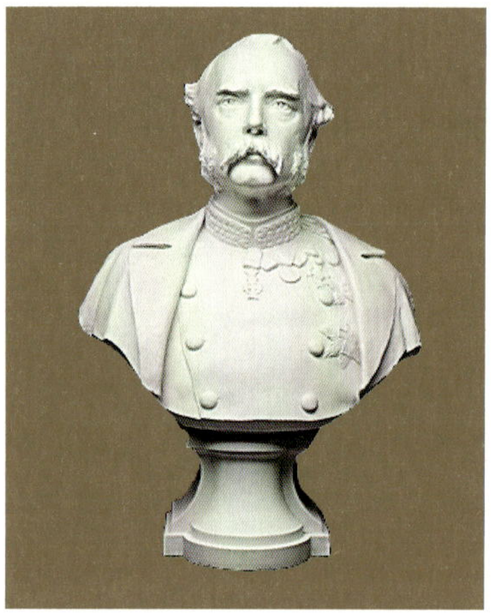

Christian IX
Nineteenth century
Marble
H. 66 cm
Amalienborg Palace, Copenhagen
Inv. A3-935

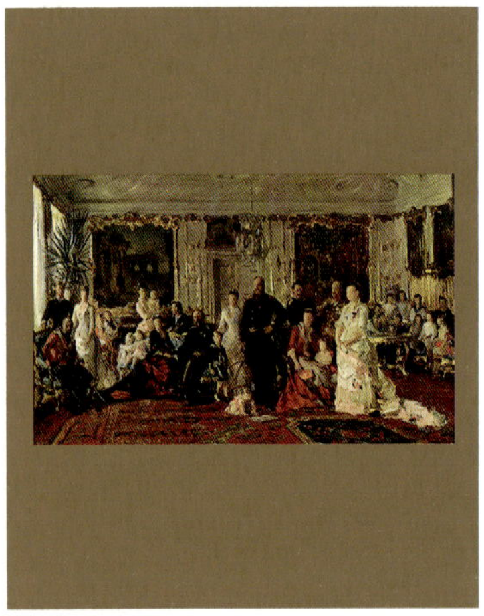

The Royal Family of Christian IX
1868
Laurits Tuxen (1853–1927)
Oil on canvas
82 × 115 cm (inc. frame)
Det Nationalhistoriske Museum,
Frederiksborg Castle, Hillerød
Inv. A 6818

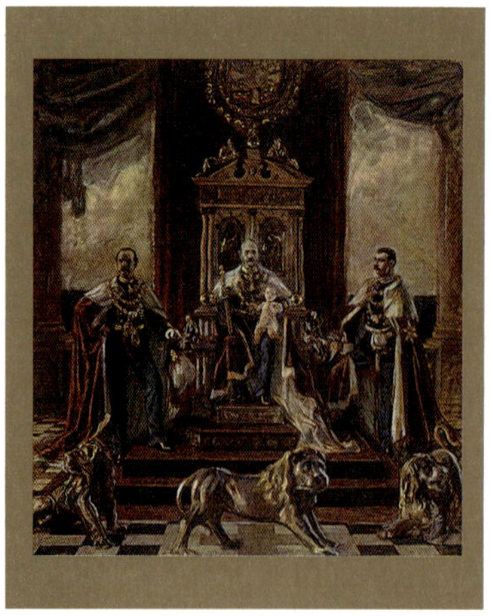

Four Generations of Danish Kings
c. 1901
Laurits Tuxen (1853–1927)
Oil on canvas
150 × 138 cm (inc. frame)
Det Nationalhistoriske Museum,
Frederiksborg Castle, Hillerød
Inv. A 6806

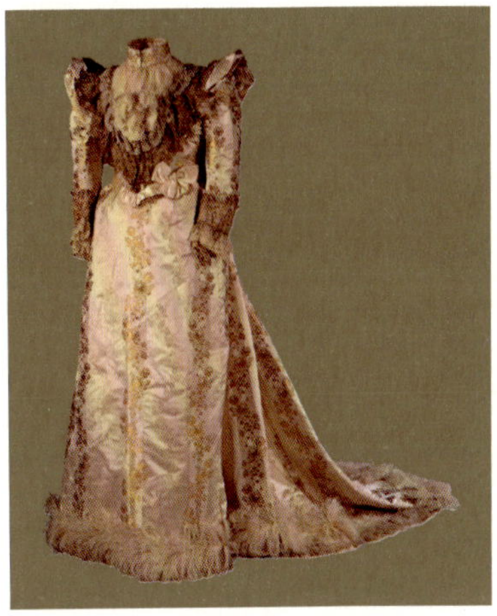

Ball gown belonging to Queen Louise
H. 210 cm
Amalienborg Palace, Copenhagen
Inv. A2-319 abj

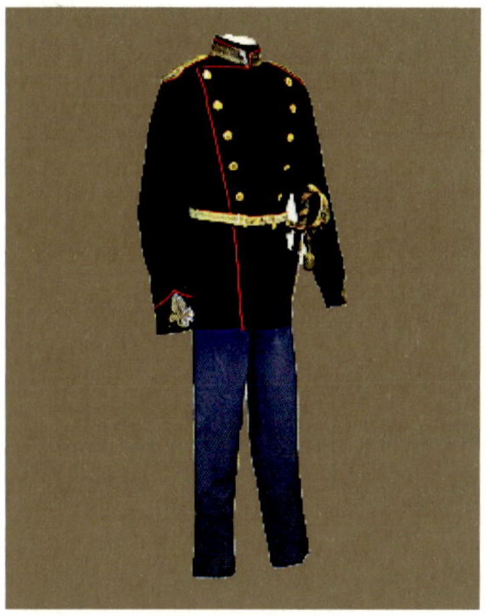

Uniform belonging to Christian IX
Nineteenth century
H. 210 cm
Amalienborg Palace, Copenhagen
Inv. A1-1762 abdefgi

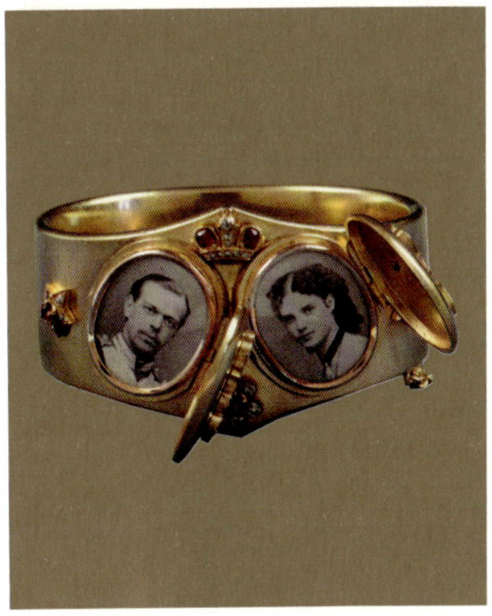

Bracelet with two miniature portraits: Czar Alexander III and Empress Maria Feodorovna
Nineteenth century, Saint Petersburg
Samuel Arndt (1845–1890)
Gold, diamonds, ruby
H. 3.9 cm
Amalienborg Palace, Copenhagen
Inv. A3-25

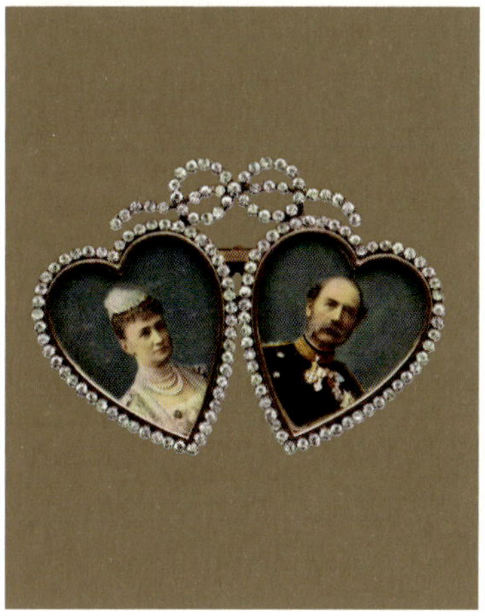

Souvenir locket with miniature portraits of Christian IX and Louise of Hesse-Kassel
1904
Anton Michelsen (1809–1877)
Painted miniature, gold, enamel, diamonds
6 × 12.5 cm
Amalienborg Palace, Copenhagen
Inv. A3-948

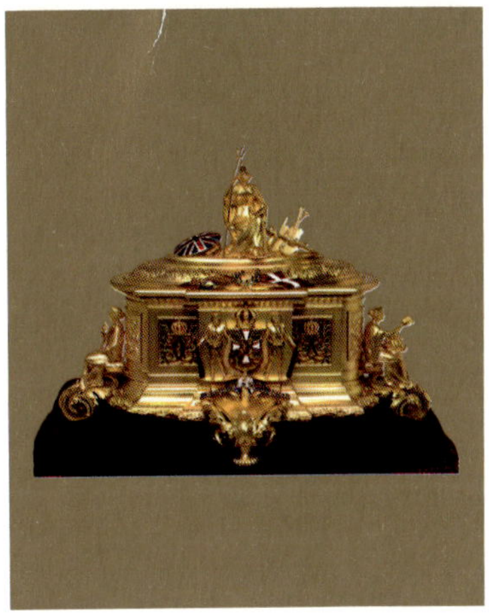

Gift case for the golden wedding anniversary of Christian IX and Queen Louise
1892
Hunt and Roskell / Late Storr and Mortimer, London
Gold, enamel
21 × 14 cm
Amalienborg Palace, Copenhagen
Inv. A1-1711 ab, property of Her Majesty the Queen

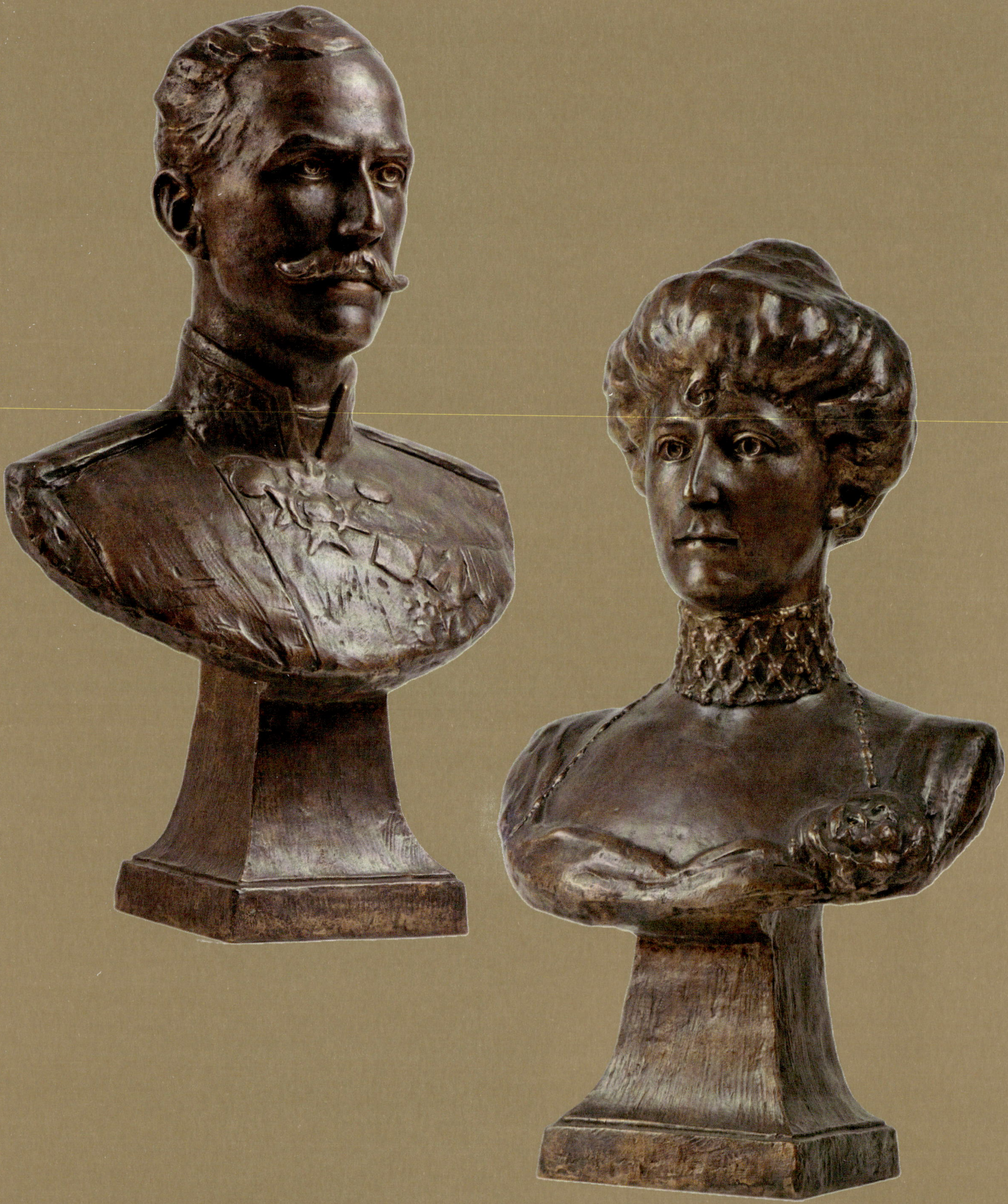

NORWAY

Haakon VII (1872–1957) and Maud (1869–1938)

King Haakon VII of Norway and Queen Maud
Early twentieth century
Lars Utne (1862–1922)
Royal Palace, Oslo

The new Norwegian monarchy and its context

Widar Halén

From time immemorial, Norway has been ruled by kings. Dating to 1103, the coat of arms of the kingdom—gules with lion d'or—is one of the oldest in Europe. Initially the personal armes of the oldest royal family, in about 1280 the lion was endowed with a crown and took up the axe of King Olav II (Saint Olav).

According to *Heimskringla* ("History of the Kings of Norway") by Snorri Sturluson (1177–1240) published en 1899, the most venerable Norwegian royal lineage can be traced back to Odin and the Norse gods. Twenty-seven royal generations later, in 872, King Harald I Hårfagre (Harald I Finehair, c. 865–931) unified Norway into a single kingdom. Governed as it still is today by one of his successors, Harald V (born in 1937), the history of the intervening royal dynasties runs from the unification of the kingdom through the contrasting roles of king and Church in the Middle Ages, the death in 1387 of Olav IV (the last representative of the historic royal line), and on to the Kalmar Union (1388–1450). Then comes the period of union with Denmark (1450–1814), and the aftermath of the Napoleonic wars, when Norway was unified with Sweden (1814–1905), ending with the current constitutional monarchy founded in 1905. Thus Norwegian royal history must be seen as a key to the understanding of the country.

The Norwegian constitution of May 17, 1814, is one of the most democratic in Europe. Irrevocably abolishing the nobility, Article 5 nonetheless affirms that "the person of the king is sacred and inviolable. The responsibility devolves to his council." The anonymous author of the Norwegian *The King's Mirror* dating to c. 1250 explains that to serve and honor the king is to pay homage to God. Royal dominion and that of the supreme leader of the Church are in both cases of divine origin. Today, when the royal house is no longer founded on divine grace but on election by the nation as stipulated in the 1905 referendum, this may seem a surprising concept. But, if it is seen simply as a description of the king's immunity and exceptional status, its significance for modern Norway is more readily understood. It was on this basis then that the Norwegian people chose Prince Carl of Denmark and Princess Maud, daughter of King Edward VII and Queen Alexandra of Great Britain, as king and queen of Norway. The king took the name Haakon VII and

Coronation of King Haakon VII and Queen Maud in Trondheim Cathedral, June 22, 1906
c. 1908
Gabriel Kielland
(1871–1960)
Statsbygg, Oslo

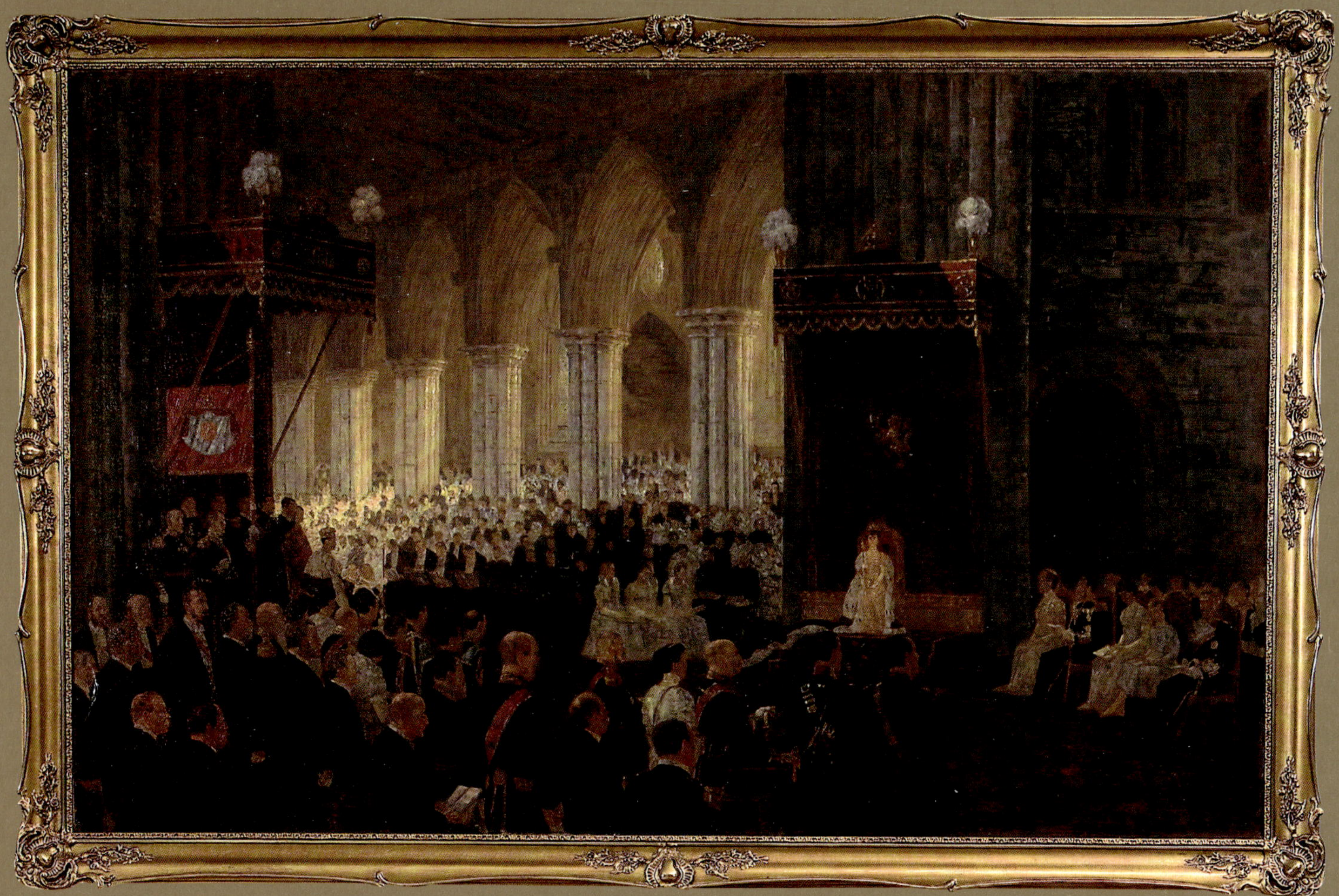

his monogram "HVII" was soon being brandished as a symbol of freedom, particularly during World War II. During that period, the king led his country from exile in London. Refusing to submit to the Nazis, by the time he celebrated his seventieth birthday in 1942, he had become the figurehead of national independence. The president of the Norwegian Parliament, Carl J. Hambro, centered his congratulatory speech on Article 5 of the constitution, affirming the hallowed nature of the king: "This fact means inter alia that the influence of the king arises from his person and is not political. From the infallible fidelity of King Haakon to the country that chose him and that he chose; from his indomitable will to serve it, always and without stint; from his sterling courage, unflappable patience, and unshakable resilience that have turned him into a rallying point for his distressed people. No government could have been what he has been for Norway. A government is partisan; it represents a class, a group, a political organization, only one section of the population. The king is the living symbol of the unity of the people and of its sovereignty." This respect for the person of the king forms a keystone of the administration of a monarchy and still remains strong in regards the current king, Harald V.

The kings of the sagas, like those who succeeded them, had to prove the legitimacy of their line and ensure the benevolence of the people and the establishment. The new king who entered Norwegian territory on November 25, 1905, fulfilled both these conditions. Through a common grandfather, Christian IX of Denmark, both King Haakon VII and Queen Maud boasted descent from King Christian I (1450–1481) of Denmark. As with many Norwegians, moreover, they could also trace their line back to the unifier of the kingdom, Harald I. The benevolence of all was thus assured: the royal couple had been elected by the country's elite, while the people had opted for a monarchy in a plebiscite on November 13, 1905, with 79 percent voting in favor.

It was an era in which kings and emperors still took an active role on the national and international political stage. For Norway, which had only recently severed its union with Sweden, it was of extreme importance that European royalty provided cast-iron guarantees to Carl, a son-in-law of the British sovereign, Edward VII. International support from the reigning dynasties of Europe proved a great asset for Norway and the new king. Haakon VII and Queen Maud were first cousins, and their respective families were related to almost all the royal houses of Europe. The king's mother, Queen Louise of Denmark, was daughter of Carl XV of Sweden and Louise of the Netherlands, and her father, King Frederik VIII, was the brother of Queen Alexandra of Great Britain (Maud's mother), Dagmar of Russia, and King George of Greece.

Since then the constitution has reined in the monarch's personal power, but some executive power remains in the hands of the king, though everyday business is now handled by the government. Today, the government oversees every royal decision and people speak of the king signing and the prime minister countersigning the order of the day. If the king's freedom to act was subsumed in 1905, this does not mean that the sovereign, using his experience or his long practice of government, exerts no influence.

While monarchs do not follow an independent policy in Norway, they have been characterized by an ability to adapt to circumstance and by an enduring vision of their role as bastions of the constitution. It is an approach that requires more than just passive observation: it presupposes tact, courage, and perspicacity, as Haakon VII declared in 1905: "I have understood the value of the constitution in the eyes of the Norwegian people. It is to the constitution, still and always, that I have attached myself."

It is today difficult to picture the warmth of feeling that gripped Norwegians in 1905 as they undertook their velvet revolution and took leave of King Oscar II of Sweden. Independence had been long in the making, the path being paved by major authors such as Henrik Ibsen and Bjørnstjerne Bjørnson, and by artists such as Johan Christian Dahl, Adolph Tidemand, and Hans Gude, who taught their fellow citizens to be proud of the Norwegian landscape. In the decorative arts and architecture, Gerhard Munthe, Lars Kinsarvik, and Henrik Bull launched the neo-Viking "dragon style" inspired by ancient stave churches and *dragons* as an authentically Norwegian idiom. Fully a thousand years after the Viking era, the exploits of Fridtjof Nansen and Roald Amundsen in the polar ice were hailed as examples of Norwegian courage and stamina. The artists who provided the superb illustrations for the edition of Snorri Sturluson's *Heimskringla* published in 1899 even lent the illustrious kings the features of Nansen and Amundsen.

It was a period in which Europe resounded to demands for independence, encouraging smaller states to assert their original identity. When the king of Denmark, Christian IX, was informed on November 18, 1905 of the choice of Prince Carl as sovereign of Norway, the aging monarch was so moved that "warm tears fell one after the other." The prince promptly declared: "With the authorization of His Majesty the King, my most respected grandfather, I agree to become king of Norway as Haakon VII, bestowing upon my son the new forename of Olav." Two days later, the king proclaimed his motto: "All for Norway," later taken up by his son Olav V and grandson Harald V.

On November 24, he set out for Kristiania (today Oslo) and, on November 25, the new royal family disembarked on Norwegian soil at the foot of the historic royal fortress of Akershus. The fog lay thick and the air was slashed by heavy flurries of snow, but the royal couple and little Prince Olav made their entrance into the capital in an open-top barouche, passing beneath gates of honor and trotting up flag-lined avenues to the pealing of church bells and amid scenes of popular jubilation that seemed never-ending. That same day, in unabated fog and snow, the palace balcony began its existence as the linchpin between the royal family and their people. King Haakon lifted up the crown prince, then three years old, showing him to the assembled crowd. At that very moment, the sun pierced the clouds and shone down on the teeming square and the royal family. It was on this same balcony in 1945 that the people came in droves to greet their king on his return from exile in Britain. From there, too, was his death and the accession of his son Olav announced in 1958, as was the accession to the throne of Olav V's successor, his son Harald V, in 1991. But, more even than these events, the royal palace balcony is associated with the homage paid to the king each year by the thousands of schoolchildren who parade beneath it on the national holiday of May 17.

King Haakon was the founder of the modern, democratic Norwegian monarchy, in which the king is a symbol, while the country is ruled by the government and parliament. The symbol of the unity and independence of the country, he was dubbed "king of the people," a moniker that stemmed from the forthright and sober manner he adopted in the performance of his duties and that he passed

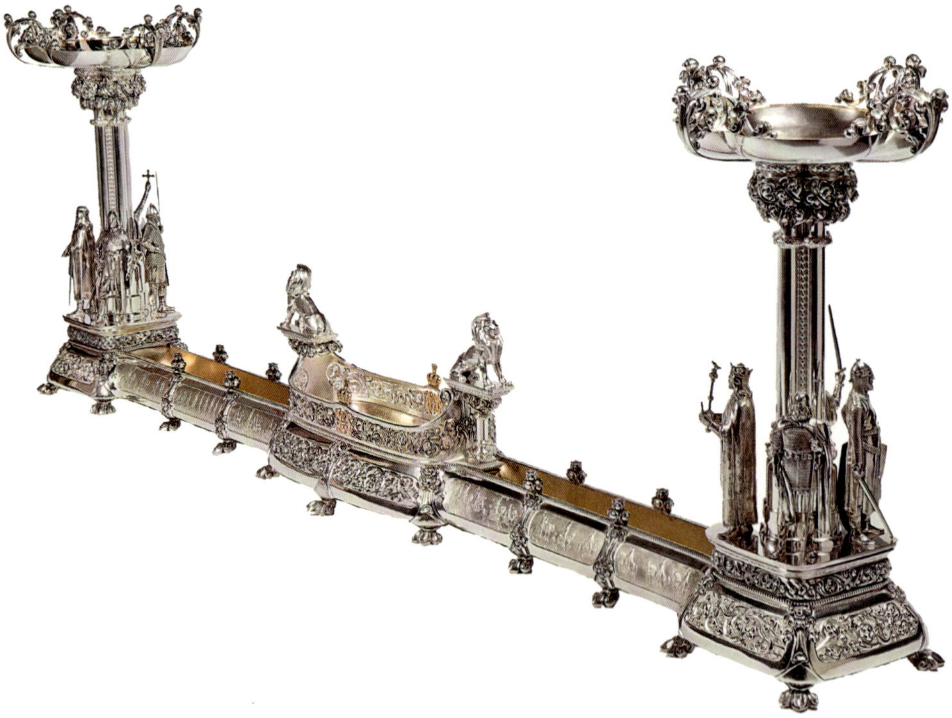

Neo-Viking style table centerpiece offered to Queen Maud for her birthday and coronation, November 26, 1905 by the ladies in Kristiania
c. 1905, Oslo
Lars Utne (1862–1922)
and Pritz Torolf
Jacob Tostrup Manufactory
Royal Palace, Oslo

on to his son and grandson. Surrounded by a modest court, his unsophisticated tastes went down well with Norwegians and formed a model for his successors.

Queen Maud was rather different. Renowned in Britain for her luxurious lifestyle, she, too, adapted to her new station with grace. Nicknamed "Her Royal Shyness" among the family, she was of a timid, reserved nature and had envisaged a less public existence with her Prince Carl, who had not originally numbered among the claimants to the crown. The prospect of becoming queen of Norway had initially dismayed and overwhelmed her, but she soon learned to love her adoptive country. It reminded her, moreover, of Scotland, "as well much by its inhabitants as by its landscapes," as she was wont to say. Queen Maud was keen on sport, a horsewoman and tennis player. In her youth she had been something of a tomboy (she was known as Harry) and she took ample opportunity in Norway to enjoy outdoor activities, including the national sport of cross-country skiing. It has been said that Norwegians are born with skis on their feet, and it was Fridtjof Nansen in person who introduced the royal family to the sport on its arrival in the country. Private photographs of the royal couple and the little prince on skis were soon circulating, earning them a place in the heart of every Norwegian. Nothing could have done more to ensure their popularity in the first years of their reign. It was in Kongsseteren—a chalet in Voksenkollåsen donated by the people to the royal couple in 1910—where she could ski and toboggan that Queen Maud felt most at ease. In early photographs, she appears slight and thin, frail even, but proud and independently minded. Extremely refined, she exuded class, but was not blessed with a crowd-pleasing personality. Yet her efforts also played their part in the history of the monarchy and she did her best to earn the trust of the Norwegians and forge the kind of personal entente that binds a people to its royal family.

Conserving close links with Great Britain throughout her life, she spent every autumn at Appleton House in Norfolk, where she was to pass away on November 20, 1938. On November 26, her birthday, and exactly thirty-three years after her arrival in Norway, her coffin, conveyed by *The Royal Oak,* disembarked on the Oslo quayside to full honors. The lead in the newspaper *Adresseavisen* perhaps best expresses the feelings of the Norwegian people as they mourned: "If King Haakon is the founder of the new kingdom of Norway, Queen Maud was the wife who followed him faithfully to his new land and who was able to build for herself—without fuss and eschewing the superficiality and showiness of court life—an existence as a queen without reproach, through her appearance, her presence, and her steadfastly unique personality."

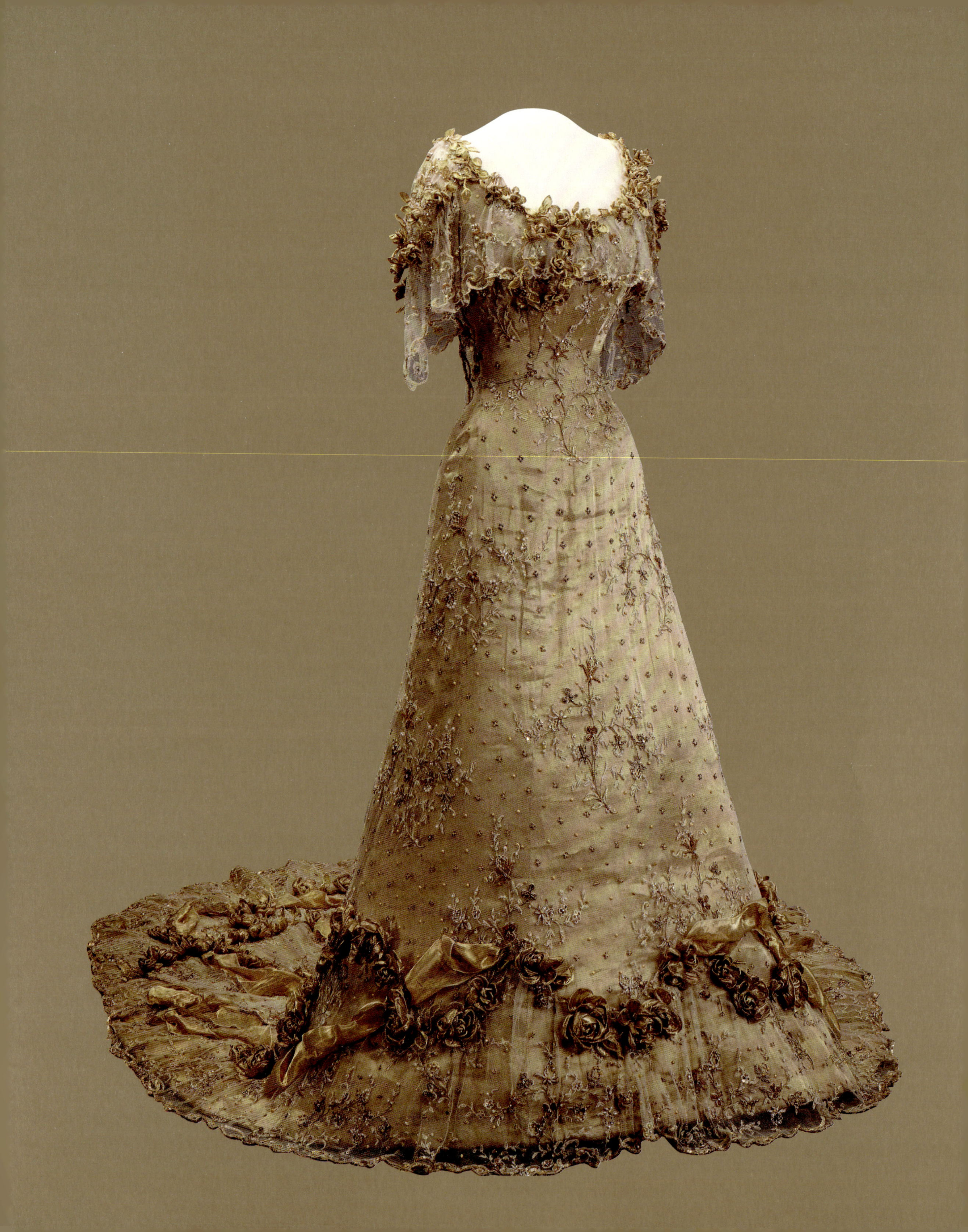

Queen Maud of Norway and her gorgeous wardrobe

Anne Kjellberg

Queen Maud's dress sense was unerring. Keeping a weather eye on women's fashion, the looks she chose were always those that best her. She thus created a modern and personal style that befited her role as queen as much as her private life.

A substantial proportion of this wardrobe has been preserved, and today it constitutes one of the most interesting royal collections in all Europe. Unlike many other extant royal collections, it includes not only attire worn at official ceremonies and on other public occasions, but also everyday clothes, sportswear, and accessories of every kind.

The majority of Queen Maud's garments were made by British tailors (such as the Ladies' Tailors), court dressmakers, or one of the famous French and British couture houses. Her coronation gown of 1906 was the fruit of a collaboration between the London house of Vernon and Silkehuset in Norway, an expedient greeted enthusiastically in her new homeland. As queen, however, she seldom wore garments entirely made in Norway, save for sportswear. She was presented with a number of Norwegian folk costumes as gifts, but the use to which they were put is not recorded.

Queen Maud's dressmakers numbered among the finest of the age, as is the case with Morin-Blossier, for example, one of the foremost Parisian couture houses at the turn of the century and supplier to many sovereigns. When the royal family undertook an official visit to France in 1907, Queen Maud opted for a vast wardrobe from Morin-Blossier, thus ensuring she met the severest demands of fashion.

Among the suppliers appointed to the queen, the best known was the house of Worth. This couture house occupied an exceptional place in the world of fashion until the death of its founder, Charles Frederik Worth, in 1895. Its star was still high, however, when Queen Maud had the *Arlésienne* evening gown tailored for her winter 1912–13 wardrobe. Towards the end of her life, Queen Maud ordered a further series of elegant outfits from Worth. Surviving drawings of the models show how she would intervene personally to alter details in line with her personal taste.

Thus, in collaboration with a select handful of couture houses, Queen Maud forged her own unique her own unique style.

Queen Maud's evening gown
1906
Morin-Blossier
The National Museum of Art Architecture and Design, Oslo

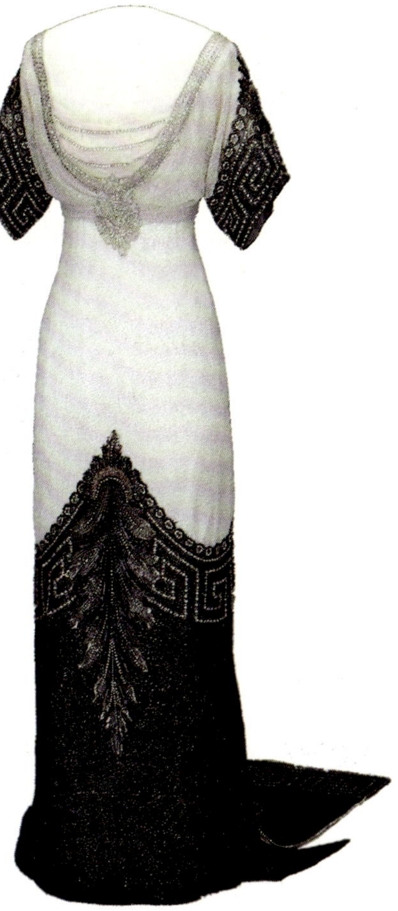

***Arlésienne* evening gown, winter 1912–13 collection**
1912
Worth, Paris / London
The National Museum of Art Architecture and Design, Oslo

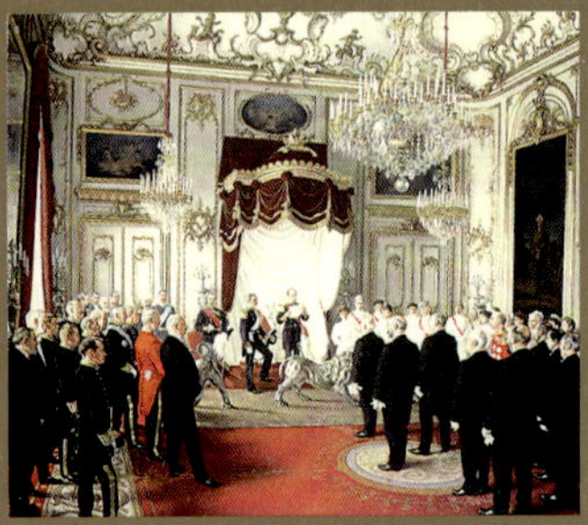

Haakon VII (1872–1957), King of Norway
1907
Paul Fischer (1860–1935)
Oil on canvas
14 × 154 cm (inc. frame)
Det Nationalhistoriske Museum,
Frederiksborg Castle, Hillerød
Inv. A 1822

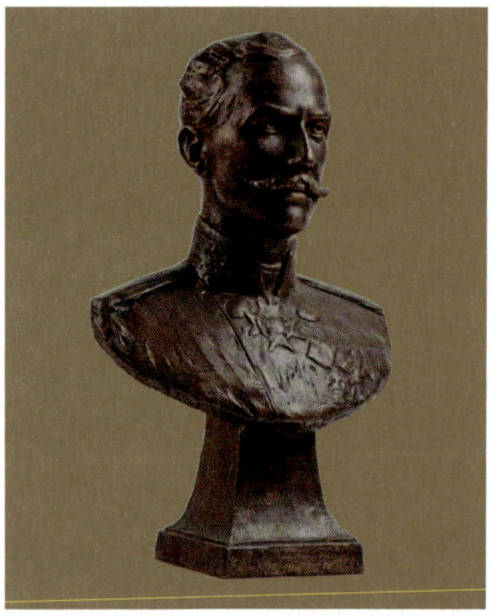

King Haakon VII of Norway
Early twentieth century
Lars Utne (1862–1922)
Bronze
H. 80 cm
Royal Palace, Oslo
Inv. DKS.025720

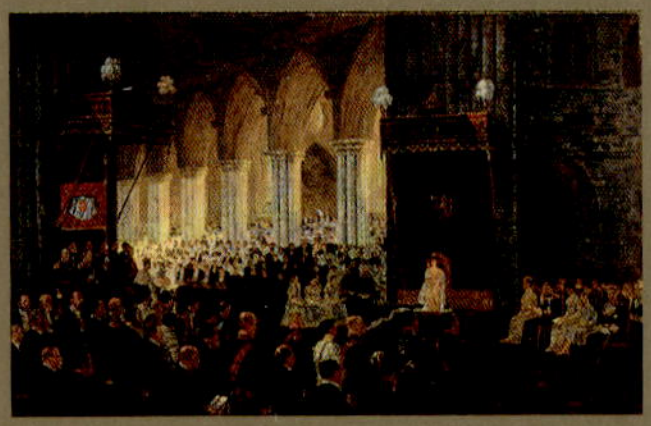

Coronation of King Haakon VII and Queen Maud in Trondheim Cathedral, June 22, 1906
c. 1908
Gabriel Kielland (1871–1960)
Oil on canvas
158 × 235 cm (inc. frame)
Statsbygg, Oslo
Inv. STG.000210

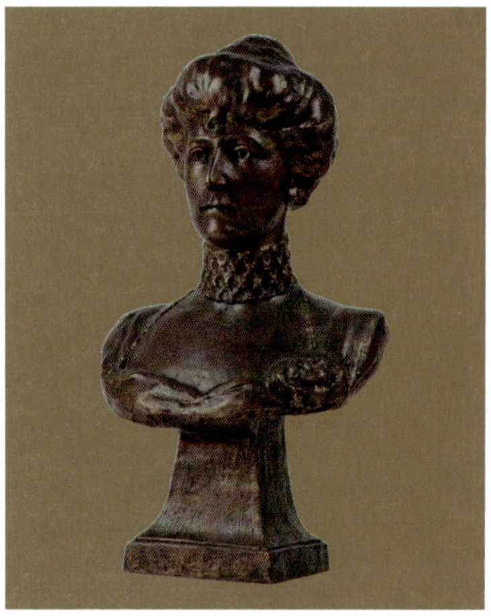

Queen Maud (1869–1938), Wife of King Haakon VII
Early twentieth century
Lars Utne (1862–1922)
Bronze
H. 81.5 cm
Royal Palace, Oslo
Inv. DKS.025719

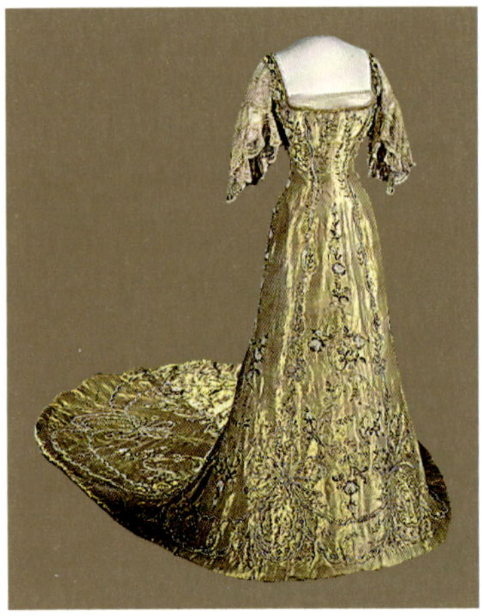

Queen Maud's coronation gown
1906
Vernon, London,
and Silkehuset, Kristiana (Oslo)
Gold lamé and lace with gilded metal embroidery, gold sequins, pearls, and artificial diamonds
H. (with train) 252 cm
The National Museum of Art, Architecture ans Design, Oslo
Inv. OK-1962-0001

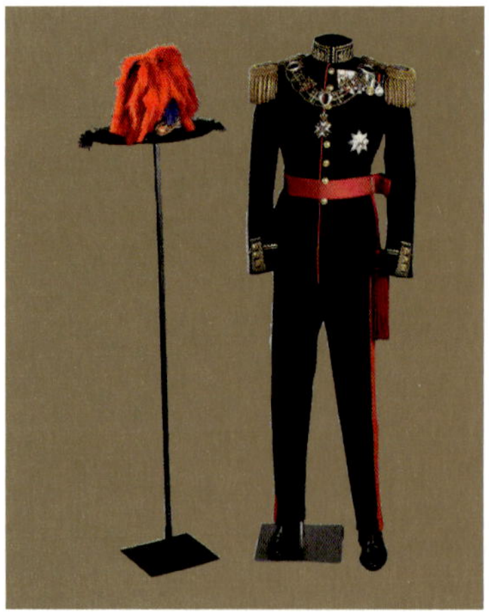

Uniform of King Haakon VII
The Norwegian Armed Forces Museum, Oslo
Inv. FMU.013578, 77 and 80-83

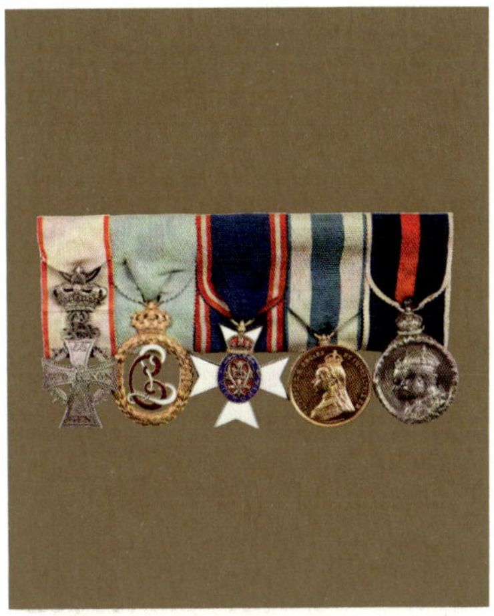

Medals belonging to King Haakon VII
Royal Palace, Oslo

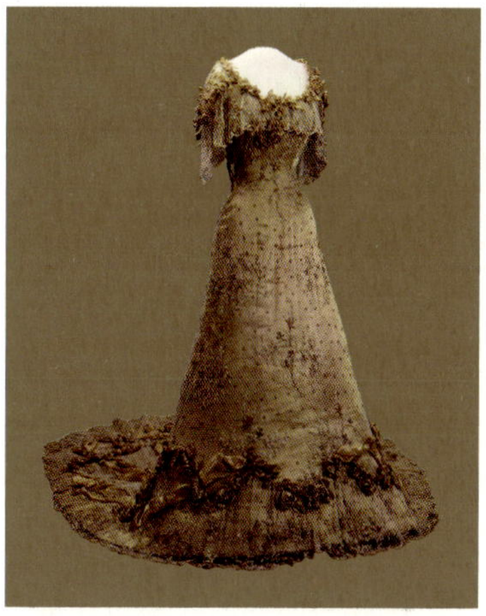

Queen Maud's evening gown
1906, Paris
MORIN-BLOSSIER
Gold lamé covered with tulle, gilded metal embroidery, sequins, pearls, and artificial diamonds
L. (with train) 252 cm
The National Museum of Art, Architecture ans Design, Oslo
Inv. OK-1962-0002

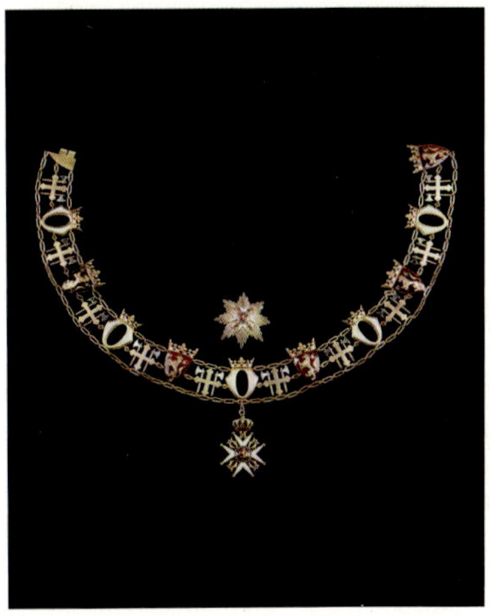

Grand cross and chain of the Royal Norwegian Order of Saint Olav
Royal Palace, Oslo

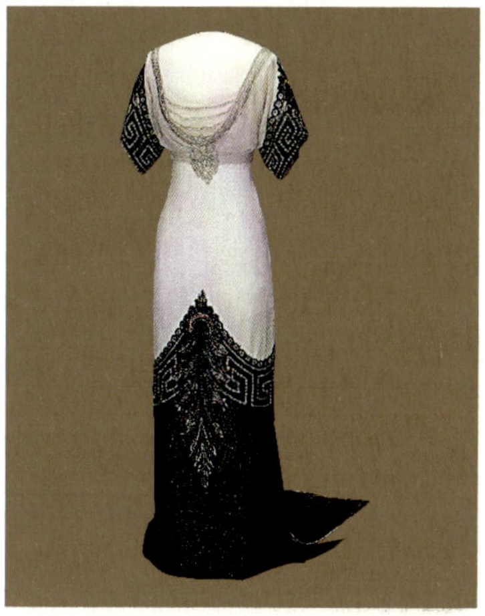

***Arlésienne* evening gown, winter 1912–13 collection**
1912
WORTH, Paris / London
Silk covered with tulle, embroidered with white, black, and silver pearls
L. (with train) 175 cm
The National Museum of Art, Architecture ans Design, Oslo
Inv. OK-1991-0201

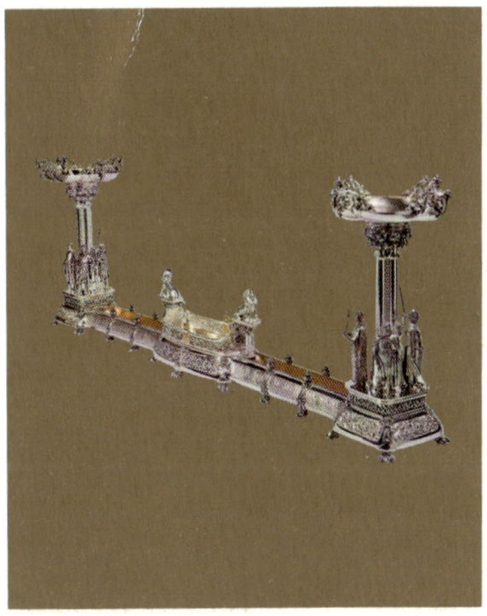

Neo-Viking style table centerpiece offered to Queen Maud for her birthday and coronation, November 26, 1905 by the ladies in Kristiania
c. 1905, Oslo
LARS UTNE (1862–1922) and PRITZ TOROLF, JACOB TOSTRUP manufactory
Silver
110 × 300 cm
Royal Palace, Oslo
Inv. DKS.016041

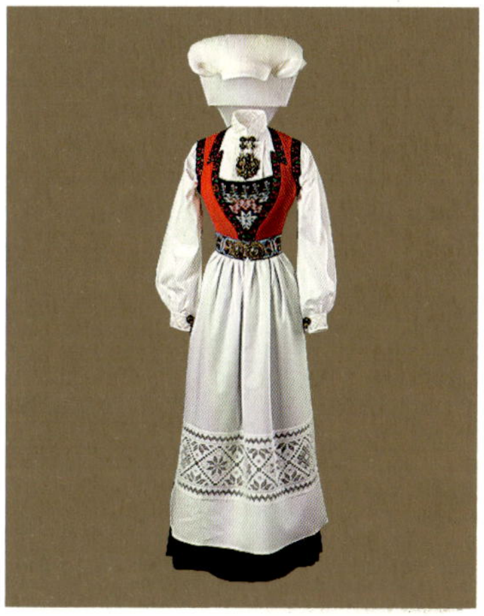

Traditional costume belonging to Queen Maud
1906–10, Hardanger (Norway)
Wool, linen, embroidered with pearls and silver
L. 141 cm
The National Museum of Art, Architecture ans Design, Oslo
Inv. OK-1962-0087 a-k

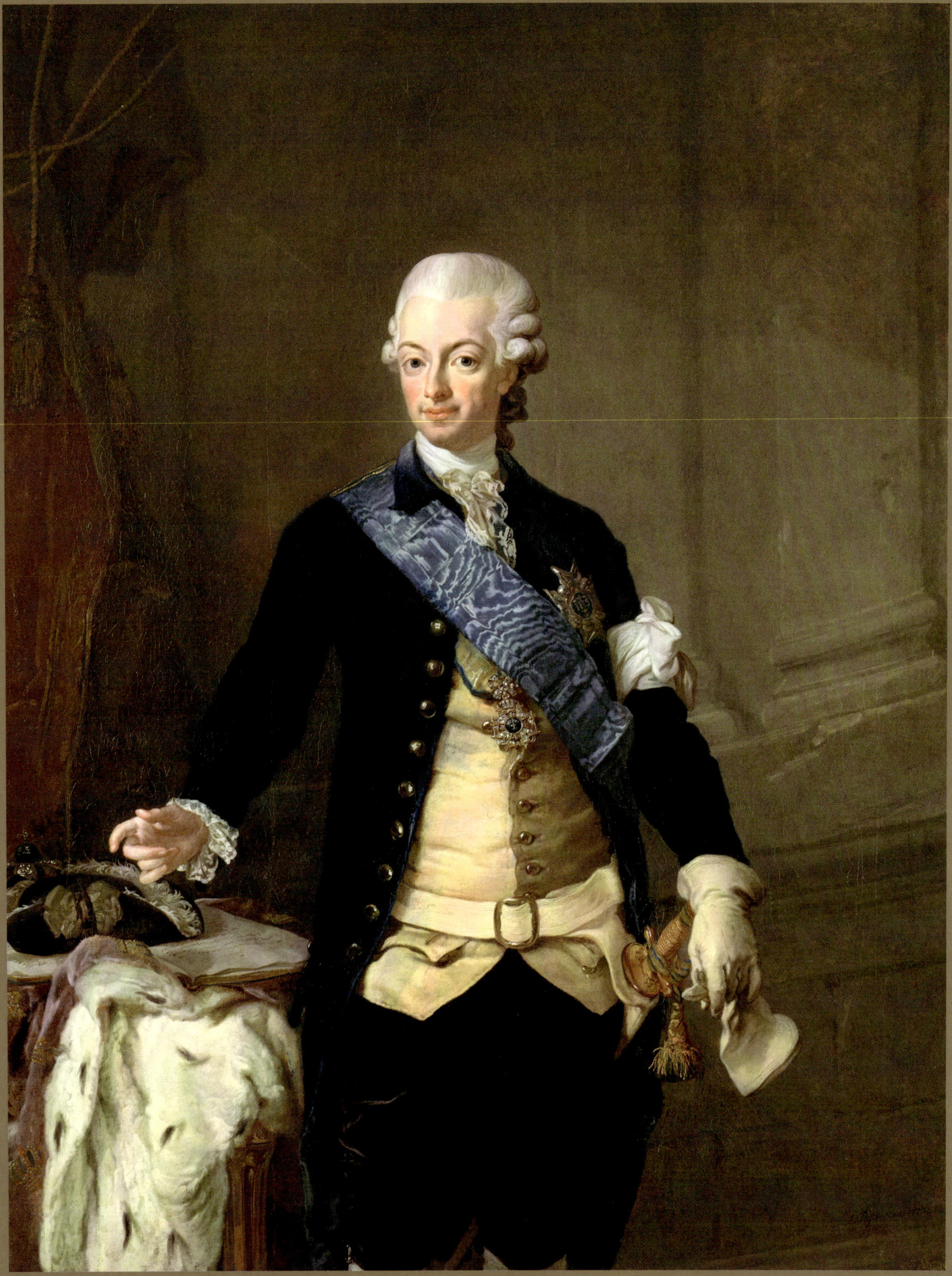

SWEDEN

Gustav III (1746–1792)

Gustav III, King of Sweden
1777
Lorens Pasch the Younger
(1733–1805)
Nationalmuseum,
Stockholm

Gustav III, a theatrical reign

Magnus Olausson

King Gustav III
After a marble
by Johan Tobias Sergel
(1740–1814)
Nationalmuseum,
Stockholm

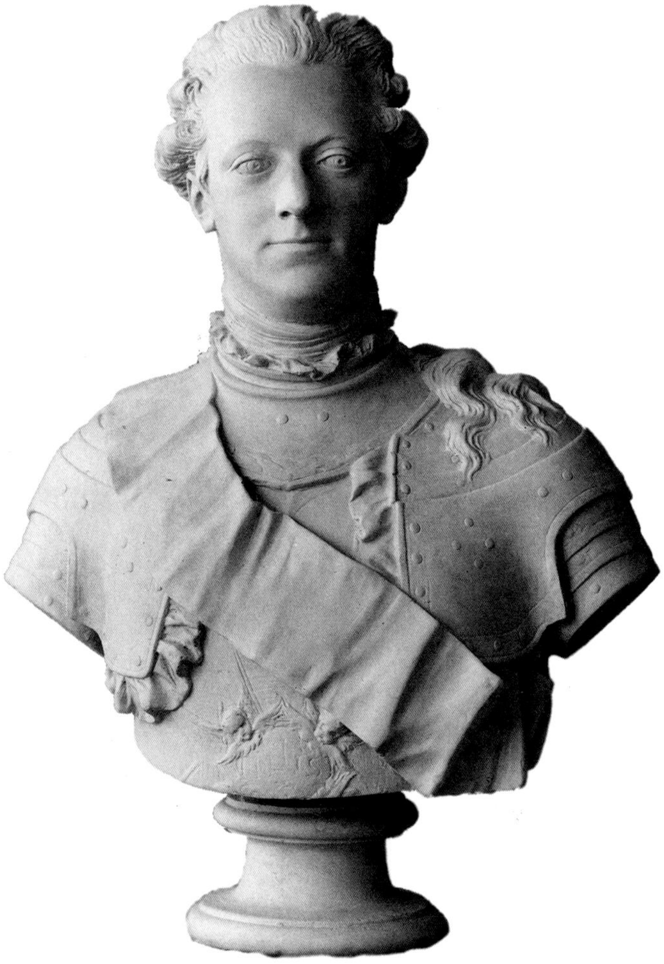

Gustav III is one of the most fascinating Swedish monarchs because of his complex nature and wide-ranging talents. Signs of his fondness for make-believe and tendencies to theatrics were already visible at an early age. In 1849 the historian Erik Gustaf Geijer revealed the king's notorious duplicity, while, in our time, the emphasis is still often placed on his unreliable temperament and supposed inability to tell real life from pantomime. Few Swedish sovereigns, however, proved better suited to the role of king. This was of course his most salient talent, as Erik Lönnroth has convincingly proved, but not his only one, since he was also a writer, theater director, and architect. In the king's personality, however, these diverse roles were inseparable. Thus, to appreciate Gustav III the statesman, one needs to understand Gustav III the artist. Many of Gustav's Swedish biographers, particularly Beth Hennings, note how a fertile imagination, while it might achieve a great deal in the field of culture, was bound to prove dangerous in the exercise of the royal office. The ease with which Gustav III could flip from one thing to another was itself not without political risk. The backs of incoming diplomatic letters and rough drafts of correspondence awaiting dispatch are often embellished with sketches for landscape gardens or venues for entertainments. As Gustav III was unlikely to need to save paper, it is a habit that speaks volumes about how he thought and behaved.

On a more positive note, it is clear that art and architecture allowed Gustav to relax when he felt overwhelmed by affairs of state, as one gleans from statements by the king and his entourage. Although on the face of it incompatible, artist and statesman were interdependent facets of his makeup. The king's attitudes to architecture, painting, and theater tell of an authentic enthusiasm for the arts compounded by manifest egomania and a drive to raise the nation's profile.

Turning to Gustav III the statesman, the same mix of motivations emerges. In spite of the criticism to which they were subjected in political circles, the king was never to abandon his idiosyncratic, often utopian views. Appointed to direct the country's foreign affairs, over the years Chancellor Ulric Scheffer could only look on aghast as the king acted in an increasingly ungovernable manner, to the point of replacing his minister in diplomatic correspondence with powers abroad. On a visit to St. Petersburg in summer 1777, Scheffer had already experienced difficulties in coming to terms with royal conduct liable to upset the diplomatic apple cart for allies and adversaries alike. Catherine II seems to have become aware of this predicament, and so, as far as the demands of protocol allowed, she spoke candidly of politics only with Scheffer and remained close-lipped on the matter in the presence of Gustav III. At the same time, of course, since royal marriages were arranged in accordance with political circumstance, Gustav III's competitors on the international scene (including, as a matter of fact, the empress of Russia) were also close relations: Catherine II was his cousin, Friedrich II of Prussia was his maternal uncle, and Christian VII of Denmark was his brother-in-law.

Gustav's father, Adolf Fredrik, duke of Holstein-Gottorp and onetime prince-bishop of Lübeck, had been elected crown prince of Sweden in 1743. He had been adopted by King Fredrik I, who had no heir, with the aim of placating Czarina Elizabeth following Sweden's defeat in the war against Russia in 1741–43. His union the following year with Princess Luise Ulrike of Prussia was a purely political act, though in fact the connection proved felicitous. Following a miscarriage, a son, Gustav, arrived on January 24, 1746, an event greeted with joy in Sweden, since he was the first crown prince to be born since the boy who became Charles XII in 1682.

The little prince's childhood was overshadowed by the power struggle opposing the states of the realm and its monarch. Sweden's constitution bestowed the right to direct the education of the crown prince on the Riksdag and on political representatives. Gustav was to prove the first victim of this policy: while in the daytime tutors such as the highly cultivated chancellor, Carl Gustaf Tessin, and, even more so, the former ambassador to Paris, Carl Frederik Scheffer, would expatiate on the parliamentary system and lambast royal absolutism, come

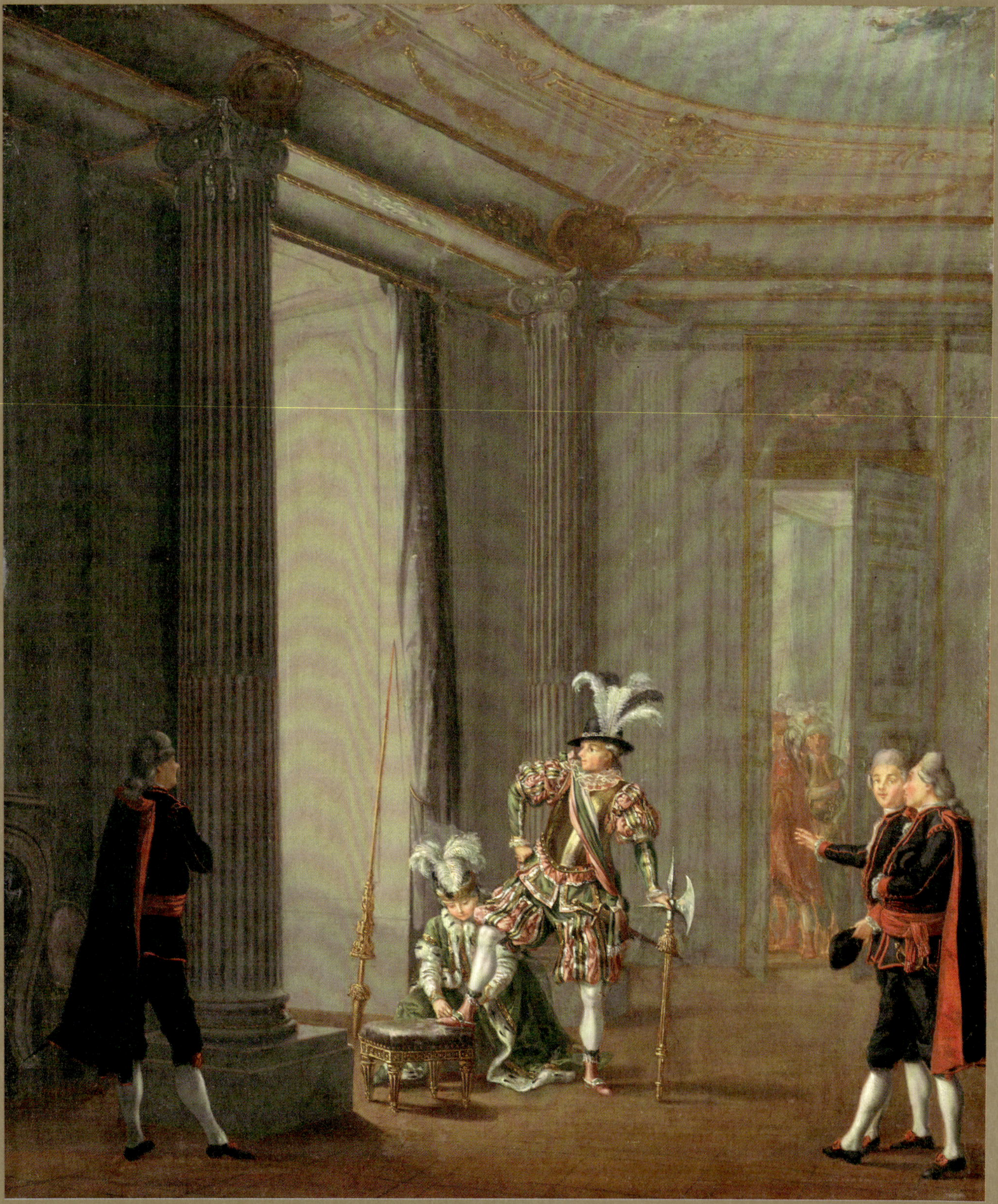

supper the prince would have to listen to his parents complaining about the stranglehold exerted by the assemblies. This ambiguous situation accentuated Gustav's hypersensitivity, and he turned to the theater as a means of escape. He was often discovered declaiming and performing on stage. He had begun to write plays in French when no more than ten, taking the roles himself until a relatively advanced age, abandoning the habit only when a French ambassador managed to convince him that it was improper. The king continued to pen the occasional drama, however, often on themes from national history, and to throw court festivals featuring magnificent carrousels.

In this context, the tone of the account the future Gustav III left of his youth and his relations at court during his later years as crown prince is only to be expected: "Since my earliest years, I had been brought up at the most turbulent court there has ever been and was initiated into the secrets of politics and the affairs of state at an age when others are still in short trousers. I was moreover soon au fait with all the malevolence and spite that minds set against one another are capable of dreaming up." Such experiences would make anyone—as Gustav III wryly noted—"either insane or exceptionally wise." His stormy relationship with his mother, the pitfalls of political horse-trading, and internecine intrigue at court all colored his attitude to life and placed an unbearable psychological burden on the crown prince. Even his much loved "China Castle" which had been a safe haven since he was a child, was to become a bone of contention. "Can peace and pleasure exist outside the China Castle?" he wondered. Banning him from this earthly paradise was the subtlest weapon chosen by his parents in raising him. It is just possible that Gustav III felt a warm glow of revenge come over him when, following the break with his mother in 1778, he was in turn to forbid her access to Drottningholm, the castle she had loved so much.

A court needs to be entertained and enchanted—a fact Gustav III had learned from Louis XIV. The reason is far from petty: The nobility must be made dependent on royal power, so that it simply does not have the opportunity to indulge in political shenanigans. Louis XIV had endured aristocratic rebellion during the Fronde and was determined never to repeat the experience. Some of the Sun King's tricks were rather subtle. In her notorious correspondence, his sister-in-law Elisabeth Charlotte, princess Palatine, describes how the monarch's expression alone would convey whether a given interlocutor was in his good books—or his bad. *Panem et circenses* also proved a motto as valid at court as for the populace, and every instant of Louis XIV's daily routine had been transformed into a theatrical performance. When in 1773, however, his cousin Catherine II was informed how Gustav, following his illustrious predecessor's example,

Gustav III dressing for the Role of Espladiant in "La Prise de la Roche Galtare" by Amadis de Gaule, Performed at the Carrousel of 1779 at Drottningholm Castle
1779
Pehr Hilleström the Elder
(1732–1816)
Nationalmuseum, Stockholm

had instituted morning receptions at which the court would pay the sovereign homage as he dressed (a ceremony reminiscent of the traditional French *levée*), she was quick to poke fun at her Swedish relative's archaic notions. In her eyes, Gustav was little better than a fop straining to imitate all things French. For him, however, this was no fashion, but an urge to articulate the might of an absolutist monarchy—something that might be called, in more modern terms, a "choreography of power."

These ceremonies were perpetuated in his various pleasure pavilions, initially at Drottningholm, and then at Gripsholm. Handwritten by the king, the rules and regulations detail the procedure: once the royal hair had been duly combed and curled, the monarch would receive his first visitors. After bowing and scraping, they would be permitted to remain present as he changed out of the royal nightshirt. Then, as the king assisted by chamberlains and pages continued his toilette, other worthies would be admitted. Pages would hand him a water basin for his ablutions and then dress him, while chamberlains presented the hat, gloves, and sword, as well as the blue ribbon of the Royal Order of the Seraphim. The king would then saunter among his attendants, addressing a word or two to those he wished to honor, before halting at the bedside to listen to reports from the general staff, and moving on to the council or to an audience.

A strict order of precedence and the most rigorous etiquette also regimented the "courts" the king held for courtiers, dignitaries, and members of the diplomatic corps once a week, generally on Tuesdays, which concluded with the king dining in public at a *grand couvert*. For the most part, guests just whiled away the time waiting for the royal couple to make their appearance. Such occasions were usually graced by a Gustav III "sumptuously attired, wearing the insignia of the orders of knighthood, as well as diamond-studded buttons and buckles; admittedly, it looked a little overdone, but he always seemed quite at ease." Tottering on her high heels, the queen, on the other hand, appeared stiff and walked with difficulty. She made one courtier in particular think of "a parade-ground horse with a good long neck, but a lolloping gait."

Once the "court" had finished, the public *grand couvert* could be served. Most of the personalities present had to remain standing while the king and queen sat, though, in deference to their rank, those who had married dignitaries of the kingdom—namely members of the council and Her Majesty's principal ladies-in-waiting—were permitted to perch on stools placed in a semicircle at one end of the table. From time to time Gustav III would beckon one of them over to have a word—as can be seen in the painting by Pehr Hilleström entitled *Stockholm Castle on New Year's Day 1779*.

View of the Stockholm Royal Palace
XVIIIe siècle
ELIAS MARTIN
(1739-1818)
Nationalmuseum, Stockholm

"Grand Couvert" at Stockholm Castle on New Year's Day 1779
1779
PEHR HILLESTRÖM THE ELDER
(1732–1816)
Nationalmuseum, Stockholm

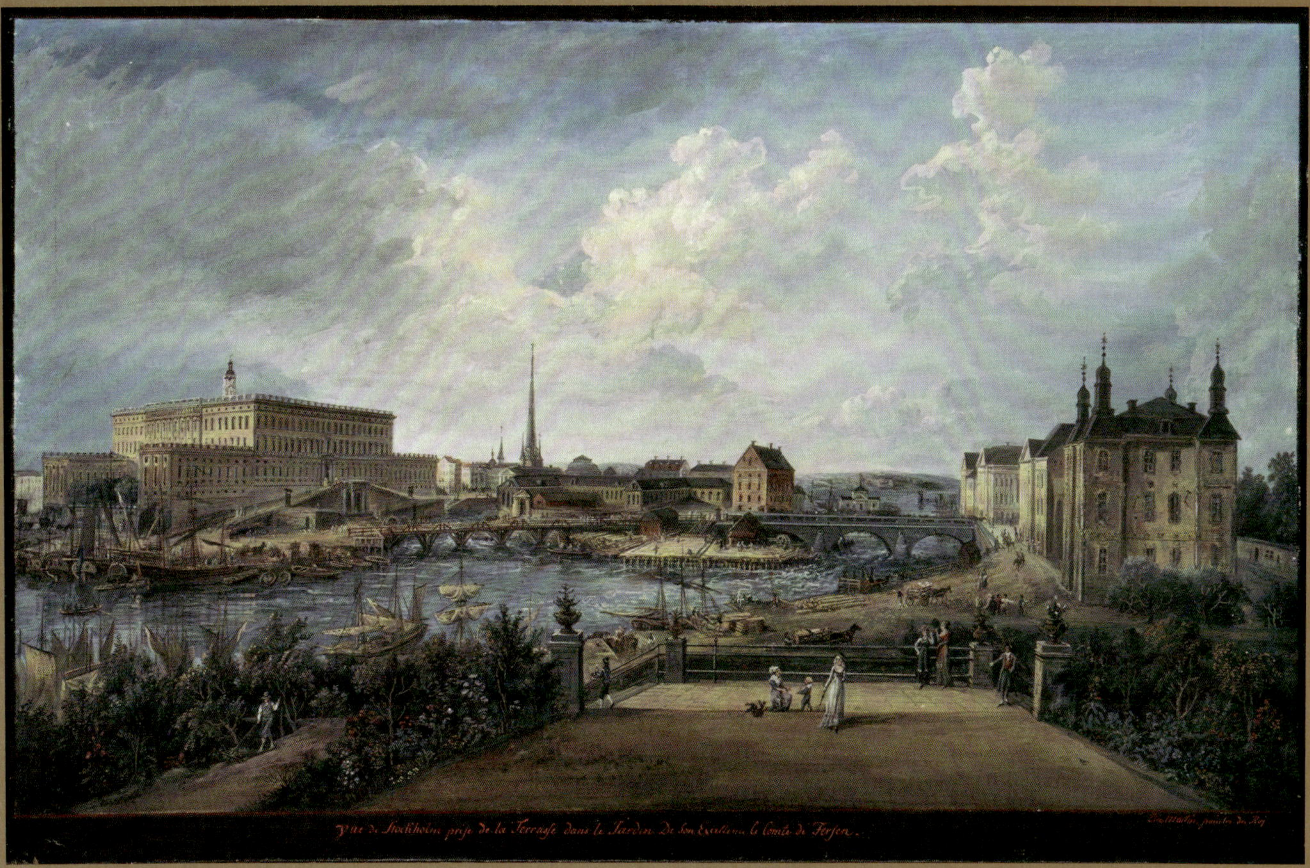
Vue de Stockholm prise de la Terrasse dans le Jardin De son Excellence le Comte de Fersen.

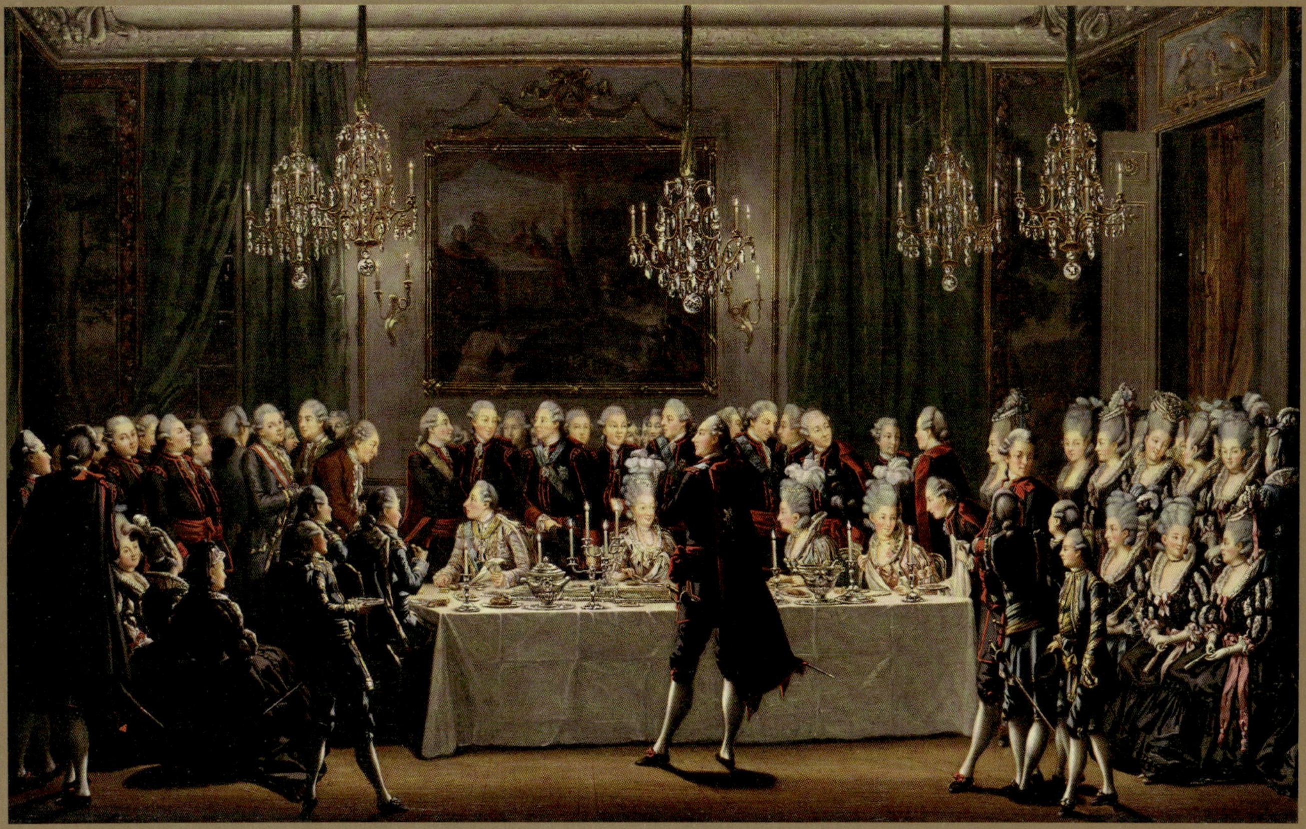

His mother, Luise Ulrike, loomed large in Gustav III's life. He inherited her acute intelligence and impetuous temperament, as well as a lively interest in culture and the arts, with a particular penchant for France. But his mother's authoritarian and egoistical nature was also a prominent source of the traumas that dogged Gustav in later life. The contradictory feelings she felt for her son—a potent combination of passion and emotional coldness—unhinged him. Thus, at an early age, Gustav learned how to avoid open conflict with his mother, often showing great finesse in this regard.

Of more easygoing temperament, his father Adolf Fredrik never really counted in Gustav's existence. As soon as he ascended the throne in 1771, Gustav III gradually distanced himself from his mother in a process that culminated in a dramatic rupture seven years later.

Compared to the rest of the family, Gustav III's wife, Queen Sofia Magdalena, of Danish origin, would have seemed like an exotic bird. Her self-absorption, compounded by the cold shoulder she received from her mother-in-law, Luise Ulrike, jeopardized all chance of satisfactory relations between king and queen. During the first nine years of the marriage, indeed, the couple eschewed intimacy. When, in summer 1775, it transpired that Gustav III's young sister-in-law, Hedvig Elisabet Charlotta, wife of the future Charles XIII, would never produce an heir to the throne, Gustav had to bite the bullet and attempt a rapprochement with his wife. As go-between he chose the master of the royal horse, Adolf Fredrik Munck, who also benefited from the confidence of the queen. Judging from the report Munck later composed concerning this delicate mission, the royal spouses were subjected to a degree of psychological and physical coercion. When consummation did finally take place, it was less due to any sincere feelings of affection on either side than to the imperative of supplying an heir to the crown. Relations between Gustav III and Sofia Magdalena were eventually smoothed over, however, and on February 1778 came the reward: the queen fell pregnant. The subsequent chain of events is a matter of record: court gossip; tactless accusations on the part of the queen mother, and the definitive break between mother and son. During the whole sorry episode, however, the king at least remained loyal to his wife. In 1780 she miscarried, but later gave birth to a second son, baptized Karl Gustav. The family's joy proved short-lived, however, as, six months later, this child also died.

The first-born son, the crown prince, the future Gustav Adolf IV, whose upbringing might have united the family, was, on the contrary, yet a further apple of discord. Gustav III wanted to start preparing the prince for his monarchical duties from an early age, while Sofia Magdalena did all she could to keep the

Queen Sofia Magdalena (1746–1813) of Denmark and Norway, Wife of Gustav III
1768
Lorens Pasch the Younger
(1733–1805)
Nationalmuseum,
Stockholm

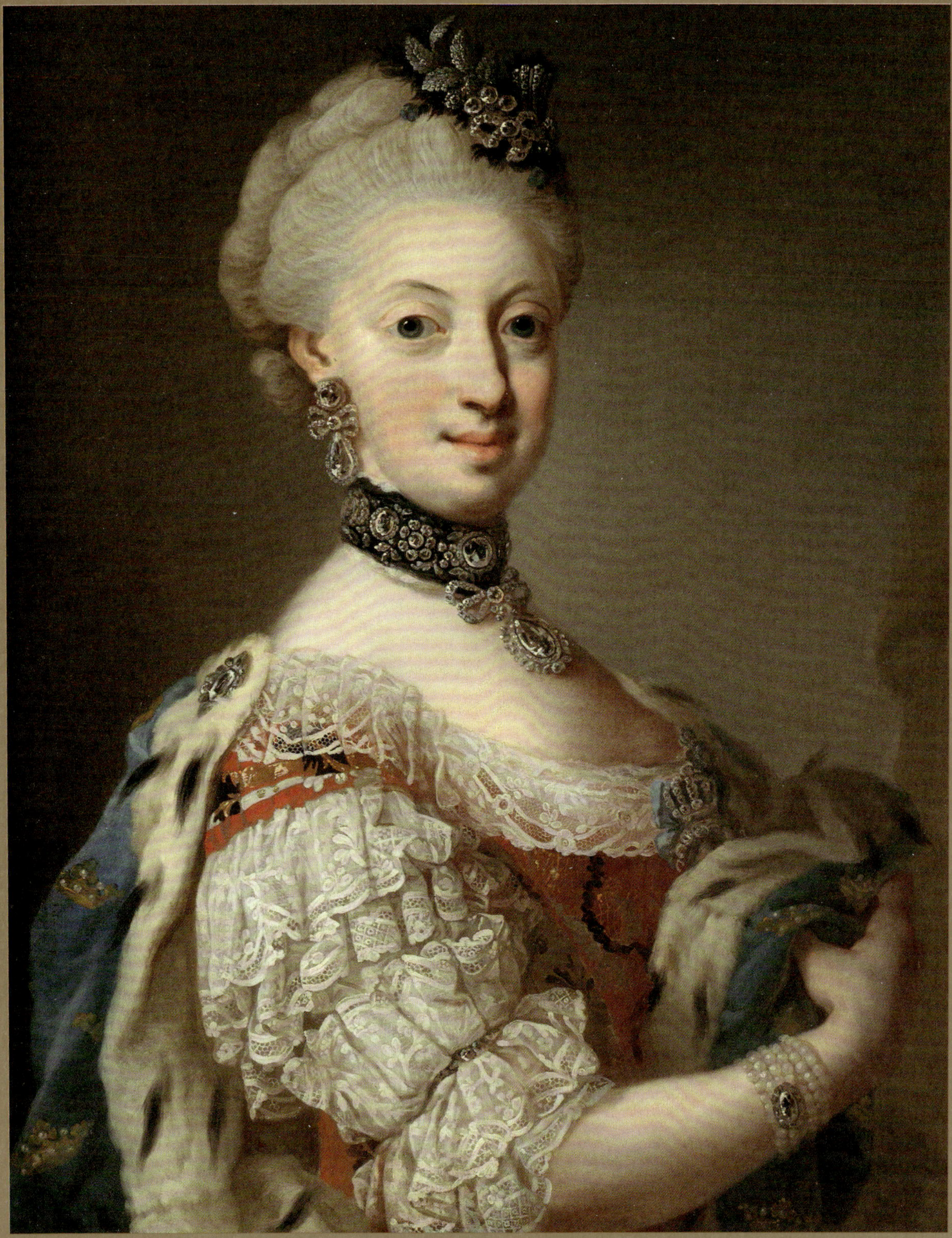

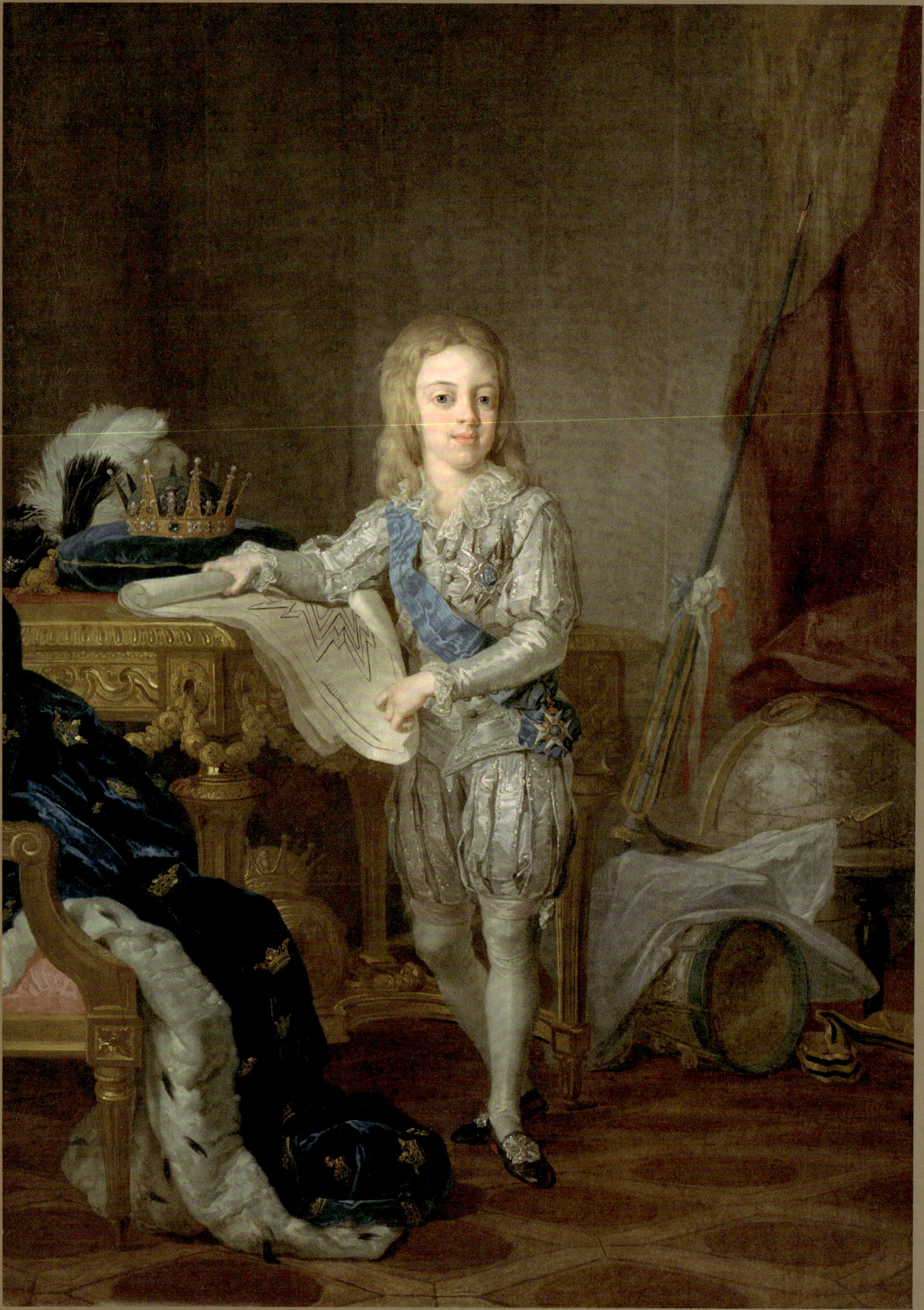

boy out of the public eye. When scarcely more than eight, Gustav Adolf would accompany his father as he crisscrossed the country, inspecting military exercise camps in Skåne or the university town of Uppsala, even venturing as far as Finland. The boy was present at the last three Riksdags, and even sat, at the age of twelve, on the kingdom's council. Thus father and son grew close, which to some extent made up for the lack of warmth Gustav III had experienced in his family as a child.

Would it have been possible for a monarch such as Gustav III to have a private life, even when it came to something as intimate? It seems unlikely. Thus the question arises as to whether one can speak of Gustav III other than as an official persona. The king's whole life took place in the spotlight, as if held up for inspection, to the point that, when interpreting official documents—chock-full as they are of conventional language and rhetoric—distinguishing genuine spontaneity, affection, and love from mere show is a challenge. In spite of much scholarly work in the archives, Gustav III seems destined to remain an enigmatic figure.

Displaying all the trappings of classical drama, a veil of tragedy and incompleteness hangs over the life of Gustav III. His fate was sealed in 1792 at the masked ball in the opera house, when, ignoring an anonymous letter that should have warned him off, he chose instead to brave the danger. Did Gustav III think himself invulnerable? Or did he simply believe that it was his destiny to die a violent death, as a fortuneteller had once predicted? No one will ever know.

Gustav Adolf IV (1778-1837), Son of Gustav III
1787
PEHR KRAFFT THE ELDER
(1724-1793)
Nationalmuseum, Stockholm

Gustav III and the theater

Lena Rangström

Gustav III and Countess Luise Ulrike of Fersen in front of the Drottningholm Carrousel, 1785
1785
Pehr Hilleström the Elder
(1732–1816)
Nationalmuseum, Stockholm

One could say that the reign of Gustav III happened between two visits to the theater. It was during a theater performance in Paris 1771 that the young crown prince got the message that his father the king had died—and that he himself was to put on his mantle. And the terminal point was set on March 16, 1792, at the fateful masked ball at the Royal Opera in Stockholm—when surrounded by black domino capes and white masks he met his Ravaillac in the shape of Captain Anckarström. The years betweens these events—the Gustavian era—comprised a golden age in Swedish cultural history. The royal theaters were founded on his initiative, the beginning of the national museum was laid out, academies were established, and the fine arts flourished. Famous artists, composers, stage designers, and actors were called to Sweden. And the feverishly active king himself created many different roles: architect, playwright, actor, and director. No other Swedish king had such great interest in the theater and no other patronized it like him. His aim was to create a national Swedish opera with inspiring motifs taken from Swedish history and introducing Swedish as a stage language. During this flourishing period, the costumes of the royal theaters were also known for their splendor. And Gustav III himself took an active part in creating the costumes—both for the theater and for the many tournaments and carousels that were performed during his reign—and in ceremonial life at court. The reign of "the theater king" has never ceased to enchant, especially during the summer performances at the Gustavian opera at Drottningholm.

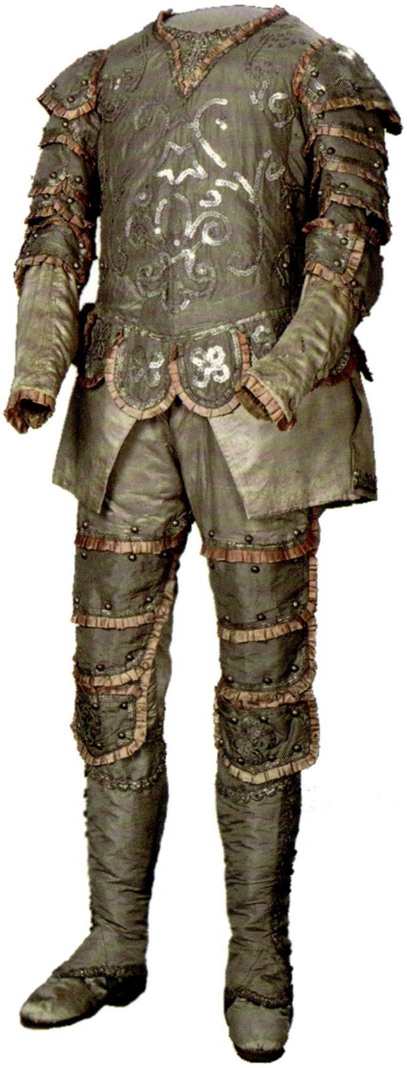

Theatrical costume worn by Gustav III for the opera Armida
Royal Palace, Stockholm

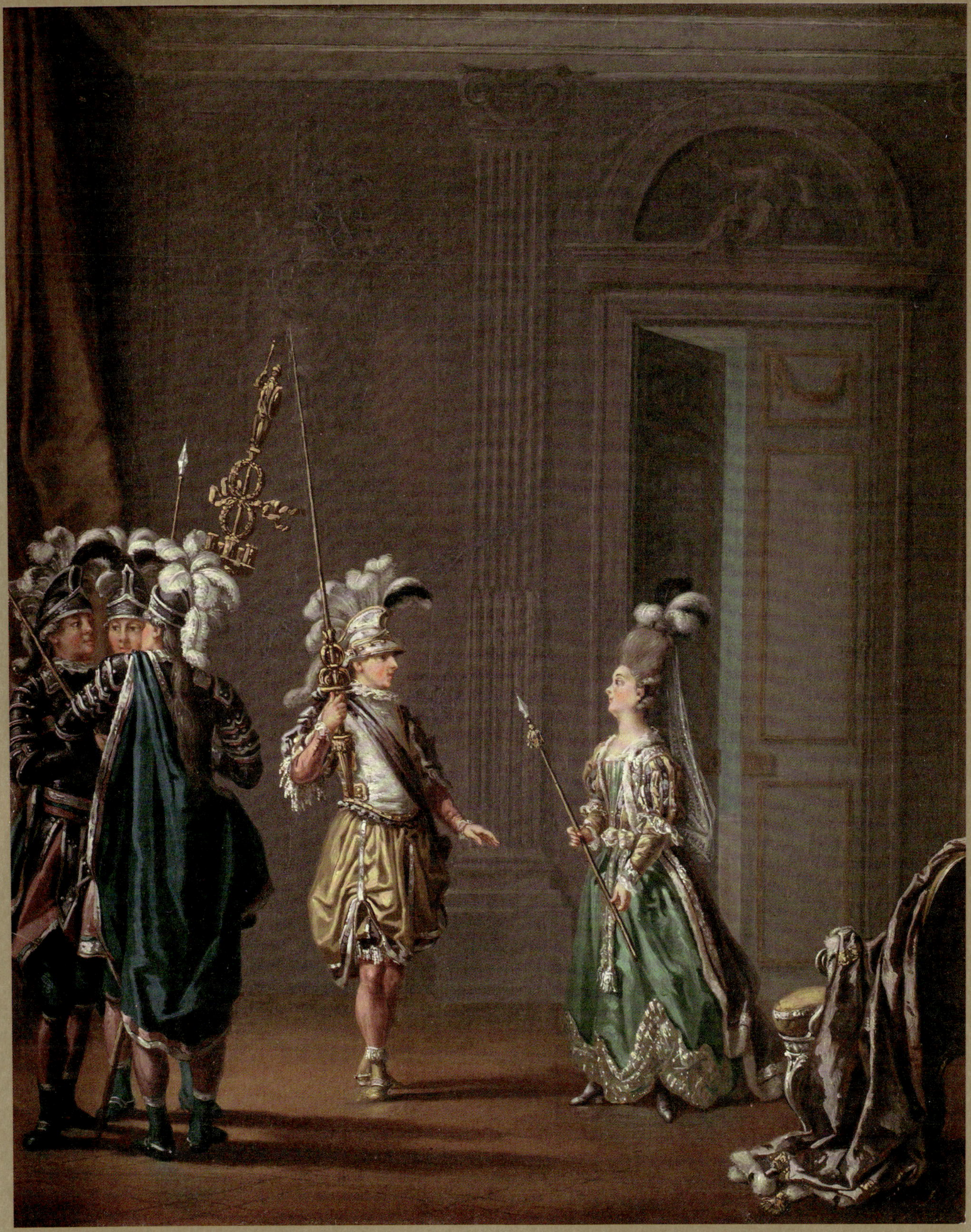

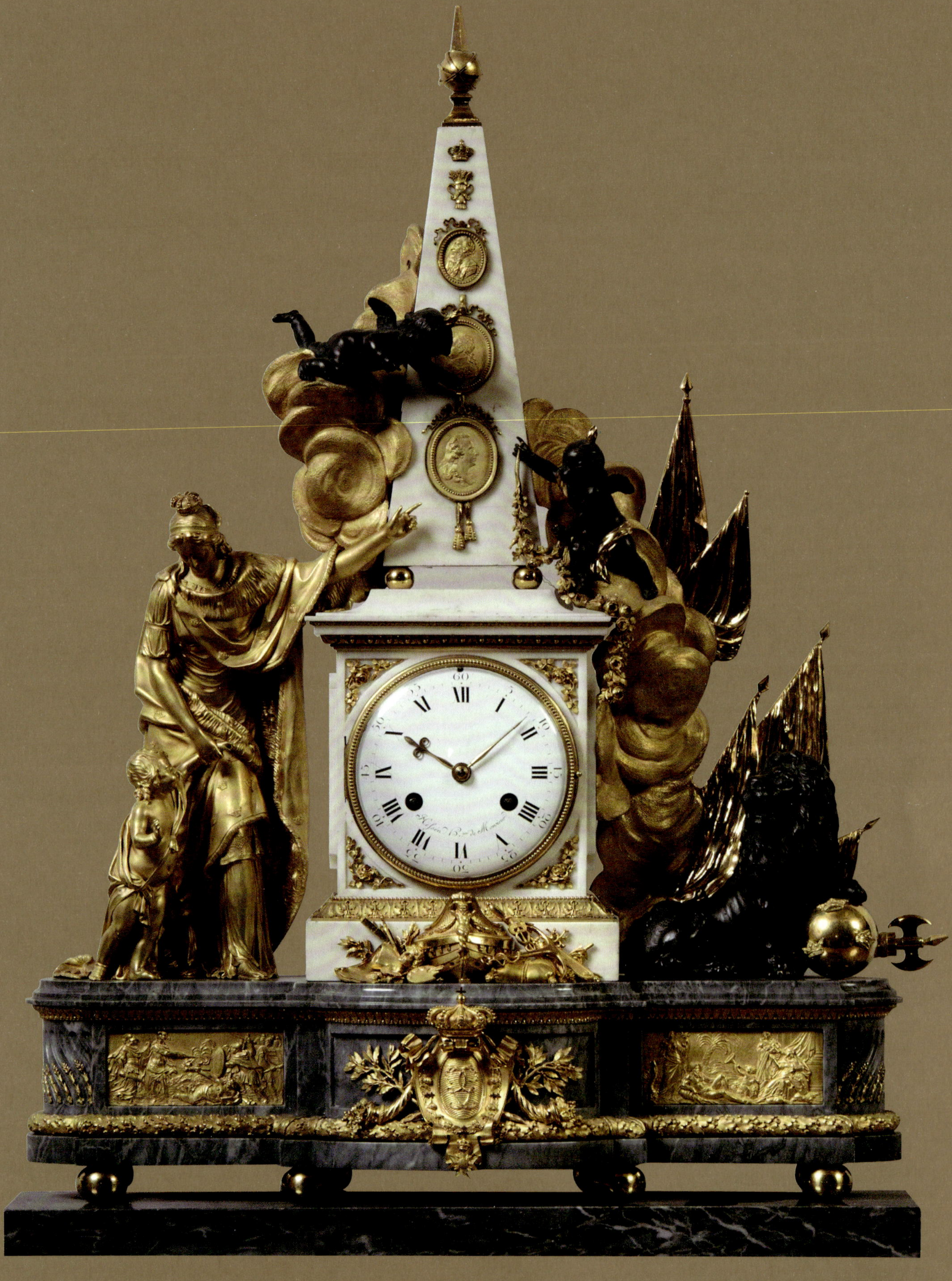

Swedish dynastic clock

Lars Ljungström

In 1783, Gustav III, eager to experience the grandeur of antiquity for himself, embarked on a journey to Italy. On his return he made a detour via Paris and Versailles, where his time was monopolized by political obligations. Gustav already knew the French royal family; a friendship had grown up between them while he was still crown prince. In 1772 Louis XV had afforded him backing for his *coup d'état.* At the time of his voyage to France, Gustav had hoped to cement these cordial relations, which might prove beneficial if the growing tension between Sweden and Denmark ever led to war.

In the cultural field, the king by now enjoyed a securely established image as the descendant of the preeminent kings of Sweden. Among the gifts he received in Paris was a splendid clock that perfectly sums up the image of his celebrated forebears. Placed one above the other on the obelisk of immortality appear portraits of Gustav I Vasa, Gustav II Adolf, called the Great or the Lion of the North, and Gustav III; Sweden itself, with the features of a woman, points out these paragons of princely virtue to the young prince.

Tradition has it that this clock was presented to the sovereign by the Swedish community in Paris. The figures represented correspond to those ancestors the king most admired, so its creator, whoever he was, must have been well informed. In the same year, 1784, its creator, the Swedish watchmaker André Hessen, was appointed "clock and watchmaker cum gentleman of the bedchamber to Monsieur," brother of the king of France.

It is equally possible that the present depiction was inspired by a courteous comment on the part of the marquis of Montesquiou-Fézensac when Gustav visited the French Academy. On that day enthroned as a member of the academy, Montesquiou concluded his acceptance speech by an allusion to how a number of leaders concerned with public welfare had left their palaces to lend an ear to impartial arguments, and that, wherever he went, this worthy heir to the two Gustavs would be sure to receive acclaim from all quarters.

Obelisk clock with medallions of three generations of Swedish kings: Gustav I, Gustav II, and Gustav III
1784
Messin (clockmaker)
Royal Palace, Stockholm

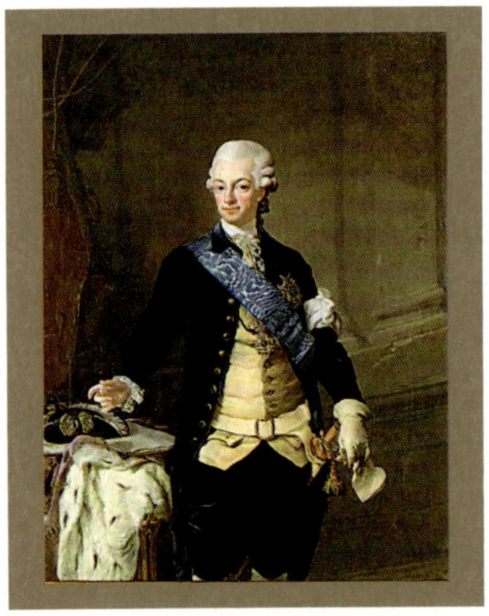

Gustav III (1746–1792), King of Sweden
1777
Lorens Pasch the Younger
(1733–1805)
Oil on canvas
224 × 149.5 cm (inc. frame)
Nationalmuseum, Stockholm
Inv. NM 2346

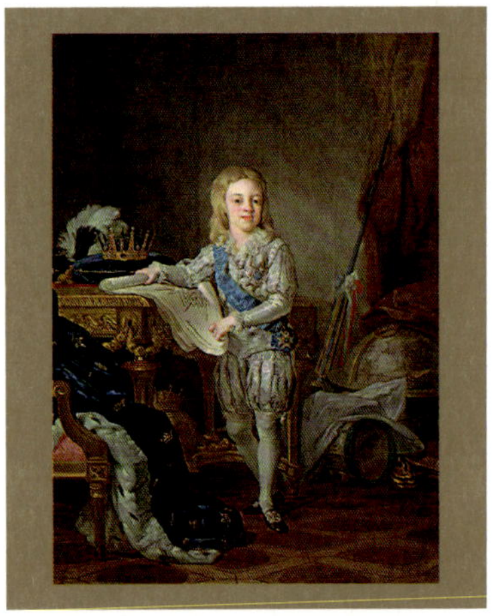

Gustav Adolf IV (1778-1837), Son of Gustav III
1787
Pehr Krafft the Elder
(1724-1793)
Oil on canvas
181 × 127 cm
Stockholm, Nationalmuseum
Inv. Grh 831

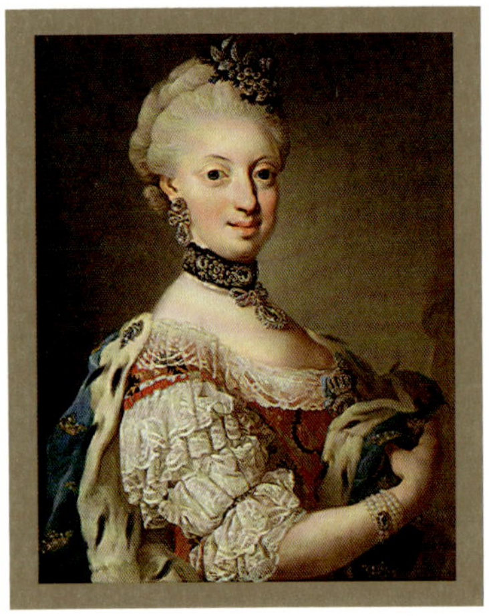

Sofia Magdalena (1746–1813), Queen of Denmark and Norway, Wife of Gustav III
1768
Lorens Pasch the Younger
(1733–1805)
Oil on canvas
89 × 73 cm (inc. frame)
Nationalmuseum, Stockholm
Inv. Grh 439

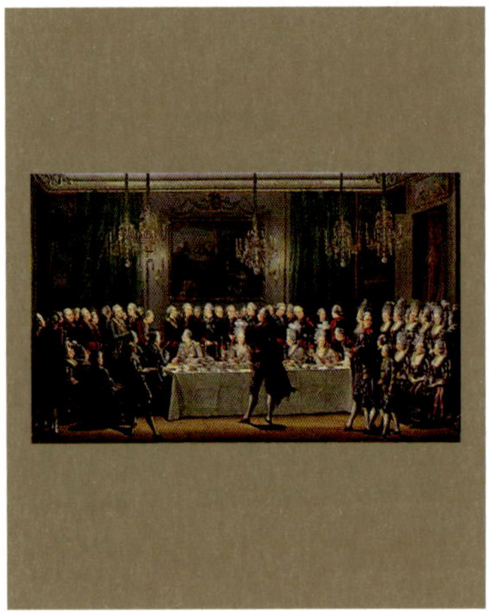

"Grand Couvert" at Stockholm Castle on New Year's Day 1779
1779
Pehr Hilleström the Elder
(1732–1816)
107.5 × 142 cm (inc. frame)
Oil on canvas
Nationalmuseum, Stockholm
Inv. NMDrh 499

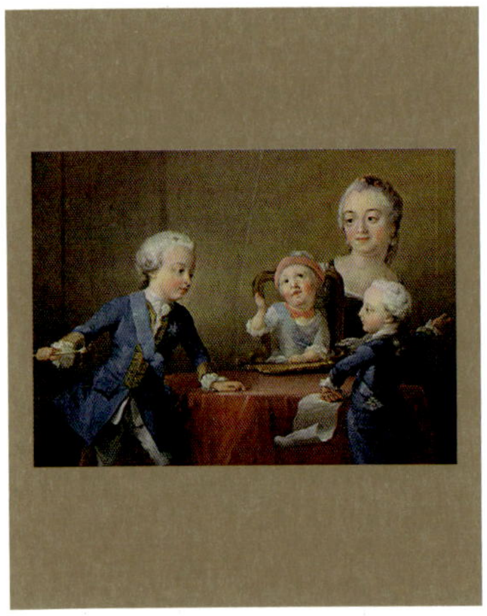

"Prelude to Glory", Queen Luise Ulrike of Prussia (1720–1782) and her Children: Gustav III and his Brothers
1752
Johann Pasch (1706–1769)
and Gustaf Lunberg (1695–1786)
Oil on canvas
44 × 59 cm
Nationalmuseum, Stockholm
Inv. DRH 500

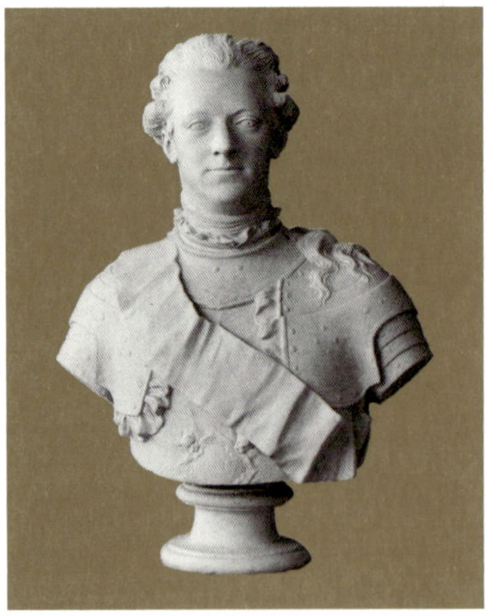

King Gustav III
Model after a marble
by Johan Tobias Sergel (1740–1814)
H. 76 cm
Nationalmuseum, Stockholm
Inv. Grh 3948

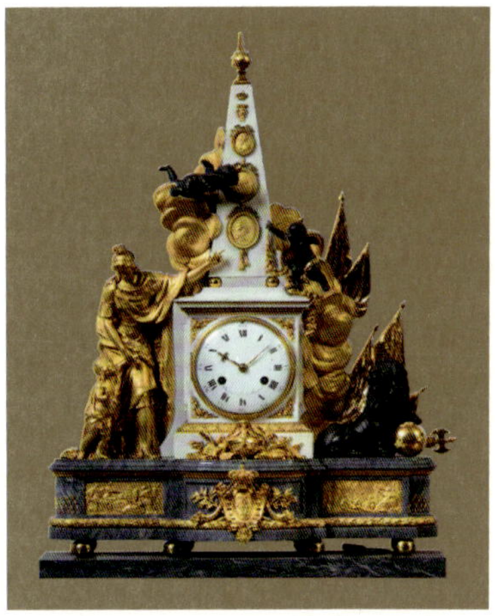

Obelisk clock with medallions of three generations of Swedish kings: Gustav I, Gustav II, and Gustav III
1784
Messin (clockmaker); André Hessen (1745–1805) (movement)
Bronze
85 × 61 × 24 cm
Royal Collections, Royal Palace, Stockholm
Inv. HGK 54

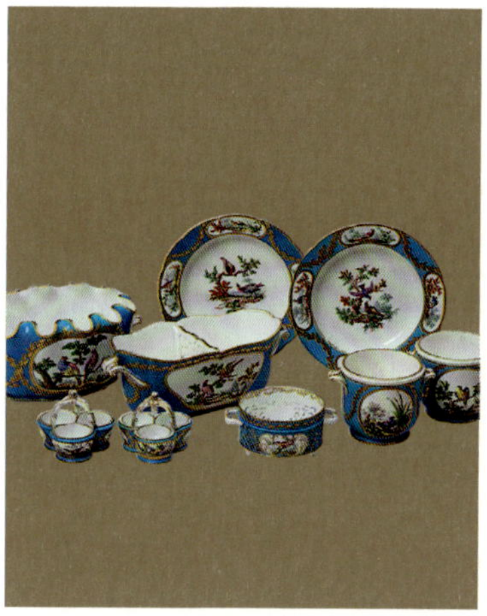

Items of the celestial blue dinner service offered by Louis XV to Gustav III during his visit to France
1775
Sèvres Porcelain Manufactory
Royal Collections, Royal Palace, Stockholm
Glass bowl, inv. HGK 17
Two plates, inv. HGK 136 and 123
Liqueur cooler, inv. HGK 105
Two spice boxes, inv. HGK 44-45
Cheese dish, inv. HGK 103
Two liqueur coolers, inv. HGK 60 and 62

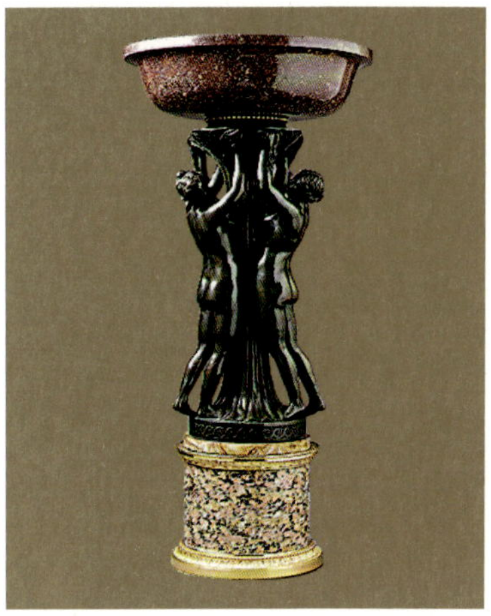

Basin carried by the Three Graces
c. 1780
Luigi Valadier (1726–1785)
Marble
66 x 32.5 cm (total)
Royal Collections, Royal Palace, Stockholm
Inv. HGK 35

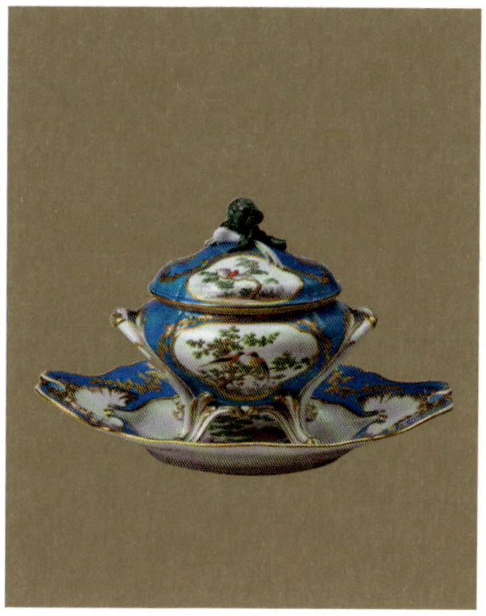

Soup tureen and celestial blue serving platter
1775
Sèvres Porcelain Manufactory
D. 29 cm
Royal Collections, Royal Palace, Stockholm
Inv. HGK 1 and 8

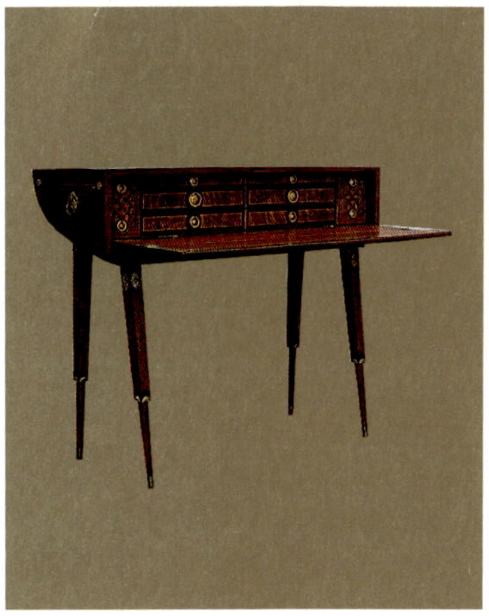

Travel writing desk
Second half of the eighteenth century
Georg Haupt (1741–1784)
Veneering
95 × 115 × 44 cm
Royal Collections, Royal Palace, Stockholm
Inv. HGK 910

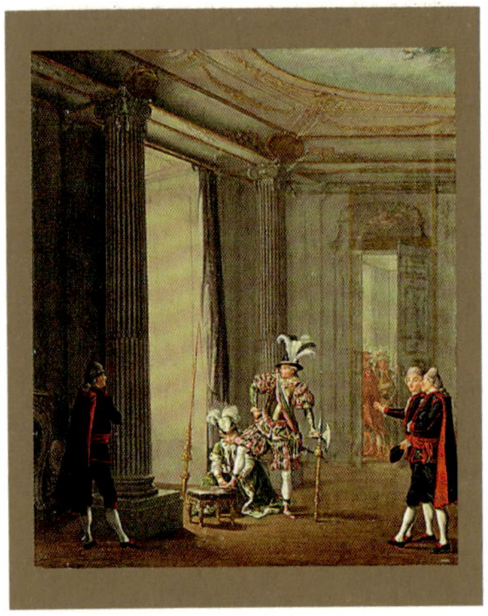

Gustav III dressing for the Role of Espladiant in "La Prise de la Roche Galtare" by Amadis de Gaule, Performed at the Carrousel of 1779 at Drottningholm Castle
1779
Pehr Hilleström the Elder
(1732–1816)
Oil on canvas
87.5 × 74.5 cm (inc. frame)
Nationalmuseum, Stockholm
Inv. GRH 265

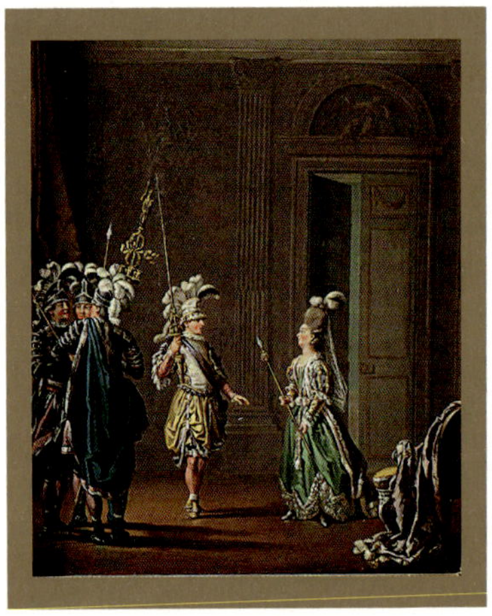

Gustav III and Countess Luise Ulrike of Fersen in front of the Drottningholm Carrousel
1785
Pehr Hilleström the Elder
(1732–1816)
Oil on canvas
61.5 × 52 cm
Nationalmuseum, Stockholm
Inv. Grh 1755

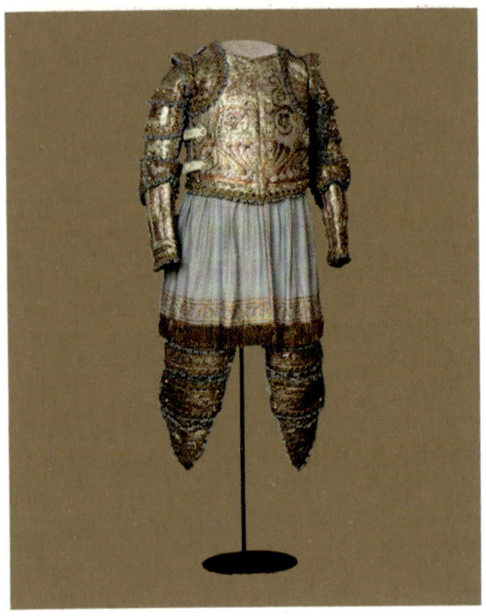

***Theatrical costume worn by Gustav III for the opera* Gustav Vasa**
Eighteenth century
H. 85 cm
Royal Palace, Stockholm,
H. M. the King of Sweden

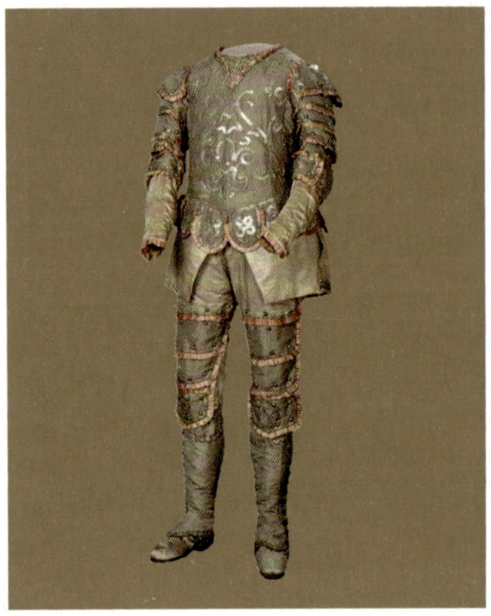

***Theatrical costume worn by Gustav III for the opera* Armida**
Eighteenth century
H. 85 cm
Royal Palace, Stockholm,
H. M. the King of Sweden

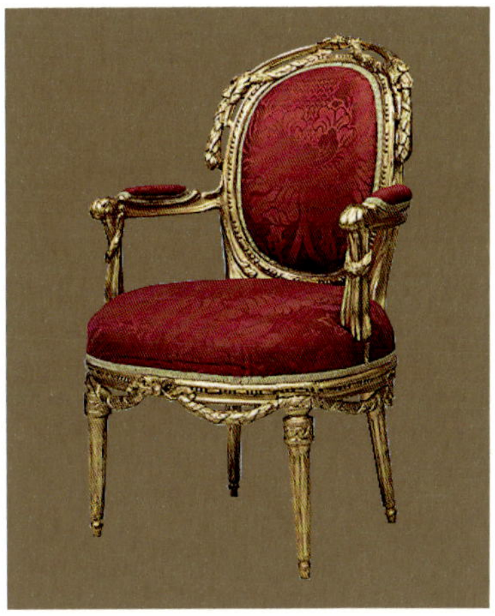

Theater dressing room armchair
Stockholm
Eighteenth century
99 × 62 × 63 cm
Royal Collections, Royal Palace, Stockholm
Inv. HGK 5605

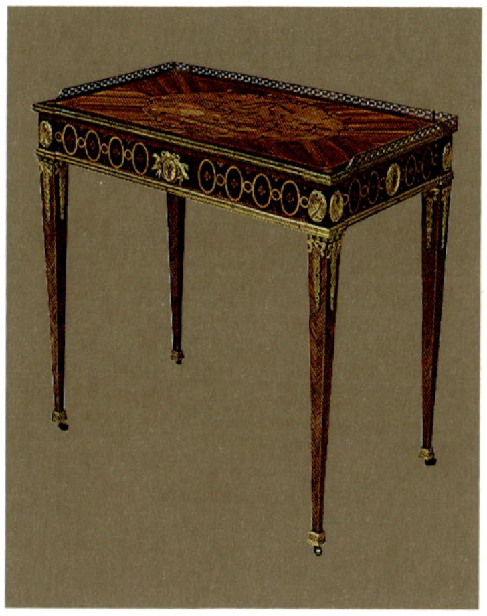

Theater dressing room dressing table
Stockholm
Eighteenth century
74.7 × 74.5 × 43.5 cm
Royal Collections, Royal Palace, Stockholm
Inv. HGK 1331

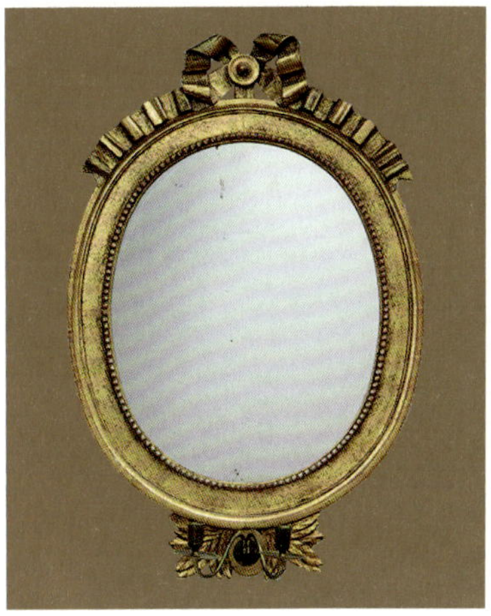

Dressing room mirror
Stockholm
Eighteenth century
78 × 51.5 cm
Royal Collections, Royal Palace, Stockholm
Inv. HGK 292

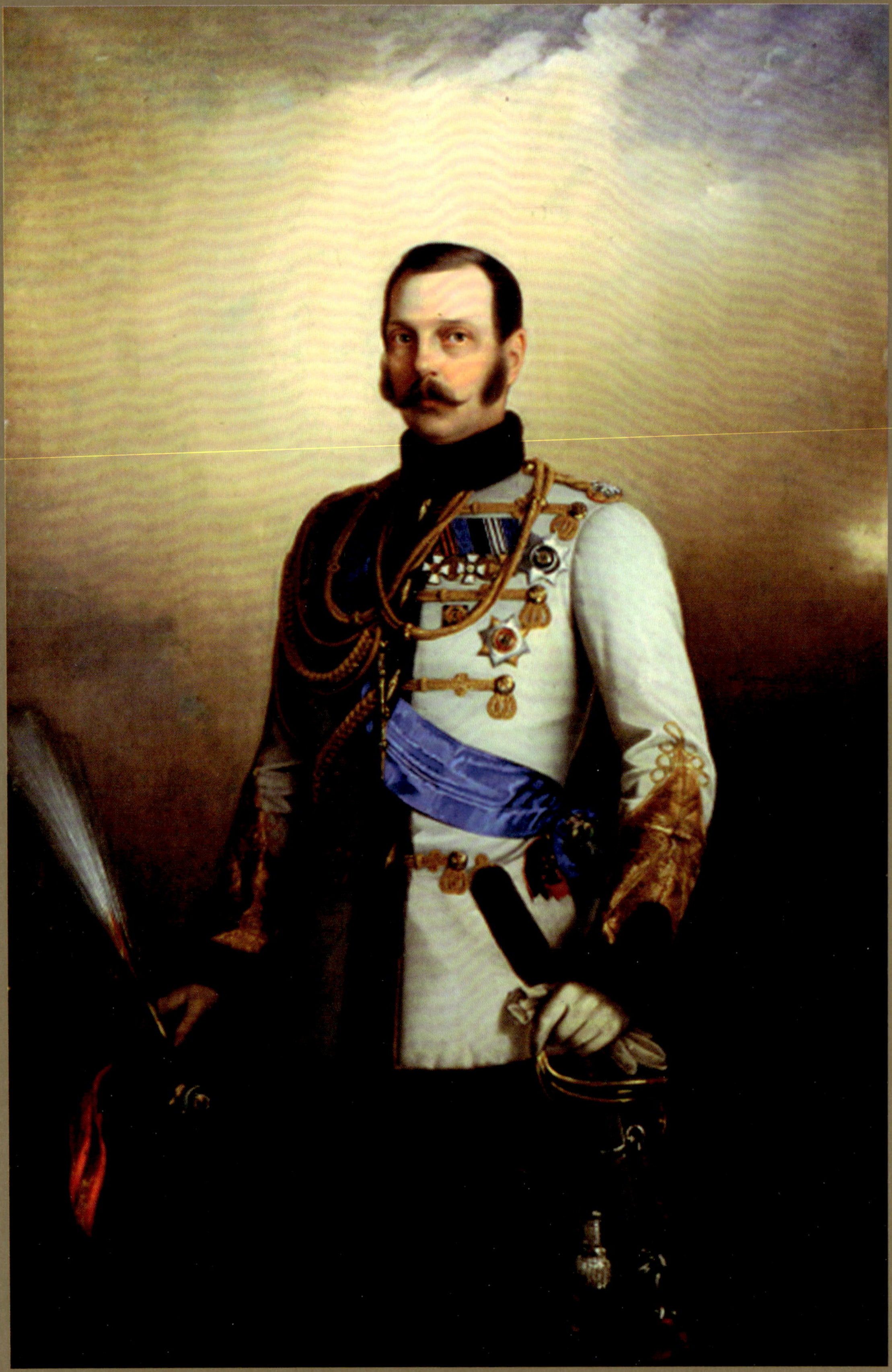

RUSSIA

Alexander II (1818–1881)

Czar Alexander II
in the uniform of
the Hussar Regiment
of the Imperial Guard
1860
Nikolai A. Lavrov
(1820–1875)
Tsarskoye Selo
Palace Museum,
Pouchkine

Alexander II, known as the "Liberator" Emperor of Russia

Wilfried Zeisler

"The abolition of serfdom allowed Russia to see a hitherto unsuspected side to the long underrated Alexander II, who, from the very beginning of his reign, acquired merits equal to those of his two most notable and celebrated predecessors in Russian history, Peter I and Catherine the Great."
Hélène Carrère d'Encausse

The eldest son of Emperor Nicholas and Empress Alexandra, née Charlotte of Prussia, Grand Duke Alexander benefitted from an exhaustive education under the watchful eye of the Romantic poet Vasily Zhukovsky (1783–1852). At the time of his grand tour of Europe, the czarevitch fell for the charms of Princess Marie of Hesse (1824–1880), as a passage from his journal (April 4, 1840) describes: "I am unable to say what I felt the instant I took my Marie in my arms for the first time. I will never in my life forget the angelic expression in her eyes during those moments."

Their wedding was duly celebrated in St. Petersburg in 1841, and Marie, converted to the Orthodox Church, became Maria Alexandrovna. Eight children were born to the union, many allying themselves to European courts: Denmark (Nicholas, later Alexander), Mecklenburg-Schwerin (Vladimir), England (Maria), Hesse-Darmstadt (Sergei), and Greece (Paul). With his hands on the levers of power from as early as 1840, the young Alexander, while more open-minded than his father, nevertheless remained wedded to the core ideas of empire—"Orthodoxy, autocracy, nationality"—which, on his deathbed in 1855, Nicholas I had demanded he uphold. Once emperor, Alexander II brought an end to the Crimean War, negotiating an honorable peace for a defeated Russia under the terms of the Treaty of Paris (1856).

As Wladimir Berelowich underlines, the country then had to resolve the intractable question of serfdom: "Since the reign of Catherine, the situation of the feudal peasantry had gradually become a major political headache." This national peculiarity, which sparked regular uprisings, was the inspiration for Gogol's *Dead Souls* (1842) and Turgenev's *A Sportsman's Sketches* (published between 1847 and 1852), both pretexts for an uncompromising critique of serfdom which supposedly

Empress Alexandra Feodorovna (1798–1860), Mother of Czar Alexander II, in Russian Costume
After 1834
P. Hesse (after F. Krüger)
Tsarskoye Selo Palace Museum,
Pouchkine

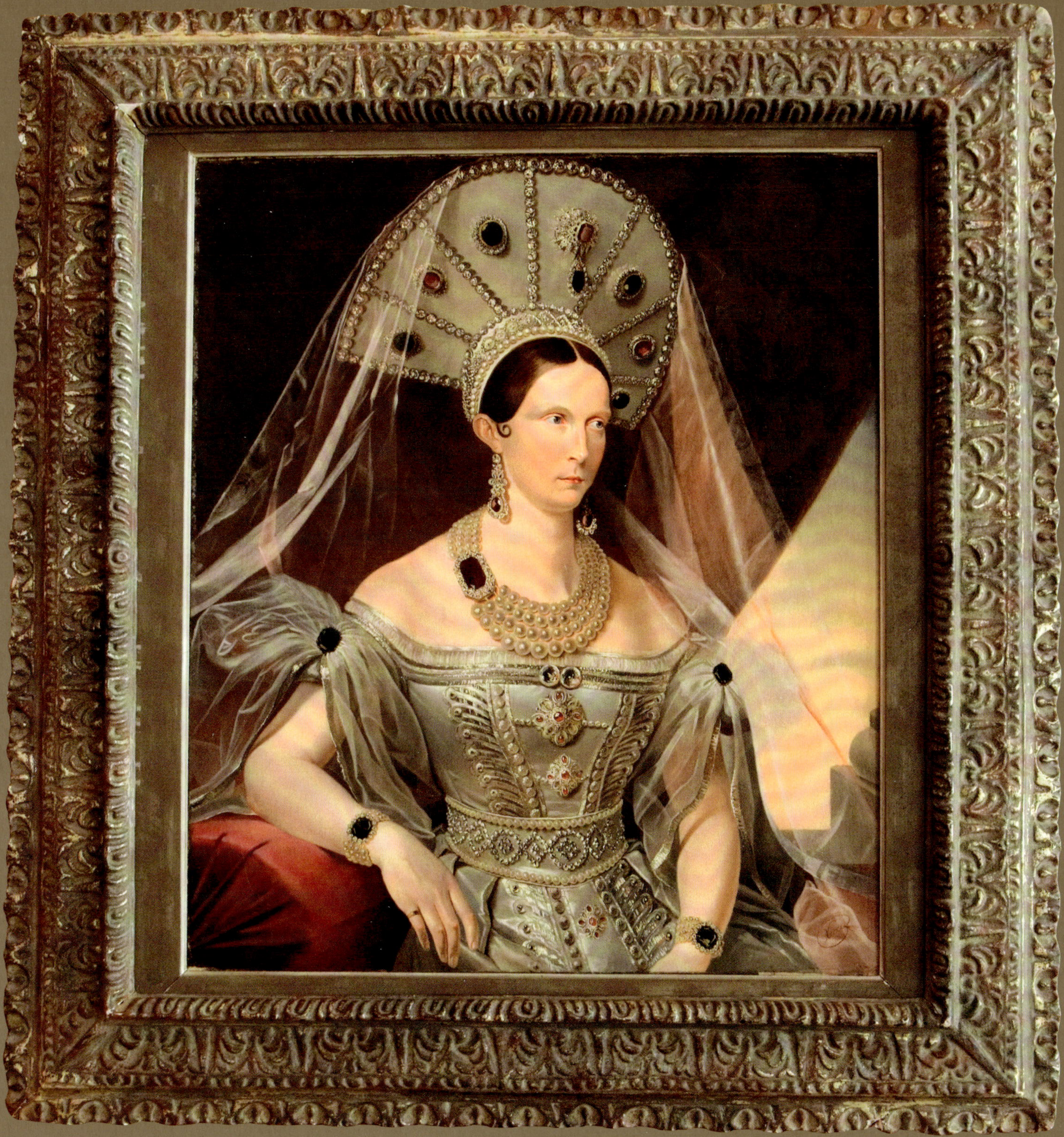

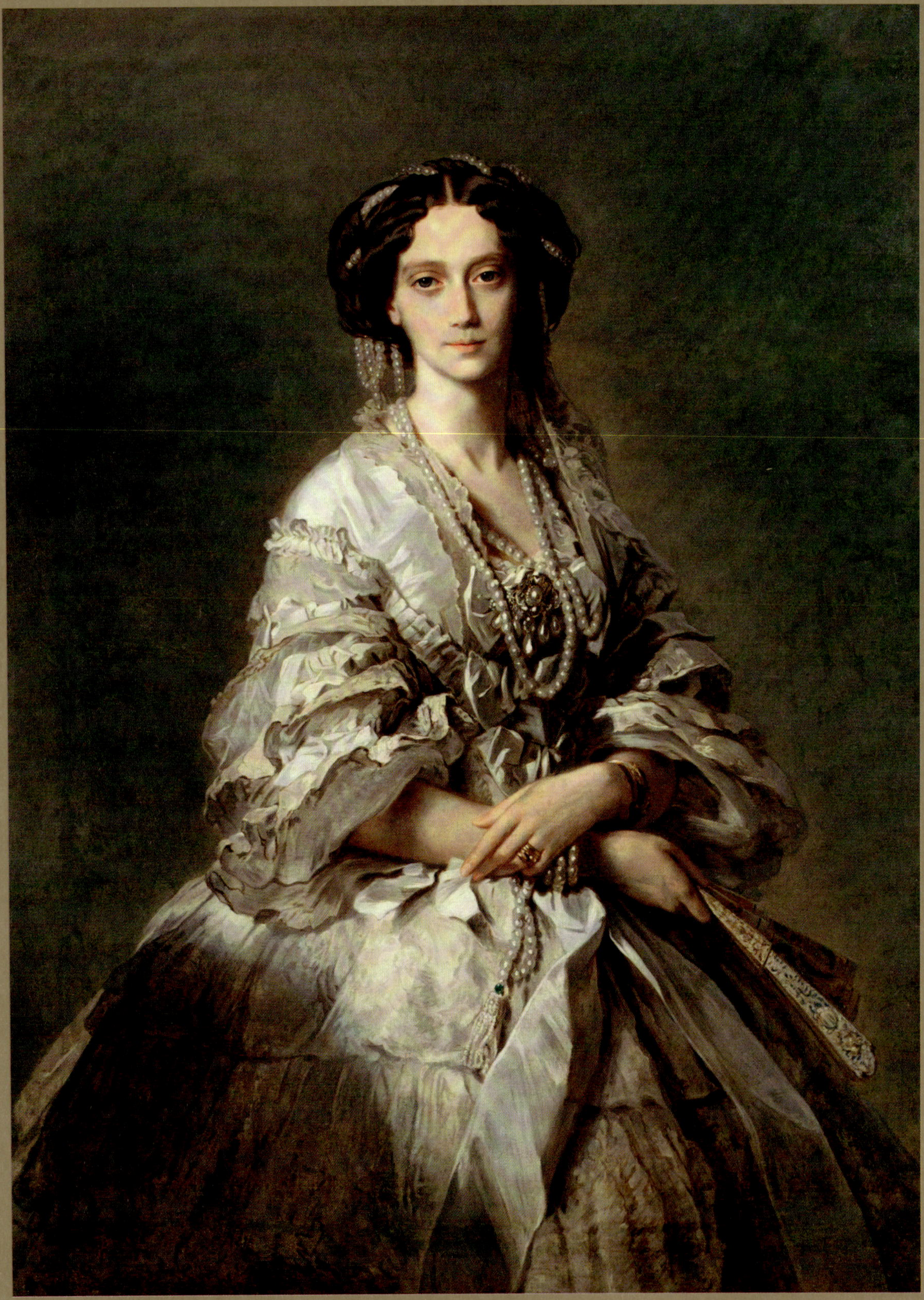

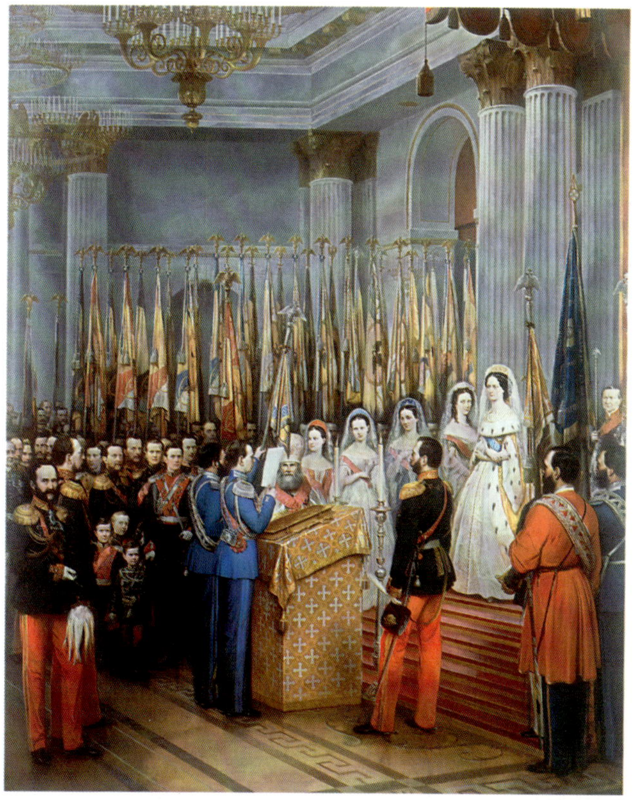

Grand Duke Nicholas Alexandrovich's Oath of Loyalty, in the hall of St. George, Winter Palace, September 8, 1859
1867
Gottfried Willewalde (1818–1903)
Tsarskoye Selo Palace Museum, Pouchkine

influenced Alexander II. The question of emancipation was all the more topical in that it was endowed with international scope: slavery had been abolished in France in 1848 and was stoking the fires of civil war in the United States.

Urged to reform by a section of the intelligentsia and certain members of the imperial family, Alexander II, convinced that any such initiative was better "coming from the top," on July 1858 freed the crown's "souls," followed by those of the nobility by a ukase of February 19/March 3, 1861, thereby manumitting more than 50 million subjects.

In spite of these reforms, rural society in the counties of Russia (the *mir*) remained under the thumb of the nobility, which organized the collective management of the land and its redistribution to the newly freed peasants (approximately 4 hectares each)—the latter not even being permitted to exploit the land as they saw fit. The peasantry had 49 years to reimburse the state that had advanced the requisite funds to the nobility, while the latter remained the most important landowner with 103 million hectares compared with 17 million hectares for the former serfs. The ruling class also dominated the *zemstvo*, a new local assembly elected by indirect suffrage from 1864, responsible for overseeing the local budget, highways, healthcare, and education, which Alexander II also intended to reform.

Censorship also slackened its grip, and universities won greater autonomy. Reform of the legal system, inspired by European models, preached equality for all and offered increased independence to the judges. Finally, the army, too, was modernized. It was a thirst for freedom that even surfaced in the arts, when, in 1863—when the official Salon in Paris had to vie with the new Salon des Refusés—fourteen artists denounced the diktats of establishment painting, left the benches of the academy, and struck out to capture the unvarnished reality of modern Russia. One of these "rebels," a talented portraitist of the time, Ivan Kramskoy (1837–1887) became instrumental in founding the group of realists known as the "Wanderers."

Such liberalization, aided and abetted by an expanding and increasingly industrialized Russian economy, restored the international prestige of the empire. Although a Germanophile, Alexander II, influenced by Prince Alexander Gorchakov

Empress Maria Alexandrovna (1853–1920), Wife of Czar Alexander II
After 1857
After Franz Xaver Winterhalter (1805–1873)
Palace Museum, Gatchina

Tea service (and détails) with views of the Gatchina Palace and grounds
1860–70,
Saint Petersburg Imperial Manufactory
Palace Museum, Gatchina

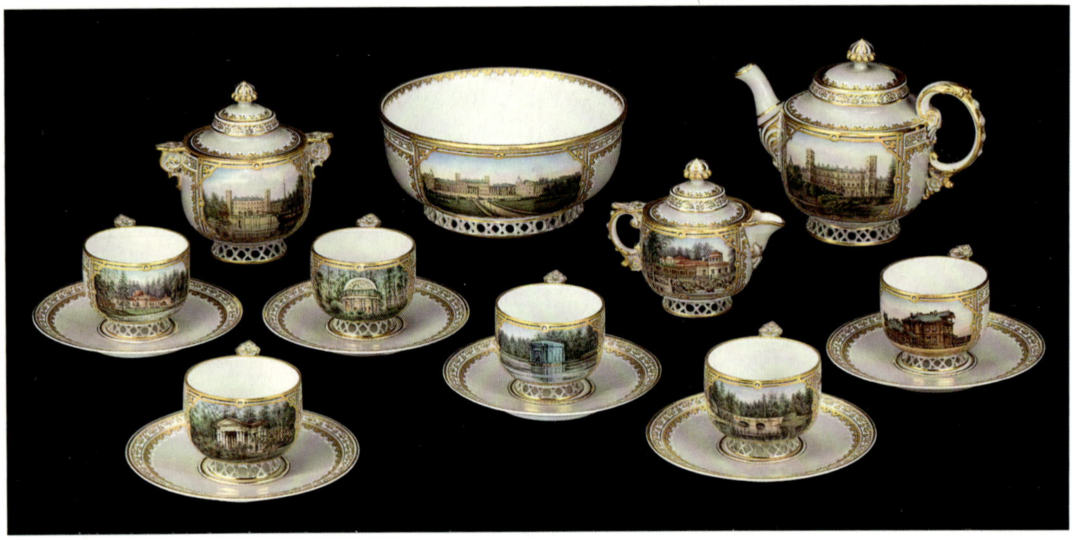

(1798–1883), a pro-France diplomat, attempted an unprecedented reconciliation with the regime of Napoleon III, but following acts of repression in Poland the plan came to naught. Allied to the court of Prussia through his mother, on the fall of the French empire Alexander II seized the opportunity to make good his interests at the London Conference in 1871. Two years later he formed with Germany and Austria-Hungary the League of the Three Emperors that afforded Europe a measure of stability, later jeopardized by the ratification of the 1891 Franco-Russian Alliance.

On the home front, the reforms, considered too slow or not far-reaching enough, fostered the rise of radical movements, such as nihilism, the stock characters of which Turgenev paints in *Fathers and Sons* (1862). In 1866 the first attempt on Alexander II's life—and, what was worse, by a Russian citizen—left the sovereign nonplussed and doubtful as to the continuation of reform. Conservatives preaching a return to the good old days of order demanded the reforms be rolled back, only exacerbating the claims of nihilists and populists. The secret society Land and Liberty split into two factions and, on August 26 / September 7, 1879, the emperor was condemned by a group calling itself The People's Will. Determined to complete his allotted task, however, Alexander II prepared one final reform to pave the way for parliamentary government in Russia. The sovereign then planned to withdraw from affairs of state and set up house publicly with Ekaterina Dolgorukova (better known under the name Katia; 1847–1922), a princess who had been his companion since 1866 and whom he had recently married. But terrorism put an end to both the emperor, assassinated in March 1881, and his last great project, which was buried, together with the "Liberator," by his son Alexander III.

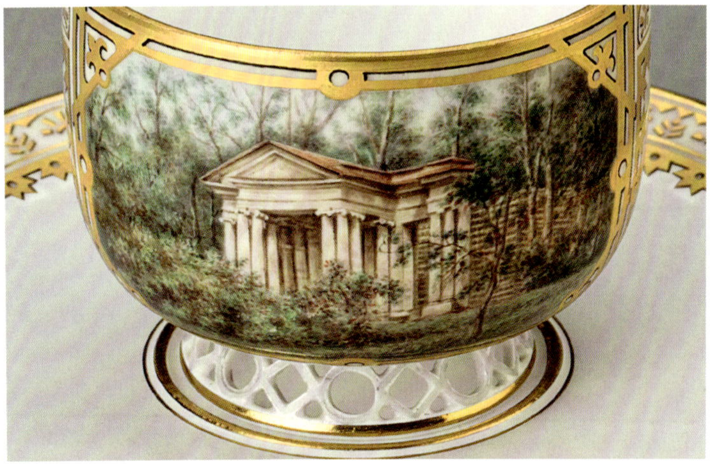
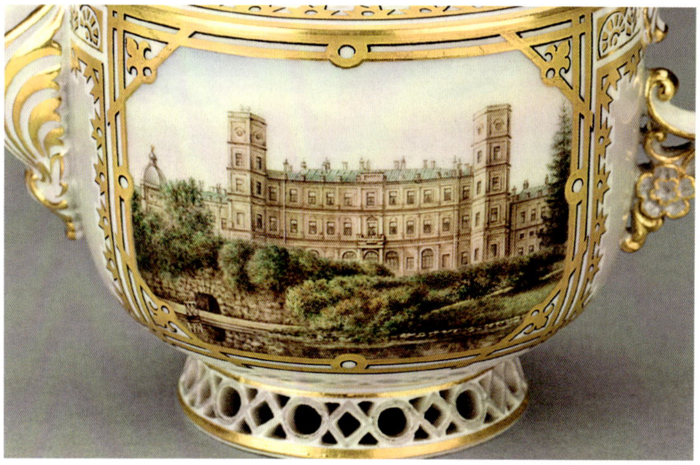
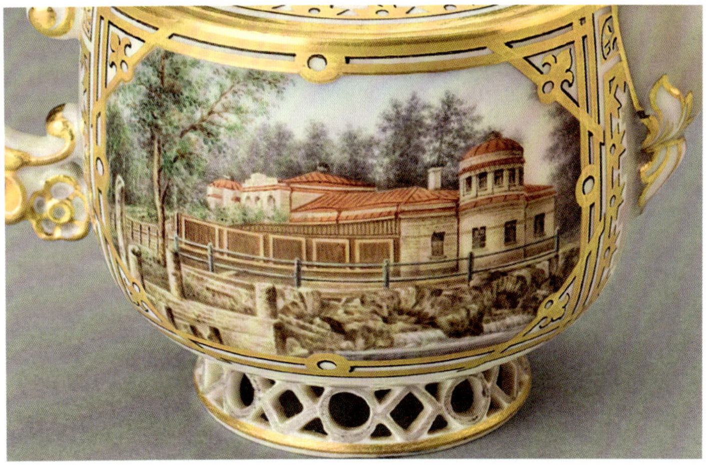
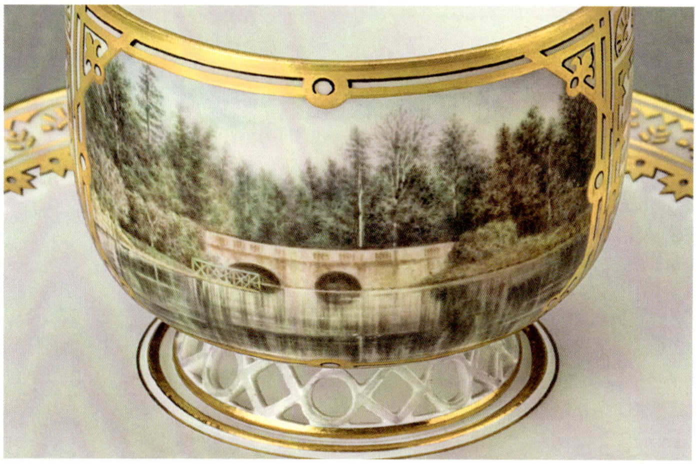
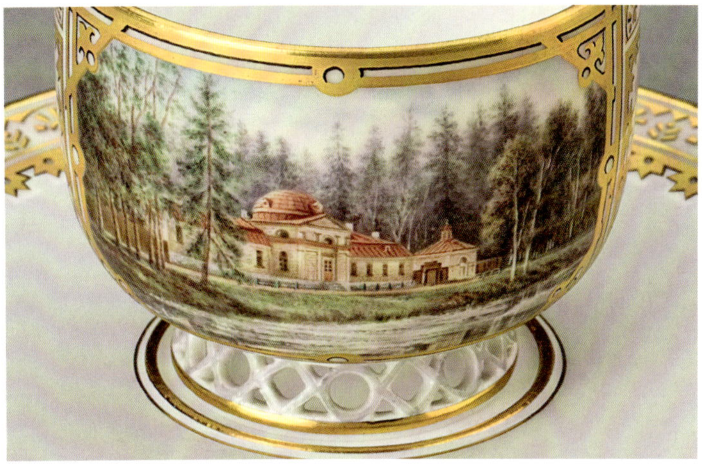
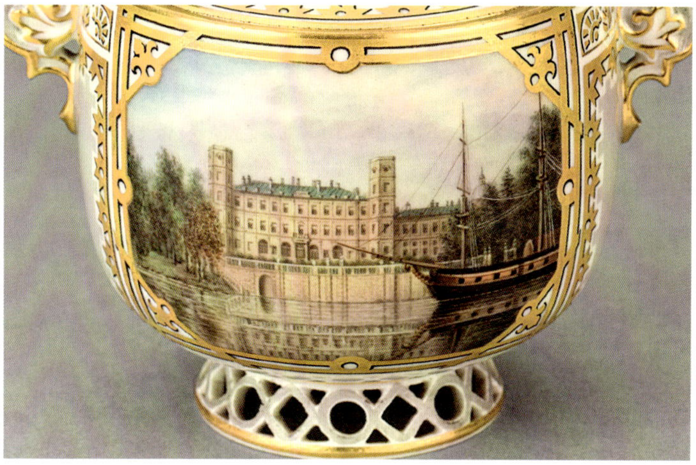
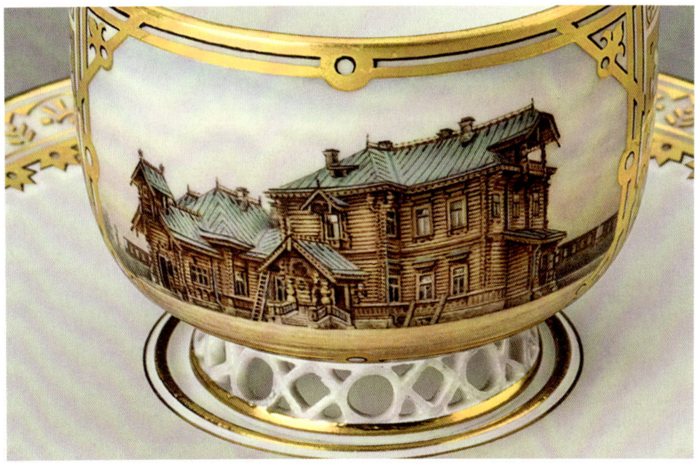
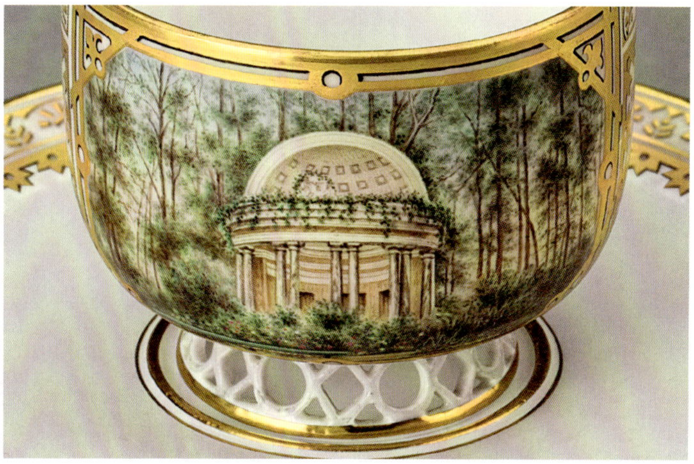

Russians and the Riviera during the reign of Alexander II

Wilfried Zeisler

Grand Duke Nicholas Alexandrovich (1843–1865), son of Czar Alexander II, in the uniform of the Hussar Regiment of the Imperial Guard
1868
Georg Botman
Tsarskoye Selo Palace Museum, Pouchkine

Grand Duke Alexander Alexandrovich (1845–1894), son of Czar Alexander II and future Alexander III, in the uniform of the Imperial Guard
1867
Sergei Zarianko (1818–1871)
Tsarskoye Selo Palace Museum, Pouchkine

"Nice, at that time, comprised a colony from abroad that represented the cream of European high society—sovereigns, princes of blood, millionaires, and the great and the good of all nations. The location was enchanting and, further heightening its prestige, the empress of Russia and her house afforded the foreign colony a touch of class." Philippe Palasi

Before a more direct railway line on which ran what some called the "train of the grand dukes" entered service, Empress Alexandra Feodorovna would arrive from Italy by sea. She took quarters in Nice during the winters of 1856–57 and 1859–60, seeking out the climate that had so delighted her in the Crimea, that future "Russian Riviera" whose cachet she had assured. First staying at the Villa Avigdor with a retinue of 102, she then moved into the Villa De Orestis. Although accompanied or joined later by her children and members of the Russian court—such as Grand Duchess Elena Pavlovna,

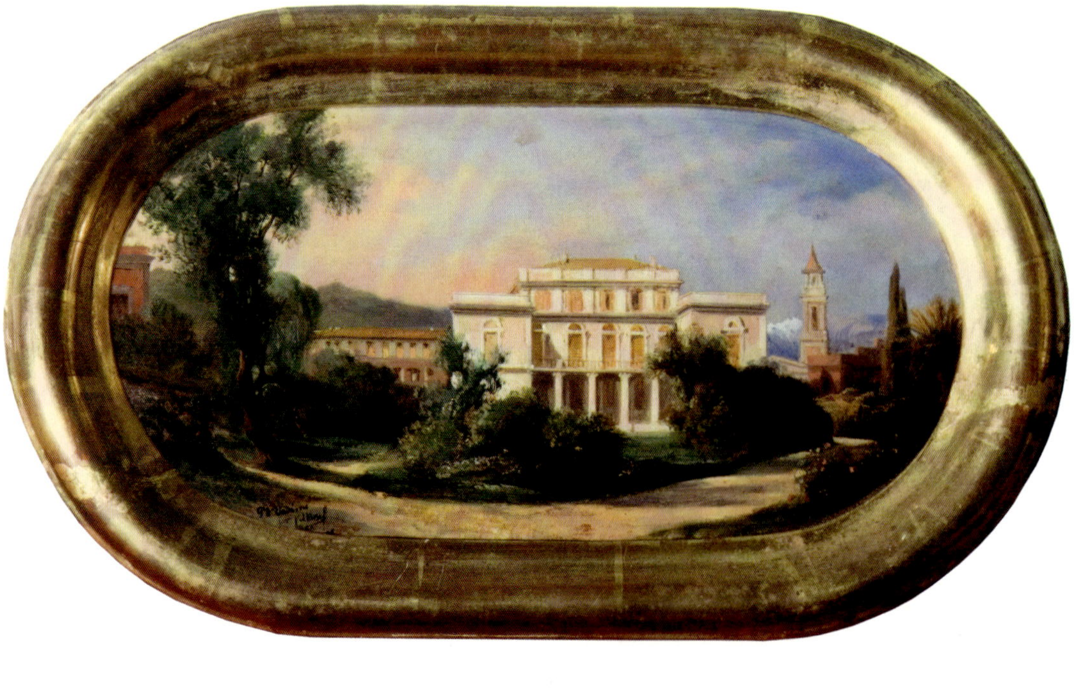

Villa Orestis on the Promenade des Anglais in Nice where the Empress Maria Alexandrovna Stayed in 1857 and 1859–60, Followed by Queen Isabella II of Spain in 1882
1853
Musée d'Art et d'Histoire, Palais Masséna, Nice

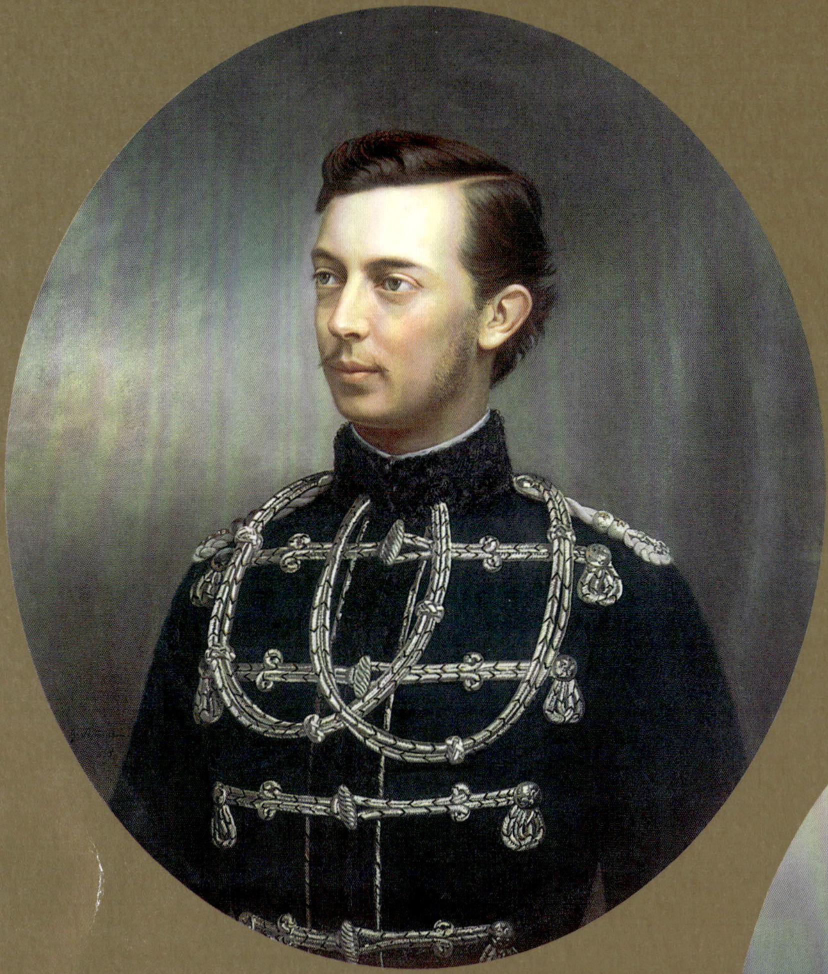

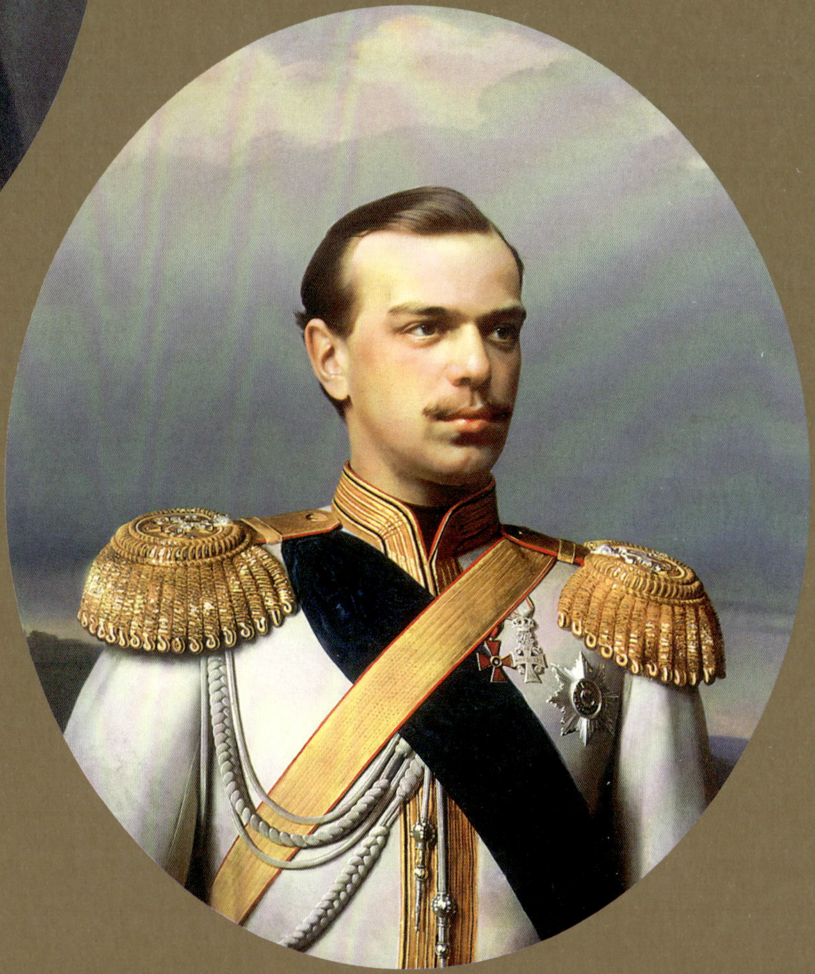

born Princess Charlotte of Württemberg (1807–1873), *habitué* of the coast who was at the time known as the "Juno of the North" or Grand Duke Constantine (1827–1892)—the holidaying sovereign would not neglect more official obligations. In 1857 she received King Vittorio Emanuele of Italy for luncheon, while Grand Duchess Elena Pavlovna (resident of the Villa Bermond) threw a dinner for forty in her honor, together with an open-air dance.

That same year, the empress offered her backing to the foundation of the first Russian church in Nice, whose inauguration in 1860 heralded the sprouting of many a colorful onion dome up and down the coast. When the city had been attached to France, and while the two great nations were trying to stabilize their relations, Emperor Napoleon III and Empress Eugénie met Alexandra Feodorovna on their way back to Paris (June 1, 1860).

Thus, during such sojourns diplomacy, politics, and leisure proved closely intertwined. In October 1864, when Alexander II was staying in the Villa Peillon with his family, a discussion with Napoleon III was organized and followed by a dinner. After the emperor departed, Maria Alexandrovna remained on in Nice with her eldest son, Czarevitch Nicholas (1843–1865), whose brilliant education and broadmindedness had made him "the hope of Russia." He was hoping to benefit from the Mediterranean climate to recover from a riding accident that had probably been poorly treated—the origin perhaps of the bone tuberculosis that carried him off in 1865. On his death, the emperor and his family hurried over, including the new heir, Grand Duke Alexander (1845–1894), the future Alexander III, and his brother's betrothed, Princess Dagmar of Denmark (1847–1928), his future wife, Maria Feodorovna.

The Riviera and the city of Nice, where the emperor erected a commemorative chapel on the site of the villa in which his son had passed away, thus sealed the political fate of the empire. It also partially explains the special place the French Riviera occupied in the hearts of Russians of all classes, from the empress to poets such as Fyodor Tyutchev (1803–1873): "Nice! That sea! That midday sun! / Oh! How their splendor moves me! / Like a wounded bird, life / Wishes to leave this earth but cannot / She has no élan, no zest, / Her two wings hang broken; / She trembles, bolted to the ground, / Of a restless hue" (1864).

The imperial presence inevitably made a profound impression on the local population. By September 1864, even before the empress accompanied by the emperor, traveling incognito, had arrived, the grand marshal of the palace had to arrange everything for their stay in the Villa Peillon and its 15-hectare park. Quarters for a retinue of fifty-four people had to be unearthed and a substantial body of personnel had to be recruited from the vicinity who, after each imperial visit, would receive, in addition to their wages, numerous gifts—as did the local worthies. There is much evidence of the manna these repeated stays would rain down on the regional economy. In 1857 one Nice tradesman pleaded for authorization to post an imperial eagle in his shop window, while from 1865 several businesses in the district (sculptor, marquetry maker, baker, grocer, olive-oil manufacturer, dressmaker, milliner) began to display endorsements as suppliers "by appointment" to the court. The Paris luxury trade also reaped the benefit of rich Russians stopping off on the way to the Riviera. In 1859 Empress Alexandra, followed in 1864 by Empress Maria Alexandrovna, for example, patronized the jeweler Mellerio *dits* Meller on rue de la Paix. In 1879–80, the empress, weakened by disease and mortified by the unwelcome presence of the emperor's mistress at court, placed an order with Boucheron on her way to Cannes on her last voyage to the Riviera. It was in addition precisely to attract such well-heeled tourists that Prince Charles III of Monaco (1818–1889) laid out the city of Monte-Carlo, commissioning François Blanc to develop the Société des Bains de Mer, the famous casino, and the Hôtel de Paris.

On the death of Alexander II, his widow, now Princess Yurovsky, and her legitimate children settled in France, where the children of Maria Alexandrovna and their families were already habitués. It was these grand dukes and grand duchesses, heirs to the fashion launched by their parents, who set an imperial seal on Riviera chic during the Belle Époque.

Inspired by such figures, and by the hive of activity that surrounded their arrival in the city, Jean Lorrain's 1862 novel *Les Noronsoff* tells of an imaginary family settling into Nice when an uncle of the last of the line acquires an opulent villa. With a touch of exaggeration, the writer plunges the reader into a spiral of outlandish luxury: "A legion of Parisian tapestry-makers and a cloud of Italian workmen, mosaicists from Turin and sculptors from Genoa, heralded

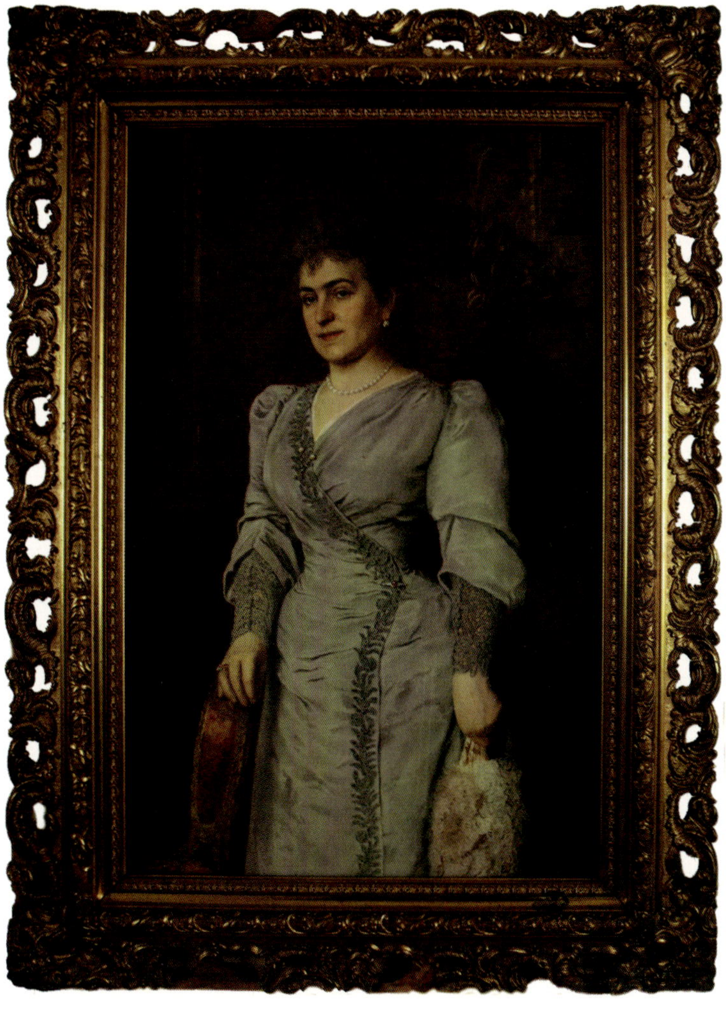

Princess Ekaterina Mikhailovna, née Princess Dolgorukova, known as Katia (1847-1922), Second Wife of Czar Alexander II
c. 1890
STEPHAN FEDOROVICH ALEXANDROVSKI (1842–1906)
Palace Museum, Pavlovsk

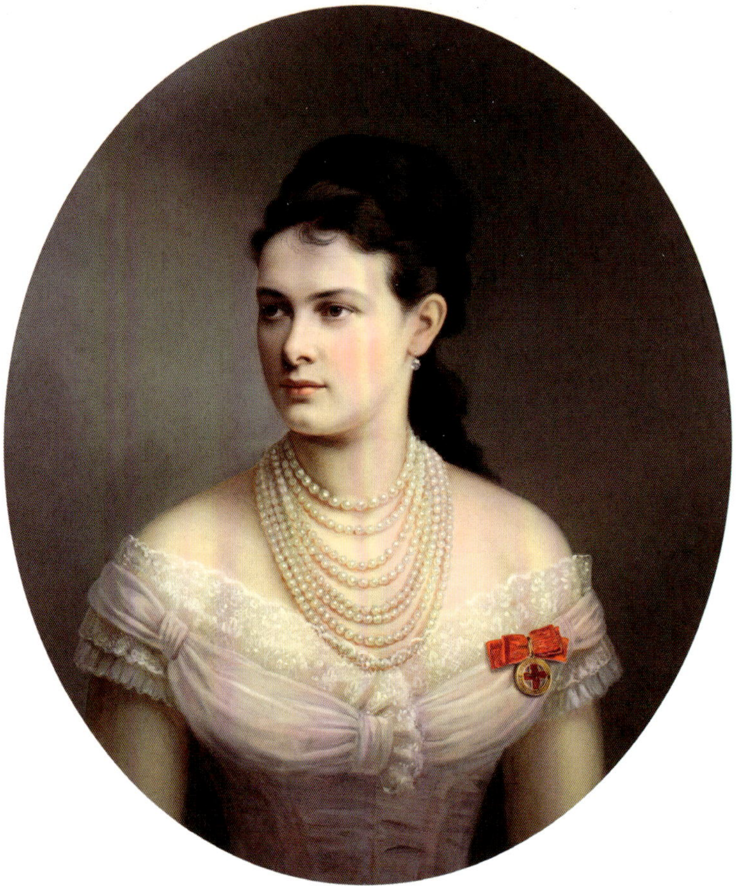

Grand Duchess Maria Pavlovna (1854–1920), née Marie of Mecklenburg-Schwerin, Wife of Grand Duke Vladimir Alexandrovich, Daughter-in-law of Alexander II
Last quarter of the nineteenth century
Palace Museum, Gatchina

the master's homecoming; the memory of the ostentation and luxury deployed by earlier denizens was to pale into insignificance before the sophistication and refinement of the décor and furniture of the new owner. The only subject of conversation thereabouts was a swimming pool dug in the villa's onetime billiard room and a red porphyry pool embedded in pink marble flagstones where the long-awaited Noronsoff would bathe. . . . There was talk, too, of a trelliswork cabinet in gilt tracery all bedecked in Vieux Saxe flowers the like of which neither Chantilly nor Versailles ever knew, an exquisite and mannered folly in the Louis XV style, like those one sees in Munich and Potsdam." The novel does however allude to some recognizable aspects of Nice and the Riviera of the period: "(...) people only went into town to do their shopping; the landau parked for hours in front of the jewelers on quai Saint-Jean-Baptiste and quai Masséna, lengthy conversations in the shopfronts of Morgan's and Lacloche's. (...)"

Grand Duchess Elena Pavlovna (1806–1873), née Friederike Charlotte Marie of Württemberg, Wife of Grand Duke Michael Pavlovich, Aunt of Alexander II
After 1862
After Franz Xaver Winterhalter (1805–1873)
Palace Museum, Pavlovsk

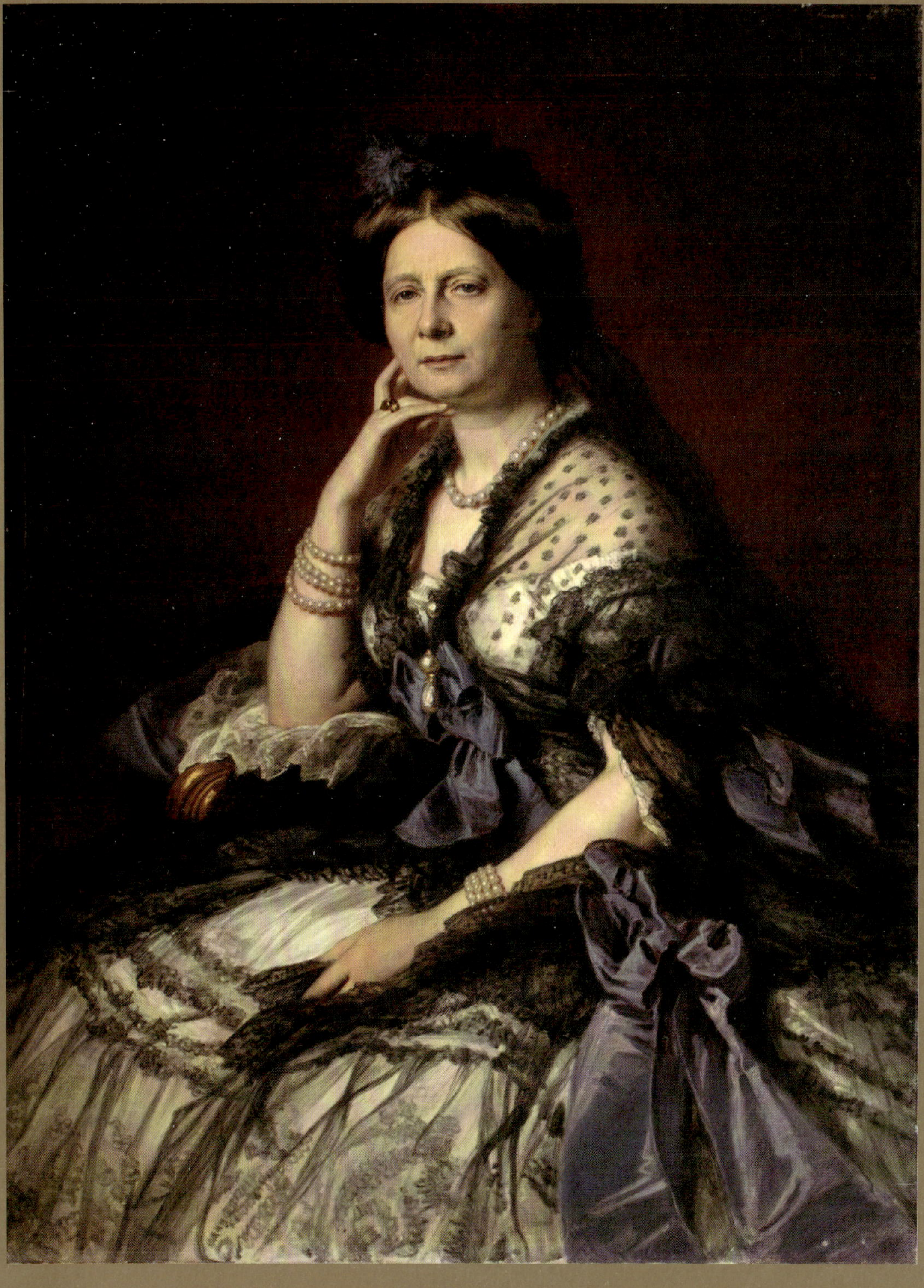

Emperor Alexander II and the official summer residence at Tsarskoye Selo

Ludmila Kanaeva

Come summertime, the imperial court of Russia, one of nineteenth-century Europe's most dazzling, would set off from St. Petersburg and follow Emperor Alexander II to the suburban imperial residence of Tsarskoye Selo, not far from the capital of the empire. There, from early in the eighteenth century, an imposing group of palaces and parks had sprung up, including the Great Palace of Tsarskoye Selo (since renamed the Catherine Palace), built between 1752 and 1756 by the city's architect, Bartolomeo Rastrelli, and the Alexander Palace, built between 1792 and 1796 to plans by Giacomo Quarenghi.

The exalted owners of the residence had amassed a remarkable collection of paintings and decorative art. Comprising works by European, Oriental, and Russian masters, it reflected the tastes of successive emperors and the imper-ial family. Empress Maria Alexandrovna (Maximilienne-Wilhelmine-Augusta-Sophie-Marie, princess of Hesse-Darmstadt until her conversion to Orthodoxy), who adored Tsarskoye Selo as much as her imperial husband, also had a passion for lapis lazuli. One of the most sumptuous ceremonial interiors in the whole Great Palace, the so-called "Lyon" drawing room, thus boasts furniture and chandeliers adorned with the semiprecious stone set off with gilded bronze. Created in the early 1860s to designs by the architect Ippolito Monighetti (1819–1878), immediately after their installation they acquired a reputation for being parti-cularly exquisite and precious.

From the middle of spring until late fall, life at the imperial court centered on the residence of Tsarskoye Selo, which became the venue for a whirl of balls, masquerades, receptions, audiences, and military parades. From his accession in 1855, the life Alexander II led at Tsarskoye Selo was similar to that in St. Petersburg, and saw him taking note of ministerial reports, convening conferences, instigating political decisions, and signing urgent documents of state. Tsarskoye Selo, however, was not just another official imperial residence; it was also a home that witnessed many key events in the imperial family's life, happy and unhappy. It was there that the elder son of Alexander II, Grand Duke Nicholas Alexandrovich (1843–1865), was born. It was also at Tsarskoye Selo that Nicholas Alexandrovich spent the crucial few days before the first significant act of his official existence: the swearing of the military oath and the oaths of state. It was the custom that sons of the imperial family, on the day they attained their majority at sixteen, would take an oath to faithfully serve the czar and the motherland. Thus, on September 8, 1859, in the Winter Palace in St. Petersburg, in the presence of Emperor Alexander II, Empress Maria Alexandrovna, grand dukes and grand

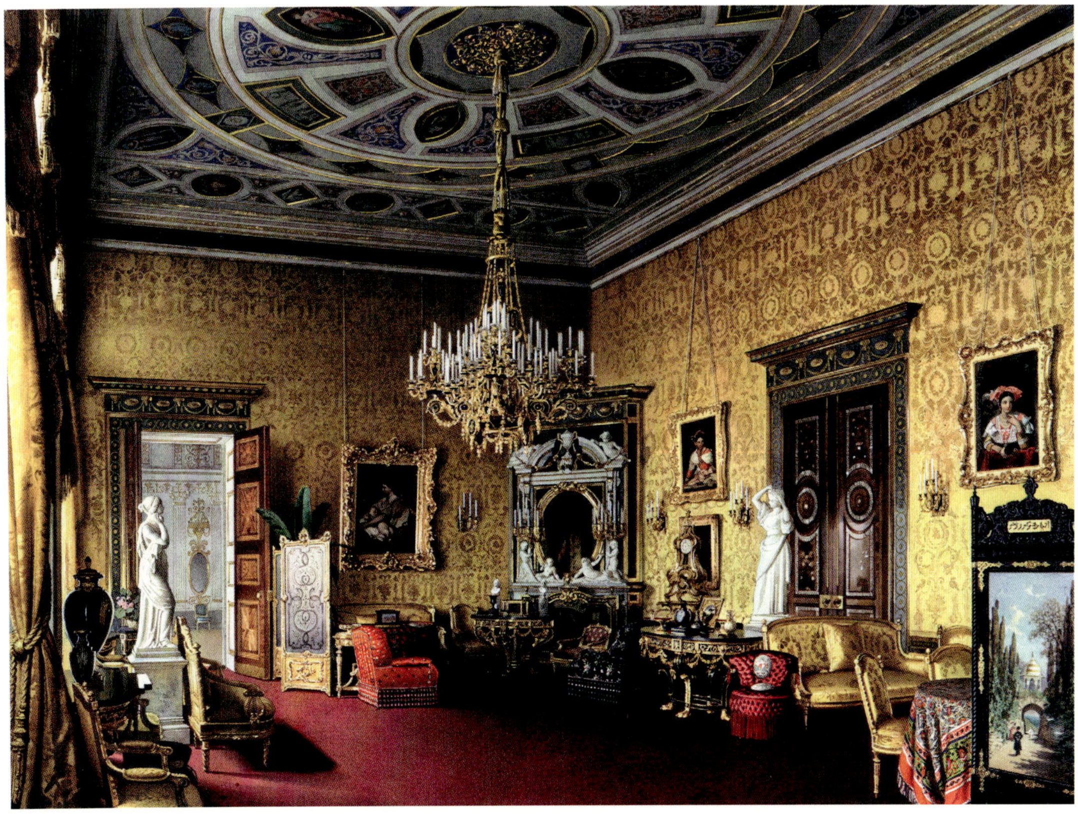

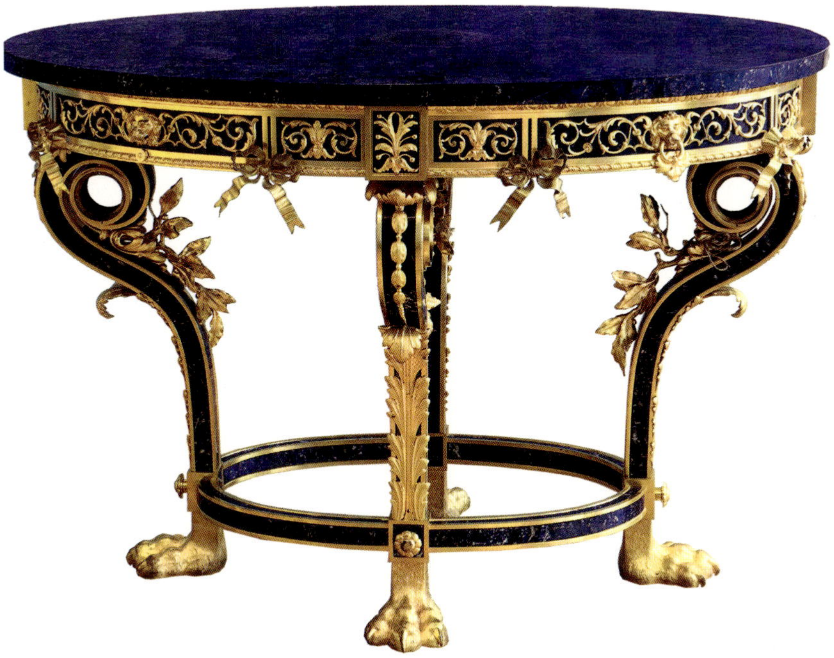

Vue of the Lyon salon decorated in Lyon silk at the Tsarskoye Selo Palace with its lapis-lazuli furnishings, created c. 1860
Tsarskoye Selo Palace Museum, Pouchkine

Table included in the lapis-lazuli furnishings, based on Ippolito Monighetti's models, ca 1860, Peterhof hard-stone cutting workshops
Tsarskoye Selo Palace Museum, Pouchkine

duchesses, the upper echelons of the civil service, the court, and the diplomatic corps, Nicholas Alexandrovich duly swore the civilian oath in the Great Church, followed by the military oath in the Hall of St. George, near the throne and beneath the colors of the Ataman regiment that bore his name. The solemn service of the oath by the heir to the throne was an event of utmost significance for the nation. To immortalize it, Alexander II commissioned a huge canvas, completed in 1861, from court artist Gottfried Willewalde. In 1867, fulfilling a second order from His Majesty, Willewalde painted another picture on the same subject, showing Alexander II's next son, Grand Duke Alexander Alexandrovich (1845–1894), swearing the oath. For many years, this pair of pictures recalling two important pages in the history of nineteenth-century Russia hung on the walls in the Great Palace at Tsarskoye Selo.

Plant holders with support (from a pair)
c. 1860
Peterhof Imperial Gem Cutters
English Store, Saint Petersburg
Tsarskoye Selo Palace Museum, Pouchkine

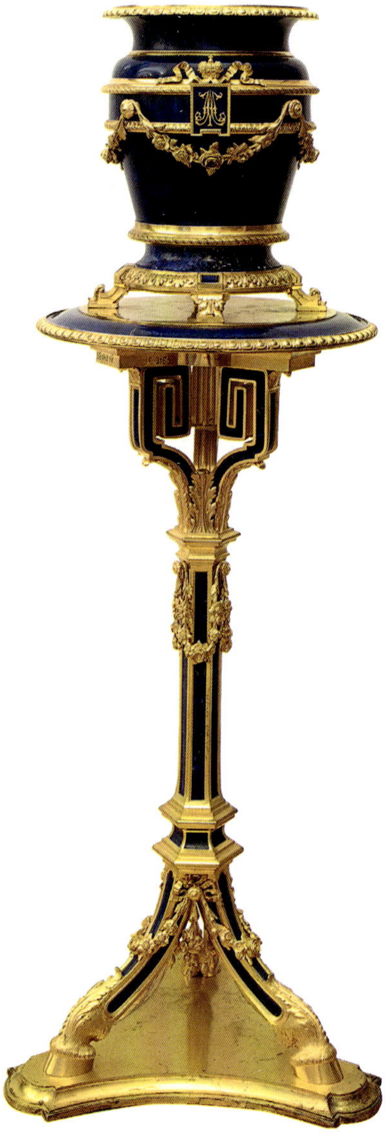

On June 12, 1864, the heir to the throne, Czarevitch Nicholas Alexandrovich, left Tsarskoye Selo to travel abroad. In the spring of 1865, the emperor received news from Nice that his son was afflicted with an incurable disease and hurried to his bedside. On April 12, 1865, in the presence of Alexander II, Empress Maria Alexandrovna, Grand Duke Alexander Alexandrovich, and the fancée of the heir to the throne, the Danish princess Marie Sophie Frederikke Dagmar (1847–1928; in 1866, she will maried Alexander Alexandrovitch, renamed Maria Feodorovna after her conversion to Orthodoxy and empress in 1881), Grand Duke Nicholas Alexandrovich expired in the Villa Bermond in Nice. Alexander II returned to Tsarskoye Selo to live out the dark days of mourning preceding his son's funeral in the Cathedral of Saints Peter and Paul in the Fortress at St. Petersburg.

By April 1868, Alexander II had been commander of the Hussar Regiment of the Imperial Guard for fifty years, and festivals for the jubilee were celebrated in Tsarskoye Selo. Alexander II had inherited his love of the army, and more generally for all things military, from his father Emperor Nicholas I. He would never miss a regimental function and attended exercises, march-pasts, and parades. He was head of many other regiments, but leading the Hussar Regiment of the Imperial Guard had acquired particular significance in his eyes.

As Emperor Alexander I had been appointed to command the regiment on April 27, 1818, when he was but ten days old, the emperor's fiftieth birthday thus necessarily coincided with

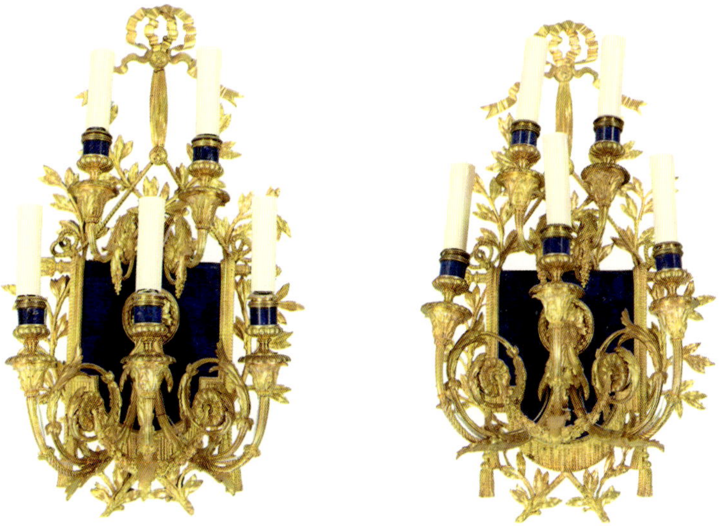

Two "appliques de lumière" from a series of eight
c. 1860
Peterhof Imperial Gem Cutters
Ippolito Monighetti (1819–1878)
Tsarskoye Selo Palace Museum, Pouchkine

half a century at the head of the regiment. While Alexander II celebrated his birthday with his family, the military jubilee was the occasion for two days of festivities at Tsarskoye Selo, the site of the regimental headquarters.

It was once again at Tsarskoye Selo on July 6, 1880, that Alexander II was married secretly for a second time, to Princess Ekaterina Mikhailovna Dolgorukaya (1847–1922), before a temporary shrine set up for the purpose in one of the apartments of the Great Palace. This proved to be Alexander's final significant act in the imperial summer residence at Tsarskoye Selo. On March 1, 1881, he was mortally wounded by shrapnel from a terrorist bomb in St. Petersburg.

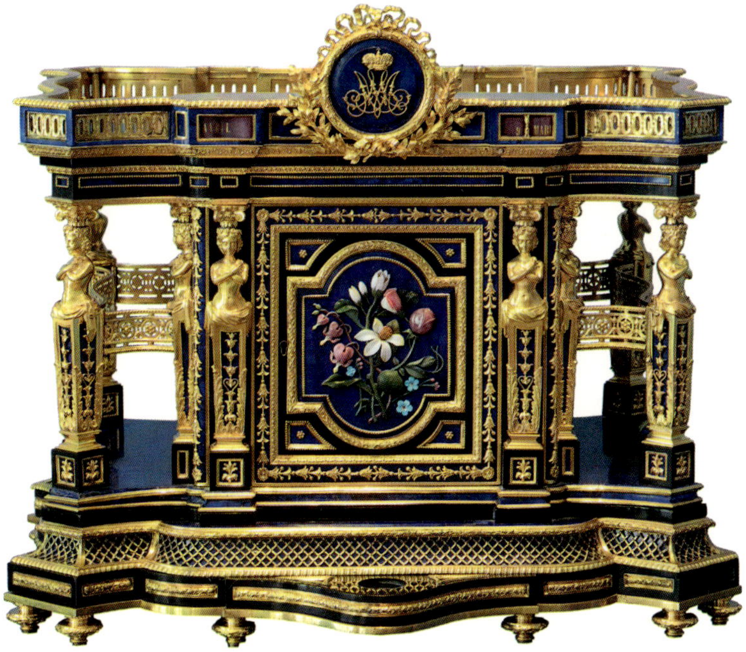

Cabinet with the monogram of Empress Maria Alexandrovna
1861
Peterhof Imperial Gem Cutters, English Store in Saint Petersburg
Tsarskoye Selo Palace Museum, Pouchkine

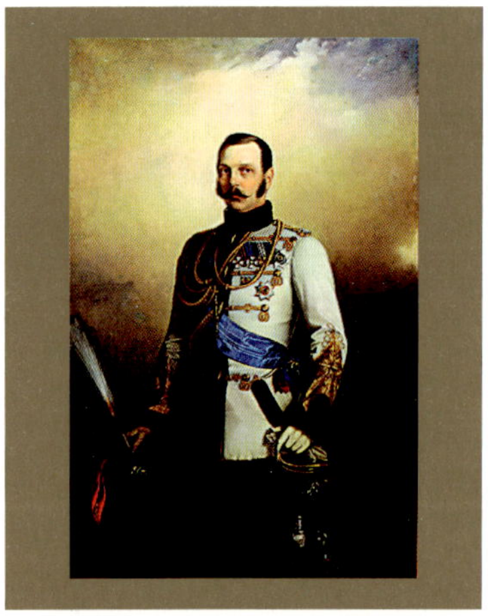

Czar Alexander II (1818–1881) in the uniform of the Hussar Regiment of the Imperial Guard
1860
Nikolai A. Lavrov (1820–1875)
Oil on canvas
181.8 × 115 cm
Tsarskoye Selo Palace Museum, Pouchkine
Inv. ED-639-X, KP-19713

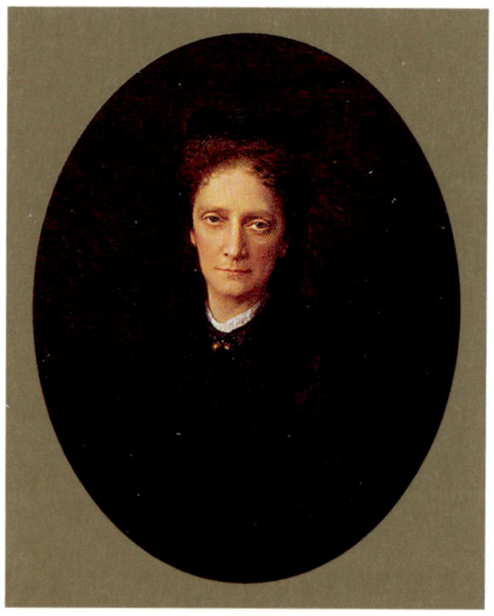

Empress Maria Alexandrovna (1805–1873)
1877
Ivan Kramskoi (1837–1887)
Oil on canvas
80 × 66 cm
Palace Museum, Gatchina
Inv. GDM-118-III, KP-2289

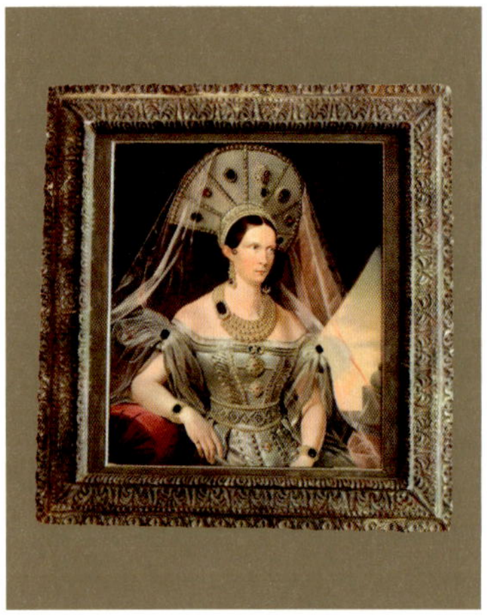

Empress Alexandra Feodorovna (1798–1860), Mother of Czar Alexander II, in Russian Costume
After 1834
P. Hesse
Oil on canvas
96 × 80 cm
Tsarskoye Selo Palace Museum, Pouchkine
Inv. ED-1206-X, KP-29441

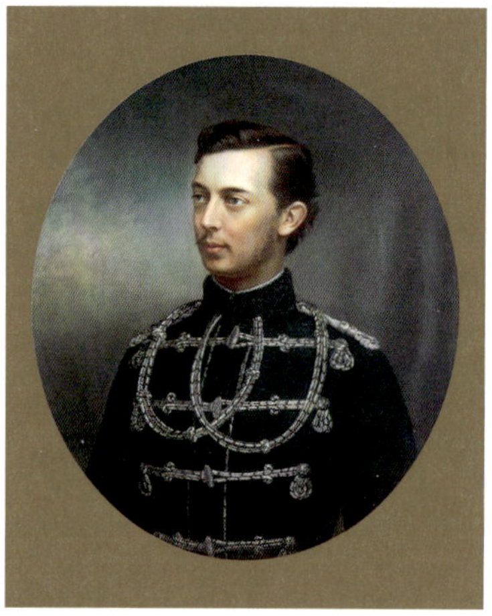

Grand Duke Nicholas Alexandrovich (1843–1865), Son of Czar Alexander II in the winter uniform of the imperial guards' hussar regiment
1868
Georg Botmann
Oil on canvas
83.9 × 69.8 cm
Tsarskoye Selo Palace Museum, Pouchkine
Inv. ED-651-X, KP-19725

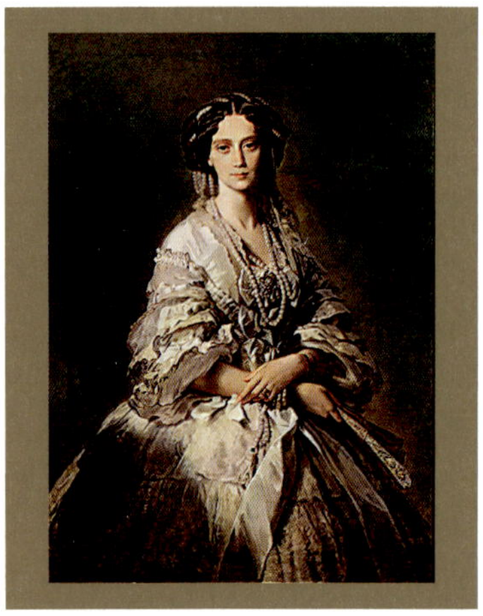

Empress Maria Alexandrovna (1853–1920), Wife of Czar Alexander II
After 1857
After Franz Xaver Winterhalter (1805–1873)
Oil on canvas
129 × 93.5 cm
Palace Museum, Gatchina
Inv. GDM-436-III, KP-7783

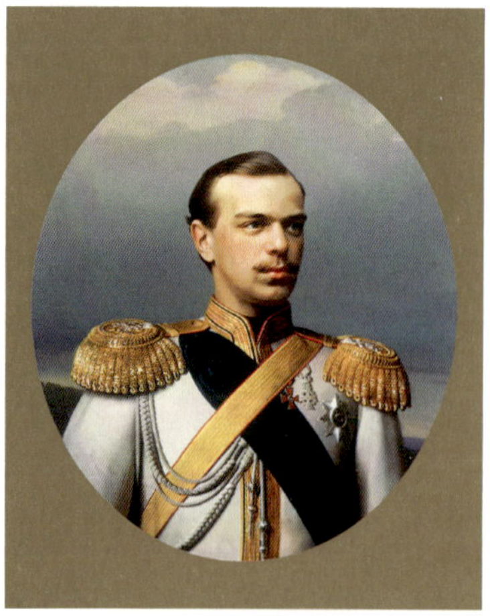

Grand Duke Alexander Alexandrovich (1845–1894), Son of Czar Alexander II and the Future Alexander III in the uniform of the imperial guards' regiment
1867
Sergei Zarianko (1818–1871)
Oil on canvas
82 × 75 cm
Tsarskoye Selo Palace Museum, Pouchkine
Inv. ED-337-X, KP-18395

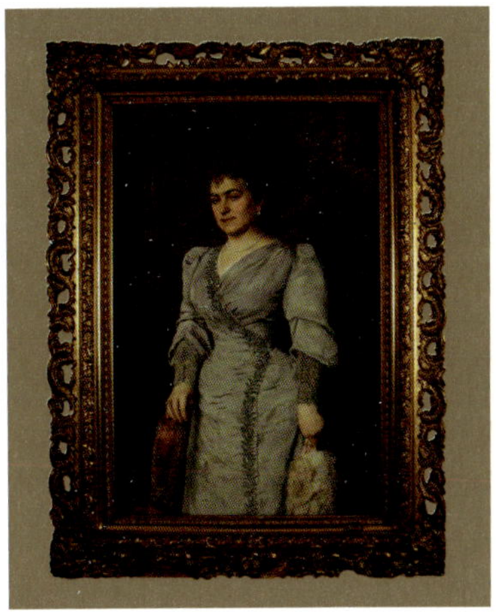

Princess Ekaterina Mikhailovna, née Princess Dolgorukova, known as Katia (1847-1922), Second Wife of Czar Alexander II
c. 1890
STEPHAN FEDOROVICH ALEXANDROVSKI
(1842–1906)
Watercolor, pastel; paper pasted on cardboard
86.7 × 55.4 cm
Palace Museum, Pavlovsk
Inv. TsKh-2960-XI

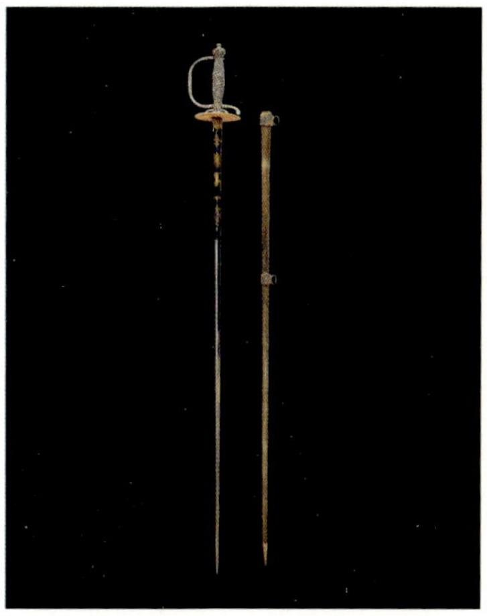

Ceremonial sword belonging to Alexander II
1880
Steel
Palais Princier, Monaco
Inv. MU000988

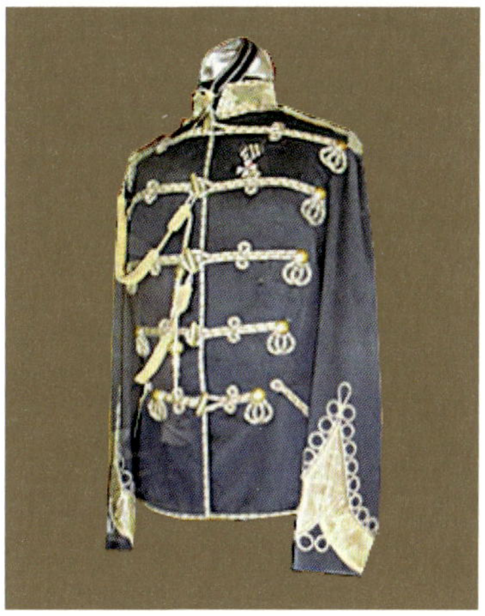

Uniform of Czar Alexander II bearing the Prussian merit award, known as the "Blauer Max"
Blue wool and gold thread braid
85 × 50 × 35 cm
Paroisse Saint-Nicolas, Nice
Inv. 42

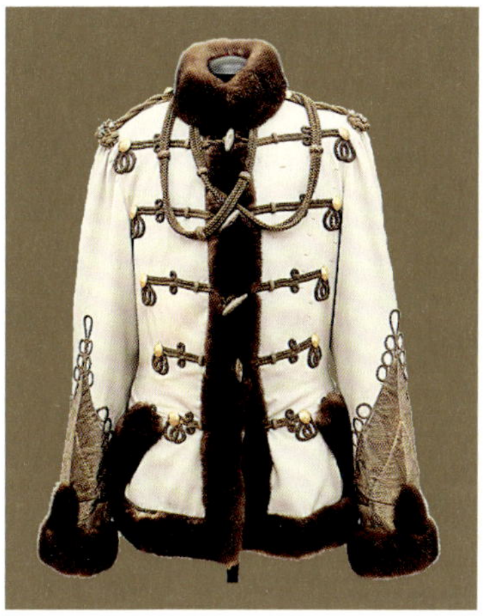

Pelisse of the imperial guards' hussar regiment
c. 1870
Wool, silk, Kamchatka beaver fur, and gold lace
70 × 43 cm
Tsarskoye Selo Palace Museum, Pouchkine
Inv. ED-197-II, ED-198-II

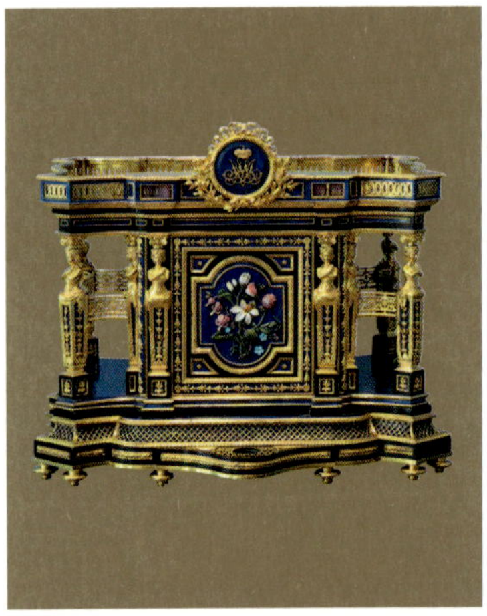

Cabinet with the monogram of Empress Maria Alexandrovna (1853–1920)
1861
Peterhof Imperial Gem Cutters,
English Store in Saint Petersburg
Lapis lazuli, jasper, opal, turquoise, marble, rhodonite, velvet, silk, gilded bronze
41.5 × 47.5 × 39 cm
Tsarskoye Selo Palace Museum, Pouchkine
Inv. ED-159-IV

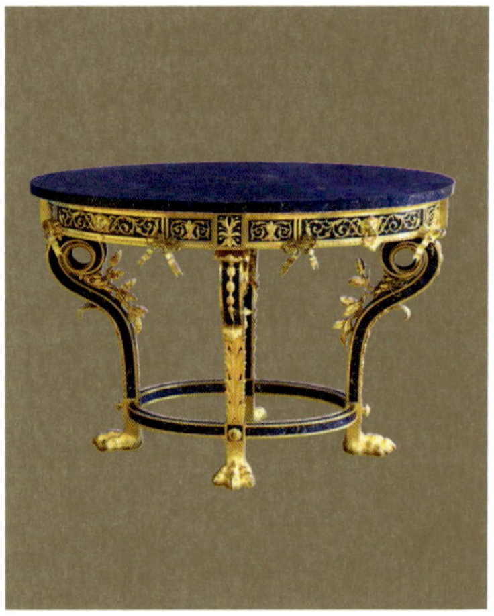

Pair of oval tables
c. 1856
Ippolito Monighetti (1819–1878)
Peterhof Imperial Gem Cutters,
English Store in Saint Petersburg
Lapis lazuli, gilded bronze
123.5 × 85.5 × 84.5 cm
Tsarskoye Selo Palace Museum, Pouchkine
Inv. ED-136-IV et ED-137-IV

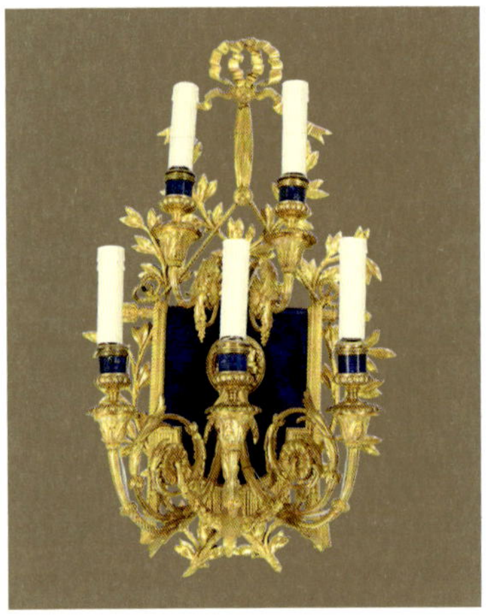

Two "appliques de lumière" from a series of eight
c. 1860
Ippolito Monighetti (1819–1878) (?)
Peterhof Imperial Gem Cutters,
English Store in Saint Petersburg
Lapis lazuli, gilded bronze
59 × 34 cm
Tsarskoye Selo Palace Museum, Pouchkine
Inv. ED-150-IV, KII-8756
and ED-158-IV, KII-8760

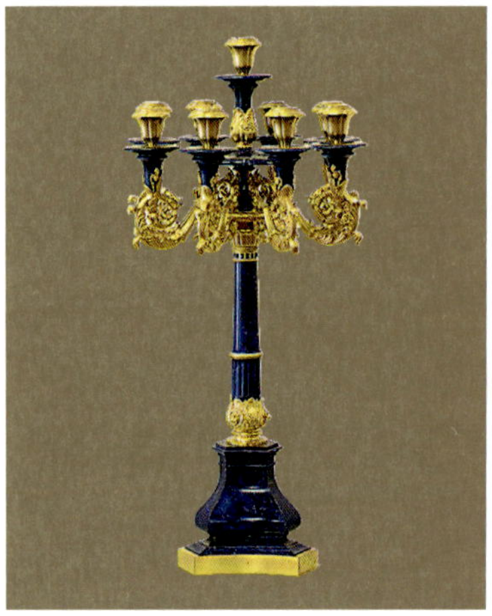

Pair of candelabras
c. 1860-1870, Saint Petersburg
Peterhof Imperial Gem Cutters,
English Store in Saint Petersburg
Lapis lazuli, gilded bronze
84 × 40 × 40 cm
Tsarskoye Selo Palace Museum
Inv. ED-1a46-IV, KII-8742
and ED-147-IV, KII-8743

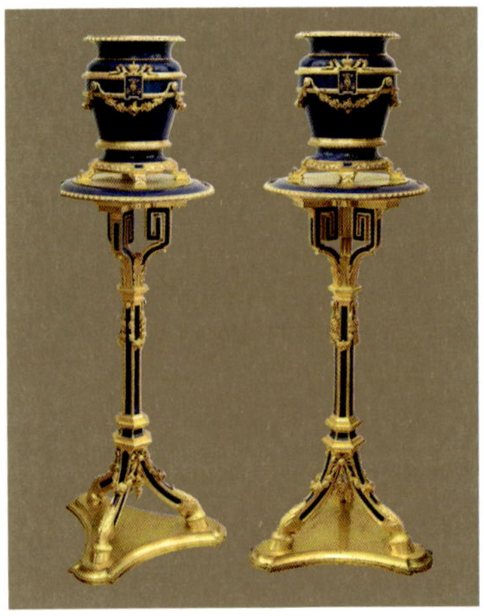

Pair of plant holders with supports
c. 1860
Peterhof Imperial Gem Cutters,
English Store in Saint Petersburg
Lapis lazuli, gilded bronze
133 × 40 × 40 cm
Tsarskoye Selo Palace Museum, Pouchkine
Inv. ED-142/1-IV KP-8748/1,
ED-142/2-IV, KP-8748/2,
ED-143/1-IV, KP-8749/1,
ED-143/2-IV, KP-8749/2

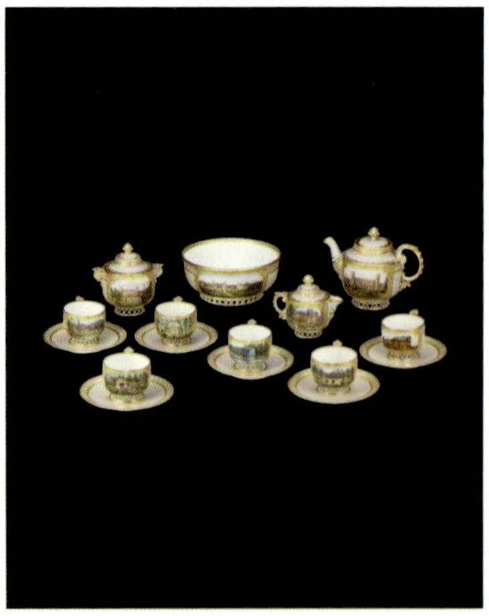

Tea service with views of the Gatchina Palace and grounds
1860–70, Saint Petersburg Imperial Manufactory, Porcelain
Palace Museum, Gatchina
Six cups and saucers
Inv. GDM -38-I- KP -1906, -48-I- KP -1938, -50-I- KP -1940, -52-I- KP -1942, -39-I- KP -1910, -49-I- KP -1939, -51-I- KP -1942, -53-I- KP -1943, -46-I- KP -1936, -56-I- KP -1946, -47-I- KP -1937, -55-I- KP -1945
Teapot and cover
Inv. GDM -40-I- KP -1911/1-2
Cream pot and cover
Inv. GDM -41-I- KP -1912/1-2
Sugar bowl and cover
Inv. GDM -42-I- KP -1913/1-2

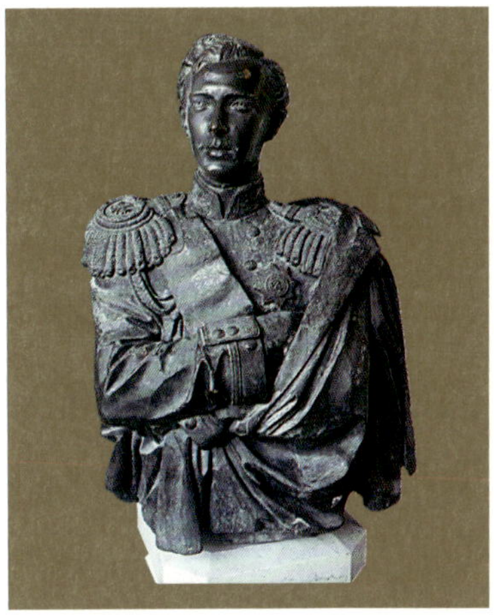

Grand Duke Nicholas Alexandrovich
c. 1870
Aleksandr Opekushin (1838–1923)
Bronze
93 × 60 × 50 cm
Tsarskoye Selo Palace Museum, Pouchkine
Inv. ED-34-VIII

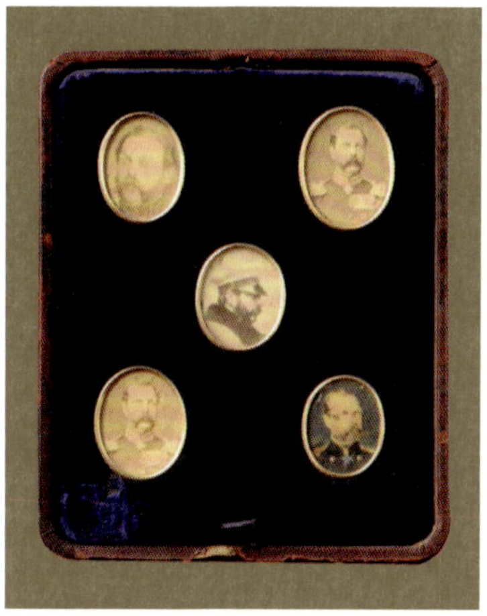

Five medallions representing photographic portraits of Czar Alexander II
12 × 15 cm
Paroisse Saint-Nicolas, Nice

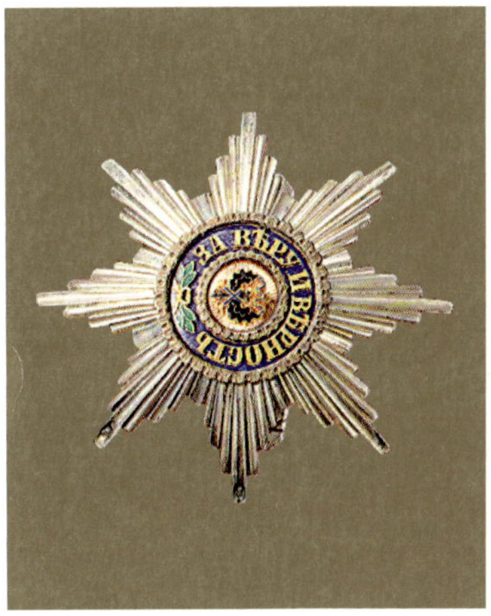

Star of the Order of Saint Andrew belonging to Alexandre II
Paroisse Saint-Nicolas, Nice

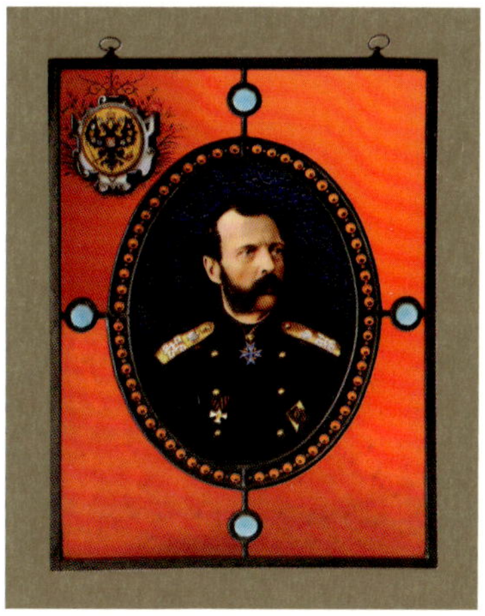

Czar Alexander II
c. 1870
Stained-glass window
Glass and lead
57 × 43 cm
Paroisse Saint-Nicolas, Nice
Inv. 39

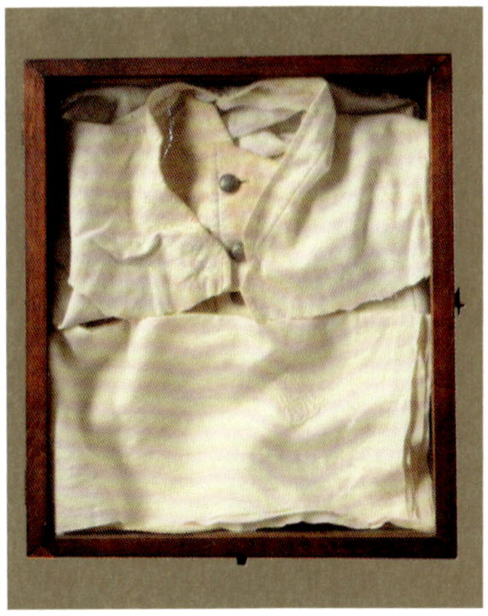

Shirt and waistcoat worn by Alexander II on the day of his assassination, 13 March 1881
5 × 35 × 32 and 5 × 37 × 29 cm
Paroisse Saint-Nicolas, Nice
Inv. 40-41

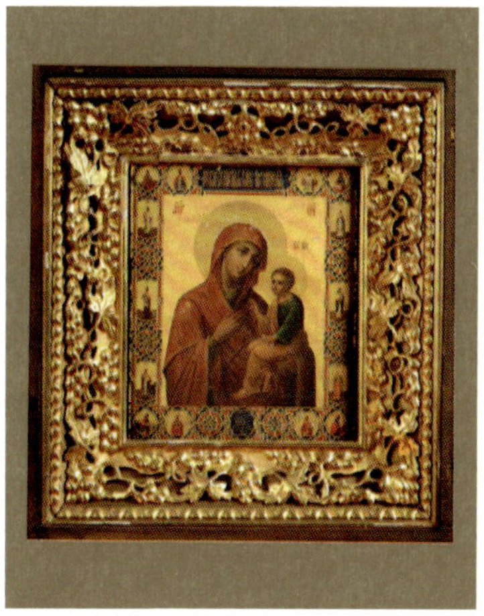

Icon offered by Empress Alexandra, mother of Alexander II, to celebrate the founding of the Russian cathedral in rue Longchamp, Nice, in 1860
Painting on wood; metal
68 × 61 cm (inc. frame)
Paroisse Saint-Nicolas, Nice
Inv. 6

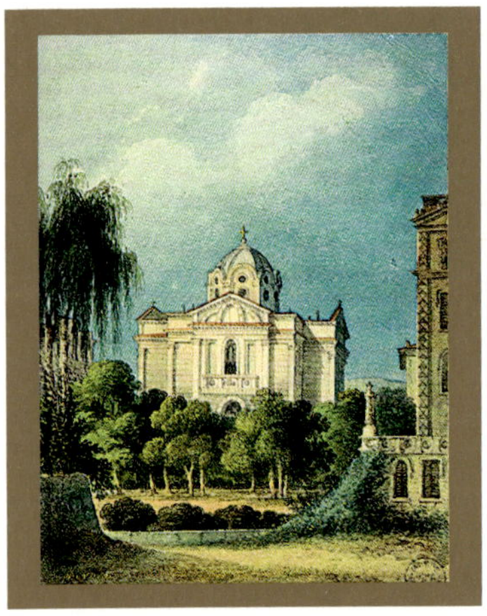

First Russian Church Commissioned by Czarina Alexandra Feodorovna, Inaugurated January 1859 in the Presence of Grand Duke Constantine and Grand Duchess Maria, Princess of Leuchtenberg, Rue Longchamp, Nice
1860
Carlo Meraga
Watercolor
28.5 × 22 cm
Musée d'Art et d'Histoire,
Palais Masséna, Nice
Inv. MAH-381

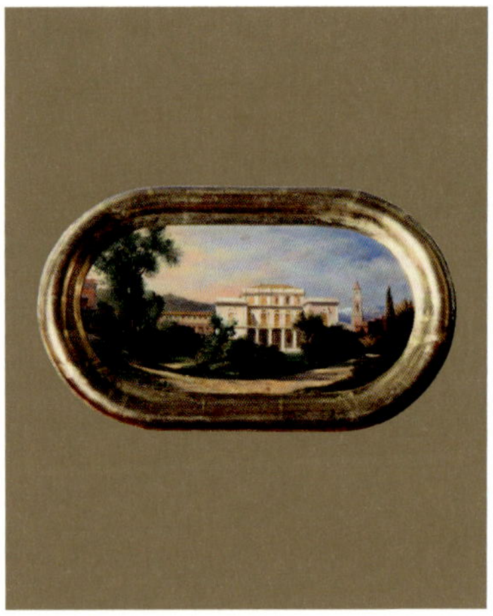

Villa Orestis on the Promenade des Anglais in Nice Where the Empress Maria Alexandrovna Stayed in 1857 and 1859–60, Followed by Queen Isabella II of Spain in 1882
1853
Oil on board
25 × 35 cm
Musée d'Art et d'Histoire,
Palais Masséna, Nice
Inv. MAH-9161

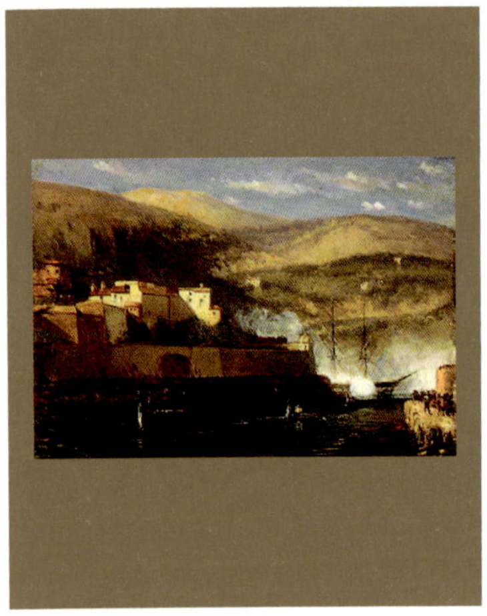

The Mortal Remains of Grand Duke Nicholas, Czar of Russia, Leave Villefranche-sur-Mer for Saint Petersburg, 1865
1865
Hendrick Leys (1815–1869)
Oil on canvas
55.5 × 69 cm
Musée d'Art et d'Histoire,
Palais Masséna, Nice
Inv. MAH-5930

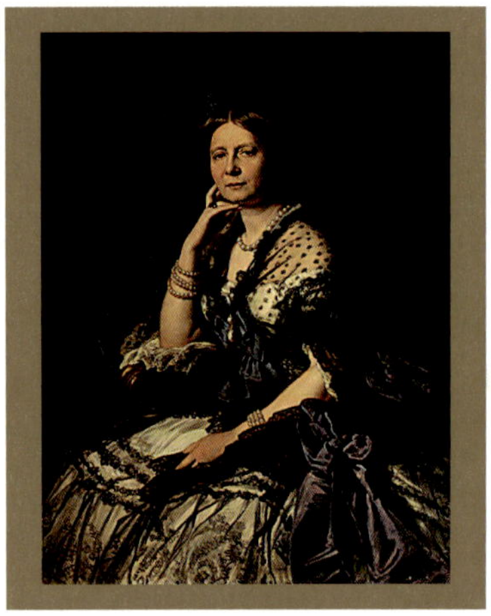

Grand Duchess Elena Pavlovna (1806–1873), née Friederike Charlotte Marie of Württemberg, Wife of Grand Duke Michael Pavlovich
After 1862
After Franz Xaver Winterhalter (1805–1873)
Oil on canvas
123.3 × 90.5 cm
Palace Museum, Pavlovsk
Inv. TsKh-2467-III

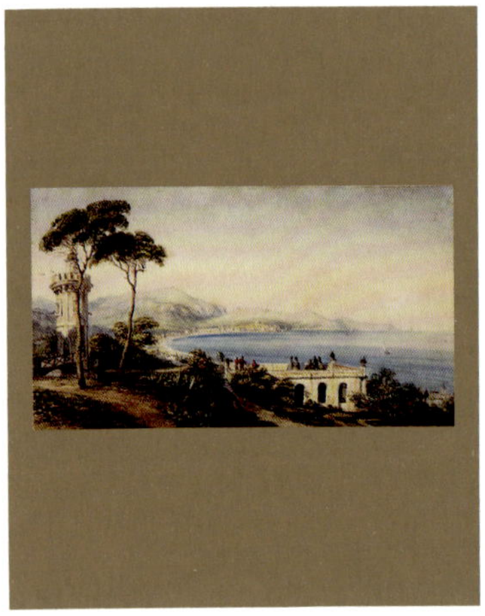

Empress Maria Alexandrovna Admiring the View from the Villa Gastaud, Sainte-Hélène District, Nice
1864
Hercule Trachel (1820–1872)
Watercolor
27.5 × 47.5 cm
Musée d'Art et d'Histoire,
Palais Masséna, Nice
Inv. MAH-10224

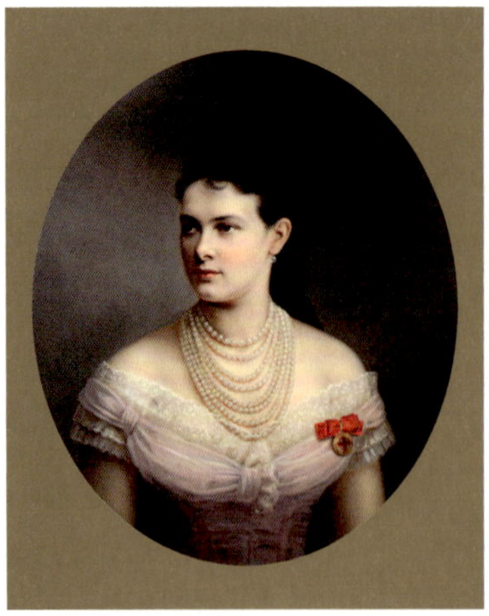

Grand Duchess Maria Pavlovna (1854–1920), née Marie of Mecklenburg-Schwerin, Wife of Grand Duke Vladimir Alexandrovich
Last quarter of the nineteenth century
Oil on canvas
75 × 62.5 cm
Palace Museum, Gatchina
Inv. GDM-455-III, KP-12436

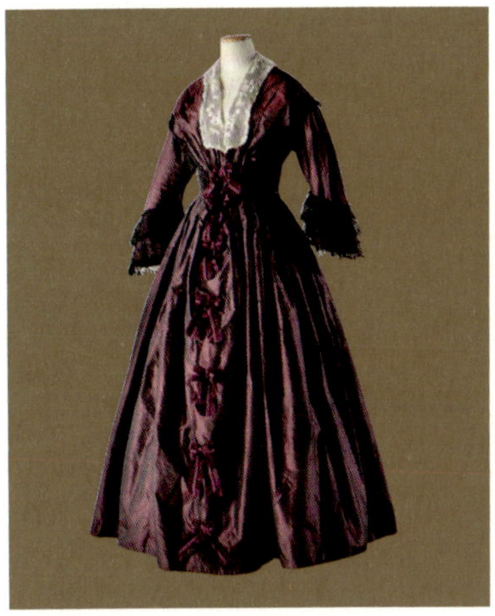

Afternoon gown
c. 1856
Russian (?)
Mauve taffeta; scarf-effect bodice with dual-flounced black lace pagoda sleeves; skirt on crinoline, seven double rosette knots on the front of the waist hem
Museo Daphné – Musée de la Mode et du Parfum, San Remo

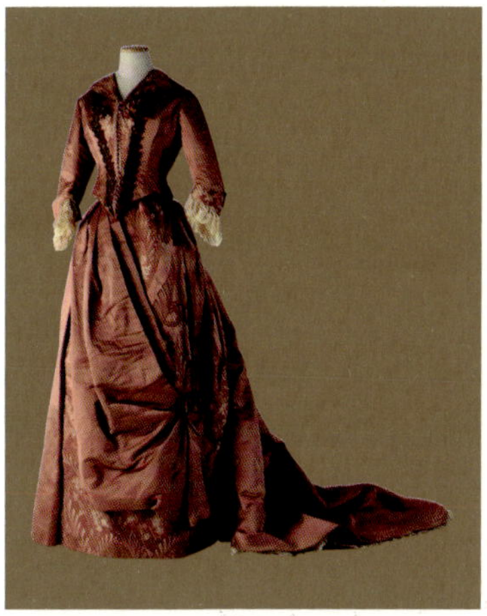

Gown and bustle from the wardrobe of Princess Obolensky
c. 1880
Mauve satin brocaded with floral patterns; whalebone bodice with three-quarter sleeves and cuffs; skirt with satin train, pinned with a satin rosette
Museo Daphné – Musée de la Mode et du Parfum, San Remo

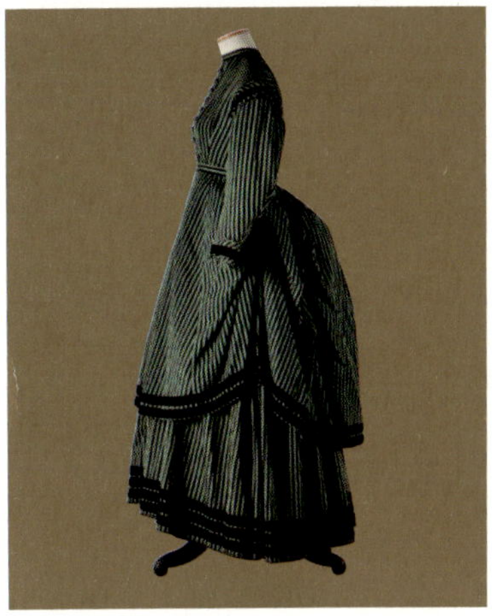

Promenade outfit
c. 1870
Three-piece gown of green and black striped wool; front-buttoning bodice forming a bunched up polonaise tunic behind; round skirt; shoulders and cuffs decorated with a black velvet ribbon, the polonaise with two ribbons and the skirt with three ribbons
Museo Daphné – Musée de la Mode et du Parfum, San Remo

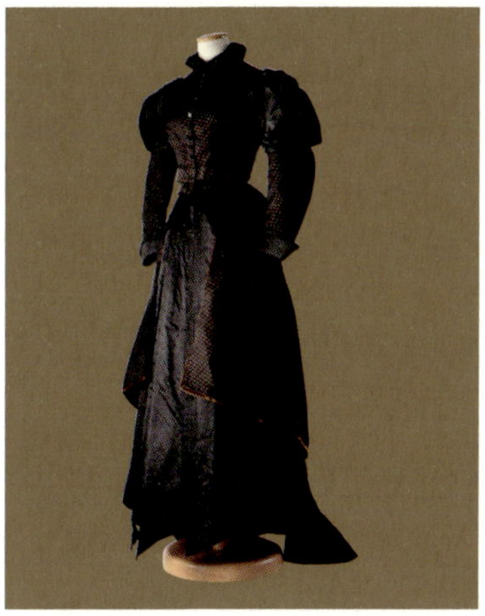

Evening gown
c. 1892
Three-piece gown, skirt, bodice and petticoat; satin in two stippled tones; contrasting sleeves, cuffs and skits; embroidery on the collar, cuffs, and waistband
Museo Daphné – Musée de la Mode et du Parfum, San Remo

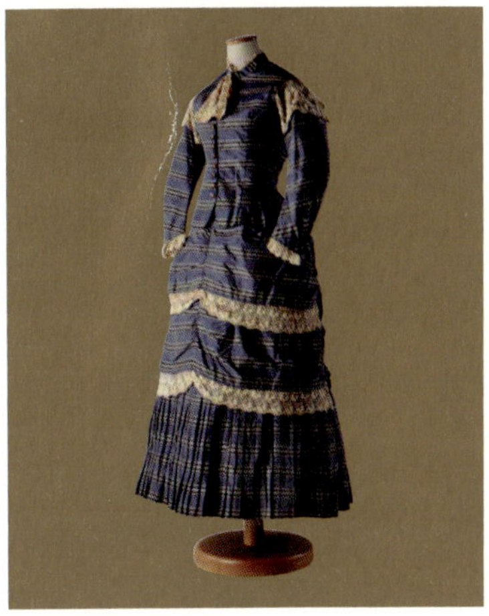

Promenade outfit
c. 1878
Striped silk and light blue tartan; short jacket and pleated skirt with large flounces; hanging effect with two rows of white embroidered flounces in front; pouf hanging behind
Museo Daphné– Musée de la Mode et du Parfum, San Remo

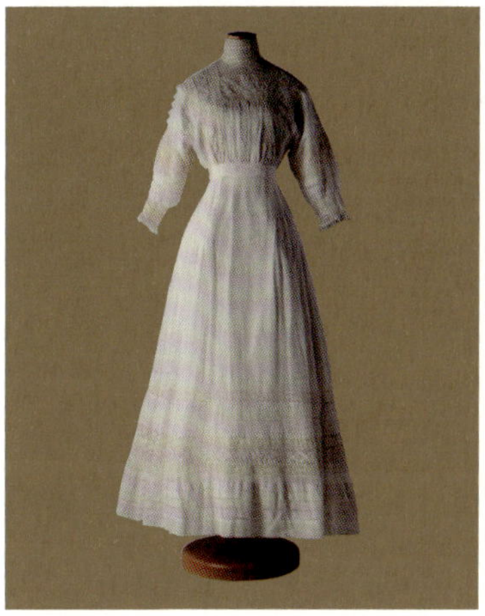

Summer gown from the wardrobe of countesses Alexandra and Elizabeth Olsoufieff
Early twentieth century
White Embroidered white cloth with lace inserts; rising collar, embroidered shoulder straps, puff sleeves with flat pleats and embroidered cuffs; flared skirt with pleats and lace inserts
Museo Daphné – Musée de la Mode et du Parfum, San Remo

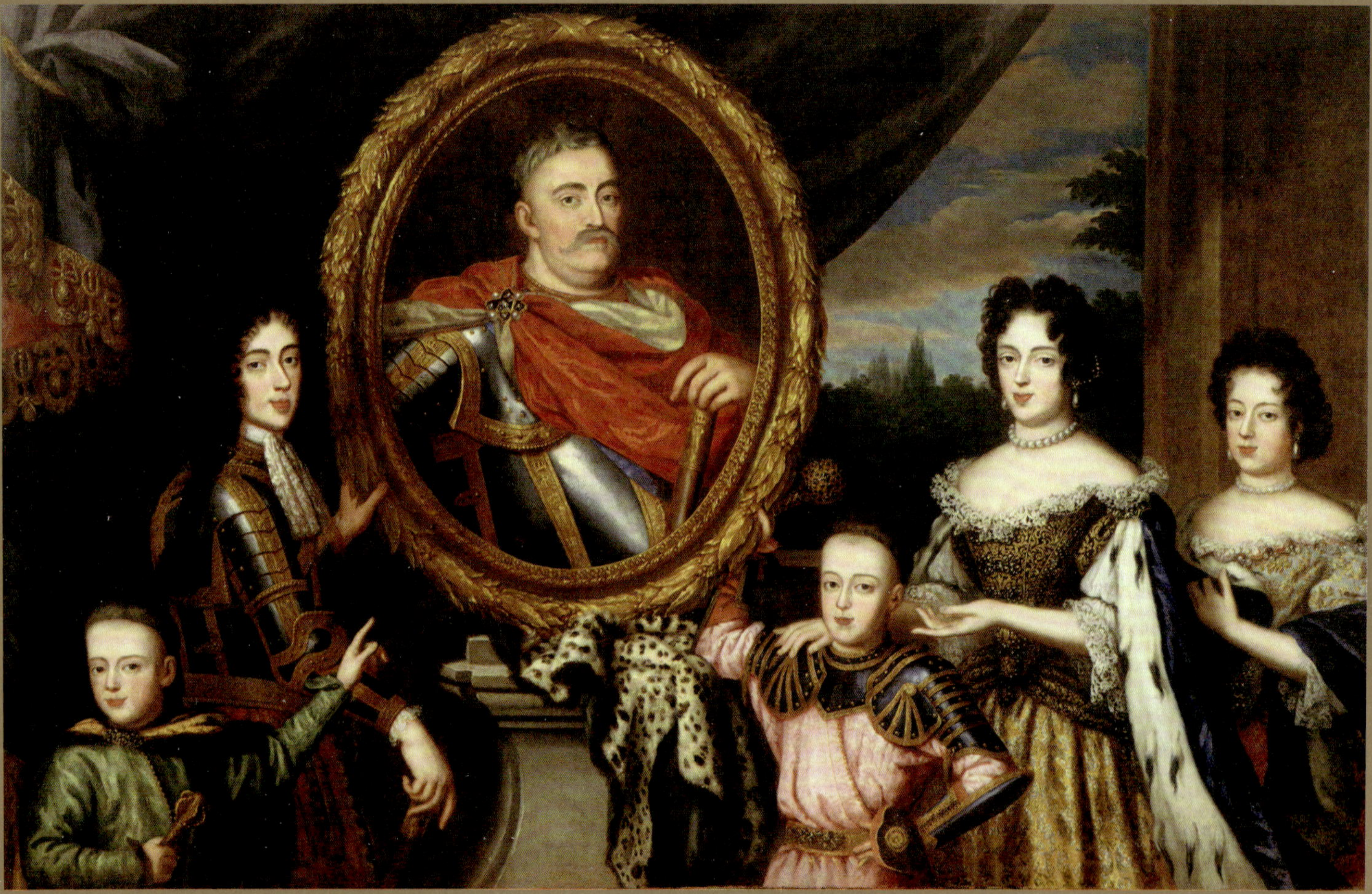

POLAND

Jan III Sobieski (1629–1696)

King Jan III Sobieski and Family
1691, Rome
Henri Gascar (1635–1701)
Wawel Royal Palace, Krakow

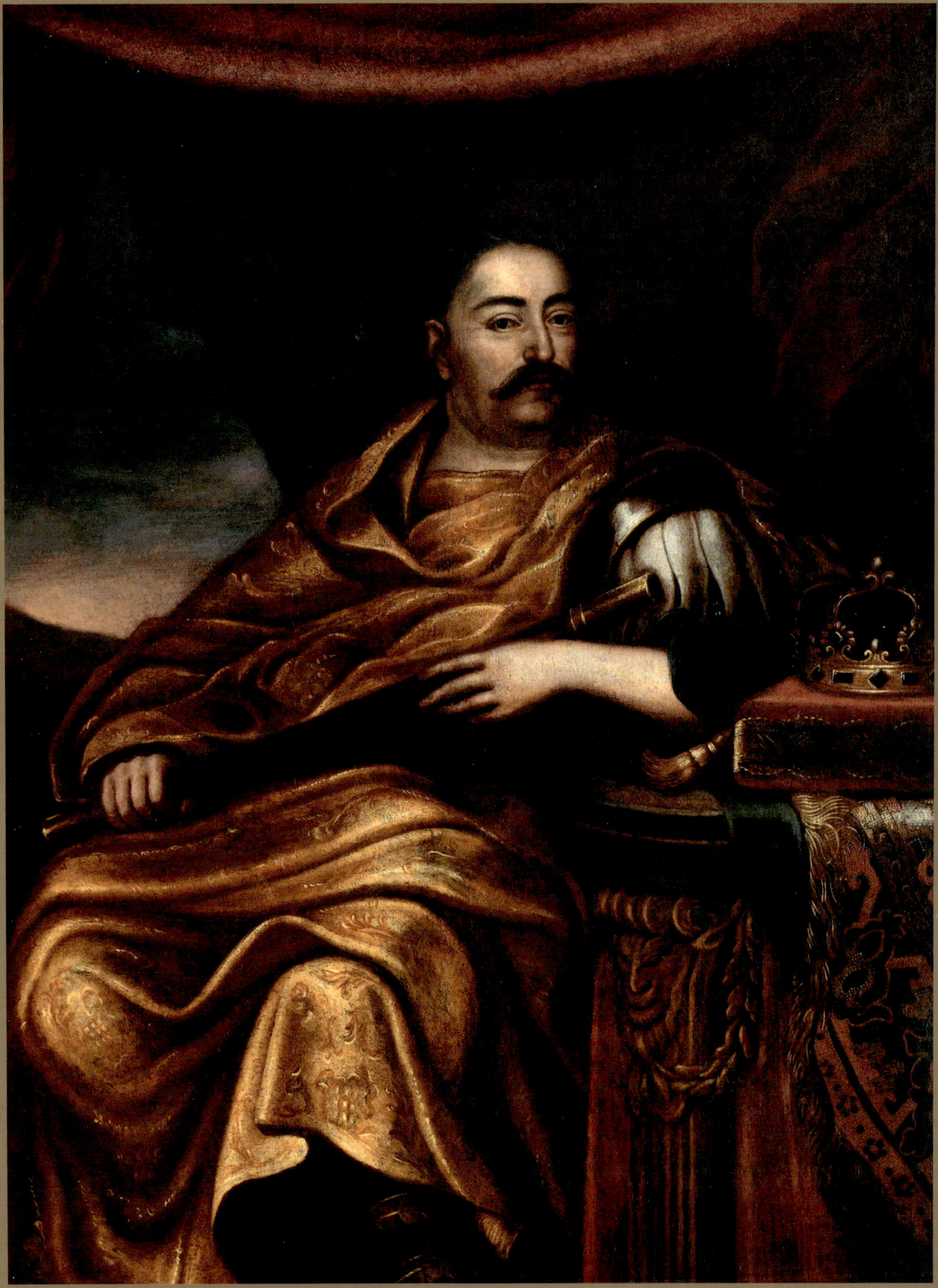

Jan III Sobieski and Marie Casimire d'Arquien

Marta Golabek

On December 22, 1673, Madame de Sévigné wrote the following to her daughter: "The grand marshal, the husband of Mademoiselle d'Arquien, is at the head of an army against the Turks; he has lately gained . . . complete victory over them. . . . After so distinguished a victory, it is not in the least doubted that he will be declared king, especially as he is at the head of such an army, and that fortune generally declares in favor of numerous battalions. This piece of news has given me pleasure."

Indeed, these were the circumstances that accompanied the assumption of the crown by Jan Sobieski (1629–1696), a successful soldier and a representative of the Polish nobility. The battle mentioned was the famous confrontation with Turks that took place on November 11, 1673, by the walls of Chocim fortress. Sobieski was then a commander in chief and he led his troops promptly to a resounding victory. Popularity and authority were the new characteristics linked with the commander's name. On May 21, 1674, he was entrusted with the crown of the Commonwealth of Two Nations, Poland and Lithuania. His reign lasted twenty-two years and was the last illuminated period in early modern Polish history, even though the times were eventful and harsh. In national historiography, Jan III Sobieski is one of the most appreciated monarchs, a perfect embodiment of a skillful warrior, a sensible man of state, a patron of the arts and sciences, a caring father, and a passionate admirer of a beloved woman. Due to his international military successes, he has become a symbol of the significance of their homeland for generations of Poles. This particular emotion was most intense during the nineteenth century, when Poland lost its independence and desperately searched for cultural and historical identity. For people of this period, who often could not speak their national language freely, Sobieski was surrounded by a romantic legend that placed a man of flesh and blood with virtues and vices on a pedestal. Even today it is difficult to separate the canon from the apocrypha. Surely, every Pole questioned about Sobieski would pronounce a couple of praiseworthy sentences, and each and every one would be able to describe the most characteristic features of his appearance.

Jan III Sobieski (1629–1696)
1676
Alexandre Jan Tricius
(1620–1692/98)
Wilanów Palace Museum, Warsaw

Sobieski was born into a noble family with firm traditions. His father Jakub was a holder of key public functions and enjoyed the trust of the royal court. The family's fate was strongly determined by two factors, the location of its estates—in Ruthenia near the southeastern borders of the country—and its military prowess. Due to these factors, they were hardened in battles aiming to chase away Turks and Tatars, the invaders from the south. Hence, not one of Sobieski's ancestors lost his life in the battlefield against the aforementioned opponents. This led to a certain way of thinking about the role of noble Samartian men and the ideals that determined their attitude toward public obligation. *"O, quam dulce et decorum est pro patria mori"* was the motto that Teofila, Sobieski's mother, engraved in her son's mind. This quotation from Horace's ode was carved on the memorial tomb of Sobieski's grandfather, Stanislaw Zólkiewski, who died in 1620 from wounds received in a battle against the Turks. Jan was raised and educated according to his father's strict will. The program was designed to prepare him for a future public role, both military and political. After years of university studies in Krakow, he traveled through western Europe: Germany, France, England, and the United Provinces of the Netherlands. The voyage ended in 1648, when Sobieski was called to begin his military career. Years had passed; the situation in Poland was becoming worrying. The Seym (parliament of nobles) was becoming more and more an arena for chaotic and aggressive debates, rather than a place to come to a collective agreement on treasury issues, taxes to fund a reliable army, and the launch of practical foreign policy. Sobieski quickly made quite a dazzling career and became one of the first confidants to Marie Louise Gonzaga, the French-born queen of Poland. He supported her political plans and projects even though they were neglected by the nobles. Sobieski got more and more involved and his ties with the court grew stronger. This was undoubtedly because of love, Sobieski having been struck by a genuine *coup de foudre*. He and Marie Casimire d'Arquien first met in Warsaw in the spring of 1655. She was a beautiful and smart young lady, one of the ladies in waiting who had traveled to Poland with the queen in 1646. This is how a delightful story of love entangled with politics started. Despite many trials and long periods of separation, the story of those two must have been guided by the lively Cupid, who clearly wished to unite the lovers. Their example may serve as a convincing argument for belief in destiny; the love was fortunately fulfilled by their marriage in 1665. Sobieski's letters to his beloved Marysienka are delightful evidence of their passion. Their content seems almost impossible to have been written by the man who was trained as a ruthless warrior and politician: "My prettiest wife, the greatest solace of my heart and soul, so deeply, my golden lady, thine beauty has gotten into my head that I could not close my eyes the entire night."

Marie Casimire Louise de la Grange d'Arquien (1641–1716), Wife of Jan III Sobieski
Seventeenth century
Alexandre Jan Tricius (1620–1692/98)
Wilanów Palace Museum, Warsaw

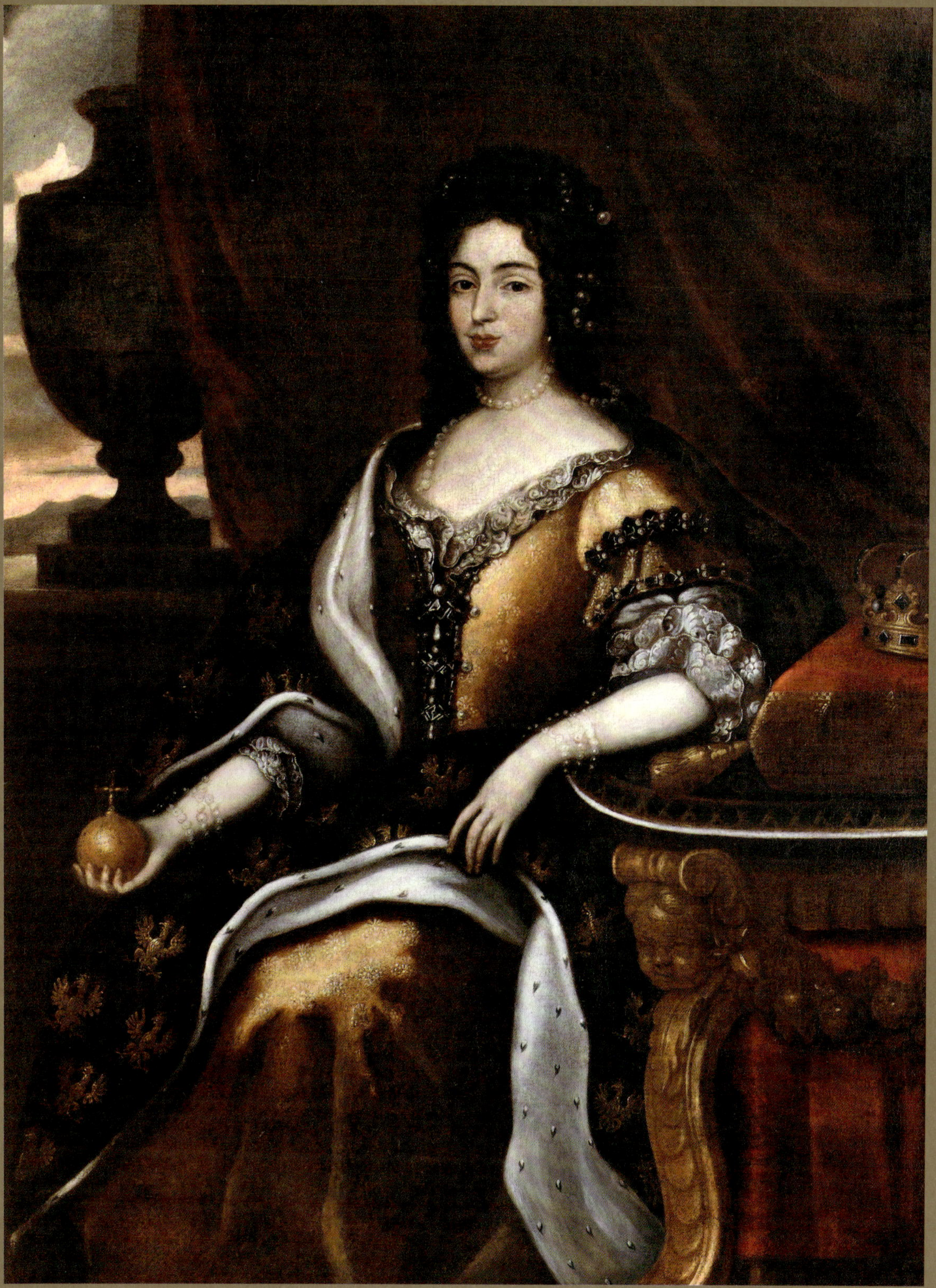

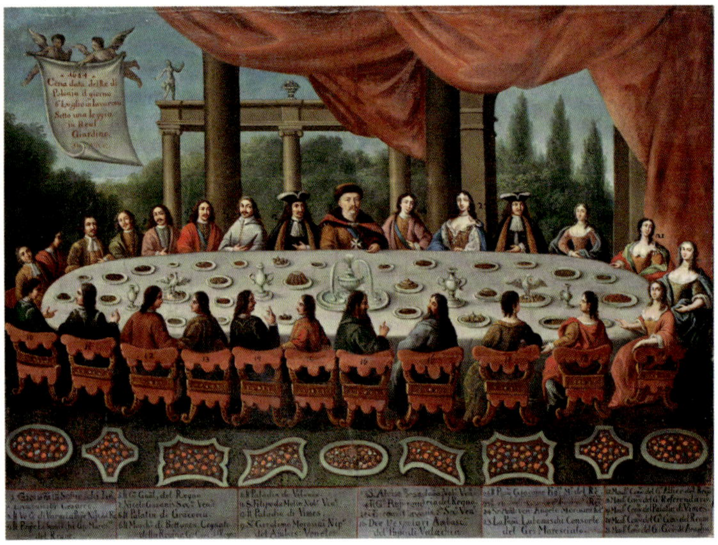

The couple had another great challenge before them; it came together with Sobieski's election of 1674. They were to become the king and the queen of the Commonwealth of Two Nations, a country which still participated in the international political chess tournament. Their reign started dynamically and with a master plan of conducting general reforms aiming at strengthening the centralized power. One of the means to achieve this plan was the establishment of a dynasty, a hereditary power that would ensure continuity in politics. The couple was blessed with children, four of whom managed to live into adulthood. There were three sons, Jakub Ludwik, Aleksander Benedykt, Konstanty Wladyslaw, and one daughter, Teresa Kunegunda, the future wife of the elector of Bavaria. Sobieski did his best to supply his children with special education and preparation for their future roles as potential sovereigns. As it was customary in early modern Europe, they were considered a *sui generis* investment in future political plans and aims. But apart from that, there was also something else in the parents' relationship with their children. It was love, sensibility, care, and a sincere joy to spend time in their company. A rare quality in royal family members. It surprises us when we read that the king liked to watch his children play draughts, observe them dancing, or simply go out with them to the garden and enjoy the view of nature. This valiant and victorious soldier, whose iconography cites imperial antiquity, was a caring and preoccupied father, who would make every effort to ensure a profitable life for his children.

Banquet in Jaworow for Jan Sobieski after his Victory at the Battle of Vienna
c. 1685
Frans Geffels
National Museum, Wroclaw

The dynastic plans became consolidated after the most conspicuous event in Sobieski's military career, the Battle of Vienna in 1683. After a complete switch in the political direction of the court, which mainly relied on its relations with France,

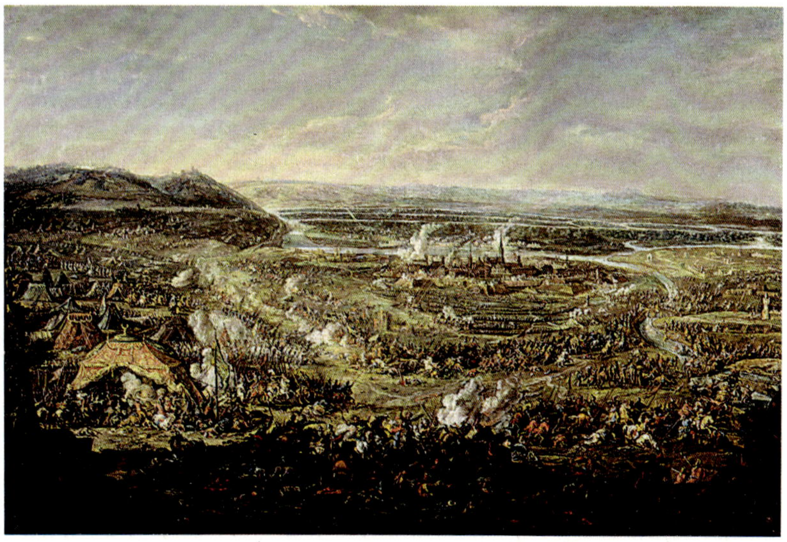

Sobieski decided to react to emperor Leopold I's claim, rushing to the imperial capital to liberate it from the Turkish invaders. The Polish king was the perfect commander for this challenge, as he had passed days, weeks, and months in the battlefield and was undoubtedly the most experienced person in confronting the Ottomans. He knew their strong and weak points, he was aware of their strategies. It is no surprise that on September 3, 1683, in Stettelsdorf, after a *consilium bellicum,* all the key leaders of the imperial and German armies—Charles, duke of Lorraine; Maximilian II Emmanuel Wittelsbach; and Prince Georg Friedrich of Waldeck—chose Jan III Sobieski to command their forces. The united forces fought a great battle on September 12. It ended with a complete Turkish defeat and the flight of Grand Vizier Kara Mustafa. It is necessary to recall here the legendary Polish cavalrymen, the so-called hussars, whose armor was equipped with wings, a well-known and characteristic motif. Their massive attack, which took place in the key moments of the battle, definitely influenced its spectacular results. The following days, Sobieski wrote two famous letters whose content was disseminated all over Europe. The first one was addressed to the queen, Marie Casimire, anxiously awaiting news in Krakow, and read: "The one and only solace of my heart, the most beautiful and most beloved Marysienka, God our Lord, may he be hailed for eternity, gave victory and glory to our nation that was not heard of in centuries." The other letter written on the 14th September in the Grand Vizier's tents was addressed to Pope Innocent XI. It commenced with words paraphrasing the famous quotation of Caesar: *Beatissimo Padre, Venimus, Vidimus, Deus Vicit....* In the absolute heyday after the Vienna victory, Sobieski truly believed that his plans would be achieved. His deeds were extolled through the written word,

The Battle of Vienna
Late seventeenth century
Dutch School
Fine Arts Academy,
Krakow (on deposit to
the Wawel Royal Palace)

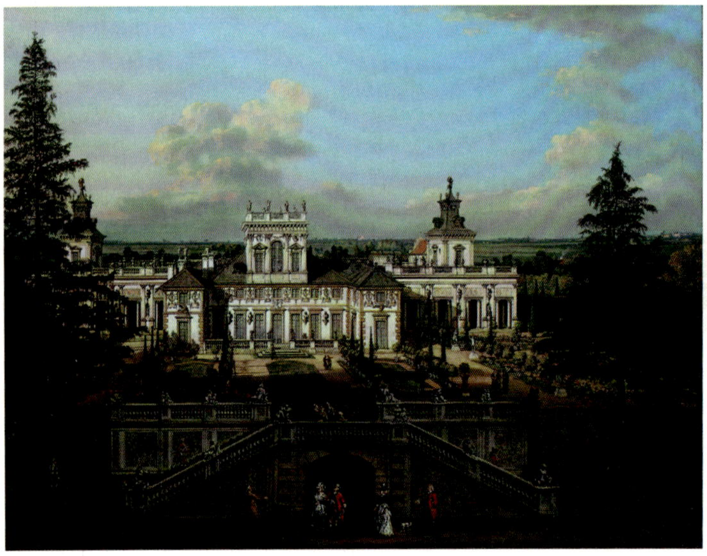

paintings, prints, and sculptures. He himself decided to implement a very concrete iconography in the recently erected suburban residence of Wilanów. A modest manor house was enlarged and enhanced with a complex decoration. From the front elevation it was dedicated to the glorification of the great warrior. The interior declared the prosperous years to come and the golden age to be revived. Finally, the garden façade promised that all this would be attained during the Sobieskis' reign.

The royal castle in Warsaw was the state residence. The royal castle in Krakow was the monument of the nation and the venue of Sobieski's coronation. The king's favorite residence, fortunately extant today and unique evidence of the past, was and still is Wilanów, situated right in the southern suburbs of Warsaw. A monument of architecture, art, and the mindset of our predecessors, it makes an exceptionally attractive topic for research. All the more as it was built strictly according to Sobieski's taste, the king being actively engaged in the process of its construction and decoration. It tells us so much about its founder and sheds more light not only on his military talents, but also his erudition and ideals. What you see in the apartments are scenes from Virgil's *Georgics*, which praise a simple life in harmony with nature. In the library there are painted figures of two major disciplines of human thought, Theology and Philosophy. The ceilings are guarded by the mythological gods ruling over the harmonious changes of seasons and the passing of day onto night. In Wilanów, Sobieski could take off his arms, put aside his soldier's vigilance, and enjoy the simple life of a landlord, which he longed for so much. It was here that he rejoiced in the company of his friends and family. A spoken tradition states that he himself planted trees in the Wilanów garden.

Love, war, politics, patriotism, and devotion to high ideals: all these features can be found in the figure of King Jan III Sobieski. He constitutes a perfect combination of all the characteristics typical of a Polish Sarmatian, a noble with all the qualities specific to the cultural mixture that existed on the boundary between East and West. Yet Sobieski was a man of European stature. We like him so much because he embodies a certain ideal to which we aspire: a Pole —a European, not devoid of national identity.

View of the Wilanów Palace from the garden
1776
BERNARDO BELLOTTO
(1722-1780)
Royal Palace,
Warsaw

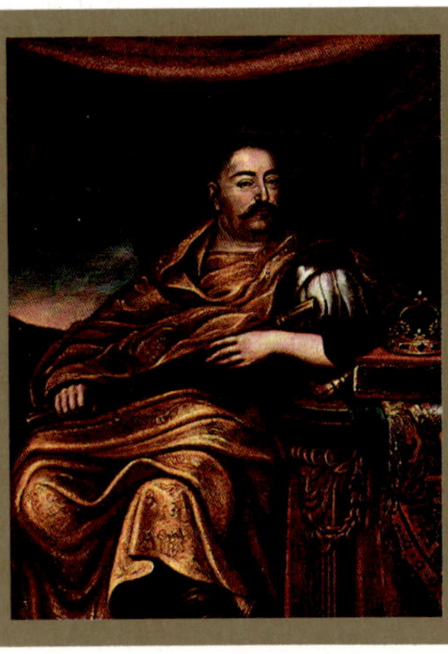

Jan III Sobieski (1629–1696)
1676
ALEXANDRE JAN TRICIUS (1620–1692/98)
Oil on canvas
162 × 114 cm
Wilanów Palace Museum, Warsaw
Inv. 1953

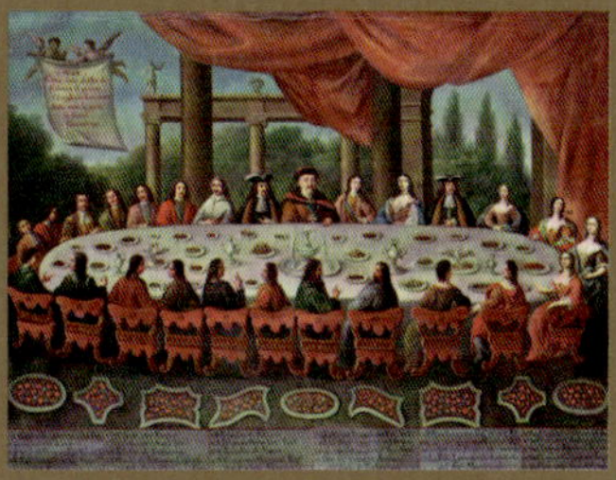

Banquet in Jaworow for Jan Sobieski after his Victory at the Battle of Vienna
c. 1685
FRANS GEFFELS
Oil on canvas
95 × 135 cm
National Museum, Wroclaw
Inv. MNWr.VIII-201

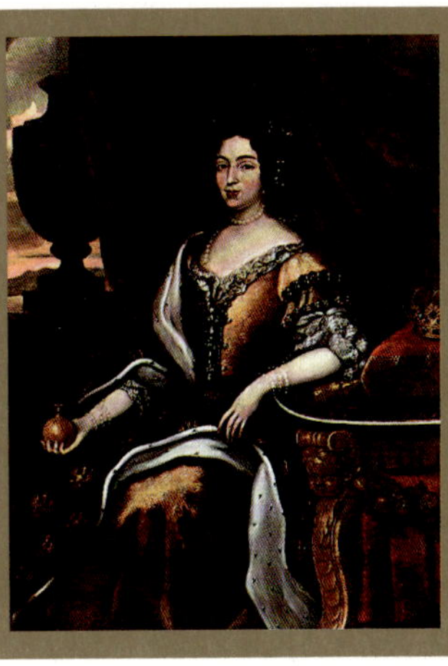

Marie Casimire Louise de la Grange d'Arquien (1641–1716), Wife of Jan III Sobieski
Seventeenth century
ALEXANDRE JAN TRICIUS
(1620–1692/98)
Oil on canvas
160 × 114 cm
Wilanów Palace Museum, Warsaw
Inv. 1584

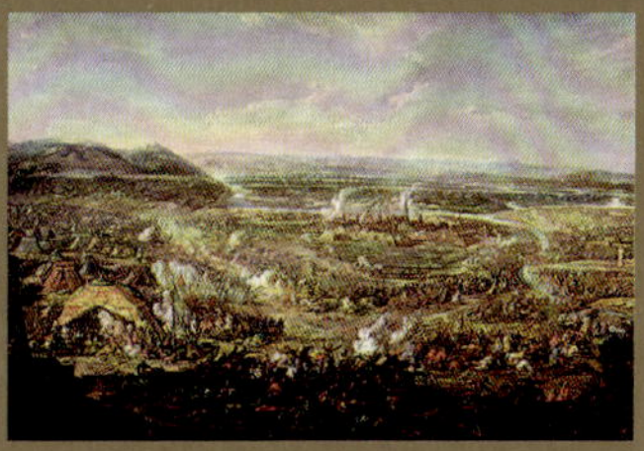

The Battle of Vienna
Late seventeenth century
Dutch School
Oil on canvas
97 × 142 cm
Fine Arts Academy, Krakow
(on deposit to the
Wawel Royal Palace)
Inv. dep344

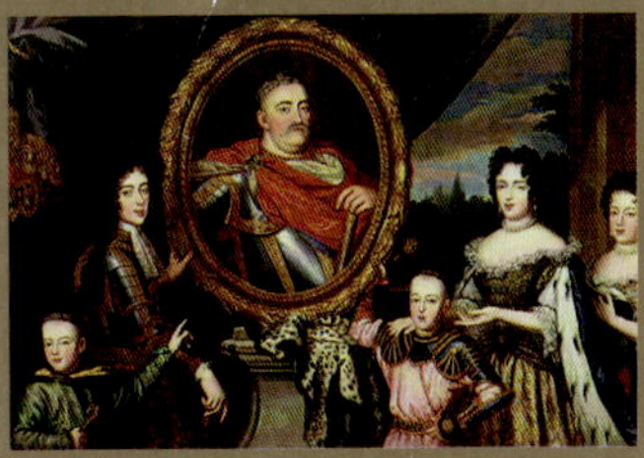

King Jan III and Family
1691, Rome
HENRI GASCAR (1635–1701)
Oil on canvas
151 × 232 cm
Wawel Royal Palace, Krakow
Inv. 3222

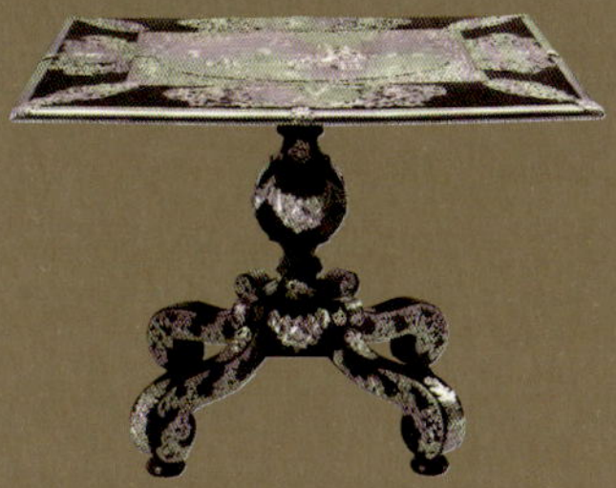

Table given to Jan III Sobieski after his victory in Vienna
Last quarter of the
seventeenth century
SAMUEL SCHNEEWEISS, Augsburg
Silver and ebony
approx. 75 × 100 × 83 cm
Jagellon University Museum, Krakow
Inv. MUJ 7500

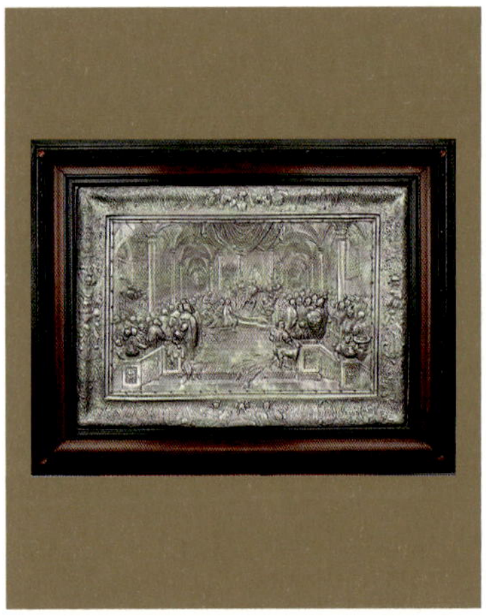

Jan III Sobieski received by the Emperor after the Battle of Vienna
1883
Baruch Dornhelm (1858–1928)
Silver
87 × 120 cm
Wilanów Palace Museum, Warsaw
Inv. 5677

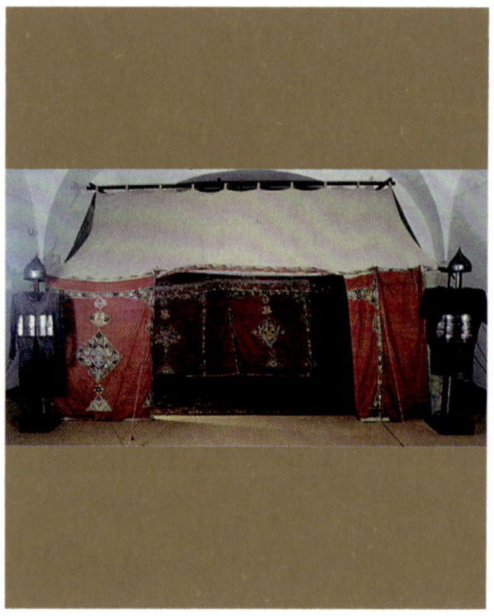

Turkish tent
Late seventeenth century
Topkapi Palace workshop, Istanbul
Linen, satin, leather
310 × 565 × 280 cm
Wawel Royal Palace, Krakow
Inv. 2537/1-3

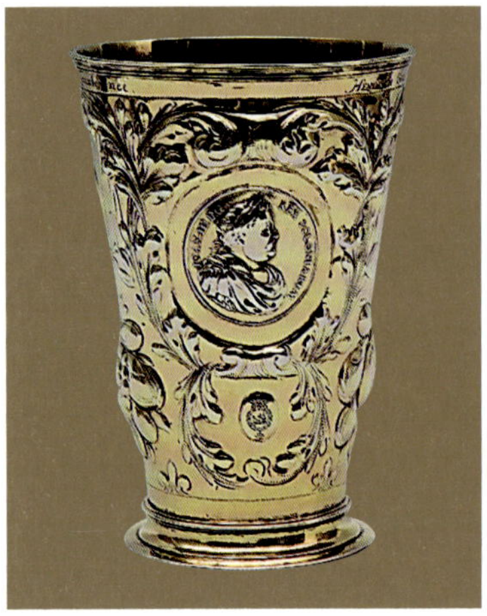

Cup with medallion depicting Jan III Sobieski
Johann Gottfried Hall
Silver
H. 20.6 cm
Wilanów Palace Museum, Warsaw
Inv. 3781

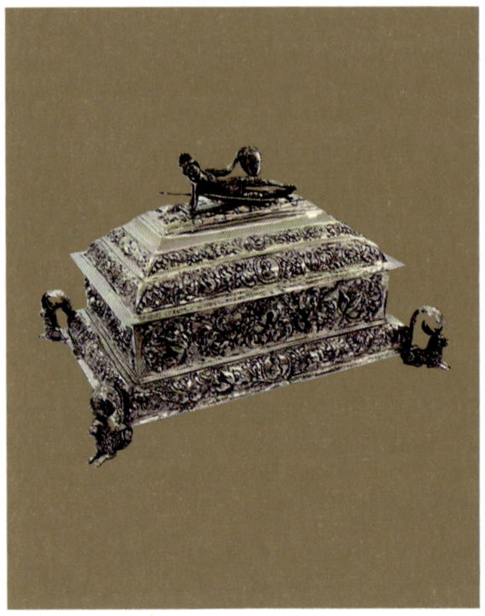

Ink well belonging to Jan III Sobieski
c. 1700, Danzig
Nathanael Schlaubitz
(active 1690–1726)
Silver
27 × 48 × 35 cm
Wilanów Palace Museum, Warsaw
Inv. 3865

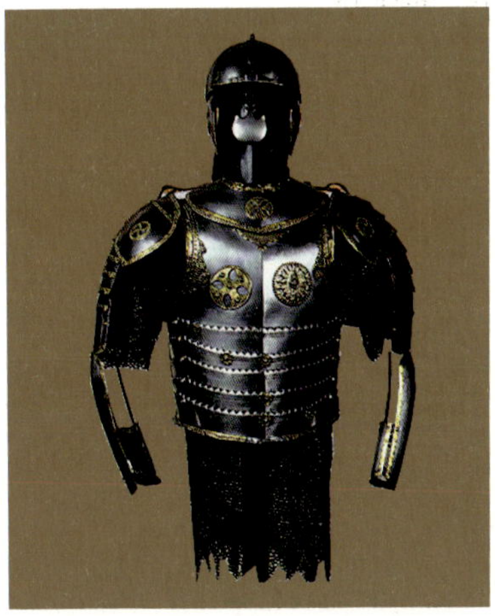

Hussar armor
First half of the seventeenth century
Poland
Steel, copper, leather, silk
Wawel Royal Palace, Krakow
Inv. 1304/1-7
Helmet
H. 34 cm
Breastplate
H. 51 cm

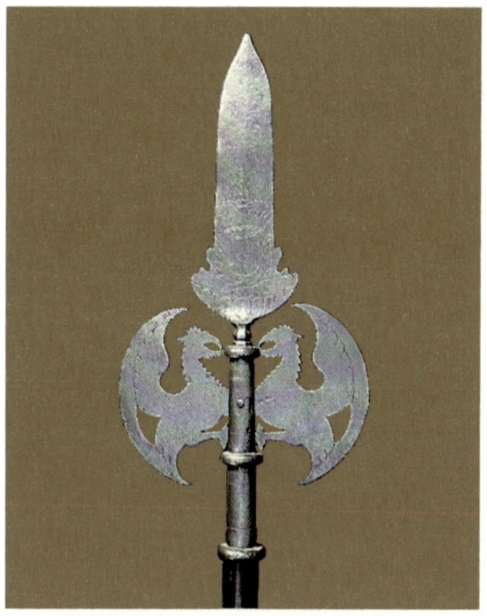

Lance
1673, Poland
Steel, wood
L. 250 cm
Wawel Royal Palace, Krakow
Inv. 358

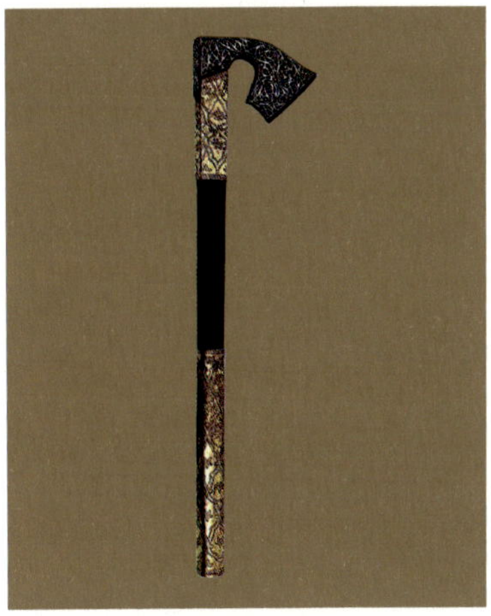

Small axe
Second half of the seventeenth century
Iron
L. approx. 100 cm
Wilanów Palace Museum, Warsaw
Inv. 5662

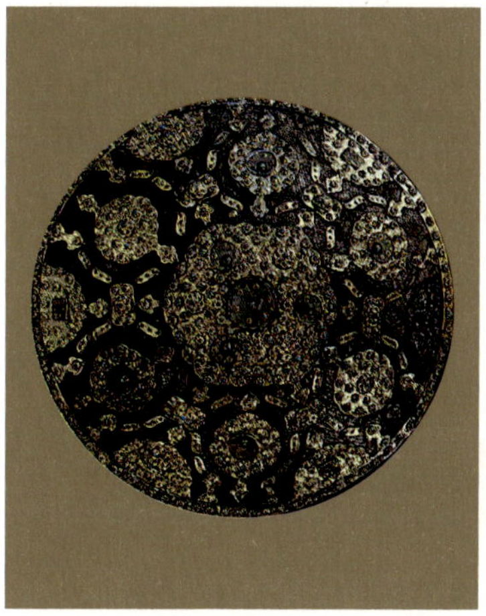

Shield
Seventeenth century
Turkey
Wood, silver, silver thread, velvet, nephrite, jadeite, turquoise
44.2 × 62.9
Wawel Royal Palace, Krakow
Inv. 358

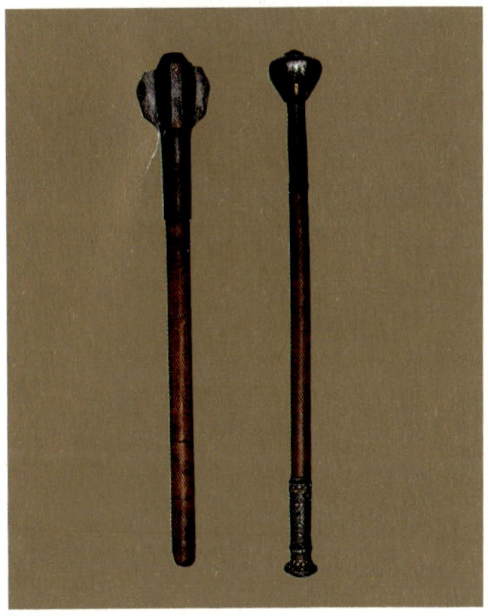

Maces
Second half of the seventeenth century
Iron
L. approx. 100 cm
Wilanów Palace Museum, Warsaw
Inv. 5673 and inv. 5674

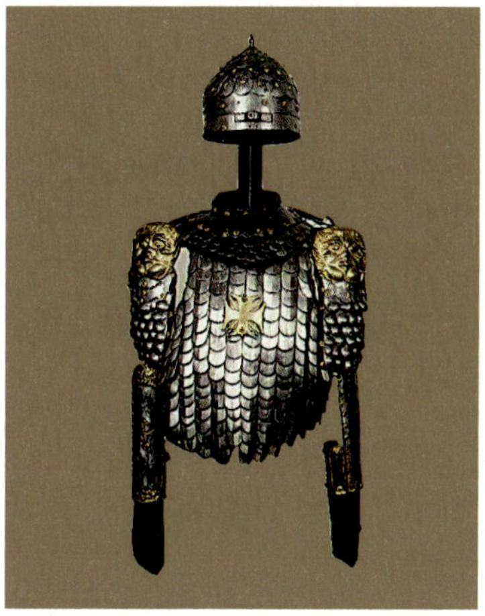

Armor
Mid-eighteenth century
Poland
Steel, copper, leather, silk
Wawel Royal Palace, Krakow
Inv. 4709/1-7
Helmet
H. 23.5 cm
Breastplate
H. 59.6 cm

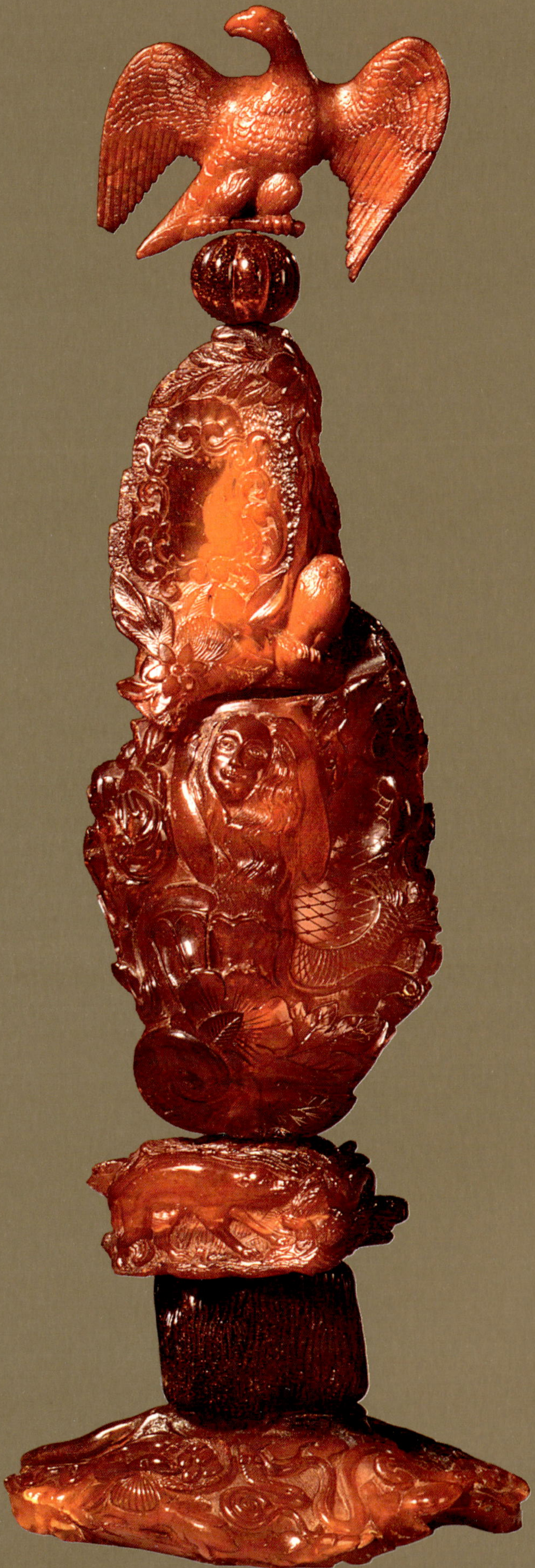

PRUSSIA

From Friedrich I (1657–1713) to Friedrich Wilhelm IV (1795–1861)

Eagle and amber, two emblems of Prussia
Post 1700, Königsberg
Deutsches Historisches Museum,
Berlin

From king “in” Prussia to king “of” Prussia the rise of the Prussian monarchy

Samuel Wittwer

On the death of his father in 1688, Friedrich III became prince-elector of Brandenburg, a position his family, the Hohenzollers, occupied for more than 270 years. Friedrich joined his long line of forefathers as one of the nine members of the college responsible for electing the emperor of the Holy Roman Empire. Each of the nine electors would be offered an honorary post by the emperor, though generally these were exercised only on the occasion of the coronation. The electors acted as arch-chamberlains in the imperial household; for instance, it was the princes of Brandenburg who presented the imperial scepter at the crowning of the emperor—hence its appearance on their coat of arms. This particularly prestigious distinction also meant that the prince of Brandenburg had the honor of handing the new emperor his finger basin and napkin at the coronation banquet.

Since the sixteenth century, the prince-electors of Brandenburg had also been dukes of Prussia. The duchy of Prussia, with Königsberg as its capital, was situated on the shores of the Baltic Sea and was a dependency of the kingdom of Poland until 1660. Prussia and Brandenburg remained, however, geographically distinct territories. In spite of such distinctions, the Hohenzollern—like all German electors in the eyes of royal houses outside the empire—seemed to stand on a lower rung of the hierarchical ladder. Hence the unstinting diplomatic efforts on the part of Friedrich Wilhelm, known as the Great Elector and father of Friedrich III, to be treated as one of their own by European monarchs. This attempt to elevate his status among the sovereigns of Europe failed not only due to his role as prince-elector, but also because in the duchy of Prussia he was essentially a tributary of the king of Poland. The situation changed little when in 1660 the kingdom of Poland was deprived of the duchy of Prussia, which became a sovereign territory in its own right. Friedrich III thus pursued his father's policy and harbored the even greater ambition of becoming a real king. He thus laid the stress on his close family relations with the House of Orange—his mother had been born a princess of Orange—and his ties with the English king.

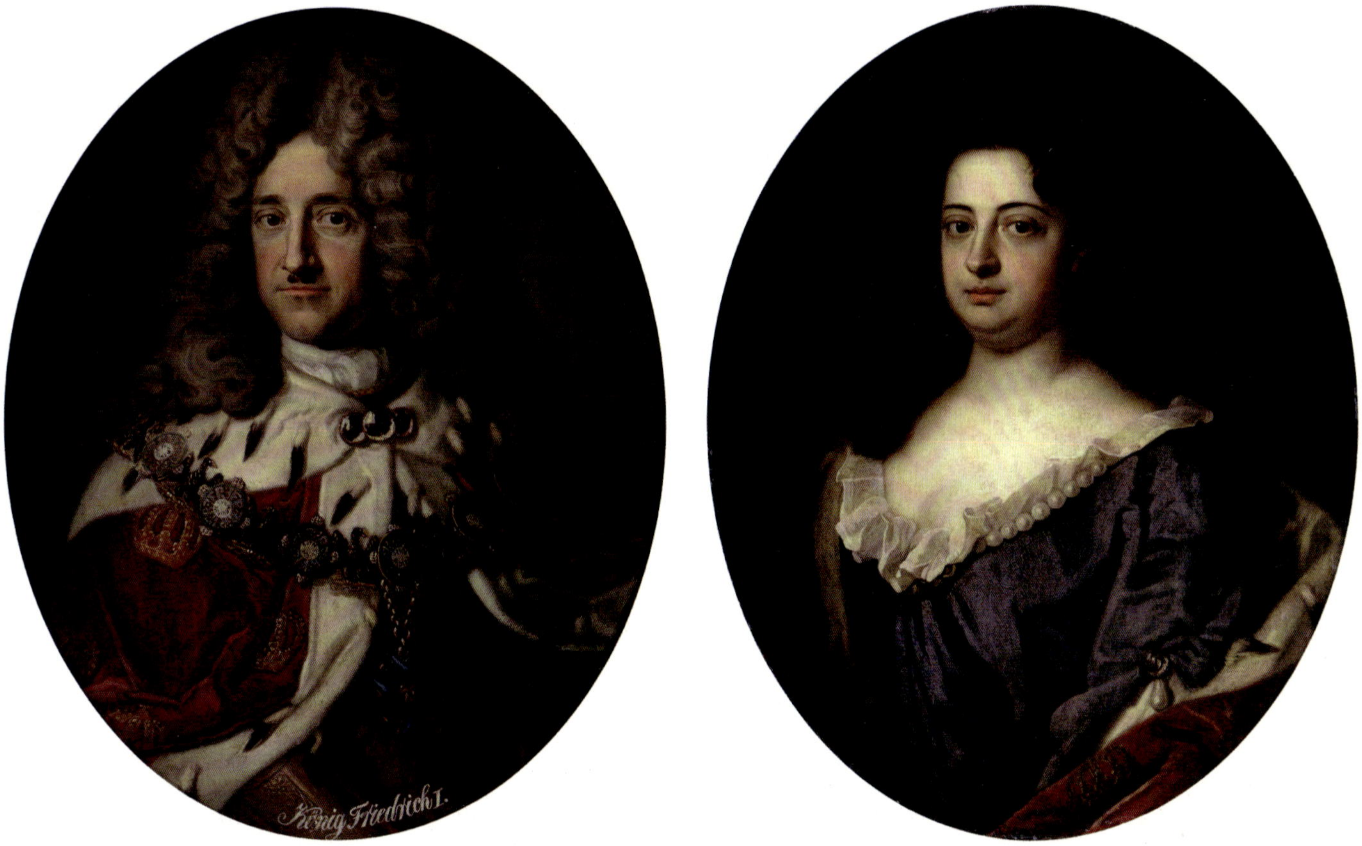

Around 1700, the power structure of the empire changed: first, in 1697, the prince-elector of Saxony was elected king of Poland; then in 1701 the prince-elector of Hanover became king of England—though his accession only actually took place in 1714. It was against this background that Friedrich's negotiating skills finally bore fruit. Granted military aid for the imminent War of the Spanish Succession by the emperor, he convinced Leopold I to recognize his status as king on November 30, 1700—though solely outside the borders of the empire. Scarcely three weeks later, the prince-elector of Brandenburg settled with his court at Königsberg in the duchy of Prussia, and preparations for the coronation got underway. On January 17, 1701, he founded the Order of the Black Eagle, crowning himself king "in" Prussia the following day, in the company of his wife Sophie Charlotte, princess of Hanover and sister of the future king of England, George I. In agreement with the emperor, Friedrich III, now King Friedrich I, was authorized to continue using the title even on returning to the principality of Brandenburg. However, as Prussia remained a mere duchy, he could not be styled King Friedrich "of" Prussia. The same applied to his southern neighbor,

Friedrich I (1657–1713) and Queen Sophie Charlotte (1668–1705), King and Queen in Prussia
Early eighteenth century
Friedrich Wilhelm Weidemann
Stiftung Preußische Schlösser und Gärten Berlin-Brandenburg, Berlin

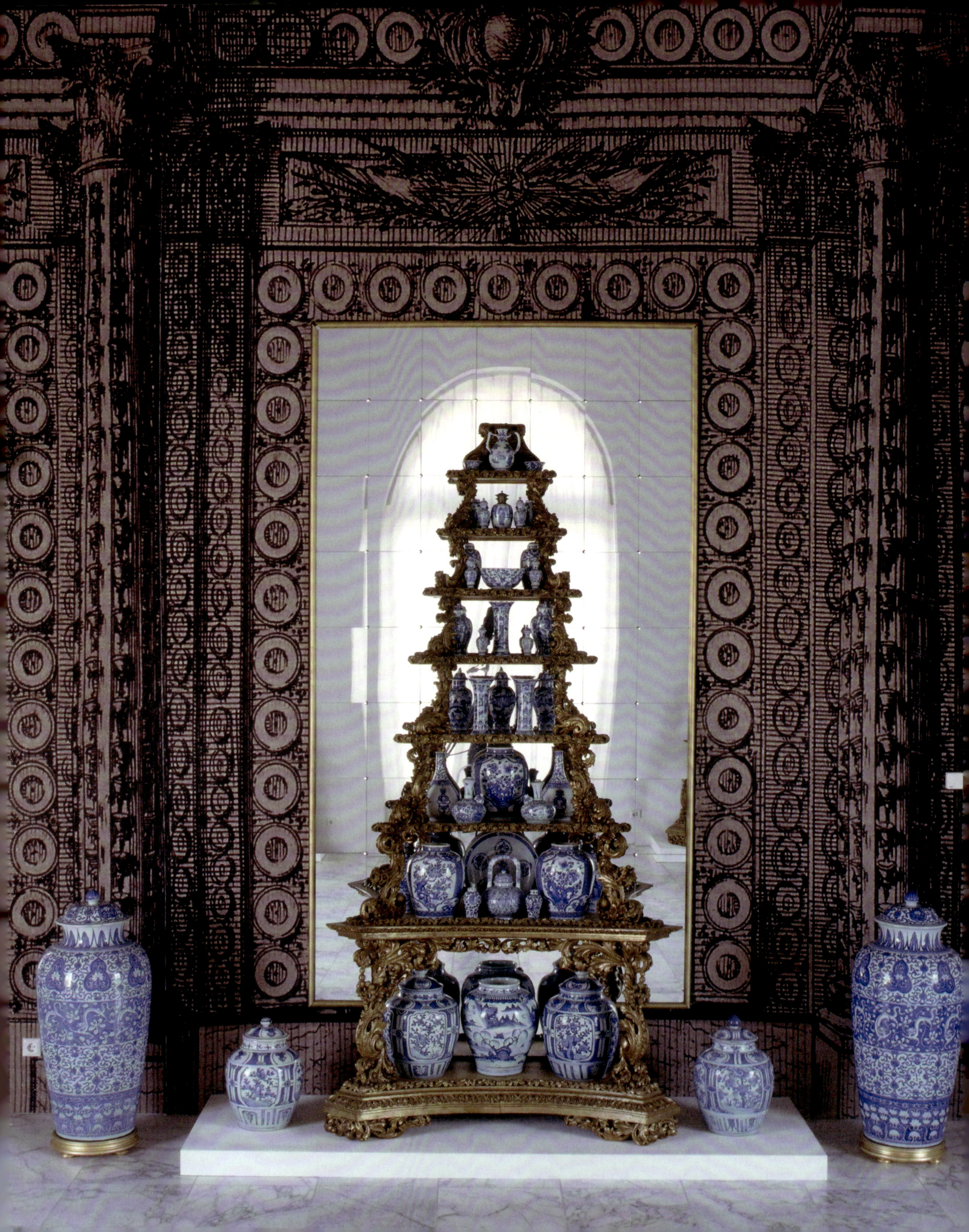

Elector Friedrich August of Saxony when he became king "in" Poland outside the borders of the empire—though in the latter case the expedience derived from the fact that it was impossible to transform the electoral system of the Polish kingdom into a hereditary monarchy.

On the death of Friedrich I in 1713, he was succeeded as prince-elector of Brandenburg and king "in" Prussia by his son Friedrich Wilhelm I, who had married a cousin, Sophie Dorothea of Hanover, daughter of the future King George I, in 1706. Thanks to a raft of reforms and after reinforcing the army, Friedrich Wilhelm I laid the foundations of a highly organized government that colored the image of Brandenburg-Prussia for several generations. Moreover, with his wife's support, he implemented a successful matrimonial policy for the majority of his fourteen children, allying his house closely with the German electorates of Ansbach, Bayreuth, Schwedt, Hesse-Kassel, and Brunswick-Wolfenbüttel. One of his daughters, Luise Ulrike, even became queen of Sweden (she'll be the mother of the king-to-be Gustav III of Sweden).

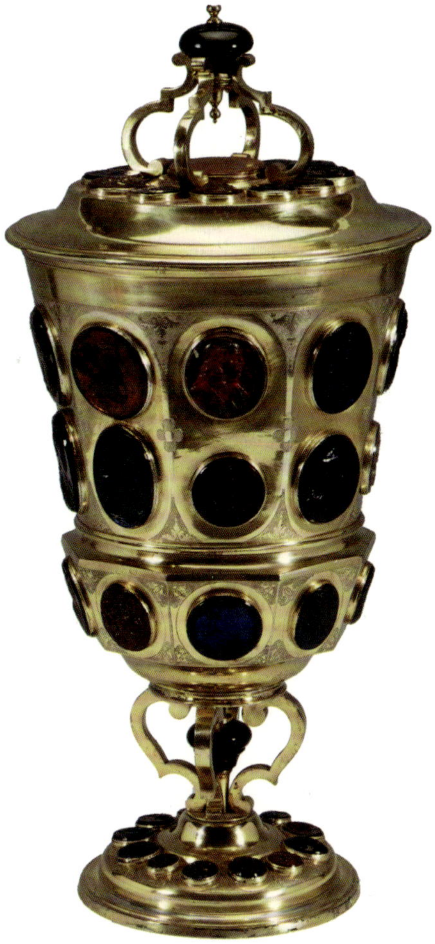

Large ceremonial cup featuring the portraits of the great historical personages
Nineteenth century, Berlin
Kunstgewerbemuseum, Berlin

In 1740, he was succeeded by his eldest son, who became the most famous sovereign of the Hohenzollern dynasty as Frederick the Great. Unlike his ancestors, Friedrich II engaged in three wars against the Habsburg imperial house, promoting Brandenburg-Prussia into one of the foremost European powers. At the time of what is known as the "first partition of Poland" in 1772, having acquired the northwestern part of the country up to the Baltic coast (thus linking Prussia and Brandenburg), Frederick the Great could change his style of address, at last becoming king "of" Prussia. As a logical consequence of the rise of House of Hohenzollern, the creation of the Prussian monarchy in 1701 heralded a further shift in power in the empire and more widely in Europe, while the electoral dignity waned in importance compared to the office of king. As Friedrich II and his wife Elisabeth Christine of Brunswick-Bevern had no children, it was his nephew Friedrich Wilhelm II who succeeded him after a reign of forty-six years. Eleven years later, in 1797, the son of the latter, Friedrich Wilhelm III, ascended to the throne of Prussia.

The Chinese Porcelain Room in the palace at Oranienburg
Created in 1695
Stiftung Preußische Schlösser und Gärten Berlin-Brandenburg, Berlin

He had married Luise of Mecklenburg-Strelitz, niece of Queen Charlotte of England. In 1815, the victory of Prussia and its Austrian, Russian, and British allies over Napoleon promoted Prussian preeminence among the German states, as well as furthering the royal house's marriage policy: Bavaria, Saxe-Weimar, Mecklenburg-Schwerin, and the Netherlands all forged close family ties with Prussia, while in 1825 one of the Prussian princesses became the czarina. In 1858, for reasons of health, his elder brother, King Friedrich Wilhelm IV of Prussia, had to submit to the regency of his younger brother Wilhelm, who became king of Prussia three years later as Wilhelm I, as well as the first German emperor after the Franco-Prussian War of 1871. His son Friedrich III followed by his grandson Wilhelm II bore the title of emperor until the revolution of 1917 brought the demise of the Prussian monarchy.

So, in a little more than two hundred years, the Hohenzollerns did not only establish and consolidate the monarchy, but also ensured an enduring position in Europe through war, marriage, and political maneuver, so elevating their homeland from a minor German state into a significant European power.

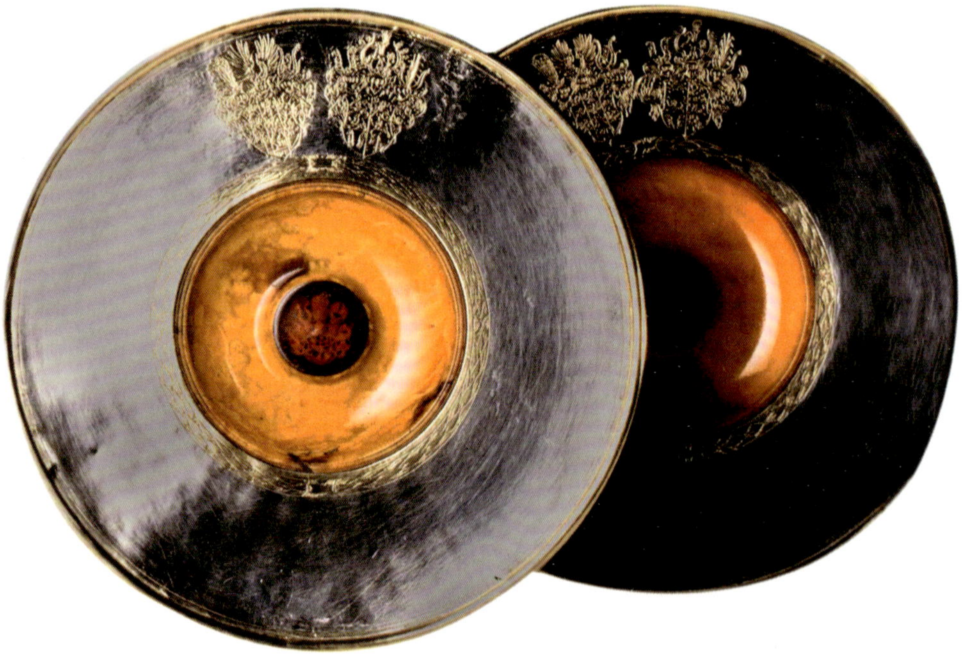

Two amber plates with the arms of Brandenburg, a gift from the elector of Brandenburg to the king of Denmark
1585
Rosenborg Castle, Copenhagen

Amber, the gift of the kings of Prussia

Hans Ottomeyer

Fished primarily from the waters of the Baltic Sea, collected on the surface solely from its coasts, amber was long a prerogative of sovereigns. Its prestige sprung from regal regulations enshrined in the Teutonic Order in Prussia in the twelfth century and was reiterated in 1660 with the transfer of royal status as kings of Poland onto the prince-electors of Brandenburg, who were later to become kings of Prussia.

In law, amber, like any treasure trove uncovered at a depth "beyond that of a plow shear," was treated as a mining resource. No material then could have been better placed than amber to become the typical Prussian diplomatic gift. Amber did not have to be purchased by the monarch with tax revenue, but was legally part and parcel of his sovereign status and possession of the land, and consequently was simply the monarch's property. At the time, amber was thus considered "one of the noblest boons from the kingdom of His Royal Majesty," petition presented by the guild of amber turners (Bernsteindrechsler) to Friedrich the Great on 1747. It is noteworthy how the various states of amber were viewed differently over the centuries. For pharmaceutics, white amber, and until the sixteenth century objects made from it tended to be placed on permanent display or were confined to personal use to treat various ailments or to alleviate pain (rosaries, knife handles).

Duke Albrecht of Prussia (1490–1568) of the House of Hohenzollern-Ansbach and Bayreuth, who first married Dorothea of Denmark in 1526 and in 1550 took as his second wife Anna Maria of Brunswick-Lüneburg, followed by his son Albrecht Friedrich (1553–1618) and his wife Marie Eleonore of Jülich-Cleves-Berg (1550–1608), regularly had large pieces of amber worked into articles to be presented as diplomatic gifts to neighboring courts.

Under Duke Albrecht, amber became a most significant factor in the public finances, with extensive exports to Persia and Turkey through Russia swelling the coffers. Prestigious gifts such as those to the court in Moscow also served as diplomatically couched appeals in favor of the sovereign status of the then duchy of Prussia.

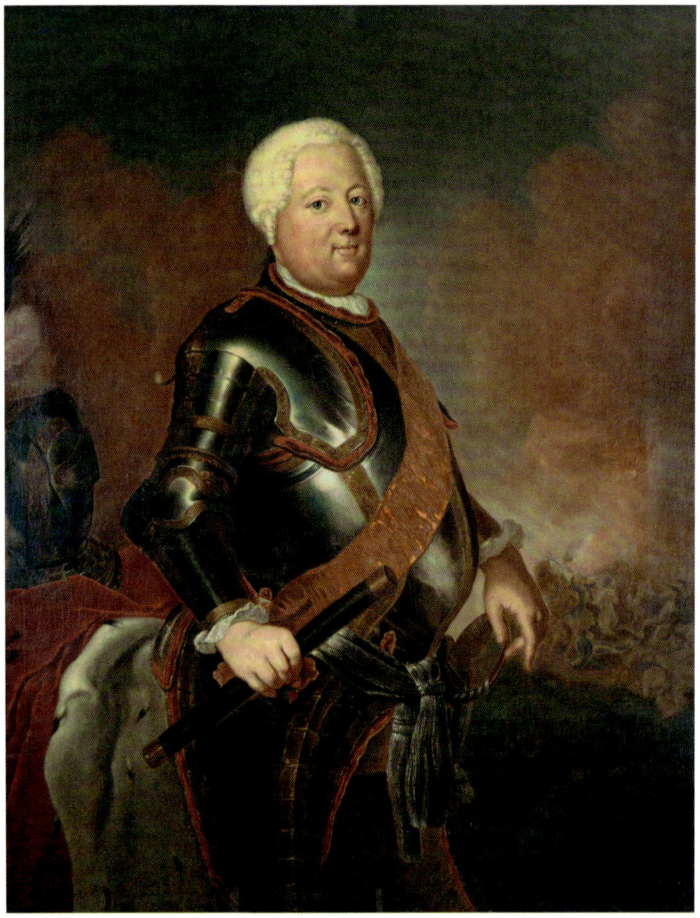

When Friedrich Wilhelm, the Great Elector, came to the throne (reigned 1640–1688), amber continued to feature in diplomatic gifts to princely courts, and it was during his reign that Prussia was finally recognized as a sovereign duchy by the terms of the Treaty of Oliva in 1660. In connection with this event, but dated to after 1647, the year of the wedding, the double miniature portrait of the prince-elector with his first wife Luise Henriette of Orange (1627–1667) carved in amber represents an ideal couple sporting the coronation insignia from the honorary bequest of 1640. The most likely occasion for the presentation of such a commemorative effigy to a court with which Brandenburg enjoyed close family ties was the wedding in 1649 between the sister of the prince-elector, Hedwig Sophie, and the landgrave of Hesse-Kassel, Wilhelm VI.

Friedrich Wilhelm I (1688–1740), King in Prussia
After Antoine Pesne (1683–1757)
Stiftung Preußische Schlösser und Gärten Berlin-Brandenburg, Berlin

Elector Friedrich Wilhelm of Brandenburg's impressive gifts to Emperor Leopold I can plausibly be seen as setting the tone for Prussia's ascent to the heights of a full-fledged kingdom. Indeed, with its covered back, seat, and armrests, the amber armchair combines all the characteristics of a throne. Designed by Nicolaus Thurau in 1677, it can be ascribed to Winfried Baer, Gottfried Wolfram, and Christoph Maucher. The sizable drawing in Berlin corresponds to a multitude of fragments of the no longer extant throne whose hybrid design was executed in amber relief of various hues. Once belonging to the treasury (*Kunstkammer*), it is now housed in the Kunsthistorisches Museum, Vienna. There is also evidence of an order for a "triad" in amber for Versailles in 1679—an ensemble comprising console-table and mirror in an amber frame, together with a pair of sconces; from the same year comes a mirror frame with episodes from Ovid's *Metamorphoses*, while the following year saw the execution of a table for King William III of England, mention of which appears in archives for 1692.

Commissioned from Danzig (Gdansk), these attractively crafted components of diplomacy have inevitably proved vulnerable to the ravages of time. Amber pieces were mounted with adhesive to a substructure or wooden armature, and over decades the difference in the expansion coefficients of the two materials forces them apart. Thus, from among the many gifts Elector Friedrich III of Brandenburg presented on the occasion of his coronation as "king in Prussia" in 1701 to European sovereigns whose ranks he thus joined there remains but a solitary box in Gotha.

Prussian diplomatic gifts in amber should be seen in the light of the delicate balancing act performed by the European powers during the sixteenth and seventeenth centuries, when Brandenburg deployed every means—political, military, and diplomatic—to carve out a new role for itself. The period signaled the onset of the rational reorganization of the state, a process that gathered pace in the modern era. Since the primary aim was to concrete the sovereignty of the nation—essential to its sense of identity—pomp and circumstance proved less prevalent than at other courts. Obtaining such sovereignty depended on assent from European monarchs, so their good offices had to be obtained through diplo-matic ploys. Thus, reigning sovereigns in Vienna, Moscow, and Copenhagen, as well as in France, Dresden, and Krakow, were all to receive opulent gifts in amber, outward manifestations of Prussia's claims to regal power and status.

The nature of these amber articles changed markedly over time: items for personal use or intended to take their place in a treasury were gradually replaced by ceremonial objects, reserved for private apartments in royal residences, among which sumptuous pieces of furniture had pride of place. An amber cabinet commissioned from Königsberg and presented by Friedrich Wilhelm I to the elector of Saxony and king of Poland, August II, on his visit to Berlin in May 1728 provides a perfect illustration.

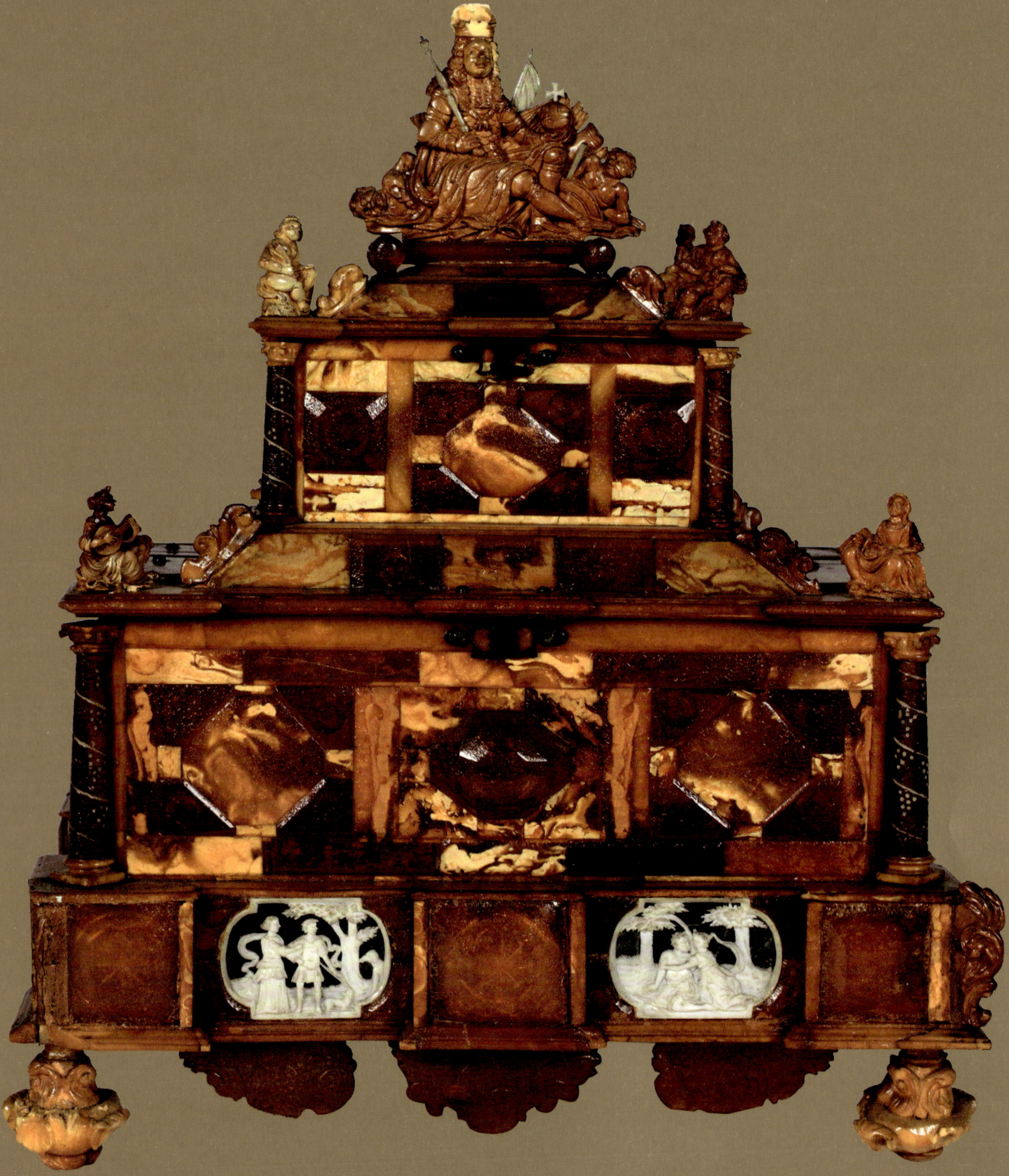

An official role can also be assigned to that furniture intended less for the owner's private use than to express through a language of nonverbal signs and enshrined hierarchies the claims and position of the state. By respecting every nuance in this code, a patron could establish a pecking order in society and convey his political objectives. Ensuring a role in the Holy Roman Empire and asserting sovereignty as expressed by royalty were explicit political objectives to be articulated not only verbally, but also through architecture, as well as by how the sovereign appeared at his court and elsewhere, and by the gifts he exchanged.

While such formal expressions today require elucidation and interpretation, at that time they appeared self-evident. Essential accessories in the mise-en-scène of the life of the state, over the years they acquired a significance that is still perceptible nowadays. Peaceful in nature, their principal objective was to proclaim the rank of a given state with respect to the others. The process was materialized in acts of "conspicuous consumption," performed before other heads of state or their representatives, or for the benefit of guests who would recount what they had seen thereafter. Each fresh innovation, each subtly modified gesture added to the gradual accretion of experience. Thus the now disappeared Amber Room occupied a special place in Prussian–Russian (and then German–Russian) relations, whose significance runs much deeper than its bare material value and whose popularity is, after due consideration, readily understandable.

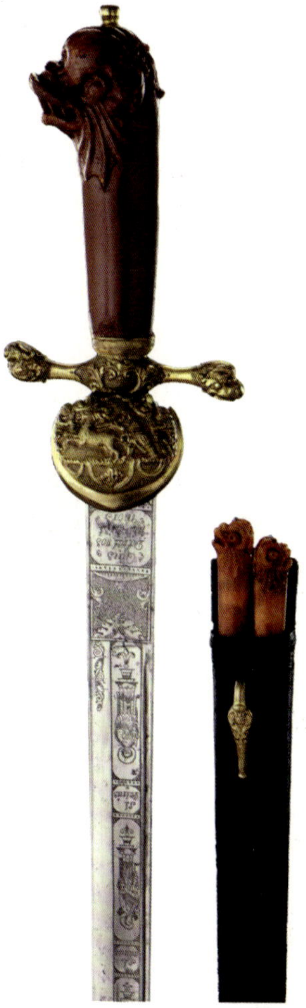

Knife with amber handle, for serving stag
Late seventeenth century–early twentieth
Staatliche Kunstsammlungen Dresden – Rüstkammer, Dresden

Casket in amber mounted with the figure of King Friedrich I
1701, Danzig
Stiftung Schloss Friedenstein, Gotha

Though the impressive material culture of the baroque era remains evident to all today, gauging the political import of the conception of self-representation it has bequeathed (in the form of "total works of art," in a special use of space, and an iconography rich in pathos) and its precise value as evidence from history, remains nonetheless a challenge.

The system according to which European sovereigns and princes acted as reciprocal guarantors and offered their neighbors gifts in the shape of rare products from their seas or mountains or precious articles of craftsmanship can be observed in many places, and constitutes the fundamental structure of the culture of the court gift.

Cup for the Festival of the White Rose

Samuel Wittwer

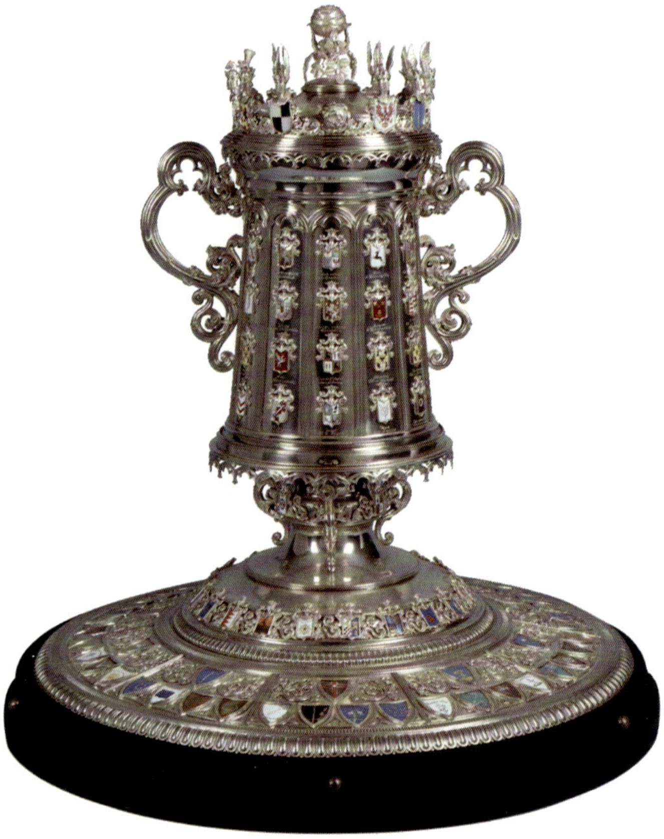

Commemorative cup for the Festival of the White Rose
1830
Johann Georg Hossauer, after Karl Friedrich Schinkel
Stiftung Preußische Schlösser und Gärten Berlin-Brandenburg, Berlin

This substantial ceremonial cup played an important part in one of the most sumptuous festivals ever organized by the Prussian royal house: the Festival of the White Rose held on July 13, 1829 in Friedrich II's New Palace, built in Potsdam from 1763 to 1769, and provided for the occasion with facilities for a "medieval" tournament.

The pretext for these entertainments was a visit by Princess Charlotte of Prussia, elder daughter of the king of Prussia, Friedrich Wilhelm III. In 1817 she had converted to Orthodoxy and taken the name Alexandra Feodorovna in order to marry Grand Duke Nicholas of Russia, second brother of Czar Alexander I. Following the death of the czar in 1825, her husband ascended to the Russian throne as Nicholas I. Although throughout the eighteenth and nineteenth centuries Prussian princesses had always maintained good relations with the courts to which they were allied, this marriage, which was intended simply to cement the friendship between the two fathers concerned—who had joined forces against Napoleon—had special political significance. All eyes were thus turned on the couple as they made their way to Berlin in 1829 on the occasion of the wedding of one of the czarina's brothers. While the czar stayed for only a brief time, Alexandra Feodorovna stayed on for a few weeks with her family, residing in the "New Palace" in Potsdam. Her thirty-first birthday falling during this period, the Prussian court, orchestrated by the czarina's uncle, Duke Karl of Mecklenburg-Strelitz, laid on a feast in keeping with her exalted rank. As Alexandra had been given the nickname "Blanche fleur" when she was a child, a suitable white flower was chosen as her emblem. The moniker derived from the main character in a novel set in the medieval period, *Der Zauberring* by Friedrich de la Motte-Fouqué, published in 1812, and one of the former Princess Charlotte's favorite books. As befitted the story, the birthday celebrations included knightly tournaments staged for the benefit of the many members of German nobility attending, followed by a performance in the castle's theater, and concluding with a ball. Thousands of curious private citizens also made their way from Berlin to Potsdam to admire the spectacle. That same year a printed commemorative album appeared with lithographs showing the various episodes of the festival.

Not long afterwards, court goldsmith Johann Georg Hossauer (who had already provided the decorations for the "Order of the Rose" at the gala, as well as a solid silver model of the flower) was commissioned by Karl of Mecklenburg-Strelitz to produce a cup to commemorate the czarina's thirty-second birthday. In return, the czarina commissioned Hossauer to make a second cup as a gift to her uncle, the prime mover behind the festival. The king of Prussia then ordered a third for himself. Drawings of the designs of all three pieces (displaying minor variants) were executed by the architect Karl Friedrich Schinkel.

The work exhibited is the cup Alexandra Feodorovna gave to Karl II of Mecklenburg-Strelitz. Presenting in a Gothic style the coats of arms of the families taking part in the festival, it materializes the bonds between the Prussian royal house and the German nobility.

Alexandra Feodorovna (1798–1860), Wife of Nicholas I, née Princess Charlotte of Prusse (1798–1860), Daughter of Friedrich Wilhelm III
1817
Franz Gerhard von Kügelgen (1772–1820)
Palace Museum, Gatchina

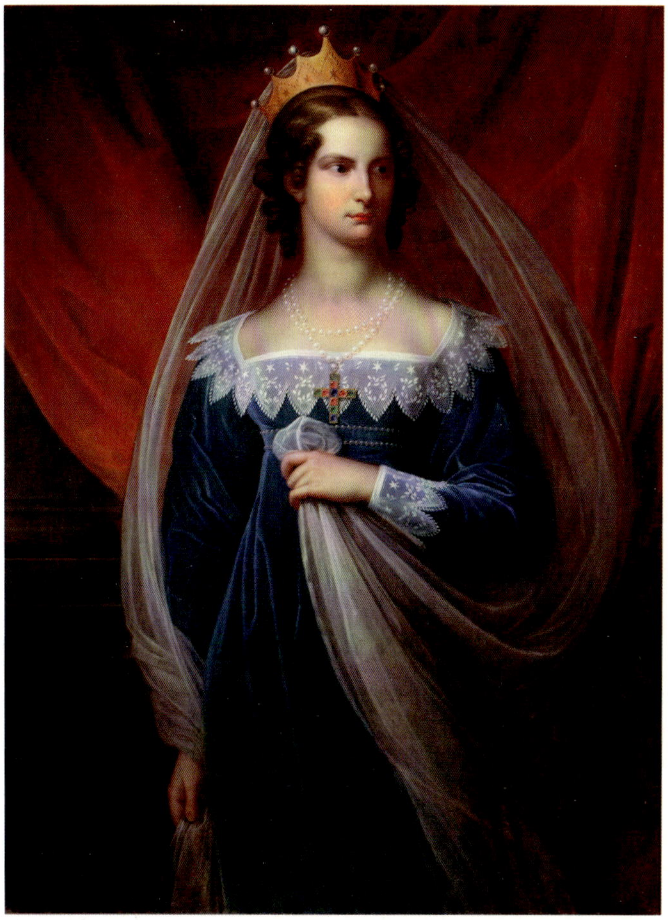

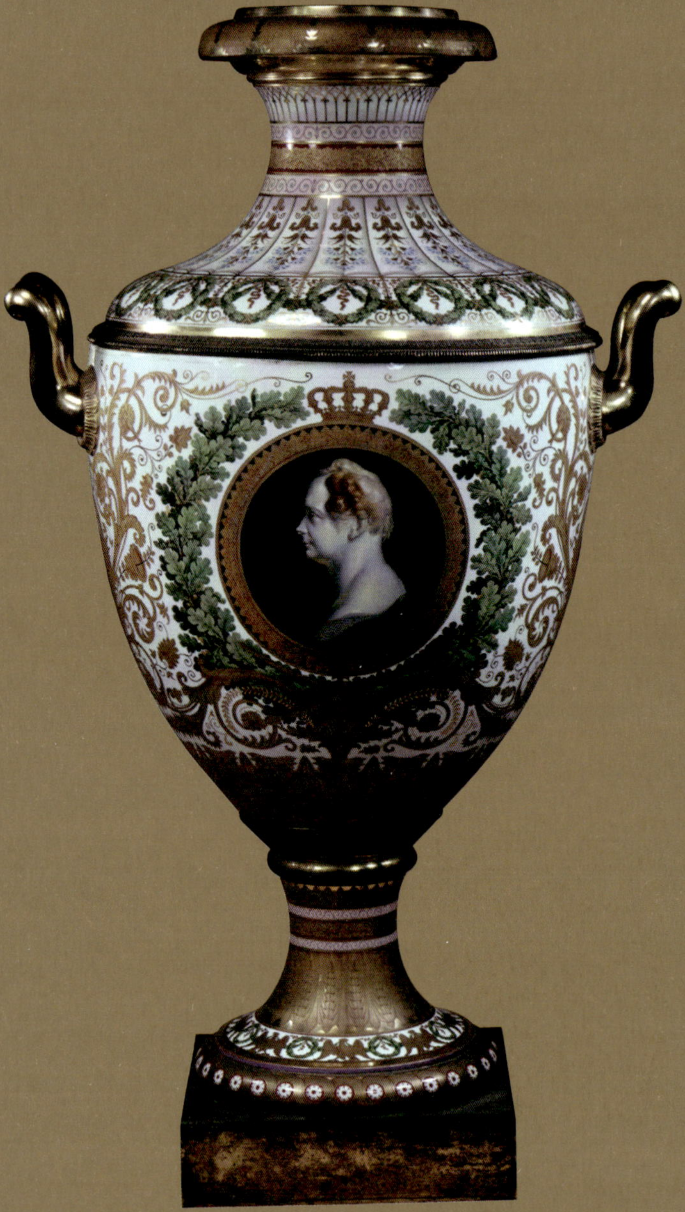

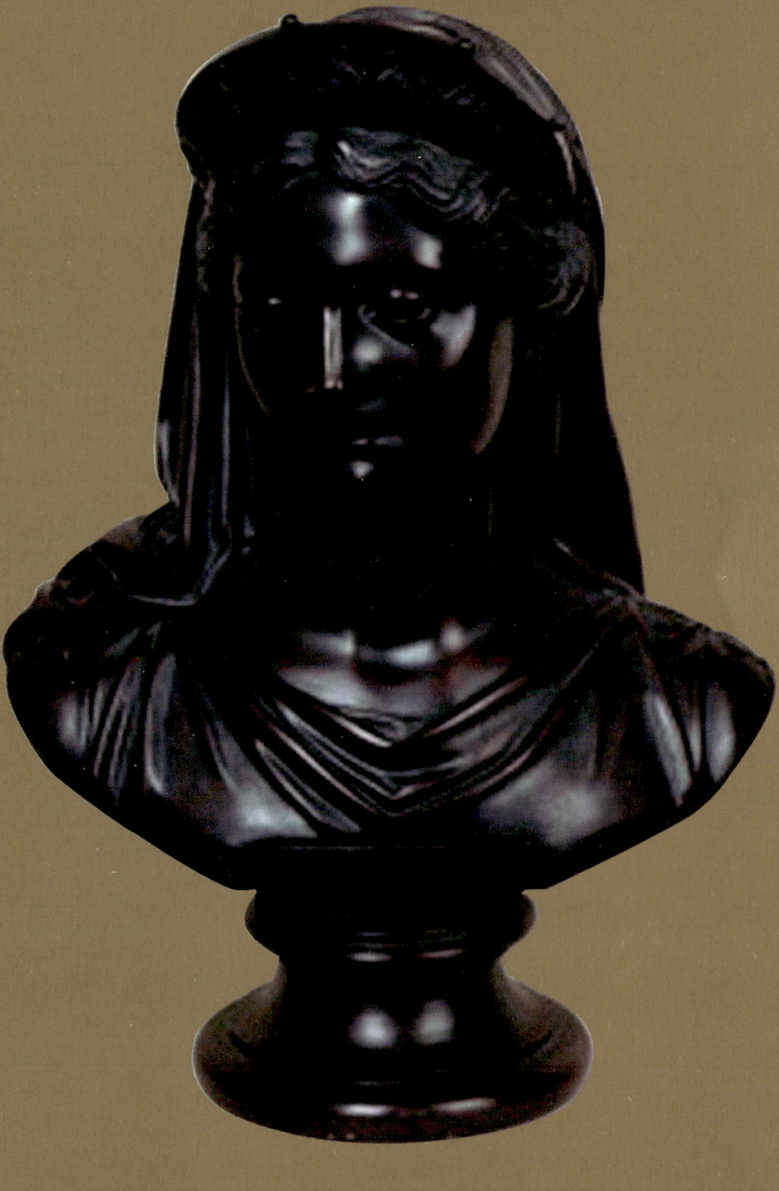

Monumental vase with the portrait of Friedrich Wilhelm IV (1795–1861) on one side and a tribute from the people on the other
1841
Royal Manufactory
Stiftung Preußische Schlösser und Gärten Berlin-Brandenburg, Berlin

Queen Luise of Prussia (1776–1810)
1818
Christian Daniel Rauch
Stiftung Preußische Schlösser und Gärten Berlin-Brandenburg, Berlin

Friedrich I (1657–1713), King in Prussia
Early eighteenth century
Friedrich Wilhelm Weidemann
Oil on canvas
75 × 59.5 cm
Stiftung Preußische Schlösser und Gärten Berlin-Brandenburg, Berlin
Inv. SPSG GK I 3813

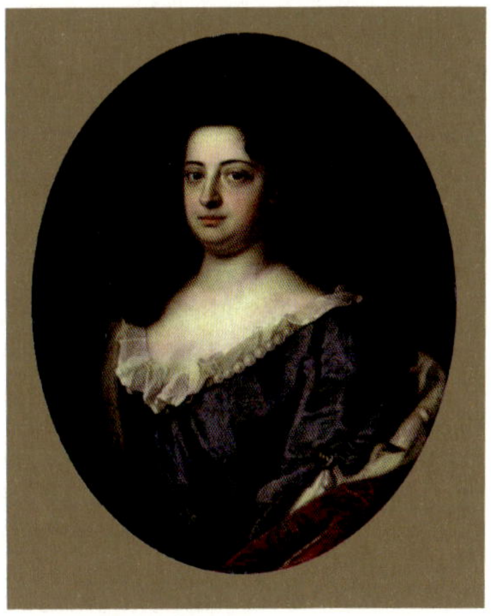

Queen Sophie Charlotte (1668–1705), Second Wife of Friedrich I
Early eighteenth century
Friedrich Wilhelm Weidemann
Oil on canvas
75 × 59.5 cm
Stiftung Preußische Schlösser und Gärten Berlin-Brandenburg, Berlin
Inv. SPSG GK I 3816

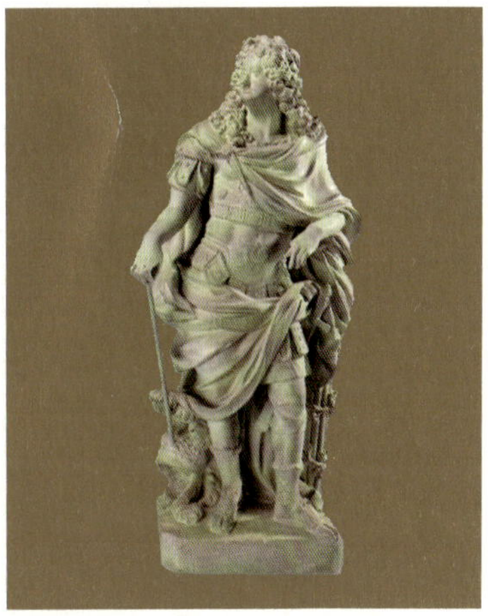

Statuette of Friedrich I depicted as Louis XIV, after the marble in the Prussian Fine Arts Academy
Plaster
H. 60 cm
Kunstgewerbemuseum, Berlin
Inv. Hz 2784 /2011, 101

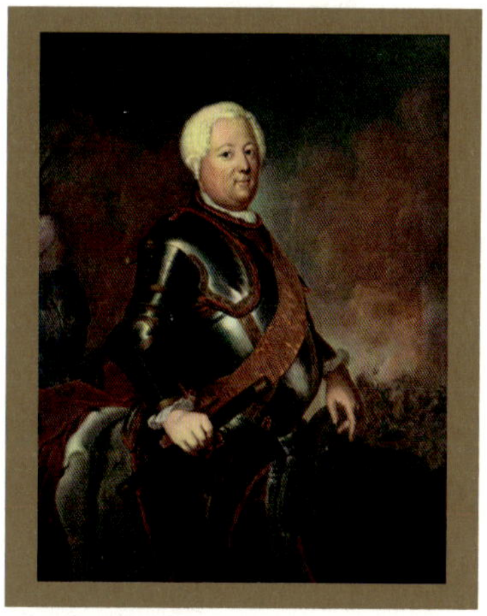

Friedrich Wilhelm I (1688–1740), King in Prussia
After Antoine Pesne (1683–1757)
Oil on canvas
149 × 118 cm (with frame)
Stiftung Preußische Schlösser und Gärten Berlin-Brandenburg, Berlin
Inv. SPSG GK I 50046

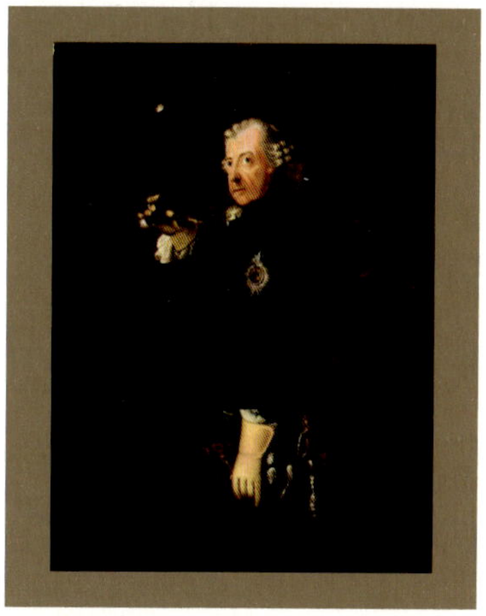

Friedrich II (1712–1786), Known as Frederick the Great, Son of Friedrich Wilhelm I, King in Prussia, who became King of Prussia in 1772
Johann Heinrich Franke
Oil on canvas
137 × 100 cm
Stiftung Preußische Schlösser und Gärten Berlin-Brandenburg, Berlin
Inv. SPSG GK I 30089

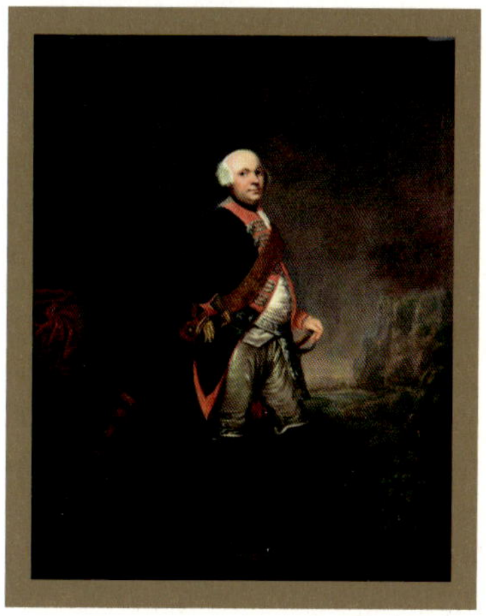

Friedrich Wilhelm II (1744–1797), King of Prussia
After Anna Dorothée von Schröder
Oil on canvas
158 × 129 cm
Stiftung Preußische Schlösser und Gärten Berlin-Brandenburg, Berlin
Inv. SPSG GK I 5091

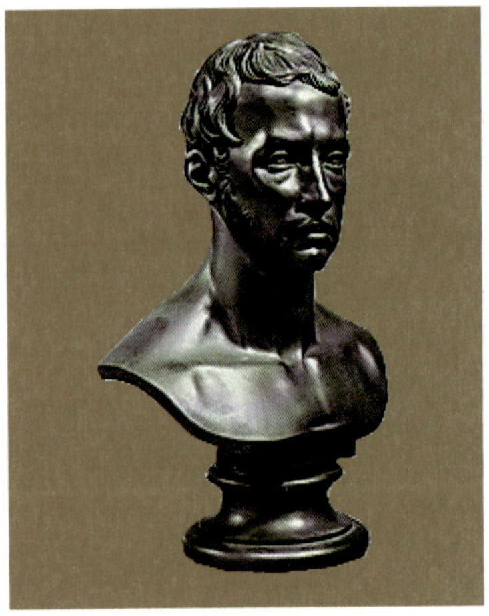

Friedrich Wilhelm III
1818
Berlin bronze
H. 56 cm
Stiftung Preußische Schlösser und Gärten Berlin-Brandenburg, Berlin
Inv. Skulpt.slg. 1533, GK III 2877

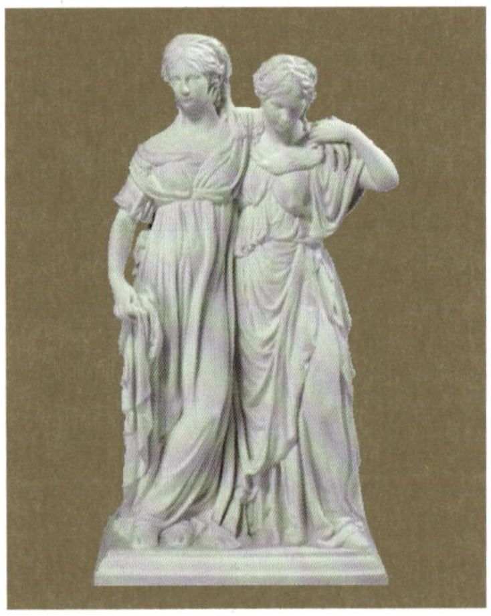

Double Portrait of Princess Luise (1776–1810) and her Sister, Princess Friederike of Prussia, Commissioned by Friedrich Wilhelm II
1795, Berlin
Johann Gottfried Schadow (1764–1850)
Berlin Royal Manufactory
Bisque porcelain
54.5 × 30.5 × 20 cm
Kunstgewerbemuseum, Berlin
Inv. 1998, 13

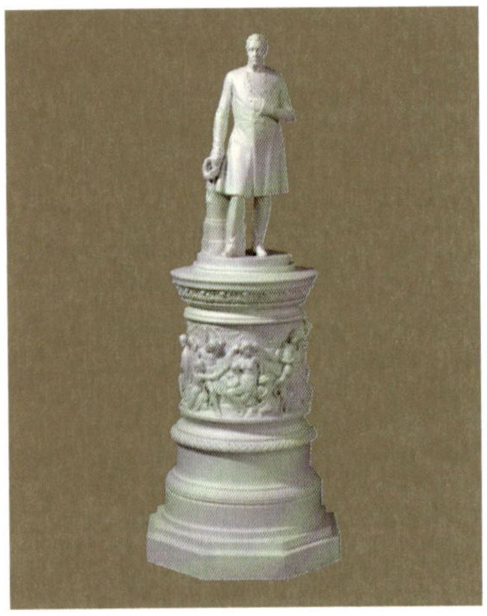

King Friedrich Wilhelm III
1858, Berlin
Berlin Royal Manufactory
Bisque porcelain
H. 76.3 cm
Kunstgewerbemuseum, Berlin
Inv. O-1965.19a-d

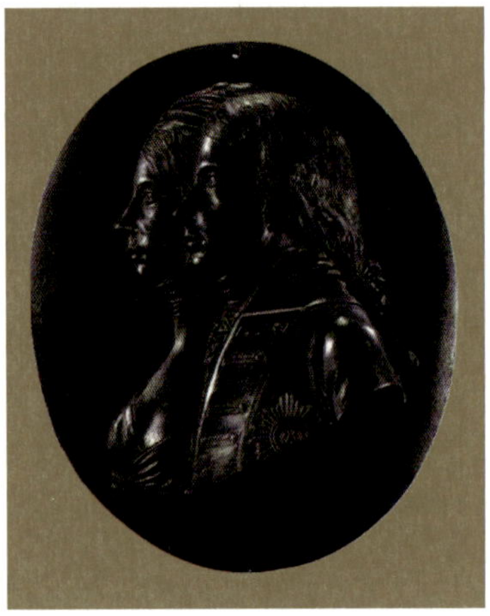

Oval medallion with the profiles of Friedrich Wilhelm III (1770–1840), son of Friedrich Wilhelm II and Luise
Berlin bronze
27.5 × 21.5 cm
Kunstgewerbemuseum, Berlin
Inv. WBI 22

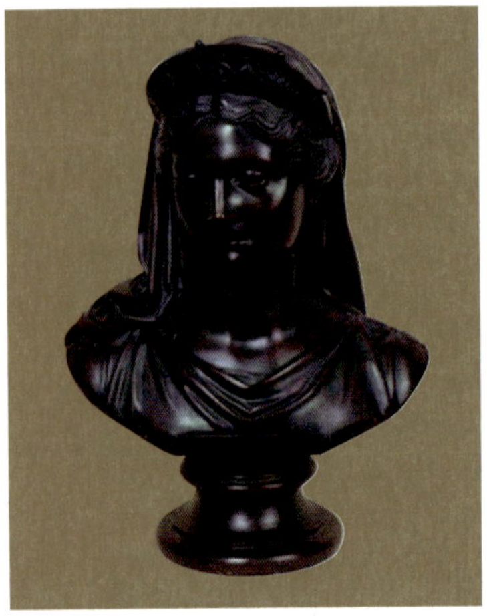

Queen Luise of Prussia (1776–1810)
1818
Stiftung Preußische Schlösser und Gärten Berlin-Brandenburg, Berlin
Inv. SPSG, Skulpt.slg. 4149

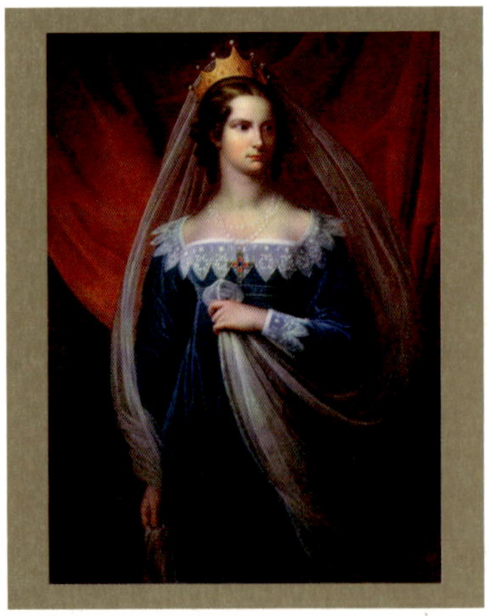

Princess Charlotte of Prussia (1798–1860), Daughter of Friedrich Wilhelm III
1817
Franz Gerhard von Kügelgen (1772–1820)
Oil on canvas
115 × 85 cm
Gatchina Palace Museum
Inv. GDM-114-III-KP-2285

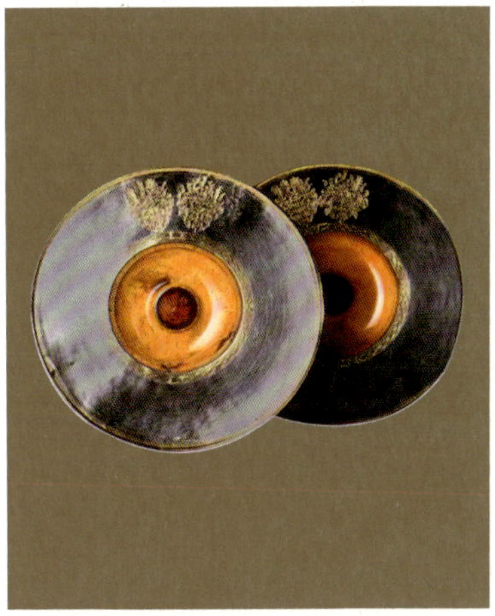

Two plates with the arms of Brandenburg, a gift from the elector of Brandenburg to the king of Denmark
1585, Berlin
Andreas Kniffel (silversmith)
Amber, engraved silver
D. 20.5 cm
Rosenborg Castle, Copenhagen
Inv. 1-14 and 1-15

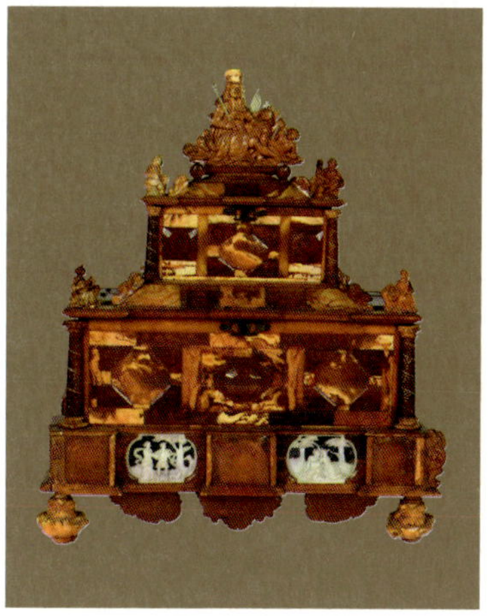

Casket mounted with the figure of King Friedrich I
1701, Danzig
Amber
Stiftung Schloss Friedenstein, Gotha
Inv. K 137

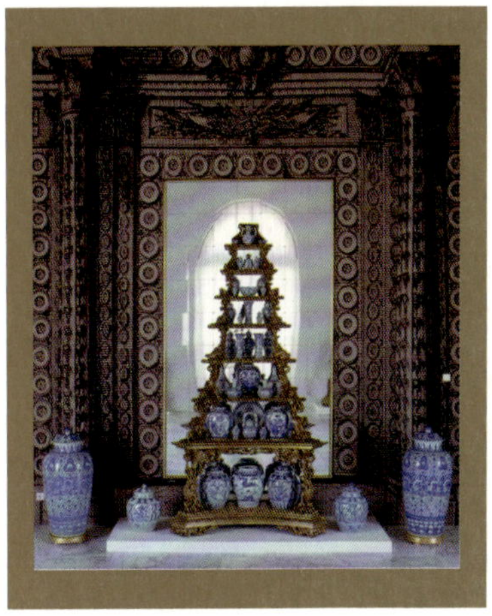

The Chinese Porcelain Room in the palace at Oranienburg
1695
China porcelain
300 × 145 × 75 cm
Stiftung Preußische Schlösser und Gärten Berlin-Brandenburg, Berlin
Inv. SPSG GK I V2246

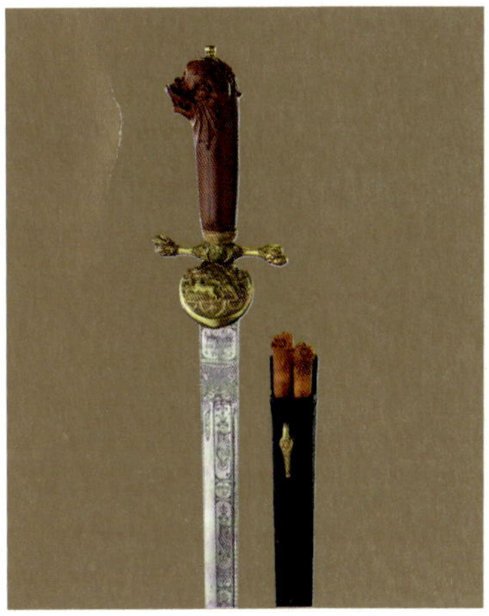

Knife with amber handle, a gift of Friederich Wilhelm of Prussia to Augustus II, King of Poland, Prince of Saxony
Late seventeenth century
Amber and steel
L. 67.3 cm
Staatliche Kunstsammlungen Dresden – Rüstkammer, Dresden
Inv. X 437

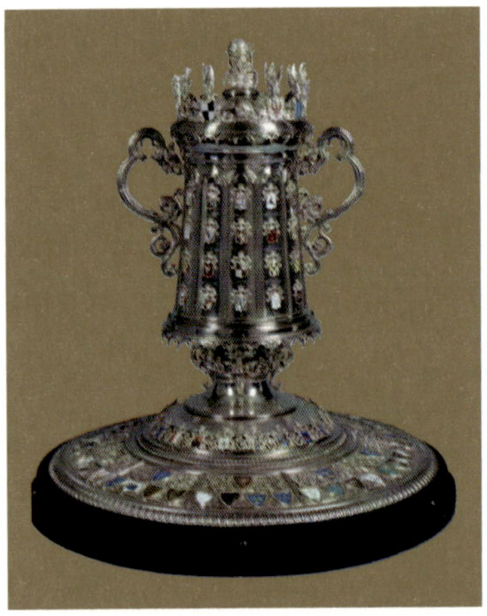

Commemorative cup for the Festival of the White Rose
1830
Johann Georg Hossauer,
after Karl Friedrich Schinkel
Silver
Stiftung Preußische Schlösser und Gärten Berlin-Brandenburg, Berlin
Inv. SPSG X 3168

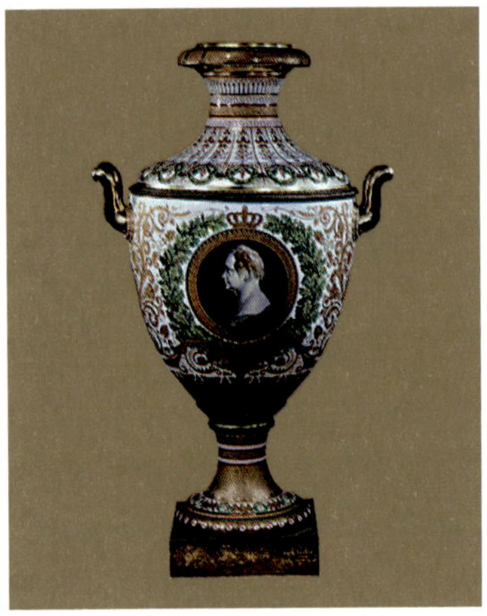

Monumental vase with the portrait of Friedrich Wilhelm IV (1795–1861) on one side and a tribute from the people on the other
1841
Berlin Royal Manufactory
Porcelain
Stiftung Preußische Schlösser und Gärten Berlin-Brandenburg, Berlin
Inv. SPSG XII 8099

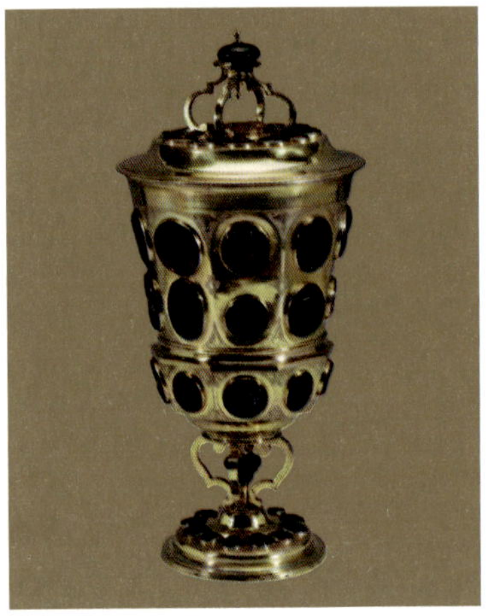

Large ceremonial cup featuring the portraits of the great historical personages
Nineteenth century, Berlin
Gilded silver
H. 45 cm
Kunstgewerbemuseum, Berlin
Inv. S 563

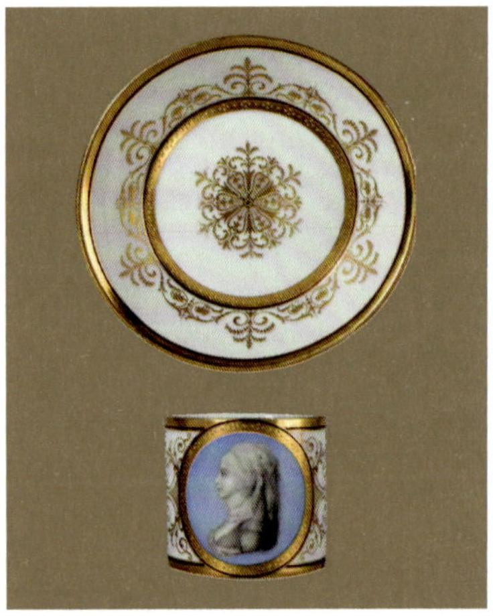

Cup with the profile of Queen Luise of Prussia (1776-1810)
c. 1796
Berlin Royal Manufactory
Porcelain
H. (cup) 6 cm; D. (saucer) 13 cm
Kunstgewerbemuseum, Berlin
Inv. Hz 516 (HM 10789)

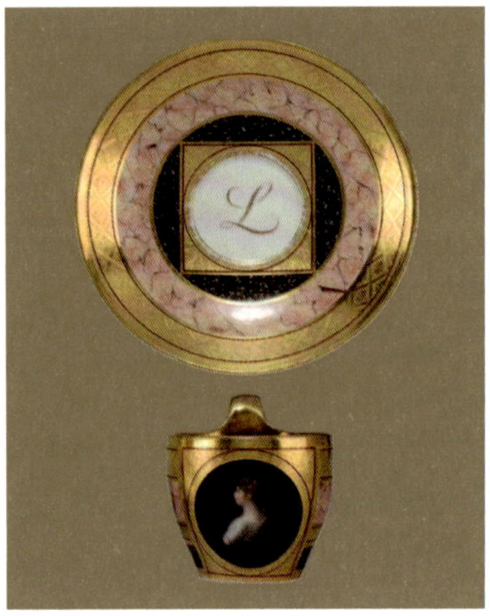

Cup with the portrait of Queen Luise of Prussia (1776-1810)
Post 1810
Berlin Royal Manufactory
Porcelain
H. (cup) 10.5 cm; D. (saucer) 19.5 cm
Kunstgewerbemuseum, Berlin
Inv. Hz 552 (HM 10784)

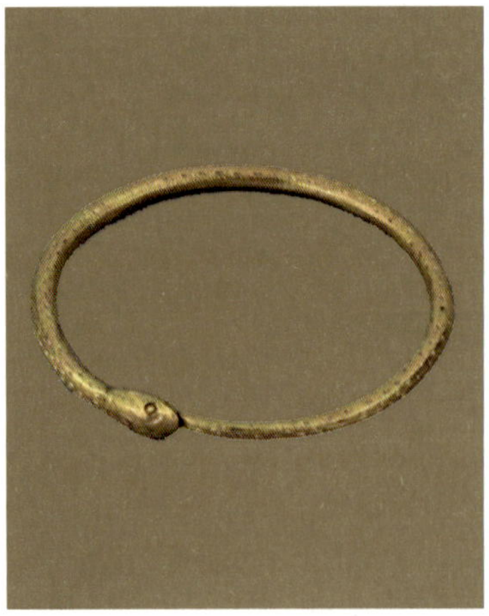

Bracelet in the form of a serpent belonging to Queen Luise of Prussia for six charms
D. 4.1 cm
Kunstgewerbemuseum, Berlin
Inv. SMS, H 7425 (O 1974, 112)

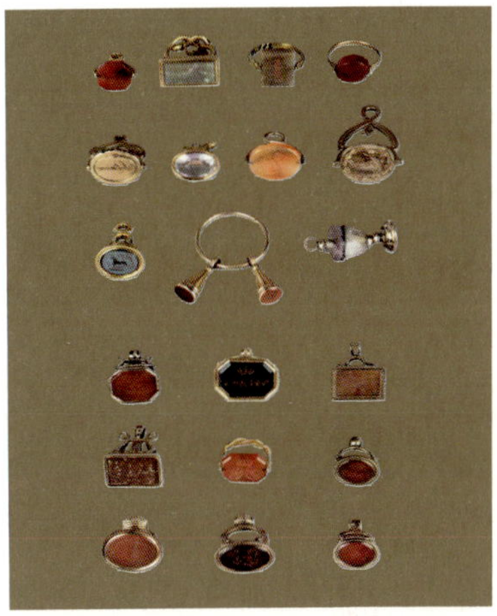

Eighteen charms belonging to Queen Luise and three signet rings
Kunstgewerbemuseum, Berlin
Inv. HM 7403 and 07,
7409 to 7420, 7422 to 7426

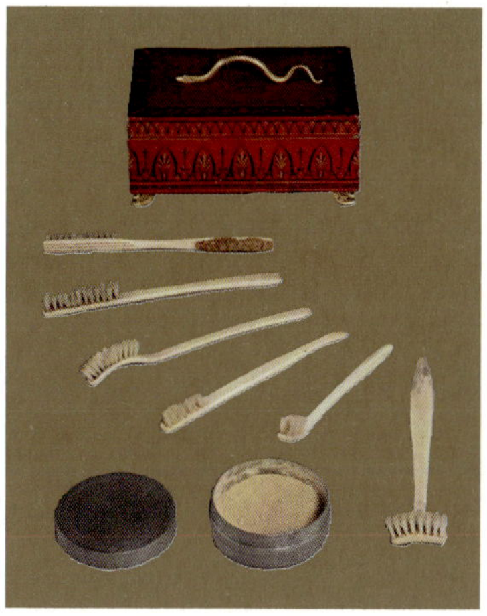

Dental hygiene set belonging to Queen Luise of Prussia
Kunstgewerbemuseum, Berlin
Inv. HM 7601 and HM 7619

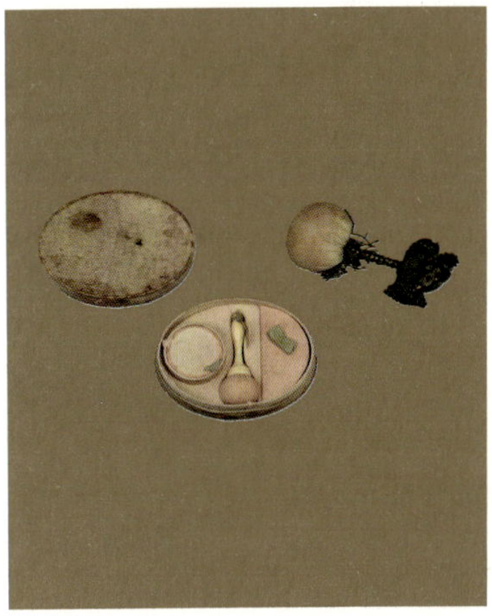

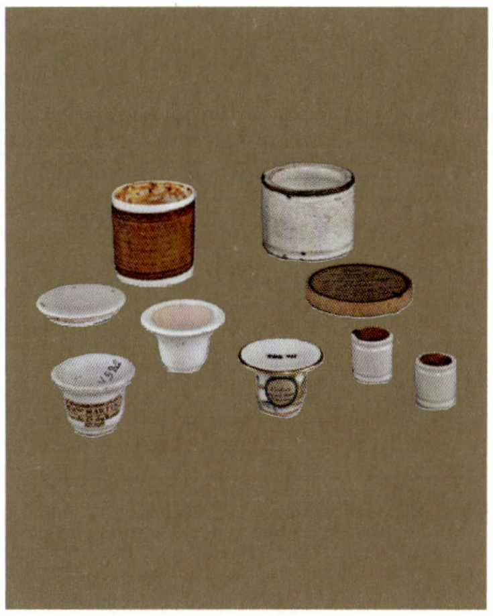

Toilette set belonging to Queen Luise of Prussia
Paris
Kunstgewerbemuseum, Berlin
Inv. HM 7605, 7606,
7611, 7613, 7620, 7621

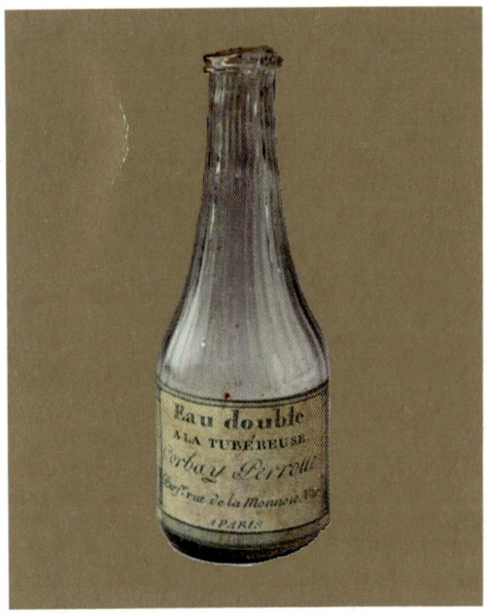

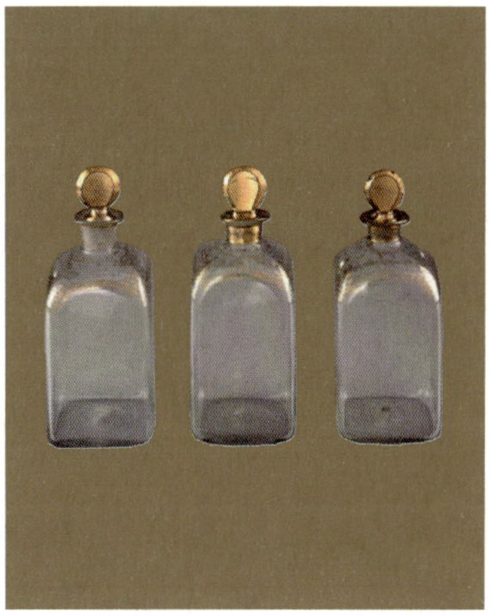

"Eau de toilette" from Paris, three bottles with gold caps and a recipe in English for rose milk belonging to Queen Luise of Prussia
Kunstgewerbemuseum, Berlin
Inv. HM 7604 anf HM 7622

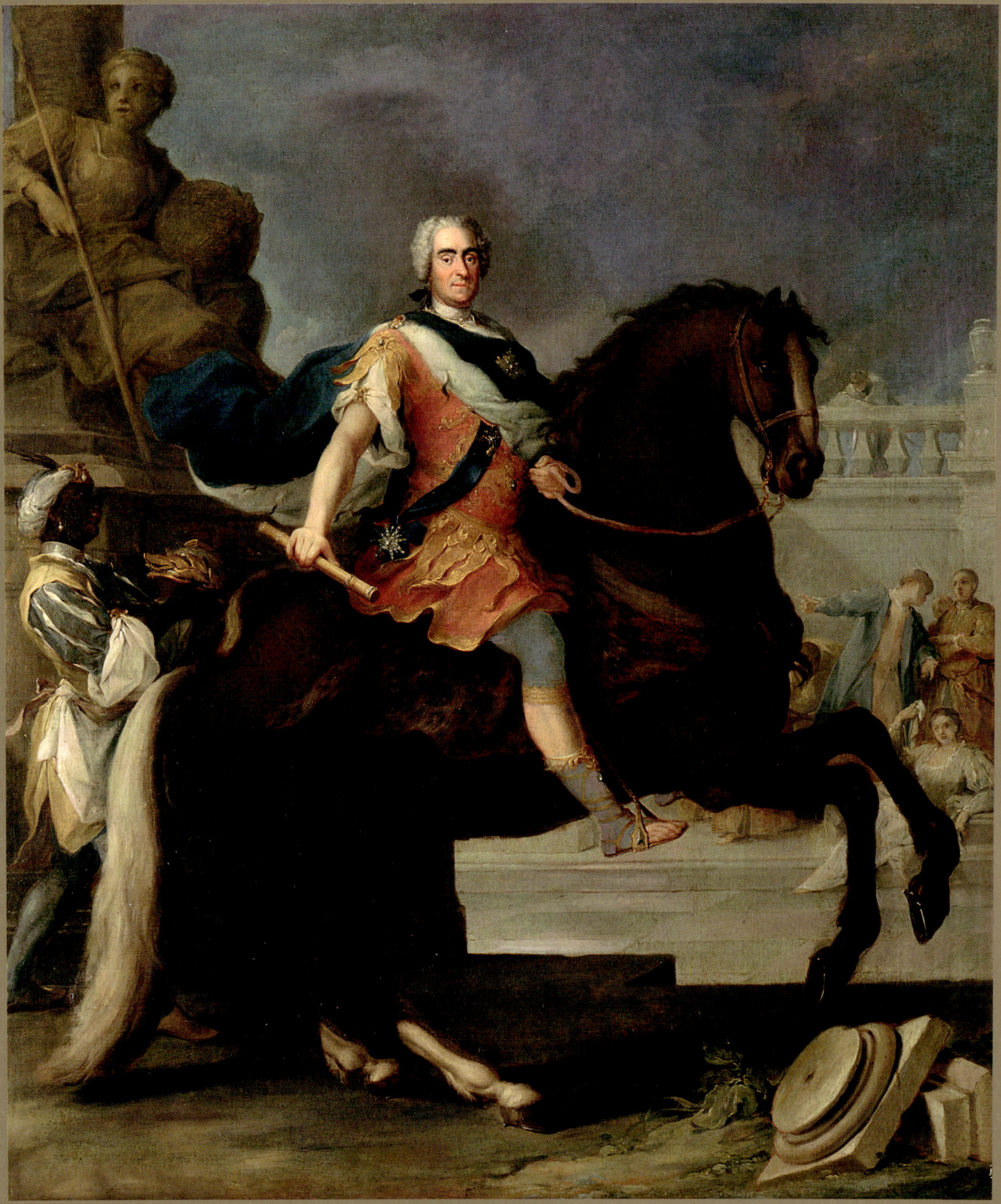

SAXONY

Augustus the Strong (1670–1733)

Augustus the Strong, Prince-Elector of Saxony and King of Poland under the name of Augustus II
c. 1728
Staatliche Kunstsammlungen Dresden, Gemäldegalerie Alte Meister, Dresden

Augustus the Strong, Prince-Elector of Saxony and King of Poland

Dirk Syndram

In Dresden, on May 12, 1670, Prince Johann Georg III and his wife Anna Sophia, daughter of the king of Denmark, were blessed with a son, whom they christened Friedrich Augustus. Nobody would have dreamed at the time that Augustus the Strong as he became known would turn out to be the most popular and most famous Wettin sovereign.

Younger son of the future elector, Friedrich Augustus's chances of one day reigning over Saxon hereditary lands must have looked slim indeed. Still, he received a thorough and wide-ranging education during which he displayed far more interest in fencing, the art of war, and horsemanship than in religion, history, and languages. At the end of his schooling, his father, as was customary at the time, packed him off on a "grand tour" of Europe. The young duke sojourned in France at the court of Louis XIV between 1687 and 1689, and also traveled to Madrid, Lisbon, Genoa, Venice, Florence, and Vienna. The goal was simultaneously to perfect his princely education and to publicize his existence at various up-and-coming courts. Thus he became acquainted with the regal majesty of absolute monarchy in the baroque period in all its guises and saw for himself many of the cultural highlights of the age. In the years that followed, Friedrich Augustus took part in the empire's wars with France with courage and panache.

After a youth in which he had earned a reputation for womanizing, in 1693, Augustus the Strong married Christiane Eberhardine of Brandenburg-Bayreuth. Together they had a legitimate son, Friedrich Augustus, born in 1696, who succeeded his father as king of Poland, as Augustus III. Between 1696 and 1712, Augustus also recognized eight other children by five of his many mistresses.

In April 1694, Friedrich Augustus's elder brother Johann Georg IV died of smallpox. As he died without issue, Friedrich Augustus I was elevated to the rank of prince-elector. A man of abnormal physical strength, of farsighted views, and with a weakness for the fairer sex, he pictured himself more readily riding at the head of an army than presiding at a music salon.

In Saxony, the young elector pursued his brother's rigorous political path to absolute power, endeavoring at the same time to elevate his status as a ruler.

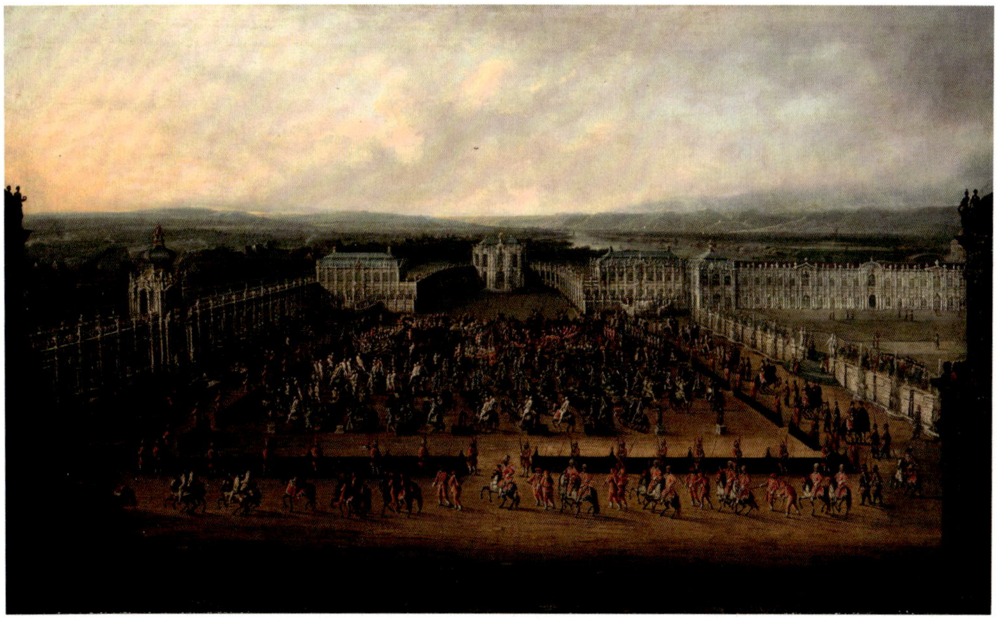

After the death of King Jan Sobieski of Poland-Lithuania, the elector of Saxony, with support from the German emperor, began to eye the Polish crown. To improve his chances, the Lutheran prince converted to Catholicism and had to convince the "magnates," the powerful Polish aristocracy, of his financial muscle. In Krakow in September 1697, Friedrich Augustus I was crowned king of Poland and grand duke of Lithuania as Augustus II. The byname "the Strong" was given to him by historians some two generations after his death.

More than two decades of war followed for Augustus II, initially against other pretenders to the Polish throne and their backers, then against the Ottoman sovereigns, and finally, in the Great Northern War (1700–21) sparked by Augustus himself, against the skillful general Charles XII, king of Sweden. Moreover, between 1715 and 1717, a violent civil war, led by a faction of the Polish-Lithuanian nobility, broke out. Between 1706 and 1709, Augustus found himself on the back foot, losing significant battles and forfeiting the Polish throne. Nevertheless, demonstrating considerable skill and perseverance, he managed to reassert his rights and, for some thirty-six years, jointly governed two countries vastly different in geography and legal system: wealthy, socially rigid, and rigorously Protestant Saxony and the noble Republic of Poland and Lithuania, hobbled by dynastic squabbling.

Augustus II is, however, remembered, not as a vanquished military leader or peripatetic monarch, but rather as a great European patron of the arts with a talent for organizing lavish entertainments, as an architectural patron of genius,

"Carrousel" in the Zwinger, 1722
Before 1725
Johann Alexander Thiele
(1685–1752)
Staatliche Kunstsammlungen Dresden, Gemäldegalerie Alte Meister, Dresden

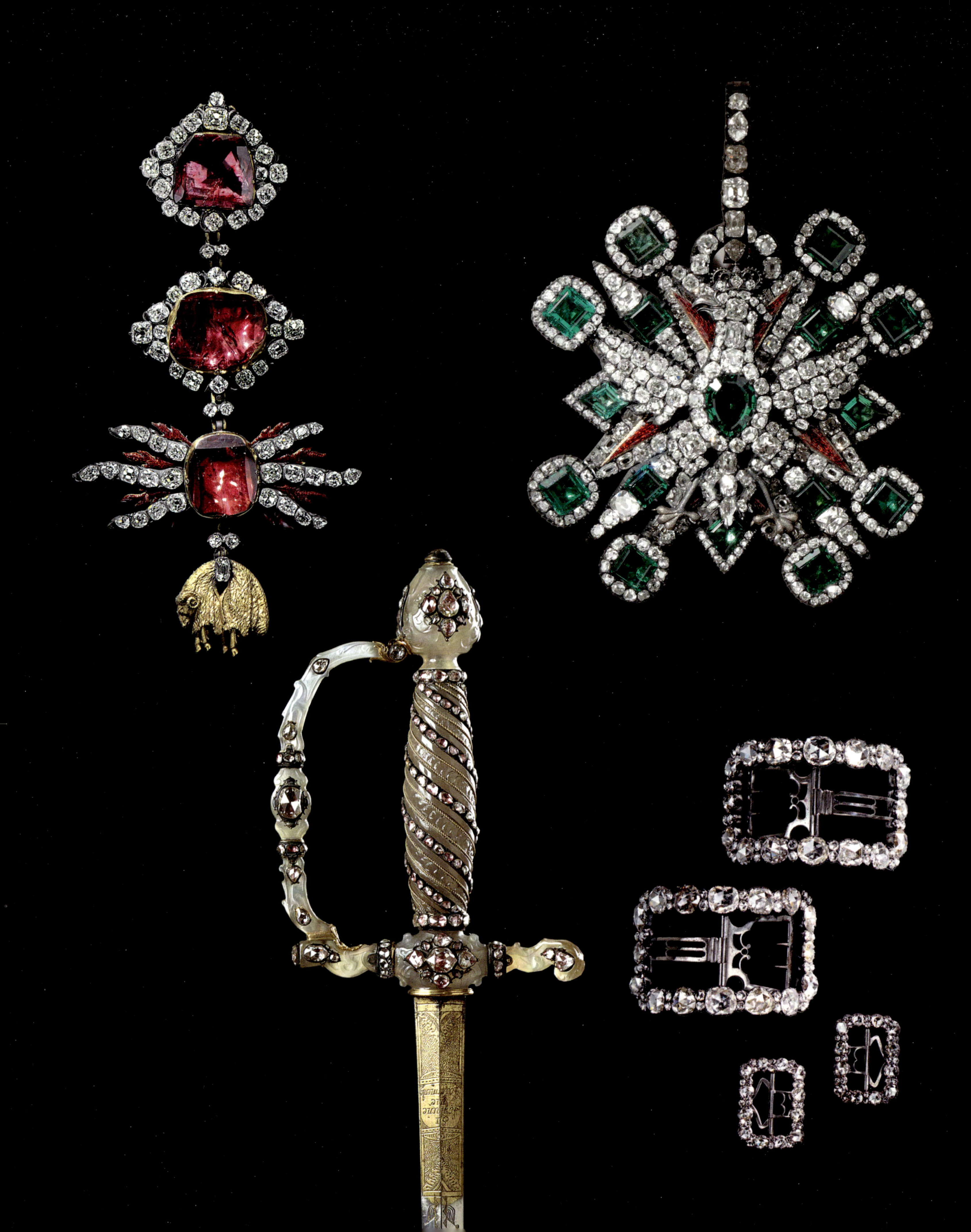

and as a clairvoyant founder of museums—one of the first to sense the perennial power of the arts. His singularly creative imagination, extravagant yet focused, led the elector-king, wearing his gentleman-architect's hat, to practice an art he had learnt early on with considerable success. He was also receptive to other artistic genres and possessed a gift for spotting talent. Knowing how and when to offer support, by rewarding long-term contracts, he attracted some first-rank painters and sculptors to the court, as well as architects and goldsmiths.

It was a period in which royal splendor was expressed not only in architectural grandeur and sumptuous banquets, but also through a prince's deportment and mien, his magnificent attire, and opulent ornaments or jewelry. By combining a genuine fascination for beauty with his ideas of majesty, Augustus the Strong lived up to contemporary expectations of perfection.

He was rightly regarded as one of the greatest jewelry connoisseurs among the princes of his age, as evidenced by his private treasury of which he was so fond. While the gilt coffee service created by Johann Melchior Dinglinger between 1697–98 and 1701 constituted yet another masterpiece for his new royal majesty, the golden coffeepot is also a groundbreaking artifact in which the unique idiom of Dresden baroque is clearly formulated for the first time.

During the first half of Augustus's reign the inevitable drain on the public purse caused by war and the high cost of his ephemeral courtly events had a negative impact primarily on his architecture projects. They also affected the reconstruction of the palace at Dresden that its new function as a royal residence and a catastrophic fire in 1701 had rendered particularly urgent. The first major plan actually carried out (1705–08), the "Turkish Palace," (the current Taschenberg

Order of the Golden Fleece
1772, Dresden
Workshop of Johann Melchior Dinglinger (1664–1731)
Staatliche Kunstsammlungen Dresden, Grünes Gewölbe, Dresden

The Polish Order of the White Eagle
1746
Johann August Jordan
Staatliche Kunstsammlungen Dresden, Grünes Gewölbe, Dresden

Sword
1722–33, Dresden
Johann Melchior Dinglinger (1664–1731)
Staatliche Kunstsammlungen Dresden, Grünes Gewölbe, Dresden

Pair of diamond-encrusted garter buckles and **shoe buckles**
1782–89, Dresden
Christian August Globig
Staatliche Kunstsammlungen Dresden, Grünes Gewölbe, Dresden

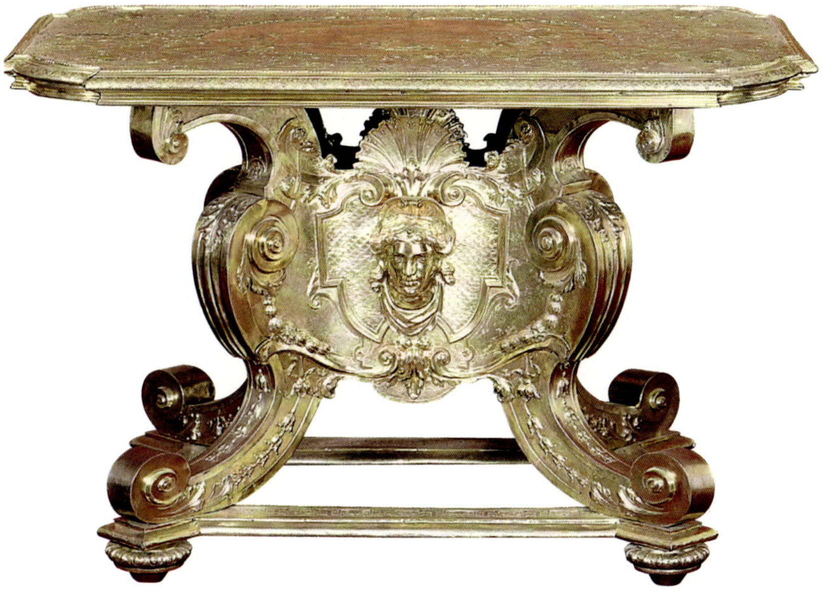

Table decorated with the seasons represented by Mars, Ceres, Neptune, and Aeolus
1708–10, Augsburg
Albrecht Biller
Staatliche Kunstsammlungen, Dresden

Saber decorated with Moor's head
First quarter of the seventeenth century, Germany; Istanbul (blade)
Staatliche Kunstsammlungen Dresden, Rüstkammer, Dresden

Palace built for his favorite, Countess Cosel), was followed by the project for the Zwinger between 1709 and 1719. Begun as an orangery under the direction of the architect Matthäus Daniel Pöppelmann and the sculptor Balthasar Permoser, it was soon being envisaged as the first element in a new castle, before ending up as a backdrop to baroque festivals. These rapid shifts in allotted function are typical of Augustus's ingenious yet pragmatic mindset.

When in about 1717 the situation in the kingdom of Poland-Lithuania began to brighten and the longed-for family ties between the House of Wettin and the imperial House of Habsburg were sealed, Dresden could finally flourish as a royal seat in the true sense. The ambitious plans for a new residence were abandoned and replaced by rebuilding projects. In two years, the chief architect Pöppelmann and the decorator Leplat created a modern interior that responded to the twin exigencies of kingly pomp and royal dwelling. At the same time, a pleasure dome was created in the city, dubbed the Dutch Palace (today, the Japanese Palace), as well as a new opera house in the Zwinger that ensured that Dresden was a prominent musical center for decades.

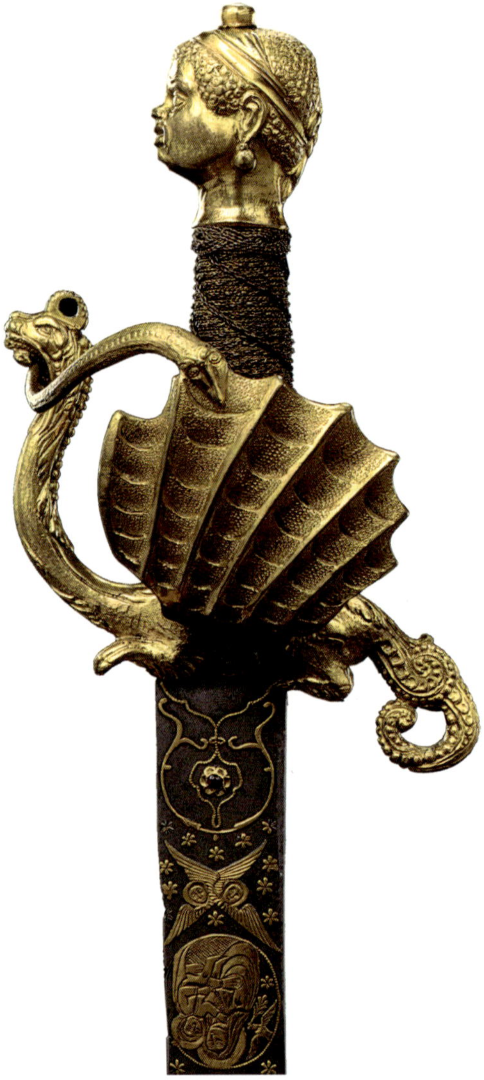

The year 1719 signaled a watershed in the reign of Augustus the Strong, with seven weeks of uninterrupted junketing on the occasion of the wedding of his son, at which the king appeared splendidly arrayed in nine ensembles of jewels unique in all Europe.

Augustus subsequently decided to have the outskirts of his city-residence laid out in fittingly regal fashion, including the gardens at Großsedlitz, with the Friedrich's castle (1719–27), the palaces on the water and in the mountains at Pillnitz (1720–22 and 1723–24), the hunting lodge at Moritzburg (1723–27), and at Übigau (1724–26). Each of these castles served as a setting in which the elector-king and his court, hunts, and festivals could all be seen to their best effect.

The final decade of Augustus's life was colored by a cultural policy that might almost be described as visionary. In these years, his elevation to the kingship of Poland served to motivate and justify a growing quantity of artworks, which in the 1720s began to be separated into various collections. The result was carefully differen-

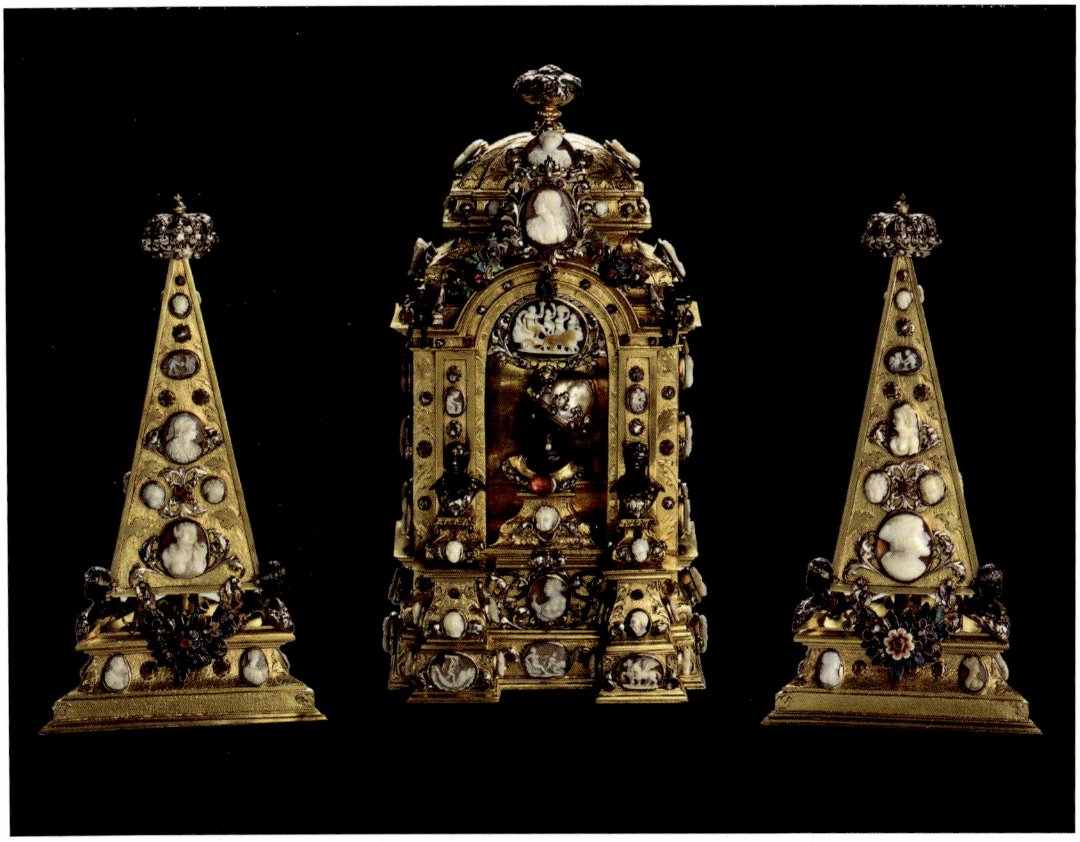

tiated, specialized holdings covering various fields of the arts and sciences following a logic that anticipates many aspects of the modern conception of a museum. Much was displayed in the pavilions and galleries of the Zwinger, converted for the occasion into a "Royal Palace of the Sciences." The treasury in the Green Vault was reorganized as a single artistic space and developed into the largest and most modern collection of treas-ures of the eighteenth century that was open to the public.

Augustus died of diabetes in Warsaw on February 1, 1733. At his death, a number of projects remained unfinished, but his efforts had already raised the profile of the city of Dresden and its residence, which, thanks to him, both still shine brightly in the consciousness of Europe.

"Triumphs" in architectural form
1701–05, Dresden
Johann Heinrich Köhler
Staatliche Kunstsammlungen Dresden, Grünes Gewölbe, Dresden

The Green Vault of Dresden, treasury of Augustus the Strong

Dirk Syndram

Between 1723 and 1724, Augustus the Strong—under the direction of his principal court architect, Matthäus Daniel Pöppelmann, designer of the Dresden Zwinger—had a magnificent structure built for his vast collection: comprising carved consoles, mirrors, and varnished and painted woodwork, it stood in three rooms of the Geheime Verwahrung (the secret repository) located on the ground floor of the residence's west wing. The works transformed the Schatzkammer, or treasury, of the elector-king's ancestors—inaccessible for the most part until that time—into a glorious showcase for his collections of gold- and silverwork, curios, and jewels.

By the late sixteenth century, these rooms, owing to their vaulted ceilings partly decorated in stucco and with architectural elements painted copper-green, had acquired the name Grünes Gewölbe (Green Vault). Later, the Renaissance painting disappeared behind precious baroque cladding in mirror glass and only the name survived.

Inevitably the three halls proved too small to house Augustus the Strong's ever expanding collection of treasures. Thus, in 1727, the sovereign himself sketched a substantial project for their enlargement that saw them extending to eight rooms in which a subtly orchestrated mise-en-scène displayed collections that were opened to the public in 1729. From the start, then, collections and museum design formed a single, inseparable unit. The presentation of the pieces on consoles and tables depended on the materials concerned, while the interior decoration of the great halls had to suit—be it in terms of color or form—the works displayed within.

Thanks to this incomparable treasure trove—composed of diamonds, rubies, sapphires, and emeralds, and unique pieces by the goldsmith and jeweler Johann Melchior Dinglinger, the museum of the Green Vault quickly acquired a reputation as "a fairy palace of unbounded splendor" (Arthur Schopenhauer, 1804).

Until Dresden was razed by bombs in 1945, the space and structure of the collections in the Green Vault remained nearly unchanged. Following extensive works that saw the five surviving rooms restored and the three destroyed ones rebuilt, today the jewel shines as brightly as ever. A unique example of the art of the late baroque treasury, the Grüne Gewölbe lives on as the one of oldest museum collections in Europe.

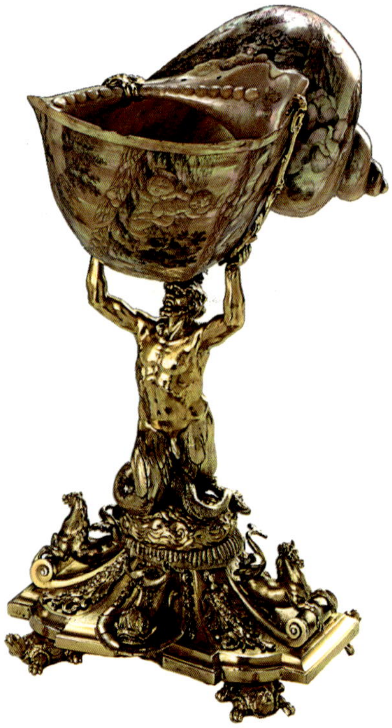

Nautilus with silver mounting
Second half of the seventeenth century
Cornelis van Bellekin
Mounting
1724, Dresden
Johann Heinrich Köhler
Staatliche Kunstsammlungen Dresden, Grünes Gewölbe, Dresden

Meissen porcelain

Ulrich Pietsch

The discovery of European hard-paste porcelain by Johann Friedrich Böttger in January 1708 and the rapid establishment of a firm to produce it, the Königliche Porzellan-Manufaktur in Dresden in January 1710, laid the foundations for the unprecedented monopoly exercised by the prince-elector of Saxony and king of Poland, Augustus II. His passion for Chinese and Japanese ceramics soon saw him amass the greatest European collection of East Asian and Meissen porcelain of the time, displayed in spectacular fashion in a gigantic porcelain palace—the famous Japanisches Palais in Dresden.

Made in the Albrechtsburg at Meissen, where hard-paste porcelain remained a jealously guarded secret, the production of the royal manufactory was not just destined for the personal use of the king: it was also sold at the famous Leipzig fair.

A bestiary (some of it life-size) by modelers Johann Joachim Kaendler and Gottlieb Kirchner, together with the first great table service for the Saxon-Polish court, are some of the highlights of the early output of the manufactory. The many decorations painted on the coffee, tea, and chocolate services by Johann Gregorius Höroldt also reflect Augustus's penchant for chinoiserie. The reign of his son Augustus III, from 1734 to 1763, heralded the production of figurines for decorating the dessert services of the nobility, corresponding to a new vogue for displaying figure groups in cabinets.

At that time, Meissen porcelain often constituted part of a diplomatic gift, in this manner becoming widely known throughout Europe as a status symbol. Meissen held on to its ceramic supremacy until the end of the Seven Years' War in 1763, when it began to be ousted by the Sèvres manufactory.

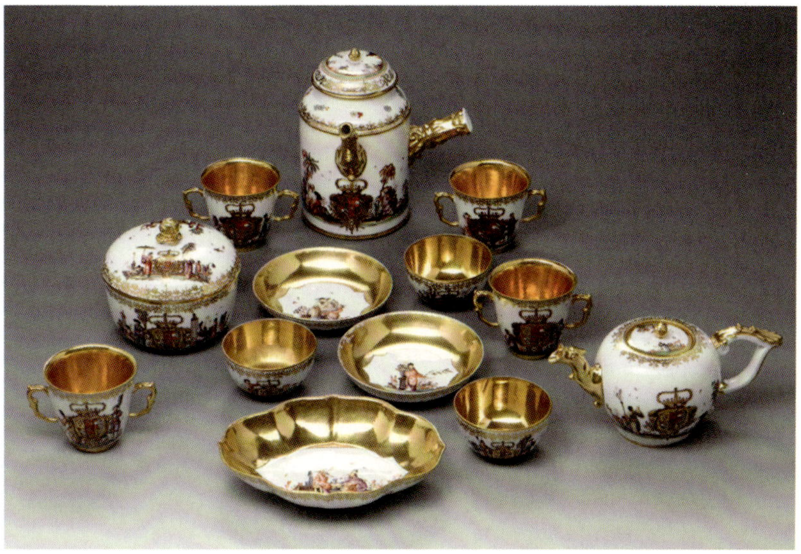

Tea service with the arms of Parma for Isabella Farnese
c. 1728
Meissen
Staatliche Kunstsammlungen Porzellansammlung, Dresden

Festivals at the court of Augustus the Strong

Jutta Charlotte von Bloh

As well as music, opera, ballet, banquets, illuminations, fireworks, and great hunts, Dresden boasts a venerable cultural festival tradition, including tournament entertainments, carrousels, masquerades, water parades, and sleigh rides. On his accession to the throne of Poland in 1697, Augustus II had the princely residence of Dresden provided with spaces for hosting such events—the most celebrated being the Zwinger—and new parade rooms in the palace, in which splendid royal festivals could be staged. In keeping with the fame of the king whose star stood high in the European firmament at the time, the royal wardrobe featured sumptuous garments, some woven entirely in gold thread.

In 1709—in echo of his model Louis XIV, the Sun King—Augustus II played the personification of the sun god Apollo in an allegorical "procession of the gods" during an evening joust that included tilting at the ring. To amuse the ladies, Augustus had introduced running at the ring using slender French-style lances in entertainments at court. On the occasion of a "Carrousel of the Four Corners of the World," the king donned the costume of an African chief.

In 1719 the festivities thrown in Dresden for the wedding of the crown prince to Maria Josepha of Habsburg, the emperor's daughter, centering on "jousting between the seven planets," lasted for over a month. This planetary entertainment proved the zenith of the late baroque culture of the festival. The bride sailed up the Elbe on a gilded boat built along the lines of a Venetian gondola. For the "Festival of Mars," Augustus II again revived ancient tournament events, equipping the horses mounted for running the ring with pageantry saddles presented to him by Louis XIV in 1715. At the time of the phenomenally opulent "Festival of Apollo," Augustus led the "Carrousel of the Four Elements" as the king of fire. In 1722 he chose the role of Scaramuccia from the *Commedia dell'arte* for a "Comic Carrousel." One final example of Augustus's immense energy and creative talent is provided by the major military maneuvers staged at the camp of Zeithain in the presence of Friedrich Wilhelm I and his son, the crown prince and future Friedrich II, in 1730, which concluded with a fireworks display and a grand concert on the Elbe featuring the full complement of court musicians.

Goblet (from a set of four) decorated with the arms of Saxony and of the Polish Order of the White Eagle, commissioned by Augustus the Strong the marriage of his son, the future Augustus III
1719, Dresden
Johann Jacob Irminger (1635–1724)
Staatliche Kunstsammlungen Dresden, Rüstkammer, Dresden

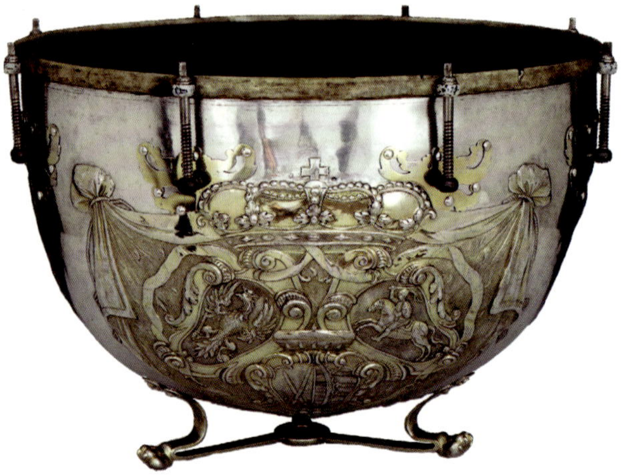

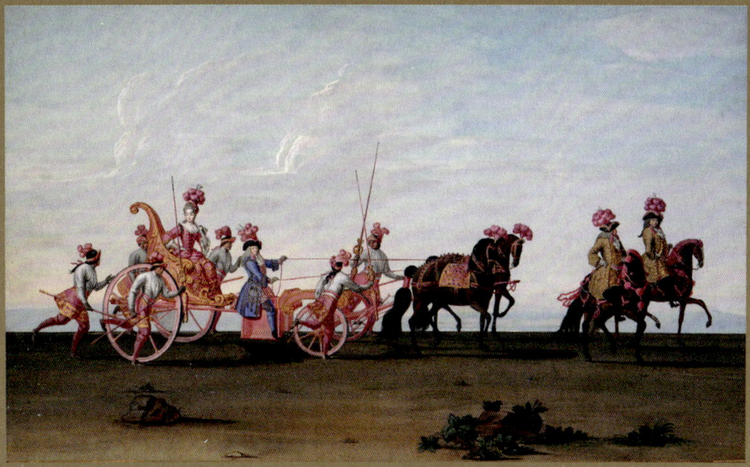

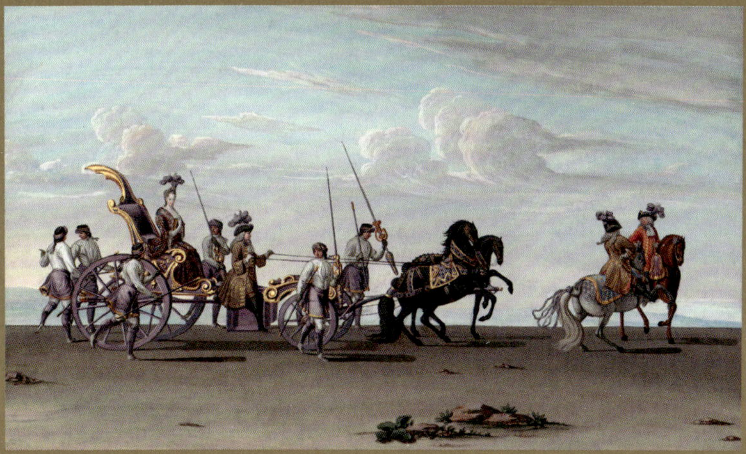

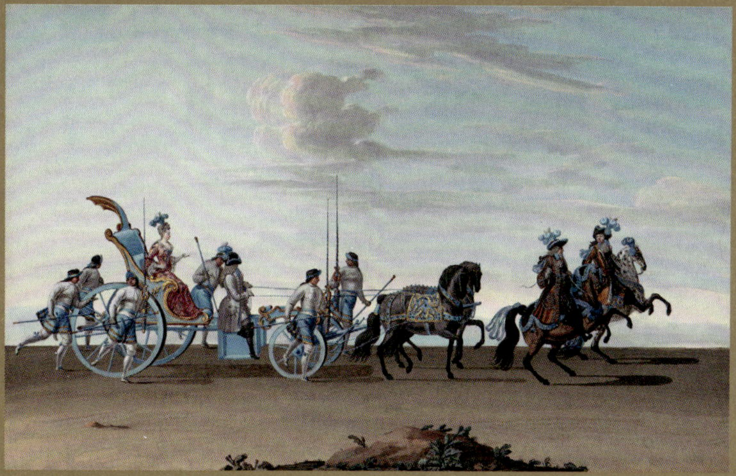

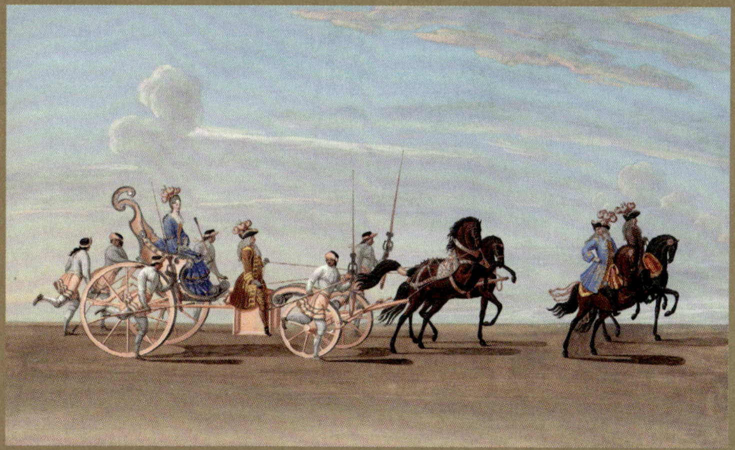

"Ladies Jousting", Dresden, June 6, 1709: Countess Cosel with King Frederik IV of Denmark and Augustus the Strong; Lady Haugwitz, "Lady-Chamberlain"; Countess of Pflug, High Court Marshal; Lady Prebenau, Guardian of the Royal Treasures
1710, Dresden
Johann Samuel Mock (c. 1687–1737)
Staatliche Kunstsammlungen Dresden, Kupferstich-Kabinett, Dresden

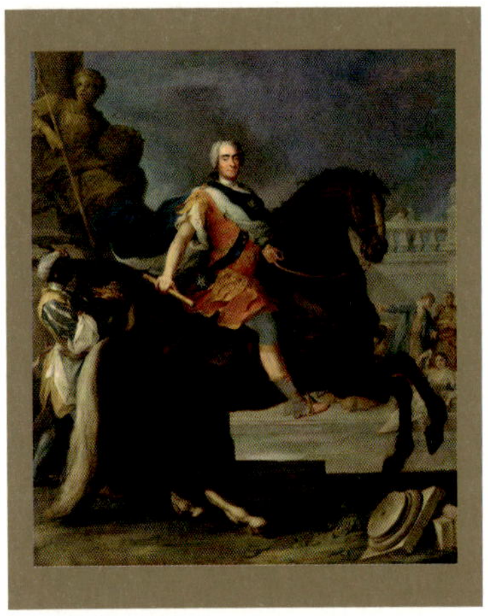

Augustus the Strong (1670-1733) on Horseback, King of Poland under the name of Augustus II
c. 1728
Oil on canvas
139 × 116.5 cm
Staatliche Kunstsammlungen Dresden, Gemäldegalerie Alte Meister, Dresden
Inv. 2005/01

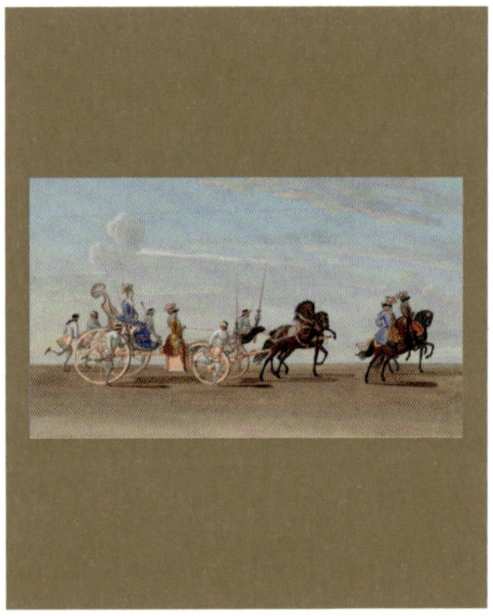

Lady Prebenau, Guardian of the Royal Treasures, during Ladies Jousting, Dresden, June 6, 1709
1710, Dresden
Johann Samuel Mock (c. 1687–1737)
Gouache, highlighted in white and gold, black lead
58.5 × 91.3 cm
Staatliche Kunstsammlungen Dresden, Kupferstich-Kabinett, Dresden
Inv. Ca 198 BI 13

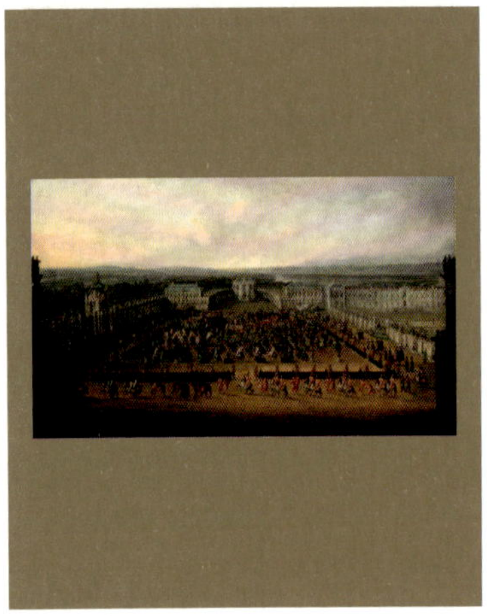

"Carrousel" in the Zwinger, 1722
Before 1725
Johann Alexander Thiele (1685–1752)
Oil on canvas
106 × 168 cm
Staatliche Kunstsammlungen Dresden, Gemäldegalerie Alte Meister, Dresden
Inv. Gal.3604

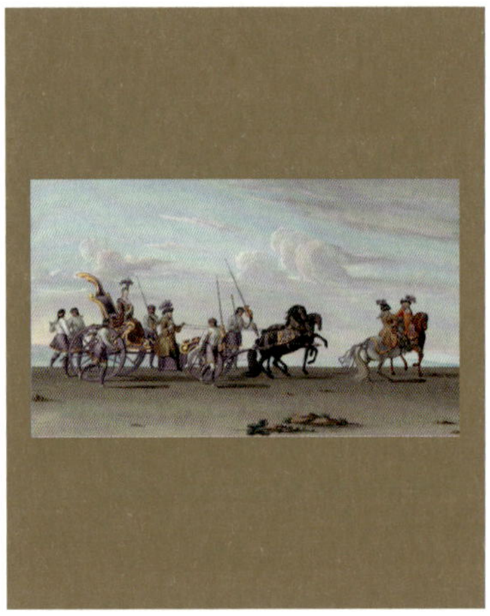

Lady Haugwitz, "Lady-Chamberlain," during Ladies Jousting, Dresden, June 6, 1709
1710, Dresden
Johann Samuel Mock (c. 1687–1737)
Gouache, highlighted in white and gold, black lead
58.5 × 91.6 cm
Staatliche Kunstsammlungen Dresden, Kupferstich-Kabinett, Dresden
Inv. C 198 Bl 8

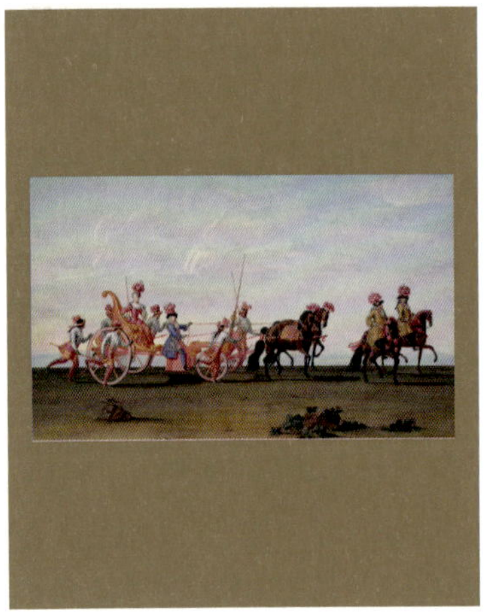

Countess Cosel with King Frederik IV of Denmark and Augustus the Strong during Ladies Jousting, Dresden, June 6, 1709
1710, Dresden
Johann Samuel Mock (c. 1687–1737)
Gouache, highlighted in white and gold, black lead
58.5 × 91.3 cm
Staatliche Kunstsammlungen Dresden, Kupferstich-Kabinett, Dresden
Inv. Ca 198 Bl 23

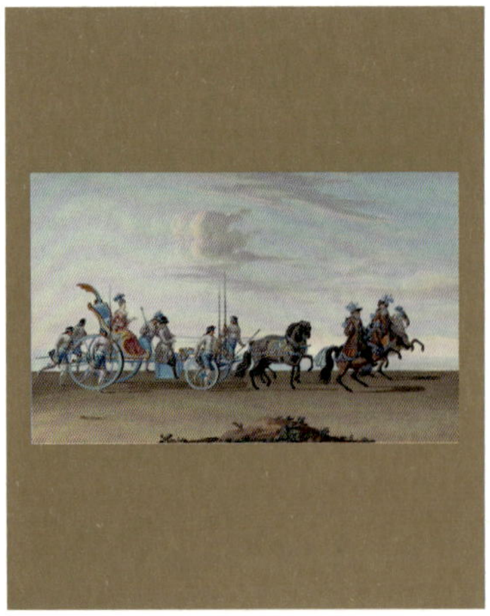

Countess of Pflug, High Court Marshal, during Ladies Jousting, Dresden, June 6, 1709
1710, Dresden
Johann Samuel Mock (c. 1687–1737)
Gouache, highlighted in white and gold, black lead
58.5 × 91.3 cm
Staatliche Kunstsammlungen Dresden, Kupferstich-Kabinett, Dresden,
Inv. Ca 198 BI 18

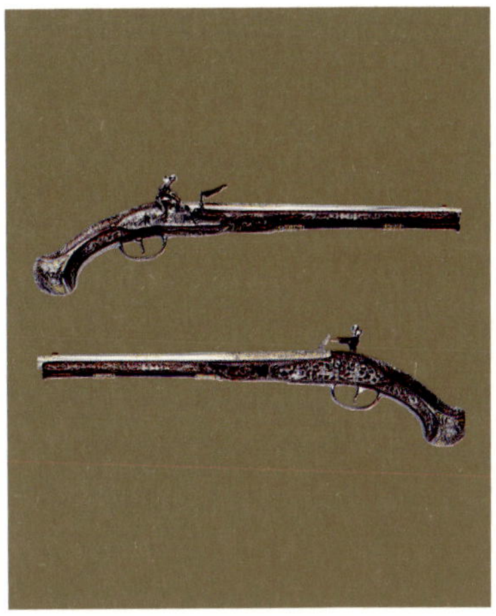

Pair of pistols, gift from Louis XIV to Augustus the Strong
c. 1690, Paris
Bertrand Piraube
(active 1670–1682); plate signed "Piraube aux galleries à Paris"
Polished, engraved, and partially gilded iron; butt in walnut and silver incrustations
L. 52.5 cm
Staatliche Kunstsammlungen Dresden, Rüstkammer, Dresden
Inv. J1419-1420

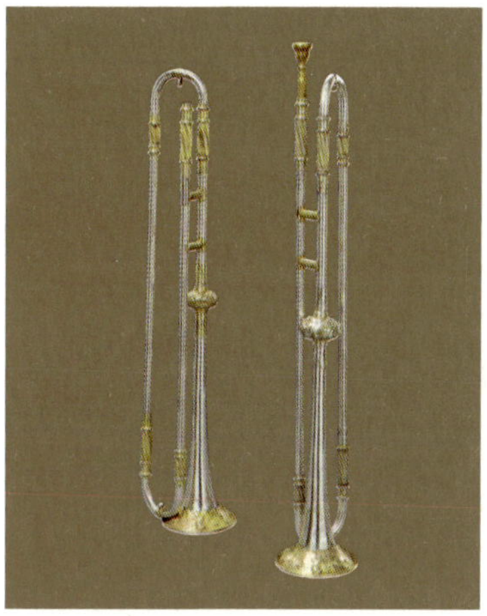

Two of the four bugles (in a series of twelve) used at official ceremonies in the court of Saxony
1753, Dresden
Christian Friedrich Riedel
(1703–1784) and
Heinrich Leopold Schmey
Partially gilded silver
L. 65.8 cm
Staatliche Kunstsammlungen Dresden, Kunstgewerbemuseum, Dresden
Inv. 37458 a1, a2, b1, b2

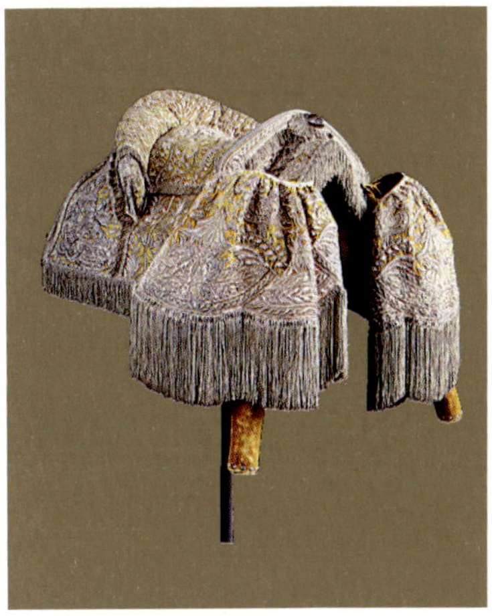

Parade saddle, gift from Louis XIV to Augustus the Strong: saddle, cover, holster covers, and a pair of pistol holsters
1715, Paris
Wood, leather, linen, and horse hair; iron and gilded brass; silk velvet lining, embroidery, braid, and fringes in gold and silver thread
133 × 98 cm
Staatliche Kunstsammlungen Dresden, Rüstkammer, Dresden
Inv. L25

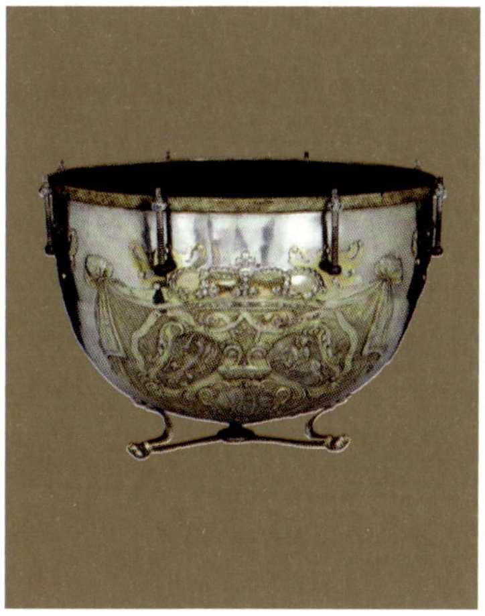

Goblet (from a set of four) decorated with the arms of Saxony and of the Polish Order of the White Eagle, commissioned by Augustus the Strong for the marriage of his son, the future Augustus III
1719, Dresden
Johann Jacob Irminger (1635–1724)
Partially gilded silver, calf's leather
43.5 × 58.5 cm
Staatliche Kunstsammlungen Dresden, Rüstkammer, Dresden
Inv. P298

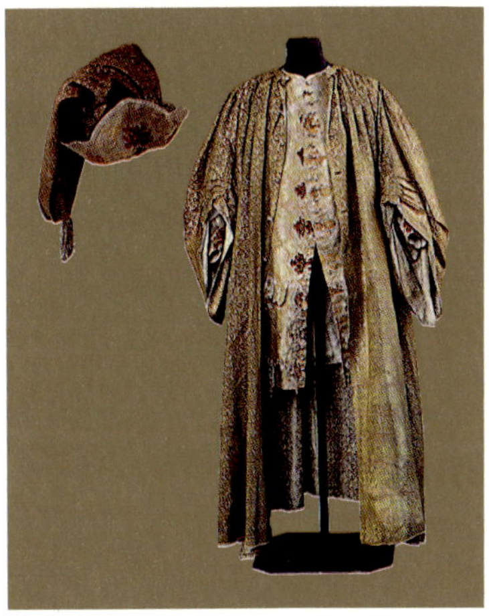

Gown and hat from the wardrobe of Augustus the Strong
1727–33, Lyon (?)
Gold cloth, velvet brocade
L. (gown) 390 cm
Staatliche Kunstsammlungen Dresden, Rüstkammer, Dresden
Inv. i.33

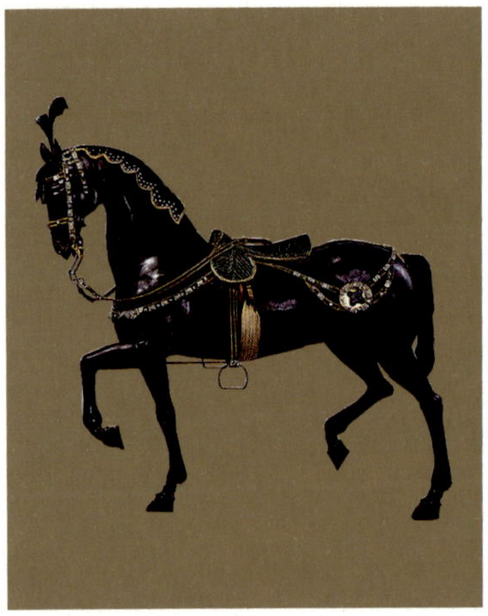

Life-size horse
Nineteenth century, Dresde
Wood, hair, iron
Ceremonial harness: commissioned by Prince Johann Georg IV of Saxony in 1709, transformed for Augustus the Strong
1691–94, Meisse, and 1709
Attributed to
Johann Abraham Schneider
Gilded silver, precious stones, diamonds, gilded brass, gilded iron, leather
Staatliche Kunstsammlungen Dresden, Rüstkammer, Dresden
Inv. PF0013, L0013 and L0607

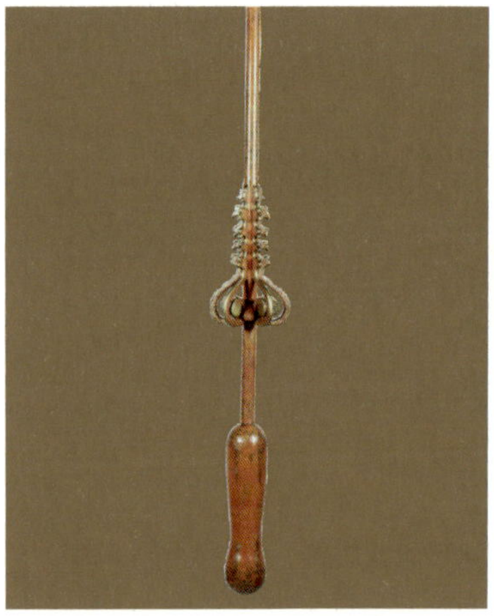

Jousting lance
1719, Dresden
Martin Schnell
Wood, lacquerware, gilded bronze
L. 270 cm
Staatliche Kunstsammlungen Dresden, Rüstkammer, Dresden
Inv. R282

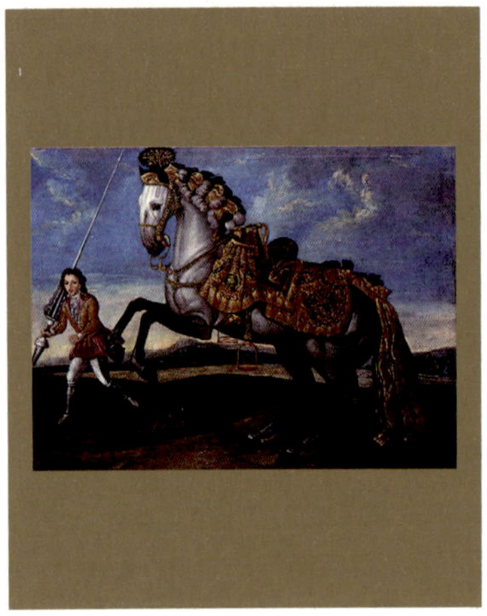

Lance porter and ceremonial horse harnessed for jousting, Dresden, 1719
c. 1719
Oil on canvas
113.8 × 139.9 cm
Staatliche Kunstsammlungen Dresden, Rüstkammer, Dresden
Inv. H85

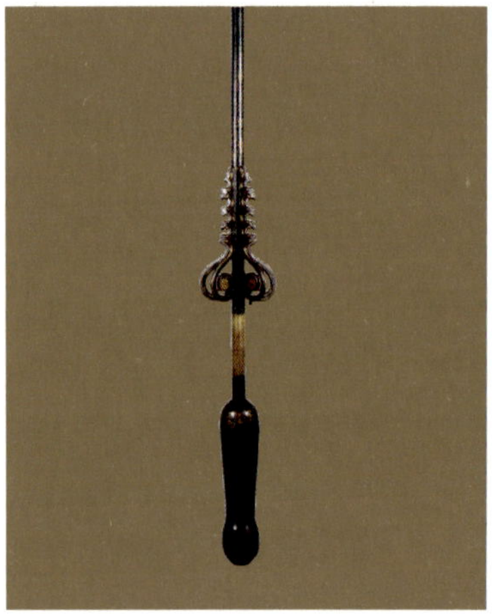

Jousting lance: commissioned by Augustus the Strong for the jousting tournament in honor of Frederik IV of Denmark in 1709 and for the princely wedding in Dresden, 1719
1709 and 1719, Dresden
Martin Schnell
Wood, lacquerware, iron
L. 270.5 cm
Staatliche Kunstsammlungen Dresden, Rüstkammer, Dresden
Inv. R280

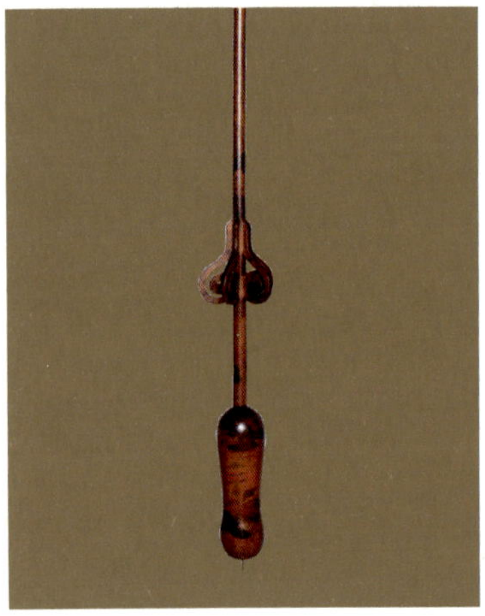

Jousting lance commissioned for the princely wedding in Dresden, 1719
c. 1719, Dresden
Martin Schnell
Wood, lacquerware, iron
L. 264 cm
Staatliche Kunstsammlungen Dresden, Rüstkammer, Dresden
Inv. R284

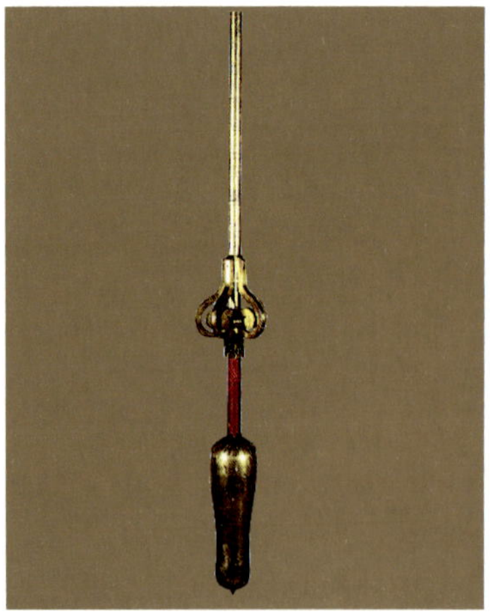

Jousting lance: commissioned by Augustus the Strong for the princely wedding in Dresden, 1719 and the "Four Elements Carrousel" in 1719
1709 and 1719, Dresden
Wood, gilded bronze, velvet
L. 247 cm
Staatliche Kunstsammlungen Dresden, Rüstkammer, Dresden
Inv. R287

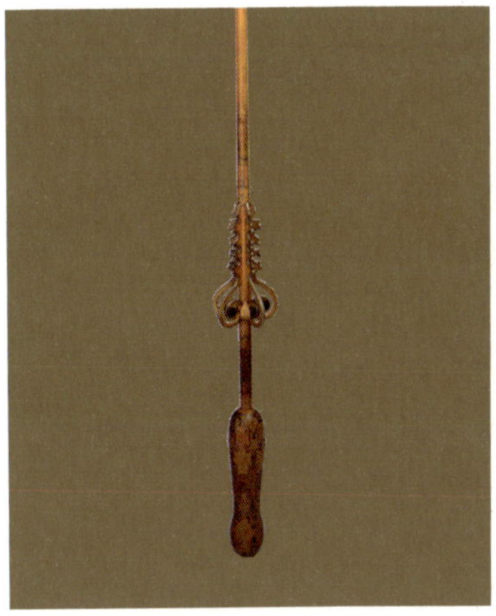

Jousting lance
1719, Dresden
Martin Schnell
Wood, lacquerware, iron
L. 270.5 cm
Staatliche Kunstsammlungen Dresden, Rüstkammer, Dresden
Inv. 282

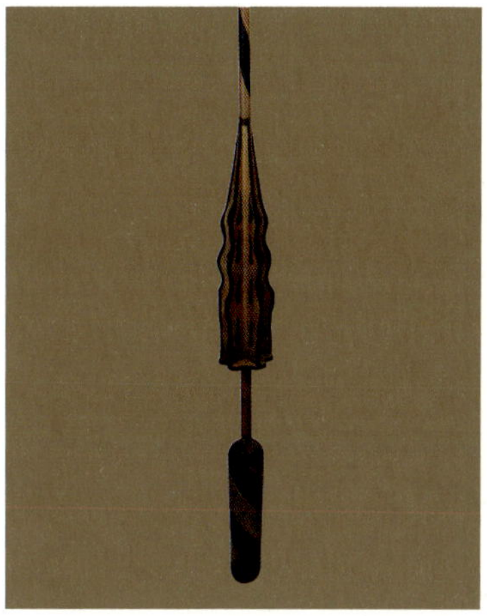

Jousting lance
First quarter of the eighteenth century, Germany
Wood, iron
L. 279 cm
Staatliche Kunstsammlungen Dresden, Rüstkammer, Dresden,
Inv. R319

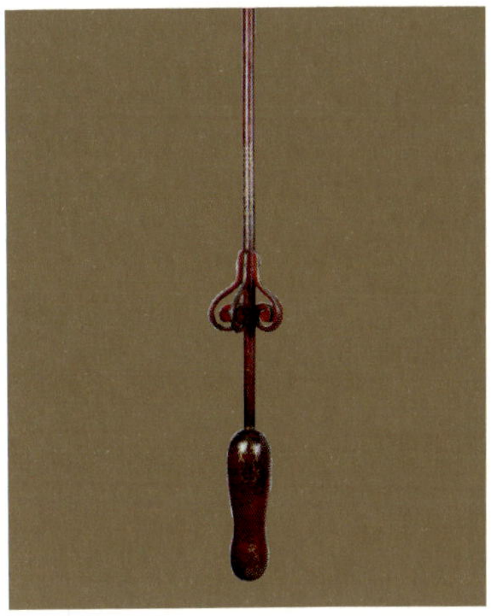

Jousting lance
1709, Dresden
Martin Schnell
Wood, lacquerware, iron
L. 262 cm
Staatliche Kunstsammlungen Dresden, Rüstkammer, Dresden
Inv. R283

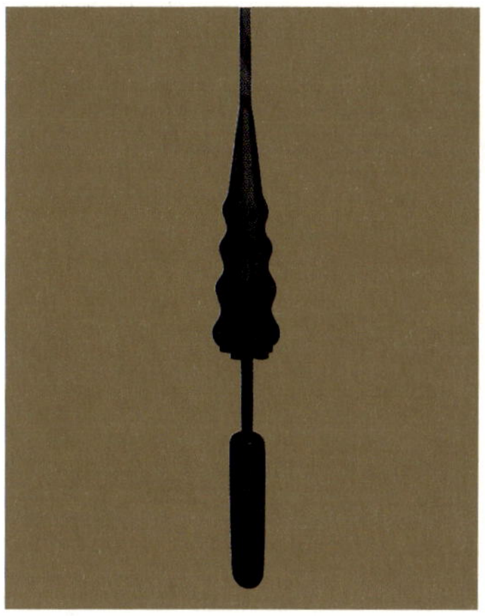

Jousting lance
First quarter of the eighteenth century, Germany
Wood, iron
L. 280 cm
Staatliche Kunstsammlungen Dresden, Rüstkammer, Dresden,
Inv. R326

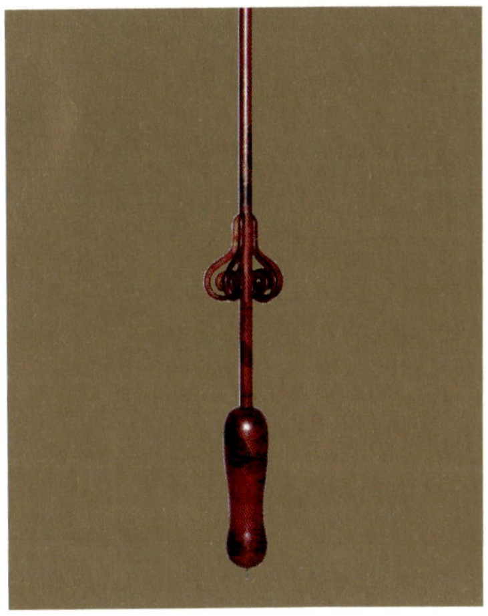

Jousting lance
1719, Dresden
Martin Schnell
Wood, lacquerware, iron
L. 262.5 cm
Staatliche Kunstsammlungen Dresden, Rüstkammer, Dresden
Inv. R285

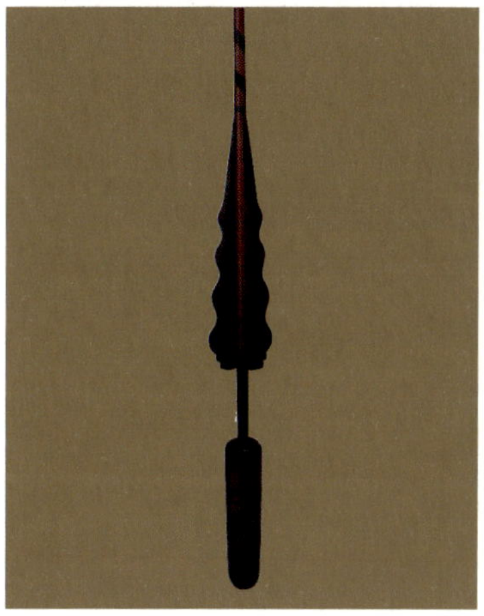

Jousting lance
First quarter of the eighteenth century, Germany
Wood, iron
L. 278 cm
Staatliche Kunstsammlungen Dresden, Rüstkammer, Dresden
Inv. R317

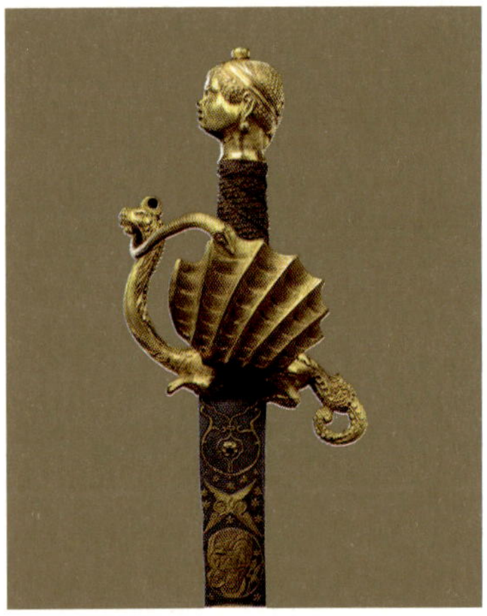

Saber decorated with Moor's head
First quarter of the seventeenth century, Germany; Istanbul (blade)
Gold damasked blade, ruby, gilded brass
L. 109 cm
Staatliche Kunstsammlungen Dresden, Rüstkammer, Dresde
Inv. Y 26

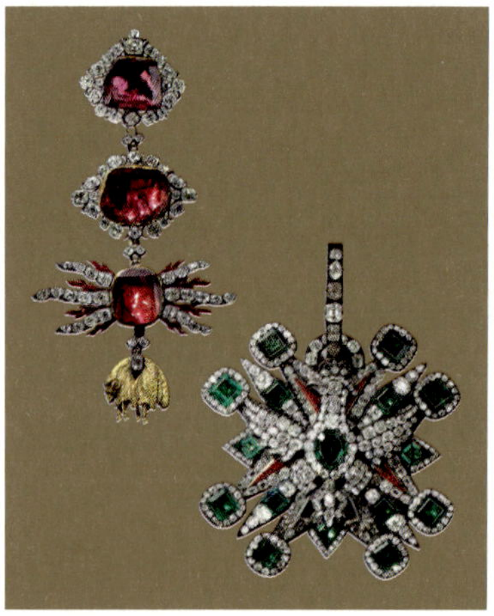

Order of the Golden Fleece
1772, Dresden
JOHANN MELCHIOR DINGLINGER (1664–1731)
Gold and ruby
17.9 × 9.5 cm
Staatliche Kunstsammlungen Dresden, Grünes Gewölbe, Dresden
Inv. VIII 122

The Polish Order of the White Eagle, 1746
JOHANN AUGUST JORDAN
16 emeralds, 342 diamonds, gold, silver, enamel, 10.4 × 7.8 cm
Staatliche Kunstsammlungen Dresden, Grünes Gewölbe, Dresden
Inv. VIII 143

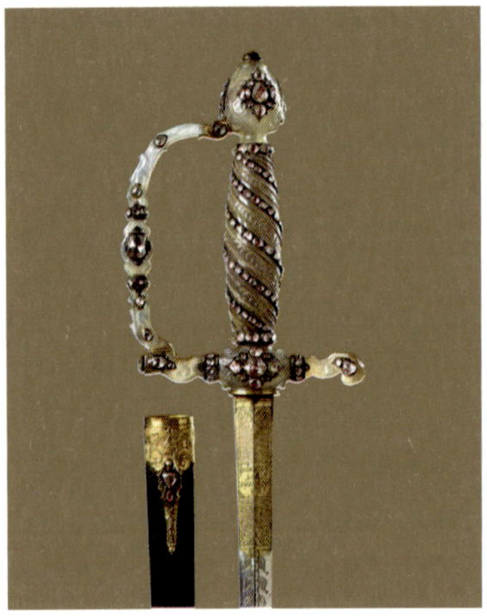

Sword
1722–33, Dresden
JOHANN MELCHIOR DINGLINGER (1664–1731)
Damascened steel, 241 pink diamonds
L. 84 cm
Staatliche Kunstsammlungen Dresden, Grünes Gewölbe, Dresden
Inv. VIII 257

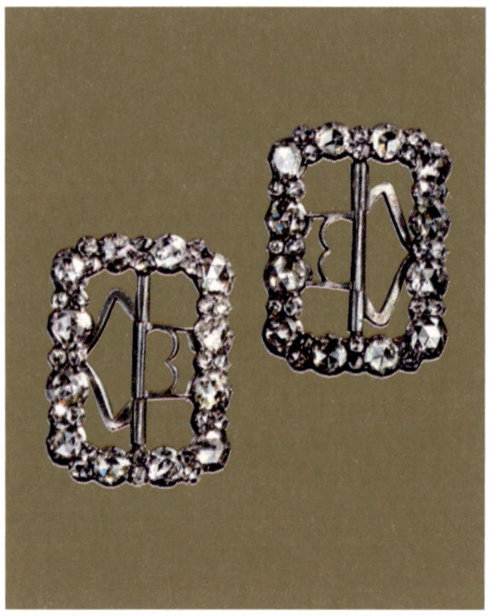

Pair of diamond-encrusted garter buckles
1782–89, Dresden
CHRISTIAN AUGUST GLOBIG
24 large diamonds, 48 small diamonds, silver, gold, steel
4.3 × 3 cm
Staatliche Kunstsammlungen Dresden, Grünes Gewölbe, Dresden,
Inv. VIII 14/1-2

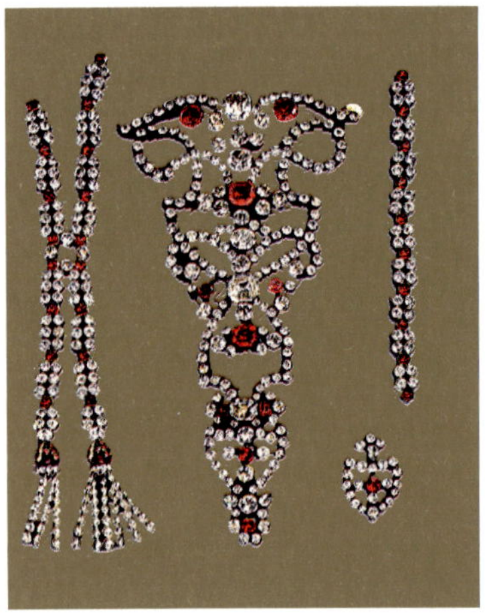

Parure for bustier
Late seventeenth–early eighteenth century
Crystal, glass, silver, brass; partially silver-plated copper
29 × 16 cm (corset)
Staatliche Kunstsammlungen Dresden, Grünes Gewölbe, Dresden
Inv. V 155 b

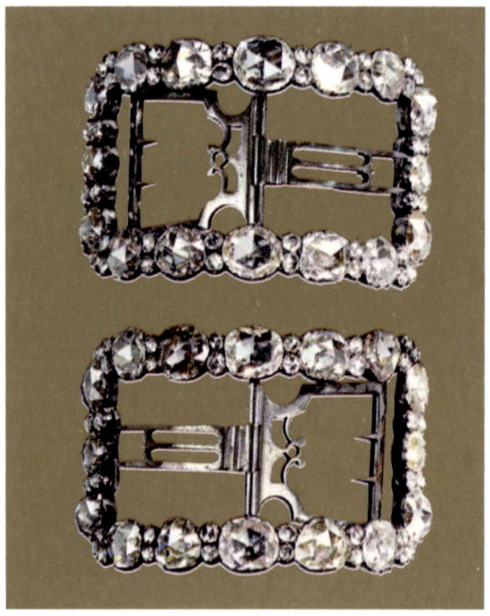

Pair of diamond-encrusted shoe buckles
1782–89, Dresden
CHRISTIAN AUGUST GLOBIG
32 large diamonds, 72 small diamonds, silver, gold, steel
8.5 × 6 cm
Staatliche Kunstsammlungen Dresden, Grünes Gewölbe, Dresden
Inv. VIII 12/1-2

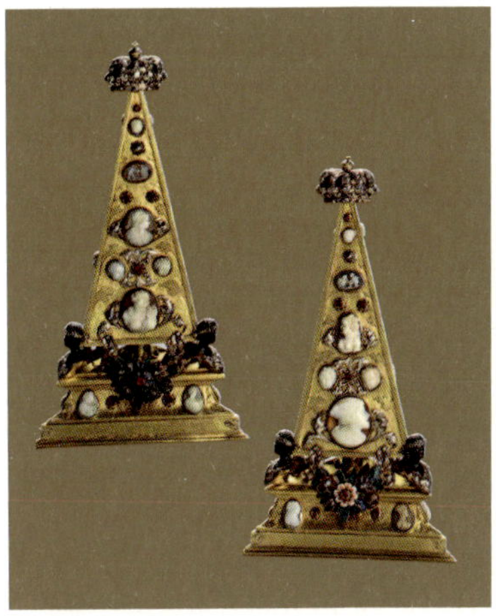

Two "Triumphs" in obelisk form
1701–05, Dresden
Johann Heinrich Köhler
Gilded silver, enamel, cameos, precious stones
H. 16.6 cm
Staatliche Kunstsammlungen Dresden, Grünes Gewölbe, Dresden
Inv. VI 41 and inv. VI 42

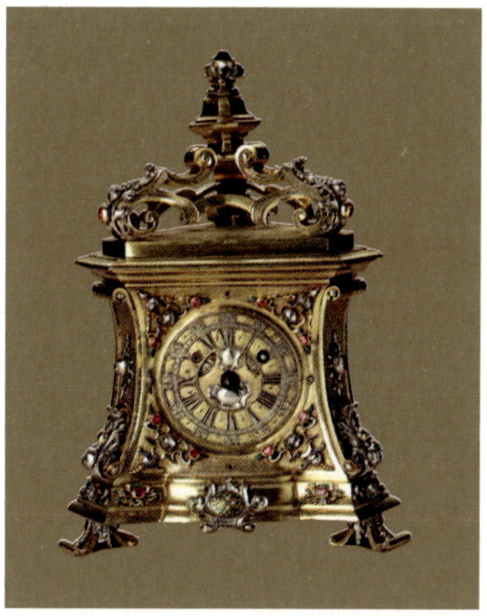

Table clock
1721–25, Dresden
Johann Christof Dünnebier, clockmaker; Gottfried Reiche the Younger, silversmith
Gilded silver, precious stones; wood and leather (case)
13.3 × 9.5 cm
Staatliche Kunstsammlungen Dresden, Grünes Gewölbe, Dresden
Inv. VI 44, Inv. E 50

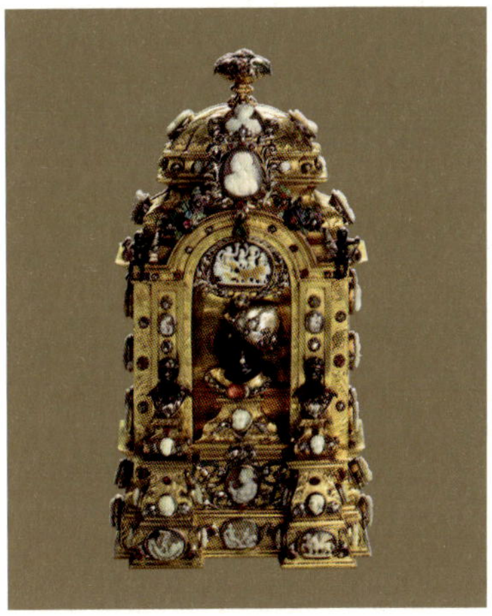

"Triumph" architectural centerpiece
1701–05, Dresden
Johann Heinrich Köhler
Gilded silver, enamel, cameos, precious stones
H. 20 cm
Staatliche Kunstsammlungen Dresden, Grünes Gewölbe, Dresden
Inv. VI 40

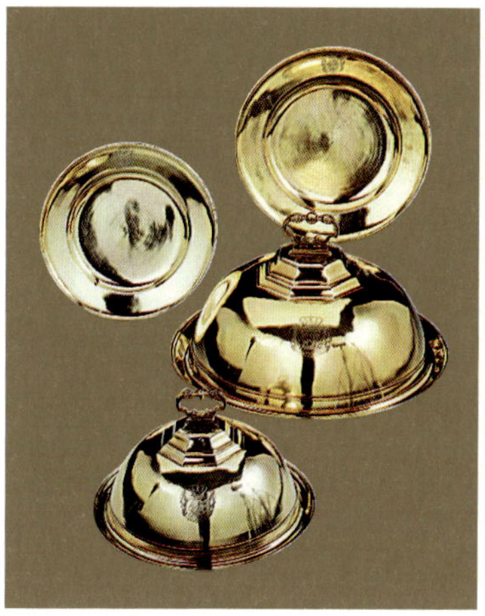

Items from Augustus the Strong's vermeil service
1718–30, Augsburg
Gottlieb Menzel; Christian Winter
Gilded silver
Staatliche Kunstsammlungen Dresden, Grünes Gewölbe, Dresden
Large table dome and platter
D. (platter) 47 cm; D. (dome) 42.5 cm; H. (dome) 25.9 cm
Inv. 1992/1-2
Small table dome and platter
D. (platter) 32.4 cm;
D. (dome) 28.7 cm; H. (dome) 19.6 cm
Inv. 1992/11 and 15
Large platter
D. 39.3 cm
Inv. 1992/13

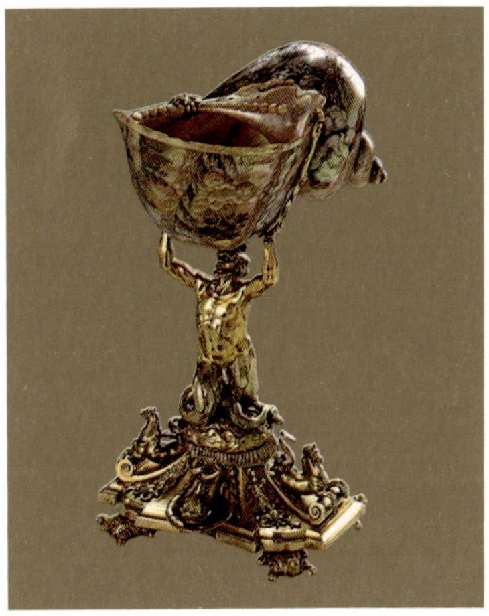

Nautilus with silver mounting
Second half of the seventeenth century
Cornelis van Bellekin
Mounting
1724, Dresden
Johann Heinrich Köhler
Staatliche Kunstsammlungen Dresden, Grünes Gewölbe, Dresden
Inv. III 142

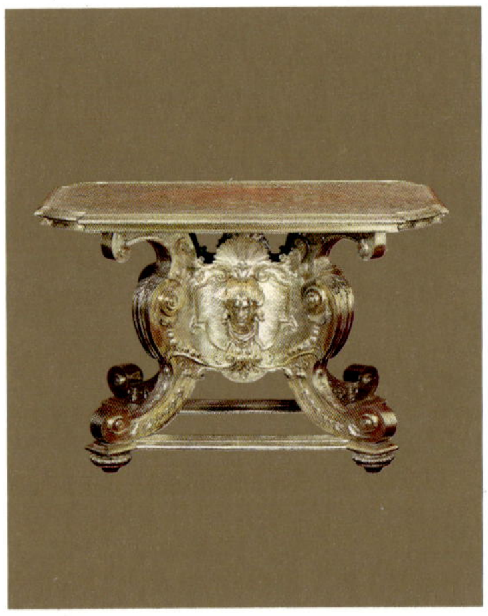

Table decorated with the four seasons represented by Mars, Ceres, Neptune, and Aeolus
1708–10, Augsburg
Albrecht Biller
Wood and silver
80.5 × 120 cm
Staatliche Kunstsammlungen Dresden, Grünes Gewölbe, Dresden
Inv. 37532

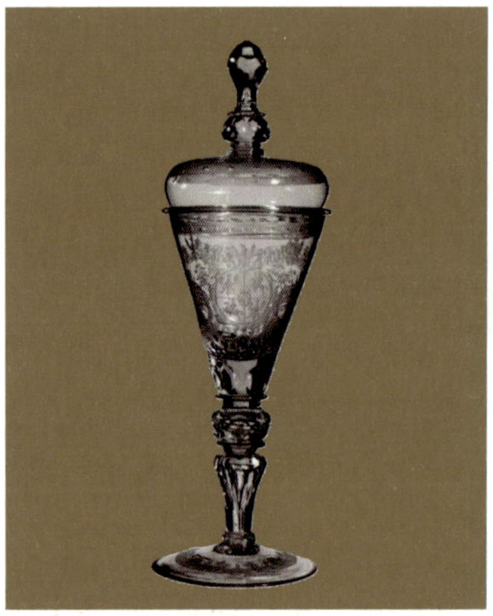

Cup with cover
c. 1713, Dresden
Glass
H. (with cover) 38.3 cm
Staatliche Kunstsammlungen Dresden, Kunstgewerbemuseum, Dresden
Inv. 37141

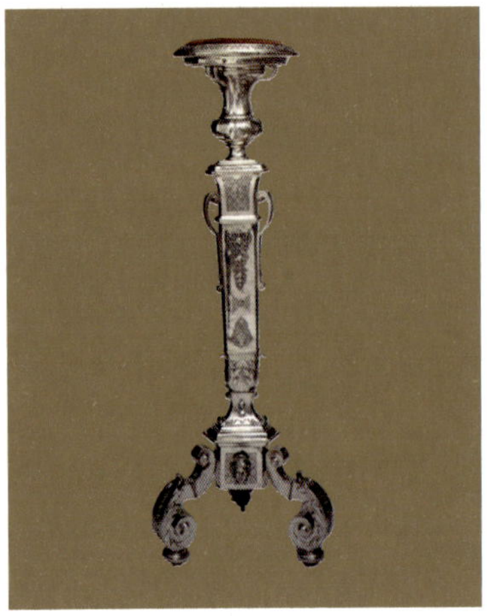

Occasional table
c. 1720, Augsburg
Mickaël II Heckel
Silver, velvet
H. 115 cm
Staatliche Kunstsammlungen Dresden, Rüstkammer, Dresden
Inv. P346

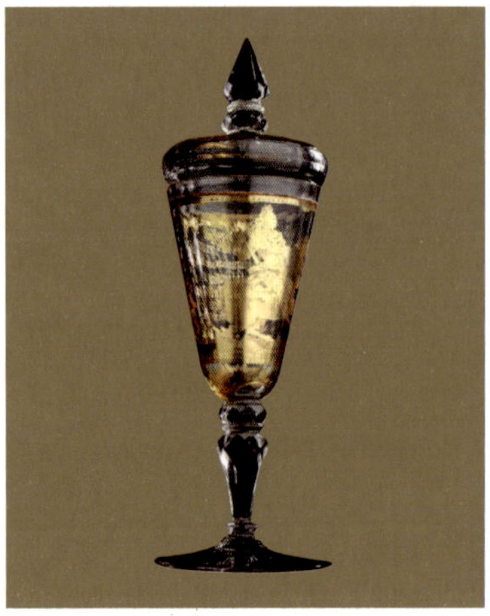

Cup with cover
1721–22, Bohemia
Glass
H. (with cover) 27.8 cm
Staatliche Kunstsammlungen Dresden, Kunstgewerbemuseum, Dresden
Inv. 47845

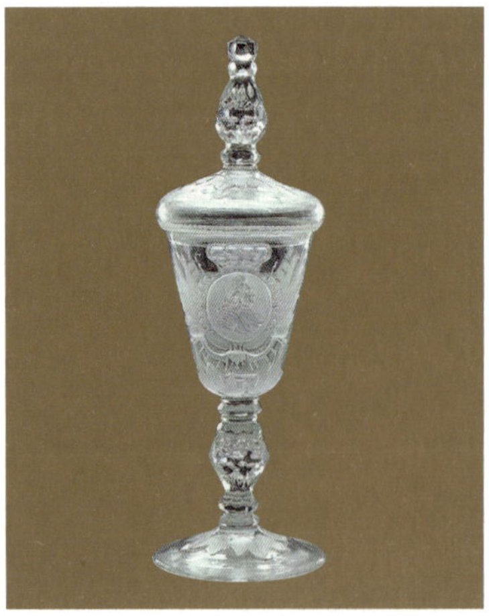

Covered cup with a portrait of Augustus the Strong with the crowned monogram "FAR"
1728–30, Dresden
Johann Christoph Kiessling
Glass
H. 44.1 cm (with cover)
Staatliche Kunstsammlungen Dresden, Kunstgewerbemuseum, Dresden
Inv. 37168

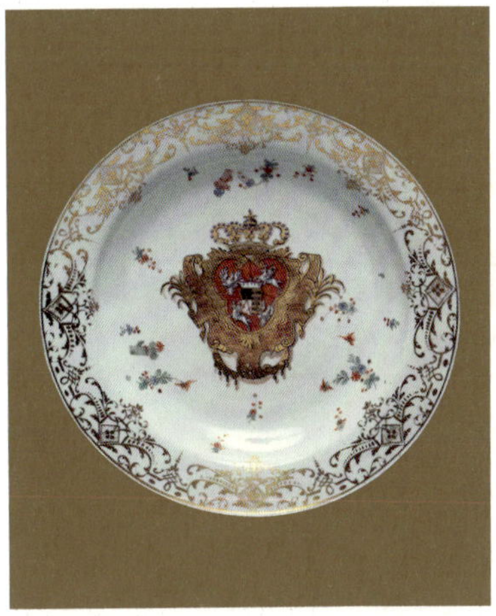

Large coronation service dish with the arms of Saxony
c. 1734
Meissen porcelain
D. 44.8 cm
Staatliche Kunstsammlungen Dresden, Porzellansammlung, Dresden
Inv. PE 1279

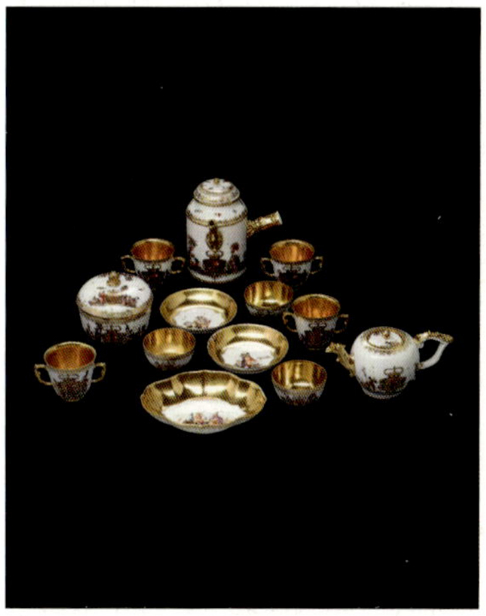

Tea service with the arms of Parma for Isabella Farnese
c. 1728
Meissen porcelain
Staatliche Kunstsammlungen Dresden, Porzellansammlung, Dresden
Two chocolate cups
H. (cup) 6.5 cm; D. (saucer) 12 cm
Inv. PE 1506 e-g-l-m
Two tea bowls and saucers
H. 4.2 cm
Inv. PE 1506 i-j-n-o
Teapot and saucer
H. 8.5 cm; L. (saucer) 17.4 cm; W. (saucer) 13.4 cm
Inv. PE 1506 b, d
Chocolate pot
H. 16.5 cm
Iinv. PE 1506 a

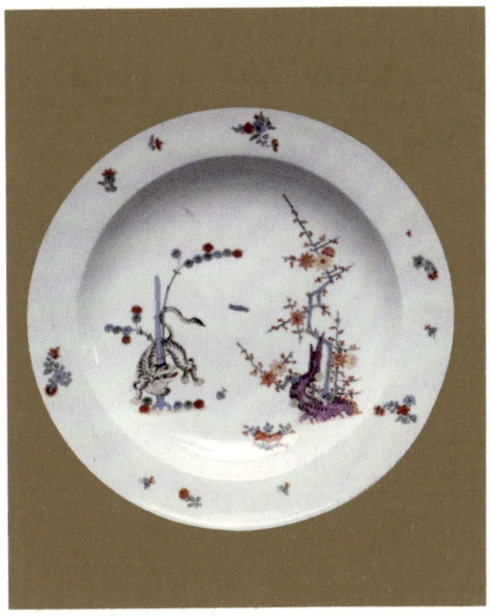

Dish
1740–60
Meissen porcelain
5.7 x 34 cm
Staatliche Kunstsammlungen Dresden, Porzellansammlung, Dresden
Inv. PE 1196

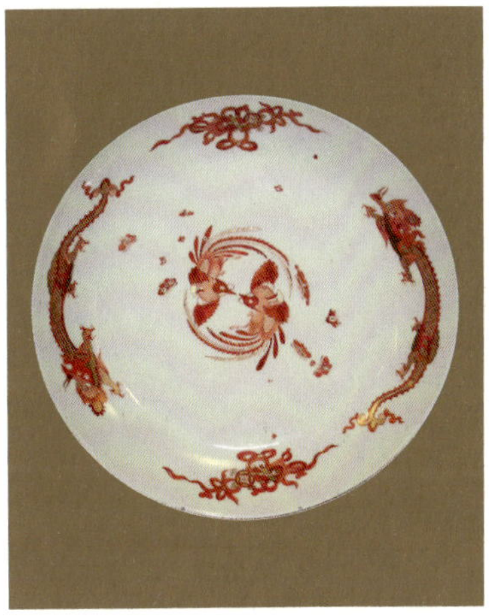

Dish with red dragon decoration
c. 1740
Meissen porcelain
4.5–4.7 x 29.7 cm
Staatliche Kunstsammlungen Dresden, Porzellansammlung, Dresden
Inv. PE 1188f

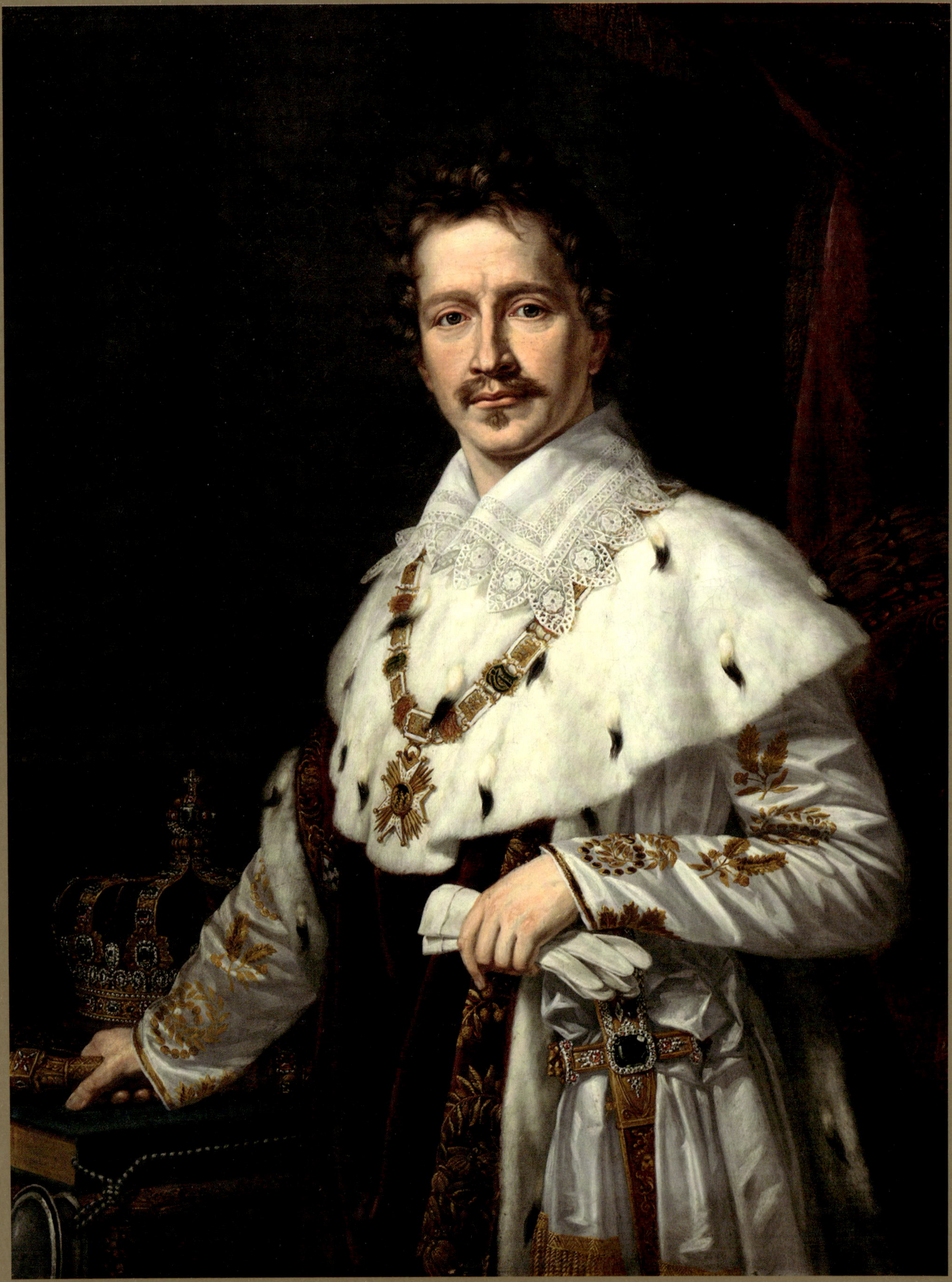

BAVARIA

Ludwig I (1786–1868)

Ludwig I, King of Bavaria, 1825–48
After 1826
Joseph-Karl Stieler
(1781–1858) workshop
Bayerische Verwaltung
der staatlichen Schlösser,
Gärten und Seen,
Munich

Ludwig I, King of Bavaria

Lorenz Seelig

The House of Wittelsbach reigned over Bavaria without interruption from 1180 to 1918, but no member of the dynasty left a deeper imprint on the architectural landscape and artistic heritage of Munich as King Ludwig I.

The prince was born in Strasbourg on August 25, 1786. His father, Count Palatine Maximilian Joseph of Pfalz-Zweibrücken-Birkenfeld, scion of a junior branch of the Wittelsbachs, had served as a colonel in the Royal Alsace regiment of the French army. In 1789 the Revolution forced Maximilian Joseph to flee Alsace with his family. A landless prince until then, in 1799 he took up the reins of power in Munich as prince-elector of Bavaria-Palatinate, henceforth reigning over extensive territories in the south and the west of the empire.

In 1804 Ludwig undertook a first journey to Italy, where he was filled with enthusiasm not only for classical antiquity but also for contemporary neoclassical art. He would thereafter often sojourn in Rome, treating the German artists he spent time with as his equals.

Thanks to its alliance with Napoleon, in 1806 Bavaria was elevated into a kingdom. Henceforth a royal prince, Ludwig felt it incumbent upon him to officially pursue the policies of his father that had favored the French. That same year, he embarked on a protracted visit to the court of the emperor in Paris; he was especially impressed by the artworks in the Musée Napoléon—spoils of war that had been amassed from every region in Europe.

None of this, however, prevented Ludwig from adopting a hostile attitude towards Napoleon. To proclaim his nationalist German convictions, he had his portrait painted in a traditional *altdeutscher* jacket[1], even though the wearing of such garments was officially outlawed in Bavaria. The wavy blade of his sword was also in the *altdeutscher* (old German) style.

Queen Therese of Bavaria (1792–1854), Wife of Ludwig, King of Bavaria
1833
Pino Bauer,
(1781–1858)
Bayerisches Nationalmuseum, Munich

Furthermore, to outflank Napoleon's matrimonial gerrymandering—his sister, Augusta Amélie, had married Napoleon's son-in-law, Eugène de Beauharnais, in 1806—Ludwig took as his wife Therese, princess of Saxe-Hildburghausen, in 1810. On the occasion of the wedding a horserace was held on the Theresienwiese that then stood at the gates of Munich, the origin of the famous Oktoberfest beer festival, which has taken place every year since on the "Wiesn." Ludwig and

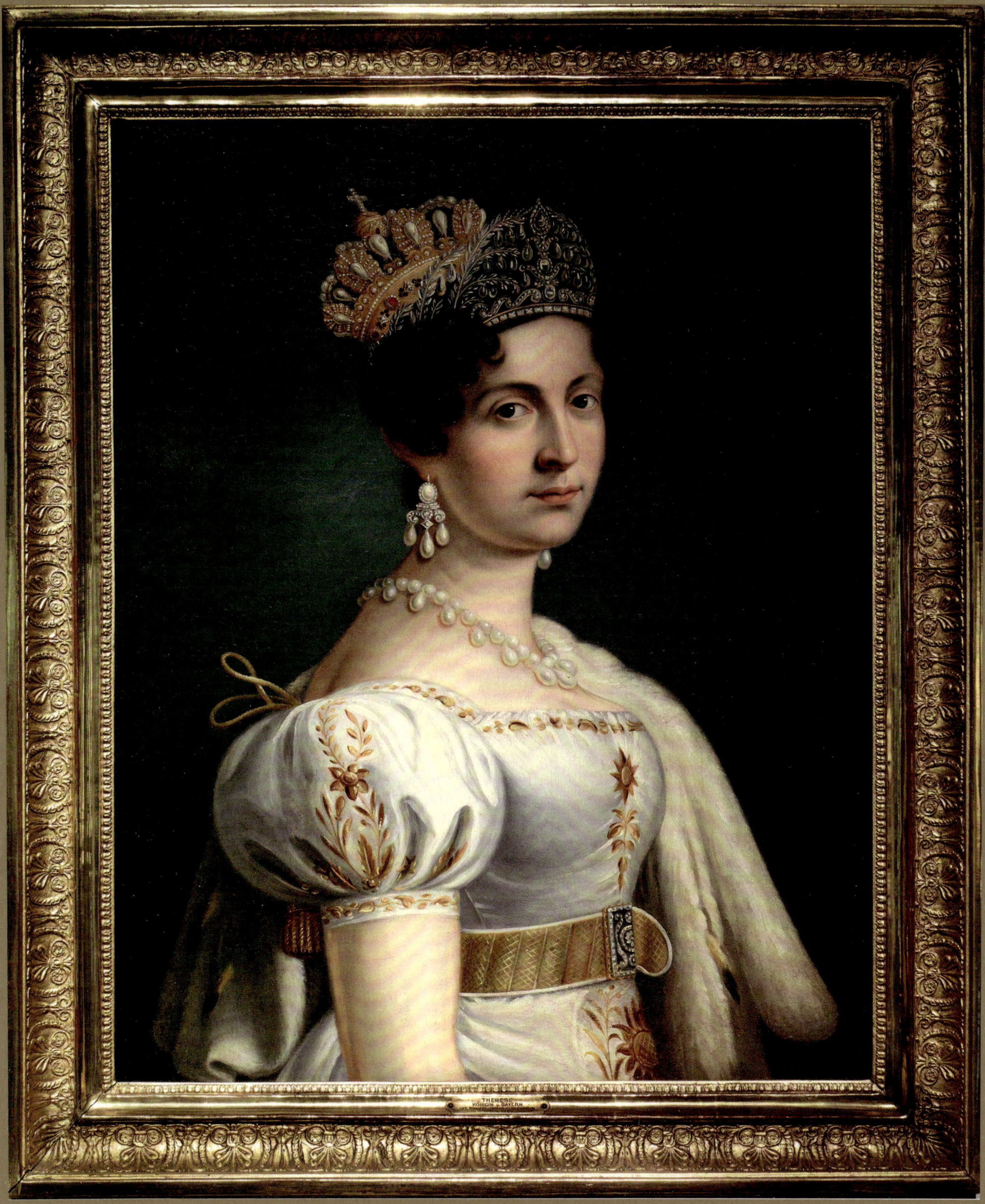
THERESE
KÖNIGIN v. BAYERN

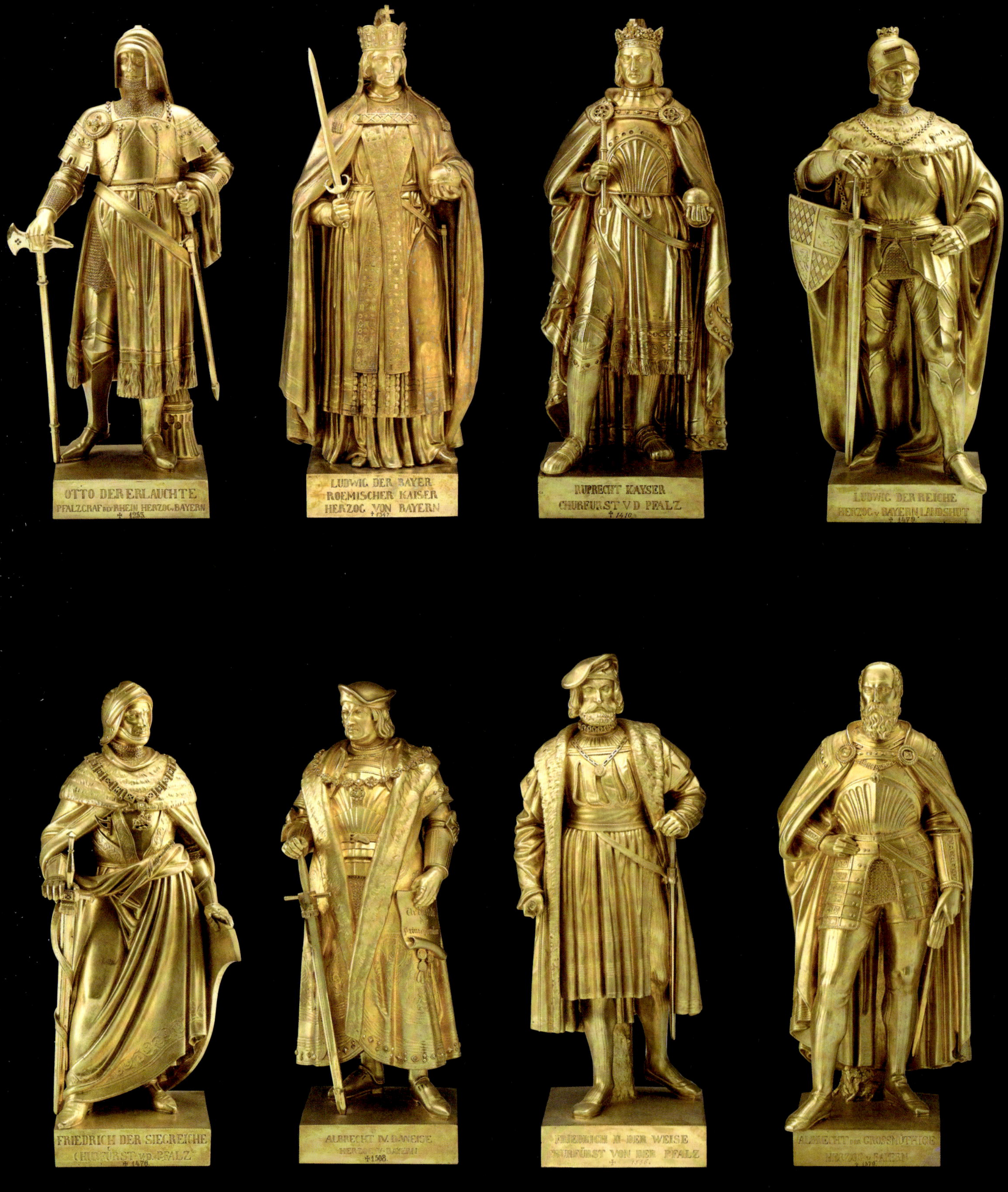
OTTO DER ERLAUCHTE
PFALZGRAF BEY RHEIN HERZOG v. BAYERN
† 1253
LUDWIG DER BAYER
ROEMISCHER KAISER
HERZOG VON BAYERN
RUPRECHT KAYSER
CHURFURST V D PFALZ
† 1410
LUDWIG DER REICHE
HERZOG v BAYERN LANDSHUT
† 1479
FRIEDRICH DER SIEGREICHE
† 1476
ALBRECHT IV. D. WEISE
† 1508
DER WEISE
CHURFÜRST VON DER PFALZ
ALBRECHT DER GROSSMÜTHIGE

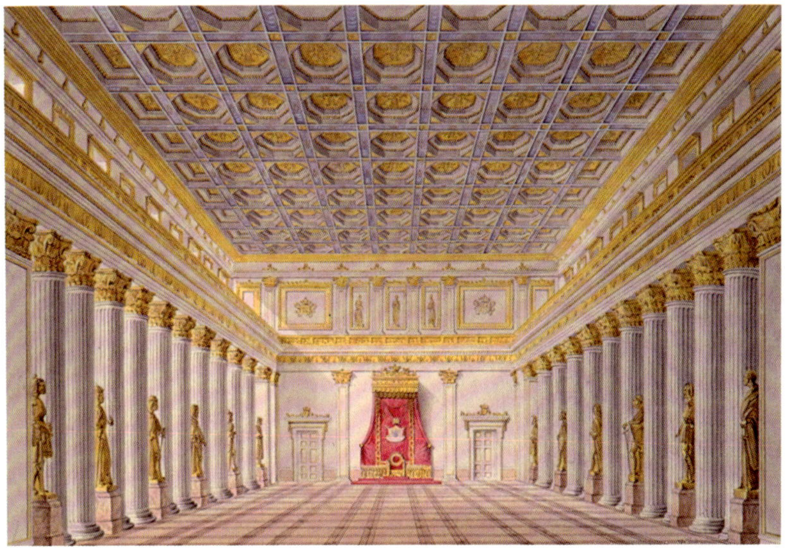

Inside view of Louis I's throne room in the Festsaalbau with statues of the sovereigns of the House of Wittelsbach
c. 1842
Heesische Hausstiftung,
Museum Schloss Fasanerie,
Eichenzel

Therese's union was blessed by nine children, thereby ensuring the Wittelsbachs' survival. The depiction of the couple's children on porcelain cups made by the Nymphenburg manufactory articulates a dynastic statement, while a silver relief from Augsburg (a preeminent goldworking center) immortalizes the arrival of Therese before the city cathedral for the baptism of Princess Mathilde in 1813.

In 1818 Crown Prince Ludwig made a decisive contribution to framing the country's progressive constitution. As a result, Bavaria became the first kingdom in the German Confederation to institute a constitutional monarchy. His long awaited accession to the throne in 1825 allowed him not only to further realize his political goals, but also to make substantial advances on his artistic projects. In the wake of the profound upheavals occasioned by the Napoleonic age, it became clear to Ludwig that the now considerably enlarged kingdom of Bavaria stood on a solid base and that the second quarter of the century would represent an era of peace. Once king, Ludwig I embraced the "monarchical principle," regarding his ministers as virtual servants. After five years of relatively liberal government, these autocratic tendencies gathered steam in 1830, a chaotic year that also saw disorder breaking out in Bavaria. The positively tumultuous years of 1846–48 concluded with Ludwig I's abdication. When, in 1847, he attempted to naturalize the supposedly "Spanish" dancer known as Lola Montez (she had in fact been born in Ireland), whom he was intent on elevating to the rank of countess of Landsfeld, conflict arose with the ministry, while popular protests were further stoked in spring 1848 by news of the outbreak of the revolution in Paris. Faced with unavoidable concessions and the diminished power these entailed, on March 19–20, 1848 the king announced that he was renouncing the throne

Otto the Illustrious (850-912), Palatine Count of the Rhine; Emperor Ludwig of Bavaria (1282-1347); Rupprecht I (1309-1390), King of the Holy Roman German Empire; Ludwig the Rich (1417-1479), Duke of Bavaria-Landshut; Friedrich the Victorious (1425-1476), Palatine Prince Elector; Albert IV the Wise (1447-1508), Duke of Bavaria; Friedrich II the Wise (1482-1556), Palatine Prince Elector; Albert the Magnanimous (1528-1579), Duke of Bavaria; sovereigns of the House of Wittelsbach
c. 1842, Munich
Ludwig Schwanthaler
(1802-1848)
(after the drawing of)
Bayerische Verwaltung
der staatlichen Schlösser,
Gärten und Seen,
Munich

in favor of his son Maximilian. Discharged, the monarch lived out the final two decades of his life as a private citizen, his building plans left unfinished. Dying in Nice on February 29, 1868, Ludwig was interred at the Benedictine abbey of St. Boniface in Munich, in whose construction he had played a notable role by supporting the restoration of religious practice and by favoring the reestablishment of the monastic communities disbanded during the period of secularization.

Art and its links with religion and history had occupied a preponderant place in the sovereign's ideas and plans, and it was thanks to Ludwig that Munich became an artistic metropolis of European status. He had already started amassing a significant collection of antiques in 1810. The foundation stone of the Glyptothek, after plans by his favorite architect, Leo von Klenze, was laid in 1816, though the inauguration of what became the first museum of ancient and contemporary sculpture open to the public to be built in Germany took place only in 1830.

Ludwig displayed similar determination in acquiring an exceptional ensemble of paintings that he added to the Wittelsbachs' long-held collections. An idealized gallery, the Alte Pinakothek, designed during the second decade of the nineteenth century, was erected between 1826 and 1836–42 to plans by Klenze. From 1827, the king had excellent copies of selected works from the Alte Pinakothek reproduced on porcelain plates made by the Nymphenburg manufactory. As the Alte Pinakothek was being built, the king envisaged the construction of a gallery for nineteenth-century art located nearby, the Neue Pinakothek. This saw the light of day from 1846 to 1853 after plans by August von Voit.

These innovative museums, which the king financed partly from his own purse, as was the case with many of his projects, were integrated into grandiose urban schemes. The Glyptothek was joined by the Art Exhibition Building (1838–45), today the State Collections of Antiquies, and the Propyläen (1854–62), which together form the striking Propylaea (royal square). The constructions in the neoclassical style—especially the Propyläen—reflect the philhellenism of Ludwig, who wanted Munich to be known as "Athens on the Isar."

Laid out by Klenze from 1816, Ludwigstrasse, which opened the historic city to the north, blossomed into the impressively grand boulevard of the young kingdom, on which stood (and in some cases still stand) palaces and ministry buildings, the Odeon concert hall, the library of state and court, the university—transferred to Munich in 1826—as well as the Ludwigskirche. An eye-catching vanishing point to this triumphal way is formed by the Siegestor (triumphal arch), erected in remembrance of the victory over Napoleonic France.

Ludwigstrasse starts out by, on the one side, the Feldherrnhalle (1841–44), built in emulation of the Loggia dei Lanzi in Florence, and, on the other, the nearby

Residenz, to which Ludwig added two gigantic wings after designs by Klenze. The royal couple's state and private apartments (with an interior laid out by Klenze) were located up on the piano nobile of the Königsbau (1826–35) situated to the south. Significant space is given over to murals representing scenes from the *Song of the Nibelungen*[2], as well as to subjects from Greek and German verse. Ludwig was keen that the apartments of state should be open to the public on certain days of the week so as to enlighten the people through the arts.

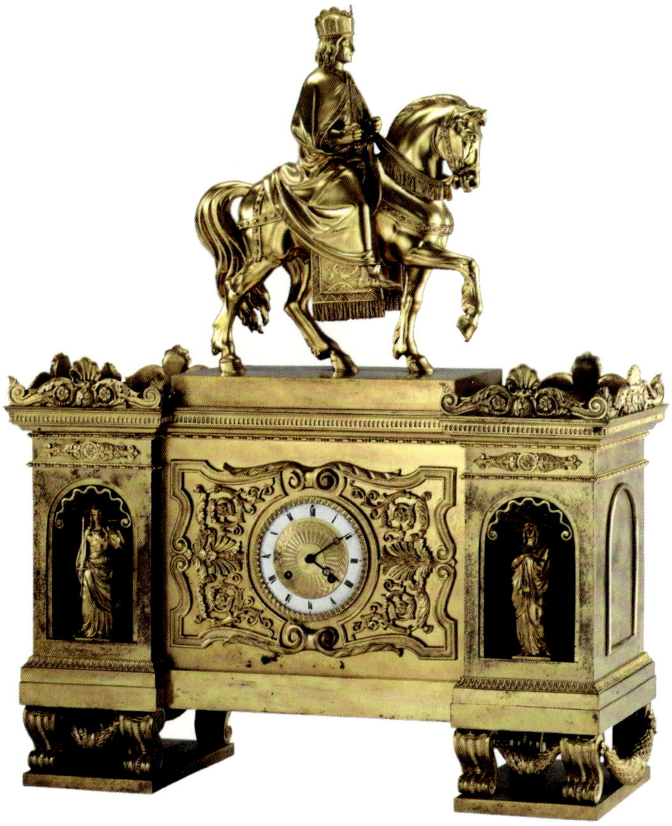

The largest hall in the Festsaalbau (1832–42) to the north of the Residenz was the throne room with its dynastic program. On each side stood six larger than life-size bronze statues of the most important sovereigns of the House of Wittelsbach realized after models by Ludwig von Schwanthaler. These figures were also reproduced in the form of statuettes. The three imperial rooms (Kaisersäle) and the other rooms of the Festsaalbau boasted bronze clocks designed by Schwanthaler and Klenze, one representing Ludwig the Bavarian (Louis IV), the only Wittelsbach emperor of the Middle Ages. The pictures in Ludwig I's Schönheitengalerie (Gallery of Beauties), for which the portrait of Lola Montez by Joseph Stieler was intended, originally also hung in two rooms of the Festsaalbau.

The preeminent role was allotted to the monuments projected by Leo von Klenze and his rival Friedrich von Gärtner—each evidence of Ludwig's program to raise national awareness. In 1807 he set his cap on a project for a pantheon to house the marble busts of "Germans who had distinguished themselves in some glorious manner." The peripteral Doric temple of the Valhalla ("Hall of the Slain") near Regensburg on the Danube was actually erected only in 1830–42, however. Devoted exclusively to the glorious history of the kingdom, the Bayerische Ruhmeshalle, erected on the Theresienwiese in Munich from 1843 to 1853, plays host to *Bavaria*, a bronze statue some 60 feet high. The bust portraits in this "Hall to the Glory of Bavaria" also feature historical figures from the territories of Swabia and Franconia, annexed to Bavaria only in 1802–03. Through art, then,

Clock with the figure of Ludwig of Bavaria on horseback (1282–1347)
1840–42
Leo von Klenze (1784–1864) and Ludwig Schwanthaler (1802–1848)
Bayerische Verwaltung der staatlichen Schlösser, Gärten und Seen, Munich

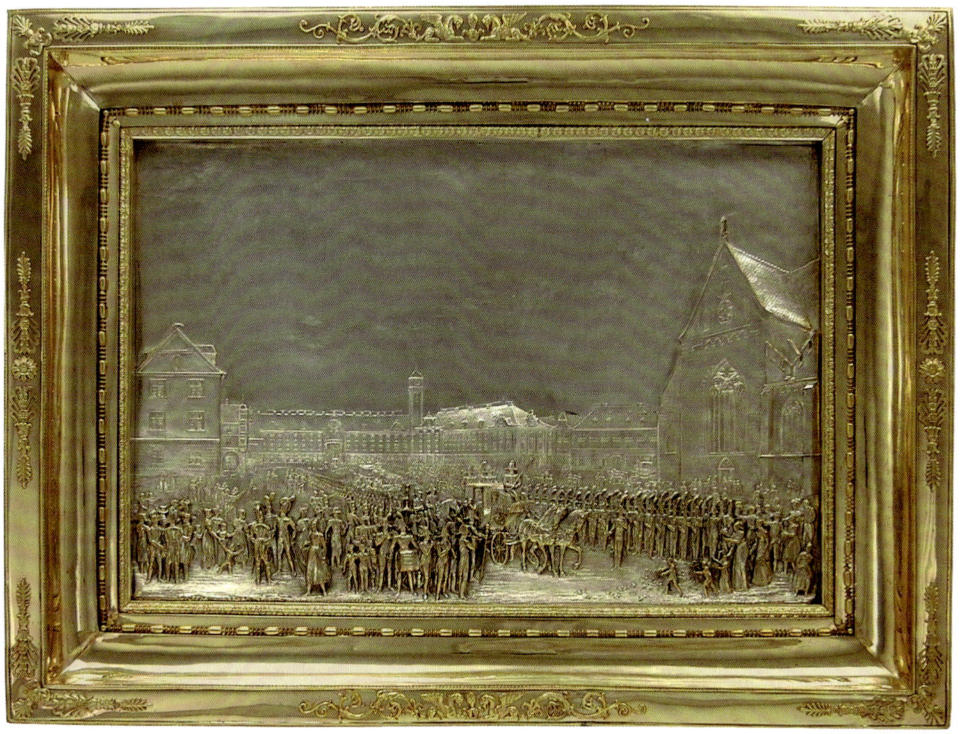

Silver panel depicting the arrival of the Royal Princess Therese (1792–1854) at Augsburg Cathedral for the baptism of Princess Mathilde in 1813
1826–33, Augsburg
Johann Georg Kröner (1790–1869) and Alois Simpert Eschenloher (c. 1785–1837), based on the drawing of Georg Haevel (active 1801–29)
Bayerisches Nationalmuseum, Munich

Ludwig can be seen favoring the integration of territories only recently acquired by the Bavarian state.

The Befreiungshalle (Hall of Liberation) erected near Kelheim from 1842 to 1863 forms, on the contrary, a purely architectural monument. The sculpted decoration of victories carrying bronze shields inside the rotunda surmounted by a colossal dome is confined to a series of statues to the glory of the military heroes of the Liberation of 1813–15.

As in so many of his constructions, the royal patron here fuses architectural planning with the political experience of his years when crown prince. A passionate building entrepreneur, a visionary urbanist, and a tireless collector, Ludwig's avowed objective in artistic policy was to establish his land as a "kingdom of the arts."

1. *Altdeutscher Rock.* Traditional costume that came to prominence in Germany in 1813-1815, at the time of the war of liberation. As a symbol of national and anti-French sentiment, it was adopted in opposition to the Empire style that was seen as a French import. Harking back to the styles of the 16th century and the Reformation, the most important component of the fashion for men was a long, waisted jacket with a wide shirt collar with several points, worn with ample trousers, and sometimes a velvet beret. Though the fashion was popularized by the eminent figure of Crown Prince Ludwig—the future Ludwig I—it was thought of as provocative and mutinous, and was partially prohibited by the decree of Carlsbad.

2. German medieval epic considered in the 19th century as a national saga relating the history of the country's emergence.

Otto I (1815-1867), King of Greece

Lorenz Seelig

A tireless admirer of ancient Greece as the cradle of Western civilization, Ludwig I of Bavaria had backed the Orthodox Christian Greeks in their war of independence with all his might. In 1829–30, Russia, England, and France declared the independence of Greece from the Ottoman Empire. As the future monarch did not belong to such exalted European dynasties, the three protective powers proposed a tribute to Ludwig I of Bavaria's philhellenism: his younger son, Otto (1815–1867), would become king of the Hellenes. The Greek national assembly approved the choice and so, in 1833, Otto made his entrance into Nauplia. In 1835, having attained his majority, he ascended the throne in Athens, capital of the new kingdom. The insignia and coats of arms of Greece were based on Bavarian models, while the administration, army, and justice departments, as well as secondary and tertiary education, were all founded on modern lines, thanks above all to assistance from Bavarian civil servants and officials. In 1837 Otto founded the University of Athens, while Karl Friedrich Schinkel of Berlin drew up plans for a residence on the Acropolis in 1834; the building was finally constructed in the east of the city from 1836 to 1843 to designs by the Munich architect, Friedrich von Gärtner.

Following a putsch in 1862 Otto I left the country with his wife Amalie of Oldenburg, without, however, ever formally abdicating. Flanked by their Greek court, the childless couple retreated to the Neue Residenz in Bamberg. Thus Ludwig I's dream of establishing a second Wittelsbach branch in Greece was never fully realized.

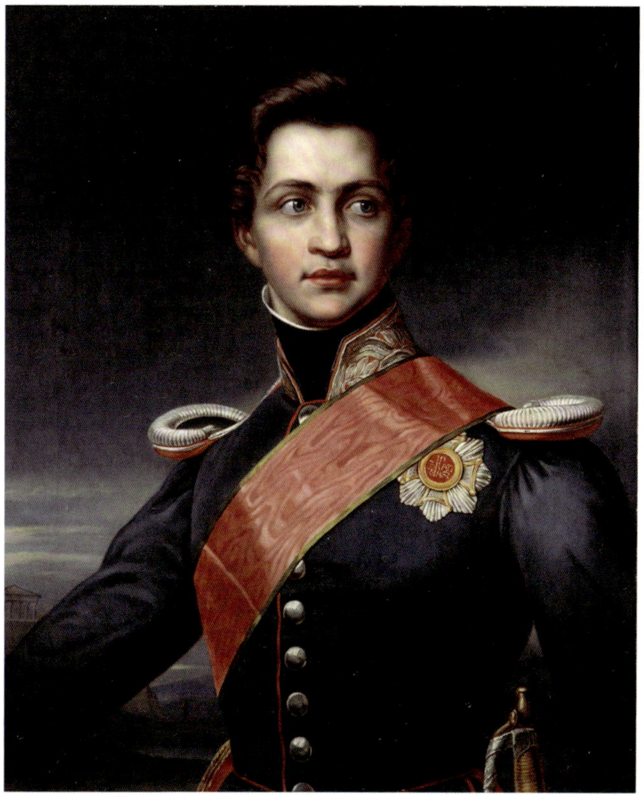

Otto I (1815-1867), King of Greece, Son of Ludwig I of Bavaria
1832
Joseph-Karl Stieler
(1781–1858)
Bayerische Verwaltung der staatlichen Schlösser, Gärten und Seen, Munich

Ludwig II of Bavaria (1845-1886)

Uwe Gerd Schatz

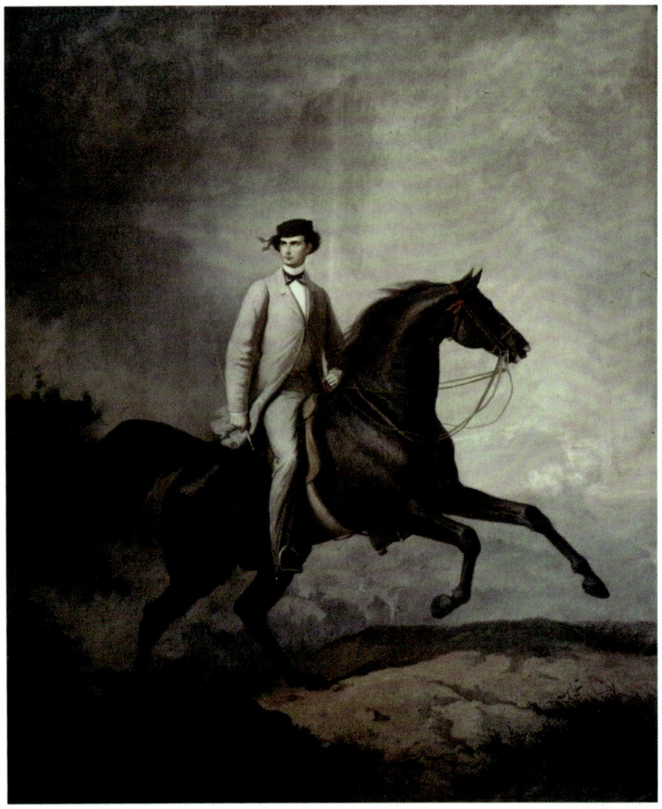

Ludwig II of Bavaria (1845–1886) on Horseback in the Mountains
1864
Feodor Dietz
(1813–1870)
Bayerische Verwaltung der staatlichen Schlösser, Gärten und Seen, Munich

Ludwig II's birthday (on August 25, 1845) coincides with the feast day of Saint Louis, the thirteenth-century king of France whose descendants were to become the Bourbons. Furthermore, King Louis XVI had acted as godfather to Ludwig I of Bavaria at his baptism in Strasbourg in 1786. For Ludwig II, such exalted ties with the Bourbons acquired almost mystic significance. In 1864, after the unexpected death of his father Maximilian II, Ludwig became, aged just eighteen, the youngest sovereign prince in all Europe at the time.

Roundly beaten by Prussia in 1866, Bavaria forfeited its independence and Ludwig II his sovereignty. Constituting the great drama of the king's life, this unhappy event colored all his subsequent acts. Part of Ludwig's history dreamworld in which he could continue living as a true king, Neuschwanstein was designed as a monument to the memory of the Christian monarchs of the Middle Ages, while the copy of Versailles on the island of Herrenchiemsee was also to act as a "temple to the glory" of the Sun King and his successors. As Ludwig wrote himself one day, it was his desire to live in an idealized, monarchical, poetic isolation in which he would be allowed to compose an inextricable mix of reality and fiction—even if this meant exceeding his financial means. After 1855, the foreign banks with which he held his debts threatened seizure. It was Ludwig's categorical refusal to reach an accommodation that explains and seemed to justify his overthrow. Interned on June 12, 1886, in the castle at Berg, he drowned the very next day in Lake Starnberg in circumstances that remain obscure.

Ludwig II is the most famous representative of the German romantic ideal, who, by extending protection to Richard Wagner, continued the glorious Wittelsbach tradition of patronage. For French poet Paul Verlaine, Ludwig II of Bavaria was "the only true king of this century." On August 1, 1886, his castles into which he had declared no stranger should be admitted were opened to the public.

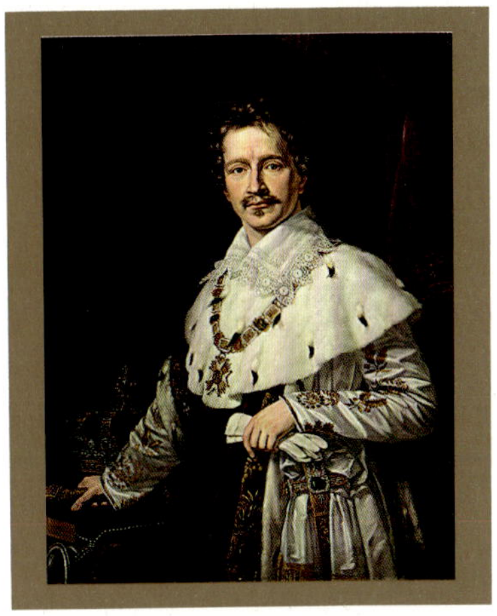

Ludwig I (1786–1868), King of Bavaria, 1825–48
After 1826
Joseph-Karl Stieler
(1781–1858) workshop
Oil on canvas
123 × 95 cm (inc. frame)
Bayerische Verwaltung
der staatlichen Schlösser, Gärten
und Seen, Munich
Inv. ResMü G 1284 (property of
Wittelsbacher Ausgleichsfond) /
Munich Residenz

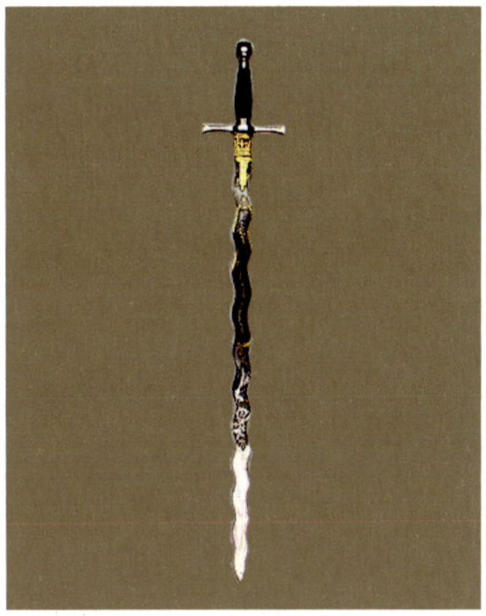

Sword belonging to Ludwig I (1786–1868)
c. 1814
Partially gilded iron, ebony
L. 97 cm
Bayerisches Nationalmuseum,
Munich
Inv. W 2848

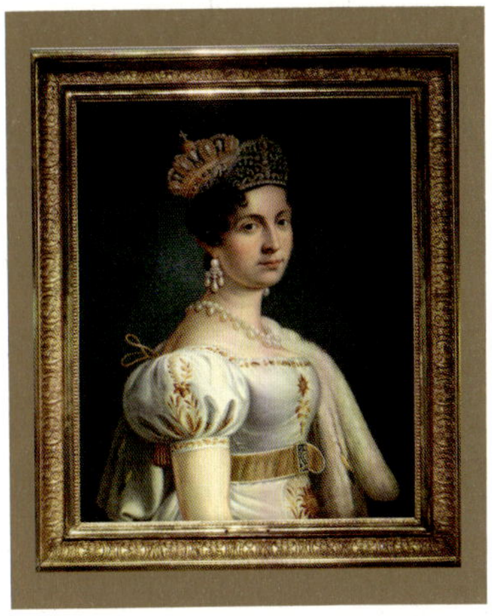

Queen Therese of Bavaria (1792–1854)
1833
Pino Bauer, after
Joseph-Karl Stieler (1781–1858)
Oil on canvas
89.5 × 73.5 cm (inc. frame)
Bayerisches Nationalmuseum,
Munich
Inv. 93/518

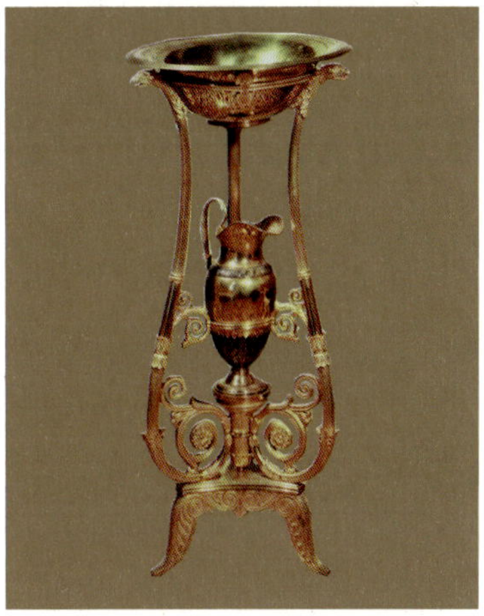

Washstand belonging to Ludwig I (1786–1868)
1835
Leo von Klenze (1784–1864),
designer, Franz Sales Sauter
(1791–1875), caster, Joseph Weber
(1799–1868), silversmith
Gilded bronze (mounting),
gilded silver (ewer and basin)
88 × 40 cm (mounting) ;
39 × 30.5 cm (basin)
Bayerische Verwaltung
der staatlichen Schlösser,
Gärten und Seen, Munich
Inv. ResMü M 855, 601, 606 /
Munich Residenz

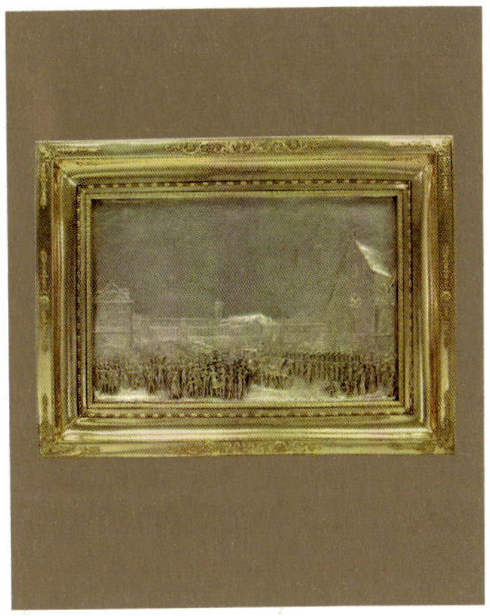

Silver panel depicting the arrival of the Princess Royal Therese (1792–1854) at Augsburg Cathedral for the baptism of Princess Mathilde in 1813
1826–33, Augsburg
Johann Georg Kröner (1790–1869)
and Alois Simpert Eschenloher
(c. 1785–1837), based on the drawing
of Georg Haevel (active 1801–29)
Partially gilded silver
55 × 71 cm
Bayerisches Nationalmuseum,
Munich
Inv. R 6193

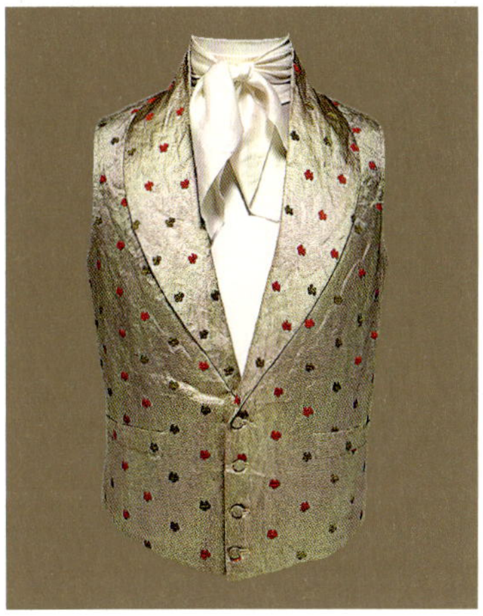

Waistcoat belonging to Ludwig I (1786–1868)
Taffeta, wool, and silk
63 × 43 cm
Bayerisches Nationalmuseum,
Munich
Inv. T.5375

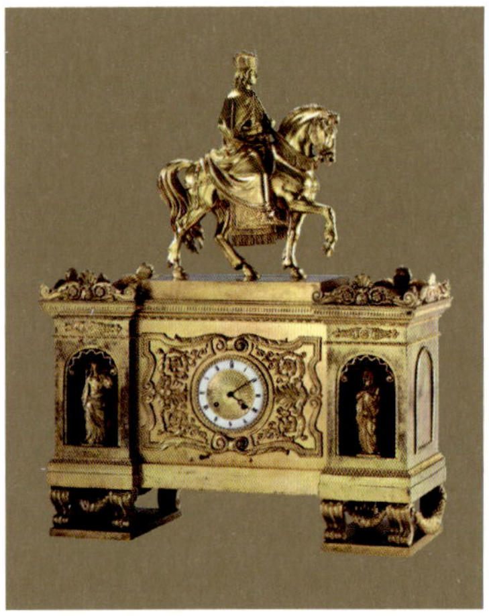

Clock with the figure of Ludwig of Bavaria on horseback (1282–1347)
1840–42
Leo von Klenze (1784–1864) and
Ludwig Schwanthaler (1802–1848)
Gilded bronze
77 × 60 × 20 cm
Bayerische Verwaltung
der staatlichen Schlösser,
Gärten und Seen, Munich
Inv. ResMü U 53 / Munich Residenz,
royal buildings, king's apartments,
study, S. 125

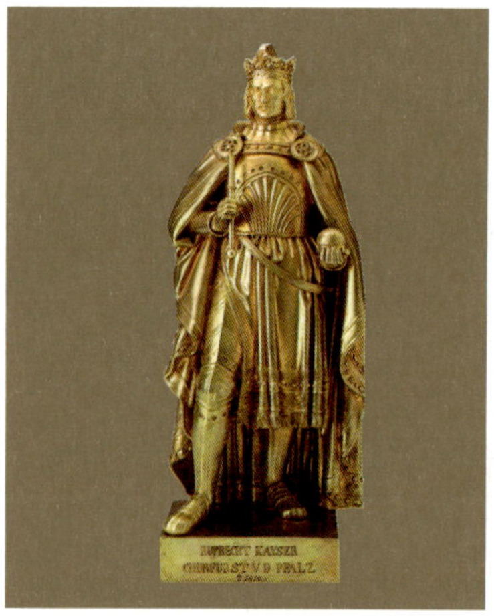

Ruprecht I (1309–1390), King of the Holy Roman Empire
c. 1842, Munich
Ludwig Schwanthaler (1802–1848),
sculptor; Johann Baptist Stiglmaier
(1791–1844), caster
Gilded bronze
53 × 20 × 17 cm
Bayerische Verwaltung
der staatlichen Schlösser,
Gärten und Seen, Munich
Inv. ResMü P II 80 / Munich
Residenz

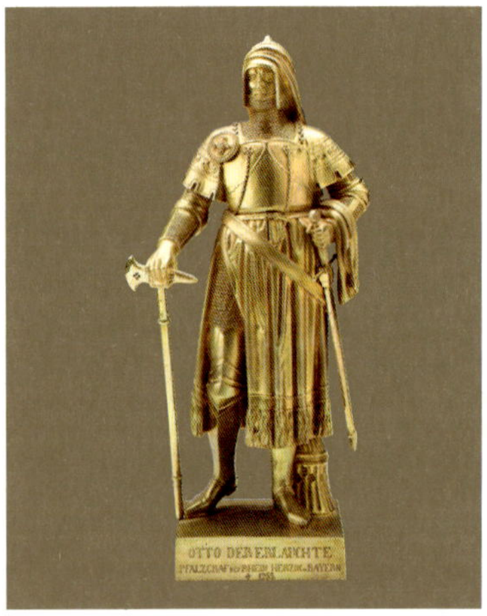

Otto the Illustrious (850–912), Palatine Count of the Rhine
c. 1842, Munich
Ludwig Schwanthaler (1802–1848),
sculptor; Johann Baptist Stiglmaier
(1791–1844), caster
Gilded bronze
45 × 23 × 17 cm
Bayerische Verwaltung
der staatlichen Schlösser,
Gärten und Seen, Munich
Inv. ResMü P II 78 / Munich
Residenz

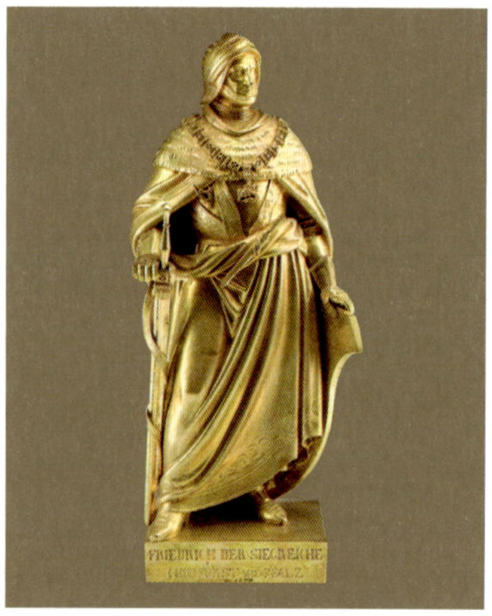

Friedrich the Victorious (1425–1476), Palatine Prince Elector
c. 1842, Munich
Ludwig Schwanthaler (1802–1848),
sculptor; Johann Baptist Stiglmaier
(1791–1844), caster
Gilded bronze
51 × 22 × 17 cm
Bayerische Verwaltung
der staatlichen Schlösser,
Gärten und Seen, Munich
Inv. ResMü P II 81 / Munich
Residenz

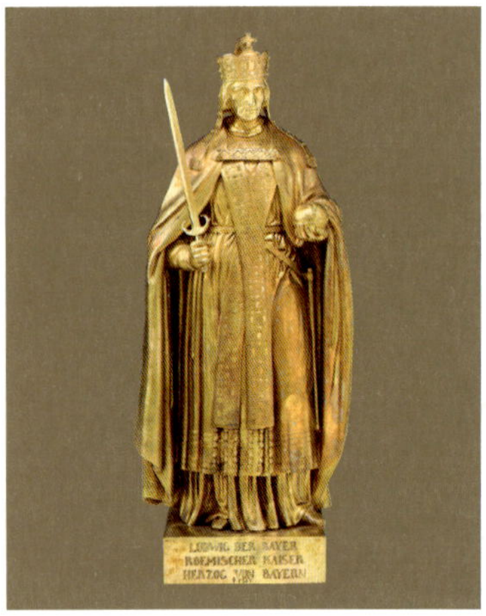

Emperor Ludwig of Bavaria (1282–1347)
c. 1842, Munich
Ludwig Schwanthaler (1802–1848),
sculptor; Johann Baptist Stiglmaier
(1791–1844), caster
Gilded bronze
55 × 22 × 16 cm
Bayerische Verwaltung
der staatlichen Schlösser,
Gärten und Seen, Munich
Inv. ResMü P II 79 / Munich
Residenz

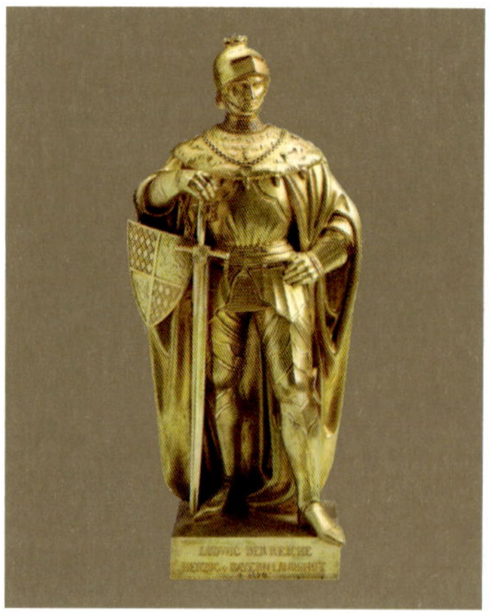

Ludwig the Rich (1417–1479), Duke of Bavaria-Landshut
c. 1842, Munich
Ludwig Schwanthaler (1802–1848),
sculptor; Johann Baptist Stiglmaier
(1791–1844), caster
Gilded bronze
53 × 24 × 18 cm
Bayerische Verwaltung
der staatlichen Schlösser,
Gärten und Seen, Munich
Inv. ResMü P II 82 / Munich
Residenz

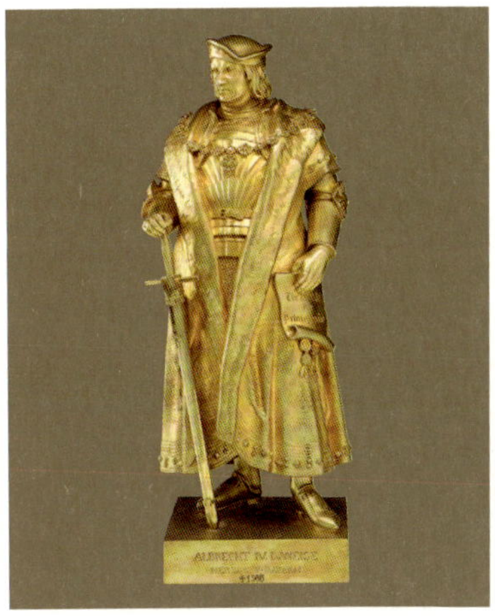

Albrecht IV the Wise (1447–1508), Duke of Bavaria
c. 1842, Munich
Ludwig Schwanthaler (1802–1848), sculptor; Johann Baptist Stiglmaier (1791–1844), caster
Gilded bronze
49 × 17 × 16 cm
Bayerische Verwaltung der staatlichen Schlösser, Gärten und Seen, Munich
Inv. ResMü P II 83 / Munich Residenz

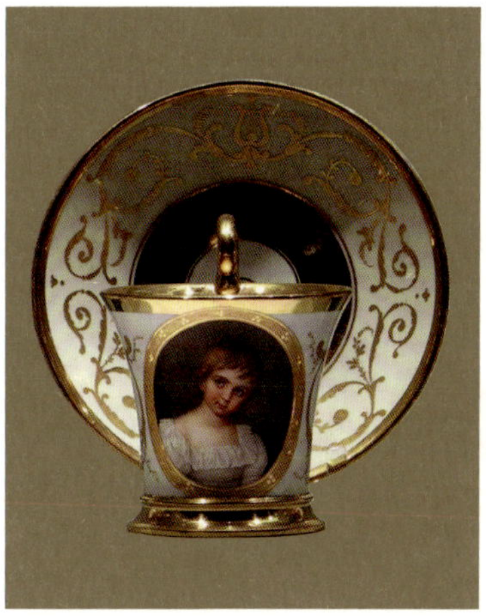

Cup and saucer with the portrait of Ludwig I (1786–1868), in Bavarian Household Cavalry uniform
Nymphenburg porcelain
Munich, Bayerisches Nationalmuseum
Inv. Ker 3652-3662

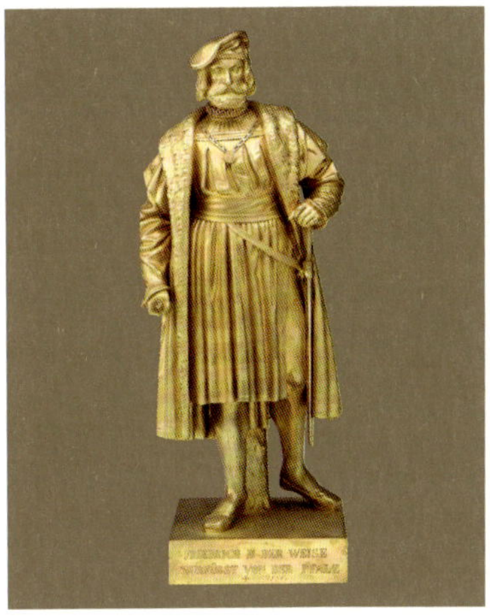

Friedrich II the Wise (1482–1556), Palatine Prince Elector
c. 1842, Munich
Ludwig Schwanthaler (1802–1848), sculptor; Johann Baptist Stiglmaier (1791–1844), caster
52 × 19 × 16.5 cm
Bayerische Verwaltung der staatlichen Schlösser, Gärten und Seen, Munich
Inv. ResMü P II 84 / Munich Residenz

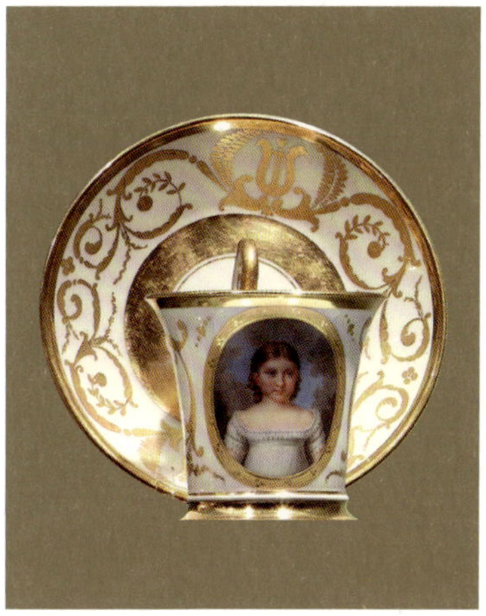

Cup and saucer with the portrait of Queen Therese of Bavaria (1792–1854), Princess of Saxe-Hildburghausen
Nymphenburg porcelain
Bayerisches Nationalmuseum, Munich
Inv. Ker 3650-3660

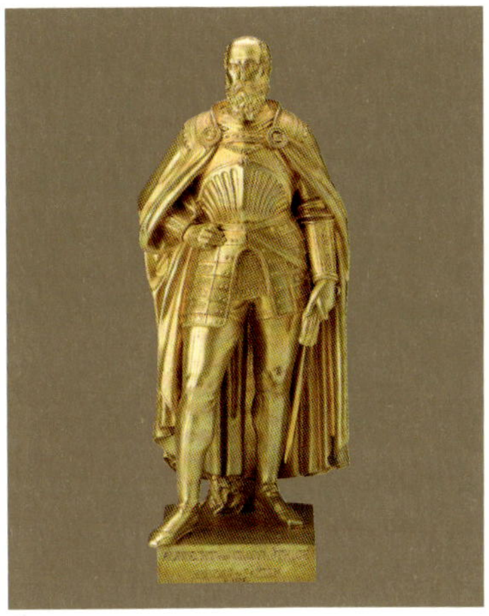

Albrecht the Magnanimous (1528–1579), Duke of Bavaria
c. 1842, Munich
Ludwig Schwanthaler (1802–1848), sculptor; Johann Baptist Stiglmaier (1791–1844), caster
Gilded bronze
50.5 × 18 × 17 cm
Bayerische Verwaltung der staatlichen Schlösser, Gärten und Seen, Munich
Inv. ResMü P II 85 / Munich Residenz

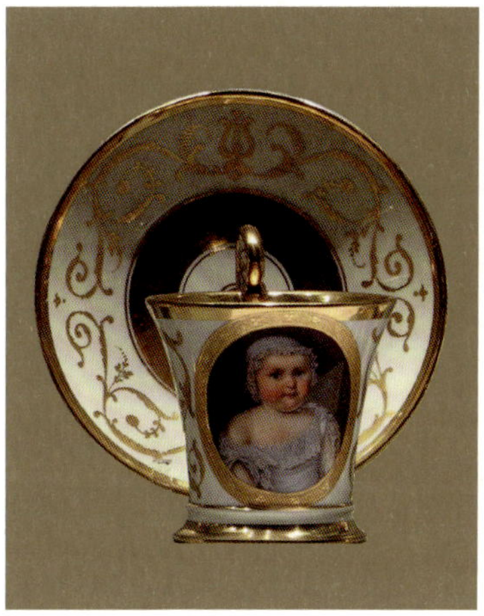

Cup and saucer with the portrait of Crown Prince Maximilian (1811–1864)
Nymphenburg porcelain
Bayerisches Nationalmuseum, Munich
Inv. Ker 3654-3664

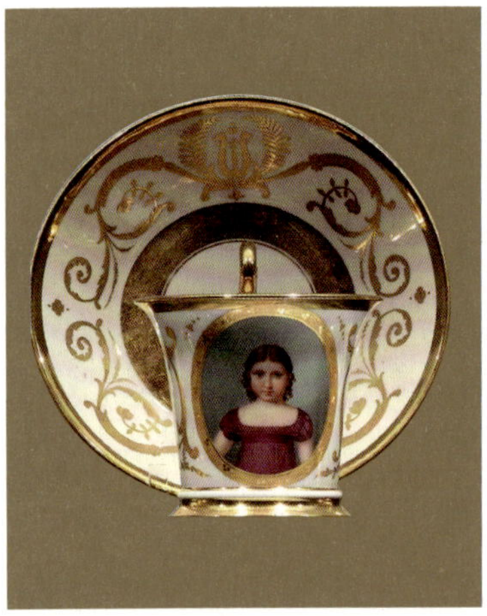

Cup and saucer with the portrait of Princess Mathilde Karoline Frederik (1813–1862), future wife of Grand Duke Ludwig III of Hesse (1808–1877)
Nymphenburg porcelain
Bayerisches Nationalmuseum, Munich
Inv. Ker 3646-3656

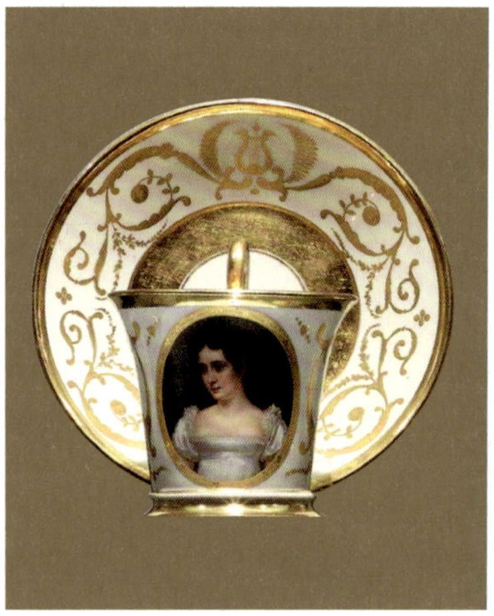

Cup and saucer with the portrait of Princess Adelgunde Auguste Charlotte (1823–1914), future wife of Duke Francesco V of Modena, Archduke of Austria-Este (1819–1875)
Nymphenburg porcelain
Bayerisches Nationalmuseum, Munich
Inv. Ker 3647-3657

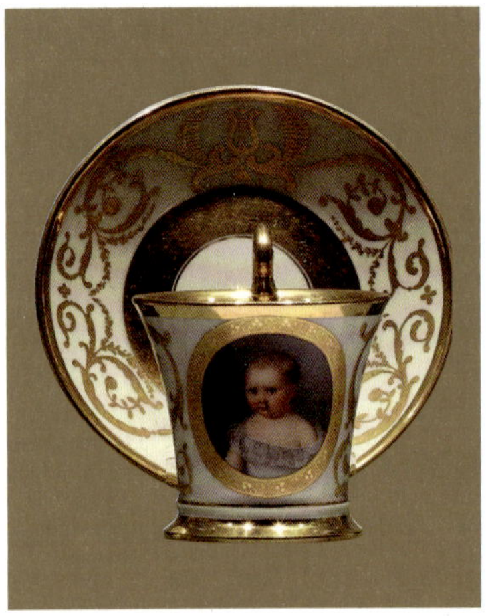

Cup and saucer with the portrait of Prince Otto Friedrich Ludwig (1815–1867), future king of Greece
Nymphenburg porcelain
Bayerisches Nationalmuseum, Munich
Inv. Ker 3653-3663

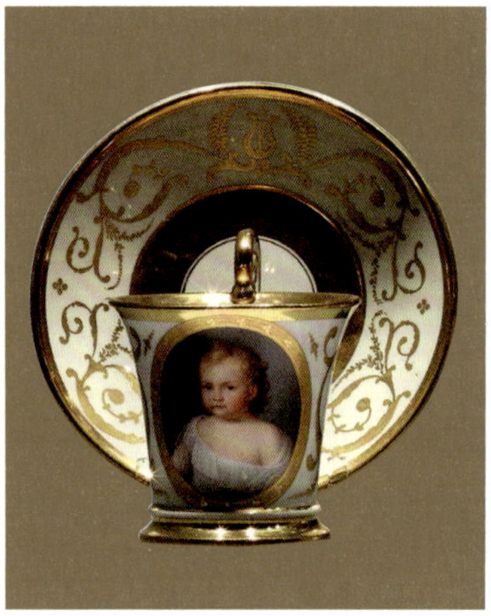

Cup and saucer with the portrait of Princess Hildegard Luise Charlotte (1825–1864), future wife of Archduke Albrecht of Austria (1817–1895)
Nymphenburg porcelain
Bayerisches Nationalmuseum, Munich
Inv. Ker 3651-3661

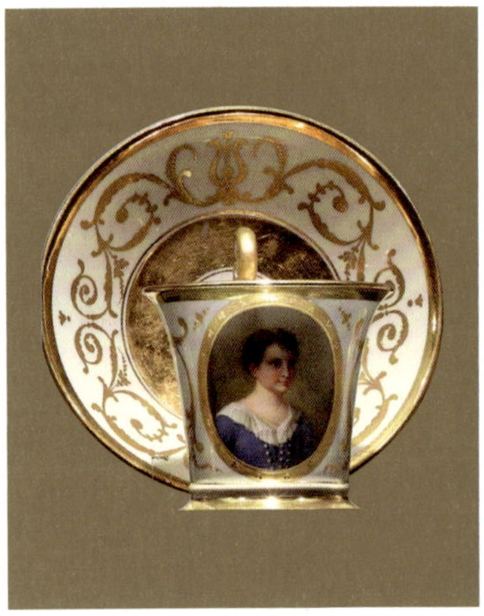

Cup and saucer with the portrait of Prince Luitpold (1821–1912), future crown prince
Nymphenburg porcelain
Bayerisches Nationalmuseum Munich
Inv. Ker 3649-3659

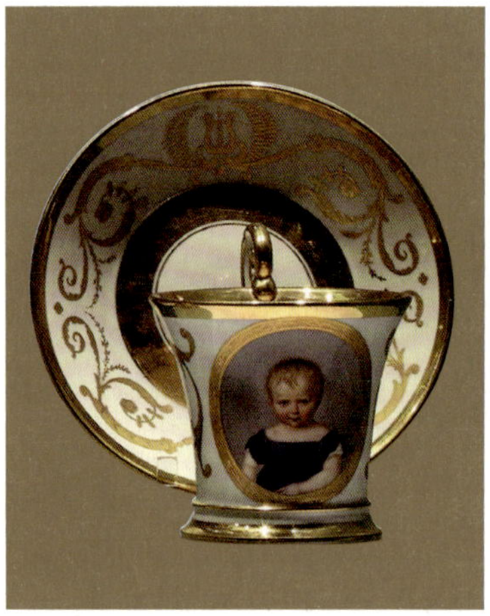

Cup and saucer with the portrait of Princess Alexandra Amalie (1826–1875), future abbess in Munich and Würzburg
Nymphenburg porcelain
Bayerisches Nationalmuseum, Munich
Inv. Ker 3655-3665

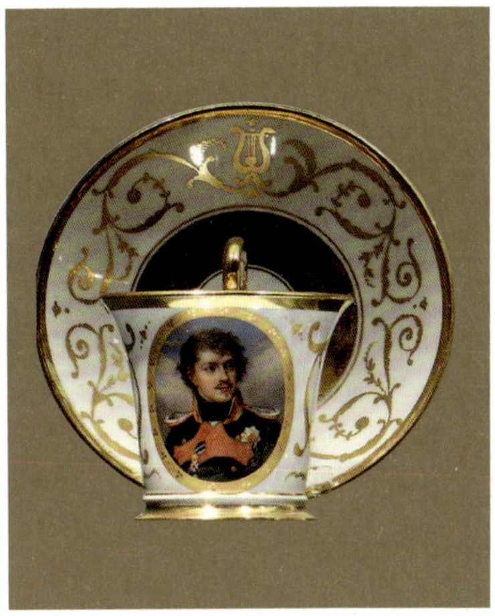

Cup and saucer with the portrait of Prince Adalbert Wilhelm (1828–1875)
Nymphenburg porcelain
Bayerisches Nationalmuseum, Munich
Inv. Ker 3648-3658

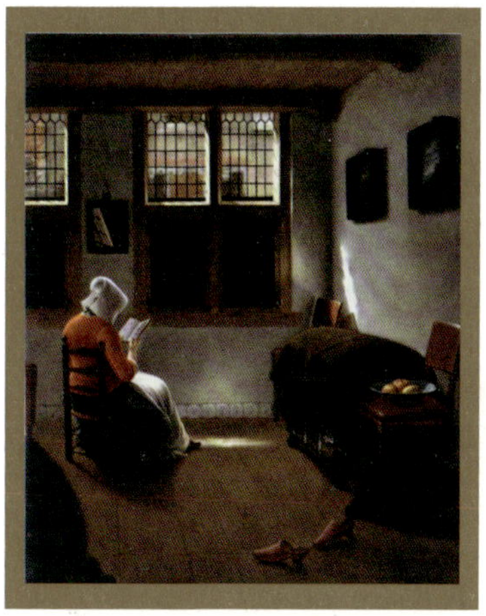

Woman Reading, after Pieter Janssens Elinga (1623–1682)
c. 1860
Otto Wüstlich (1819–1886)
Painted porcelain
38 × 30 cm
Bayerische Verwaltung der staatlichen Schlösser, Gärten und Seen, Munich
Inv. ResMü K IV 170 (WAF) / Munich Residenz

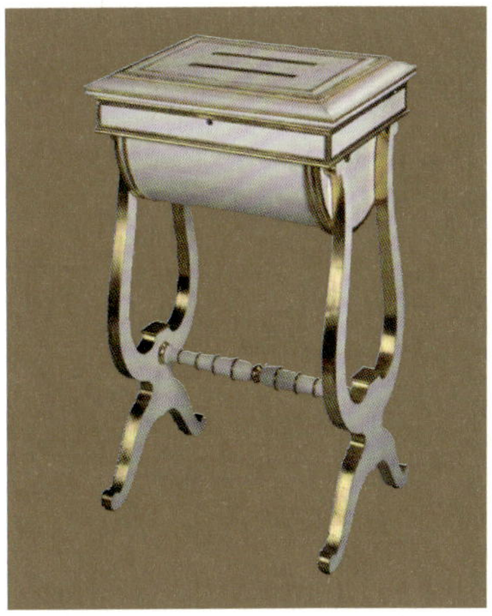

Table-letter case belonging to Queen Therese
1835–36
Attributed to Leo von Klenze (1784–1864)
Spruce, beech, white, partially gilded veneering, brass
82.5 × 49.5 × 39.5 cm
Bayerische Verwaltung der staatlichen Schlösser, Gärten und Seen, Munich
Inv. ResMü M 706 / Munich Residenz

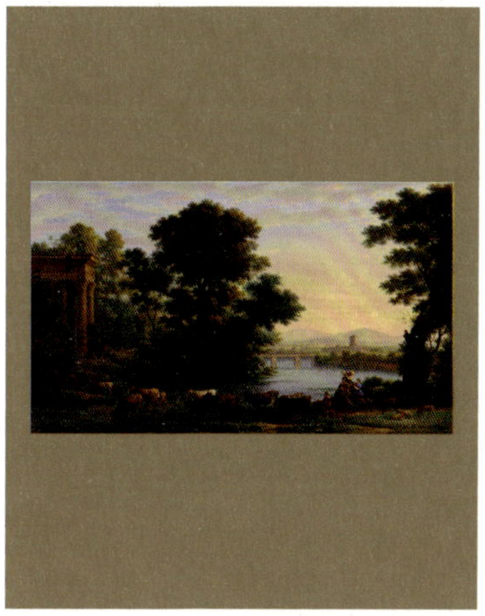

Agar and Ishmael in the Desert, after Claude Lorrain (1600–1682)
1833
Carl Friedrich Heinzmann (1795–1846)
Painted porcelain
24.3 × 39 cm
Bayerische Verwaltung der staatlichen Schlösser, Gärten und Seen, Munich
Inv. ResMü K IV 72 (WAF) / Munich Residenz

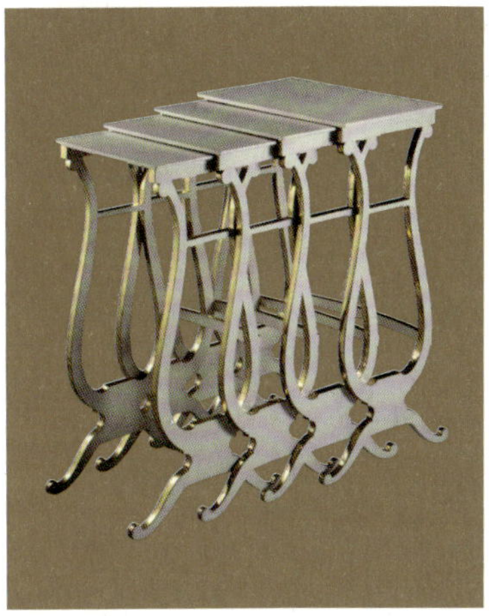

Four stowaway tables from the study of Queen Therese
1834–35
Melchior Frank (1783–1855)
Linden, white and partially gilded veneering, brass
Table a: 77 × 46.5 × 30.5 cm; table b: 76 × 41.5 × 30.5 cm; table c: 74.5 × 37 × 30.5 cm; table d: 73.5 × 32.5 × 30.5 cm
Bayerische Verwaltung der staatlichen Schlösser, Gärten und Seen, Munich
Inv. ResMü M 121 / Munich Residenz

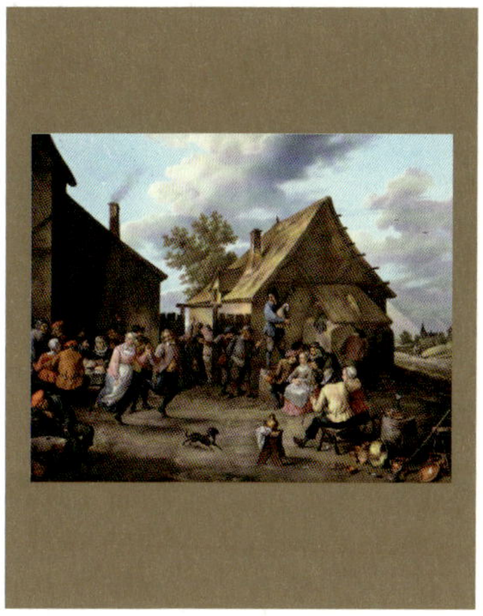

Rural Dance in Front of a Tavern, after David Teniers (1610–1690)
1837
Carl Le Feubure (1805–1886)
Painted porcelain
32.5 × 28 cm
Bayerische Verwaltung der staatlichen Schlösser, Gärten und Seen, Munich
Inv. ResMü K IV 60 (WAF) / Munich Residenz

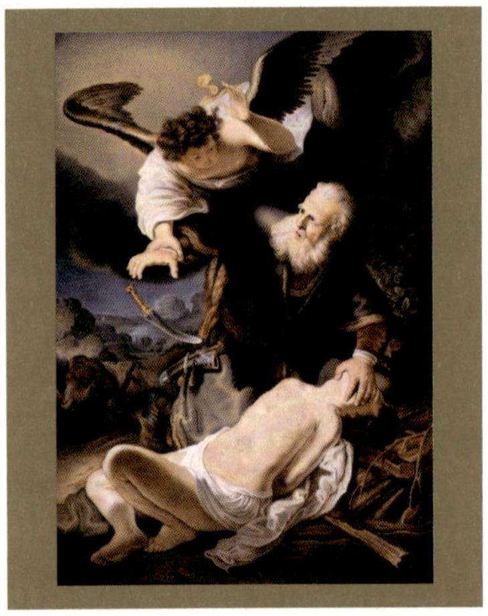

The Sacrifice of Isaac, after Rembrandt (1606–1669)
1843
Philipp Kristfeld (1797–1874)
Painted porcelain
28.5 × 20.5 cm
Bayerische Verwaltung der staatlichen Schlösser, Gärten und Seen, Munich
Inv. ResMü K IV 89 (WAF) / Munich Residenz

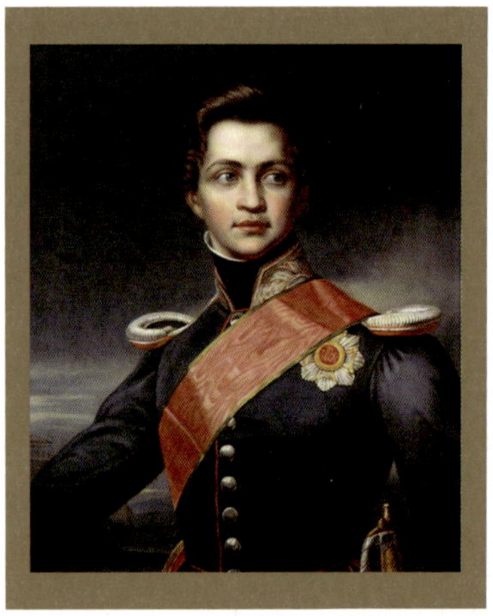

King Otto I of Greece (1815–1867), son of Ludwig I of Bavaria
1832
Joseph-Karl Stieler (1781–1858)
Oil on canvas
97 × 83 cm (inc. frame)
Bayerische Verwaltung der staatlichen Schlösser, Gärten und Seen, Munich
Inv. ResMü G 0410 / Bamberg Residenz

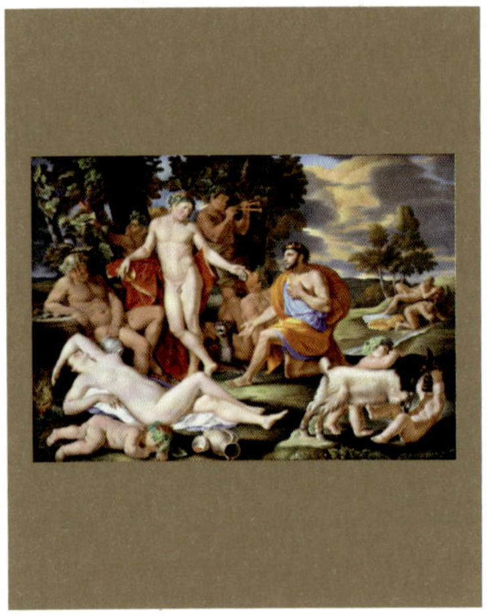

Midas and Bacchus, after Nicolas Poussin (1594–1665)
1843
Philipp Kristfeld (1797–1874)
Painted porcelain
22 × 30 cm
Bayerische Verwaltung der staatlichen Schlösser, Gärten und Seen, Munich
Iinv. ResMü K IV 93 (WAF) / Munich Residenz

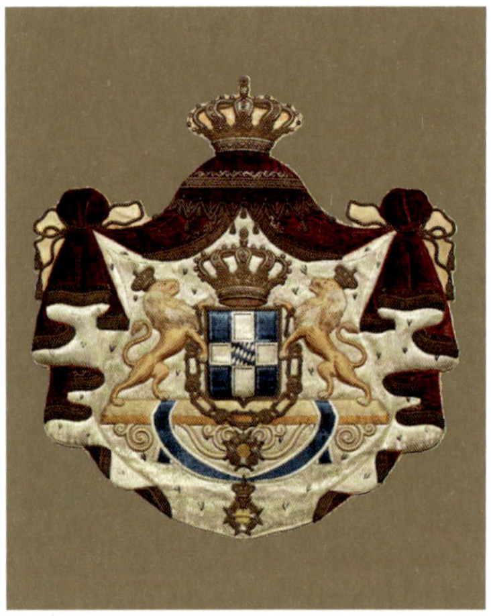

The Greek royal coat of arms
c. 1835
Embroidered silk velvet, gold and silver appliqué lace
67 × 61 cm
Bayerisches Nationalmuseum, Munich
Inv. T 5451

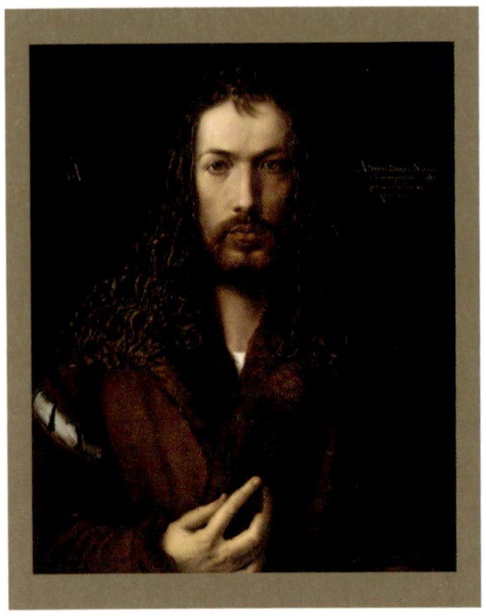

Self-Portrait of Albrecht Dürer in 1500, after Albrecht Dürer (1471–1528)
c. 1845
Christian Adler (1787–1850)
Painted porcelain
28.5 × 22.5 cm
Bayerische Verwaltung der staatlichen Schlösser, Gärten und Seen, Munich
Inv. ResMü K IV 1 (WAF) / Munich Residenz

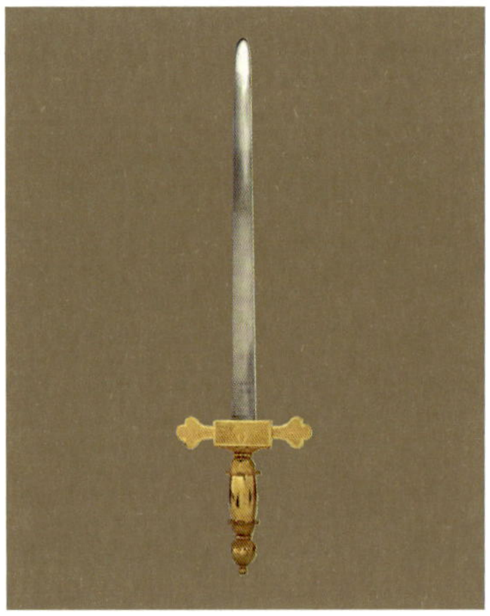

Sword of King Otto I of Greece (replica)
c. 1835, Athens
Matthias Wimmer
Iron, gilded brass, steel
L. (max) 78 cm
Bayerisches Nationalmuseum, Munich
Inv. T 5449

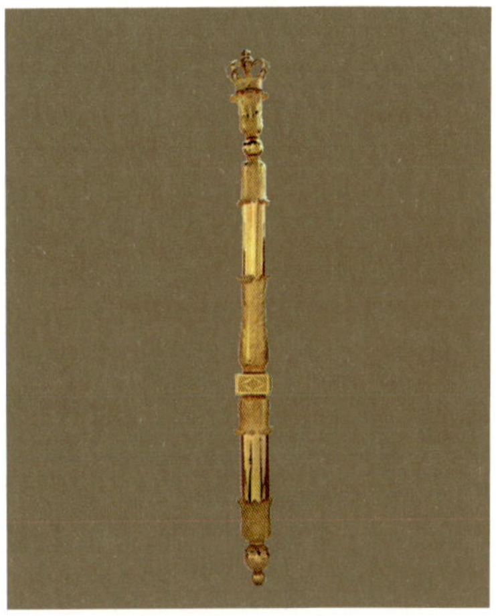

Scepter of King Otto I of Greece
(replica)
c. 1835
Gilded brass, steel
L. (max) 75.5 cm
Bayerisches Nationalmuseum, Munich
Inv. T 5450

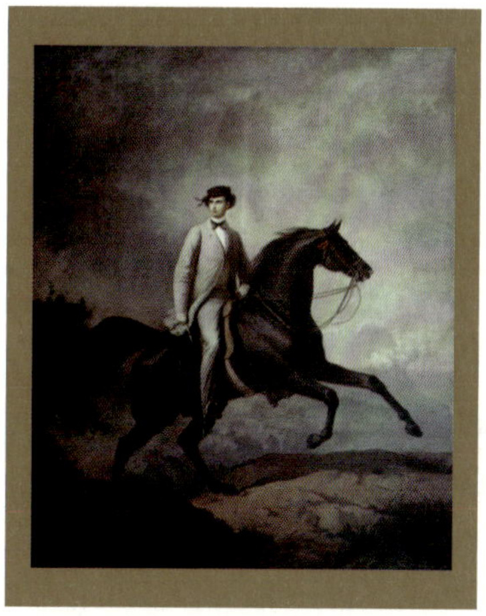

Ludwig II of Bavaria (1845–1886) on Horseback in the Mountains
1864
Feodor Dietz (1813–1870)
Oil on canvas
97.3 × 83.5 cm (inc. frame)
Bayerische Verwaltung der staatlichen Schlösser, Gärten und Seen, Munich
Inv. 7 (BSV) / Nymphenburg Castle, Marstallmuseum

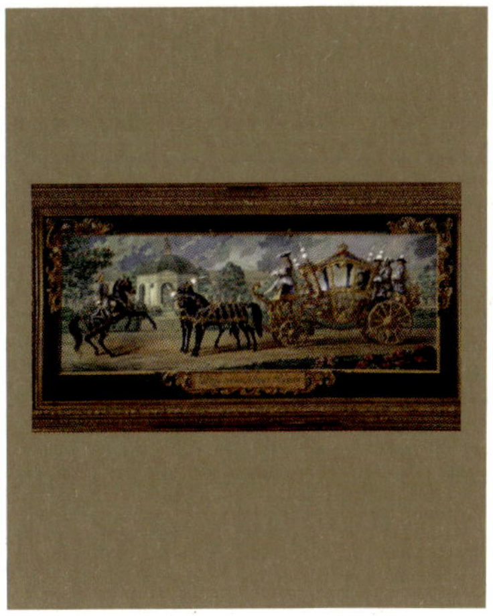

King Ludwig II (1845–1886) in the Ceremonial Coach of Emperor Karl VII (1697–1745)
c. 1867, Munich
Franz Seitz (1817–1883)
Pencil, pen, gouache on paper
67 × 180 cm (inc. frame)
Bayerische Verwaltung der staatlichen Schlösser, Gärten und Seen, Munich
Inv. W 13 (WAF) / Nymphenburg Castle, Marstallmuseum

Ink well belonging to Ludwig II (1845–1886)
c. 1869
Franz Seitz (1817–1883)
Gilded bronze, silver, porcelain
24 × 35 × 13 cm
Bayerische Verwaltung der staatlichen Schlösser, Gärten und Seen, Munich
Inv. ResMü F.V.III, Bd. VII, folg. 1397, 1184, Kat. L-II.-Museum nr. 158 / Herrenchiemsee Castle, Ludwig II Museum

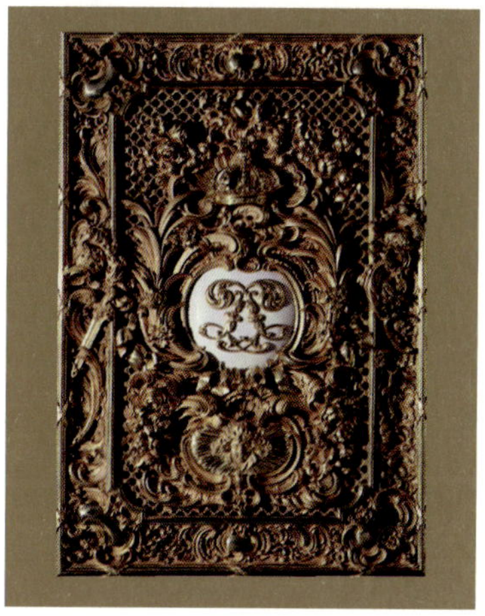

Writing case with the monogram of Ludwig II
c. 1883
Ferdinand Harrach (1821–1898)
Gilded silver
52 × 38.7 cm
Bayerische Verwaltung der staatlichen Schlösser, Gärten und Seen, Munich
Inv. L.II.-Mus. 168, Kat. nr. 297 / Herrenchiemsee Castle, Ludwig II Museum

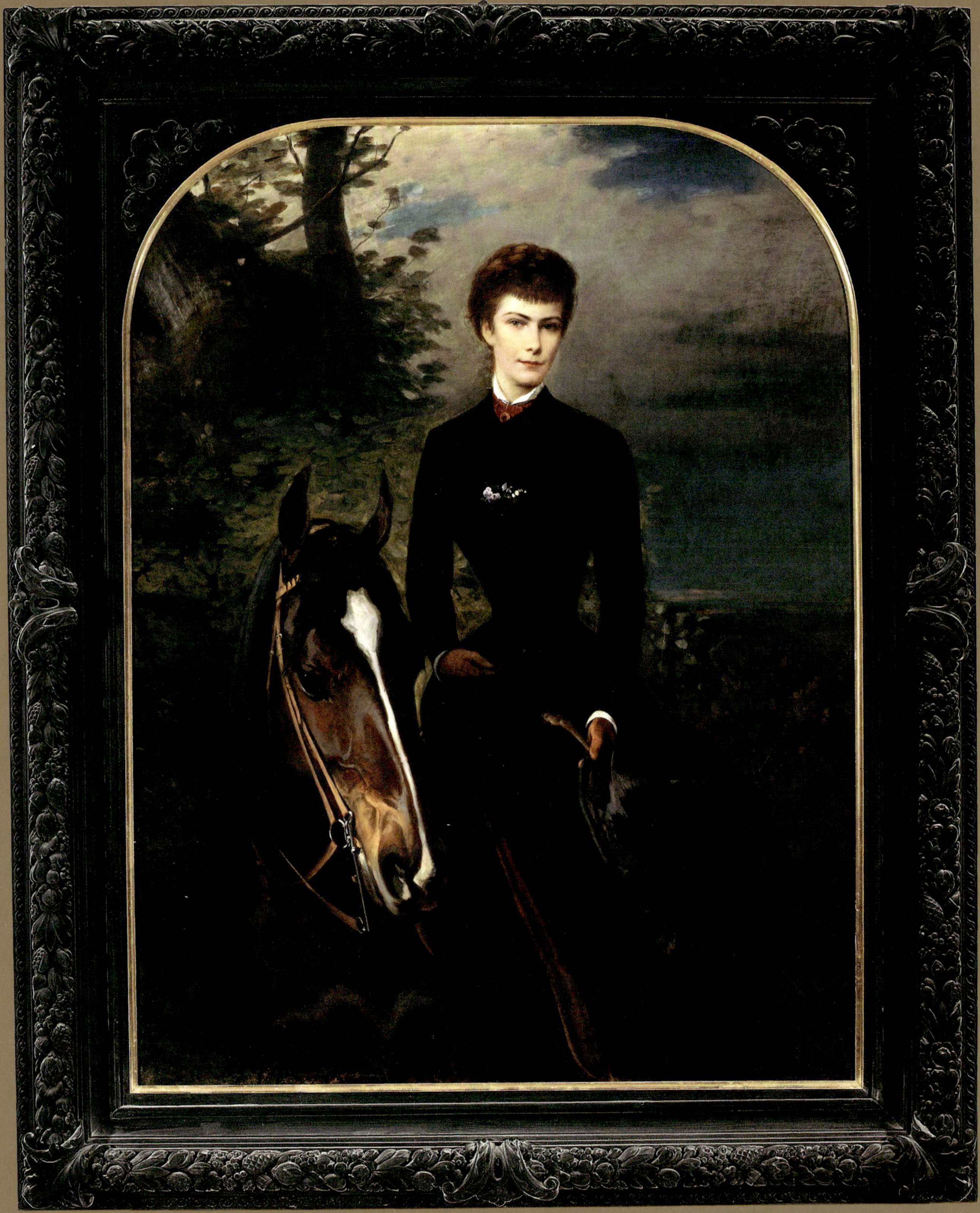

AUSTRIA

Franz Josef (1830–1916) and Elisabeth (1837–1898)

Empress Elisabeth Riding her Favorite Horse
c. 1876
WILHELM RICHTER
(1824–1892)
Eisenstadt Castle,
Esterházy Foundation

Empress Elisabeth of Austria
The myth of Sissi

Ilsebill Barta

Emperor Franz Josef I
(1830-1916)
c. 1854
Bundesmobilienverwaltung/
Hofmobiliendepot
Möbel Museum,
Vienna

Empress Elisabeth
(1837-1898)
1856
Franz Russ
Eisenstadt Castle,
Esterházy Foundation

It is today difficult to distinguish the historical figure that was Empress Elisabeth from all the legends and anecdotes, the fact and fiction—as well as the private diaries, poems, pictures, and even films. Contemporary descriptions too succumb at least partly to the legend that sprung up around the character of the Austrian empress, who herself expended considerable energy in constructing her myth.

Empress Elisabeth of Austria, daughter of Duke Maximilian of Bavaria, was born in Munich in 1837, and married her cousin, Emperor Franz Josef I, her elder by seven years, in 1854. Between the engagement and the wedding, Elisabeth received many gifts from the emperor, as her parents were not well enough off to afford a suitable trousseau. Among these presents appears a blue velvet coat trimmed in sable, together with a muff of the same material, a silver traveling set and a painting depicting Elisabeth side-saddle on her favorite horse at Christmas 1853, a picture subsequently copied and altered on many occasions.

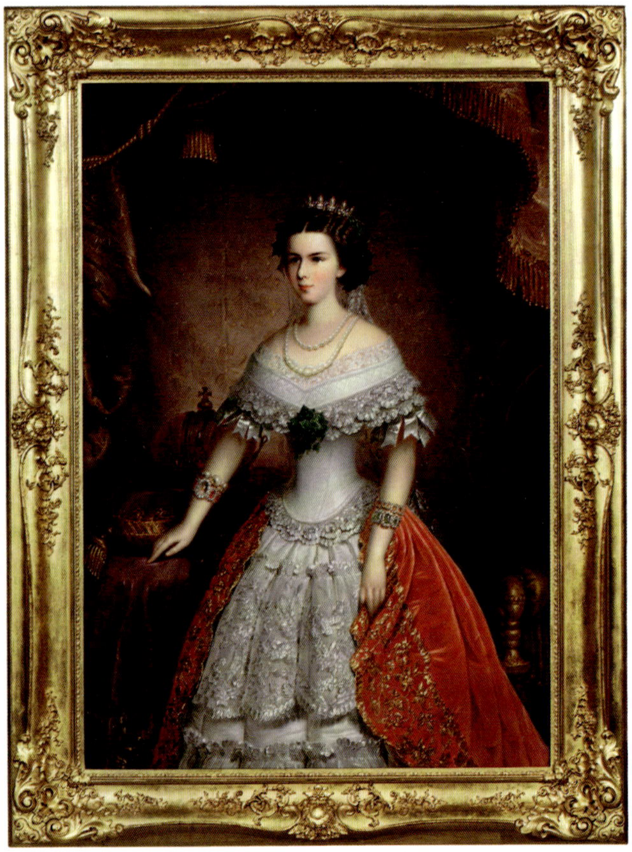

Riding had been one of her great passions since childhood, and Empress Elisabeth had a Europe-wide reputation for being adroit in the saddle. She would not only ride when out hunting but also enjoyed dressage and demonstration riding. In England, she took part in great meets, outdoing most of the men in horsemanship.

Transported to Vienna in twenty-five boxes and suitcases, her trousseau is documented in a precise inventory. Four

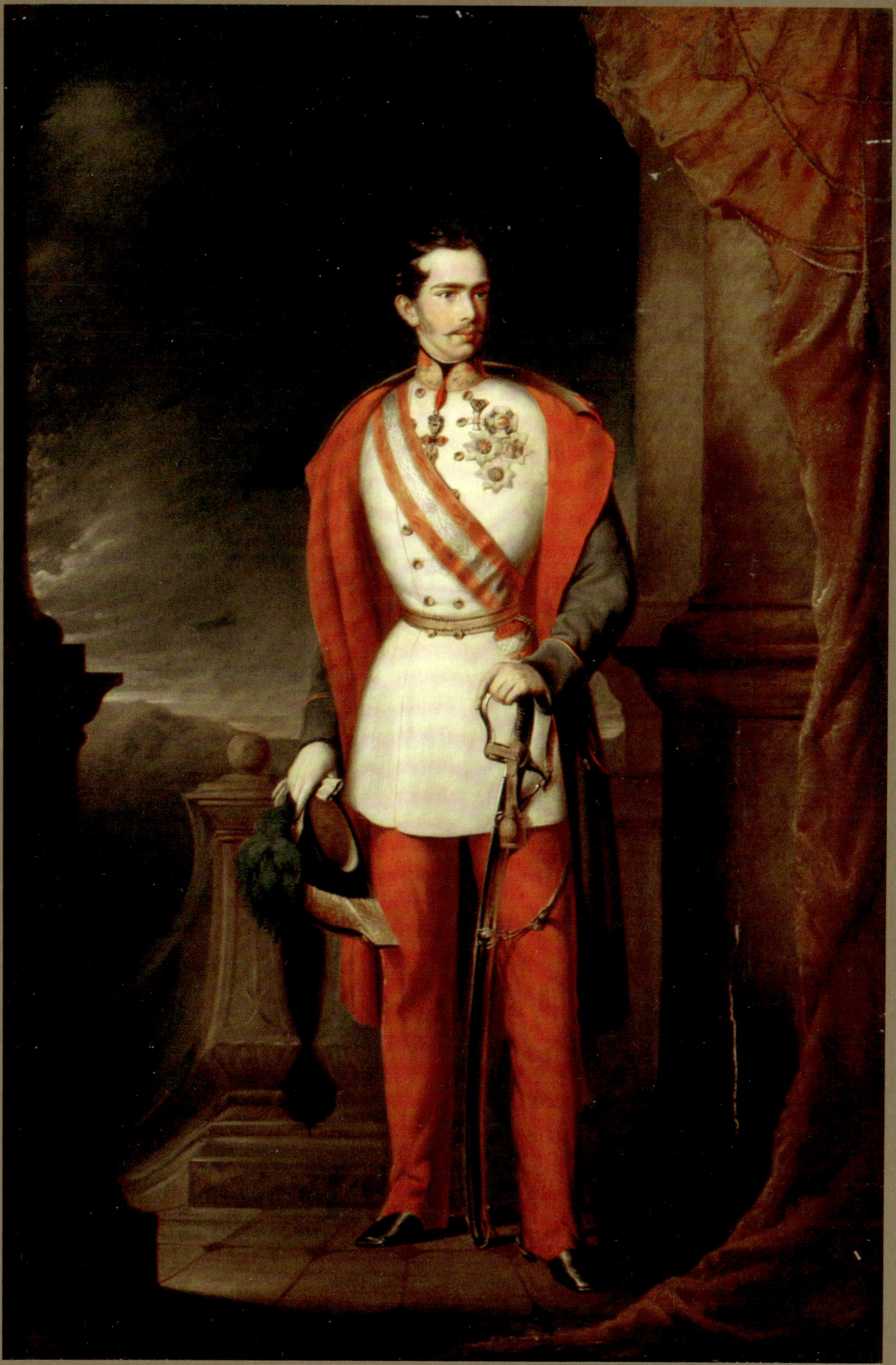

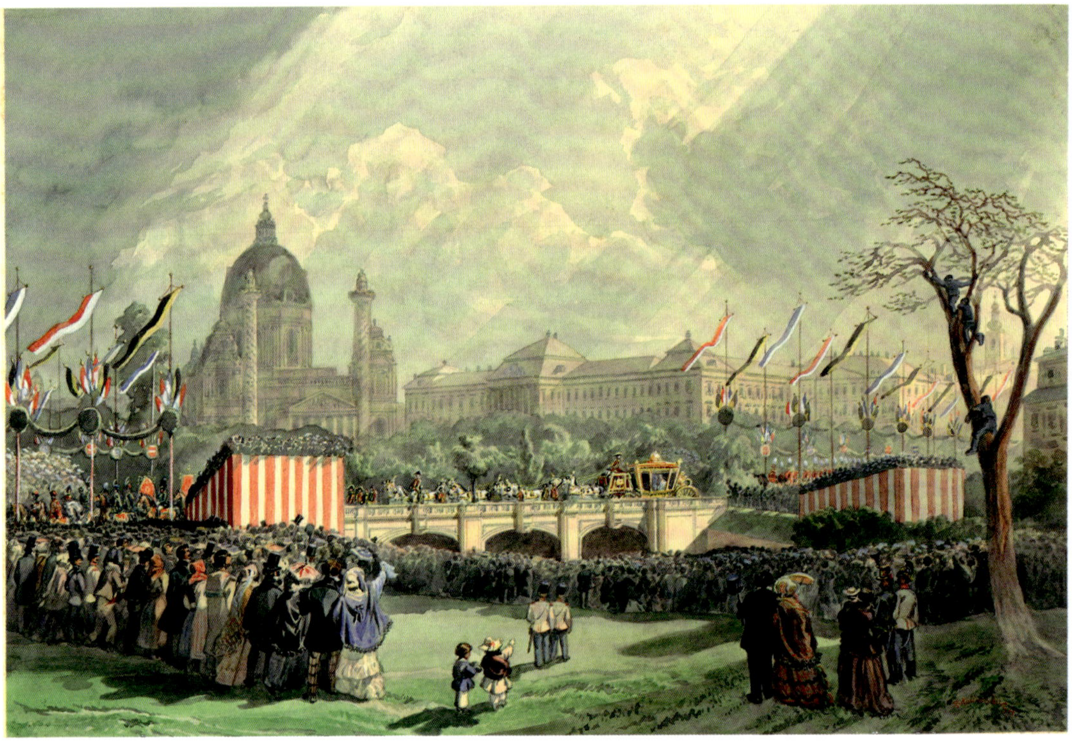

ballgowns, including two white, one pink and another sky-blue with white roses, seventeen dress-gowns with train, as well as the wedding-dress in silver moiré with a coat, and the white and pink satin and tulle dresses comprising her court wardrobe. Completing the wardrobe for solemn occasions, there were also fourteen silk gowns and nineteen summer dresses embellished with floral embroidery. The bride herself took note of three ample crinolines, four corsets, three riding corsets, and one hundred and forty-four lace and cambric chemises, as well as thirty-six nightgowns, one hundred and sixty-eight pairs of cotton and silk socks, one hundred and thirteen pairs of shoes, sixteen hats, two umbrellas, two fans, and six parasols, together with a mass of toiletry articles.

Never was a bride more rapturously greeted than Sissi in Vienna. The bells of Viennese churches announced the arrival of the emperor's wife-to-be on April 22, 1854, at four in the afternoon. The emperor leaped on the boat even before it could be tied up and gathered his fiancée up in his arms. The streets were lined with people from all walks of life joyously welcoming the Bavarian duchess. After Sissi was presented to her close family, the emperor handed over the wedding presents, among which were an engagement gift of a diamond crown and a dazzling emerald-studded bodice. That evening a great gala dinner served on the

Princess Elisabeth Visiting the Saint Charles Church in Vienna
1854
Franz Kaliwoda
Eisenstadt Castle,
Esterházy Foundation

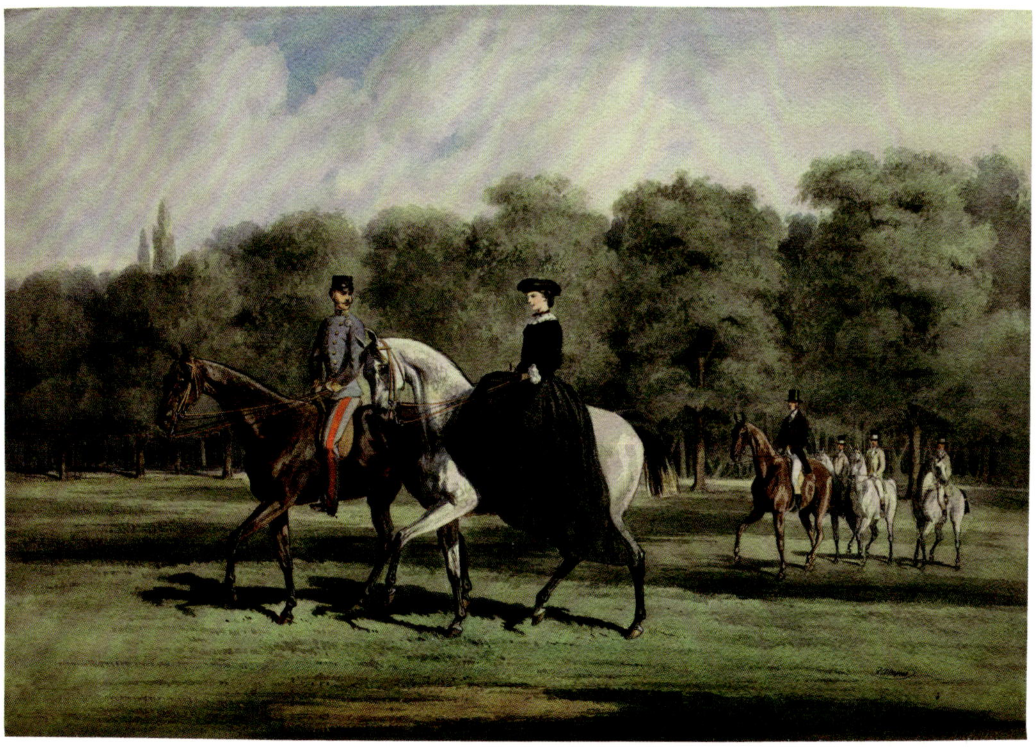

so-called "Grand Vermeil" service was thrown in Elisabeth's honor at the palace of Schönbrunn. The following day, the wedding carriage drawn by eight horses trotted into the Vienna Hofburg. The wedding took place on April 24 at seven o'clock in the evening in the church of St. Augustine lit for the occasion by fifteen thousand candles. The angelic beauty of the new empress was lauded in lengthy paeans of tribute. The happiness of the couple, blessed in early years by the birth of three children—Sophie, who died prematurely, Gisele and Crown Prince Rudolph—was marred though by endless rows with the intransigent mother-in-law, who was determined to forbid Sissi all political activity or influence whatsoever at the Hofburg where she felt increasingly suffocated. Perhaps partly due to the emperor's extra-conjugal affairs, from about 1860 the couple's relationship deteriorated. Elisabeth took refuge in an ailment that probably originated in depression, leaving Vienna for a series of journeys and cures that lasted almost two years. As the years passed, Elisabeth took the decision—in what was a very unusual and scandalous departure for a sovereign—to remove herself forever from life at court, where she had played an active role on the political level only once, in 1867, at the time of the conciliation with Hungary. Free of all responsibilities and duty, she could henceforth devote herself, in addition to bringing up

The Emperor and Empress on Horseback
c. 1854
ZAMNIO
Eisenstadt Castle,
Esterházy Foundation

her daughter Marie Valerie, almost exclusively to traveling, horseriding, looking after her pets, reading, writing poems, and keeping herself trim and attractive. In an effort to fulfill the only role granted her—namely to perpetuate the Habsburg name and show herself as the beautiful wife ever ready to fly to the emperor's side—she fine-tuned her figure and appearance in a cult of the body that became more and more extreme, not to say costly and eccentric. Elisabeth's neurotic desire was not really directed towards any sexual relationship, but was rather the expression of an exacerbated narcissism; an "entirely overwhelming and passionate love of her own body" and its representation, as her niece Marie Larisch recalled: "She adored her beauty as a pagan does his idols and would kneel before it. The sight of the perfection of her body afforded her aesthetic delight; and anything that might jeopardize this perfection she found unbearable on an artistic level, and it repulsed her... She had made it her life's duty to remain young and her mind was entirely fixed on the best means to maintain her beauty."

She had a gym installed in each palace, complete with bars, rings, and dumbbells. Daily exercise, hours of horseriding practice—to the point of being able to perform circus acts—endless walks and fencing, together with draconian diets and notebooks detailing her figure and weight, meant she kept a youthful silhouette and a 19-inch waist. Expensive cosmetics for face and body masks in conjunction with baths attempted to preserve her skin from the effects of aging, but she refused to use either make-up or strong scents.

Elisabeth's increasing obsession with her physical appearance (which in several regards anticipates the cult of the body as that came to the fore at the turn of the century) reached a climax with the almost ritual cult she dedicated to her hair: her long, chestnut-brown tresses that reached down to her feet were combed and dressed for three hours every day by the onetime hairdresser of the Burgtheater, Fanny Feifalik, and every three weeks underwent a day-long deep-clean with precious essences, cognac, and eggs.

The intricate braid was comprised of a crown made up of nine parts that formed a plait in three sections above the temples, whence the hair was swept back. At the end the braids were gathered up and attached by a fine velvet ribbon interlaced to either side to support the weight of the hair. She wears this famous, oft-imitated "crown" in the well-known picture showing her with diamond stars in her hair. Elisabeth confessed to her reader Christomanos that she felt that her hair was "like a foreign body on her head." This splitting of the ego—a phantasmatic desire focusing on a truly fetishized part of the body—is clearly a manifestation of hysteria that transpires more openly still in Sissi's later poems addressed to her great mass of hair.

Elisabeth, Empress of Austria, with her hair loose
1864
Franz Xaver Winterhalter
(1806-1873)
Kunsthistorisches Museum, Vienna

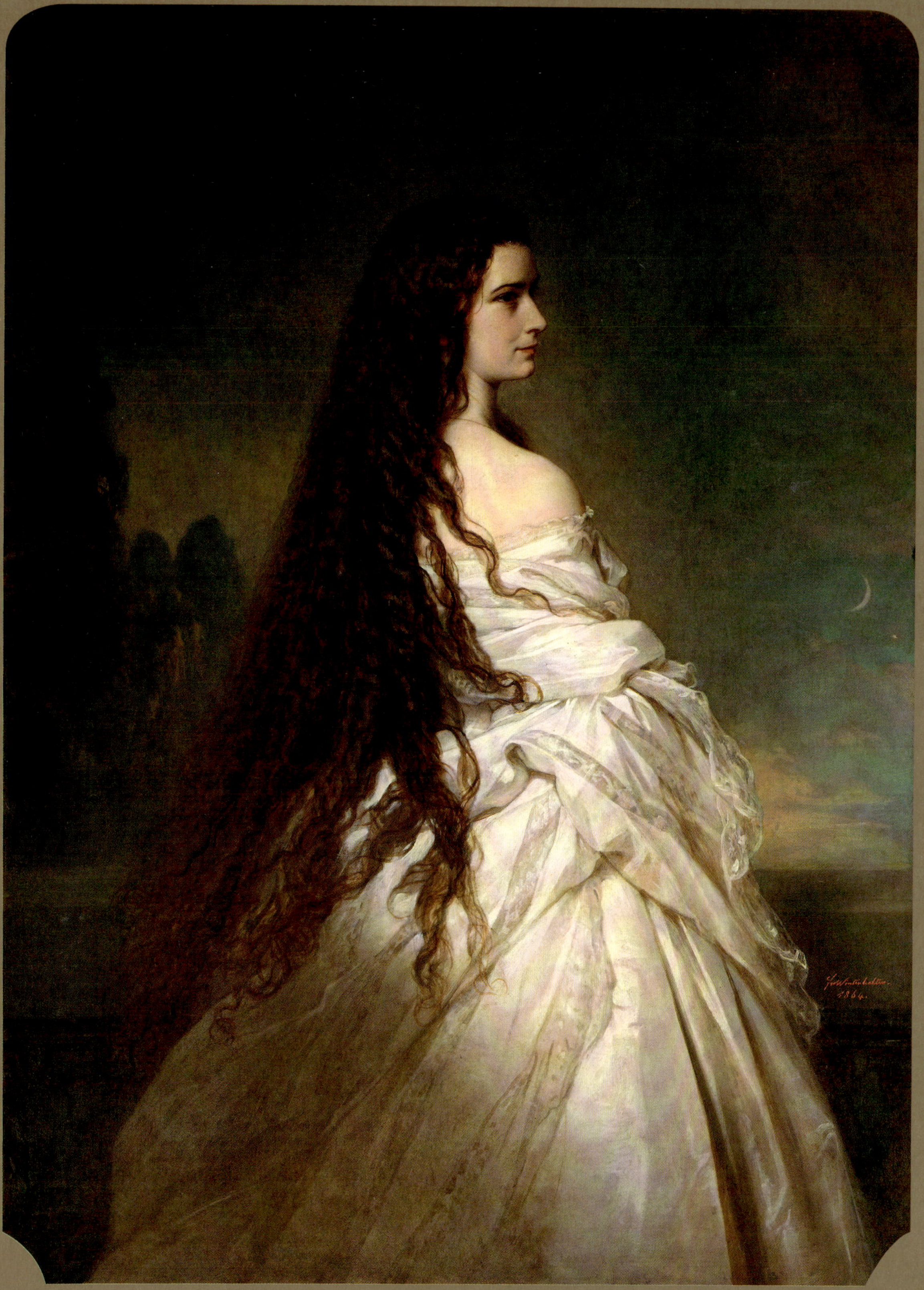

"Wishes
By my hair I would fain die,
All my life, all my strength,
All my blood, the best nectar,
Those I would pass into my locks...
O that my existence would pass
In a silken wave of golden curls,
Rolling, ever richer, ever deeper,
Until I fall asleep, exhausted, on that other side".

Sissi wrote poems for a prolonged period. Her idol was Heinrich Heine, to whose memory she raised a monument in the Achilleion Palace on Corfu. She copied out collections of her own poems some six times, entrusting their publication to various individuals, who were instructed to issue them only seventy years after her death. The Swiss Republic also received a copy that was printed precisely after this lapse of time...

In the last years of her life, more particularly after the death of her only son, Crown Prince Rodolph, in 1889, Elisabeth became a loner, almost constantly traveling with a maid of honor from the court, and was scarcely ever to be seen in Vienna.

In 1898, while staying in Geneva, she was stabbed with a file by the anarchist Luigi Lucheni. The posterity and myth of Empress Elisabeth of Austria as a woman wholly out of the ordinary were consolidated in contemporary eyes in the 1950s by the *Sissi* movies with Romy Schneider.

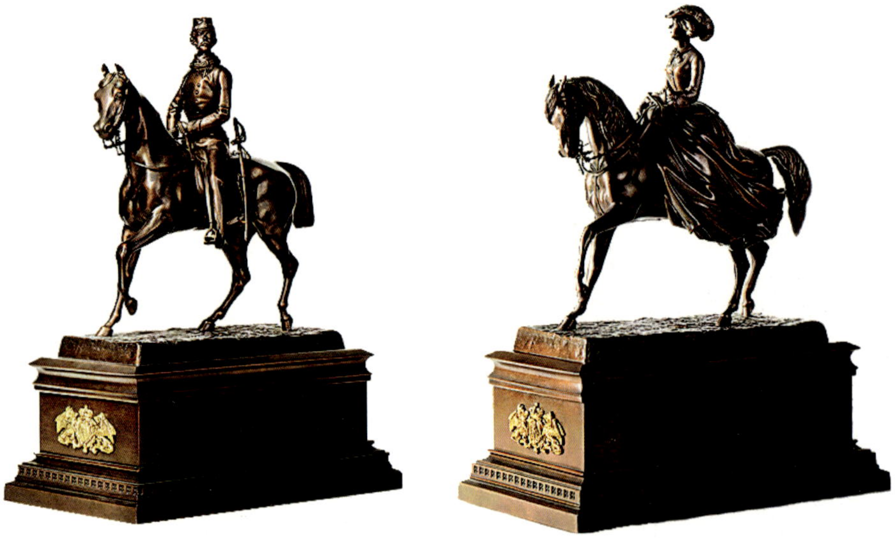

Emperor Franz Josef and Empress Elisabeth on Horseback
F. Sauter
Mid-nineteenth century
Eisenstadt Castle,
Esterházy Foundation

The famous ruby parure of the empress

On the occasion of the imperial couple's silver wedding anniversary in 1879, the painter Georg Raab, for whom Empress Elisabeth as queen of Hungary had already sat, carried out this portrait of the empress and queen represented wearing her famous ruby parure. Immortalizing forever the image of a truly fascinating beauty, this picture is the last portrait she ever posed for. She was forty-two.

For one *soirée* given at the Hofburg for five thousand guests, the empress wore a fur-trimmed pearl-gray court gown with a long train superbly embroidered with gold. Those who witnessed the spectacle all averred how her diamond and ruby-studded bodice shone with a thousand fires.

The sumptuous ruby parure she wears comes from the estate of Marie-Antoinette and comprises a diadem, a necklace, a corsage, and earrings. Emperor Franz Josef had it remounted, presenting it to his wife as a wedding gift in 1854. The ensemble belonged to the jewelry that was the private property of the Habsburgs of which there has been no trace since 1918.

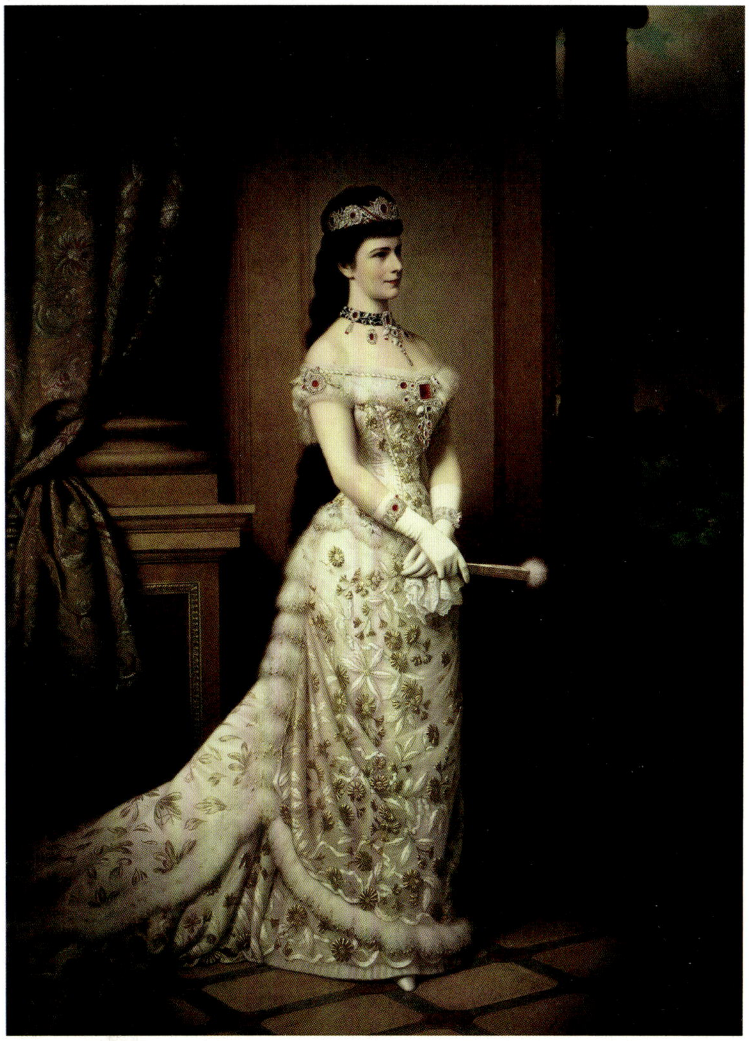

Empress Elisabeth in Her Ruby Parure
c. 1879
Georg Raab
Bundesmobilienverwaltung / Hofburg Wien, Sisi-Museum, Vienna

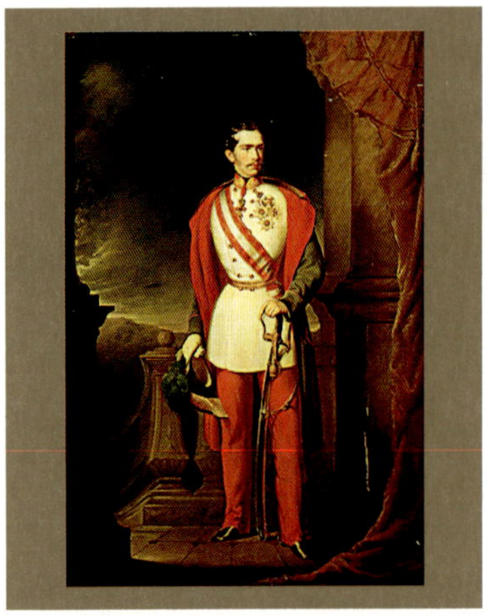

Emperor Franz Josef I
c. 1854
Oil on canvas
266 × 185 cm (inc. frame)
Bundesmobilienverwaltung /
Hofmobiliendepot Möbel Museum,
Vienna
Inv. MD 056434, MD 057965

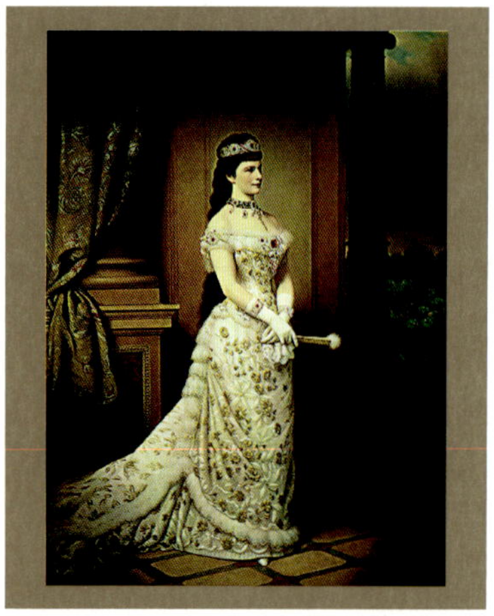

Empress Elisabeth in Her Ruby Parure
c. 1879
Georg Raab
Oil on canvas
260 × 191 cm (inc. frame)
Bundesmobilienverwaltung /
Hofmobiliendepot Möbel Museum,
Vienna
Inv. MD 043548, Inv. MD 043609

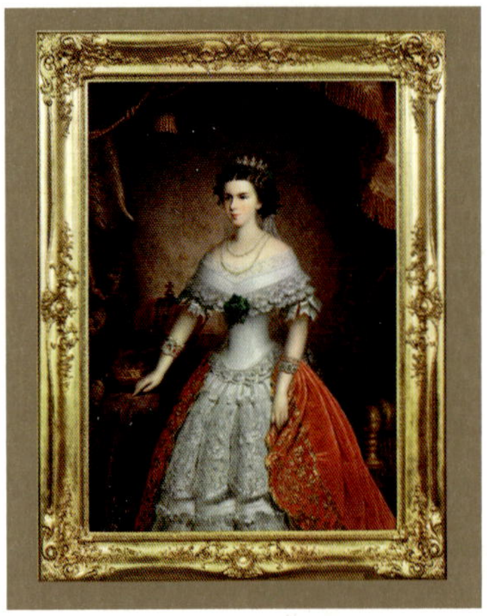

Empress Elisabeth
1856
Franz Russ
Oil on canvas
194 × 144 cm
Eisenstadt Castle,
Esterházy Foundation
Inv. B485

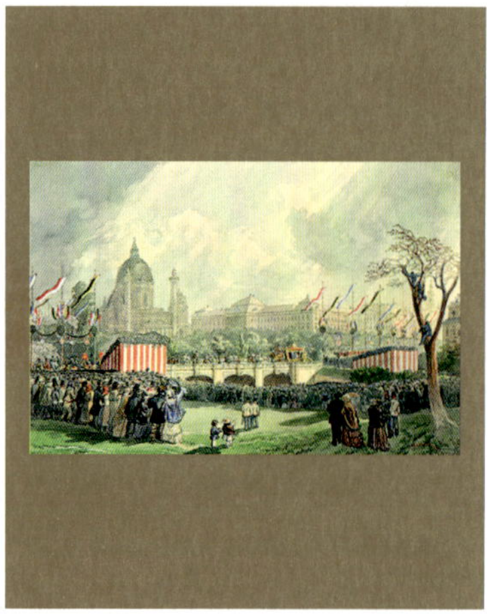

Princess Elisabeth Visiting the Saint Charles Church in Vienna
1854
Franz Kaliwoda
Watercolor
65 × 78 cm (inc. frame)
Eisenstadt Castle,
Esterházy Foundation
Inv. B612

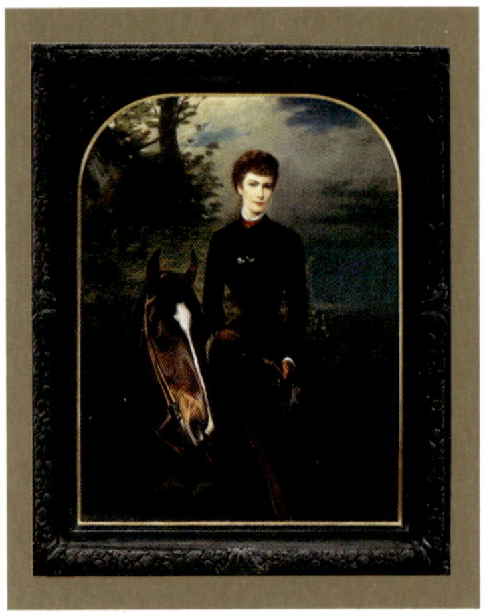

Empress Elisabeth Riding her Favorite Horse
c. 1876
Wilhelm Richter (1824–1892)
Oil on canvas
127 × 96 cm
Eisenstadt Castle,
Esterházy Foundation
Inv. B37

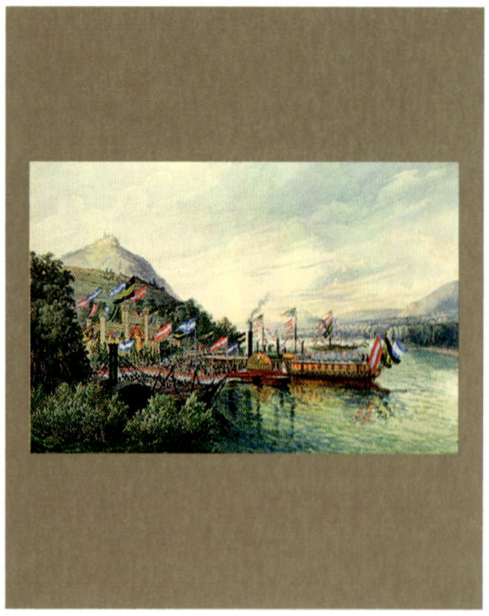

Princess Elisabeth Arriving in Vienna by Boat
1854
Franz Kaliwoda
Watercolor
65 × 78 cm (inc. frame)
Eisenstadt Castle,
Esterházy Foundation
Inv. B611

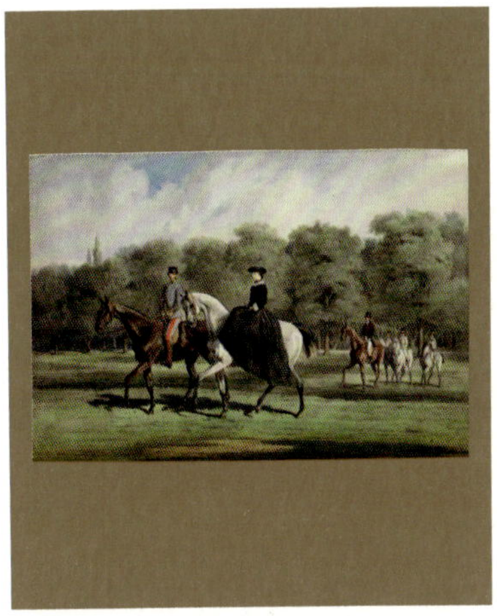

The Emperor and Empress on Horseback
c. 1854
Zamnio
Watercolor
65 × 78 cm (inc. frame)
Eisenstadt Castle,
Esterházy Foundation
Inv. B613

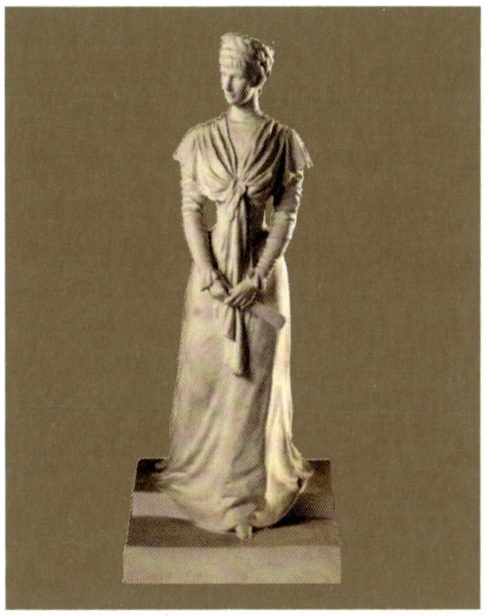

Empress Elisabeth
1906
Hermann Klotz (1850–1932)
Bisque porcelain from
the Vienna manufactory
46 × 24.5 × 19 cm
Vienne, Bundesmobilienverwaltung /
Silberkammer, Hofburg Wien
Inv. MD 047537/000

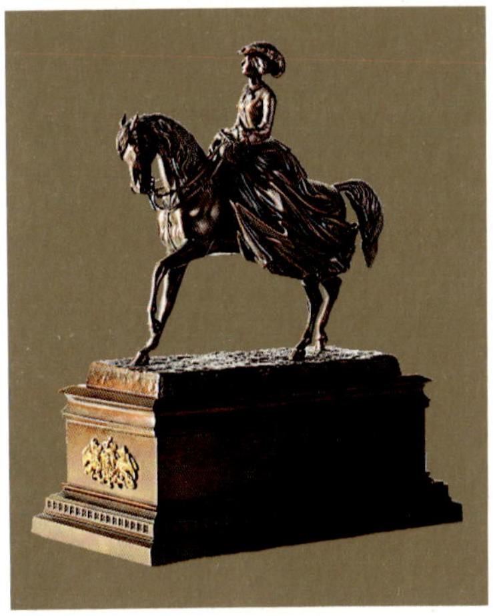

Empress Elisabeth on Horseback
Mid-nineteenth century
F. Sauter
Bronze
50.3 × 37.8 × 22.6 cm
Eisenstadt Castle,
Esterházy Foundation
Inv. SK 1

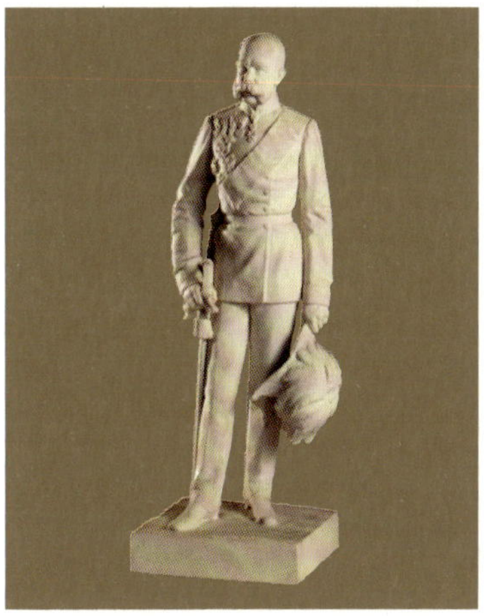

Emperor Franz Josef
1906
Hermann Klotz (1850–1932)
Bisque porcelain from
the Vienna manufactory
H. 48 cm
Vienne, Bundesmobilienverwaltung /
Silberkammer, Hofburg Wien
Inv. MD 047536/000

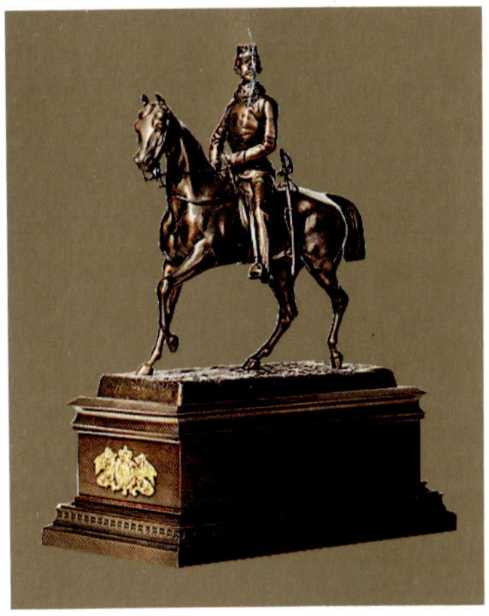

Emperor Franz Josef on Horseback
Mid-nineteenth century
F. Sauter
Bronze
52.2 × 37.8 × 22.6 cm
Eisenstadt Castle,
Esterházy Foundation
Inv. SK 2

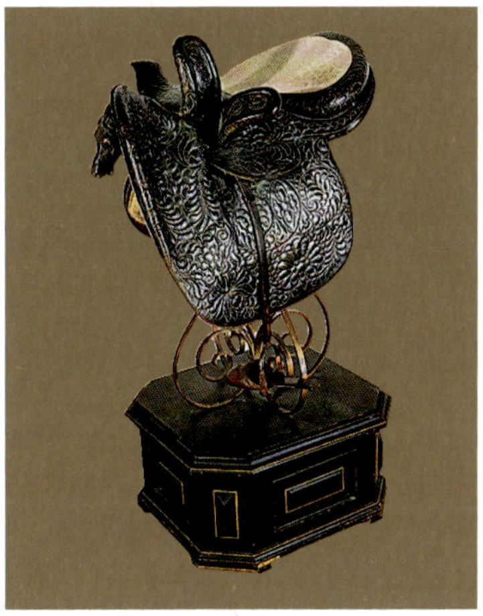

Saddle belonging to the empress
c. 1855
Casimir Foltz
Leather, wood, metal
100 × 100 cm
Kunsthistorisches Museum,
Wagenburg, Vienna
Inv. G298

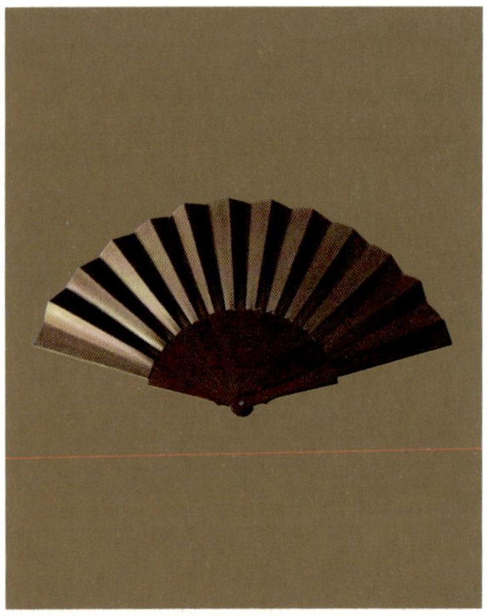

Fan belonging to the empress used during horse-riding
Second half of the nineteenth century
Rodeck Brothers, Vienna
Leather
45 × 55 cm
Bundesmobilienverwaltung / Hofmobiliendepot Möbel Museum, Vienna
Inv. MD 071503/000

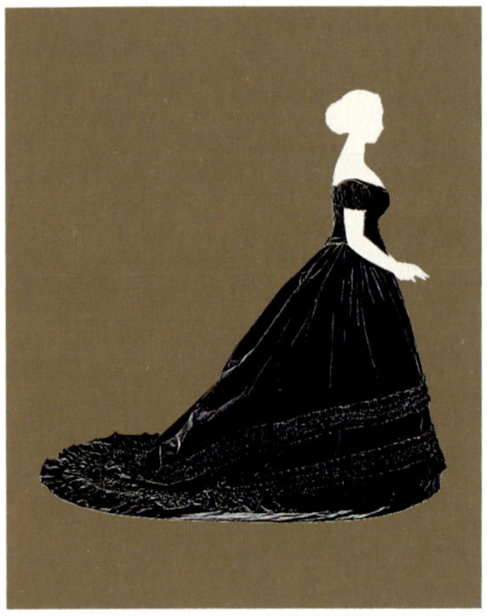

Empress Elisabeth's black gown
c. 1860
H. approx. 170 cm
Kunsthistorisches Museum, Wagenburg, Vienna
Inv. 126/001

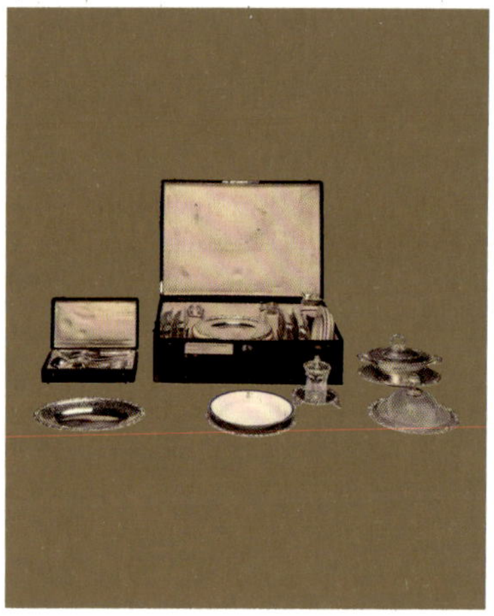

Travel service belonging to Empress Elisabeth
1832, Vienna
Stephan Mayerhofer
Bundesmobilienverwaltung / Silberkammer Hofburg, Vienna
Wood case
covered in leather, silver, glass, porcelain (interior)
21.5 × 61 × 45.5 cm
Inv. MD 180374/026 and 027
Two plates
Porcelain
D. 24.7 and 26.2 cm
Inv. MD 180374/001 and 002
Sauceboat
Silver
8.7 × 27.5 cm
Inv. MD 180374/003 and 004
Oval dish
Silver
2.7 × 26.8 × 20.7 cm
Inv. MD 180374/005
Salt cellar
Silver
4.8 × 9.4 × 7.5 cm
Inv. MD 180374/010
Egg cup
Silver
H. 5.5 cm
Inv. MD 180374/011
Small covered dish and platter
10.5 × 14 cm
Inv. MD 180374/012, 013 and 014
Cutlery case
6.8 x 30.2 × 17.8 cm
Inv. MD 180374/028 and 029
Two spoons
Silver
L. 22.7 cm
Inv. MD 180374/019
Two knives
Silver
L. 25.8 cm
Inv. MD 180374/022
Two forks
Silver
L. 21.2 cm
Inv. MD 180374/023

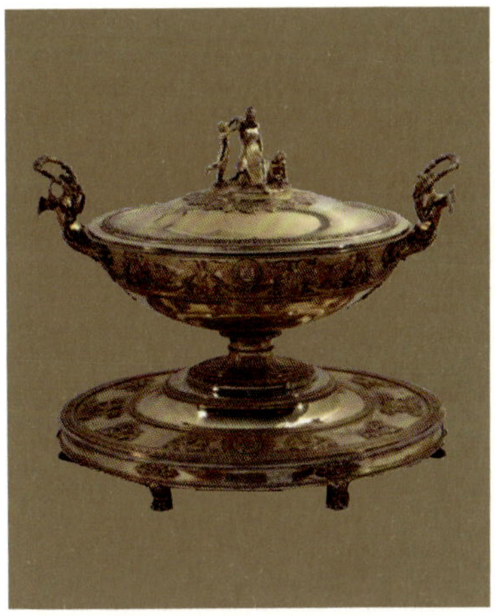

Terrine from Napoleon I's "Grand Vermeil" service
1808, Paris
Martin-Guillaume Biennais (1764–1843)
Gilded silver; "F.I.A." (Franz I of Austria) monogram, against Napoleonic arms
H. (total) 56.5 cm
Bundesmobilienverwaltung / Silberkammer, Hofburg, Vienna
Inv. MD 180435/038 and Inv. MD 180435/039

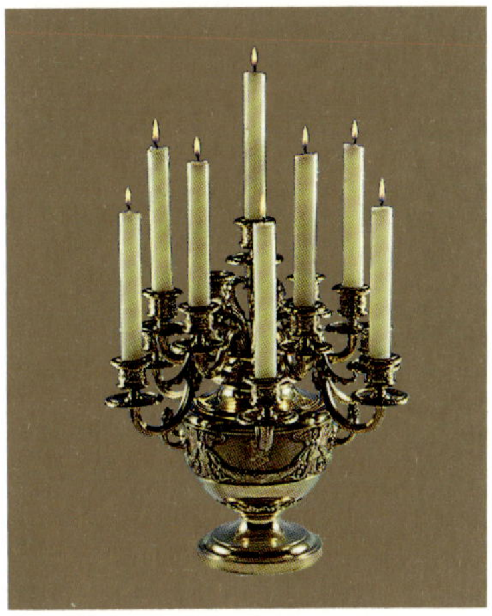

Two candelabras
1854
Josef Carl Klinkosch (1822–1888), Vienna
Gilded silver
34 × 38 cm
Bundesmobilienverwaltung / Silberkammer Hofburg, Vienna
Inv. MD 180435/097

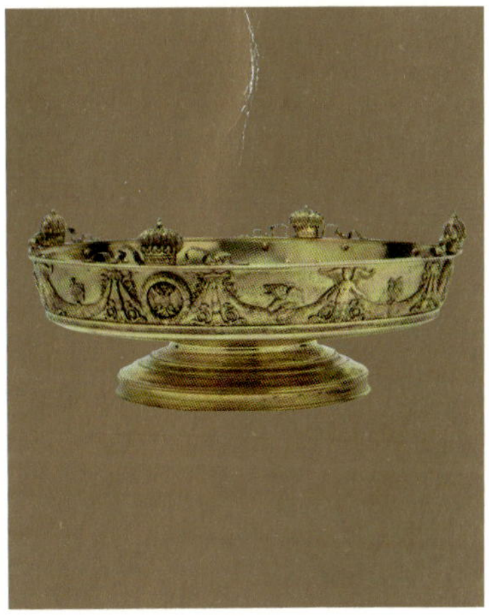

Cup
c. 1850
"F.I.A." (Franz I of Austria) monogram
Josef Carl Klinkosch (1822–1888), Vienna
Gilded silver
22 × 52 cm
Vienna, Bundesmobilienverwaltung / Silberkammer Hofburg
Inv. MD 180435/100

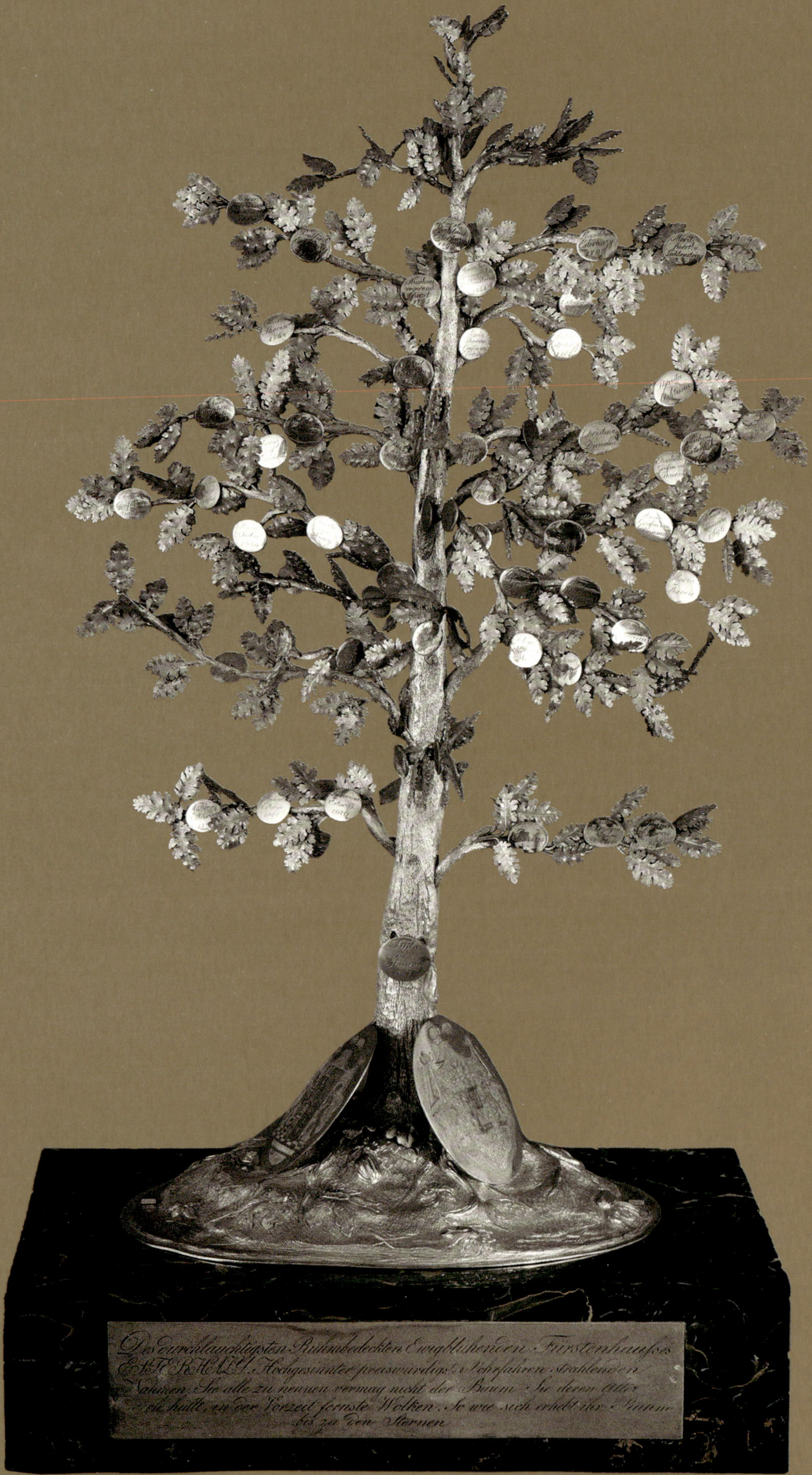
Des durchlauchtigsten Ruhmbedeckten Ewigblühenden Fürstenhaußes
ESTERHÁZY Hochgesinnter preiswürdigster Vohrfahren strahlenden
Nahmen. Sie alle zu nennen vermag nicht der Baum : Sie deren Alter
sich hüllt in der Vorzeit fernste Wolken. So wie sich erhebt ihr
bis zu den Sternen

ESTERHÁZY

Nikolaus II (1765–1833)

Esterházy Family Tree
1812, Vienna
Johann Ignatz Fautz
(active 1774–1812)
Forchtenstein Castle—
Treasure Vault, Esterházy
Foundation

Prince Nikolaus II Esterházy
Art and collecting, or how to win royal status

Stephan Körner

Nikolaus II Esterházy (1765–1833)
1793
Martin Knoller (1725–1804)
Eisenstadt Castle, Esterházy Foundation

Uniform of the Hungarian Guard
1905–10
Kunsthistorisches Museum, Wagenburg, Vienna

In July 1821, at the coronation of King George IV of England, in the Gothic gloaming of Westminster Abbey, a few sunbeams conducted Sir Walter Scott's gaze to Prince Nikolaus II Esterházy: "The box assigned to the foreign Ambassadors presented a most brilliant effect, and was perfectly in a blaze with diamonds. When the sunshine lighted on Prince Esterházy, in particular, he glimmered like a galaxy."

Prince Nikolaus II Esterházy wore a Hungarian gala uniform embellished and embroidered with pearls and diamonds in what was a dazzling symbol of his rank and authority. The aigrette on his hat alone, adorned with some 4,000 brilliants, bore testimony to the huge wealth of the Esterházy house. *The Gentleman's Magazine* also recorded the noble and imposing appearance of the Hungarian grandee. As the representative of his sovereign, Emperor Franz I of Austria, the prince occupied a special niche in European aristocracy at the time of the coronation. During these summer days, London high society played host to a cordial, easygoing, witty, and intelligent Nikolaus, and he was often to be spotted at the court of George IV. Indeed, the two men maintained a warm friendship lasting many years and shared a passion for the arts and architecture—as well as for beautiful women. The prince, then aged fifty-six, was fascinated by the deployment of royal pomp and circumstance at a coronation that proved to be the most magnificent in British history.

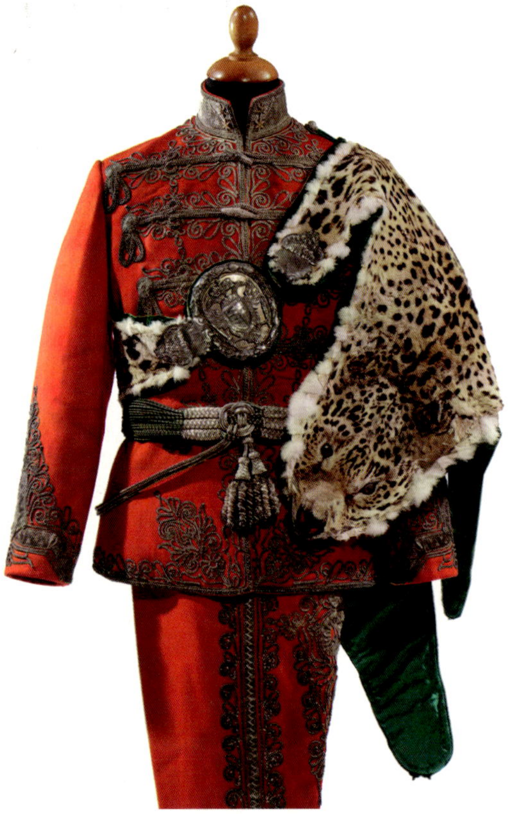

Nikolaus II was brought up in the second half of the eighteenth century with the idea that nothing could be better than being an Esterházy prince. For a century, the family had been an integral part of the

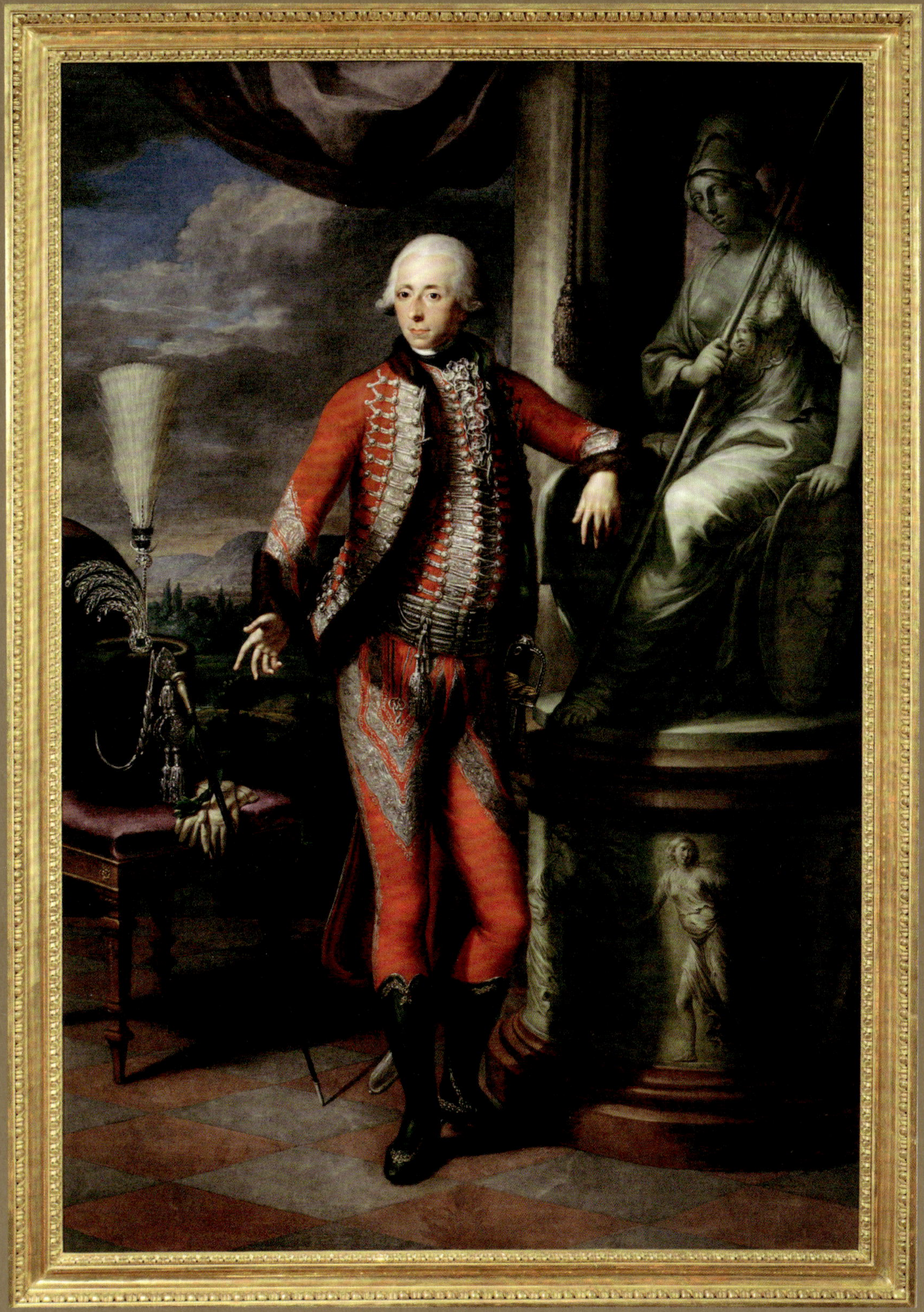

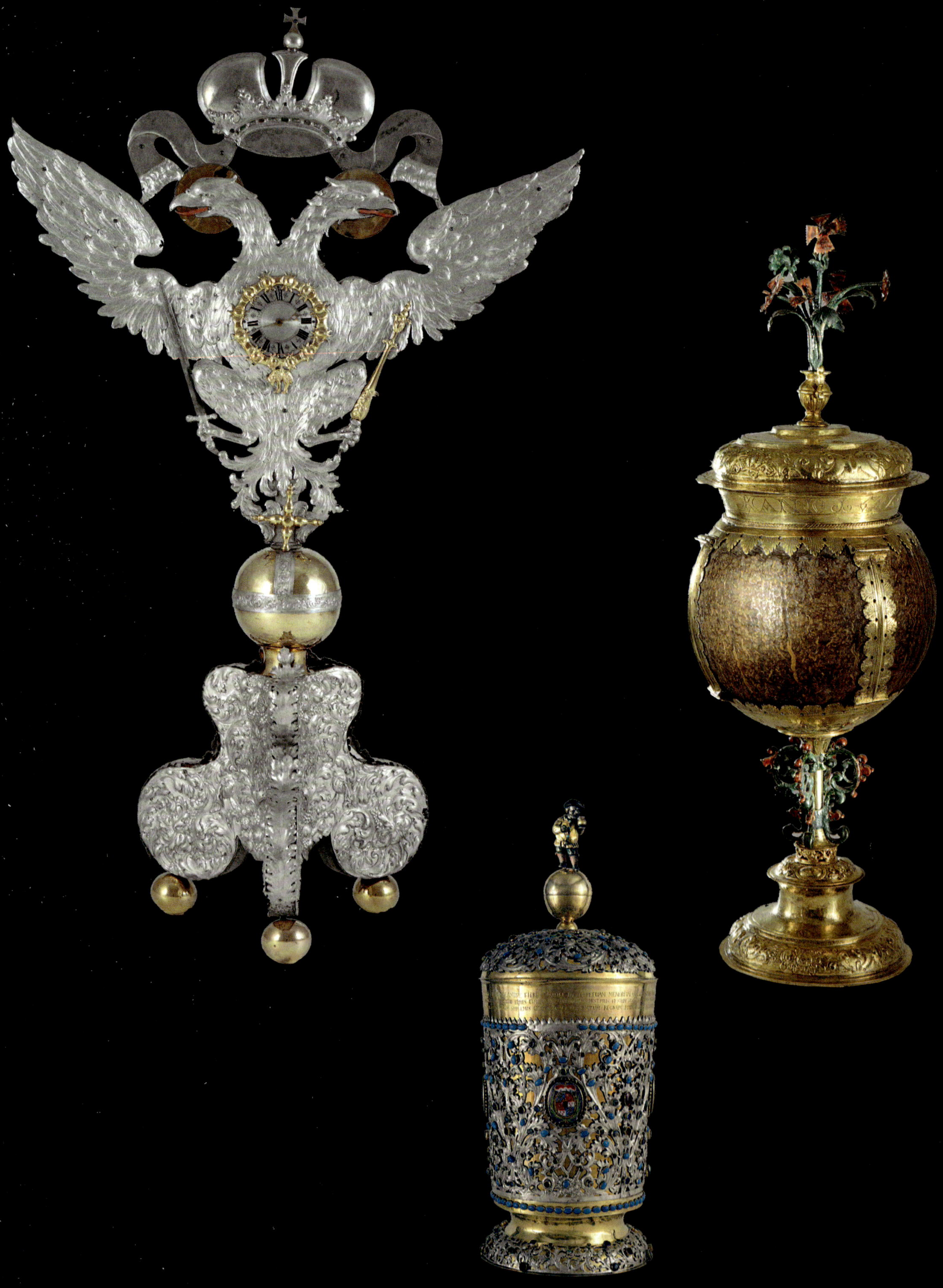

destiny of Hungary: in addition to being the greatest landowners in the kingdom, as faithful helpmates to the Habsburg emperor, the Esterházys were appointed viceroys, ambassadors, and bishops. Their zone of influence extended from south of Lake Balaton to the very gates of Vienna. In accordance with Hungarian law, the Esterházys, lords over almost 300,000 subjects, reigned with the panache of sovereign princes. They had recourse to apparently unlimited resources, which since the seventeenth century had also often been invested in art. The prince's study in the castle at Forchtenstein contained works of art, precious articles, and curios: scientific instruments, too, such as the gilt Bacchus automaton in pride of place amid fabulous silver furnishings of legendary opulence.

Crown Prince Nikolaus II had been educated at the court of his grandfather, Prince Nikolaus I (1714–1790), at the castle of Eszterháza. In this residence, known as the "Hungarian Versailles," the child was brought up as befitted his station in life and with an enduring love of music. The celebrated Joseph Haydn was music director, and his work and fame has earned his patrons an enviable place in the history of music.

The Esterházys had already become renowned, not only for the quality of their artistic collections, but also for the manner in which they broadcast their exalted rank and for stage-managing magnificent festivals. Johann Wolfgang von Goethe had already spoken in glowing terms of the Esterházy "fairy realm," when in 1764 Prince Nikolaus I, nicknamed the *"Practliebende"*—the "lover of splendor"—further burnished the family glory by organizing the heinously expensive illuminations at the coronation of Emperor Franz I in Frankfurt.

This was the first chapter in what proved a meteoric rise: in very short order, thanks to a taste for collecting art and a dazzling court, the Hungarian dynasty ascended to the summit of European nobility. It is in this context that the young crown prince Nikolaus II, aged 28, who became an ambassadorial envoi at the coronation of Emperor Franz II, made a remarkable entry on the international scene in 1792 in a sumptuous golden carriage. Nikolaus II pursued these costly efforts to acquire prestige, power, and influence during the period of social strife that extends from the Enlightenment in the late eighteenth century and the French Revolution. On obtaining his *majorat* (today we might say "trust fund"), a magnificent ceremony on the margins of the coronation proper represented him in an imperial pose in keeping with his position as *primus inter pares* and adding still greater luster to his dignity.

Without concerning himself overmuch with the financial stability and governance of his property, that same year (1764), the young prince traveled to Rome and Naples, and began collecting Italian Renaissance paintings, which

Clock in the shape of a double eagle
1680–90, Friedberg
Forchtenstein Castle—Treasure Vault,
Esterházy Foundation

Covered goblet
1698
Forchtenstein Castle—Treasure Vault,
Esterházy Foundation

Coconut mounted as a covered cup with base
1642, southern Germany
Forchtenstein Castle—Treasure Vault,
Esterházy Foundation

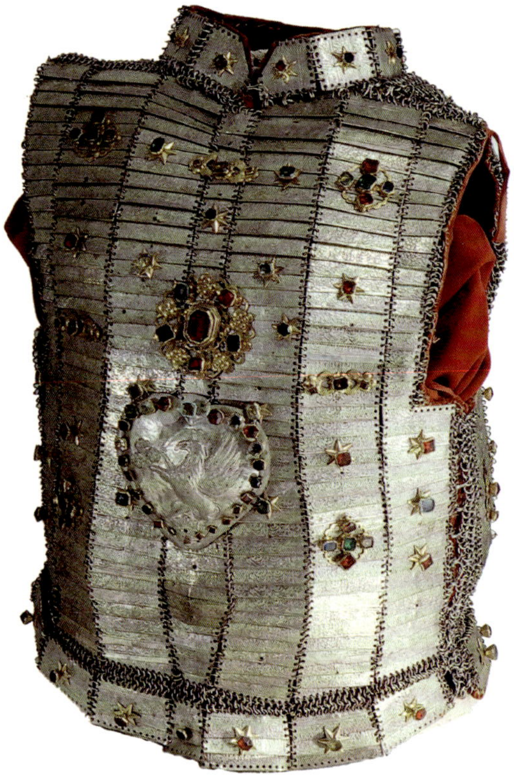

he had sent to Vienna in packing cases. On this score, the prince made intelligent use of the resources of his "fairy realm," benefitting from the aid of notable experts and amassing a spectacular collection of works by European masters.

His return home to the Esterházy castles corresponded to the beginning of a phase of aesthetic experiment and exploration of new forms of artistic expression that remodeled the cultural landscape. Seeking advice from various quarters, he adopted novel ideas in architecture and enthused over new styles, especially a revolutionary classicism that Vienna found hard to stomach. Thanks to his inexhaustibly inventive festivals and some sumptuous cuisine, Nikolaus II rapidly attracted guests from all Europe to the residence at Eisenstadt—including the legendary *ménage à trois* of Lord Nelson and the Hamiltons in 1800. Exuding irrepressible joie de vivre and nurturing an ungovernable foible for the limelight, the prince would, for instance, deck out the castle like a stage for a late medieval mummers' play.

In 1803 Nikolaus II traveled to Paris, where he discovered his future architectural models in classicism and the ideal way of displaying his collection in the recently opened Musée Napoléon. To go with the Empire furniture, drawings, gilded gala carriage, and books, the prince summoned to court the architect Charles Moreau and art expert Joseph Fischer. These two men, in conjunction with technical and economic innovations subsequently imported from London—such as a steam engine—ushered in a period of unprecedented growth in Eisenstadt, where Nikolaus set up a kind of "court of the muses." Pouring money into an orchestra and a private theater in an era when noble families in Austria and Germany were cutting back or even doing without masters of music for financial reasons, the emotionally unstable prince also played host to figures of German intellectual life from the duchy of Weimar, such as Ludwig Wieland and Heinrich Schmidt. In ten years, the director of the gallery, Fischer, purchased first-rate works of art, presenting them systematically in a picture gallery and a cabinet of drawings. Moreover, virtually cleaning out the European market, minerals, books, maps, and musical scores were collected in accordance with the most up-to-date principles.

Ceremonial armor
c. 1696
Forchtenstein Castle—
Treasure Vault,
Esterházy Foundation

Nikolaus II conceived of the Eisenstadt region as a single cultural entity: around the residence renovated by Moreau and complete with opera house and picture gallery, landscaped gardens sprung up, with hunting lodges and eye-catchers, the estate boasting a flourishing economy centered on the breeding of Swiss cattle, and, especially, on sheep, whose wool made Nikolaus the greatest producer in Europe and were the source of his vast wealth.

Allying beauty and utility, Eisenstadt greenhouses grew collections of plants that combined a taste for collecting with the interests of science and the demands of the national economy. For Nikolaus's investments were not destined solely for personal pleasure. The collections, his artistic patronage, indeed the whole court were intended to promote Esterházy in the eyes of German sovereign houses. The "consumption" of art and the state's matrimonial policy were thus directed towards the west. Even Austria's war against Napoleon and the consequent reduction in financial resources could not halt the energetic Nikolaus II, nor prevent him in 1807 from wanting to take over the theater in Vienna and recruit the celebrated actor August Wilhelm Iffland. With the purchase in 1804 of the county of Edelstetten that lay directly under the authority of the empire and the intervention of Emperor Franz I, Nikolaus II attained a rank equivalent to a German royal house, allowing him to appear on a par with the German princes.

But the Holy Roman Empire was to shatter under pressure from Napoleon, who also wanted to remove Hungary from the Habsburg sphere of influence, and Nikolaus II found himself Napoleon's preferred candidate for a Hungarian throne. Things did not, however, quite run to plan, since Napoleon's second marriage in 1810 allied him with the Habsburgs. Still, the emperor's magnificent wedding in Paris to Archduchess Marie Louise served as Nikolaus's model for the sumptuous entertainments thrown two years later to celebrate his son's wedding to Therese, princess of Thurn-und-Taxis. A family tree made of silver belonging to the treasury symbolizes the importance of the Esterházy dynastic alliances that allowed Nikolaus II, thanks to a skillfully handled matrimonial policy, to place

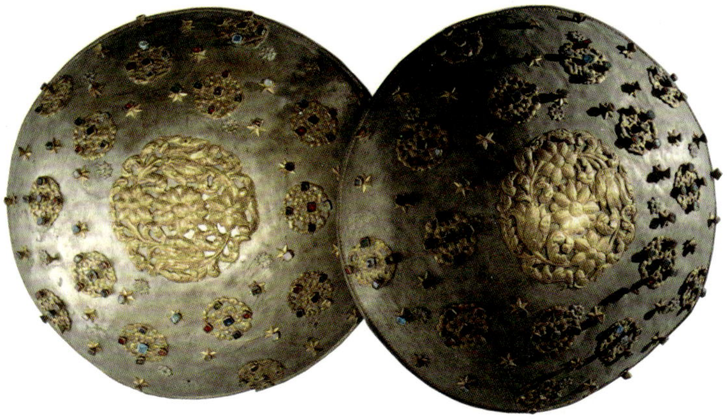

Shields
Seventeenth century, Hungary
Forchtenstein Castle—Treasure Vault, Esterházy Foundation

Charles Moreau's (1758-1840) project for the reconstruction of the Palace of Eisenstadt
1812
JOHANN CARL LUDWIG ENGEL (1778–1840)
Eisenstadt Castle, Esterházy Foundation

his house on a level with the most prestigious German lineages. If his estates held in *fideicommissum* (majorat) had not collapsed during the Austrian financial crash, no less a figure than Luigi Cherubini would have become the Esterházys' master at the chapel of Esterházy. Shortly afterwards, however, Napoleon was overthrown and the Congress of Vienna signaled a new departure for Europe.

From 1815, after the congress and following a reorganization of his finances, Nikolaus II withdrew from public life to Biedermeier Vienna, where he was to convert the Mariahilfer Palais into one of the first museums of German idealism. The public and artistic taste as reflected in the Esterházy collection was housed there; on journeys to Italy the prince had acquired sculptures by the greatest artists of the genre, such as Antonio Canova, Bertel Thorvaldsen, and Rudolf Schadow, and thus launched a new fashion. With the acquisition in the 1820s of works by hitherto largely neglected Spanish baroque masters from the London collection of Edmund Burke, his gallery attained worldwide fame. Thanks to his activities in the world of art and his talent for self-display, the family acquired the regal, almost mythical reputation that Nikolaus II consolidated as a prince-collector.

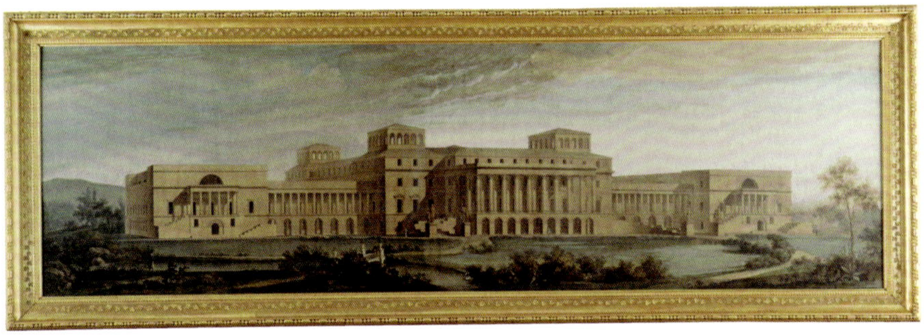

Nevertheless, nothing could slow the decline of the Austrian nobility—or that of his house. To shelter himself from its effects, the aging prince spent his remaining years on the island of Mainau on Lake Constance or in his palace in Naples. Thus could he turn his back, not only on the turbulent Vormärz period (1815–48), but also on a disastrously accelerating spiral of debt.

The prince's spectacular entrance into Westminster Abbey in 1821 sporting that gorgeous uniform awash with jewels in fact represents the last glimmer of the "fairy realm" in all its splendor. After his death in 1833, his possessions were gradually sold off at auction or frittered away by his heirs. The collection of drawings and paintings of Prince Nikolaus II Esterházy found its way into the Museum of Fine Arts in Budapest where it still hangs today. When in 1867 the Esterházy jewels fell under the gavel, the entire diamond market threatened to collapse. It was as remnants of a "spirit of an older world" that the Esterházy gems were acquired by Charles Lewis Tiffany, who provided them with new mounts. The fame of Prince Nikolaus II echoes down to our day thanks to his unbelievably rich collections: enduring evidence of his style and spectacular festivals—as well as of his diamonds, now scattered to all four corners of the earth.

Clockwork figure of Bacchus
1600, Augsburg
Forchtenstein Castle—Treasure Vault, Esterházy Foundation

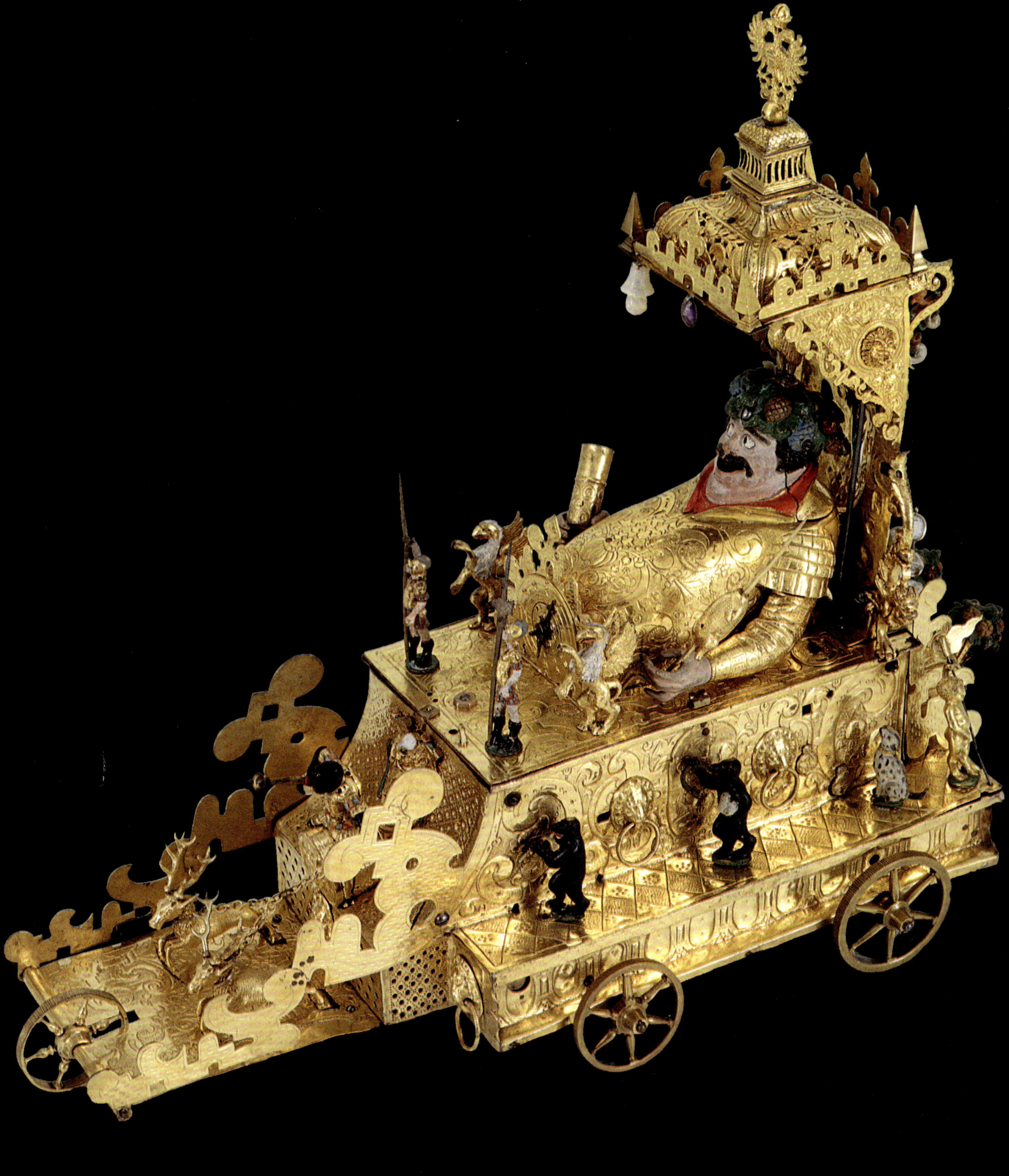

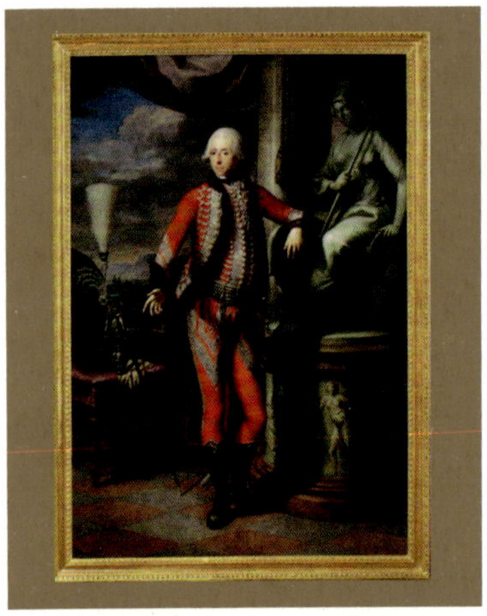

Nikolaus II Esterházy (1765–1833)
1793
Martin Knoller (1725–1804)
Oil on canvas
252 × 175 cm (inc. frame)
Eisenstadt Castle, Esterházy Foundation
Inv. B44

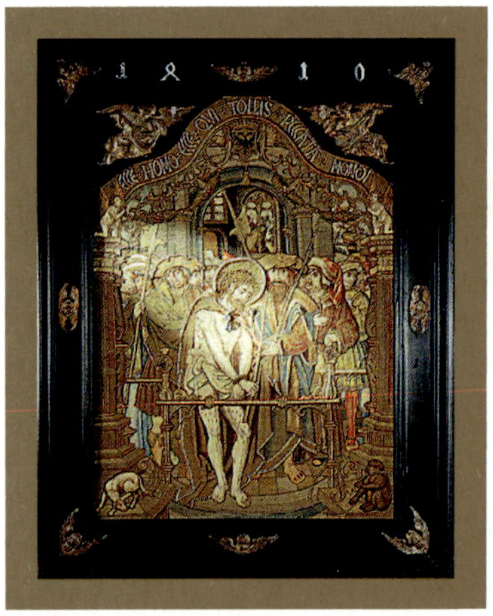

Ecce Homo
1510; seventeenth century (frame), Netherlands
Gold, silk, linen, pearls, ebony, painted
71.9 × 55.6 cm
Forchtenstein Castle—Treasure Vault, Esterházy Foundation
Inv. K 229

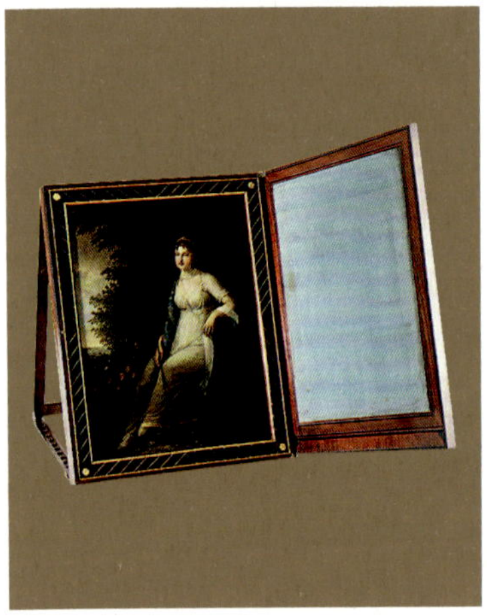

Princess Maria Hermenegilde Liechtenstein-Esterházy (1768–1845), Wife of Nikolaus II
1820, Vienna
Wood, mirror, oil painting
47.6 × 75 × 7.5 cm (open)
Eisenstadt Castle, Esterházy Foundation
Inv. M 408

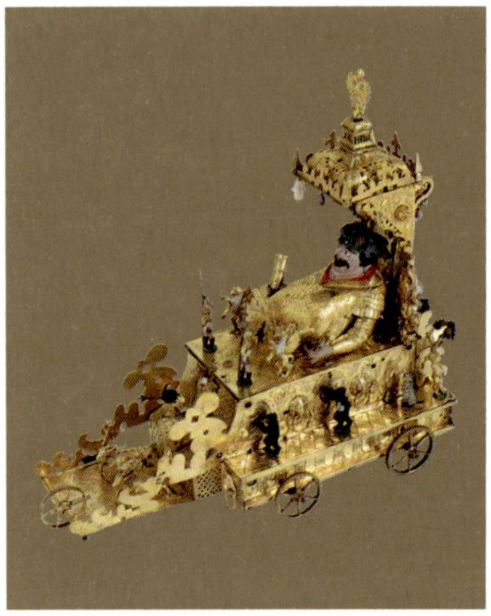

Clockwork figure of Bacchus
1600, Augsburg
Silver, gilded copper, colored enamels
52 × 57 × 25 cm
Forchtenstein Castle—Treasure Vault, Esterházy Foundation
Inv. K 170/1-2

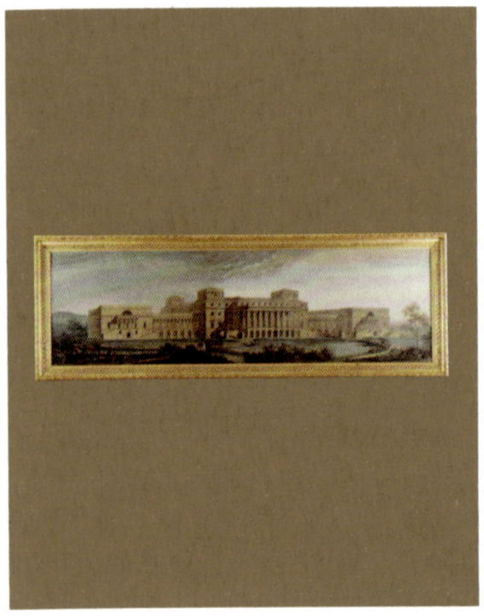

Project for the reconstruction of Eisenstadt Castle
1812
Johann Carl Ludwig Engel (1778–1840)
Tempera on paper
95 × 276 cm (inc. frame)
Eisenstadt Castle, Esterházy Foundation
Inv. B7

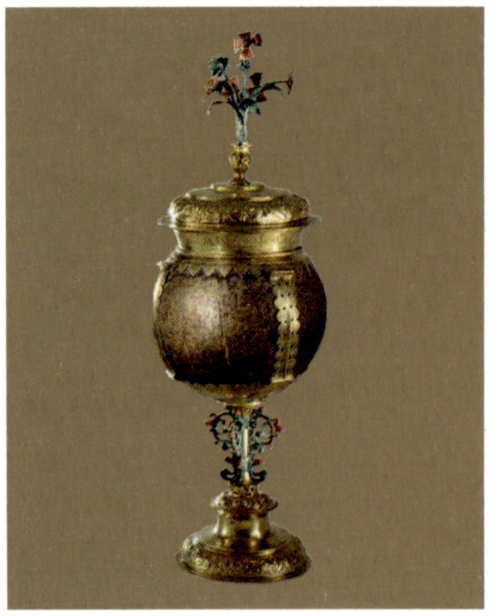

Coconut mounted as a covered cup with base
1642, southern Germany
Coconut, gilded silver, semi-precious and precious stones (ruby, topaz, turquoise), colored enamels
33 × 10.5 cm
Forchtenstein Castle—Treasure Vault, Esterházy Foundation
Inv. K 147/1-2

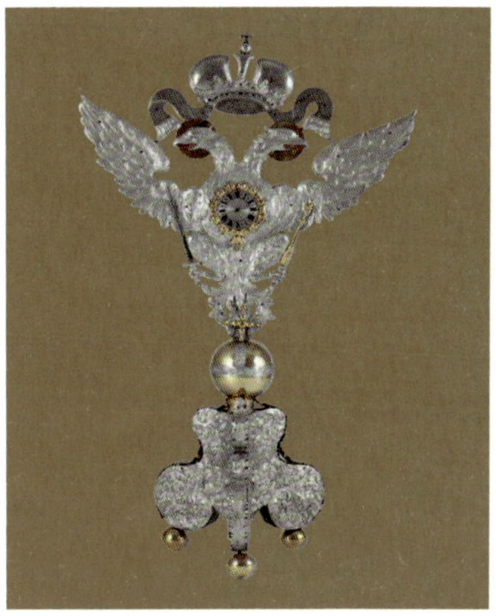

Clock in the shape of a double eagle
1680–90, Friedberg
Silver, partially gilded and silver-plated brass
108 × 65 × 35 cm
Forchtenstein Castle—Treasure Vault, Esterházy Foundation
Inv. K 205

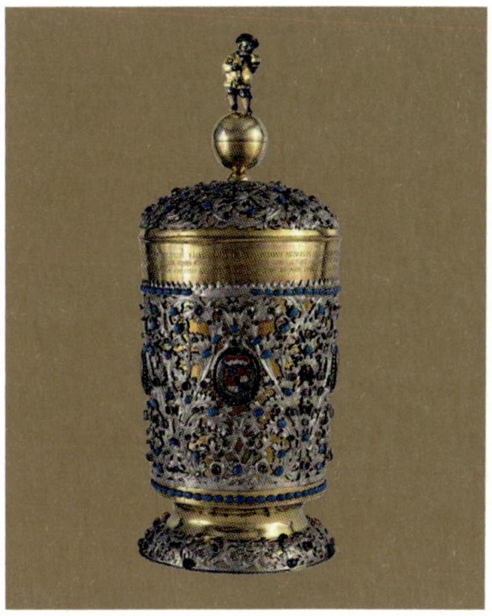

Covered goblet
1698
Silver, precious stones, glass, crystal, colored enamels
73 × 29 cm
Forchtenstein Castle—Treasure Vault, Esterházy Foundation
Inv. K 21

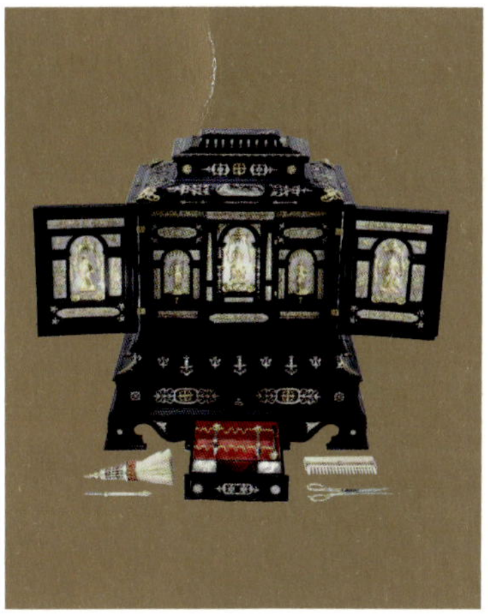

Cabinet
1690, Augsburg
Ebony, partially gilded silver
51.5 × 45.5 × 39 cm
Forchtenstein Castle—Treasure Vault, Esterházy Foundation
Inv. K 256

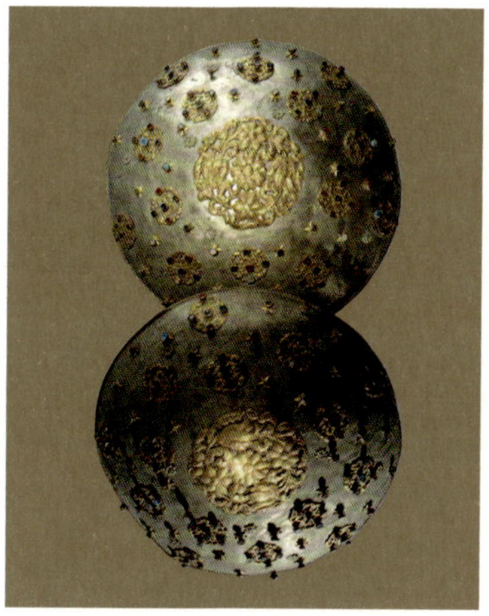

Shields
Seventeenth century, Hungary
Gilded iron, silk
10 × 53 × 10 cm
Forchtenstein Castle—Treasure Vault, Esterházy Foundation
Inv. K 19

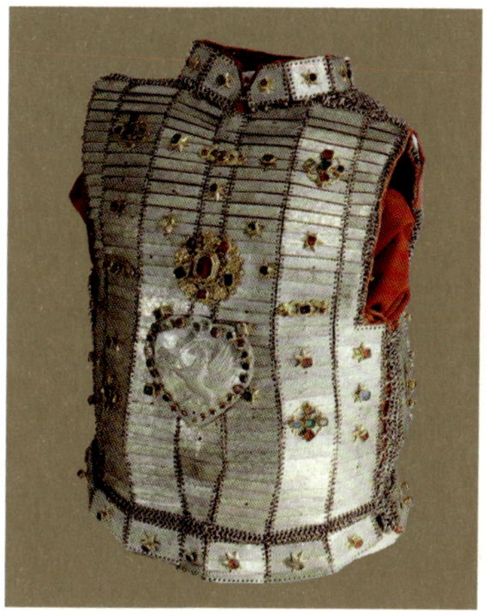

Ceremonial armor
c. 1696
Mother-of-pearl, partially gilded and silver-plated copper, iron, glass, crystal, silk
57 × 37 × 30 cm
Forchtenstein Castle—Treasure Vault, Esterházy Foundation
Inv. K 18

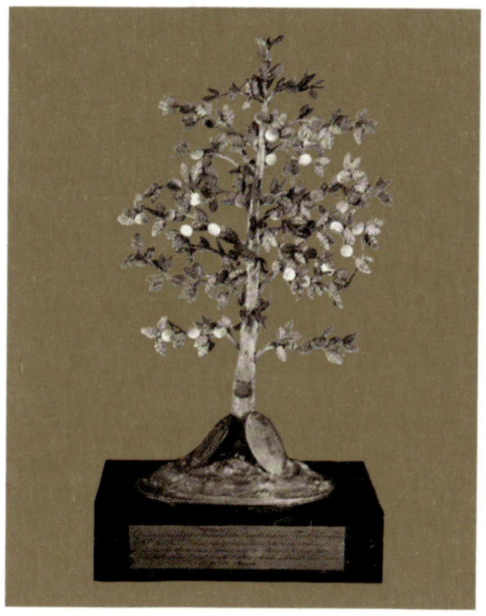

Esterházy Family Tree
1812, Vienna
JOHANN IGNATZ FAUTZ
(active 1774–1812)
Silver, marble, gypsum
81 × 43 × 31 cm
Forchtenstein Castle—Treasure Vault, Esterházy Foundation
Inv. K 797

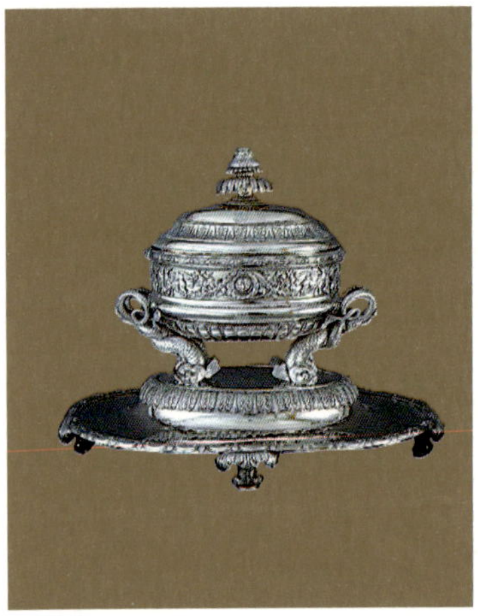
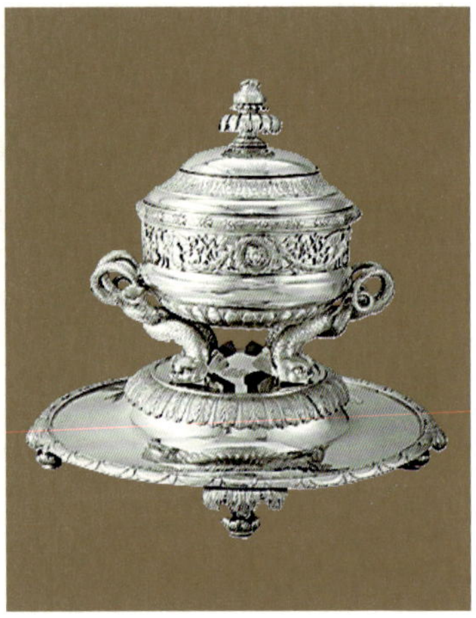
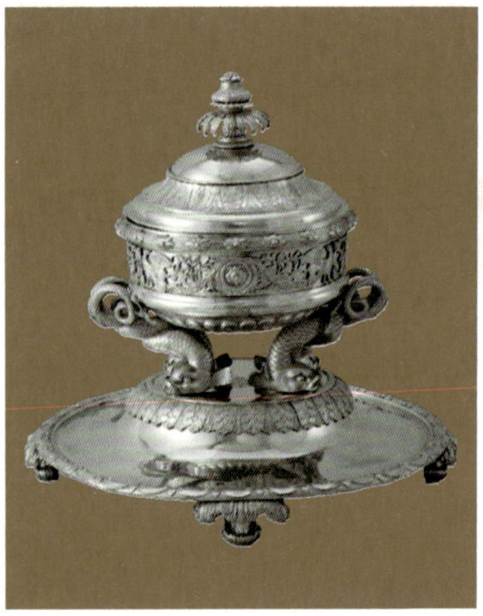
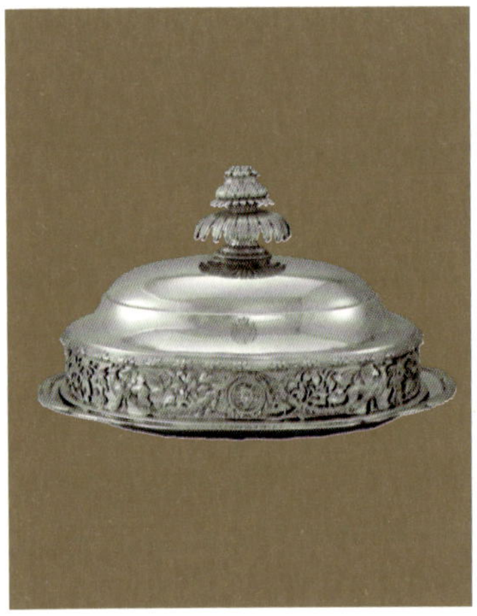
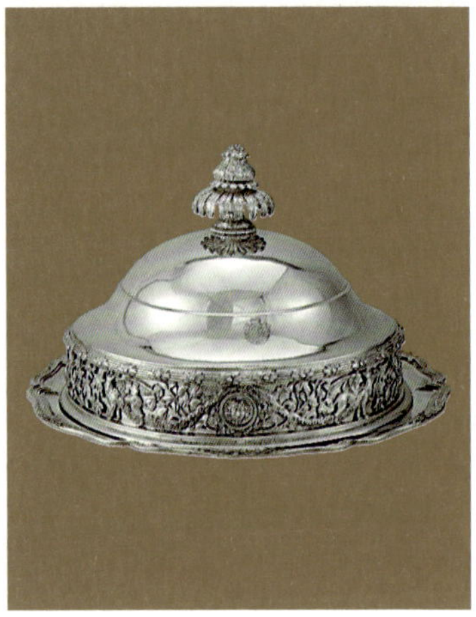
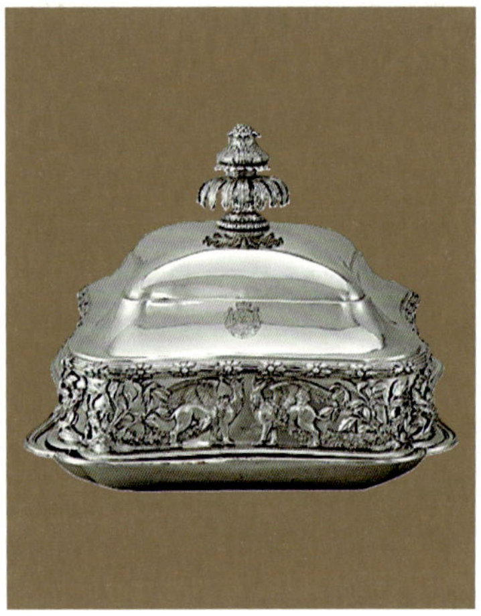

Dinner service belonging to Count Esterházy
1791–92, Vienna
Ignaz Sebastian Würth
(active 1769–1815)
Silver
Eisenstadt Castle, Esterházy Foundation
Oval terrine
51 × 62 cm
Inv. P 246/1-4
Two large round terrines
50 × 53 cm
Inv. P 244/1-4 and P 245/1-4
Two small round terrines
40 × 42 cm
Inv. P 242/1-4 and P 243/1-4
Large oval dome and platter
43 × 25 cm
Inv. P 268 and P 282
Two round domes and platters
Inv. P 265 and P 266
Two cut-away domes and platters
Inv. P 259-P 260 and P 275-P 276
Four candelabras
63.5 × 37 cm
Inv. P 145/1-4

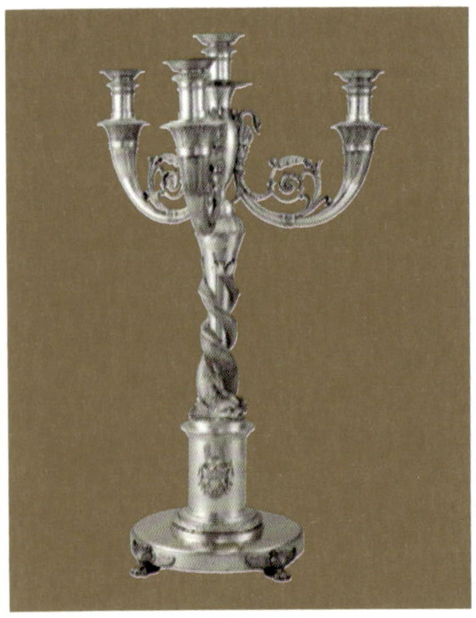
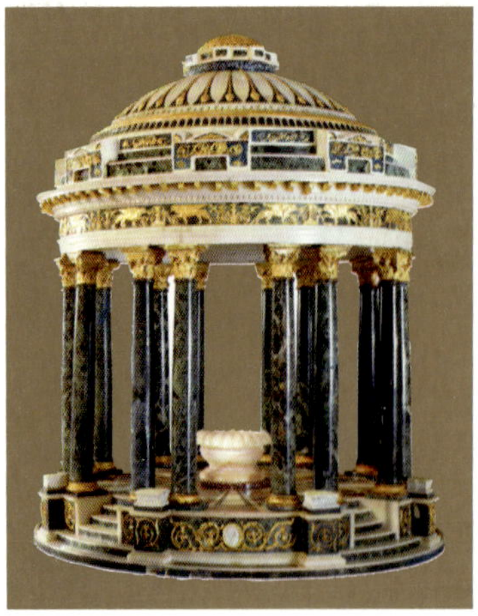

Table centerpiece in the form of a *tempietto*
c. 1820, Rome
Giacomo Raffaelli (1753–1836)
Marble, serpentine
72 × 57 cm
Eisenstadt Castle, Esterházy Foundation
Inv. P 320

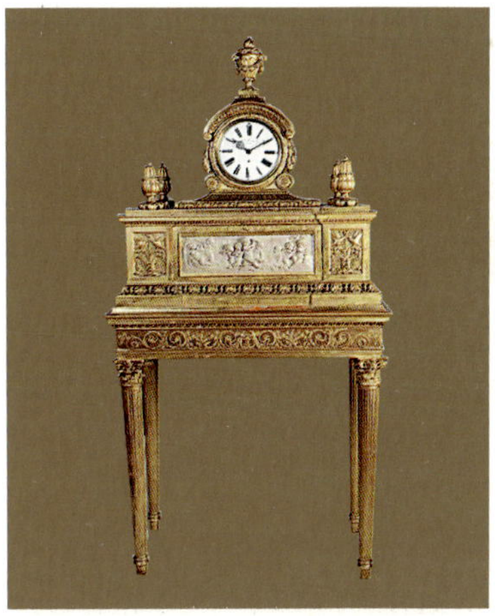

Cabinet with clock and musical mechanism featuring a composition by Joseph Haydn
c. 1793
Pater Primitivus Nimecz (clockmaker)
Wood, veneer
201 × 100 × 85 cm
Eisenstadt Castle, Esterházy Foundation
Inv. MIS 9

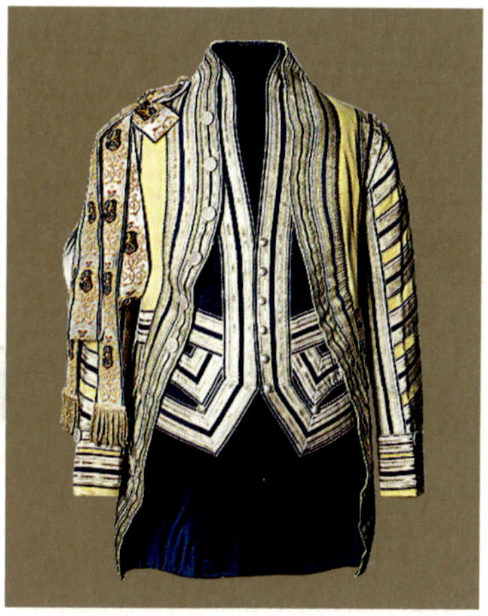

Ten liveries
Early nineteenth century, Vienna
Blue and white cloth with silver and gold braid
Forchtenstein Castle, Esterházy Foundation

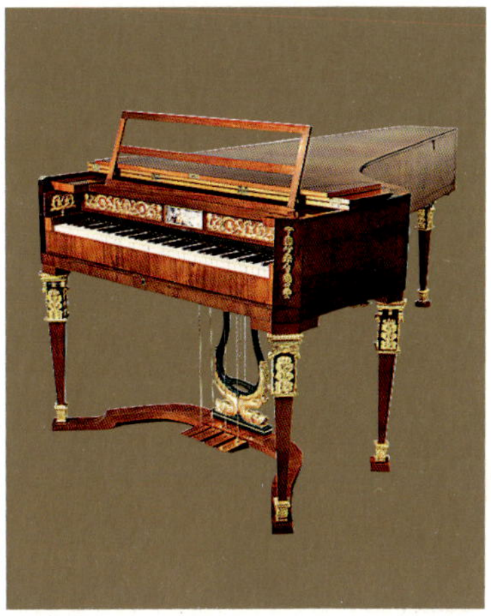

Pianoforte
Before 1805, Vienna
Matthias Müller, Vienna
Mahogany
92.3 × 117.5 × 224 cm
Eisenstadt Castle, Esterházy Foundation
Inv. MIS 8

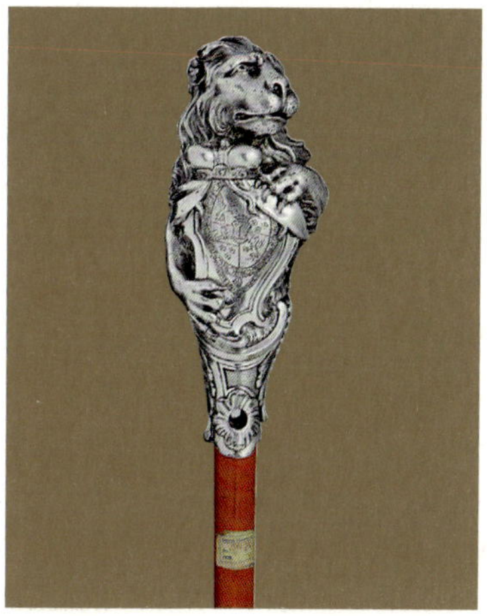

Six livery staffs and two bailiff staffs
1788, Vienna
Ignaz Sebastian Würth
Silver and wood
H. approx. 150 cm
Forchtenstein Castle, Esterházy Foundation

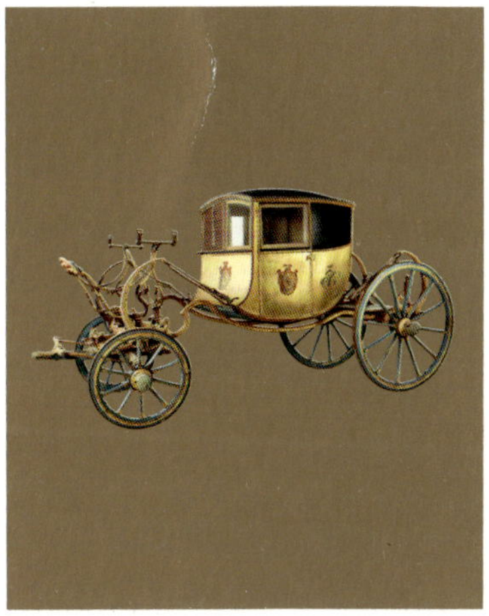

Carriage belonging to Prince Nikolaus II
c. 1785
Gilded wood, iron, leather
235 × 510 × 200 cm
Eisenstadt Castle, Esterházy Foundation
Inv. WB5

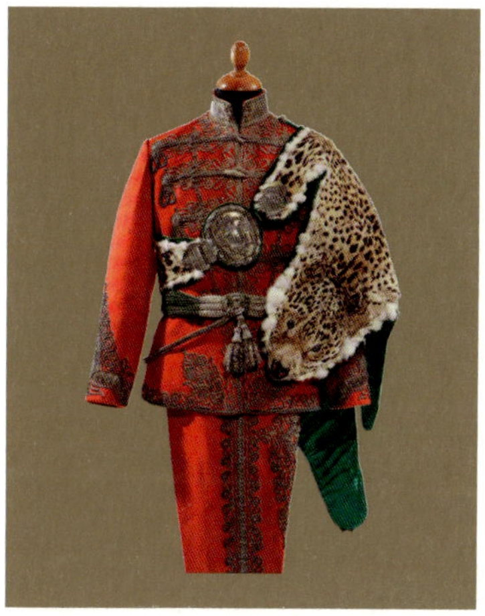

Uniform of the Hungarian Guard
1905–10
Kunsthistorisches Museum, Wagenburg, Vienna
Inv. U 1012

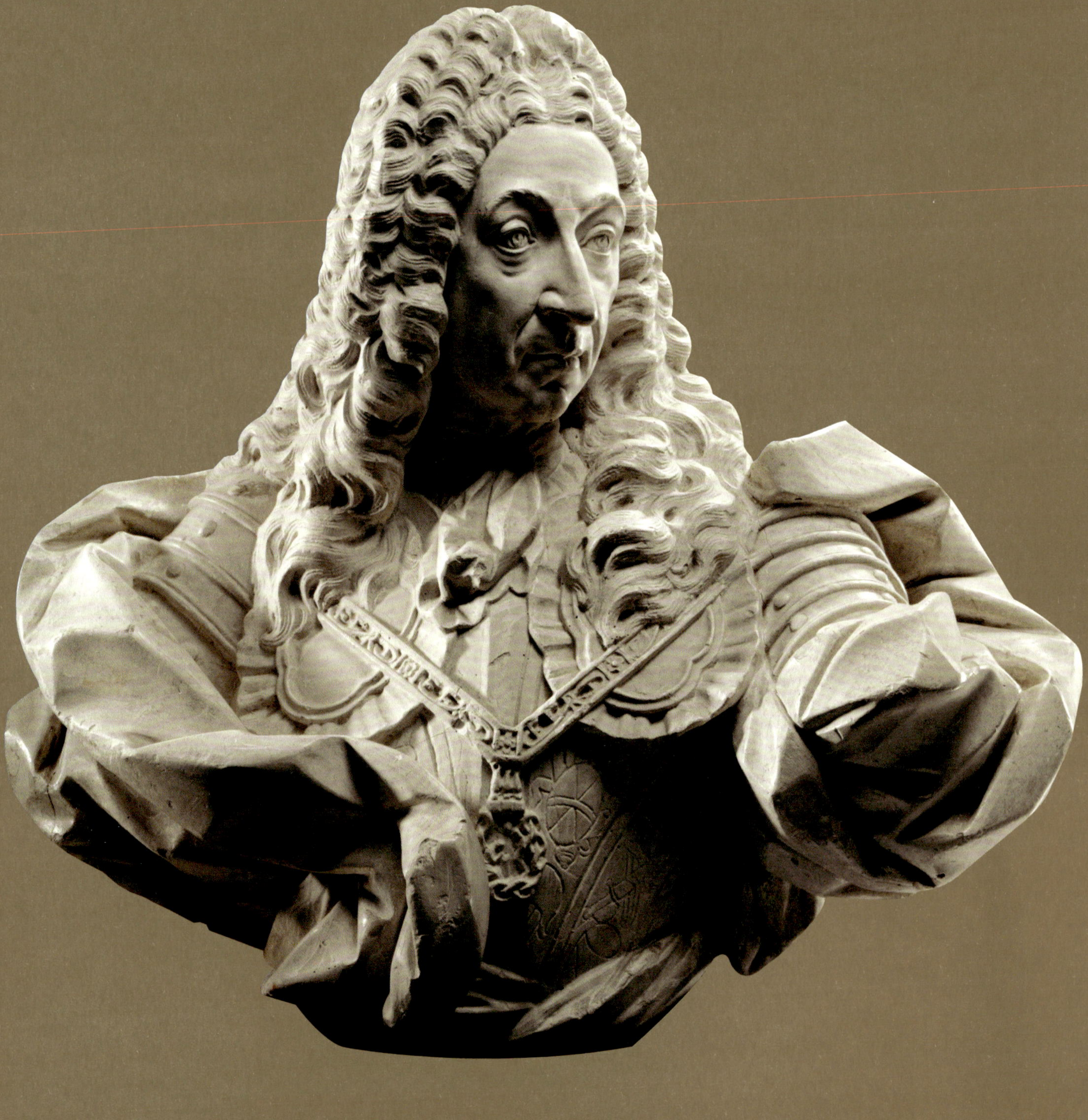

TURIN

Vittorio Amedeo (1666–1732)

Vittorio Amedeo II,
King of Sicilia
and Sardinia
c. 1730
Attributed to
Domenico Ferretti
(1702–1774)
Reggia di Venaria Reale,
Veneria Reale

Vittorio Amedeo II

Andrea Merlotti

At the turn of the eighteenth century, Vittorio Amedeo II was one of Europe's more significant sovereigns. He is, furthermore, together with Amedeo VIII, in fourteenth century, Emanuele Filiberto, in sixteenth century, and Vittorio Emanuele II, in nineteenth century, one of the most remarkable figures in the thousand-year history of the House of Savoy. When he took the throne, the states of Savoy were little better than a French protectorate: in the space of thirty years, he guaranteed them a rosy future, won them full independence, placed them at the head of the states of Italy, and promoted them into a major piece on the European political chessboard. On becoming king of Sicily in 1713 following the Peace of Utrecht, Vittorio Amedeo began implementing a raft of reforms, an aspect of his policy that was much vaunted at other European courts. Even half a century after his death, one could read in a Universal History published in 1776 by Protestant circles in Amsterdam: "The present century Europe has admired three famous legislators, each worthy of praise as much for the elevation of their genius as for the glory of their arms. And these three great sovereigns are, as everyone knows, the king of Prussia [Friedrich II], Empress Catherine II, and the king of Sardinia. Vittorio Amedeo's legislative program was far wider than that of the other two monarchs, and the wisest and most enlightened aspect of this effort indisputably concerns the new laws Vittorio Amedeo's legislation is sagacious and worthy in every regard of the present century of philosophy that has been illustrated by profoundly educated kings skilled in the art of commanding men—or rather, in that of making them happy."

By 1776, then, Vittorio Amedeo II was considered as a masterful, reforming prince, capable of undertaking and applying reforms in the full flood of the "crisis of the European conscience," and thus well before the era of what is now called "enlightened despotism."

The first king of Savoy, whose chief qualities lay in his legislative skill and military prowess, was the son of Duke Carlo Emanuele II (1634–1675) and Marie-Jeanne-Baptiste of Savoy-Nemours (1644–1724). Losing his father at a very early age, his mother was a domineering individual from under whose thumb he strove to free himself the minute he attained his majority. The conflict between mother and son was to have a decisive influence on the young sovereign's future

Vittorio Amedeo II, King of Sicilia and Sardinia (1666–1732)
1728
Martin van Meytens the Younger (1695–1770)
Reggia di Venaria Reale, Venaria Reale

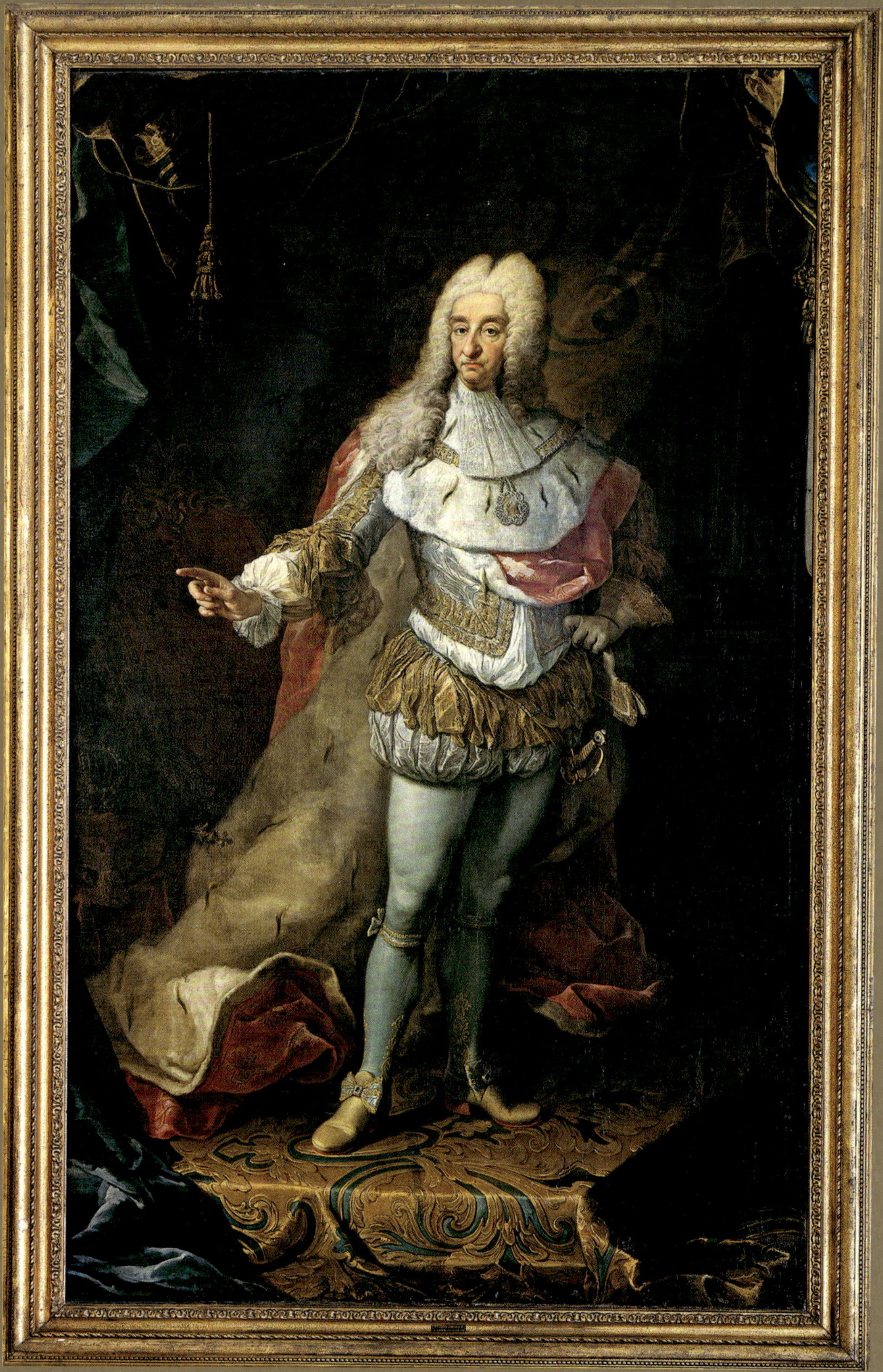

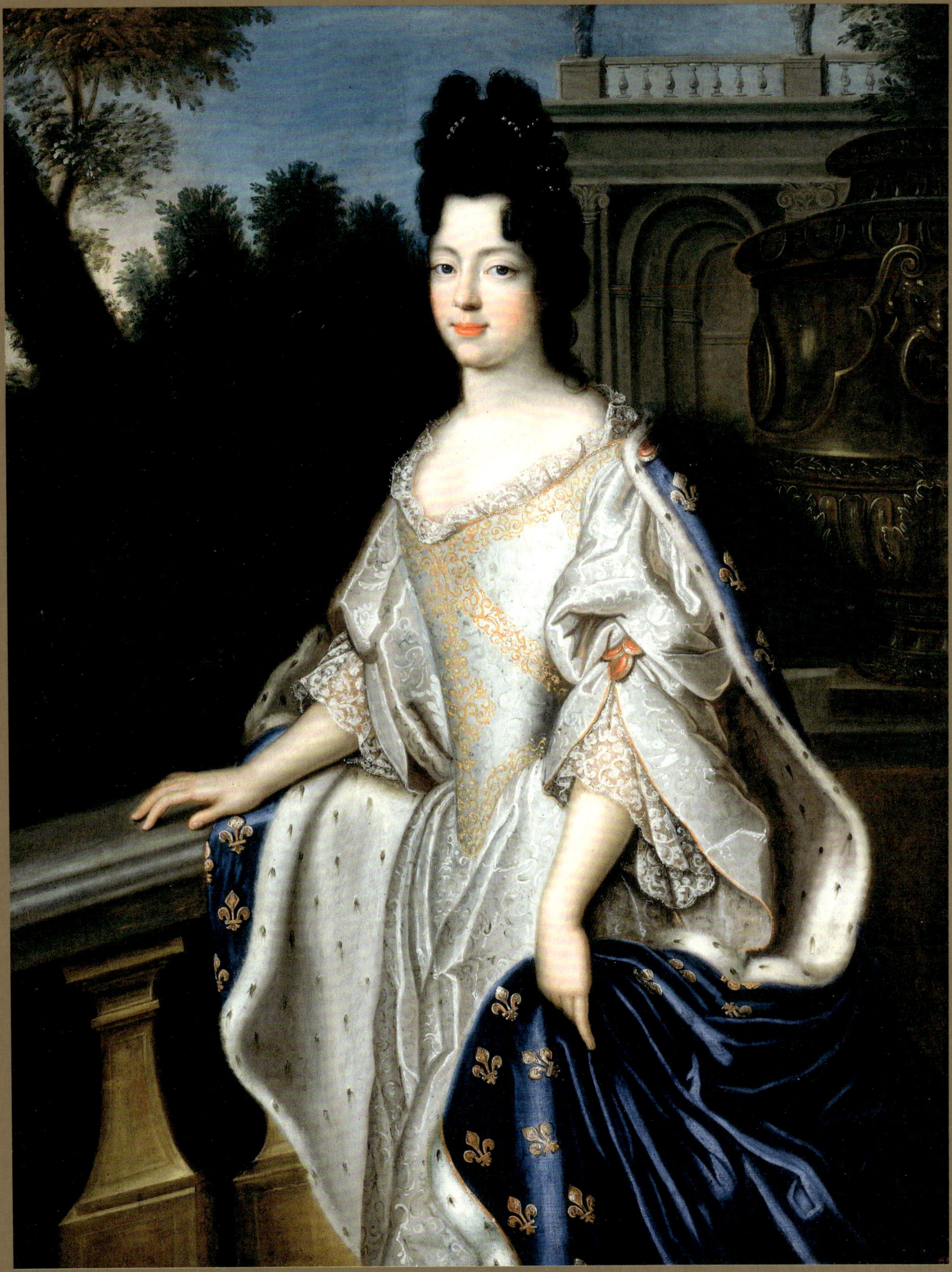

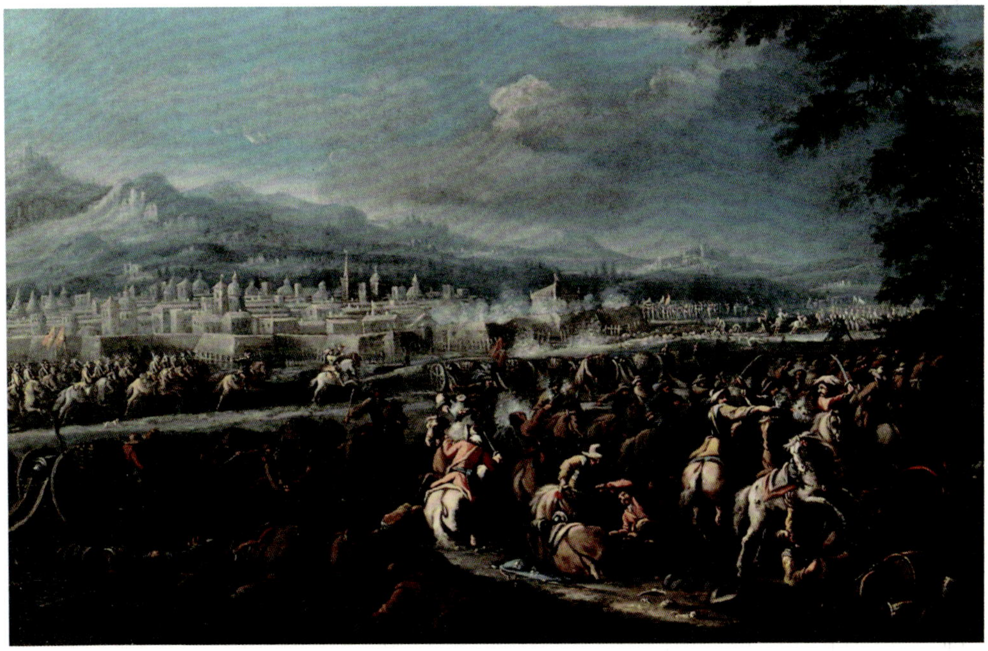

The Siege of Turin, 1706
c. 1725
Pietro Domenico Olivero
(1679–1755)
Private Collection

path. Marie-Jeanne-Baptiste would have liked to marry him to the daughter of the king of Portugal, heir to the Lusitanian kingdom, and thereby keep control of the states of Savoy, but in the face of Vittorio Amedeo's opposition the plan came to naught. Instead, in 1684, he wedded one of the two nieces of Louis XIV, Anne d'Orléans (1669–1728), daughter of Philippe d'Orléans, the Sun King's brother, and Henrietta Stuart, daughter of Charles I, king of England. This marriage afforded him the first real opportunity to apply his personal stamp on his reign. Not only did he thus gain the ear of Louis XIV, he also secured a place among the pretenders to the English crown, a role that he turned to good account in the years that followed. From a political standpoint, the marriage seemed to presage a closer alliance between France and Piedmont, but, from the 1690s, Vittorio Amedeo not only succeeded in releasing himself from the tutelage of his mother, he also avoided becoming a puppet of the mighty French monarch. In 1690 he broke the alliance with France and took up arms against Louis XIV in the War of the League of Augsburg, forcing the king to cede Pignerol (conquered by Louis XIII and Richelieu in 1630) and give the duke of Bourgogne, the young Dauphin, in marriage to his daughter, Maria Adelaide. But then he promptly joined the side of France in the War of the Spanish Succession, marrying his daughter Marie-Gabrielle to the duke of Anjou (future Felipe V of Spain). Subsequently, in what was another surprising reversal of alliances, in 1703 he allied with the Empire. By actions such as these, Vittorio Amedeo became noted among the rulers

Maria Adelaide of Savoy (1685–1712), Daughter of Vittorio Amedeo of Savoy and Anne-Marie d'Orléans (1669–1728), Wife of Duke of Bourgogne, Grandson of Louis XIV
c. 1698, French school
Galleria Sabauda, Turin

of Europe as a brilliant *condottiere*, in particular after the raising in 1706 of the siege of Turin by French troops, a triumph he earned with the help of his cousin Eugenio of Savoy. A few years afterwards, following the international negotiations that concluded with the Treaty of Utrecht, Vittorio Amedeo was crowned king of Sicily, thus obtaining a royal dignity for which Savoy had been in dispute with other Italian dynasties for around a century. Queen Anne of England provided him with decisive support, partially in compensation for the Act of Settlement promulgated in 1701 by Parliament that prohibited Catholics from acceding to the throne of England which in reality blocked the path to Anne d'Orléans, who, in the absence of such a statute, would have become queen. In 1720, following new agreements between the main European monarchs, Vittorio Amedeo became king of Sardinia, a title kept by his successors until the unifi-cation of Italy in 1861.

From 1713 to 1730, the sovereign devoted himself with characteristic energy to an intensive policy of reform. He did not hesitate, in particular, to oppose Rome so as to protect the right to name bishops and abbots in his states, a privilege which the house of Savoy had enjoyed since the fifteenth century. Rather than yielding, he went to the brink of breaking off diplomatic relations with the papacy that found itself obliged to ratify a legal settlement in 1727. He also promulgated a series of laws enabling him to exert close control over the nobility of Piedmont and reformed the secretariats of state (1717), as well as the university (1720) and the army. When, in 1728, Montesquieu visited Piedmont, the philosopher was impressed if not a little wary of a state in which the king monitored and controlled everything, and where the aristocracy kowtowed to its sovereign more than anywhere else he had been. During the years of peace, a series of important changes were made to many national institutions, some of which were sparked by the war: a new approach to tax allocation in the various territories, beginning with Savoy, continuing in Piedmont and the county of Nice (the king's successors unrolled a similar policy in the territories of Montferrat); the centralization of the bureaucracy; the redistribution of feudal titles; and the reorganization of the army into three levels of professionalism and enlistment (militias, provincial regiments with periodic conscription, and a professional standing army). Some of these transformations were discussed and drawn up between military campaigns, the acme of reform being reached with the reorganization of a body of law—in truth it resembled a compilation rather than an entirely fresh corpus of statute—culminating in the royal constitutions of 1723 and 1729. Historians have tended to stress the centralizing and rationalist tendencies of Vittorio Amedeo's policies, but this is to misuse a concept of absolutism that no *ancien régime* was ever really able to apply in its full-fledged form. Still, there can be no doubt that the reforming zeal

View of the Central Room of the Hunting Palace of Stupinigi
1798
Giovanni Battista Bagnasacco (1746–1822) and Giovanni Comandù (1777–1822)
Palazzo Reale
(on deposit to the Reggia di Venaria Reale), Turin

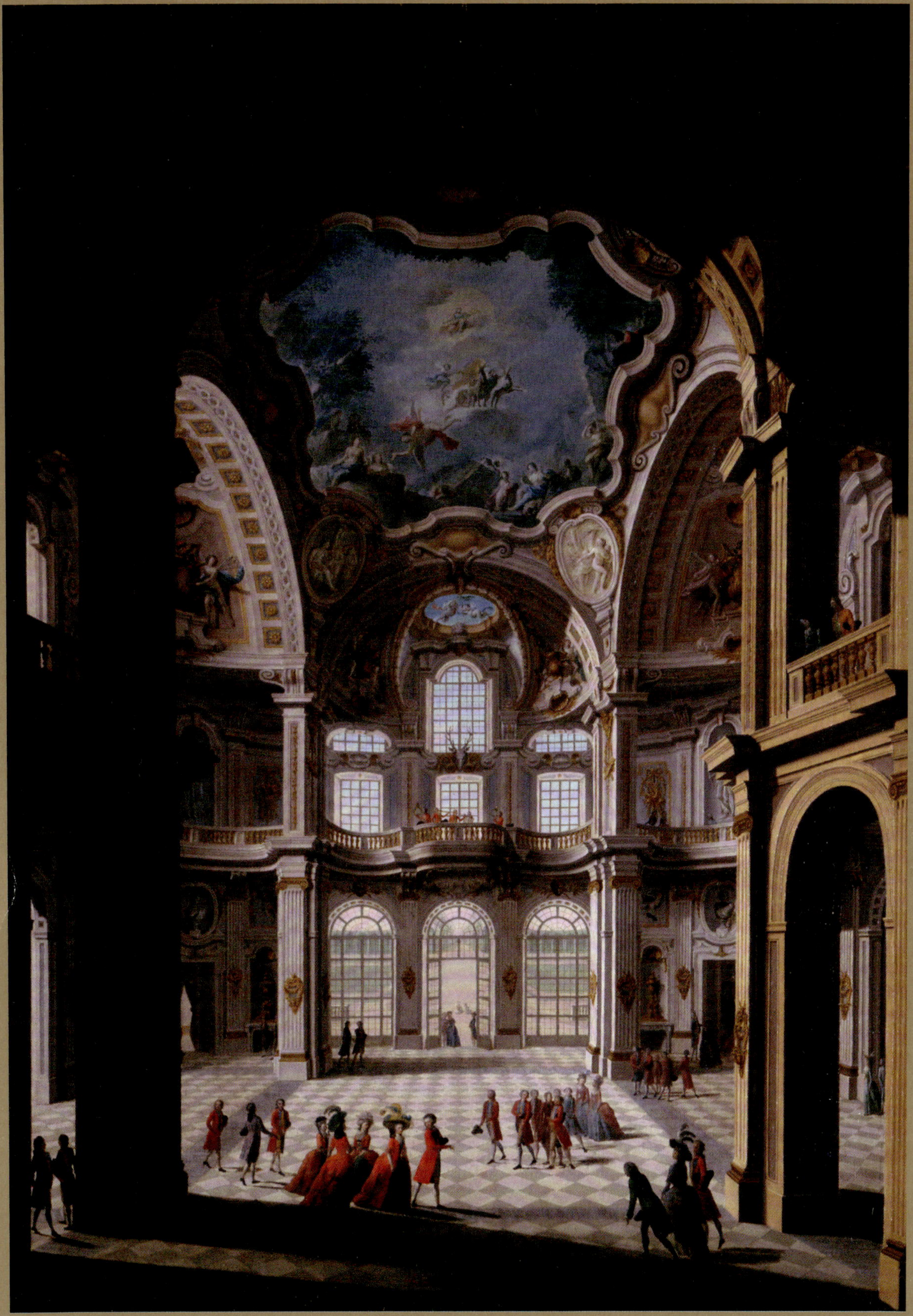

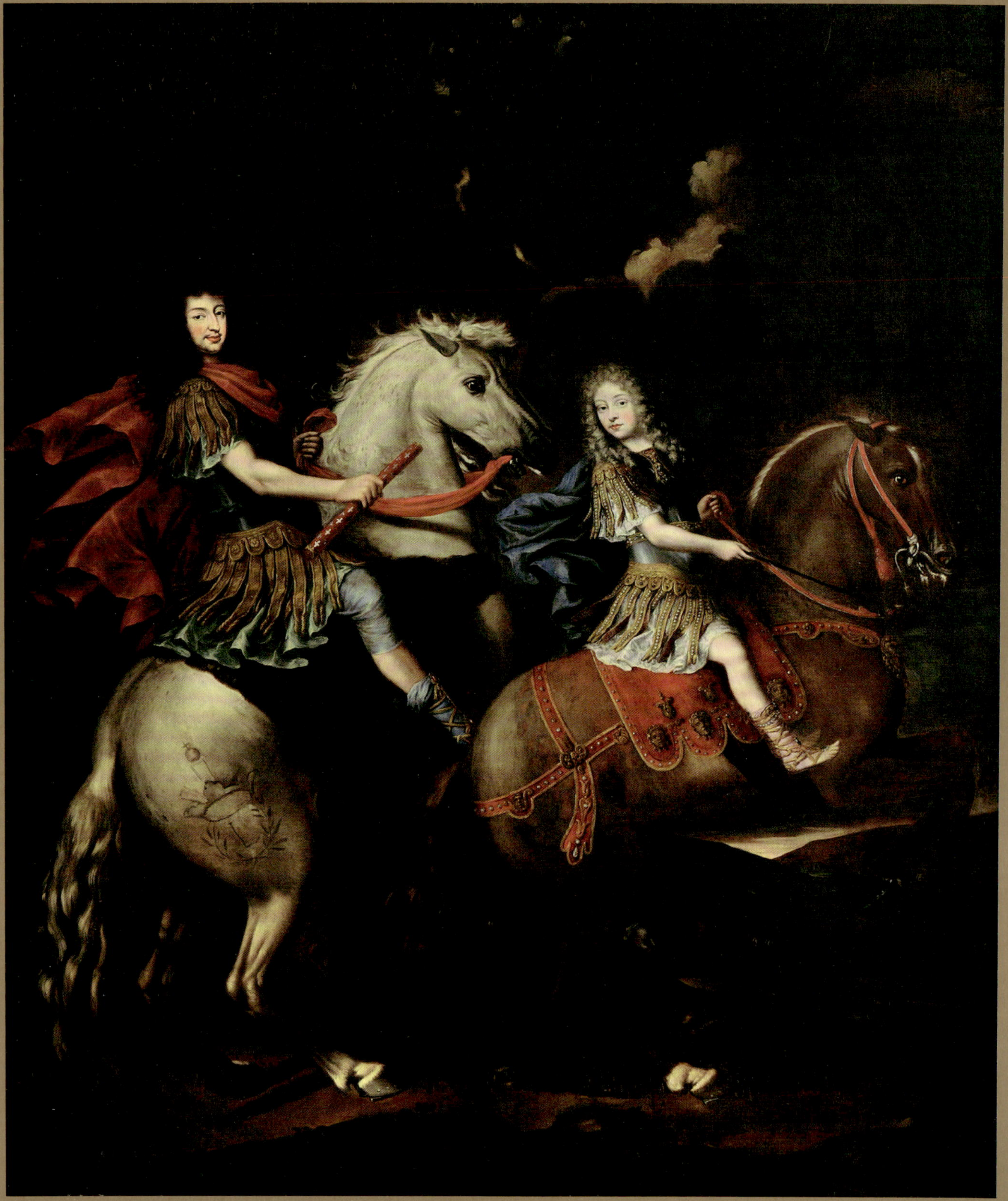

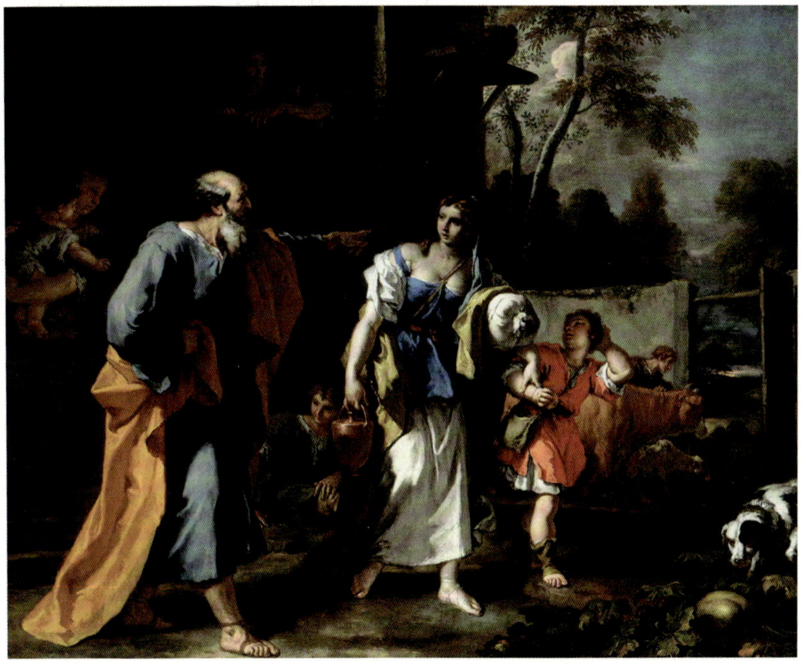

The Repudiation of Agar
c. 1724
Sebastiano Ricci
(1659–1734)
Galleria Sabauda,
Turin

of Vittorio Amedeo II was such that its thoroughness and innovative character remained intact almost until the end of the eighteenth century.

Vittorio Amedeo's end was dramatic. If acquiring power had meant facing down his mother, he lost it through opposition to his son. On September 3, 1730, in a decision that astonished every court in Europe, Vittorio Amedeo II abdicated and withdrew to Chambéry, passing the throne to his son Carlo Emanuele III (1701–1773). A year later, however, the aged sovereign accused his successor of weakness, deciding to return to Turin to take back the crown. But Carlo Emanuele had no qualms about having his father simply arrested, locking him up first in the castle at Rivoli, then in Montcalier, where he was to die on October 31, 1732, without ever setting eyes on his son again. His funeral was held in the cathedral of Turin, with a catafalque designed for the occasion by the baroque architect Filippo Juvarra, his remains languishing in situ for many years. It was only some time later that his grandson, Vittorio Amedeo III, had his corpse transferred to the basilica of Superga, erected in celebration of the victory of 1706. Let us conclude with a passage from an English historian of the mid-eighteenth century (*The Modern Part of an Universal History)*, who wrote that the great sovereign Vittorio Amedeo "was one of the most pene-trating princes in the world remarkable through all Europe for accommoda-ting his situations to his interests [and] the most extraordinary character and may be said to have been the most politic prince of his age."

Carlo Emanuele II and Vittorio Amedeo II, Princes of Piedmont
1675
G. B. Brambilla
Palazzo Madama,
Museo Civico d'Arte Antica,
Turin

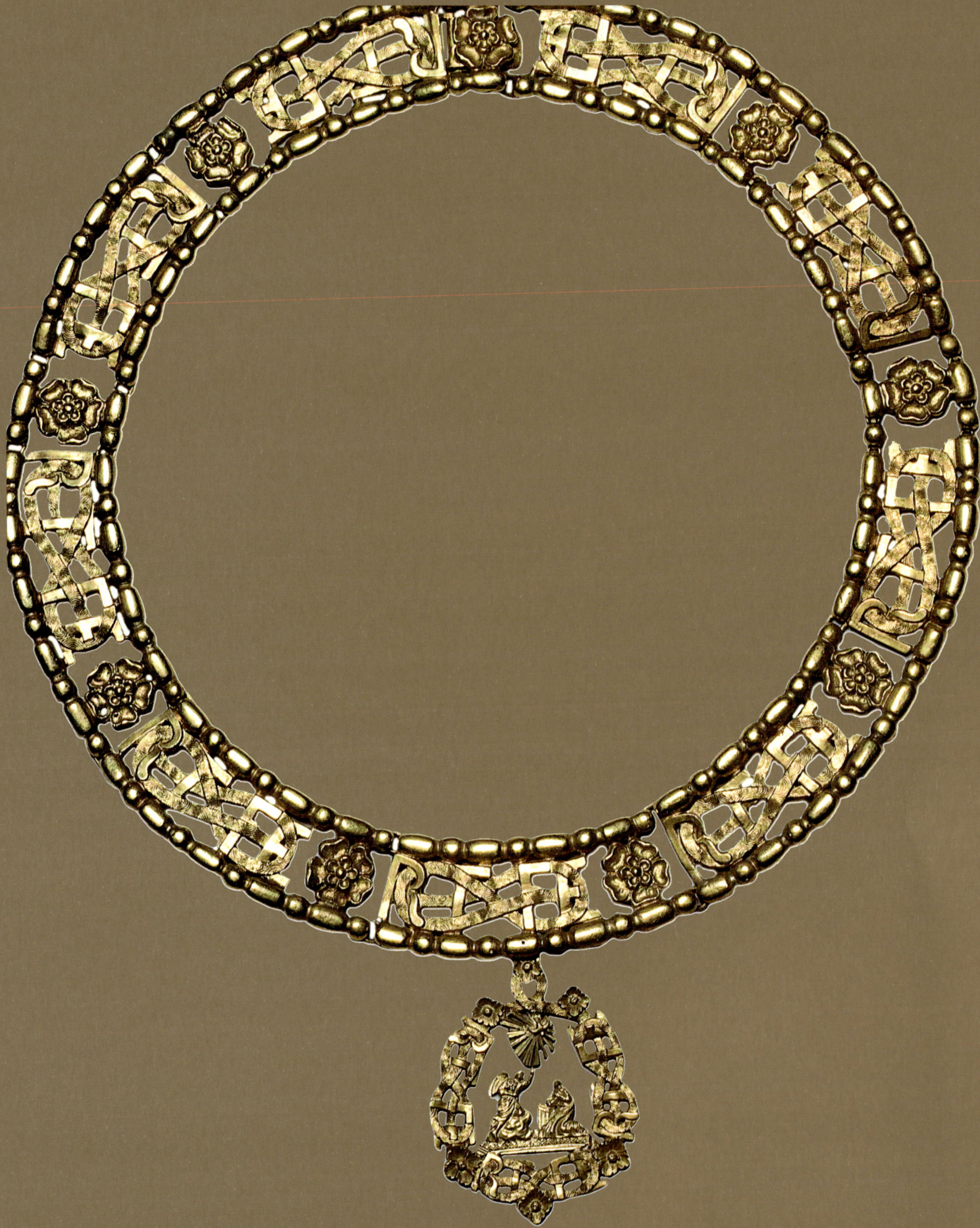

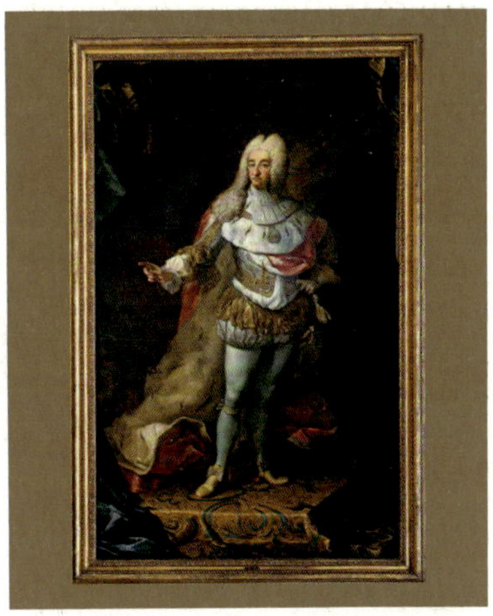

King Vittorio Amedeo II (1666–1732)
1728
Martin van Meytens the Younger (1695–1770)
Oil on canvas
278 × 180 cm
Reggia di Venaria Reale, Venaria Reale

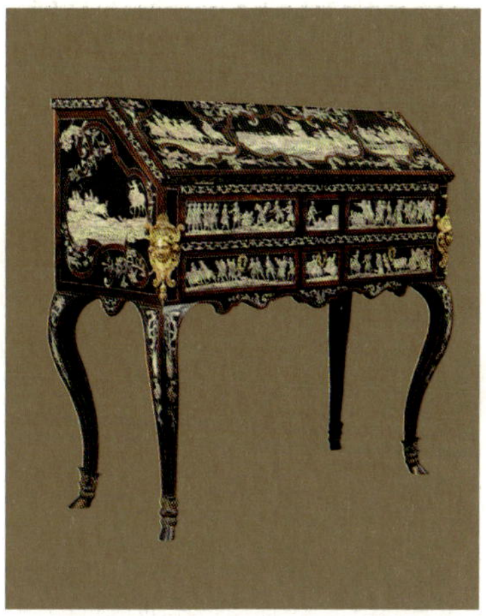

Writing desk with a depiction of the Siege of Turin of 1706 on the lid
1723
Luigi Prinotto (1715–1792)
Royal workshops of the Court of Turin
Wood incrusted with ivory
98 × 99 × 44 cm
Palazzo Reale, Turin

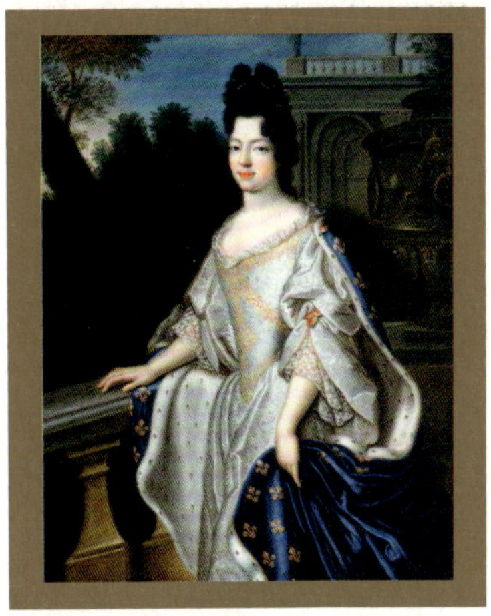

Maria Adelaide of Savoy (1685–1712), Daughter of Vittorio Amedeo of Savoy and Anne-Marie d'Orléans (1669–1728), Wife of Duke of Bourgogne, Grandson of Louis XIV
c. 1698, French school
Oil on canvas
129 × 97 cm
Galleria Sabauda, Turin
Inv. 684

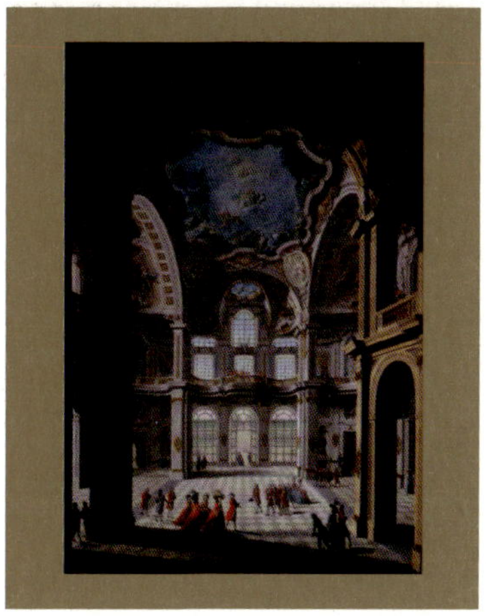

View of the Central Room of the Hunting Palace of Stupinigi
1798
Giovanni Battista Bagnasacco (1746–1822) and Giovanni Comandù (1777–1822)
Oil on canvas
233 × 165 cm
Palazzo Reale (on deposit to the Reggia di Venaria Reale), Turin
Inv. 829 DC

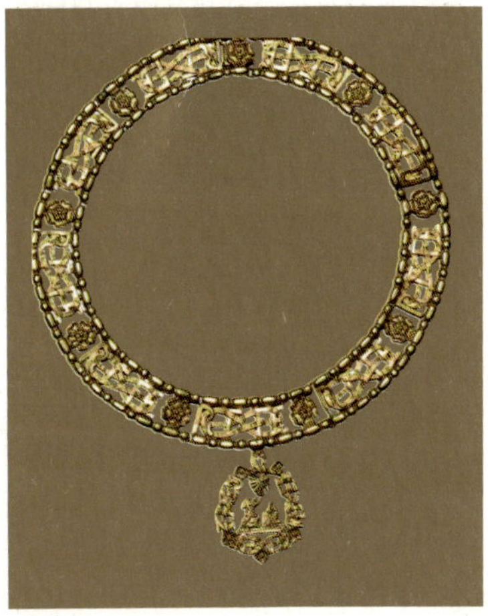

Necklace of the Order of the Santissima Annunziata
Eighteenth century
Enameled gold
35 × 30 cm
Palazzo Reale, Turin, S. N.

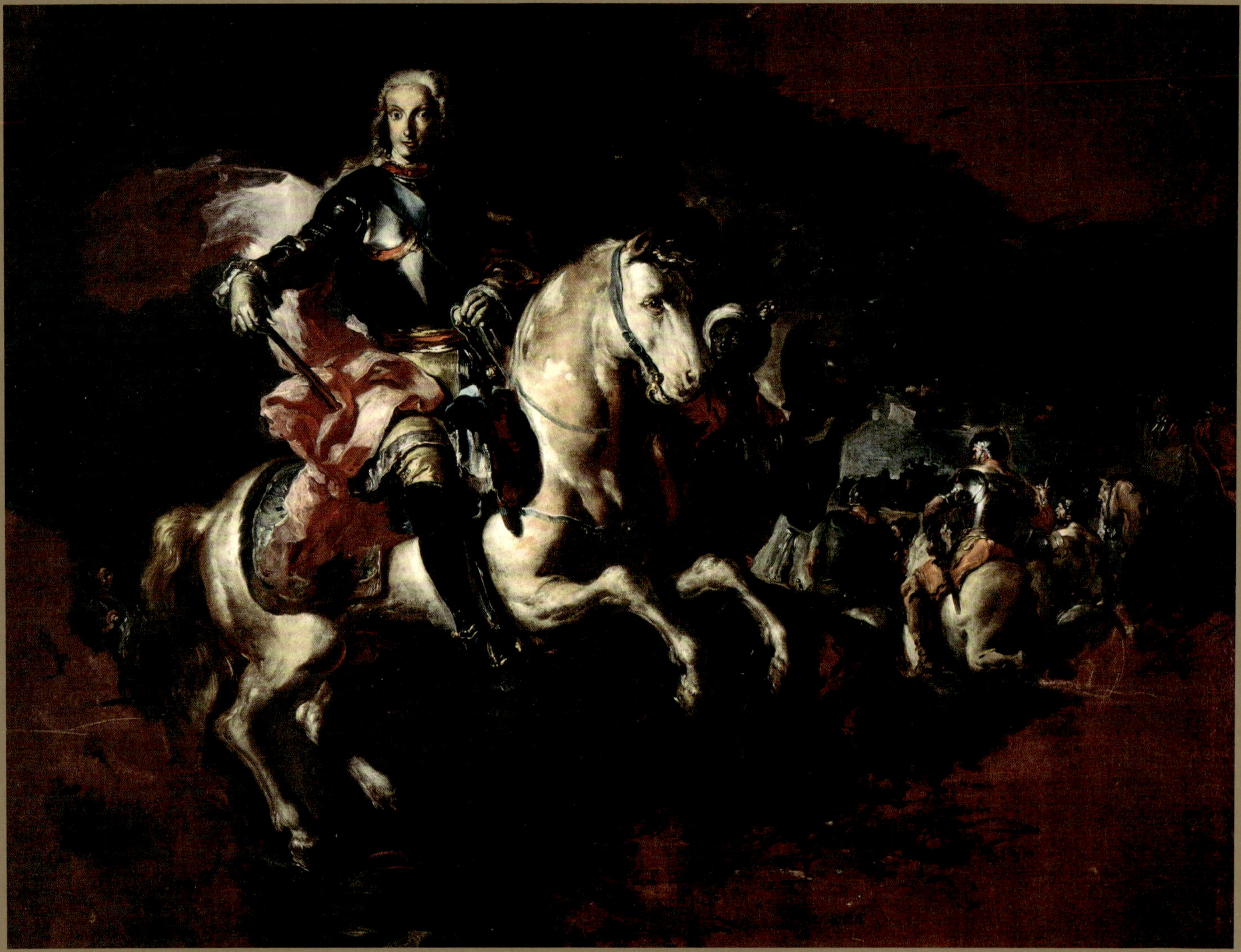

NAPLES

Carlo di Borbone (1717–1788)

The Triumph
of Carlo di Borbone,
King of Naples,
at the Battle of Gaeta
1734
Francesco Solimena
(1657–1747)
Palazzo Reale, Caserta

Carlo di Borbone, King of Naples

Imma Ascione

Carlo di Borbone's first letter to his parents, the Spanish sovereigns Felipe V and Isabella Farnese, was written from the Escorial. It is dated October 12, 1720, when Carlo di Borbone, future king of Naples and of Spain, born on January 20, 1716, was no more than four years old. The subsequent correspondence, numbering nearly a thousand letters, provides a first-rate opportunity to examine the private life of a king in every last detail.

Years later, in 1731, the Infante left Seville for Italy with an imposing retinue of ministers and advisers, including his tutor Manuel Benavides y Aragón, count then duke of Santisteban del Puerto. Disgraced in 1738, the duke was replaced in the post of prime minister by the marquis of Montealegre, one of the men Isabella Farnese had succeeding in placing in her son's entourage, together with several other trusted aides. In the first days of 1732, the royal procession arrived at Livorno, but the Infante contracted smallpox. He was only able to make his official entrance into Florence two months later, on March 9; there he was received by Grand Duke Giovanni Gastone. Seven months later, he was on the road to Parma to take possession of the states of the Farnese.

Letters from the time betray Carlo's keen interest in Italian art. Waxing lyrical about Pisa, with its great church—the "most beautiful to be seen in all Europe"—he enthused about the Medici villas of Poggio Imperiale, Castello, and Poggio a Caiano, about the Boboli gardens, the Villa di Pratolino, the Medici Chapel, and the gardens of Colorno on the outskirts of Parma.

The signing of the Treaty of Turin on September 26, 1733, and the preparations for the war that followed saw Felipe V appointing his son supreme commander of the Spanish forces in Italy: soon all was ready for the expedition to Naples. Carlo was gratified by his father's confidence and overjoyed with the title of "generalissimo" that Felipe conferred on him. In the eyes of the young prince, then but eighteen, war felt more like a day out than an onerous and dangerous duty.

Carlo di Borbone, King of Naples
Eighteenth century
Francesco Liani
(1712–1780)
Intesa Sampaolo (on deposit to the Museo San Martino), Naples

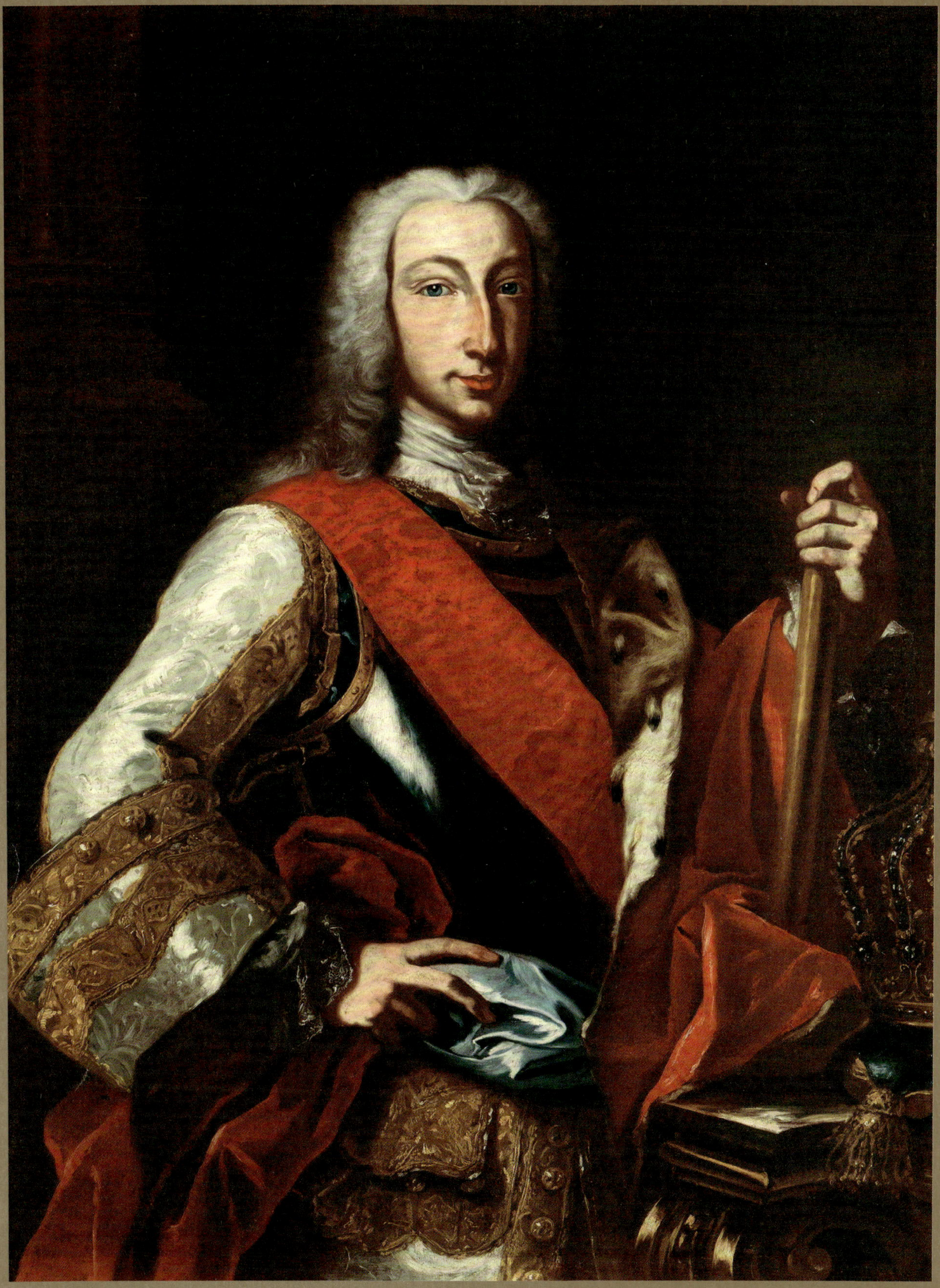

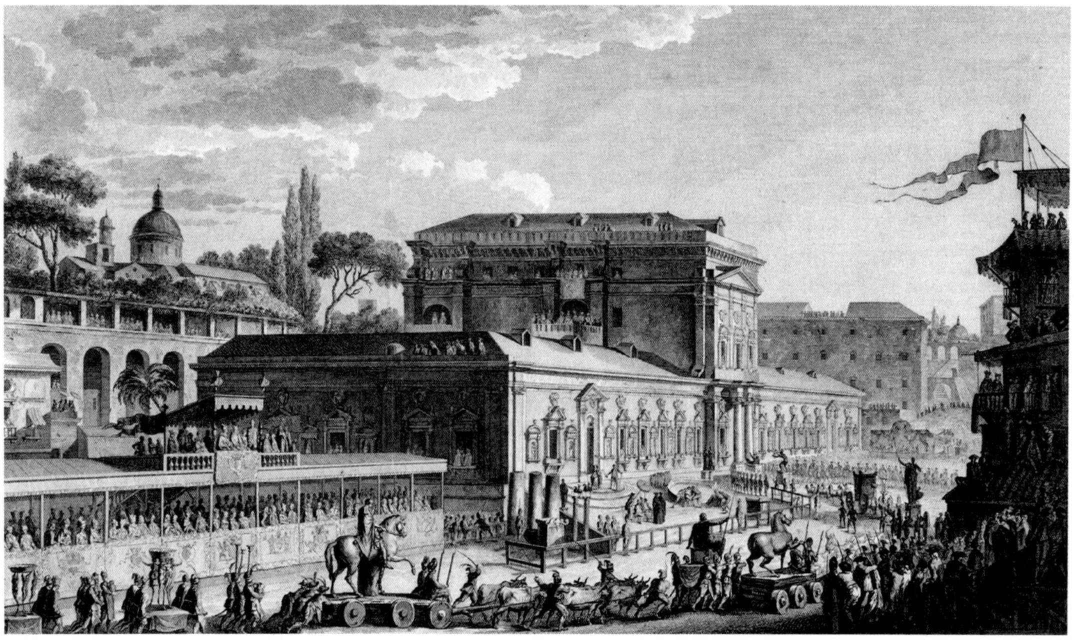

Transportation of Antiquities from Herculaneum from the Portici Museum to the Palazzo dei Regi Studi, Naples
1781–1786
RICHARD DE SAINT-NON
(1727-1791)
Picturesque journey from Naples and Sicilia, pl. 95

Entering Naples on May 12, 1734, he did not immediately find his new kingdom and capital to his liking and indeed loathed the royal palace. But he stayed on to lead the expedition to conquer Sicilia, where pockets of pro-Austrian resistance held out, setting off in January 1735. Events concluded with the all-important ceremony of his crowning as "king of the Two Sicilies" in Palermo Cathedral on July 3. The coronation sparked the onset of the most glorious, if short-lived, period in the history of the fledgling state, a veritable golden age that outstripped the aspirations of the Neapolitans. The city was then a hive of activity, with policy initiatives and buildings springing up everywhere. Carlo, too, became determined to turn the royal palace into a residence worthy of his status. This in turn signaled the start of major architectural campaigns that have left an enduring imprint on the capital, including the hunting lodge of Capodimonte, the royal palace at Portici, and the San Carlo theater, thrown up in a mere 270 days. Meanwhile, at the insistence of his parents—his mother in particular—Carlo "also had everything brought in from Piacenza and Colorno." Thus Naples filled with precious artifacts from the Farnese dynasty that were destined to form the nucleus of the city's extensive collections, hugely enriched over the decades by archaeological finds and sundry acts of court patronage.

Shortly afterwards, negotiations designed to find the young king a suitable wife began, the choice falling on Princess Maria Amelia of Saxony, daughter of the king of Poland, Augustus III, and a granddaughter of Augustus the Strong.

Maria Amelia of Saxony (1724–1760), Wife of Carlo di Borbone, King of Naples
Eighteenth century
FRANCESCO LIANI
(1712–1780)
Intesa Sampaolo
(on deposit to the Museo di San Martino),
Naples

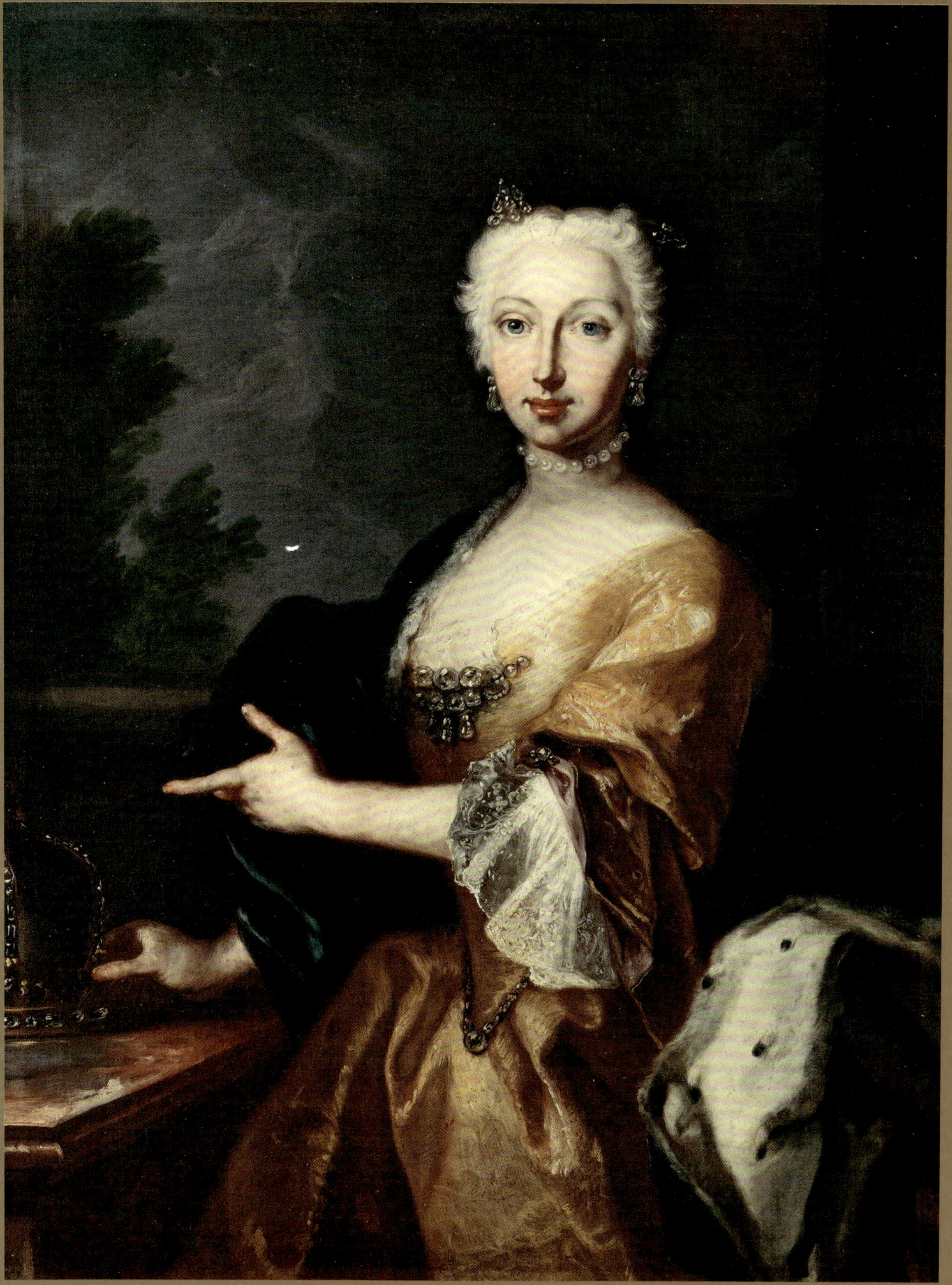

After 1740, however, state income no longer proved sufficient to cover even essential outgoings and the kingdom found itself beset by financial problems. The excessive cost of the king's own projects was subject to much criticism. In any event, the king's greatest wish was about to be realized: the queen was pregnant and an heir was in the offing. By then sixteen, Maria Amelia had begun to wield a certain political influence at court and was much loved by the common people because the Neapolitan *lazzari*—descendants of participants in Masaniello's rebellion of 1647 against the Spanish crown—thought of her as not truly Spanish. From the end of 1741, the kingdom was handicapped by endemic diplomatic and military strife. The beginning of war in Europe affected Naples, too, and it was blockaded by the British navy in August 1742. In early November 1743, the kingdom even seemed threatened by invasion, and Carlo took the head of his army and joined the Spanish forces. For almost two months, the Spanish and Neapolitan army confronted Austrian troops with hardly a shot being fired, but then, on August 11, 1744, at the Battle of Velletri, the Neapolitan forces carried the field. A landmark in its history, the kingdom of Naples now thoroughly identified with its victorious sovereign.

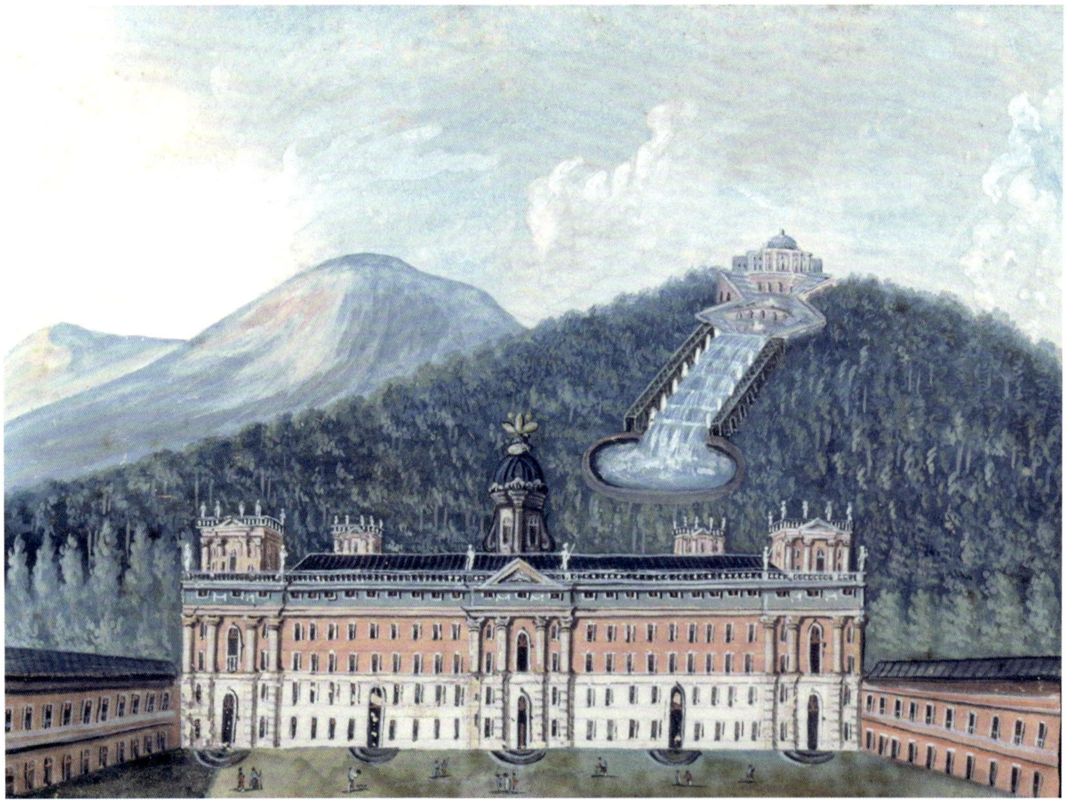

Casket depicting the royal palace of Caserta and the waterfall in the garden (détail)
Late eighteenth century
Museo di Capodimonte, Naples

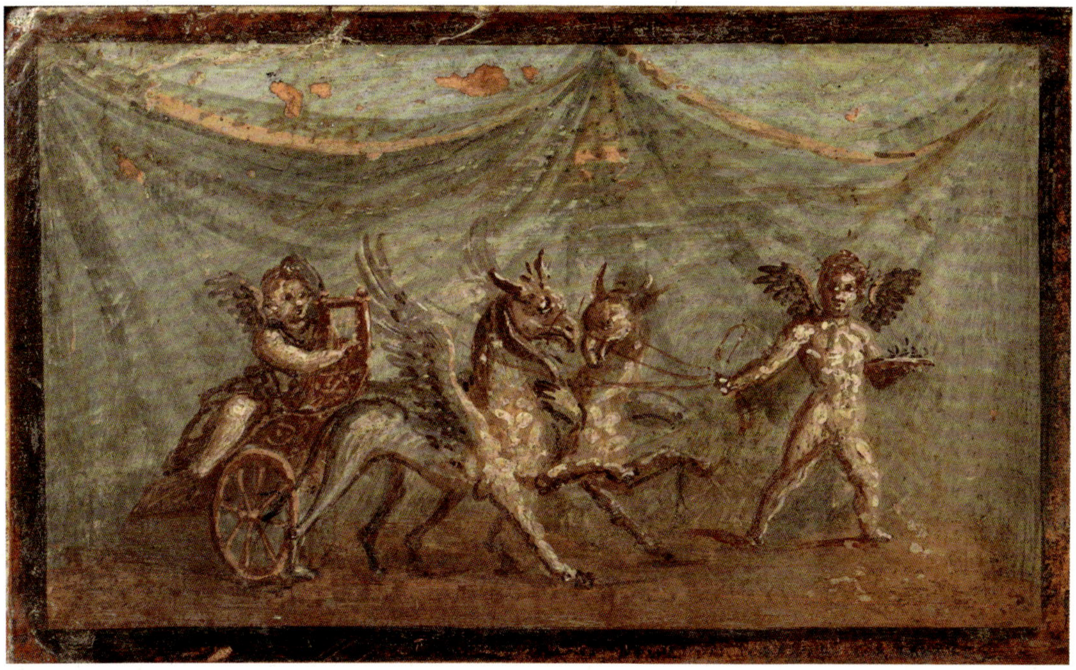

During the ten years he spent in Naples, Carlo oversaw the construction of a magnificent royal palace at Caserta, laying the foundation stone in January 1752. As regards military constructions, he erected the fort at Granatello and several other army quarters. In the capital, the sovereign ordered the construction of an imposing hospice, the Real Albergo dei Poveri, and renovated the Palazzo dei Regi Studi that housed the university, converting it into a museum.

Carlo was keen to advance archaeological excavations at Herculaneum and Pompeii, and had drawings of the uncovered objects published by the Accademia Ercolanese. A further significant artistic initiative that moreover had repercussions on trade was the creation of the royal porcelain manufactory of Capodimonte.

In October 1759, at the death of his half-brother, King Fernando of Spain, Carlo repaired to Madrid where he ascended the Spanish throne. Over the thirty years that followed, he proved an enlightened monarch who set Spain on the path towards becoming a modern state.

Fresco with cupids from a Herculaneum villa
National Archaeological Museum,
Naples

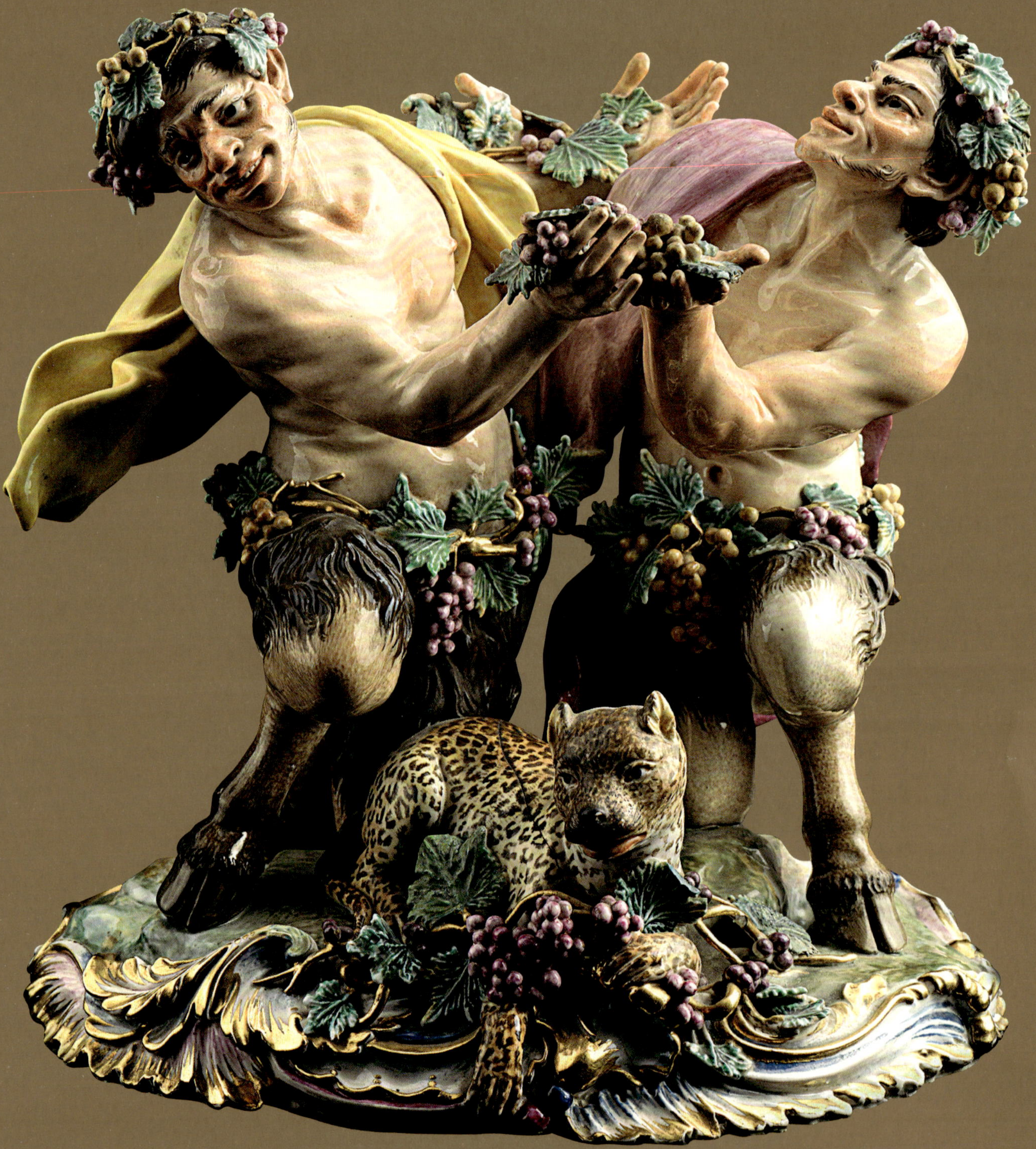

Two Satyrs
1758–65
Royal Manufactory of Capodimonte
Museo di Capodimonte, Naples

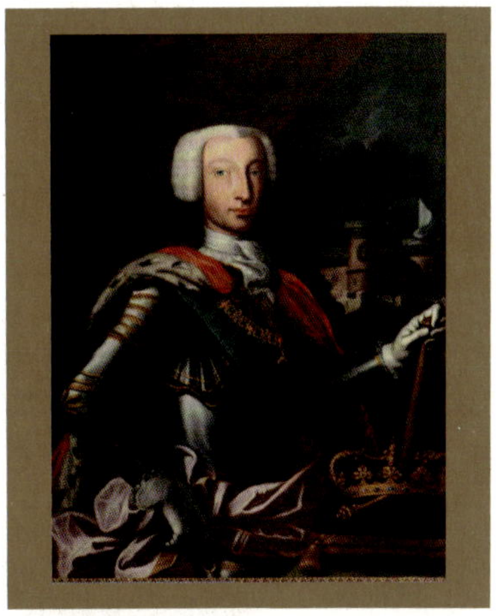

Carlo di Borbone (1716–1788), King of Naples
c. 1736
Antonio Sebastiani
Oil on canvas
102 × 76 cm
Palazzo Reale, Caserta
51/52 n.1034

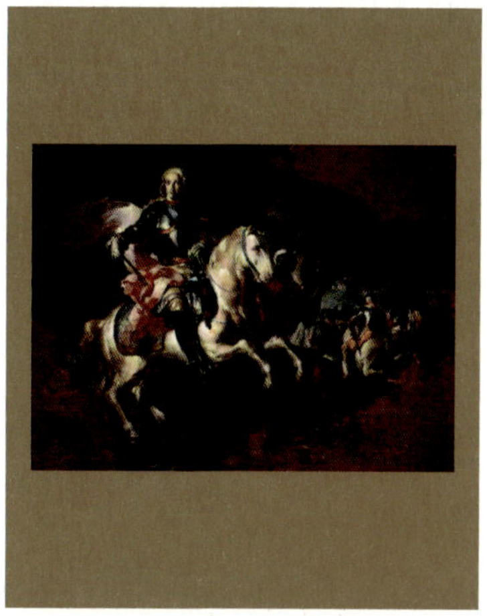

The Triumph of Carlo di Borbone at the Battle of Gaeta
1734
Francesco Solimena (1657–1747)
Oil on canvas
140 × 187 cm
Palazzo Reale, Caserta
Inv. 1977/78 n.942

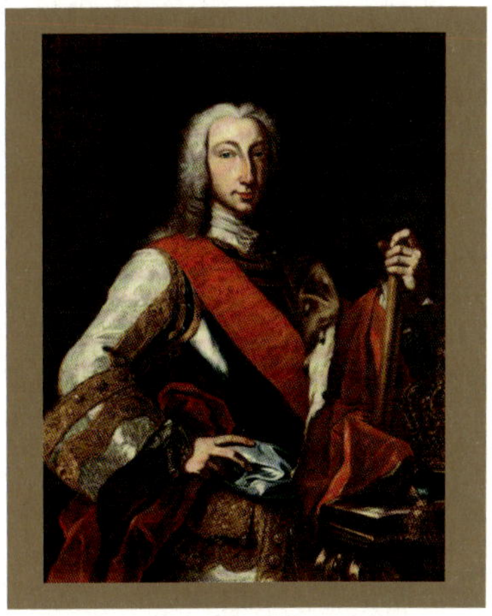

Carlo di Borbone (1716–1788), King of Naples
c. 1758
Francesco Liani (1712–1780)
Oil on canvas
120 × 65 cm (inc. frame)
Intesa Sanpaolo (on deposit to the Museo di San Martino), Naples
Inv. 281

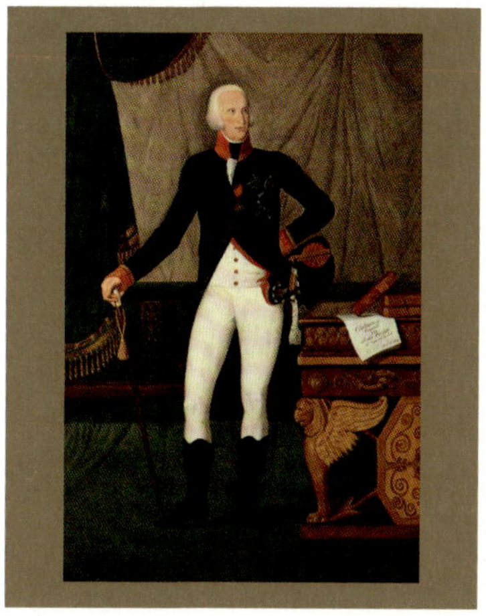

Ferdinando IV, King of Naples (1751–1825), King of the Two Sicilies, under the name of Ferdinando I
1818
Giacomo Berger
Oil on canvas
233 × 155 cm
Museo di San Martino, Naples
Inv. 50

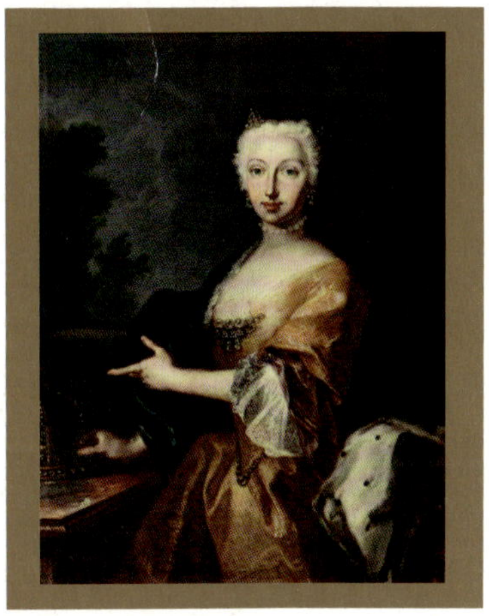

Maria Amelia of Saxony (1724–1760), Wife of Carlo di Borbone, King of Naples
c. 1758
Francesco Liani (1712–1780)
Oil on canvas
122,5 × 96 cm (inc. frame)
Intesa Sanpaolo (on deposit to the Museo di San Martino), Naples
Inv. 289

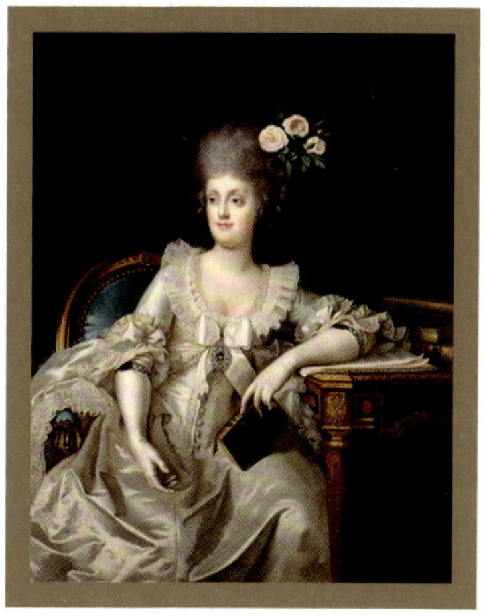

Maria Carolina of Naples (1752–1814)
Late eighteenth century–early nineteenth century
Camillio Landini (1776-1821)
Oil on canvas
133 × 105 cm
Museo di Capodimonte, Naples
Inv. OA6597

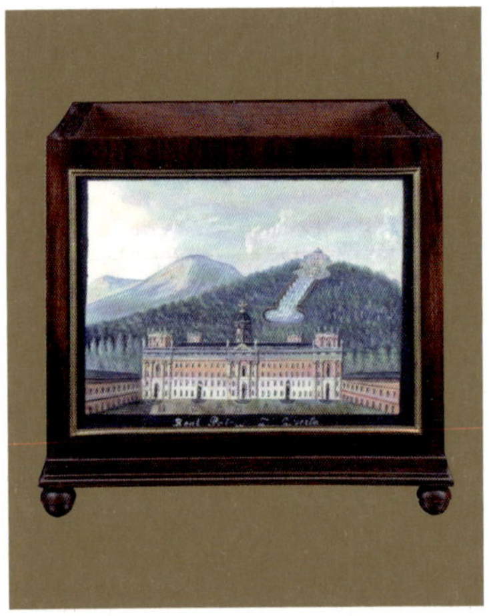

Casket depicting the royal palace of Caserta and the waterfall in the garden
Late eighteenth century
Painted wood
33 × 33 cm
Museo di Capodimonte, Naples
Inv. 2547

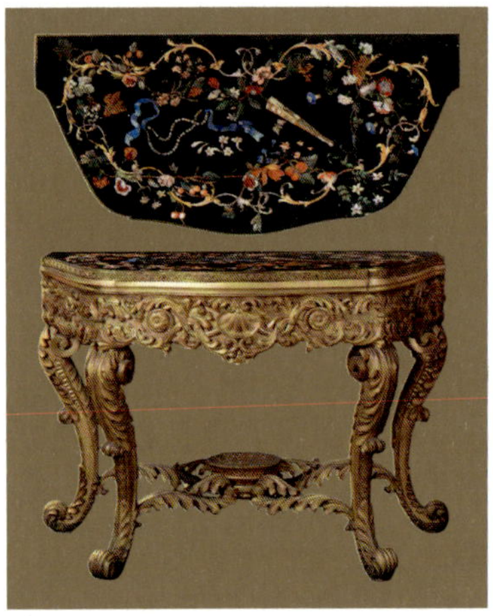

Hardstone console table
Eighteenth century (top);
nineteenth century (console table)
Royal Hardstone Workshops in Naples
Hardstone and gilded wood
approx. 133 × approx. 66 cm
Palazzo Reale, Caserta
Inv. 1951/52 n.4917

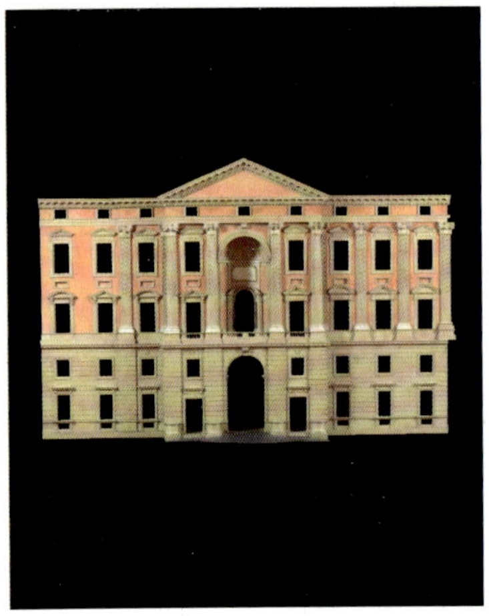

Model of the main façade of the royal palace of Caserta
1759–60
Antonio Rosz
Painted wood
75 × 215 × 50 cm
Palazzo Reale, Caserta
Inv. 1951/52 n.3887

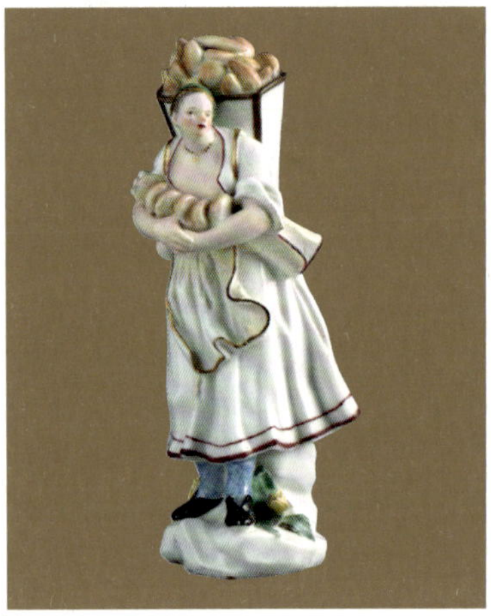

The Bread Seller
1743–59
Royal Manufactory of Capodimonte
Porcelain
H. approx. 19.5 cm
Museo di Capodimonte, Naples
Inv. OA6236

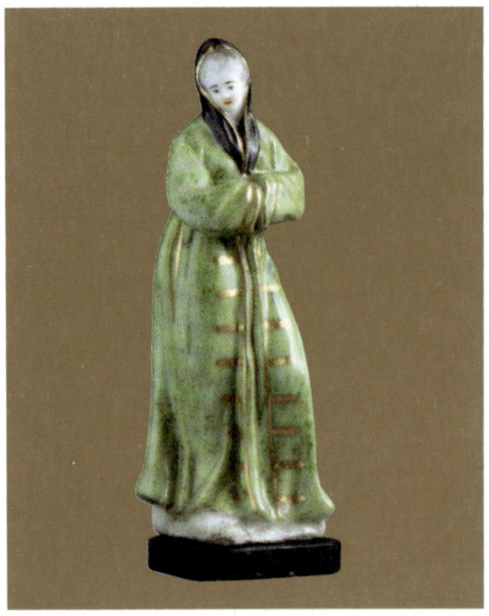

Woman in green "Marsina" costume
1743–59
Royal Manufactory of Capodimonte
Porcelain
H. 15 cm
Museo Duca di Martina, Naples
Inv. 1890

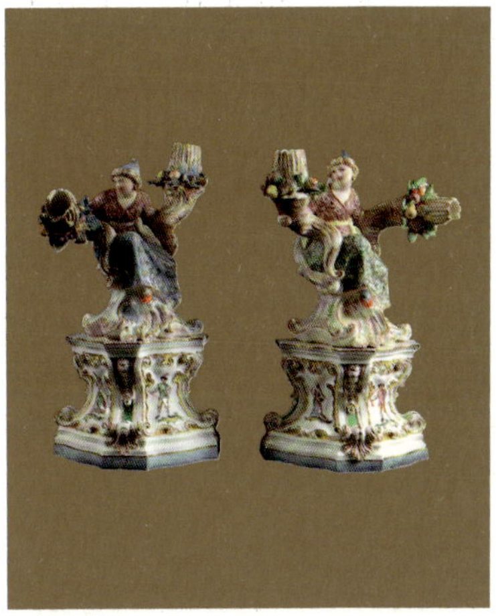

Pair of candelabras
1757–65
Royal Manufactory of Capodimonte
Porcelain
H. 29 cm
Museo di San Martino, Naples
Inv. 586

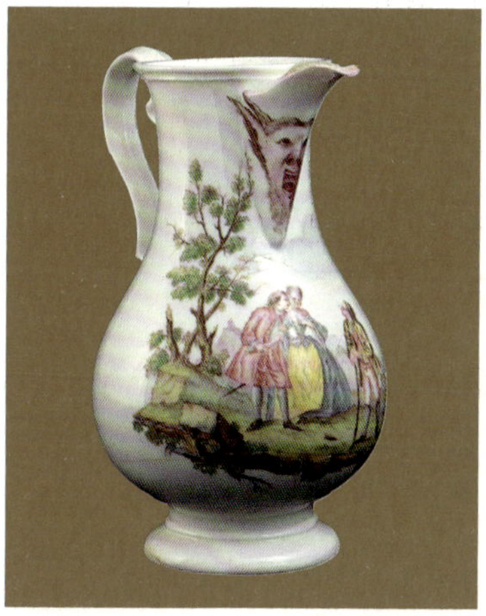

Coffee pot with courting scene
1754–57
Royal Manufactory of Capodimonte
Porcelain
H. 21.4 cm
Museo Duca di Martina, Naples
Inv. 4329

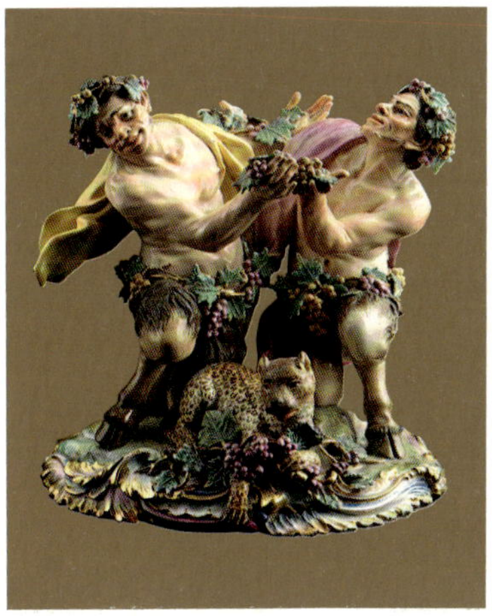

Two Satyrs
1758–65
Royal Manufactory of Capodimonte
Porcelain
H. approx. 22 cm
Museo di Capodimonte, Naples
Inv. OA6235

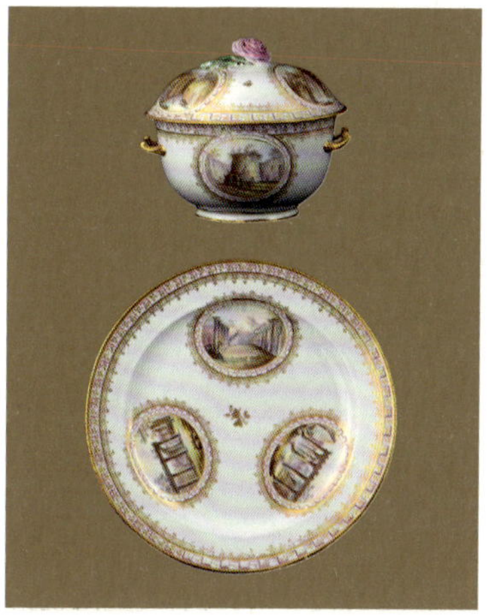

Cup and saucer
1784–88
Naples Porcelain Manufactory
Porcelain
H. 8.3 cm
Museo Duca di Martina, Naples
Inv. 1881 a and b

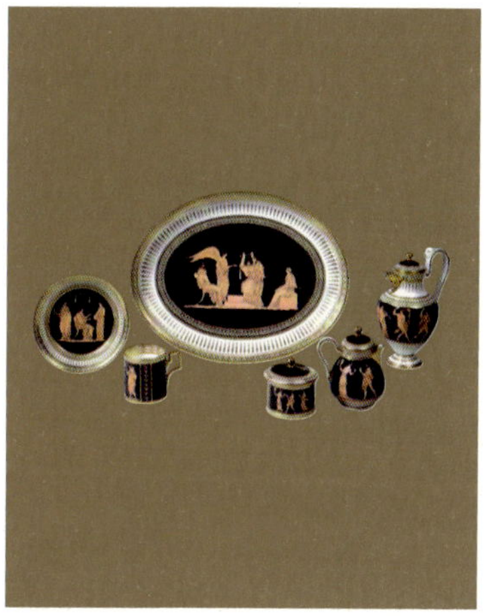

Breakfast service with an Etruscan scene: platter, cup, saucer, milk jug, sugar bowl, coffee pot
1771–1806
Naples Porcelain Manufactory
Porcelain
H. (coffee pot) 16.8 × (platter) 32.5 cm
Museo di Capodimonte, Naples
Inv. 5060-5065

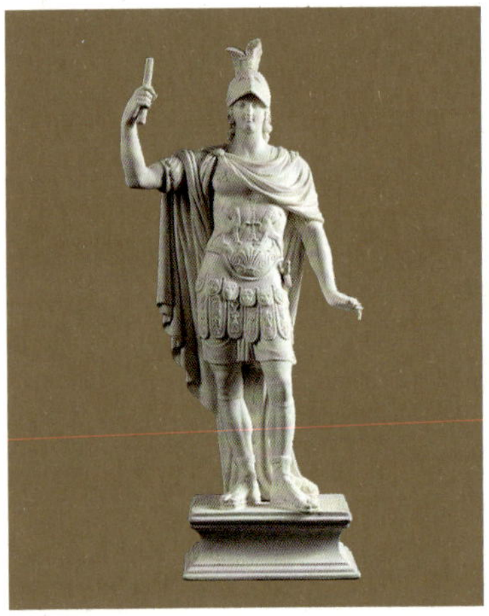

Alexander
1771–1808
Naples Porcelain Manufactory
Porcelain
H. 39 cm
Museo Duca di Martina, Naples
Inv. S 389

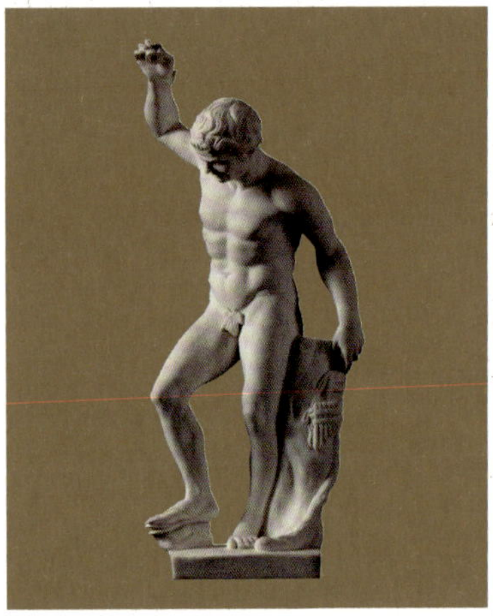

Faun
1771–1808
Naples Porcelain Manufactory
Porcelain
H. 21 cm
Museo Duca di Martina, Naples
Inv. S 392

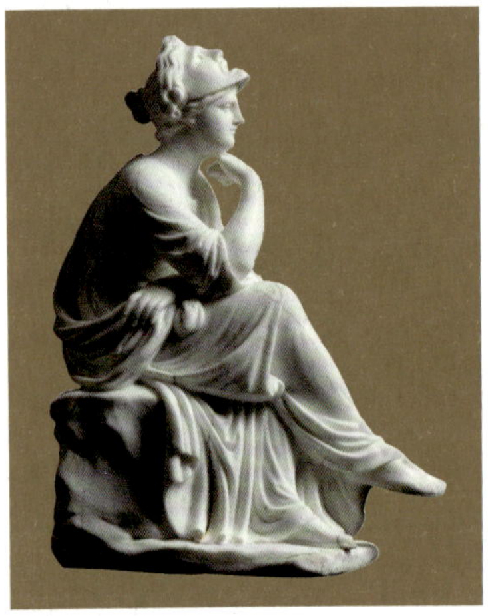

Melpomene
1771–1808
Naples Porcelain Manufactory
Porcelain
H. 22.5 cm
Museo Duca di Martina, Naple
Inv. S 99

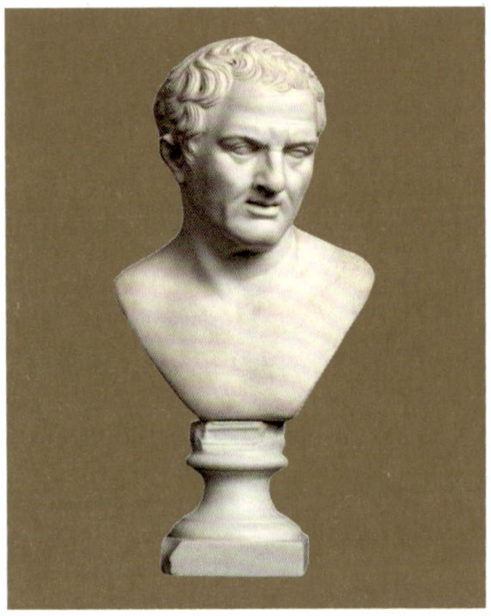

Bust of a pseudo-Philosopher
1771–1808
Naples Porcelain Manufactory
Porcelain
H. 21.5 cm
Museo Duca di Martina, Naples
Inv. S 114

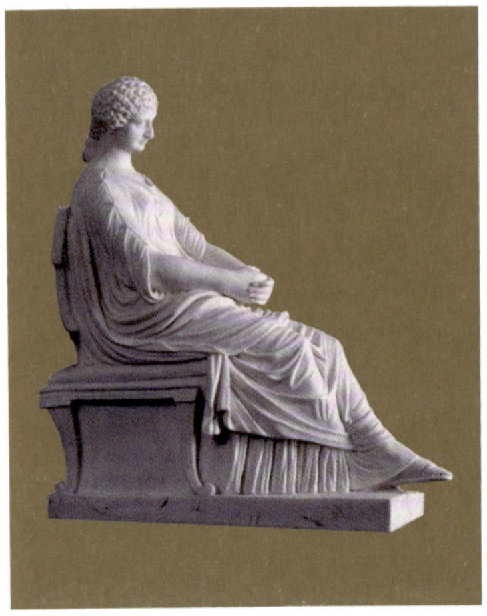

Agrippina
1771–1808
Naples Porcelain Manufactory
Porcelain
H. 25.5 cm
Museo Duca di Martina, Naples
Inv. S 41

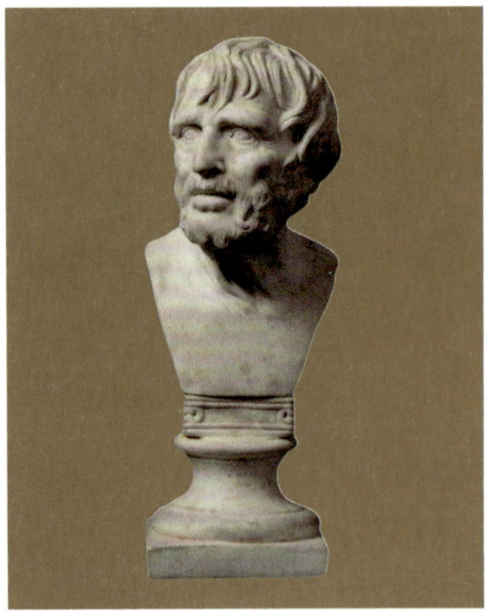

Bust of Seneca
1771–1808
Naples Porcelain Manufactory
Porcelain
H. 19 cm
Museo Duca di Martina, Naples
Inv. S 238

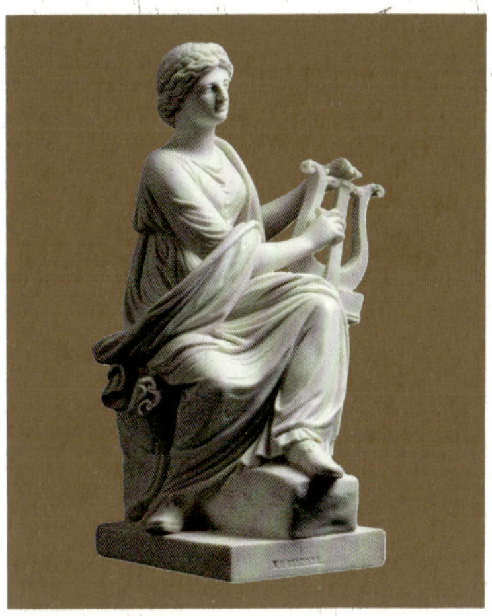

Terpsichore
1771–1808
Naples Porcelain Manufactory
Porcelain
H. 27 cm
Museo Duca di Martina, Naples
Inv. S 391

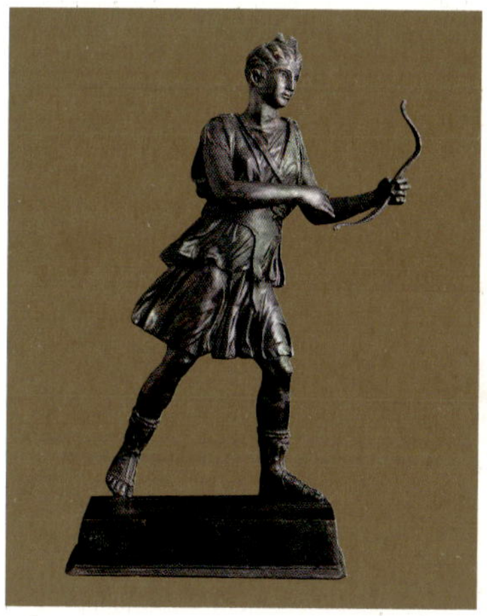

The Hunter, Diana
Marble
H. 30 cm
National Archaeological Museum, Naples,
Inv. 5024

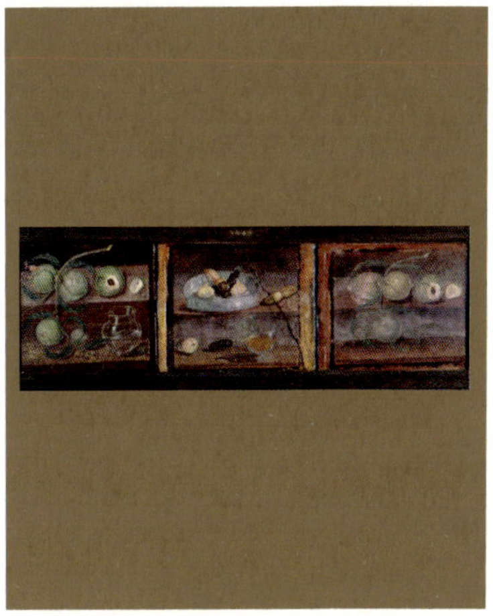

Fresco with still lifes from a Herculaneum villa
43 × 128 cm
National Archaeological Museum, Naples
Inv. 8645

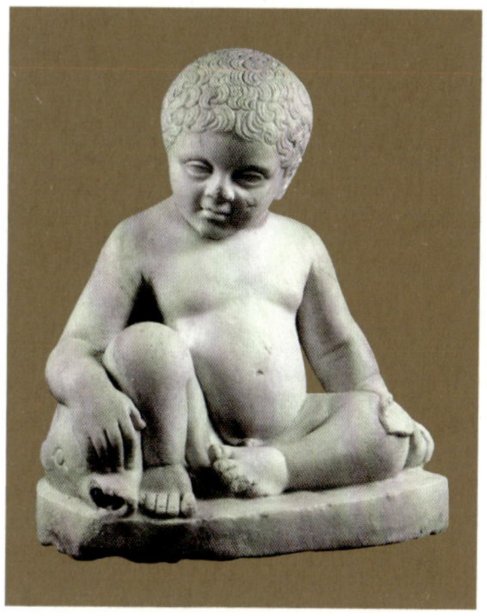

Putto from Herculaneum
Marble
H. 41 cm
National Archaeological Museum, Naples
Inv. 6112

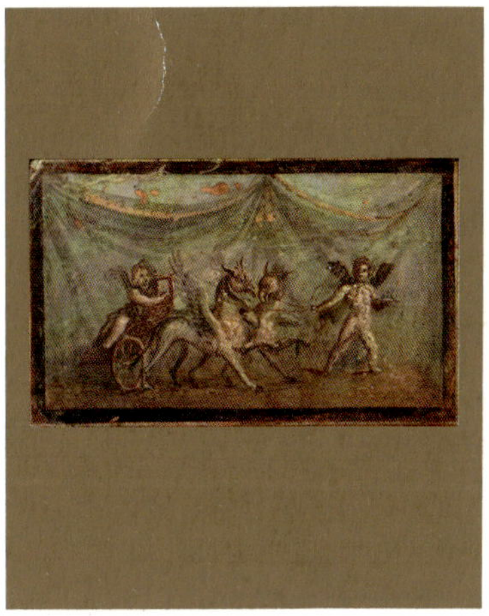

Fresco with cupids from a Herculaneum villa
30.8 × 160 cm
National Archaeological Museum, Naples
Inv. 9178

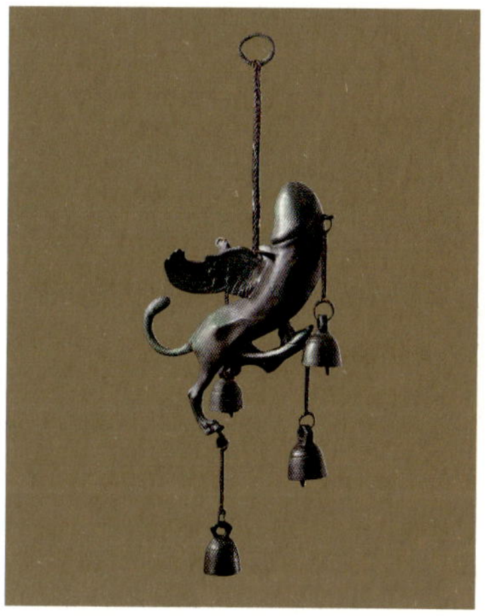

Tintinnabulum
Bronze
H. 49.5 cm
National Archaeological Museum, Naples
Inv. 27835

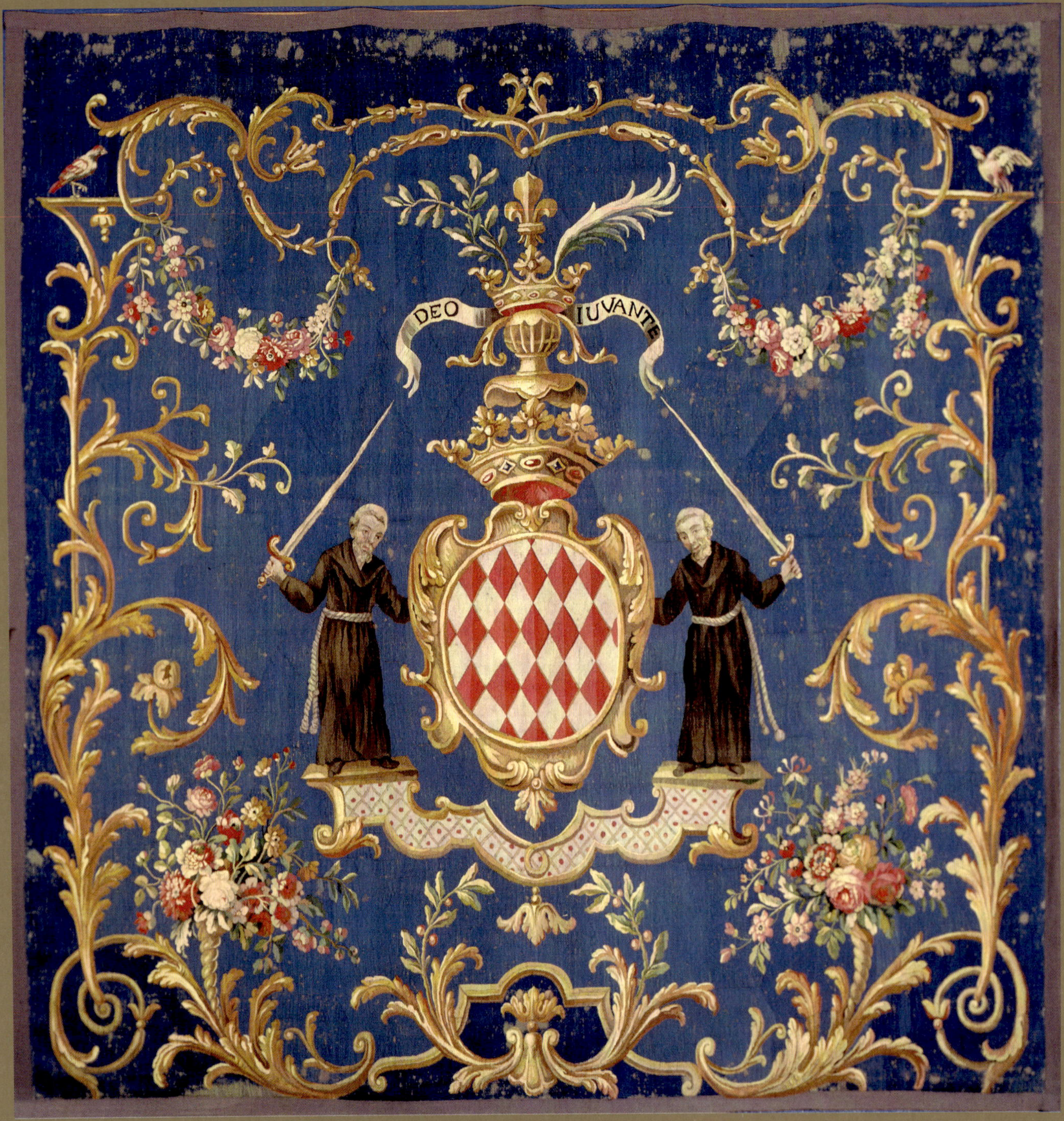
DEO
IUVANTE

MONACO

Princes from 17th to 20th century

Tapestry with the arms of the Grimaldis, princes of Monaco
Seventeenth century
Aubusson tapestry
Palais Princier,
Monaco

Jacques I of Monaco (1689–1751)
Prince and art collector

Thomas Fouilleron

Jacques I (1689–1751), Prince of Monaco
1718
Nicolas de Largillière
(1656–1746)
Palais Princier,
Monaco

Mirabilia admired by all who traveled to the Rock from the seventeenth century on, the objets d'art preserved in the palace at Monaco, attesting to the longevity and venerability of the ruling dynasty, played a role equivalent to that of royal regalia. As historiographer Jean Le Laboureur recorded in 1646: "beautiful originals, as many portraits as stories by Titian, Raphael, both Bassanos, Michelangelo, Parmigianino, Guido Reni, Albrecht Dürer . . . 'Canjage', the 'Bergamask', Caravaggio, and other famous painters." Prince Honoré II (1597–1662), the first to adopt the title of monarch in 1612, initially supplied himself with art from Italy, and then, after the Treaty of Péronne that placed the principality under the king's protection in 1641, from France. The number of pictures present in the palace rose from 44 in 1605 to 720 after his reign, reaching 1,290 on the death of Prince Antoine I

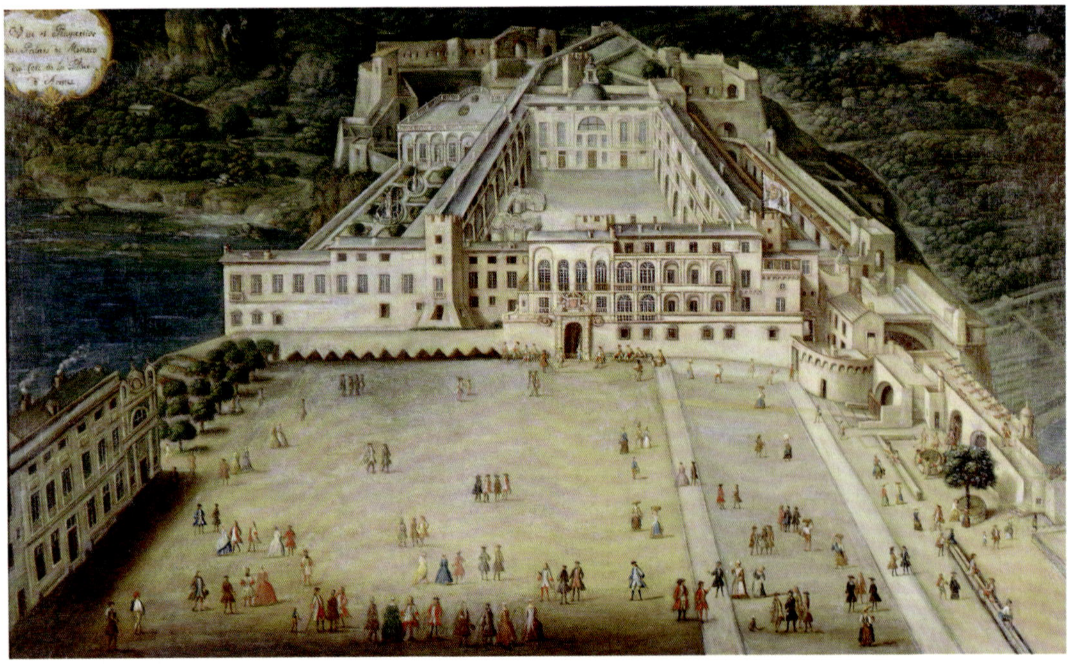

View of the Palace of Monaco from the Place d'Armes
1732
Dominique-Joseph Bressan
(1670–1746)
Palais Princier,
Monaco

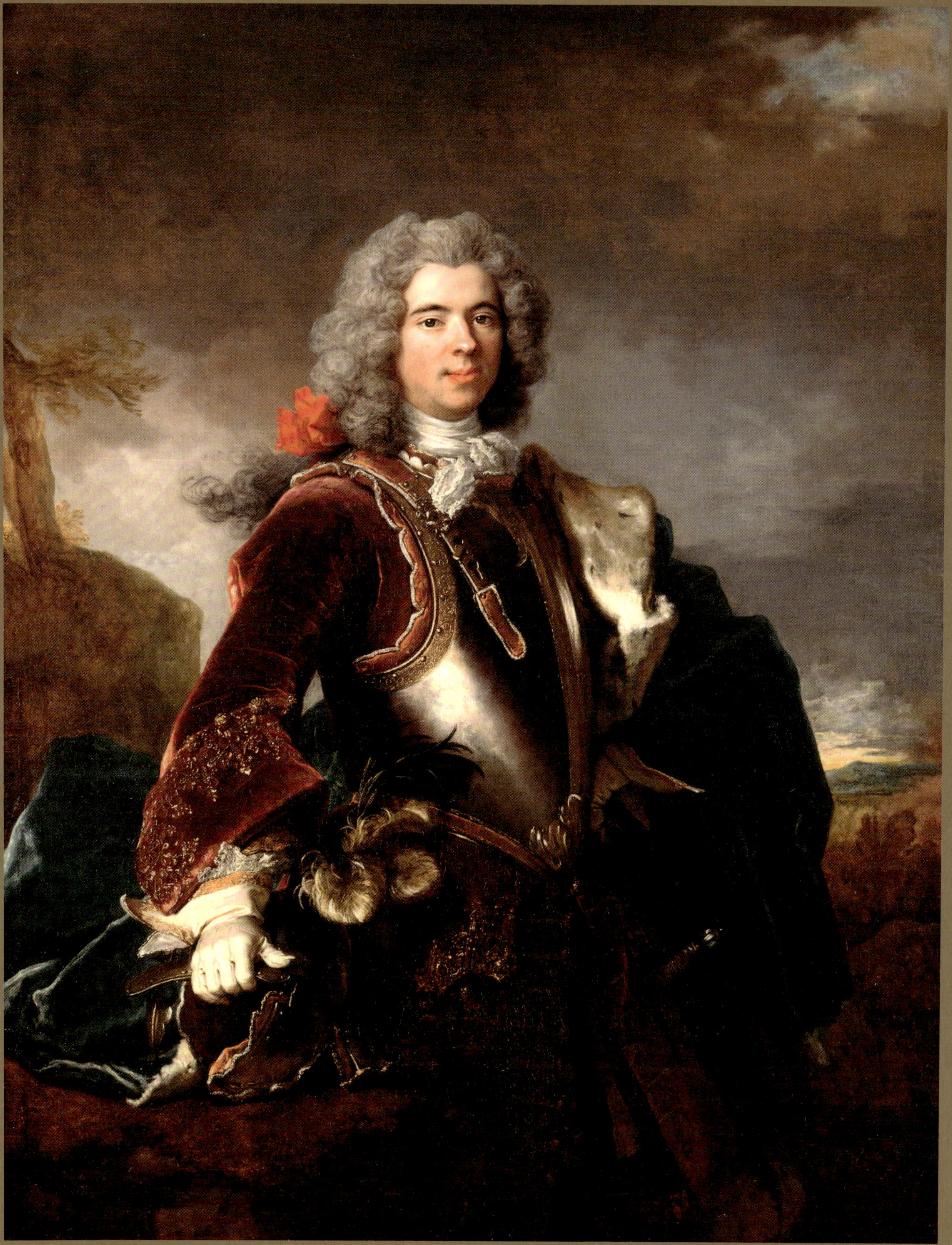

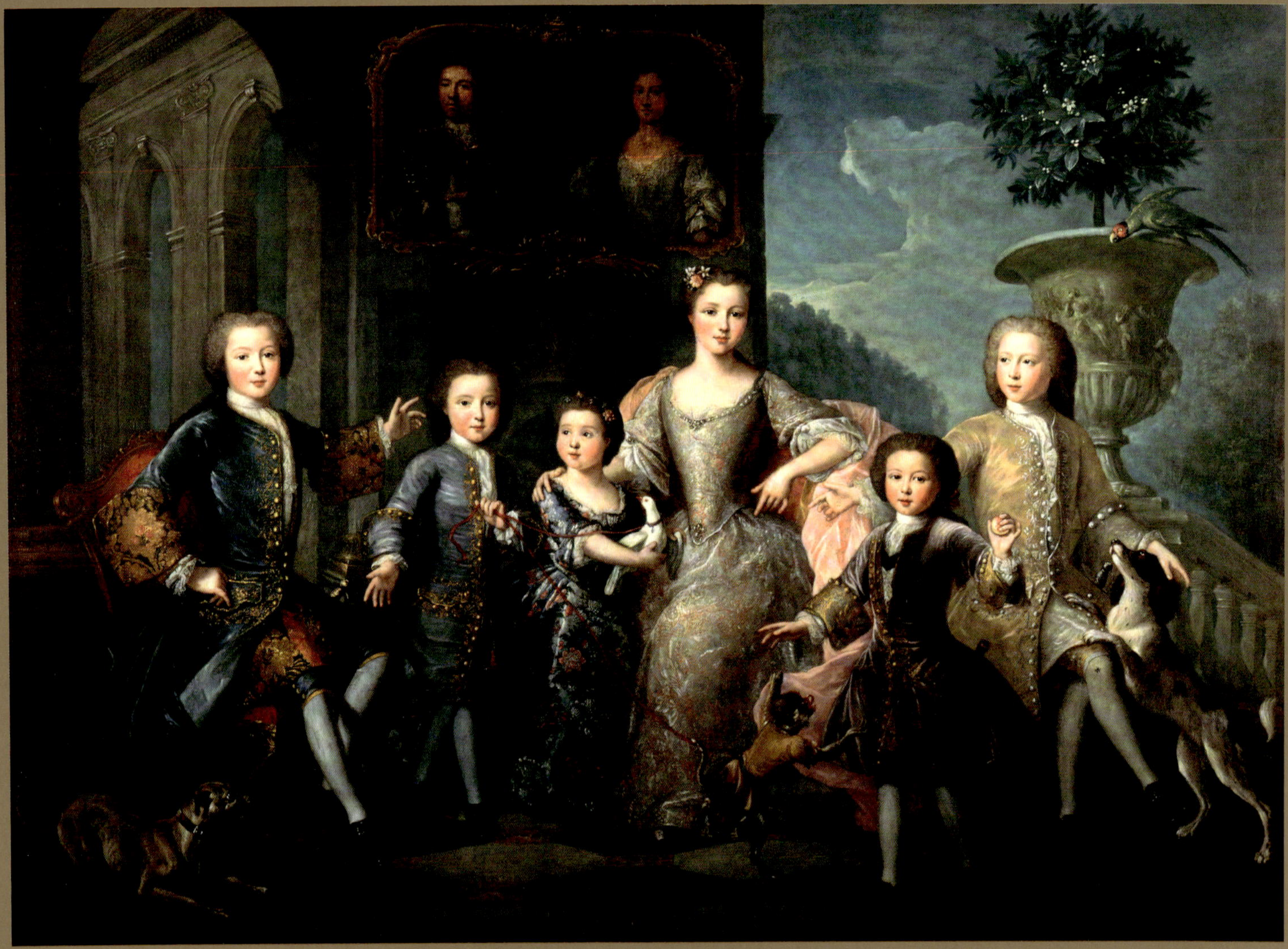

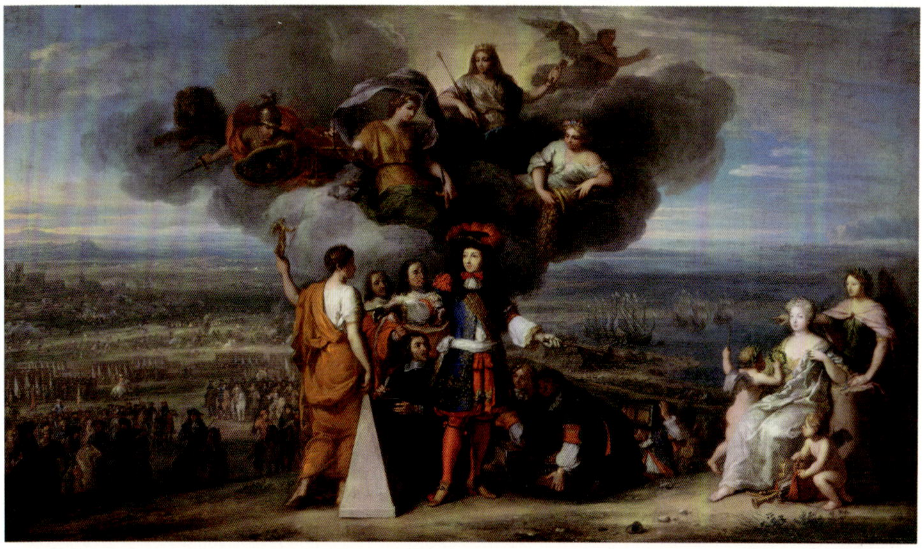

Louis XIV Declaring War on the Netherlands (1672)
Charles Le Brun (1619–1690) and Adam-François Van der Meulen (1632–1690)
Szépművészeti Múzeum, Budapest

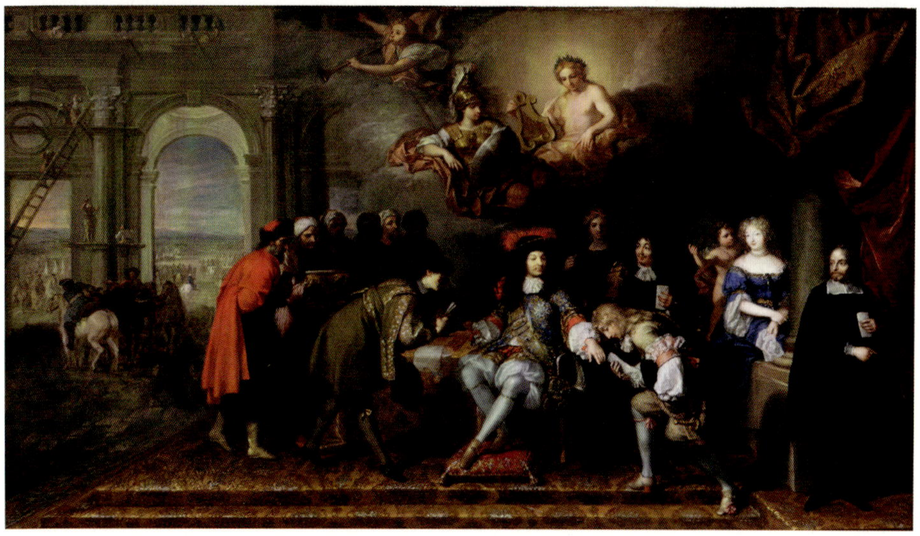

Louis XIV Receiving Ambassadors at the Signing of the Treaty of Nijmegen (1678)
Charles Le Brun (1619–1690) and Adam-François Van der Meulen (1632–1690)
Szépművészeti Múzeum, Budapest

(1661–1731), who, from 1722, fitted out a "room of conquests"—a gallery dedicated to the battles and the great warriors of the century of Louis XIV.

By marriage, his son-in-law Jacques-François-Léonor, son of Jacques de Matignon, count of Torigni, already an art lover, acquired the duchy-peerage of Valentinois, adopting the Grimaldi name and coat of arms. A sovereign prince under the name Jacques I after the death of his wife Louise-Hippolyte, in 1733 he abdicated in favor of his son, who reigned as Honoré III and brought the best part of the palatine art collection to the Hôtel de Matignon, Paris. His collection originates not only from these twin inheritances, but also from his personal taste and efforts. From the very first years of his marriage, he increased the number

The Family of the Duke of Valentinois
1733–34
Pierre Gobert (1662–1744)
Palais Princier, Monaco

of pictures, initially with copies, then with original commissions from painters, and finally with purchases from dealers. The duke of Valentinois was also keen on coins and medals, silverwork, jewels, books, modern and antique marbles and bronzes, tapestries, furniture, porcelain, and scientific instruments. This multifaceted mania for collecting—of a type more readily associated with the Renaissance than with the Enlightenment, when genuine specialized connoisseurs started to emerge—make it seem that Jacques I was "merely an inquisitive" individual. But it also reveals a will to concretize aristocratic and princely notions of superiority by placing the ruler in the dominant position symbolically in every possible domain.

Out of the some five hundred items devoted to painting in his posthumous inventory, portraiture comprises 39 percent, religious scenes 11 percent, mythological scenes 12 percent, landscapes 16 percent, and genre paintings 12 percent. Scenes from history and pictures of animals both represent less than 5 percent. Among the mythological pictures, gallant scenes represent more than half: Venus and Cupid; Venus and Mars; Venus and Adonis; the rapes of Europa, Helen, and the Sabine women; satyrs taking their pleasure with women, etc. As the duke of Luynes wrote a few days before the death of the prince, Père d'Héricourt, "Theatine and celebrated preacher . . . argues to his face and with reason that several of these pictures, though of great price, should not find space in the house of a Christian, owing to their indecency and the immodesty of their figures." He continues: "the most expensive and most beautiful came from Monaco. . . . These pictures being hugely immodest . . . M. de Valentinois was absolutely determined to burn them in their entirety and have all the unseemly figures expunged; but this he could not do without the assent of his son. Not only did M. de Monaco consent to his father's desire regarding those pictures, but he had it carried out in front of him." The genre scenes betray a liking for the Fleming David Teniers. Moreover, the Flemish school, with painters mainly from the seventeenth century, represents more than a third of the pictures; the seventeenth-century Dutch school, almost a fifth; the French school approximately a third of the painters and little more than a fifth of the pictures; the Italian school, with pictures dating for the most part from the sixteenth and early seventeenth centuries, more or less a quarter.

A prince who prides himself on collecting art must also make sure that his possessions are seen, known, and acknowledged by others. Engravings of certain works mentioning the name of the amateur in guides broadcast the quality of the collection abroad. In 1749 the *Mémorial de Paris,* for example, advises the "curious" to go and see "the Hôtel, or rather the Palace, of the duke of Valentinois. . . . One would need an entire volume to undertake a Description of all the magnificent

The Temptation of Saint Anthony
Mid-seventeenth century
David Teniers the Younger
(1610–1690)
From the collections of Jacques I
Musée des Beaux-Arts, Lille

The Country Surgeon
Mid-1660s
David Teniers the Younger
(1610–1690)
From the collections of Jacques I
Palais Princier, Monaco

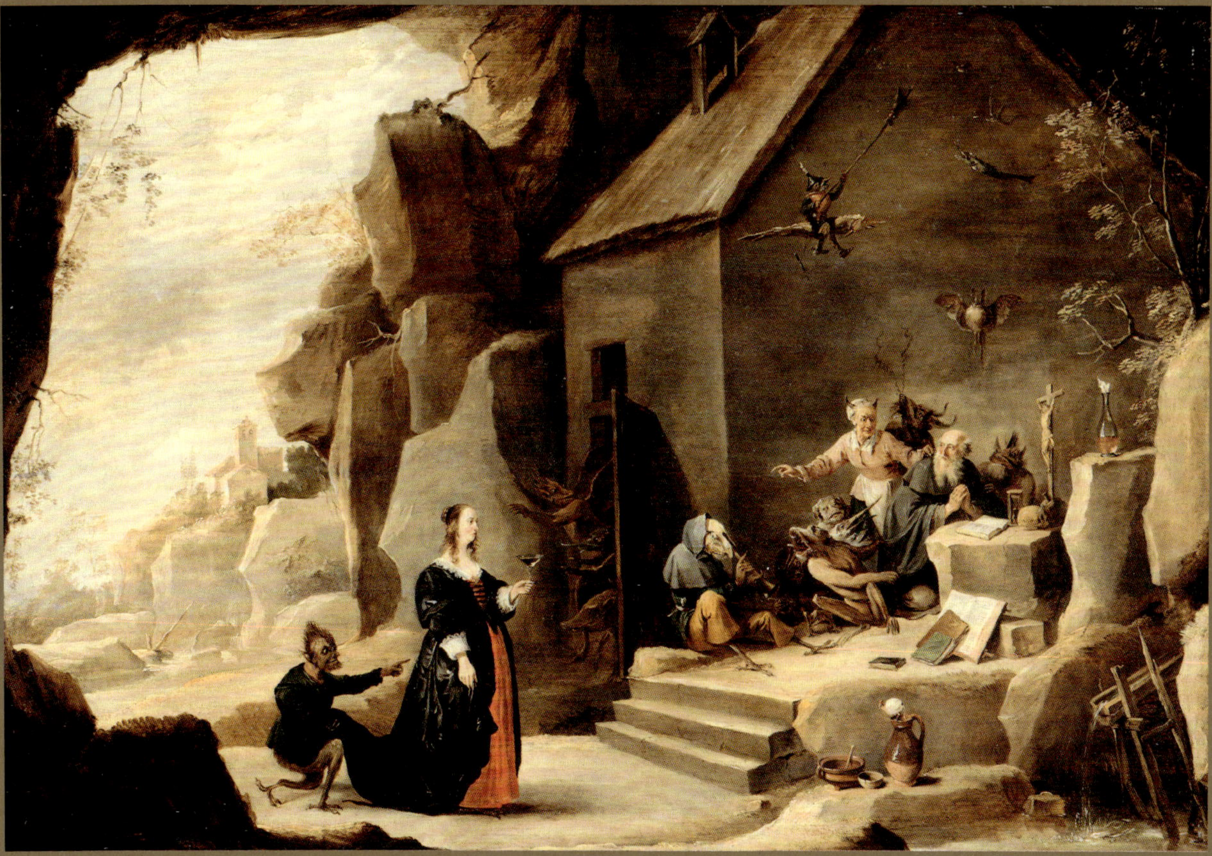

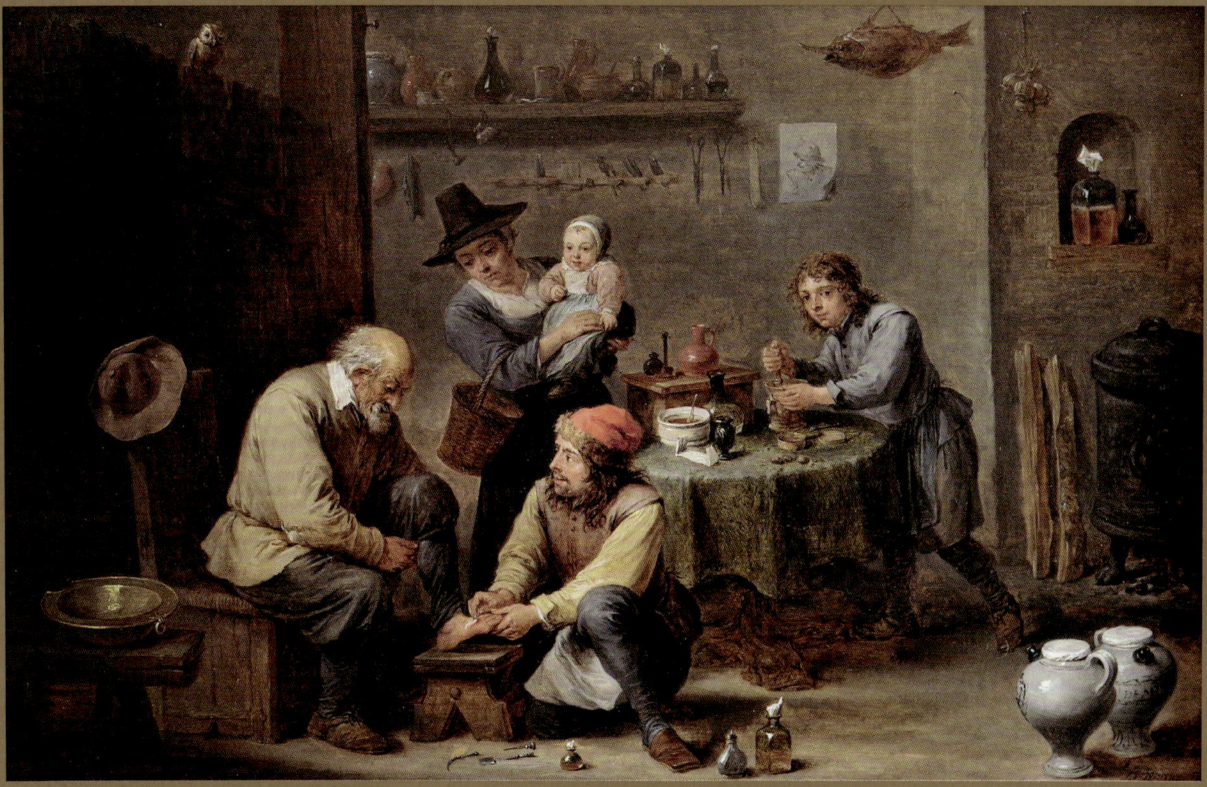

The Duke of Valentinois
1750
Jean-Baptiste Defernex
(1729–1783)
Bibliothèque Mazarine,
Paris

objects that grace its interior . . . to which few in Italy can be compared." Certain contemporaries however did not vouchsafe Jacques I the level of connoisseurship he so craved—in the sense of his being able to distinguish genuine from forgery, copy from original—because, while "M. de Valentinois was one of the *curieux* of Paris who possessed the greatest number of beautiful things . . . as they were mixed with many poor or even bad ones, his collection proclaimed the man of money, rather than the man of taste" (*Correspondance littéraire, philosophique et critique*).

Some haphazard restoration, as much as the eclectic nature of the holdings—sometimes evidence more of ostentation than of solid judgment or artistic expertise—probably prevent the prince from being fully recognized as a genuine *amateur* in the eighteenth-century sense of the word.

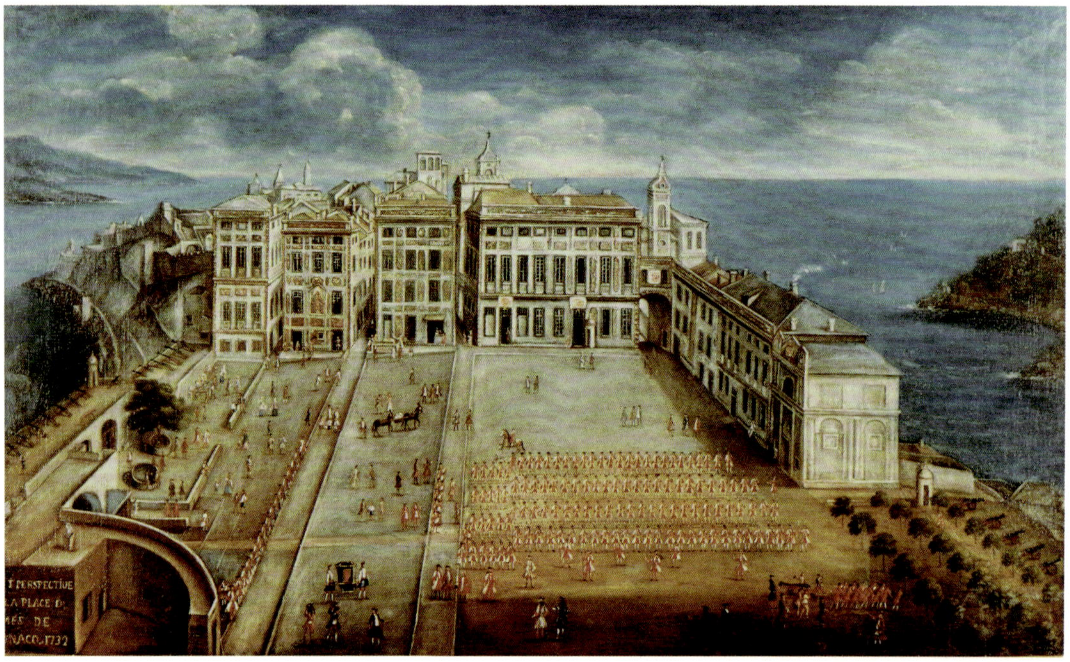

View of the Place d'Armes, Monaco
1732
Dominique-Joseph Bressan
(1670–1746)
Palais Princier,
Monaco

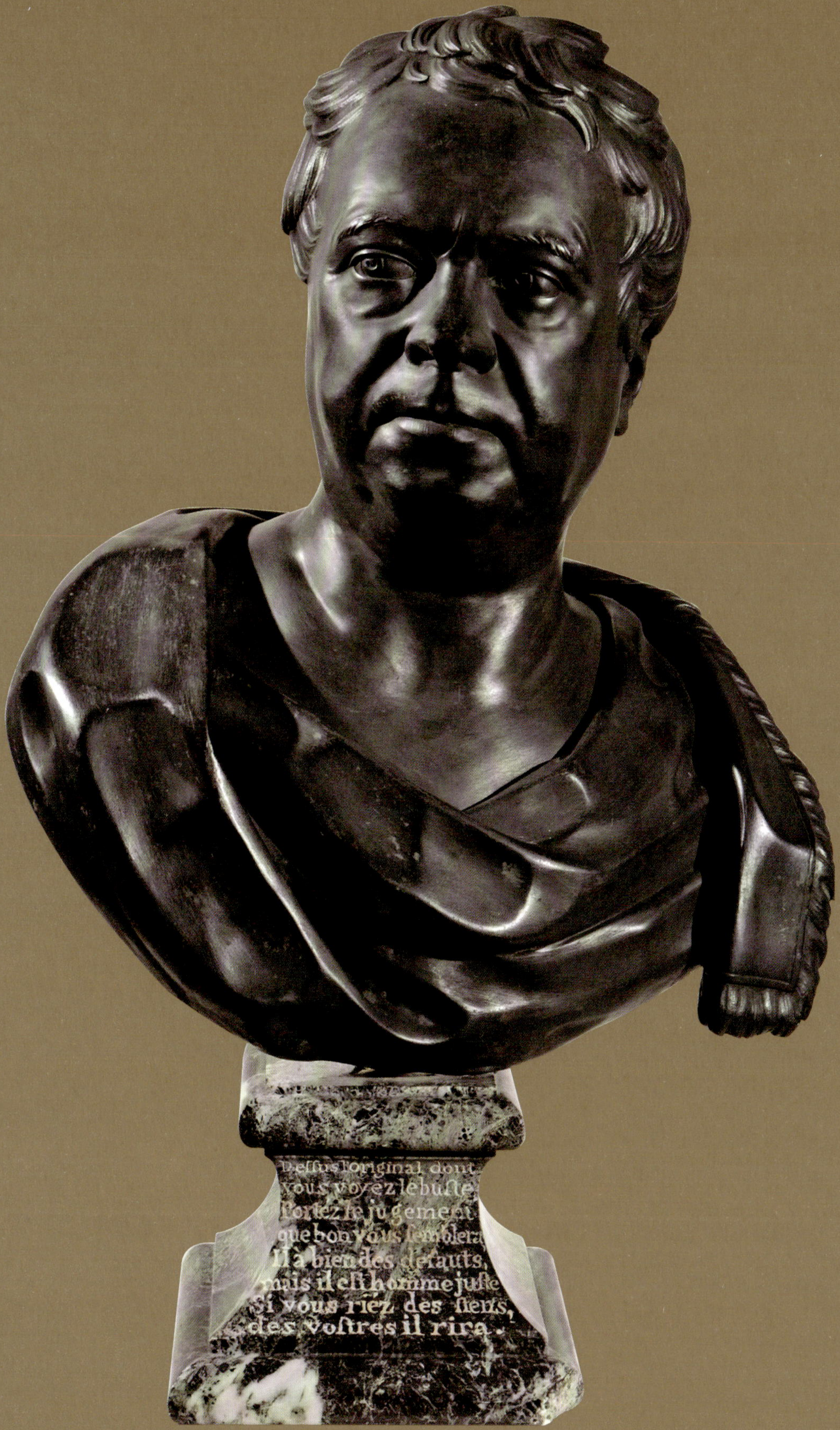
Deſſus l'original dont
vous voyez le buſte
Portez le jugement
que bon vous ſemblera
Il a bien des defauts,
mais il eſt homme juſte
Si vous riez des ſiens,
des voſtres il rira.

Prince Charles III (1818–1889), founding father of Monte-Carlo

Charles III (1818–1889)
1868
Karl Wilhelm Friedrich Bauerle (1831–1912)
Palais Princier de Monaco collection

Ascending to the throne in 1856, Prince Charles III strove to turn the principality of Monaco into a modern state, recognized internationally and furnished with all the attributes of sovereignty. With this in mind, he reformed the justice system and government, and expanded diplomatic relations. Introducing a "festival of the sovereign" in 1857, a year later he instituted a national decoration, the Order of Saint Charles. It was he, too, who, in 1881, allotted the country its national flag, revived the mint (that had fallen into disuse in 1838), began issuing the principality's own postage stamps in 1885, pushed through a policy of religious autonomy by facilitating the institution of a bishopric in 1887, and ensured that Monaco became a participant in the great international exhibitions.

But for tourists the character of Charles III remains more closely associated with the creation of a new city, baptized Monte-Carlo ("Mount Charles" in Italian). Founded in 1866 on the Spélugues plateau, the new district centered on the casino and the Hôtel de Paris, which started catering for guests in 1864. Very quickly, hotels, restaurants, cafés, villas, and apartment buildings sprung up. A place of worship was also erected, the church of Saint-Charles, consecrated in 1883.

Manifestly it was the casino, enlarged on a number of occasions, that formed the nucleus of what proved a magnet to European aristocracy. Inaugurated in 1879, the remit for the opera house had been awarded to Charles Garnier—architect of the Paris Opéra, no less—and major artists of the period furnished its interior and exterior decoration.

It is thanks to Prince Charles III that Monaco and its legendary district of Monte-Carlo secured such international glamour. At his death in 1889, however, the Monegasque sovereign could never have imagined the aura that would one day surround the principality.

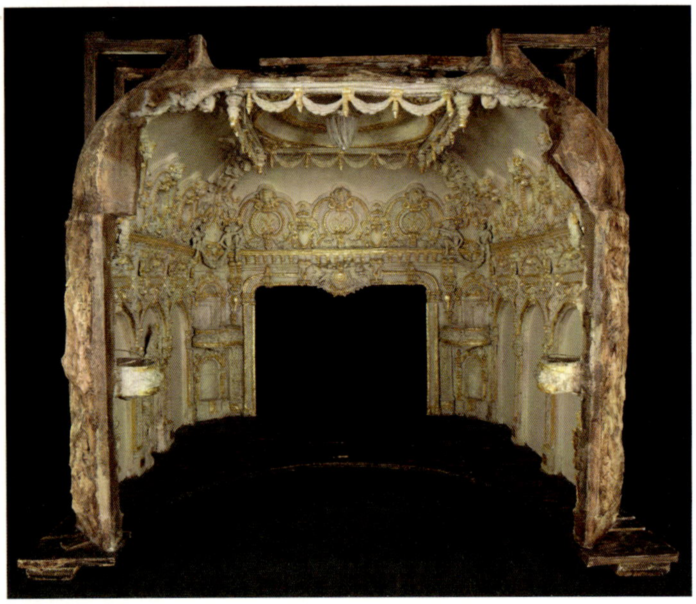

Model of the Salle Garnier, Opéra de Monte-Carlo
c. 1878
Charles Garnier (1825–1898)
Société des Bains de Mer, Monaco (on deposit to the Nouveau Musée National de Monaco)

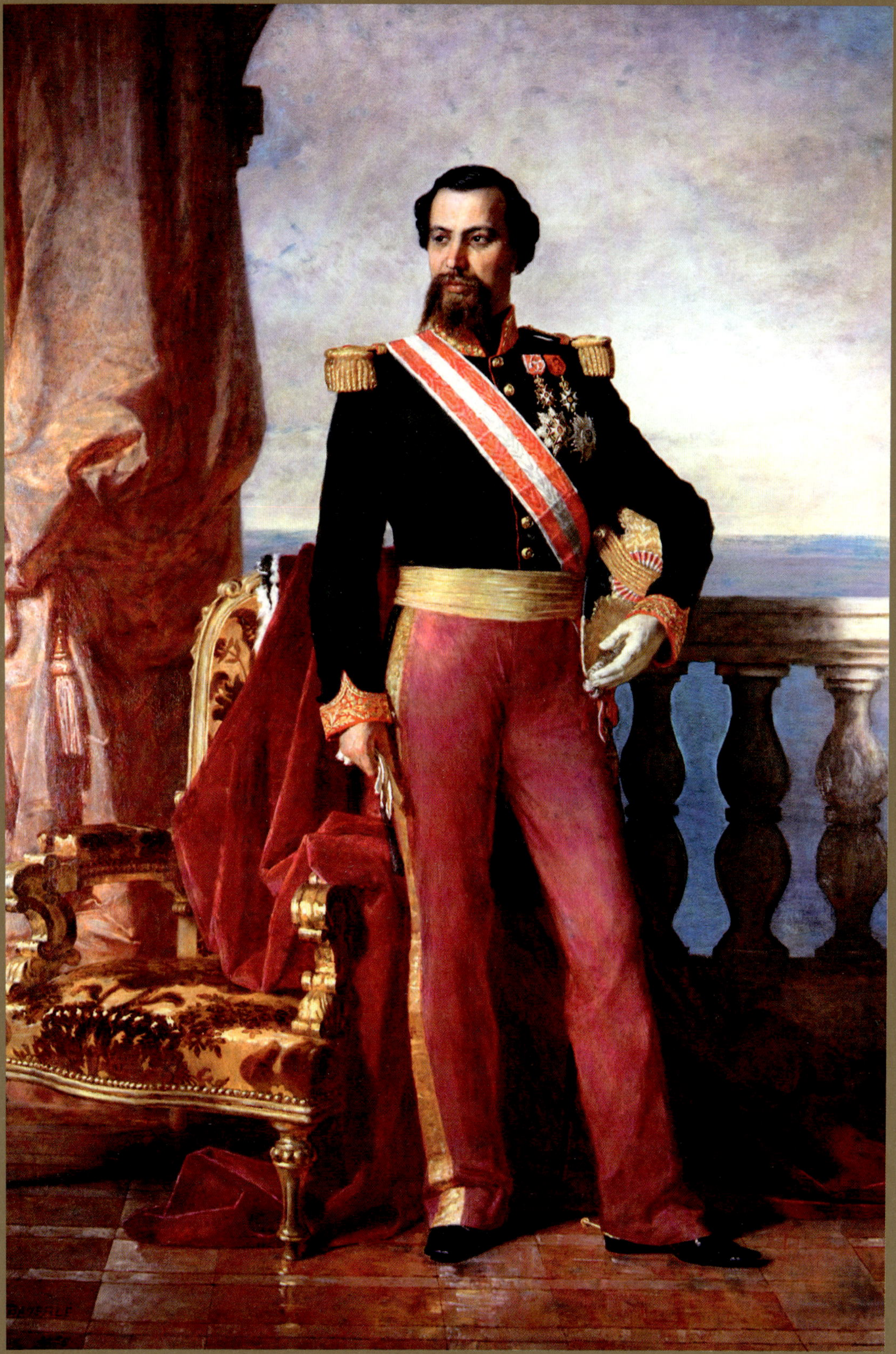

Albert I of Monaco (1848–1922), the navigator prince, and his encounter with Portugal

Jacqueline Carpine-Lancre

A reflection of their inextricable matrimonial ties, in the Europe of the monarchs it was customary to open official correspondence between male sovereigns with the formula *"Monsieur mon Cousin."* If Prince Albert was indeed the "first cousin of a sister-in-law of the Queen of Portugal," no meaningful family links have been established between the house of Braganza and the Grimaldis.

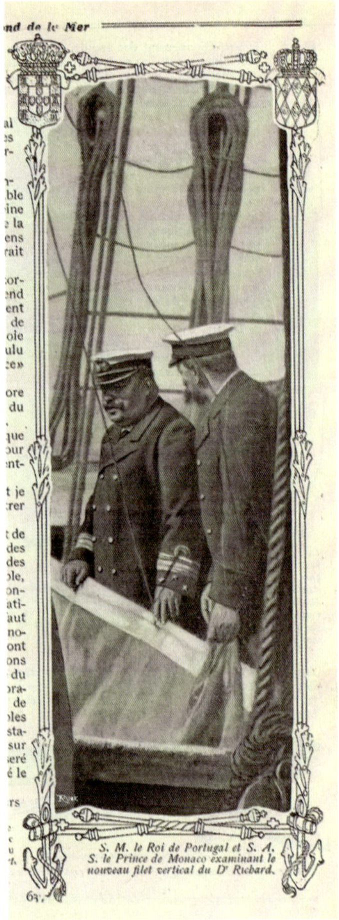

King Carlos of Portugal and Prince Albert I of Monaco aboard the second Princesse-Alice
July 1904, Lisbon
Published in Paul Portier «Le fond de la mer», *Je sais tout*, 1er a., n° 11, December 15, 1905, p. 637

Nevertheless, a special relationship between the two Catholic states of southern Europe did spring up through the personal affinities of their rulers. It is not impossible to believe, moreover, that some memory of the Portuguese Infante Henrique o Navegador (Henry the Navigator) might linger behind the title Prince Albert chose for his autobiography, *La Carrière d'un navigateur.*

The sea played a seminal role in the life and work of Prince Albert: first experiences in Lorient, followed by two years military service in the Spanish royal navy gave him his sea legs. In England, he acquired a schooner, the *Hirondelle,* which he decided, not without temerity, to sail to Monaco without waiting for clement weather. Putting in at Lisbon on December 31, 1873, he was quickly enchanted by the Tagus estuary, luxuriant scenery, and glorious monuments, such as the Belem Tower. During his stay in Portugal, he was received with the utmost courtesy by the royal couple, Luís (1838–1889) and Maria Pia (1847–1911), "charming young people who cannot have been more straightforward." Albert was also amazed by the art collections in the Palácio das Necessidades.

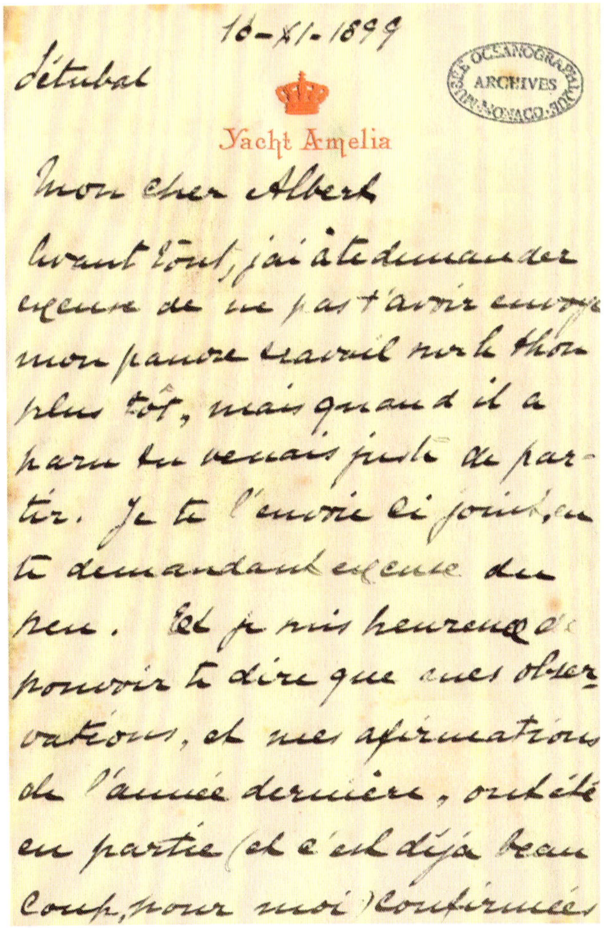

16-XI-1899
Sétubal
ARCHIVES
Yacht Amelia
Mon cher Albert
Avant tout, j'ai à te demander
excuse de ne pas t'avoir envoyé
mon pauvre travail sur le thon
plus tôt, mais quand il a
paru tu venais juste de par-
tir. Je te l'envoie ci joint, en
te demandant excuse du
peu. Et je suis heureux de
pouvoir te dire que mes obser-
vations, et mes afirmations
de l'année dernière, ont été
en partie (et c'est déjà beau
coup, pour moi) confirmées

Autographed letter from King Carlos of Portugal to Prince Albert (Setubal, November 10, 1899)
Musée Océanographique de Monaco, Archives

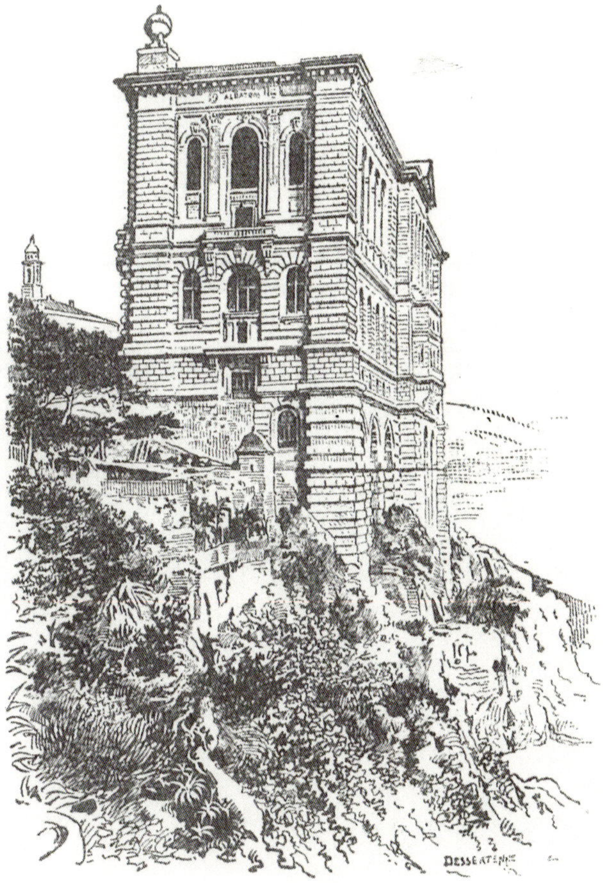

Musée Océanographique de Monaco
1910
Engraving by
Maurice Dessertenn

Five years later, he set sail on a lengthy sea voyage from Tangier to the Canary Islands, Madeira, and the Azores, before stopping off again in Lisbon where he discovered the picturesque Palácio da Pena and its flourishing park. In 1889, a few weeks after the accession of Prince Albert I in Monaco, Carlos (1863–1908), eldest son of Luís, became "King of Portugal and of the Algarve." The two sovereigns met at the conclusion of the 1894 campaign aboard a yacht especially built for oceanographic research, the *Princesse-Alice*. A profound and durable friendship struck up between the two enthusiastic mariners, who also shared a keen interest in the observation of nature and the practice of photography.

A detailed examination of the prince's yacht and the equipment aboard induced Carlos to take up oceanographic research. With four yachts, all named *Amelia*, he proceeded to undertake almost three hundred operations surveying and examining biological samples from along the coast of Portugal. From that time, the king and prince began a friendly correspondence dominated by

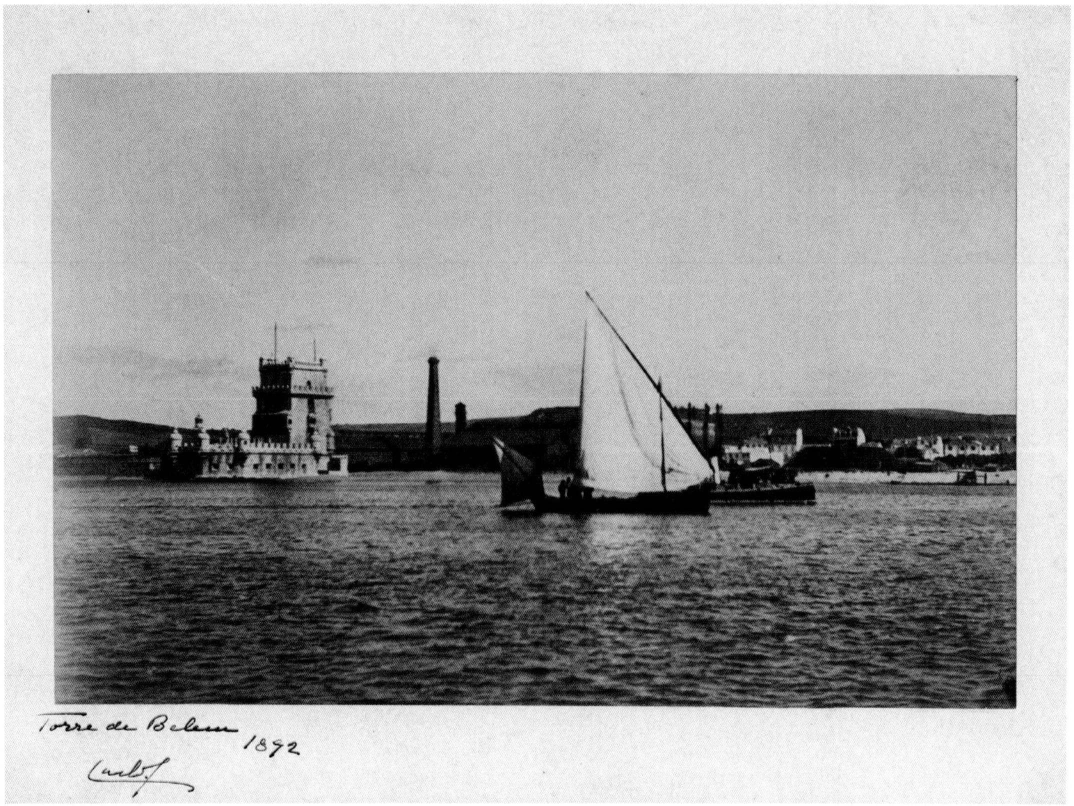

The Belem Tower in Lisbon. Photograph by King Carlos of Portugal, 1892
Musée Océanographique de Monaco collection

scientific themes, though it also deals with artistic, social, and political questions. The establishment of meteorological observatories on the Azores emerges as a major concern in their letters and conversations. From his early days at sea, the prince had become convinced that a relay station between meteorologists in North America and Europe was essential and that the Azores represented its ideal geographical location. Prince Albert was to achieve his goal only after twenty years spent lobbying heads of state, scientists, and diplomats.

On February 1, 1908, Carlos was assassinated in Lisbon, an event that greatly upset the prince. At the inauguration of the Musée Océanographique which houses animals collected by the murdered king and copies with autograph dedications of his scientific publications, due homage was paid to an "erudite, artistic, and fine monarch."

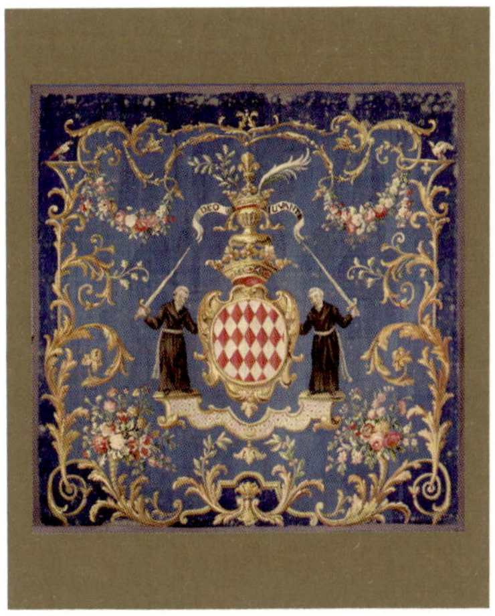

Tapestry with the arms of the Grimaldis, princes of Monaco
Seventeenth century
Aubusson tapestry
263 × 253 cm
Palais Princier, Monaco

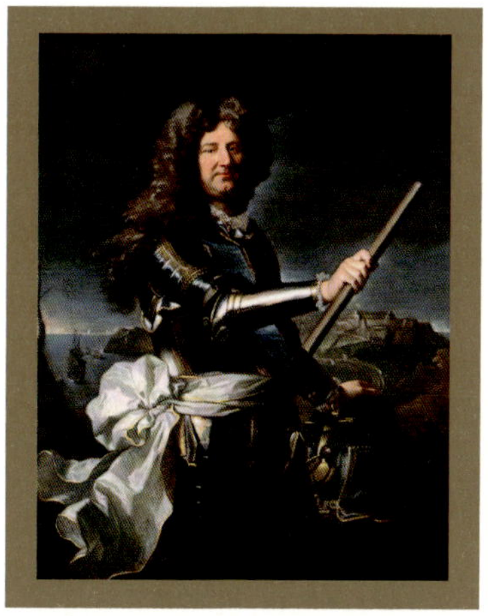

Antoine I (1661–1731)
1705
Hyacinthe Rigaud (1659–1743)
Oil on canvas
176 × 144 cm (inc. frame)
Palais Princier, Monaco

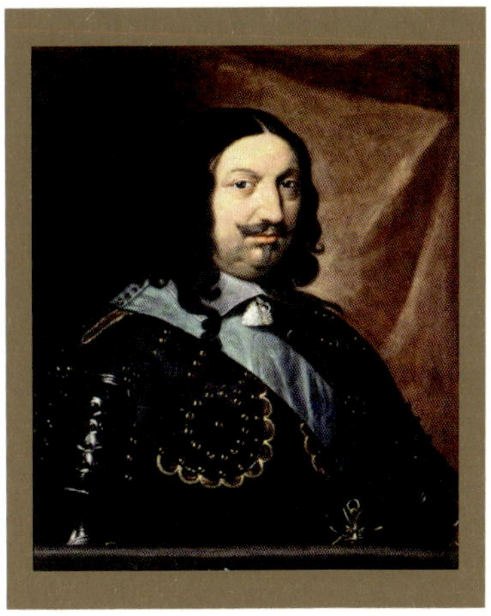

Honoré II (1597–1662)
1651
Attributed to Philippe de Champaigne (1602–1674)
Oil on canvas
72 × 58 cm
Palais Princier, Monaco

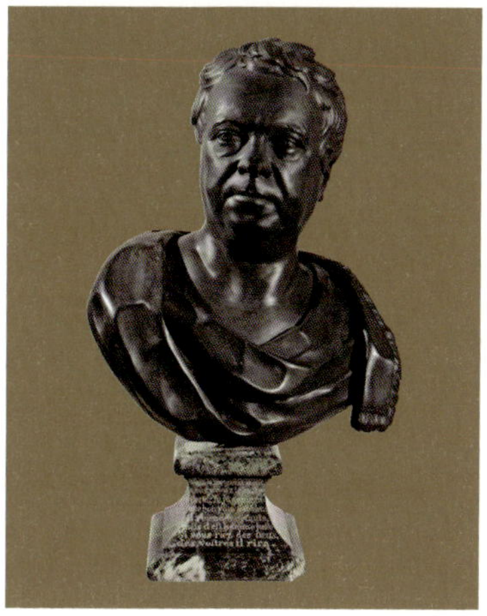

The Duke of Valentinois
1750
Jean-Baptiste Defernex (1729–1783)
Bronze
H. 64 cm
Bibliothèque Mazarine, Paris

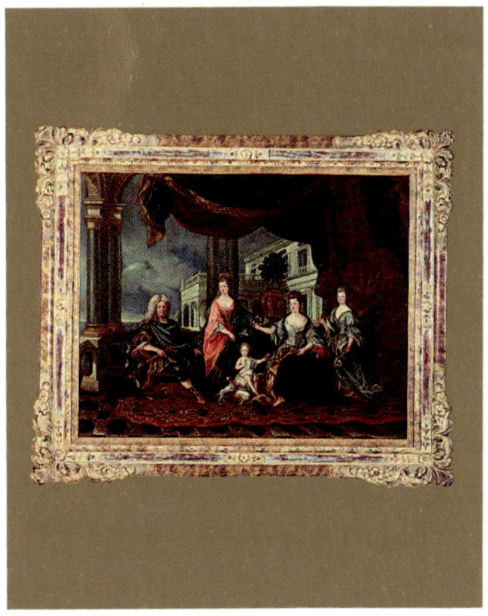

The Family of Prince Antoine I (1661–1731)
1712
Attributed to Jean-Baptiste Van Loo (1684–1745)
Oil on canvas
81.1 × 100.2 cm
Musée des Beaux-Arts, Saint-Lô

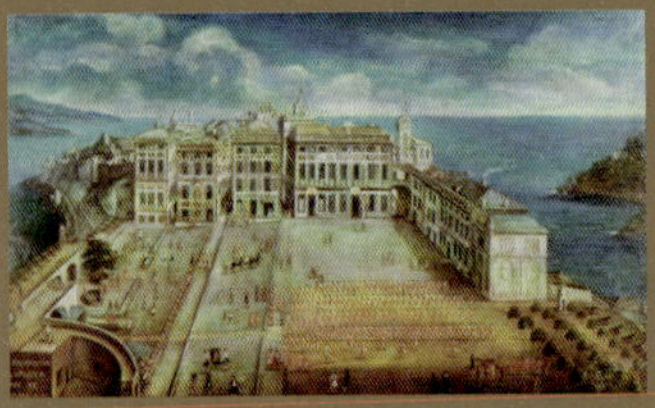

View of the Place d'Armes, Monaco
1732
Dominique-Joseph Bressan (1670–1746)
Oil on canvas
87 × 131 cm
Palais Princier, Monaco

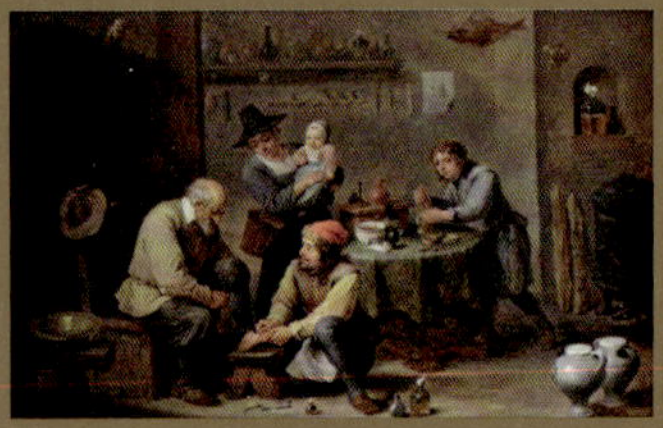

The Country Surgeon
Mid-1660s
David Teniers the Younger (1610–1690)
Oil on wood
36.8 × 50.7 cm
Palais Princier, Monaco

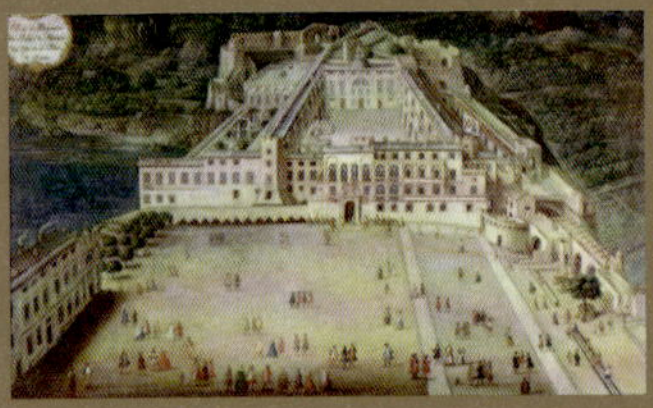

View of the Palace of Monaco from the Place d'Armes
1732
Dominique-Joseph Bressan (1670–1746)
Oil on canvas
87 × 131 cm
Palais Princier, Monaco

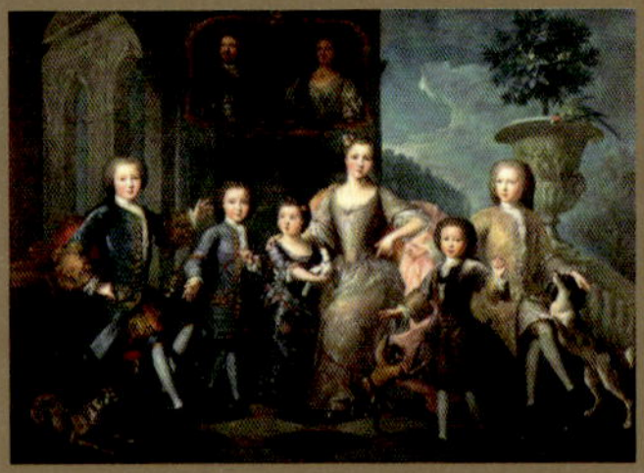

The Family of the Duke of Valentinois
1733–34
Pierre Gobert (1662–1744)
Oil on canvas
150 × 198 cm
Private collection

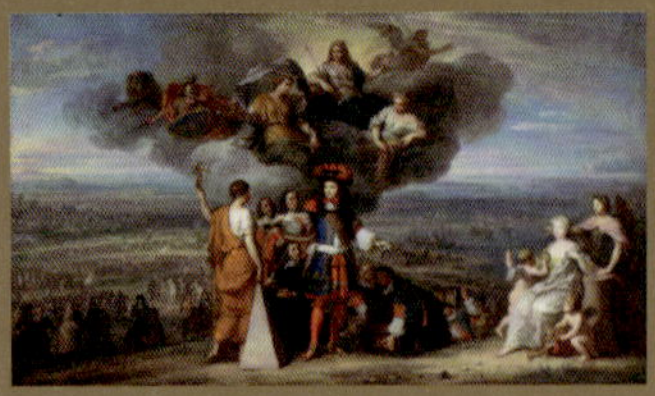

Louis XIV Declaring War on the Netherlands (1672)
Charles Le Brun (1619–1690)
and Adam-François Van der Meulen (1632–1690)
Oil on canvas
70 × 116.5 cm
Szépmüvészeti Múzeum, Budapest

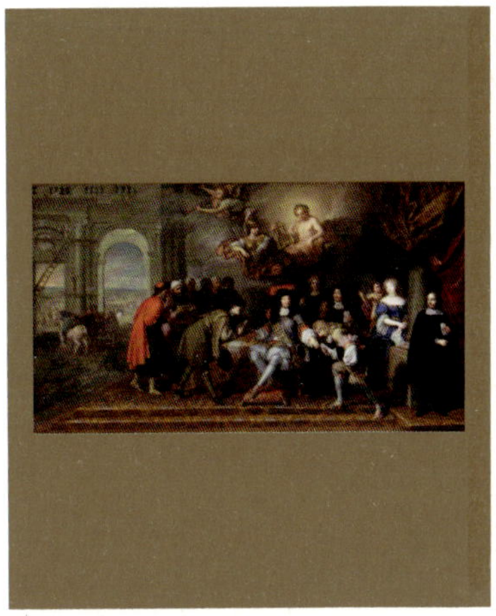

Louis XIV Receiving Ambassadors at the Signing of the Treaty of Nijmegen (1678)
CHARLES LE BRUN (1619–1690) and ADAM-FRANÇOIS VAN DER MEULEN (1632–1690)
Oil on canvas
70 × 116.5 cm
Szépművészeti Múzeum, Budapest

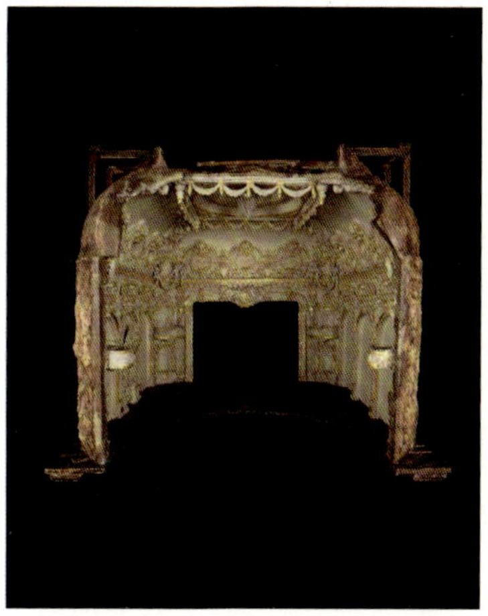

Model of the Salle Garnier, Opéra de Monte-Carlo
c. 1878
CHARLES GARNIER (1825–1898)
Polychrome, gilded model made of plaster, wood, cardboard, metal, and cloth
96 × 90.5 × 90 cm
Société des Bains de Mer, Monaco (on deposit to the Nouveau Musée National de Monaco)

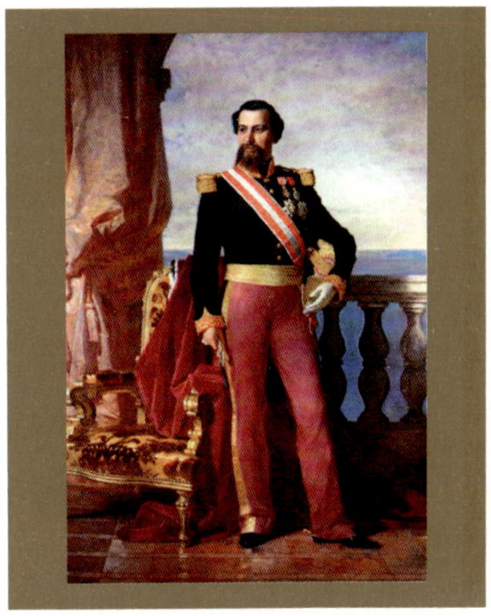

Charles III (1818–1889)
1868
KARL WILHELM FRIEDRICH BAUERLE (1831–1912)
Oil on canvas
240 × 161.5 cm
Palais Princier de Monaco collection

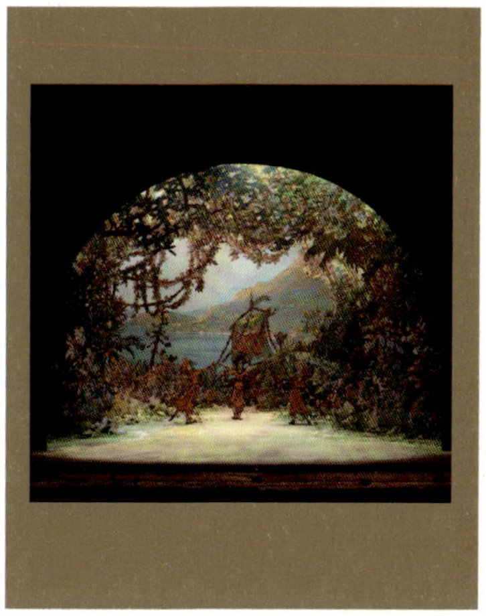

***La Côte d'Azur* ballet set**
1902
ALPHONSE VISCONTI (1856–1941)
3D set models, gouache on paper
52.5 × 50.5 × 51 cm
Société des Bains de Mer, Monaco (on deposit to the Nouveau Musée National de Monaco)

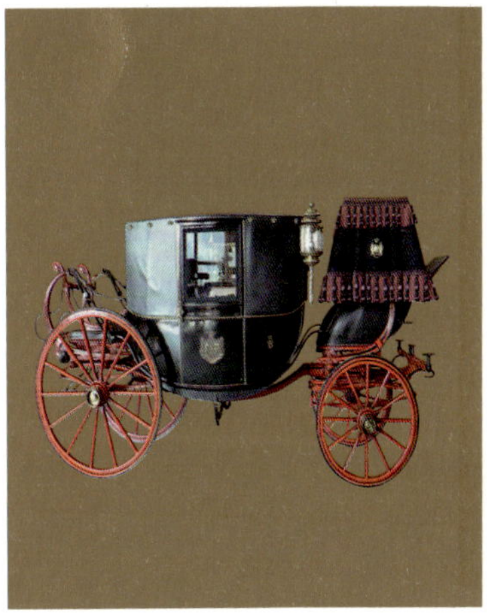

Berlin of Prince Charles III
1865–89
BINDER FRÈRES, Paris
220 × 435 × 180 cm
Collections de Voitures Anciennes de S. A. S. le Prince de Monaco, Monaco

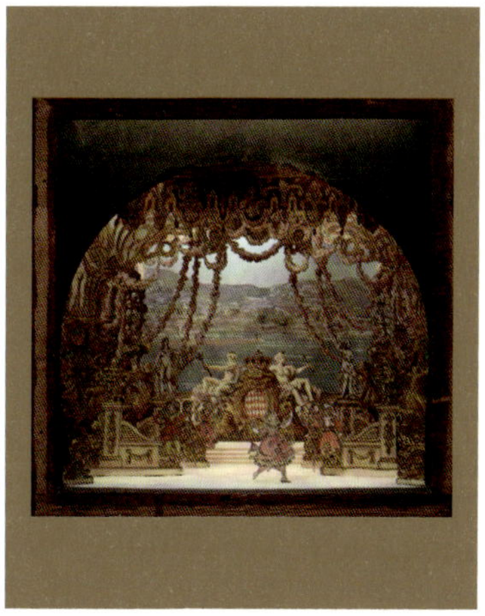

***La Côte d'Azur* ballet set**
1902
ALPHONSE VISCONTI (1856–1941)
3D set models, gouache on paper
48 × 55 × 53.1 cm
Société des Bains de Mer, Monaco (on deposit to the Nouveau Musée National de Monaco)

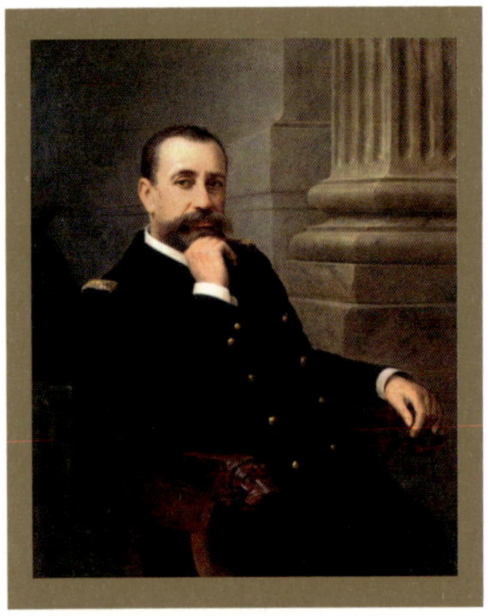

Albert I (1848–1922)
c. 1905
Ignace Spiridon (1848–after 1920)
Oil on canvas
111 × 88 cm
Palais Princier de Monaco Collection, on deposit to the Musée d'Anthropologie Préhistorique de Monaco

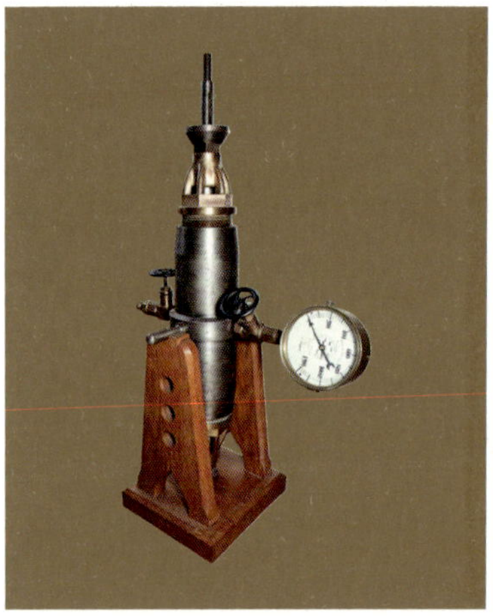

High-pressure bottle, designed by Prince Albert I
Jules Le Blanc (manufacturer)
c. 1890
97.5 × 40 cm
Musée Océanographique de Monaco, Collection

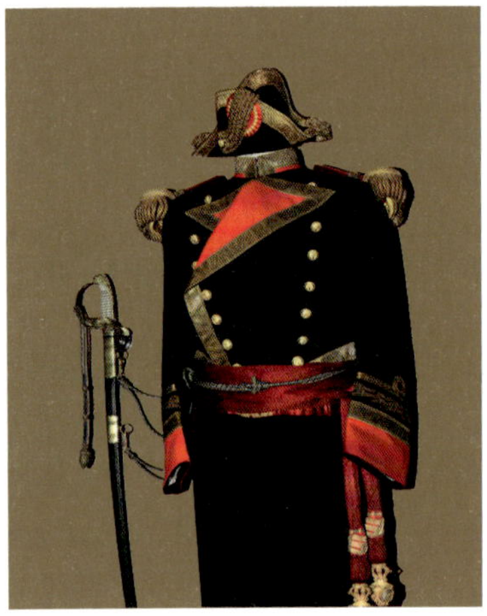

Rear admiral's Prince Albert I's Spanish Navy uniform
1912
Palais Princier de Monaco Collection, on deposit to the Musée des Princes de Monaco et de Leurs Gardes

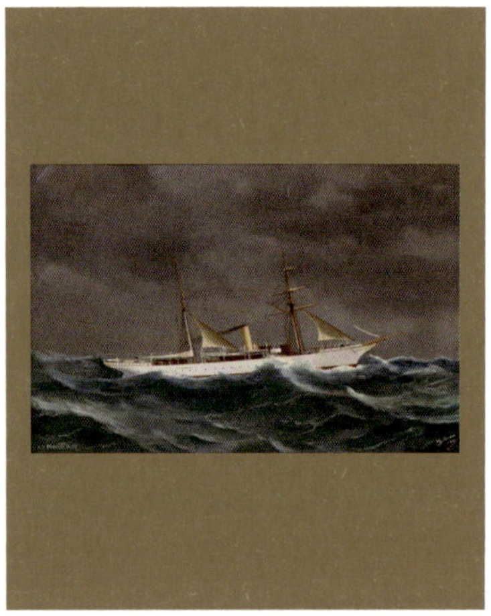

The Second* Princesse-Alice *in Heavy Weather
1909
A. de Simone
Watercolor highlighted with gouache
45 × 63 cm
Palais Princier, Monaco

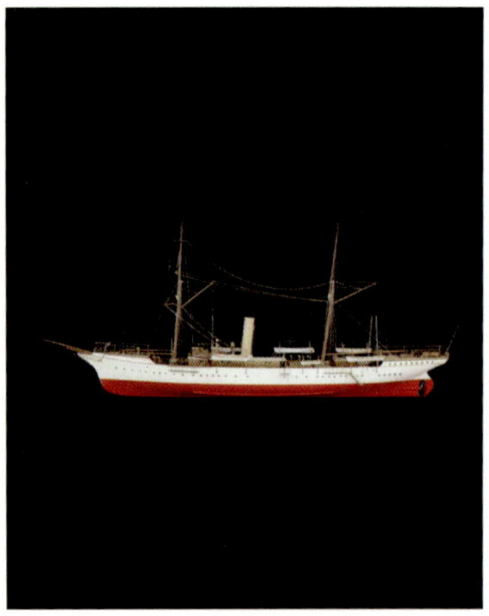

Second Princesse-Alice Model
138 × 290 × 58 cm
Musée Océanographique de Monaco, Collection

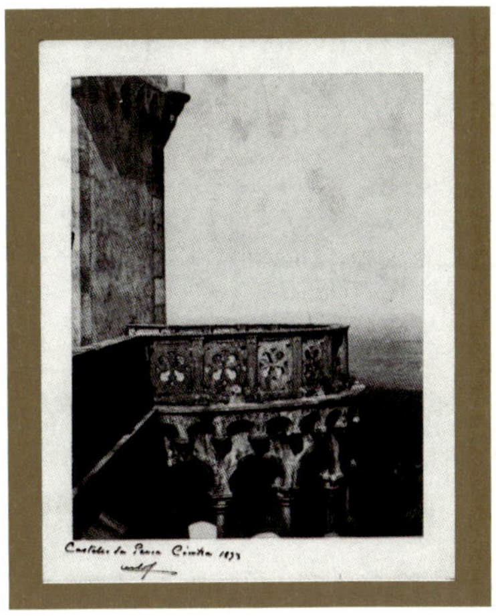

Sixteen photographs
by King Carlos I of Portugal
Musée Océanographique
de Monaco, Collection
Torre de Belem / 1892
15.9 × 24.1 cm
Fragata de Carga / Lisboa 1894
23 × 17.5 cm
Cahique / Paço d'Arcos 1894
23 × 6.5 cm
Barco do Algarve (de carga) /
Lisboa 1892
17.6 × 23.9 cm
Saveiro / Cascaes 1893
16.6 × 22.8 cm
Enviadas / Cascaes 1893
15.7 × 24.3 cm
Muleta e Enviada / Cascaes 1894
23.8 × 15 cm
Praia da Ribeira (Saveiros) /
Cascaes 1893
16.6 × 24 cm
Cahique de Carga / Lisboa 1893
22.5 × 16.3 cm
Praia da Ribeira / Cascaes 1893
23v16.6 cm
Enviada / Cascaes 1893
17 × 23.1 cm
Castello da Pena / Cintra 1893
23.4 × 17.2 cm
Muleta / Cascaes 1893
17. × 24.3 cm
Muleta / Cascaes 1893
16.6v22.3 cm
Muleta / Cascaes 1893
16.6 × 22.9 cm
Fragatas da Carga / Lisboa 1894
22.9 × 16.6 cm

ANNEX

ADRIANSEN, Inge, Lennart S. Madsen, and Carsten Porskrog Rasmussen, eds. *De slesvigske hertuger.* Historisk Samfund for Sønderjylland, 2005.

ALBERT Ier, prince de Monaco. "Discours de S. A. S. le Prince de Monaco [29 mars 1910]." In *Discours prononcés à l'occasion des fêtes d'inauguration du Musée océanographique de Monaco, 29 mars 1910-1er avril 1910.* Montrouge, Imprimerie Draeger, 1910, p. 5–11.

ALBERT Ier, prince de Monaco. *La Carrière d'un navigateur,* 150 drawings by Louis Tinayre. Paris, Hachette, 1913–14.

Alexander II and Tsarskoye Selo. Galerie Cameron / Palace-Museum of Tsarskoye Selo, 2000.

ALEXANDER OF RUSSIA. *Einst war ich ein Grossfürst.* Leipzig, Paul List Verlag, 1932.

BARKOWEZ, Olga, Fjodor Federow, and Alexander Krylow. *"Peterhof ist ein Traum..." Deutsche Prinzessinnen in Russland.* Berlin, Ed. Q, 2001.

BARBERIS, W. (gen. ed.). *I Savoia. I secoli d'oro di una dinastia europe.* Turin, 2007.

BAER, Winfried. "Ein Bernsteinstuhl für Kaiser Leopold I. Ein Geschenk des Kurfürsten Friedrich Wilhelm von Brandenburg." In *Jahrbuch der Kunsthistorischen Sammlungen in Wien 78,* 1982, p. 92–137.

BERELOWITCH, Wladimir. *Le Grand Siècle russe d'Alexandre Ier à Nicolas II.* Paris, Gallimard, 2005.

BIANCHI, Paola, Andrea Merlotti. *Le strategie dell'apparenza. Cerimoniali, politica e società alla corte dei Savoia in età moderna.* Turin, 2010.

BIANCHI, Paola. *Onore e mestiere. Le riforme militari nel Piemonte del Settecento,* Turin, 2002.

BINE-MULLER, Noëlle. *Quand les Romanov font la Côte d'Azur.* Monaco, 2009.

BJØRN, Claus. *Blot til pynt? Monarkiet i Danmark – i går, i dag og i morgen.* Fremad, 2001.

BOMANN-LARSEN, Tor. *Folket – Haakon & Maud II,* Oslo, 2004, p. 456.

BOTTINEAU, Yves. *L'Art de cour dans l'Espagne de Philippe V.* Bordeaux, 1962; Sceaux, 1993 (enlarged edition).

BRAMSEN, Bo. *Huset Glücksborg. Europas svigerfader og hans efterslægt.* 2 vols. Forum, 2002.

BUK-SWIENTY, Tom. *Dommedag Als. 29. juni 1864.* Gyldendal, 2010.

BUSK LAURSEN, Bodil, and Steen Nottelmann, eds. *Royal Copenhagen Porcelain 1775–2000.*

CARPINE, Christian. *La Pratique de l'océanographie au temps du prince Albert Ier.* Monaco, Musée océanographique, 2002.

CARPINE-LANCRE, Jacqueline, and Luiz VIEIRA CALDAS SALDANHA. *Dom Carlos I, roi de Portugal, Albert Ier, prince de Monaco: souverains océanographes,* Lisbonne, Fondation Calouste Gulbenkian, 1992.

CARPINE-LANCRE, Jacqueline. "'.... *une trace de mes anciens sillages'....* Albert Ier de Monaco et la mer." In André Z. LABARRÈRE (ed), *Monaco, port des princes.* Monaco, 1996, pp. 44–71.

CARPINE-LANCRE, Jacqueline (ed). *Albert Ier, prince de Monaco. Des œuvres de science, de lumière et de paix.* Monaco, Palais de S.A.S. le Prince, 1998.

CARPINE-LANCRE, Jacqueline. "Oceanographic sovereigns: Prince Albert I of Monaco and King Carlos I of Portugal." In Margaret DEACON (ed), Tony RICE, Colin SUMMERHAYES *Understanding the Oceans. A Century of Ocean Exploration.* Londres / New York, UCL Press, 2001, pp. 56–68.

CARPINE-LANCRE, Jacqueline. *Le Prince Albert Ier,* http://www.centrescientifique.mc, 2004.

CARPINE-LANCRE, Jacqueline. "Le prince Albert Ier de Monaco et la science." In *Archives de l'Institut de paléontologie humaine*, vol. 39, 2008, p. 13–26.

CARRÈRE D'ENCAUSSE, Hélène. *Alexandre II, le printemps de la Russie.* Paris, Fayard, 2008.

CARUTTI, Domenico. *Storia del regno di Vittorio Amedeo II.* Turin, 1863.

CASTELNUOVO, E. (gen. ed.). *La reggia di Venaria e i Savoia. Arte, magnificenza e storia di una corte europea.* Exh. cat. Turin, Reggia di Venaria, 2 vols., 2007.

CAZZOLA, Piero and Marina Moretti. *I Russi a San Remo. Tra Ottocento e Novecento.* San Remo, 2005.

CHEVALLIER, Bernard. *Douce et incomparable Joséphine.* Paris, Payot, 1999.

CLAUSEN, Inge-Lise. *Tak for dansen, Louise. Det første glücksborgske kongepar og hele deres europæiske slægt.* Aschehoug, 2003.

DEFRANCE, O. *Léopold I et le clan Cobourg.* Brussels, 2004.

DEHN-NIELSEN, Henning. *Kings and Queens of Denmark.* The Royal Danish Collections at Rosenborg Castle, 2007.

FOUILLERON, Thomas. "Miroir du prince. Le palais de Monaco vu par les voyageurs français (XVIe-XIXe siècle)." In Anne-Marie COCULA, and Michel COMBET, eds. *Châteaux, voyages et voyageurs (ses). Actes des rencontres d'archéologie et d'histoire en Périgord les 25, 26 et 27 septembre 2009.* Bordeaux, Ausonius/Université de Bordeaux III, 2010, p. 19–40.

FOUILLERON, Thomas. *Histoire de Monaco.* Monaco, Direction de l'Éducation nationale, de la Jeunesse et des Sports, 2010.

FOUILLERON, Thomas. *"Culture, sociabilité et politique des princes de Monaco, des Lumières à 1848".* Ph.D., dissertation, Université of Montpellier-III, dir. Henri Michel (dir.), 2007, 2 vols., to be published under the title *Des princes en Europe. Les Grimaldi de Monaco, des Lumières au printemps des peuples.* Paris, Honoré Champion, 2011.

FRICÉRO, E. "Les Russes à Nice au siècle passé." *Nice Historique* 3 (July–September 1952), pp. 54–82.

GAUTIER, Théophile. *Voyage en Russie.* Paris, The Document Box, 1997.

GRANDJEAN, Bredo L. *The Flora Danica Service.* Copenhagen, 1973.

GUICHARD, Charlotte. *Les aAmateurs d'art à Paris au XVIIIe siècle.* Seyssel, Champ Vallon, 2008.

HALÉN, Widar. "Le style néoviking dans l'orfèvrerie norvégienne". In *Rencontres de l'école du Louvre. L'orfèvrerie au XIXe siècle.* Paris, 1994, pp. 229–42.

HALÉN, Widar. *Dragons from the North.* Dublin/Bergen, 1995.

HAMBRO, Carl J. *Taler i Krig.* Oslo, 1945, p. 65.

HANDEN, R. *End of an Era: Victor Amadeus II and Louis XIV 1690–1696.* In R.M. HUTTON, W. (ed.), *Louis XIV and Europe,* London, 1976, p. 259–278.

HANDEN, R. "End of an Era: Victor Amadeus II and Louis XIV, 1690–1696." In R.M. Hutton (ed.), *Louis XIV and Europe.* Londres, 1976, pp. 259–278.

HEIN, Jørgen, and Gerda PETRI, , *The Royal Danish Collections: Christian VIII's Palace Amalienborg.* Amalienborgmuseet, 1999.

HEUER, P., and K. Maurice, *Europäische Pendeluhren.* Munich, 1988, p. 54.

JANSSENS, Gustaaf. "Le Roi Léopold I et le domaine d'Ardenne." In A. DIKENS, and J.-M. DUVOSQUEL, eds. *Louise-Marie, élève de Redouté, et Léopold I en Ardenne.* Brussels, 1991.

JANSSENS, Gustaaf. "König Leopold I., Freiherr von Stockmar und das Gleichgewicht in Belgien und in Europa." In Henker, M., and E. Brockhoff, eds. *Ein Herzogtum und viele Kronen. Coburg in Bayern und Europa. Aufsätze zur Landesausstellung 1997.* Augsburg, 1997.

JANSSENS, Gustaaf, and J. Stengers, eds. *Nouveaux regards sur Léopold I et Léopold II. Fonds d'archives Goffinet.* Brussels, 1997.

JENVOLD, Birgit. "Dagmar and Denmark." In Eiskonen, Satu. *Princess Dagmar – Empress Maria Feodorovna.* South Karelia Museum, 2010.

JESPERSEN, Knud J. V. *Danmarks konger og dronninger.* Gyldendal, 2008.

KAPPEL, Jutta. "Der große Bernsteinschrank. Etwas nie gesehenes und unschätzbahres". In *Bernsteinkunst aus dem Grünen Gewölbe.* Staatlichen Kunstsammlungen Dresden, Berlin and Munich, 2005, pp. 25–37.

KISTE, John van der. *Northern Crowns: The Kings of Modern Scandinavia.* Sutton Publishing, 1998.

KROG, Ole Villumsen (ed). *Flora Danica and the Royal Danish Court.* Exh. cat., Copenhaguen, Christiansborg Palace, 1990.

LABANDE, Léon-Honoré. *Les Portraits des princes et princesses de Monaco exécutés par le peintre Pierre Gobert.* Monaco, Impr. de Monaco, 1908.

LABANDE, Léon-Honoré. *Inventaires du palais de Monaco (1604-1731).* Monaco / Paris, Impr. de Monaco / Picard, 1918.

LABANDE, Léon-Honoré. *Catalogue des peintures, miniatures, aquarelles et dessins formant la collection du palais de Monaco.* Monaco, Impr. de Monaco, 1919.

LABANDE, Léon-Honoré. "L'hôtel de Matignon à Paris." *Gazette des Beaux-Arts* XIII (May–June 1935), pp. 257–70, 347–63.

LABANDE, Léon-Honoré. *Jacques Grimaldi, comte de Torigni, duc de Valentinois, prince de Monaco.* Monaco / Paris, Archives du Palais / Picard, 1939.

LERCHE, Anna, and Markus Mandal. *A Royal Family: The Story of Christian IX and His European Descendants.* Aschehoug, 2003.

LEROY-BEAULIEU, Anatole. *L'Empire des Tsars et les Russes.* Paris, Robert Laffont, 1990.

MADOL, Hans Roger. *Christian IX. Europas svigerfar.* Aschehoug, 2006.

MAGNY, Françoise, and Bruno Pons. "L'hôtel de Matignon." In *Le Faubourg Saint-Germain. La rue de Varenne.* Paris, Délégation à l'action artistique de la Ville de Paris and the Société d'histoire et d'archéologie du VIIe arrondissement / Musée Rodin, 1981.

MARCHESANI, F. *Léopold I, roi diplomate.* Brussels, 2007.

MCLEAN, Roderick R. *Royalty and Diplomacy in Europe, 1890–1914.* Cambridge University Press, 2001.

MERLOTTI, Andrea. *L'enigma delle nobiltà. Stato e ceti dirigenti nel Piemonte del Settecento.* Florence, 2000.

MICHEL, Patrick (ed). *Collections et marché de l'art en France au XVIIIe siècle. Actes de la 3e journée d'études d'histoire de l'art moderne et contemporain.* Bordeaux, Université Michel de Montaigne–Bordeaux III, 2002.

MICHEL, Patrick. *Le Commerce de l'art à Paris dans la seconde moitié du XVIIIe siècle.* Villeneuve d'Ascq, Presses Universitaires du Septentrion, 2007.

MICHEL, Patrick. *Peinture et plaisir. Les goûts picturaux des collectionneurs parisiens au XVIIIe siècle.* Rennes, PUR, 2010.

MORÁN, Miguel (ed). *El arte en la corte de Felipe V.* Exh. cat. Madrid, Museo del Prado / Patrimonio Nacional / Caja Madrid, 2002.

Morán, Miguel. *La imagen del rey. Felipe V y el arte.* Madrid, Nerea, 1990.

Netzer, Susanne. "Bernsteingeschenke in der preußischen Diplomatie des 17. Jahrhunderts." In *Jahrbuch der Berliner Museen* 35, 1993, pp. 227–246.

Nobili Vitelleschi, Amy. *The Romance of Savoy. Victor Amadeus II and his Stuart Bride.* London, 1905.

Obolensky, Alexis, Luc Svetchine, and Pierre-Antoine Gatier. *Les Églises russes de Nice.* Arles, Honoré Clair, 2009.

Olden-Jørgensen, Sebastian. *Prinsessen og det hele kongerige. Christian IX og det glücksborgske kongehus.* Gads Forlag, 2003.

Olsen, Rikke Agnete. *Kongerækken.* Lindhardt og Ringhof, 2005.

Ottomeyer, H., and P. Pröschel. *Vergoldete Bronzen.* Munich, 1986, vol. 1, p. 233.

Palasi, Philippe. "Une identification longtemps attendue: les armoiries du service Demidoff." *Gazette des Beaux-Arts* 132 (July–August 1998), pp. 47–52.

Paléologue, Maurice. *Le Roman tragique de l'empereur Alexandre II.* Paris, 1923

Petri, Gerda. *Det store guldbryllup. Guldbryllupsgaver til Christian IX og Dronning Louise 26. maj 1892.* De Danske Kongers Kronologiske Samling, 1996.

Petri, Gerda, and Peter Wessel Hansen. *Fotografi i Kongehuset / Photography in the Royal House.* De Danske Kongers Kronologiske Samling Amalienborgmuseet, 2005.

Pomian, Krzystof. "Marchands, connaisseurs, curieux à Paris au XVIIIe siècle." *Revue de l'art* 49 (1979), pp. 23–36; reprinted in *Collectionneurs, amateurs et curieux. Paris, Venise: XVIe-XVIIIe siècle.* Paris, Gallimard, 1987.

Preußen 1701. Eine europäische Geschichte. Exh. cat. DHM and the Stiftung Preußische Schlösser und Gärten Berlin-Brandenburg, Berlin, 2001, vol. 2/2, cat. II. 18 and II. 19.

Quazza, Guido. *Le riforme in Piemonte nella prima metà del Settecento.* Modena, 1957.

Ramberg, Trygve. *Med folket. Historien om vårt kongehus,* Oslo 1987, p. 62.

Reineking von Bock, Gisela. *Bernstein. Das Gold der Ostsee.* Munich, 1981, pp. 21, 28, 33.

Rodríguez Ruiz, Delfín (ed). *El Real Sitio de La Granja de San Ildefonso, retrato y escena del rey.* Exh. cat. Madrid, Patrimonio Nacional, 2000.

Rørdam, C. H. *Svundne dage.* 7 vols. Hagerup, 1916–31.

Rohde, Alfred. *Bernstein. Ein deutscher Werkstoff. Seine künstlerische Verarbeitung vom Mittelalter bis zum 18. Jahrhundert.* Berlin, 1937.

Saldanha, Luiz. "King Carlos de Bragança, the Father of Portuguese Oceanography." In Luiz Saldanha (ed.). *Publicações avulsas – Museu Bocage,* n° 2 [*One Hundred Years of Portuguese Oceanography: in the Footsteps of King Carlos de Bragança, Symposium held in Cascais 1-3 February 1996,* Pedro Ré, 1997, pp. 18–38.

Schmidtberger, Ekkehard, and Thomas Richter. *Schatzkunst 800 bis 1800 – Kunsthandwerk und Plastik der Staatlichen Museen Kassel im Hessischen Landesmuseum Kasse.* Wolfratshausen, 2001, p. 252, cat. 110.

Seelig, Lorenz. "German Silver Services at Foreign Courts – Foreign Silver Services at German Courts." In *Royal and Princely Tables of Europe: Commissions and Gifts. International Symposium.* Lisbon, Leonor d'Orey, 1999, pp. 166–79.

SILVESTRINI, Maria Teresa. *La politica della religione. Il governo ecclesiastico nello Stato sabaudo del XVIII secolo.* Florence, 1997.

SKURLOV, Valentin V., and Alexandre N IVANOV.

("Suppliers to the Court"). St. Petersburg, 2002.

STENGERS, J. *L'Action du roi en Belgique depuis 1831. Pouvoir et influence.* Louvain-la-Neuve, 1992; revised ed., 1996.

STORRS, Christopher. *War, Diplomacy and the Rise of Savoy, 1690–1720.* Cambridge, 1999.

STURLUSON, Snorri. *Histoire des rois de Norvège ou Heimskringla,* translate by Francois-Xavier Dillmann. Paris, Gallimard, 2000.

TURC, Jean-Jacques. "Les princes Honoré II et Jacques Ier numismates et collectionneurs." *Annales monégasques* 6 (1982), pp. 129–41.

VERBITSKAYA,Tatiana. . (1843–1865) ("Emperor without Empire: Grand Duke Nicholas Alexandrovich"). Moscow, 2010.

WALTON, Guy. "The Era of Louis XIV: A Turning Point in the History of Diplomatic Gifts." In *The French Court Style and its Influence.* Toronto, 1991, pp. 199–213.

WEDEL JARLSBERG, Fritz. *1905, Kongevalget.* Oslo, 1946, p. 271.

WILKENSCHILDT, Merete. *Kongelige bryllupper i Danmark gennem 500 år.* Lindhardt og Ringhof, 2002.

Zennaro, Tiziana, ed. *Genua Tempu Fà.* *Tableaux de maîtres actifs à Gênes du XVIIe au XVIIIe siècle et relations d'art et d'histoire entre la République de Gênes et la Principauté de Monaco.* Monaco. Maison d'Art, 1997.

Histoire universelle depuis le commencement du monde jusqu'à présent, Amsterdam/Leipzig, Arkstèe et Merkus, 1776, *Histoire moderne,* vol. XXIV, pp. 401–02.

The Tsar and the President: Alexander II and Abraham Lincoln, Liberator and Emancipator. The American-Russian Cultural Cooperation Foundation, 2009.

The Modern Part of an Universal History, vol. XXXVII, London, Millar, 1762, pp. 509, 516.

The Tsar and the President. Alexander II and Abraham Lincoln. Liberator and Emancipator. Exh. cat. The American-Russian Cultural Cooperation Foundation, The Oshkosh Public Museum, Oshkosh, Wisconsin, 2008, The Kansas City Union Museum, Kansas City, Missouri, 2009.

INDEX BY NAME

INDEX BY PLACE

© Alinari / Roger-Viollet: p. 312, p. 317, p. 319
© Archives du Palais Princier – G. Luci: p. 336-338, p. 342, p. 345, p. 349-352
© Archives du Palais Princier – G. Moufflet: p. 69-71, p. 205, p. 341, p. 350, p. 352
© Archives du Palais Princier – J.-M. Moll – G. Luci: p. 334, p. 349
© Bastian Krack -Bayerisches Nationalmuseum München: p. 265, p. 273, p. 275-279
© Bibliothèque nationale de France: p. 324, p. 346
© BPK, Berlin, Dist. RMN / Saturia Linke: p. 227, p. 240
© BPK, Berlin, Dist. RMN, Fotostudio Bartsch: p. 237-238, p. 240-241
© Bundesmobilienverwaltung, Hofburg Wien, Sisi-Museum. Foto: Tina King: p. 289-290
© Bundesmobilienverwaltung, Hofmobiliendepot, Möbel Museum Wien. Foto: Andreas Gugler: p. 292
© Bundesmobilienverwaltung, Hofmobiliendepot, Möbel Museum Wien. Foto: Tina King: p. 283, p. 290
© Bundesmobilienverwaltung, Silberkammer, Hofburg Wien: p. 291
© Bundesmobilienverwaltung, Silberkammer, Hofburg Wien. Foto: Andreas Gugler: p. 293
© Bundesmobilienverwaltung, Silberkammer, Hofburg Wien. Foto: Edgar Knaack: p. 293
© Bundesmobilienverwaltung, Silberkammer, Hofburg Wien. Foto: M.L. Herzberger: p. 293
© Bundesmobilienverwaltung, Silberkammer, Hofburg Wien. Foto: Marianne Haller: p. 291-292
© Château de Versailles, Dist. RMN / Jean-Marc Manaï: p. 67-68, p.79, p. 83
© Hans Thorwid /Nationalmuseum, Stockholm: p. 166, p. 168, p. 170, p. 173, p. 175-176, p. 179, p. 182, p. 184
© Hessische Hausstiftung, Kronberg i. T. (Germany): p. 267
© imedia: p. 84, p. 86-87, p. 89-90, p. 92-95
© J-J. L'Héritier: p. 205, p. 207, p. 209
© Koninklijk Huisarchief. Photo: Mr. B. Grishaaver: p. 110, p. 115-116, p. 119-123
© Koninklijk Huisarchief. Photo: Mr. E. Molenaar: p. 113-114, p. 120, p. 122-123
© Kunsthistorisches Museum, Vienna: p. 287, p. 291-292, p. 296, p. 307
© Luciano Pedicini: p. 320, p. 323, p. 325-333
© Musée royal de l'Armée et d'Histoire militaire, N° Inv KLM-MRA: 501258 et 503092. Photographe: Josse Van Den Steen: p. 108
© Musée royal de l'Armée et d'Histoire militaire, N° Inv KLM-MRA: 503453. Photographe: Josse Van Den Steen: p. 103, p. 108
© Musée royal de l'Armée et d'Histoire militaire, N° Inv KLM-MRA: 11497. Photographe: Arian Laenens: p. 108
© Museum of Fine Arts, Budapest: p. 339, p. 350-351
© Nasjonalmuseet for kunst, arkitektur og design; Stiftelsen Kunstindustrimuseet i Oslo. Photo: Teigens Fotoatelier AS: p. 162-163, p. 165
© Nasjonalmuseet for kunst, arkitektur og design. Photo: Anne Hansteen Jarre: p. 165
© Nasjonalmuseet for kunst, arkitektur og design. Photo: Teigens Fotoatelier AS: p. 164
© National Museum in Wroclaw. Photographer: Arkadiusz Podstawka: p. 216, p. 219
© Nationalmuseum, Stockholm: p. 173
© Palácio Nacional da Ajuda, António Homem Cardoso, Divisão de Documentação Fotográfica - INSTITUTO DOS MUSEUS E DA CONSERVAÇÃO, I.P: p. 31, p. 33
© Palácio Nacional da Ajuda, Henrique Ruas, Divisão de Documentação Fotográfica - INSTITUTO DOS MUSEUS E DA CONSERVAÇÃO, I.P: p. 31, p. 34, p. 37
© Palácio Nacional da Ajuda, Luisa Oliveira, Divisão de Documentação Fotográfica - INSTITUTO DOS MUSEUS E DA CONSERVAÇÃO, I.P: p. 20, p. 24-31, p. 33-37
© Palácio Nacional da Ajuda, Manuel Silveira Ramos, Divisão de Documentação Fotográfica - INSTITUTO DOS MUSEUS E DA CONSERVAÇÃO, I.P: p. 32-33
© Palácio Nacional da Ajuda, Mário Soares, Divisão de Documentação Fotográfica - INSTITUTO DOS MUSEUS E DA CONSERVAÇÃO, I.P: p. 23, p. 34
© PATRIMONIO NACIONAL: p. 43-45, p. 47, p. 49-53
© RMN (Château de Versailles) / Daniel Arnaudet: p. 41, p. 50, p. 100, p. 107
© RMN (Château de Versailles) / Droits réservés: p. 76, p. 79, p. 80, p. 82, p. 96, p. 100, p. 107
© RMN (Château de Versailles) / Gérard Blot: p. 38, p. 50, p. 63, p. 66, p. 71, p. 75, p. 81-82
© RMN (Château de Versailles) / Gérard Blot / Jean Schormans: p. 58, p. 65-66
© RMN / André Martin: p. 57, p. 64, p. 66, p. 70
© RMN / Daniel Arnaudet: p. 54, p. 64, p. 65
© RMN / Daniel Arnaudet / Jean Schormans: p. 63
© RMN / Gérard Blot: p. 66, p. 70-71
© RMN / René-Gabriel Ojéda: p. 341
© Sebastian Rosenberg: p. 190, p. 192-193, p. 198, p. 204, p. 206, p. 208, p. 235, p. 238
© State museum Pavlovsk, St. Petersburg: p. 197, p. 199, p. 205, p. 208
© The Danish Royal Collections, Amalienborg: p. 138, p. 140-142, p. 152-153
© The Danish Royal Collections, Rosenborg: p. 124, p. 127, p. 130, p. 132-134, p. 143-144, p. 147-151, p. 228, p. 239
© The Jagellonian University Museum: p. 219
© The Royal Court Photographic Archives, Oslo, Norway. Photo: Age Hojem: p. 157, p. 164
© The Royal Court Photographic Archives, Oslo, Norway. Photo: Jan Haug: p. 154, p. 160, p. 164-165
© The State Museum Preserve « Tsarskoye Selo », St. Petersburg, 2011: p. 186, p. 189, p. 191, p. 195, p. 201-207
© Victoria and Albert Museum, London: p. 72, p. 83
© Vincent Everarts / dist. La Collection: p. 101, p. 104-107, p. 108-109
© Wawel Royal Castle, Cracow. Phot. Jerzy Malinowski: p. 221
© Wawel Royal Castle, Cracow. Phot. Lukasz Schuster: p. 210, p. 219, p. 221
© Wawel Royal Castle, Cracow. Phot. Stanislaw Michta: p. 217, p. 219-221
© Wilanów Palace Museum, photo: A. Indyk: p. 221
© Wilanów Palace Museum, photo: Z. Reszka: p. 212, p. 215, p. 219-220
Archives de l'Institut océanographique: p. 347-348, p. 353
Archives départementales de la Manche, cliché Alexandre Poirier: p. 349
Archives Monte-Carlo S.B.M. en dépôt au NMNM (n° D.2010.2.52 et D.2010.2.53) © Barbara Poivan Photographie: p. 351
Archives Monte-Carlo S.B.M. en dépôt au NMNM (n° D.2010.2.71) © Barbara Poivan Photographie: p. 344, p. 351
Bayerisches Nationalmuseum, München: p. 273
Bibliothèque Mazarine, Paris. Photo: Suzanne Nagy: p. 343, p. 349
Botanisk Centralbibliotek. Photo: Rosenborg Castle: p. 146
Bruxelles, Palais royal, Liste Civile du Roi: p. 99, p. 107
Consorzio di Valorizzazione Culturale « La Venaria Reale »: p. 308, p. 311, p. 319
Deutsches Historisches Museum, Berlin: p. 222
Droits réservés: p. 313, p. 347
Esterházy Privatstiftung, Burg Forchtenstein – Esterházy-Schatzkammer; Photo: Manfred Horvath, Vienna: p. 294, p. 298, p. 300-301, p. 303-305
Esterházy Privatstiftung, Burg Forchtenstein - Jagdmonturdepot; Photo: Gerhard Wasserbauer, Wien: p. 307

Esterházy Privatstiftung, Schloss Eisenstadt - Skulpturensammlung; Photo: Gerhard Wasserbauer, Wien: p. 288, p. 291

Esterházy Privatstiftung, Schloss Eisenstadt – Musik – und Instrumentensammlung; Photo: Gerhard Wasserbauer, Wien: p. 307

Esterházy Privatstiftung, Schloss Eisenstadt – Musik – und Instrumentensammlung; Photo: National Museum from Musical Clock to Street Organ, Wien: p. 307

Esterházy Privatstiftung, Schloss Eisenstadt – Tafel – und Silberkammer; Photo: Manfred Horvath, Vienna: p. 306

Esterházy Privatstiftung, Schloss Eisenstadt – Tafel – und Silberkammer; Photo: Peter Kubelka, Wien: p. 306

Esterházy Privatstiftung, Schloss Eisenstadt – Wagenburg und Monturdepot; Photo: Peter Kubelka, Wien: p. 307

Esterházy Privatstiftung, Schloss Eisenstadt – Wagenburg und Monturdepot; Photo: Gerhard Wasserbauer, Wien: p. 14, p. 307

Esterházy Privatstiftung, Schloss Eisenstadt; Photo: Esterházy Privatstiftung, Eisenstadt: p. 284, p. 290

Esterházy Privatstiftung, Schloss Eisenstadt; Photo: Gerhard Wasserbauer, Wien: p. 280, p. 282, p. 285, p. 290-291, p. 297, p. 304

Esterházy Privatstiftung, Schloss Eisenstadt; Photo: Manfred Horvath, Wien: p. 302, p. 304

Fondation Napoléon: p. 71

Foto Roberto Goffi: p. 318

Gemäldegalerie Alte Meister, Staatliche Kunstsammlungen Dresden. Foto: Hans-Peter Klut: p. 242, p. 254

Gemäldegalerie Alte Meister, Staatliche Kunstsammlungen Dresden. Foto: Elke Estel: p. 245, p. 254

Grünes Gewölbe, Staatliche Kunstsammlungen Dresden. Foto: Jürgen Karpinski: p. 246, p. 249-250, p. 258-259

Kunstgewerbemuseum, Staatliche Kunstsammlungen Dresden. Foto: Jürgen Karpinski, Dresden: p. 255, p. 260

Kunstgewerbemuseum, Staatliche Kunstsammlungen Dresden. Foto: Klut/Estel: p. 260

Kunstgewerbemuseum, Staatliche Kunstsammlungen Dresden. Foto: SKD/Hans-Peter Klut: p. 247, p. 260

Kupferstich-Kabinett, Staatliche Kunstsammlungen Dresden: p. 253-254

Kupferstich-Kabinett, Staatliche Kunstsammlungen Dresden. Foto: Herbert Boswank: p. 253-254

Musée océanographique de Monaco – M. Dagnino: p. 352

Palazzo Madama – Museo Civico d'Arte Antica. Su Concessione della Fondazione Torino Musei © STUDIO FOTOGRAFICO GONELLA 2010: p. 316

Photo: Bayerische Schlösserverwaltung, München: p. 262, p. 266, p. 269, p. 271-275, p. 277-279

Photo Musée Masséna - Ville de Nice. Cliché Claude GERMAIN: p. 60, p. 70

Photo Musée Masséna - Ville de Nice. Cliché François FERNANDEZ: p. 67

Photo Musée Masséna - Ville de Nice. Cliché Muriel ANSSENS: p. 194, p. 208

Photo Thierry Vincent: p. 351

Photo12/Fondation Napoléon: p. 68

Photo12/Fondation Napoléon/Patrice Maurin-Berthier: p. 59-62, p. 64-70

Porzellansammlung, Staatliche Kunstsammlungen Dresden: p. 251, p. 261

Rüstkammer, Staatliche Kunstsammlungen Dresden – SLUB, DFD/ SKD. Foto: S. Bregulla: p. 256-257

Rüstkammer, Staatliche Kunstsammlungen Dresden. Foto: Elke Estel / Hans-Peter Klut: p. 255-256

Rüstkammer, Staatliche Kunstsammlungen Dresden. Foto: Hans-Peter Klut: p. 255-257

Rüstkammer, Staatliche Kunstsammlungen Dresden. Foto: Jürgen Karpinski: p. 233, p. 239, p. 248, p. 252, p. 255, p. 257-258, p. 260

Si ringrazia per la gentile concessione della foto: COMUNE DI PARMA, Assessorato alla Cultura, Settore Cultura, Pinacoteca G. "Stuard" – Musei Civici di San Paolo: p. 42, p. 50

Stiftung Preußische Schlösser und Gärten Berlin-Brandenburg: p. 225, p. 236-238, p. 240

Stiftung Preußische Schlösser und Gärten Berlin-Brandenburg / Daniel Lindner, 2011: p. 230, p. 237

Stiftung Preußische Schlösser und Gärten Berlin-Brandenburg / Jörg P. Anders: p. 237

Stiftung Preußische Schlösser und Gärten Berlin-Brandenburg / Roland Handrick: p. 225, p. 237

Stiftung Preußische Schlösser und Gärten Berlin-Brandenburg / Wolfgang Pfauder: p. 226, p. 234, p. 236-238, p. 239-240

Stiftung Schloss Friedenstein Gotha / Lutz Ebhardt: p. 232, p. 239

Su concessione della Direzione Regionale per i Beni Culturali e Paesaggistici del Piemonte, Soprintendenza per i Beni Architettonici e Paesaggistici per le province di Torino, Cuneo, Asti, Biella, Vercelli (Ministero per i Beni e le Attività Culturali), n° 829 DC et 1720 DC: p. 315, p. 319

The Museum of National History on Frederiksborg Castle. Photo: Frederiksborg/ Kit Weiss: p. 128, p. 136, p. 147, p. 152

The Museum of National History on Frederiksborg Castle. Photo: Frederiksborg/ Hans Hansen: p. 147

The Museum of National History on Frederiksborg Castle. Photo: Frederiksborg/ Hans Petersen: p. 135, p. 139, p. 147-148, p. 152

The Museum of National History on Frederiksborg Castle. Photo: Lennart Larsen: p. 131, p. 147

The Norwegian Armed Forces Museum, photo Håvard Madsbakken: p. 164

The Royal Castle in Warsaw. Photo: Andrzej Ring: p. 218

The Royal Court, Sweden. Photo Alexis Daflos: p. 178, p. 180, p. 183-185

Color separation by Bussière, Paris
Printed in Italy in June 2011 by Canale.